YOU JUST GAINED ACCESS TO
ATLAS™
YOUR ONLINE LEARNING PLATFORM!

Atlas will take you through this book and give you access to a host of additional resources, including:

- A free, full-length official practice exam with exclusive data analysis to pinpoint you strengths and weaknesses as well as thorough explanations for every problem

- Bonus lessons to build your mastery of LSAT content and extra drills to hone your newfound skills

HOW TO ACCESS ATLAS

Go to manhattanprep.com/lsat/access and follow the instructions on the screen.

Online resource access can only be granted for a single account; the guide cannot be registered a second time for a different account.

You have one year from the date of purchase to complete your registration.

D1288254

MANHATTAN PREP

LSAT Logical Reasoning

Strategy Guide

This strategy guide takes you from novice to master in Logical Reasoning.
Using a nuanced approach that emphasizes connections between question types,
this guide includes ample practice sets to help you develop both intuitive and
formal understandings of arguments and logic.

Acknowledgements

A great number of people were involved in the creation of the book you are holding.

Our Manhattan Prep resources are based on the continuing experiences of our instructors and students. The overall vision for this edition was rooted in the content expertise of Laura Damone, Dmitry Farber, Emily Madan, Scott Miller, Matt Shinners, Noah Teitelbaum, and Patrick Tyrrell, who determined what strategies to cover and how to weave them into a cohesive whole.

Laura Damone led the effort to update this edition for the new digital format of the LSAT. Christine Defenbaugh and Scott Miller provided content for these updates, and Dmitry Farber, Stacey Koprince, and Patrick Tyrell served as a sounding board during this process.

Derek Frankhouser lent his deft hand to the layout of this edition. Matthew Callan coordinated the production work. Once the manuscript was done, Laura Damone edited and Nomi Beesen proofread the guide. Carly Schnur designed the covers.

LSAT Logical Reasoning: Strategy Guide + Online Resources, 6th Edition

Retail ISBN: 978-1-5062-6566-7
Course ISBN: 978-1-5062-6568-1
Retail eISBN: 978-1-5062-6567-4
Course eISBN: 978-1-5062-6569-8

Layout Design: Derek Frankhouser

Strategy Guide Series

LSAT Logic Games
(ISBN: 978-1-5062-6562-9)

LSAT Logical Reasoning
(ISBN: 978-1-5062-6566-7)

LSAT Reading Comprehension
(ISBN: 978-1-5062-6570-4)

February 4, 2020

Dear Student,

Thank you for picking up a copy *LSAT Logical Reasoning*. I hope this book provides just the guidance you need to get the most out of your LSAT studies.

At Manhattan Prep, we continually aspire to provide the best instructors and resources possible. If you have any questions or feedback, please do not hesitate to contact us.

Email our Student Services team at lsat@manhattanprep.com or give us a shout at 212-721-7400 (or 800-576-4628 in the United States or Canada). We try to keep all our books free of errors, but if you think we've goofed, please visit manhattanprep.com/LSAT/errata.

Our Manhattan Prep Strategy Guides are based on the continuing experiences of both our instructors and our students. The authorship of the 6th Edition LSAT Logical Reasoning guide was a collaborative effort by instructors Laura Damone, Dmitry Farber, Emily Madan, Scott Miller, Matt Shinners, Noah Teitelbaum, and Patrick Tyrrell. Project management was led by Matthew Callan.

Finally, we are indebted to all of the Manhattan Prep students who have given us excellent feedback over the years. This book wouldn't be half of what it is without their voice.

And now that *you* are one of our students too, please chime in! I look forward to hearing from you. Thanks again and best of luck preparing for the LSAT!

Sincerely,

Chris Ryan
Executive Director, Product Strategy

HOW TO ACCESS YOUR ONLINE RESOURCES

Go to **www.manhattanprep.com/lsat/access** and follow the instructions on the screen.

Online resource access can only be granted for a single account; the guide cannot be registered a second time for a different account.

You have one year from the date of purchase to complete your registration.

TABLE *of* CONTENTS

Chapter 1

Logical Reasoning Overview

In This Chapter...

Logical Reasoning in the LSAT

Before we begin our discussion of the academics of the Logical Reasoning (LR) section, we'd like to spend a few moments looking at the LSAT in general and how the Logical Reasoning section works within the test as a whole.

As of September 2019, the LSAT is administered digitally in North America. When you arrive at the testing center, you'll be given a tablet, a stylus that doubles as a pen, and some scratch paper. The tablet will allow you to make certain annotations: underlining, highlighting, eliminating answers, selecting answers, and flagging questions to come back to later. Any free-hand writing or drawing must be done on scratch paper.

Every LSAT is comprised of the following sections:

Section	Questions	Scored?	Time
Logic Games	22–23	Yes	35 minutes
Reading Comprehension	26–28	Yes	35 minutes
Logical Reasoning (1)	24–26	Yes	35 minutes
Logical Reasoning (2)	24–26	Yes	35 minutes
Experimental	22–28	No	35 minutes
Essay	1 essay	No	35 minutes

The first five sections can come in any order. In previous years, the essay, formally known as the LSAT Writing Sample, was given on test day, at the testing center, and was always the last section of the exam. The Writing Sample is now administered online, can be completed from home, and does *not* have to be completed on test day. It is not factored into your overall score.

The experimental section is used for the internal purposes of the makers of the LSAT and will also not count toward your overall score. It will be an extra Logic Games (LG), Reading Comprehension (RC), or Logical Reasoning section. We do not recommend that you try to identify which section is experimental during the exam.

Of the four sections that do count toward your score, two of them will be Logical Reasoning. Therefore, Logical Reasoning is the section that will most significantly impact your performance, and it should be a priority in your studies.

You'll have 35 minutes to complete each section of the exam. If you finish a section early, you may not complete work on a different section of the exam. The digital test platform has a countdown timer to help you track your timing and a five-minute warning before the time for a section is up. Until the five-minute warning, you can hide the countdown timer by clicking on it. You can reveal it by clicking on it again. After the five-minute warning, the timer will remain visible until the end of the section. As you will see, certain Logical Reasoning questions are designed to take more time to answer than others, but based on the typical number of questions in a section, your timing for Logical Reasoning should average out to about 1:20 per question.

In all sections, every question is worth exactly one point. There is no penalty for guessing. That is, selecting a wrong answer has the same consequence as not selecting an answer at all—you will get zero points for that question. Therefore, it is to your advantage to select an answer for every single question, even if it's just a guess.

Every LSAT contains approximately 100 scored questions. Each correct answer adds one point to your raw score. This raw score is then converted to an LSAT score that fits on a scale from 120–180, and this conversion will be based on how difficult this particular test was compared to other LSAT exams.

Here's a sample conversion scale that is representative of the most recent LSATs:

Raw Score (minimum correct out of 100 total questions)	Scaled Score	Percentile Rank (the percentage of test-takers you outperformed)
99	180	99.9
95	175	99.5
89	170	97.5
82	165	91.5
74	160	80.1
65	155	63.1
57	150	44.1

The exact conversion varies a bit from exam to exam, but it is fairly consistent overall. Because you'll see approximately 100 questions, it can be helpful to think of your goal score in terms of the percentage of questions you will need to get correct (not to be confused with the Percentile Rank). For example, if your goal score is 165, it should be helpful to know that overall, you'll need to answer a bit more than 80% of the questions correctly. If you have not already, take a moment to consider your goal score and the percentage accuracy that achieving that score will require.

Now, with that goal in mind, let's turn to the purpose of this chapter: setting up your approach to Logical Reasoning.

Your Approach to Logical Reasoning

Categorization is important on the LSAT: Consider the adage "divide and conquer." To that end, it is helpful to think of the Logical Reasoning (LR) section as divided into two families:

1. Those questions in which you will be asked to *debate* what you read by identifying and exploiting a gap in the argument's reasoning, aka an assumption

2. Those questions in which you will be expected to *accept* what you read and then describe, match, or infer from that material

Knowing which family each question falls into will dramatically improve your ability to move through the LR section both effectively and efficiently.

MANHATTAN
PREP

Let's look at an example of an LSAT question that we'll work on in a later chapter:

_PT29, S4, Q2_

> Economist: To the extent that homelessness arises from a lack of available housing, it should not be assumed that the profit motive is at fault. Private investors will, in general, provide housing if the market allows them to make a profit; it is unrealistic to expect investors to take risks with their property unless they get some benefit in return.
>
> Which one of the following most accurately describes the role played in the economist's argument by the phrase "To the extent that homelessness arises from a lack of available housing"?
>
> (A)   It limits the application of the argument to a part of the problem.
>
> (B)   It suggests that the primary cause of homelessness is lack of available housing.
>
> (C)   It is offered as evidence crucial to the conclusion.
>
> (D)   It expresses the conclusion to be argued for.
>
> (E)   It suggests a possible solution to the problem of homelessness.

A Logical Reasoning question consists of three parts: the stimulus, the question stem, and the answer choices. We all know what answer choices look like, but the other two terms might be unfamiliar. The stimulus is the initial paragraph that precedes the question stem—in the example above, it begins with "Economist: To the extent..." In LR, it will be an argument or a series of statements, so we will often call it "the argument." The question stem will give us some task in relation to the stimulus—in the example above, it begins with "Which one of the..." Here are two other examples of LR question stems:

1.   The main conclusion of the argument is that...

2.   Which one of the following, if true, most strengthens the argument above?

The first example, like the question stem in the official question above, asks you to describe the argument. There is no debate required—you're asked to accept what the argument says and figure out its main point. The second example, however, does require that you debate the argument. If you want to strengthen an argument on the LSAT, you first must understand its weaknesses so that you can choose an answer that overcomes one of those weaknesses.

1

Are the two tasks related? Certainly. Both, for example, require that you understand the structure of the argument before proceeding. However, debating the argument requires a more complete understanding, because you have to understand not only what role each sentence plays, but also the important things that were left out of the argument and how those things impact the argument's strength. This is analysis you want to do right away when it's necessary and avoid completely when it's not!

That's why you should make it a habit to read the question stem first! You may end up having to reread that question stem after reading the stimulus, especially as you get started approaching LR questions in this way, but don't be deterred by this. The question stem can tell you volumes about the argument before you even begin reading it, because each type of question comes with its own bag of tricks. Knowing which tricks to be on the lookout for will help you tailor your approach to reading the stimulus. Knowing whether to accept or debate the argument will prevent you from doing unnecessary mental work. Thus, reading the question stem first is a critical component of an effective and efficient approach to the Logical Reasoning section.

(Dying to know whether you got that sample question correct? Flip to page 448 in Chapter 10 to see.)

Your Path to Success

This book is organized according to the two families discussed above, each of which represents about half of all Logical Reasoning questions. In the first half of the book, we will learn about the Assumption Family of questions—those that call for us to debate the argument by identifying gaps in reasoning.

In the second half of the book, we will tackle all of the question types outside of the Assumption Family. In that section, we'll find more variety in the tasks that we're asked to perform, but what ties them together is that we will not debate the argument.

Despite the division between questions in which we do or do not debate the argument, many of the skills you will build throughout this book are required for success on questions in both families. That is because many of the skills are not associated with a single question type. Rather, they are skills that allow you to understand and break down complicated arguments *across* question types. Thus, while you want to have a specific approach to each task the Logical Reasoning section will ask you to complete, you also want to build a more holistic understanding of the structures and conventions common to LSAT arguments on the whole.

Preparing for the LSAT

It is important to begin your LSAT preparation with a good plan. Here is some advice meant to help put you on the right path.

MANHATTAN
PREP

1. Strive for mastery.

Mastery means something far greater than simply knowing the right answer; it means maximizing the learning that you get out of every question you try. For every argument you encounter, you should be able to articulate the function of each piece of the stimulus and understand how the author supports the conclusion. If it's a question that requires a debating stance, you must be able to clearly articulate the gaps in the reasoning.

Maximizing your learning also entails consideration of the relationship between the stimulus and question stem. Once you've identified the task of the question communicated in the stem, be on the lookout for the conventions of that question type and work to predict a correct answer before moving to the answer choices.

When you reach the answers, you must carefully consider each one. Don't let yourself off the hook by saying, "Oh, this answer is obviously wrong." Imagine that you have to explain the problem to someone who thinks the answer is right. What would you say? Don't let it go until you have a great response.

Treating every piece of every question as though it has something to teach you will allow you to master the smaller skills that together make up the broad categories of argument analysis, answer choice prediction, and answer choice assessment. What's more, this approach will allow you to master those skills in far less time than you would spend if you treated each question like a race to the right answer.

2. Develop a process.

Right now, your approach to Logical Reasoning might be driven primarily by intuition. But most test-takers have a hard time getting to the score they want through intuition alone. This means that you need to develop a process for approaching question types individually, and the Logical Reasoning section as a whole, that will complement your intuition when it's working in your favor and override your intuition when it's leading you down the wrong path.

Many challenging LSAT questions make complete sense after the fact—when you review the question and see the clever shift in wording or the unexpected link between premises—but leave you feeling that you would have no better chance of getting a question like that correct the next time you see one. Though hard questions can seem this way, the reality is that every question has at least one tell: a language cue pointing to what you ought to think about and how you ought to think about it. We'll acquaint you with many of these cues over the course of this book, but the key to spotting them quickly and reliably is to approach LR questions with a consistent, reliable approach.

A good approach will help you to think about the right things at the right time. We cannot overemphasize the significance of this. There is likely no other action that you can take during your studies that will positively impact your score more than developing a sound and consistent process for every type of Logical Reasoning question. This will be a primary focus in each of the chapters to come.

3. Work from tendencies to twists.

If you were working to become a master engine builder, you likely would not begin working on the most complicated or unusual engines, nor would you attempt to learn to build all types of engines at once. Instead, you would learn to build each type of engine before moving to the next, learning both the commonalities and the differences between types and leaving the oddballs for last.

1

The same is true as you work to become a master of the LSAT. Focus on learning one question type at a time, but as you do so, work to recognize that which is unique to the particular type of question *and* that which is consistent across multiple question types. Once you've mastered the essential components of each question type and the section as a whole, you can then use your process to relate unusual challenges to that norm.

4. Integrate mixed review.

All Logical Reasoning questions test our reading and reasoning skills, but each type of question requires something unique from us. An analogy could be made to learning a variety of musical instruments. There is great commonality in what is required to understand and play each instrument, but each instrument also has its own unique characteristics that need to be understood and mastered.

The best way to master a question type, and to develop a process for it that is intuitive and automatic, is to immerse yourself in questions of just that type. Focus your energies on learning and developing strategies for one question type at a time. Spend a week doing just Assumption questions, breaking them down and seeing what is common to them. We feel that this initial focus on specific question types is the most efficient way to build mastery.

However, while question type–specific immersion is the best way to *achieve* mastery, you will need to integrate mixed review in order to *maintain* mastery. Recent research into the science of learning tells us that to carve the neural pathways that create intuition and a reflexive response, we must touch on a subject multiple times. If you study one skill for a week and then don't think about it for another three, you're likely to backslide. If you don't use it, you lose it! To prevent this from happening, we recommend that, after devoting yourself to the study of a particular question type, you then devote some time to mixed review.

This mixed review should take two forms. First, you should revisit questions from previous chapters that you found challenging, reviewing not only the question itself but the process you developed for that question type as a whole. Simply get in the habit of flagging a few items in each week's work that you want to revisit later. Second, once you've covered several question types, you should start doing mixed practice sets with a timer. Of course, this can be achieved by sitting down for a practice LSAT, but because there are times when completing an entire exam is impractical, students too often fail to integrate as much mixed practice as they should. We encourage you to break free from the strictures of the four-hour test! You can, for example, break an official LSAT into four 35-minute sections. Even half of a Logical Reasoning section, when completed and thoroughly reviewed, can cement your process for the question types it contains and build the skills necessary to switch between the processes appropriate for different question types.

While mixed review has many obvious benefits, it can also have some negative consequences if it is not approached with care. Without a conscious effort to apply process, mixed review can reinforce bad habits, particularly in the early phase of your preparation. If you have a lot of bad habits that you don't want to reinforce, it might be helpful to take a break from timed mixed practice as you build your question type–specific approaches. Integrate mixed practice exclusively by revisiting old questions untimed until you feel solid enough in your approaches to try a timed mixed set. When you do so, try the first 10 questions of an official LR section. These questions tend to be on the easier side of the difficulty spectrum, which can help you avoid reverting back to your old way of doing things instead of practicing your newly-minted approaches. Mixed review can also cause you to improperly blend together strategies for distinct question types. To combat this, think of timed mixed review as a way to practice moving from one strategy to another. Setting that intention before you begin a mixed practice set will go a long way toward correcting that tendency.

MANHATTAN
PREP

As you get closer to test day, your ability to perform well on timed mixed sets becomes more important. It makes sense, then, that as you approach test day, more of your time should be spent on this type of work than was spent in the early phase of you preparation when you were mastering individual question types. Be sure to allow plenty of space for timed sections and practice tests in your study schedule in the month(s) leading up to the test.

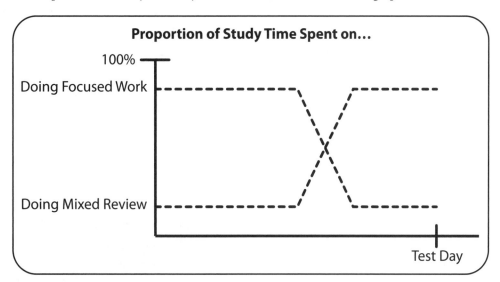

Creating the Right Mind-Set

So far, we've talked a lot about strategies for approaching the academic side of the LSAT. But did you notice that some of those strategies had to do with getting in the right state of mind? Here are a few things you can do to prime your brain for learning and get the most out of your practice:

1. Practice with purpose.

Before you embark on any LSAT endeavor, take a moment to pause and think about your goal for that point in your preparation. What are you trying to achieve? Maybe you're working to cement a process for a particular question type. Maybe you're trying to assess your ability to quickly switch gears in a mixed set. Perhaps you are setting ambitious timing goals for easier questions to buy yourself time for the harder ones. Or maybe you're combating a tendency to rush through the easier questions so you can stop making silly mistakes. Whatever your intention, take a moment to pause and articulate it. This simple action has been shown to dramatically improve your ability to achieve what you set out to do.

1

2. Be ready to improve.

You may have heard the saying "Whether you think you can or think you can't, you're probably right." While you may have seen it on a cheesy inspirational poster with a cat hanging from a tree branch, this statement has actually been borne out by science. Students who go into their studies confident that they can learn and improve outperform students who go in feeling that they're bound by their abilities. The truth is, much of what we consider "intelligence" is actually learned and not innate. The same is true for a person's ability to reason logically. Even if your intuition is constantly steering you in the wrong direction, *don't panic*. It doesn't mean that you're not a logical person or that you can't learn to reason in a more logical way. Because you will develop a systematic process for LR question types and the LR section as a whole, you can succeed on the LSAT even without a strong logical intuition at the outset of your preparation. By test day, you will likely find that the intuition you've cultivated over the course of your preparation is dramatically more logical than the intuition you came in with.

3. Love the one you're with.

At some point during your LSAT preparation, you'll probably wish that this test were already behind you. And why wouldn't you? Preparing for the LSAT is a lot of work, the stakes are high, and—let's face it—most people don't enjoy standardized tests as much as we teachers do. But the reality is that the test isn't behind you yet, and until that fine day when you never have to look at the LSAT again, it will behoove you to embrace it. Instead of thinking of the LSAT as a hurdle you have to jump over to get *into* law school, think of it as part of your preparation *for* law school. There's a reason that law schools require their intelligent, educated applicants to take this exam: It tests a skill set that you need to perform well in law school, but that many otherwise-qualified people didn't learn in their undergraduate or professional lives. Think of your LSAT preparation as an opportunity to learn these critical reading and reasoning skills that will serve you well in law school and beyond.

Chapter 2

The Argument Core

In This Chapter...

Elements of an Argument

As we've seen, in order to tackle Logical Reasoning arguments, we need to determine our task and then analyze the argument with that particular task in mind. For this first section of the book, our task will always hinge on finding the gaps, or assumptions, in an argument. In order to do that, we need to understand how arguments are put together. So, what's in an argument?

Conclusions

Every argument is designed to prove a point. That point is the argument's conclusion. Every argument also rests on one or more pieces of evidence. That evidence makes up the argument's premise or premises (there can be more than one). Sometimes, the argument's conclusion will appear in a separate sentence from the evidence. Other times, it will appear in the same sentence, as in "You shouldn't eat that apple because it's rotten." (Premise: That apple is rotten. Conclusion: You shouldn't eat that apple.)

Let's try analyzing a few examples. Underline the conclusion of each of these arguments:

1. Rum is made from sugarcane, so it is higher in calories than other alcoholic beverages.

2. It is important for children to memorize the multiplication tables. Without this knowledge, it is difficult to master higher mathematics.

3. Rabbits are mammals. All rodents are mammals, and rabbits are rodents.

4. Broccoli is more nutritious than French fries. For that reason, the school should serve broccoli more often than French fries. Nutrition, not student taste preferences, is the most important consideration in meal planning.

How did you do?

1. Rum is made from sugarcane, so <u>it is higher in calories than other alcoholic beverages.</u>

We tend to think of arguments as beginning with the premise and ending with the conclusion. While this is sometimes the case on the LSAT, it is equally common for the argument to present the conclusion first and then provide support. For this reason, we cannot rely on the position of an element within an argument to give us any clues about the element's function. What we can rely on, however, are indicator words. You will probably recognize some common conclusion indicators like "therefore" and "thus." Did you see any indicator words in the first argument? If you noticed "so," well done! Like "thus" and "therefore," the word "so" provides a clear indication that what follows is a conclusion.

2. <u>It is important for children to memorize the multiplication tables.</u> Without this knowledge, it is difficult to master higher mathematics.

Tricky! The second statement helps us to understand the importance of the multiplication tables. Why is it important to memorize those tables? Because without that knowledge, you'll be in trouble later on! That makes the first sentence

the conclusion and the second sentence the premise. While the conclusion does not logically follow from the premise (we might agree with the premise and not the conclusion), notice that the first sentence offers *no* support for the second, so we know we have identified the conclusion correctly.

3. <u>Rabbits are mammals.</u> All rodents are mammals, and rabbits are rodents.

The second sentence provides a pair of conditional statements that work together to prove the first sentence. We'll work on conditional logic throughout the book, starting later in this chapter.

4. Broccoli is more nutritious than French fries. For that reason, <u>the school should serve broccoli more often than French fries.</u> Nutrition, not student taste preferences, is the most important consideration in meal planning.

The words "for that reason" indicate that the claim in the second sentence is supported by the preceding statement. The third sentence provides an additional premise that helps us connect the conclusion to the first premise. Notice that both of the premises could be seen as opinions—how do we know what makes something more nutritious, or, for that matter, what the most important consideration in meal planning is? However, these claims have no other support in the argument, and they *provide* support for the claim in the middle. When we're given completely unsupported statements in real life, we tend to question them. On the LSAT, however, we accept the premises as given, and we analyze an argument's logic by focusing on the connection between the premises and the conclusion.

That last statement was so important that it's worth repeating: On the LSAT, we accept the premises as given, and we analyze an argument's logic by focusing on *the connection* between the premises and the conclusion.

But we're getting ahead of ourselves. Let's back up to the conclusion. Based on what you saw in the exercise above, what can you conclude about how to identify conclusions? Here are a few clues:

1. Conclusions are often indicated by language cues.

Certain language cues tend to point toward the conclusion. The traditional way to introduce a conclusion is with keywords such as "therefore," "so," "hence," "thus," "it follows that," "this suggests that," etc. However, in many cases there are no keywords to indicate the conclusion. It may simply be stated as if it were a fact. ("It's important for children to memorize the multiplication tables.") In other cases, the argument being mounted is actually a refutation of somebody else's argument. In these cases, words such as "but" and "however," which contrast the author's opinion to the opinion being refuted, can introduce the argument's conclusion. These cues are helpful, but because there is not one consistent way of flagging a conclusion, we also need to understand how the conclusion relates to the other elements of the argument.

2. Conclusions are supported by premises.

The conclusion will always draw its strength from the premises, even though it will not usually follow logically from those premises. If we've successfully identified the conclusion, we should see how it builds upon the premises, and none of the premises should seem to build on the conclusion. This relationship often presents us with another sort of language cue, in which the conclusion is connected to the premise with words such as "since" or "because" introducing the premise.

MANHATTAN
PREP

3. Conclusions are opinions.

While conclusions draw support from premises, in the end they still represent the author's opinion about the situation at hand. A premise can be an opinion, but the conclusion is *always* an opinion. Here are a few common types of conclusions:

- **Factual Claim** ("Many citizens must be submitting fraudulent tax returns.")

- **Recommendation** ("The governor should be reelected.")

- **Prediction** ("The governor will be reelected.")

- **Evaluation** ("Peaches are nutritious.")

- **Comparison** ("Peaches are more nutritious than pears.")

- **Explanation** ("The company's increased sales are due to its aggressive new ad campaign.")

Premises

If we know how to identify the conclusion, is everything else in the argument a premise? Unfortunately not. As we'll see in a moment, there can be other components of an LSAT argument. So how do we know which statements are premises? First, premises have to support the conclusion in some way. A premise will usually be a factual statement of some kind, but some premises are opinions. What all premises have in common is that, unlike conclusions, they are not supported by anything else in the argument. This might make some premises seem a little dodgy, but remember, our policy is *to accept them without question.* Why on earth would we do this? Because the LSAT is not testing our real-world knowledge, and we don't get to go and research the facts behind each argument. As we'll discuss later in this chapter, when we do question the logic of an argument, our job is simply to determine if the argument is **valid**—that is, whether the premises, if they were true, would prove the conclusion. Whether the premises themselves *are* true is for someone else to decide.

Here are a few common types of premises:

- **Simple Factual** ("Plants convert sunlight into sugars through photosynthesis.")

- **Research Results** ("A recent study demonstrated that snails move 50% slower than sloths.")

- **Principle** ("A courteous listener will not interrupt the speaker unless he or she believes that the speaker would approve of the interruption.")

- **Conditional** ("If Aisha is invited to the conference, she will attend.")

- **Alternatives** ("The dessert will feature either chocolate or fruit.")

- **Contrasting Premises** ("In some European countries, more than 50% of citizens claim to attend religious services on a regular basis. However, in the Scandinavian countries, this figure is generally lower than 5%.")

2

Complementary Premises

In some cases, two or more premises work together. We've just seen the case of contrasting premises, but we can also have premises that complement one another. Let's try adding an extra premise to a few of the premises above:

> A courteous listener will not interrupt the speaker unless he or she believes that the speaker would approve of the interruption. Eleanor interrupted Cybele to make a pun, even though she knows Cybele does not enjoy puns.

> If Aisha is invited to the conference, she will attend. She is likely to be invited as long as the conference organizers are not swayed by any of her critics.

> The dessert will feature either chocolate or fruit. Alberto is allergic to chocolate.

In none of these cases do we know exactly what will happen, but we have a stronger sense of the possibilities. (Is Eleanor a courteous listener? It depends on whether she thinks Cybele might approve of an interruption she doesn't enjoy.)

In other arguments, one premise builds on another by adding detail or showing a consequence:

> A recently opened cooking school is growing in popularity. Its enrollment is now higher than that of many more established schools.

The second premise simply shows us what this popularity looks like.

> A new programming language called Tourmaline allows programmers to adapt their previous work more quickly and flexibly. In some cases, this has led to substantial reductions in development costs.

Here, the second premise shows a consequence of the first, but it's possible that all of these elements—speed, flexibility, and cost reduction—will feed into the conclusion.

The Argument Core

At this point, we have identified the two key elements of an argument. An argument will always have a conclusion and one or more premises intended to support that conclusion. From this point forward, we will refer to this simple relationship as the argument core. We will represent the argument core using a "therefore arrow" to represent the idea that—at least in the author's mind—the conclusion follows from the premise:

$$P \;\; \text{} \;\; C$$

2

Other Elements of an Argument

So far, we've focused on the two most important elements of an argument: the conclusion and the premise(s). What other elements can an argument have?

Background Information

Some LSAT arguments will include neutral background information in an attempt to orient (or disorient) the reader before the real argument starts. Don't let this confuse you, though. We're still looking for the argument core. Take this one:

> Next week, our school board will vote on a proposal to extend the school day by one hour. This proposal will not pass. A very similar proposal was voted down by the school board in a neighboring town.

What's the conclusion? "This proposal will not pass." Why won't it pass? Because a similar proposal was voted down in a neighboring town. That's it. The first sentence doesn't add any additional strength to the argument—it just helps to explain what proposal we're talking about. In other arguments, background statements may be included to define a key term or provide other context for the argument core. Context is important, but remember that it's only there to help us understand the core.

When looking for the argument core, you want to consider just the premise conclusion relationship:

similar proposal voted   proposal will not pass
down in nearby town

Intermediate Conclusions and the "Therefore Test"

Consider the argument below. What is the conclusion?

> A new lemonade stand has just opened for business in the town square. The stand will surely fail. A popular juice store already sells lemonade in the town square, so the new lemonade stand will not be able to attract customers.

We start with background information—there's a new lemonade stand in town. But after that, the author seems to draw two distinct, if related, conclusions: 1) The stand will surely fail, and 2) the new lemonade stand will not be able to attract customers. In real life, it's fine to make one point after another, but if we want to boil an LSAT argument down to its core, we need to identify one final conclusion. If that's the case, what is the other not-so-final conclusion doing? It's supporting the main conclusion.

So which is which? Let's use what we call the **Therefore Test** to identify the final conclusion. We'll propose two possible P C relationships between our two main conclusion candidates:

Case 1: The new lemonade stand will surely fail. THEREFORE, the new lemonade stand will not be able to attract customers.

Case 2: The new lemonade stand will not be able to attract customers. THEREFORE, the new lemonade stand will surely fail.

The first case doesn't make a whole lot of sense. Sure, if the stand fails, it won't have a lot of customers—it will be closed!—but this doesn't seem like something we'd need to point out to anyone. In the second case, however, the first statement builds up to and supports the second statement. Because the stand will not be able to attract customers, it will surely fail. For this reason, the main conclusion of the argument is "The stand will surely fail." Any conclusion that supports the final conclusion is called an **intermediate conclusion.** As the name suggests, these conclusions come between the plain old premises and the final conclusion. They are always supported by at least one premise, and they support the main conclusion.

Here's the relationship in argument core form: (P) premise ➡ (IC) intermediate conclusion ➡ (C) conclusion.

popular juice store already there   ➡   new store won't be able to attract customers   ➡   new store will fail

It's important to recognize that there's a big difference between this argument and an argument with two premises. Why? Well, remember that we always accept premises as true. We don't have to extend the same consideration to intermediate conclusions. So if we're looking for holes in the argument, we can look between the premise and the intermediate conclusion *or* between the intermediate conclusion and the main conclusion. It might help to think of such an argument core as consisting of two separate arguments:

1. P ➡ IC

2. IC ➡ C

Opposing Points

Think about the arguments that you make on a daily basis (you probably make more than you realize). Sometimes you can add to your argument by conceding a point or two to the other side. In doing so, you show that you've considered other viewpoints, and you also steal the thunder of the person who might argue against you! The LSAT does this all the time. Let's revisit the lemonade argument with an added twist:

A new lemonade stand has just opened for business in the town square. The price per cup at the new stand is the lowest in town, but the store will surely fail. A popular juice store already sells lemonade in the town square, so the new lemonade stand will not be able to attract customers.

In this case, the statement that "the price per cup at the new stand is the lowest in town" is an opposing point; it is a counterpremise that would seem to support the opposite claim (that the lemonade stand will *not* fail). Notice that the contrast with the main conclusion is set up with the word "but." Here's another, slightly different example:

> A new lemonade stand has just opened for business in the town square. The columnist in the local paper writes that the stand will succeed, but it will surely fail. A popular juice store already sells lemonade in the town square, so the new lemonade stand will not be able to attract customers.

Notice again the contrast word "but." In this case, the opposing point ("The columnist in the local paper writes that the stand will succeed") is actually a counterclaim. It is directly opposed to the claim made by the author (that the stand will surely fail).

Again, the LSAT often uses opposing points to add more texture (and confusion!) to a passage. Some opposing points are counterpremises while others are counterclaims. Regardless, it'll be important that you separate the opposing points from the elements of the argument core. Don't confuse the sides! In this case, the argument core remains unchanged:

popular juice store already there ➡ new store won't be able to attract customers ➡ new store will fail

Now that we've covered the elements you can expect to find in an argument, let's test your new-found skills on a batch of official LSAT arguments.

Drill It: Identifying the Argument Core

Identify the argument core for each of the passages given below. For the purposes of this exercise, take the time to write the core, in arrow form, on your scratch paper. Be sure to check your answers against the solutions we've given (check your answer after each question to solidify your learning before attempting the next one). Your paraphrases may not always be identical to ours—that's okay. Just make sure the general P ➡ C relationship is the same.

"PT, S, Q" refers to the LSAT PrepTest from which the question was taken, the section of that PrepTest, and the question number.

1. PT7, S1, Q10

A large group of hyperactive children whose regular diets included food containing large amounts of additives was observed by researchers trained to assess the presence or absence of behavior problems. The children were then placed on a low additive diet for several weeks, after which they were observed again. Originally nearly 60 percent of the children exhibited behavior problems; after the change in diet, only 30 percent did so. On the basis of these data, it can be concluded that food additives can contribute to behavior problems in hyperactive children.

2. PT7, S1, Q20

According to sources who can be expected to know, Dr. Maria Esposito is going to run in the mayoral election. But if Dr. Esposito runs, Jerome Krasman will certainly not run against her. Therefore Dr. Esposito will be the only candidate in the election.

3. PT7, S4, Q1

In 1974 the speed limit on highways in the United States was reduced to 55 miles per hour in order to save fuel. In the first 12 months after the change, the rate of highway fatalities dropped 15 percent, the sharpest one-year drop in history. Over the next 10 years, the fatality rate declined by another 25 percent. It follows that the 1974 reduction in the speed limit saved many lives.

4. PT7, S4, Q13

The National Association of Fire Fighters says that 45 percent of homes now have smoke detectors, whereas only 30 percent of homes had them 10 years ago. This makes early detection of house fires no more likely, however, because over half of the domestic smoke detectors are either without batteries or else inoperative for some other reason.

5. PT7, S4, Q2

Some legislators refuse to commit public funds for new scientific research if they cannot be assured that the research will contribute to the public welfare. Such a position ignores the lessons of experience. Many important contributions to the public welfare that resulted from scientific research were never predicted as potential outcomes of that research. Suppose that a scientist in the early twentieth century had applied for public funds to study molds: who would have predicted that such research would lead to the discovery of antibiotics—one of the greatest contributions ever made to the public welfare?

6. PT9, S2, Q7

Waste management companies, which collect waste for disposal in landfills and incineration plants, report that disposable plastics make up an ever-increasing percentage of the waste they handle. It is clear that attempts to decrease the amount of plastic that people throw away in the garbage are failing.

7. PT9, S2, Q4

Data from satellite photographs of the tropical rain forest in Melonia show that last year the deforestation rate of this environmentally sensitive zone was significantly lower than in previous years. The Melonian government, which spent millions of dollars last year to enforce laws against burning and cutting of the forest, is claiming that the satellite data indicate that its increased efforts to halt the destruction are proving effective.

8. PT7, S1, Q24

Many major scientific discoveries of the past were the product of serendipity, the chance discovery of valuable findings that investigators had not purposely sought. Now, however, scientific research tends to be so costly that investigators are heavily dependent on large grants to fund their research. Because such grants require investigators to provide the grant sponsors with clear projections of the outcome of the proposed research, investigators ignore anything that does not directly bear on the funded research. Therefore, under the prevailing circumstances, serendipity can no longer play a role in scientific discovery.

9. PT9, S2, Q19

A university should not be entitled to patent the inventions of its faculty members. Universities, as guarantors of intellectual freedom, should encourage the free flow of ideas and the general dissemination of knowledge. Yet a university that retains the right to patent the inventions of its faculty members has a motive to suppress information about a potentially valuable discovery until the patent for it has been secured. Clearly, suppressing information concerning such discoveries is incompatible with the university's obligation to promote the free flow of ideas.

10. PT7, S1, Q7

Coherent solutions for the problem of reducing health care costs cannot be found within the current piecemeal system of paying these costs. The reason is that this system gives health care providers and insurers every incentive to shift, wherever possible, the costs of treating illness onto each other or any other party, including the patient. That clearly is the lesson of the various reforms of the 1980s: push in on one part of this pliable spending balloon and an equally expensive bulge pops up elsewhere. For example, when the government health care insurance program for the poor cut costs by disallowing payments for some visits to physicians, patients with advanced illness later presented themselves at hospital emergency rooms in increased numbers.

Solutions: Identifying the Argument Core

Below are the cores for each of the arguments and short discussions about how to identify the parts of the argument. Carefully compare your work against them, looking for different ideas, ignoring irrelevant differences in word choice.

1. PT7, S1, Q10

60% originally had behavior problems

+

only 30% had behavior problems after
decreasing additives in diet

➡ food additives can contribute to
behavior problems in hyperactive
children

Most of this argument consists of research results. Since these are facts, not opinion, we know that they are supporting premises leading to the conclusion at the end. If we had any doubt, the lovely keywords "it can be concluded" cleared it up for us!

2. PT7, S1, Q20

if Esposito runs, Krasman will not

+

Esposito will run

➡ Esposito will be only candidate in race

These two premises build upon each other. Dr. Esposito is going to run, and that lets us know that Krasman is out. From here, the author concludes that Esposito will be the only candidate. "Therefore" is another nice conclusion indicator.

3. PT7, S4, Q1

in first year after reduction,
15% drop in deaths

+

another 25% drop over next 10 years

➡ speed limit reduction has
saved many lives

The data are presented as facts, making each of them a premise. The final sentence begins "It follows that," which introduces a conclusion.

4. PT7, S4, Q13

over half of domestic detectors are
without batteries or are inoperative

 increase in detectors from 30%
to 45% does not make home fires any
less likely

The word "however" indicates a shift in direction. In this case, the argument begins with an opposing point (more smoke detectors today). The second sentence, where the "however" is introduced, provides both the conclusion and the premise. The statistic about batteries in smoke detectors is our premise, both because it's a fact and because it's introduced with the word "because," a premise keyword. The conclusion interprets the facts by evaluating the likelihood of early detection by these alarms.

5. PT7, S4, Q2

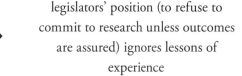

many important contributions came from research but were never predicted as potential outcomes ➡ legislators' position (to refuse to commit to research unless outcomes are assured) ignores lessons of experience

When the author presents a position held by someone else—here, some legislators—and then makes a point to disagree with it, that disagreement is almost always the main conclusion of the argument. We can be confident that is the case here, because we see both a general and a specific example of what the lessons of experience are. Those examples are premises.

6. PT9, S2, Q7

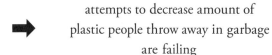

waste management reports increasing percentage of disposable plastics for disposal in landfills and incinerators ➡ attempts to decrease amount of plastic people throw away in garbage are failing

The author is drawing a conclusion on the basis of a report. Given the facts of the report, the author draws a broad conclusion.

7. PT9, S2, Q4

deforestation rate is decreasing

+

government spent millions to curb cutting and burning ➡ government efforts are proving effective

The presentation of data typically serves as a premise. The photographs provide factual data. The author provides further data by telling us what the government has spent. The only opinion, and therefore the conclusion, is the claim made by the Melonian government.

8. PT7, S1, Q24

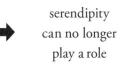

grants require investigators to provide clear outcome projections ➡ investigators ignore anything that does not directly bear on the funded research ➡ serendipity can no longer play a role

"Therefore" is just about the clearest conclusion keyword you could hope for. However, there is another conclusion here. Did you catch it? The second-to-last sentence tells us, "Because of X, Y." That kind of language sets up X to be the premise that supports conclusion Y. To figure out which of two conclusions is the final one, consider which one is supported by the other. In this case, the idea that investigators ignore extraneous information supports the idea that serendipity no longer plays a role. We can therefore be confident that the final sentence is our main conclusion.

9. PT9, S2, Q19

universities should promote free flow
and dissemination of ideas

+

universities with right to patent have
incentive to suppress information   universities should not be entitled to
                                                                        patent inventions by faculty

+

suppressing information is
incompatible with obligation to
promote free flow of ideas

Were you tricked into thinking that the final sentence is the conclusion? Be careful! The word "clearly" makes the statement sound like a conclusion, but there's no support stated in the argument. Without a supporting premise, this can't be the conclusion.

What should catch your eye more is the word "should." When an argument has just one normative statement (saying something *should* or *ought* to occur) that is almost always the conclusion, since normative statements are by definition opinions. When an argument has more than one normative statement, we must consider which is supported by the other. There are two in this argument: the first and second sentences. Of those, only the first is supported. A university should not do something because it is incompatible with another obligation and a principle.

10. PT7, S1, Q7

system gives incentive to shift costs to   solutions for reducing costs cannot be
others   found in current system

The first sentence begins with an opinion and then presents reasons for that opinion. That looks like a conclusion–premise structure. If you got lost in the final details, keep in mind that by starting with "That clearly is the lesson of…," the author is telling us that what follows will be an illustration of whatever point she just made. Each premise aims to show how the cost is pushed from health care providers and insurers onto others. That idea supports the argument's main conclusion.

Evaluating the Logic of an Argument

By now, hopefully you feel like a pro at finding the core of LR arguments. However, as we discussed in the last chapter, most LR questions will require us to *do* something with that core. In this first half of the book, we'll focus on the Assumption Family of questions. To tackle these, we'll need to evaluate the core and see what it's missing. Let's try this out on a simple argument:

the sun rises only on Mondays   the sun does not rise on Fridays

Here are two ways to think about this:

1. **The real-world approach:**

   "No way! Terrible argument! We all know that the Sun rises every day, not just on Mondays."

2. **The logical approach:**

   "Well, if we take the premise as a given truth, that the Sun rises only on Mondays, is this enough to prove the claim that the Sun does not rise on Fridays? Yes. Logically speaking, this argument is valid."

As you probably predicted, we're going to run with the second approach on the LSAT. We're only concerned with whether arguments are **valid** (meaning that the conclusion follows logically from the premises) and not with whether arguments are **sound** (meaning both valid and factually true). Since we always accept the given premises, we don't have to worry about the soundness of an argument. We just have to determine whether the argument is valid.

In fact, we usually don't even have to do that. In Assumption Family questions, the arguments will *never* be valid. If they were, we wouldn't have anything to do. Our task on these questions is to determine *why* they are not valid by identifying what these arguments take for granted. Every assumption represents a gap in the reasoning that must be bridged in order for a conclusion to follow logically from the premise(s).

Let's take a look at a flawed argument:

everyone in the room is wearing a jacket   Jim must be wearing a jacket

2

As we evaluate the logic of this argument core, we want to ask ourselves if the premise, which we accept as true for the purpose of evaluating the argument's reasoning, guarantees the conclusion to be true as well. In this case it doesn't. In fact, the argument rests on a pretty big assumption—it assumes that Jim is one of the people in the room! Notice how the assumption, when inserted into the argument, strengthens the argument:

> Everyone in the room is wearing a jacket. (Jim is a person in the room). THEREFORE, Jim must be wearing a jacket.

The assumption functions as a connecting bridge between the premise and the conclusion. In this case, adding the assumption to the argument makes the argument airtight. This will be true of some, but not all, assumptions, and the difference between those that create an airtight argument and those that don't will become important in later chapters. At this juncture, however, our focus should be on how to spot the assumptions. Sometimes, you might not see the missing piece of an argument right away. Perhaps that was true for you here. So what should you do if an argument seems pretty solid to begin with? How can you improve your chances of spotting the gaps in LR arguments? For the rest of the chapter, we'll work on exactly that. But first, we want to take a quick detour into the land of conditional logic.

Conditional Logic: Part 1

Introduction

Conditional logic is a logical structure that the LSAT tests heavily in Logical Reasoning and Logic Games. Over the course of your preparation for the LSAT, you will have many opportunities to develop your conditional logic skills. In fact, there will be an entire chapter dedicated to conditional logic later on in this book. However, because we will often reference conditional logic before then, we want to take a moment to address some of the basics now.

Conditional Logic in Logical Reasoning

Conditional logic comes up frequently in Logical Reasoning questions. Here's a very simple example to illustrate:

> When Jasmine wakes up early in the morning, she is not productive at work that day. Jasmine woke up early in the morning on Wednesday.

If the above statements are true, which one of the following must also be true?

> (A) If Jasmine was unproductive at work on any particular day, then she must have woken up early that day.

> (B) Jasmine was not productive at work on Wednesday.

This abbreviated Logical Reasoning question contains a conditional relationship. If condition X (waking up early) is met, then condition Y (unproductive at work) is guaranteed. Because we're also told that Jasmine *did* wake up early on Wednesday, we can infer that she was not productive at work on Wednesday. Answer (B) is correct.

But (A) seems like a pretty close match, doesn't it? Answer choice (A) could be true, but then again, it could be false as well. Let's explore the ins and outs of conditional logic in order to see how it could be false.

What Is a Conditional Statement?

Conditional statements have two parts:

1. The Trigger

2. The Outcome

The most common form of a conditional statement uses an If/Then structure, where "if" introduces the trigger and "then" introduces the outcome:

> IF John attends the party, THEN Mary attends as well.

We can express this using an arrow symbol:

$$J \rightarrow M$$

(trigger → outcome)

NOTE: We use an arrow symbol to indicate a conditional relationship, and we also used an arrow symbol to express "therefore" in an argument core. Their meanings are quite different, so note the difference in our notation below:

| If ... then →| Therefore ➡ |

This means that John attending the party (the trigger) is enough to guarantee that Mary will attend as well (the outcome). In other words, John's attendance is sufficient to trigger Mary's attendance. Another way to think of it is that Mary necessarily attends if John attends. You can't have John without Mary. So, we can say that John's attendance is the sufficient condition and Mary's attendance is the necessary condition. In fact, this is the formal way to refer to the two parts of a conditional statement, and the LSAT is nothing if not formal, so get comfortable with this phrasing:

Sufficient Condition: John attends the party. (The trigger is enough, or sufficient, to guarantee the outcome.)

Necessary Condition: Mary attends the party as well. (The outcome necessarily happens when the trigger occurs.)

Conditional Inferences

When you face conditional logic on the LSAT, your primary job will be to figure out what you *can* infer from the given statement(s) and what you *cannot* infer. Take the following example:

If Sally lives in Boston, then Sally lives in Massachusetts. B → M

Given the statement above, consider the following inferences. Which, if any, do you think are valid? Think about them from a commonsense standpoint based on what you know about geography:

1. If Sally does not live in Boston, then Sally does not live in Massachusetts. –B → –M
2. If Sally lives in Massachusetts, then Sally lives in Boston. M → B
3. If Sally does not live in Massachusetts, then Sally does not live in Boston. –M → –B

If you said that the third inference is the only valid inference, you are correct! The first two don't make any sense because Sally could certainly live in a different part of Massachusetts, such as Worcester or Amherst. These two bad moves, which we call illegal reversal and illegal negation, show up time after time on the LSAT. So does that one valid inference, formally known as the contrapositive.

Let's summarize all the statements in notation form:

Original Statement	B → M	
Illegal Negation	–B → –M	Invalid Inference
Illegal Reversal	M → B	Invalid Inference
Contrapositive	–M → –B	Valid Inference

In this example, we can see one of the foundational rules of conditional logic: When you're given a conditional statement, you cannot simply reverse it, nor can you simply negate it, but if you do both, you'll make a valid inference—the contrapositive. What exactly is the contrapositive?

Contrapositive: The reversed and negated version of a given conditional statement.

All other inferences are invalid! Don't be tempted to make any other inferences aside from the contrapositive. Let's practice this. Write down the contrapositive of the following conditional statement:

> If a passenger has no ticket, she cannot board the plane.

We can diagram the original statement like this:

$$-\text{ticket} \quad \rightarrow \quad -\text{board}$$

To get the contrapositive, we reverse and negate:

$$\text{board} \quad \rightarrow \quad \text{ticket}$$

Now, putting that back into English:

> If a passenger can board the plane, she has a ticket.

Revisiting Jasmine

Here's our example from earlier. Take a second now to think about why (A) is NOT a correct answer:

> When Jasmine wakes up early in the morning, she is not productive at work that day. Jasmine woke up early in the morning on Wednesday.
>
> If the above statements are true, which one of the following must also be true?
>
> (A) If Jasmine was unproductive at work on any particular day, then she must have woken up early on that day.
>
> (B) Jasmine was not productive at work on Wednesday.

If you said that (A) illegally reverses the logic, you are correct! The original statement says, "When Jasmine wakes up early in the morning, she is not productive at work that day."

2

We can symbolize this as E → –P.

Answer (A) says, "If Jasmine was unproductive at work on any particular day, then she must have woken up early on that day."

We can symbolize this as: –P → E.

Notice that this is an illegal reversal of the original. Bad inference! Couldn't there be other reasons why she was unproductive at work? Maybe her phone kept ringing. Maybe the fire alarm went off. Maybe she was sick. In any case, we can never make this inference. If we're going to reverse, we have to negate, too!

Read Like a Lawyer

There's a reason that 50% of the LSAT consists of Logical Reasoning. To succeed on these questions, it's important to cultivate the ability to spot logical flaws, inconsistent statements, and loopholes. In other words, you need to start reading like a lawyer!

First off, you need to have the right assumption-finding attitude! It's one part robot and one part detective. Once you have found the core of an argument, get to work! You should get in the habit of robotically repeating a reliable mantra: *I agree that [insert premises], but I'm not convinced that this means [insert conclusion].*

After your mantra, you might follow up with this:

> *You might be right, my good friend, but couldn't it also be that [insert other possible conclusion that could flow from the premises]?*

Or this:

> *The problem is that you simply have not explained how the fact that [premise] establishes that [conclusion]. I think you've forgotten to tell me about the connection between [part of the premise] and [part of the conclusion].*

Let's see how this looks in action.

> Unsuspecting friend: Kamasi Washington is combining the traditions of John Coltrane and Albert Ayler, two greats in jazz history. He'll surely be a jazz superstar.
>
> You: My friend, I agree that Kamasi Washington combines those traditions, but that hardly allows us to conclude that he will be a jazz superstar. You might be right, but it's also possible that the listening public is done with that sort of jazz.

MANHATTAN
PREP

Alternatively, you could have suggested that Washington might not be promoted aggressively enough, that he might not be as talented as Coltrane or Ayler, or that he may abandon jazz tradition for something else that is less appealing to jazz fans.

Let's have you try. Lawyer up and analyze this argument from your colleague:

> Anna: The last 15 measures I presented to the city council were all approved. This was the first time I presented a measure that was opposed by the mayor. That is surely why my latest measure was not approved.

Go ahead and compose your lawyerly reply.

Here's one possibility:

> Anna, I agree that this was the only measure you've presented that was opposed by the mayor, but it doesn't necessarily follow that that was the reason for the measure's rejection. Perhaps this measure was also unpopular among city council members or among the voting public. Also, can you think of any other differences in the circumstances? Did you present the measure in a different way or under different conditions? If there was some other difference, that might explain the outcome, too.

Notice that once again, we're part robot and part detective. We robotically repeat our mantra, but we have to be a bit of a detective to think of other possibilities than the conclusion we've been presented with.

Sometimes you will quickly spot a gap in the argument core. Other times, the gap will be far from obvious. In fact, you might be tempted to ignore your training and conclude that the argument makes no assumptions at all! In those cases, you may have to go into the answer choices with nothing but a general feel for what might knock the argument down. Some strong LSAT test-takers imagine that their job is to advocate for the "anti-conclusion." In the examples above, this would mean thinking about how it could be that Kamasi Washington will NOT be a jazz superstar or how it could be that the mayor's opposition was NOT the reason Anna's measure was rejected. While all we really need is a reason that we don't *have* to accept the conclusion, going in as the attorney for the anti-conclusion can be an easy way to adopt the right sort of attitude toward these arguments. See if this approach works for you.

We'll have plenty of opportunity in the next few chapters to practice reading like a lawyer. Let's start by returning to some of the arguments we've already analyzed and taking a second look at the underlying logic.

Drill It: Reading Like a Lawyer

Here are the cores we identified in the previous drill. Read each of them like a lawyer. Attack the connection between the premise(s) and conclusion. Write your criticism of the argument in the space under each one. Check your thinking against the solutions after each argument.

1. PT7, S1, Q10

60% originally had behavior problems

+

only 30% had behavior problems after decreasing additives in diet

➡️

food additives can contribute to behavior problems in hyperactive children

Notes:

2. PT7, S1, Q20

if Esposito runs, Krasman will not

+

Esposito will run

➡️

Esposito will be the only candidate in the race

Notes:

3. PT7, S4, Q1

in first year after reduction, 15% drop in deaths

+

another 25% drop over next 10 years

➡️

speed limit reduction has saved many lives

Notes:

MANHATTAN
PREP

2

4. PT7, S4, Q13

over half of domestic smoke detectors are without batteries or are inoperative increase in smoke detectors from 30% to 45% does not make home fires any less likely

Notes:

5. PT7, S4, Q2

many important contributions came from research but were never predicted as potential outcomes legislators' position (to refuse to commit to research unless outcomes are assured) ignores lessons of experience

Notes:

6. PT9, S2, Q7

waste management reports increasing percentage of disposable plastics for disposal in landfills and incinerators attempts to decrease amount of plastic people throw away in garbage are failing

Notes:

7. PT9, S2, Q4

deforestation rate is decreasing

+

government spent millions to curb cutting and burning government efforts are proving effective

Notes:

2

8. PT7, S1, Q24

grants require investigators to provide clear outcome projections investigators ignore anything that does not directly bear on the funded research serendipity can no longer play a role

Notes:

9. PT9, S2, Q19

universities should promote free flow and dissemination of ideas

+

universities with right to patent have incentive to suppress information

+

suppressing information is incompatible with obligation to promote free flow of ideas

 universities should not be entitled to patent inventions by faculty

Notes:

10. PT7, S1, Q7

system gives incentive to shift costs to others solutions for reducing costs cannot be found in current system

Notes:

MANHATTAN
PREP

Solutions: Reading Like a Lawyer

1. PT7, S1, Q10

60% originally had behavior problems

+

only 30% had behavior problems after decreasing additives in diet

food additives can contribute to behavior problems in hyperactive children

Were you suspicious about whether this study was performed correctly? There seems to be a lot of missing components (such as a control group), and if an LSAT answer choice pointed that out, it would be correct. The truth is, however, that the LSAT does not often attack the validity of a study. We'll need to dig a little deeper. Assuming that the study was done correctly and the data it provided was accurate, can you spot why the conclusion might still be flawed? Take a moment to consider that now if you didn't the first time around.

We accept that the study found that the percent of children exhibiting the problem behavior dropped from 60% to 30%, but what else other than food additives could have caused the drop? Perhaps those children's behavior would have shifted on its own! Perhaps just being aware of the bad behavior encourages children to behave better. Perhaps children are more likely to misbehave during different times of the year, such as when the opportunity to start a snowball fight presents itself. There are many alternative causes we need to rule out before we an comfortably say that we've proven the argument's conclusion.

2. PT7, S1, Q20

if Esposito runs, Krasman will not

+

Esposito will run

Esposito will be the only candidate in the race

The two premises guarantee that Esposito will run and Krasman will not, but "the only" in the conclusion is suspiciously strong. Is there anything keeping someone else from running? No. The argument is assuming that Krasman and Esposito are the only potential candidates.

3. PT7, S4, Q1

in first year after reduction,
15% drop in deaths

+

another 25% drop over next 10 years

speed limit reduction has
saved many lives

To spot the flaw here, we need to recognize the difference between correlation and causation. We are confident that the rate of deaths has decreased at the same time as the drop in speed limit. Yet can we be certain that the reduction caused the decrease in deaths? No. There are many other possible causes: other laws may have been imposed, cars may be safer, or perhaps people have become better drivers. Correlation never proves causation. We'll explore this kind of reasoning error in depth in Chapter 4.

If you thought that another flaw in this argument is that there is a shift from discussing percents (deaths dropped 15%) to the actual number of lives saved, you're not alone. However, while this sort of shift usually is a problem, in this example, a drop in the percentage of deaths does guarantee a number of lives saved. If the conclusion were about the overall number of deaths decreasing, then the shift from percents to numbers would be an issue, since the total number of drivers may have changed radically. Instead, the conclusion is simply that many lives have been saved.

4. PT7, S4, Q13

over half of domestic smoke detectors
are without batteries or are inoperative

increase in smoke detectors from 30%
to 45% does not make home fires any
less likely

There are numbers in both the premise and conclusion—it seems likely that there's a gap in how they're interpreted. Indeed, even if half of smoke detectors are not functioning, the increase in the percent of homes that have detectors should help prevent fires as long as the fraction of detectors that are not functioning has remained fairly constant. Imagine there are only 100 houses. In the past, 30 had smoke detectors, with only 15 of them working. If the number of houses with detectors climbs to 45, and half of those work—about 22—we should see more fires prevented.

A common real-world concern about this argument is whether smoke detectors actually make home fires less likely. However, that assumption is not relevant to this argument. We aren't evaluating whether smoke detectors *generally* prevent home fires. The argument is about whether the premise that half of the detectors don't function guarantees the conclusion that an increase in the number of smoke detectors has had no effect on fire prevention.

5. PT7, S4, Q2

many important contributions came
from research but were never predicted
as potential outcomes

legislators' position (to refuse to
commit to research unless outcomes
are assured) ignores lessons of
experience

MANHATTAN
PREP

This argument might seem fairly reasonable. The legislators have taken a position that seems to commit them to missing out on certain important discoveries. But look carefully at the conclusion. The author claims that the legislators are *ignoring* the lessons of experience. The legislators might be missing future research discoveries, but it is entirely possible that they're doing so after *considering* the lessons of experience. Maybe they determined that there were too few important discoveries to justify the added expense. Maybe they know that the type of research that leads to surprising discoveries is likely going to be funded by other sources. Without more information about how the legislators arrived at their current position, we can't say that they are ignoring the lessons of experience.

6. PT9, S2, Q7

| waste management reports increasing percentage of disposable plastics for disposal in landfills and incinerators | | attempts to decrease amount of plastic people throw away in garbage are failing |

This is a perfect example of a percent versus amount assumption. The argument concludes that the total *amount* of plastic thrown away has not decreased because plastic is an increasing *percentage* of total trash. Without knowing anything about the total amount of waste being sent to landfills, it's impossible to convert percents to numbers. If people are decreasing the total amount of waste being sent to landfills, then the percent of plastic could increase while the amount of plastic decreases. Here's one possibility:

	Original Amount	**New Amount**
waste (in tons)	100	50
percent plastic	20%	25%
plastic (in tons)	20	12.5

Remember, without knowing the totals, we can't use evidence based on a percent to draw conclusions about an amount.

7. PT9, S2, Q4

deforestation rate is decreasing

+

government spent millions to curb cutting and burning

government efforts are proving effective

Can we be sure the government is actually affecting the deforestation rate? No. Other things might be going on in the world, such as environmental groups stepping in, a lowering demand for the land produced by cutting and burning, or even other governments reaching out. The money may be a factor, or it may not. We can never conclude that correlation proves causation.

8. PT7, S1, Q24

grants require investigators to provide clear outcome projections investigators ignore anything that does not directly bear on the funded research serendipity can no longer play a role

The fact that a researcher is focused on a particular project does not mean she will ignore unexpected findings of that project. The researcher will, according to the premise, propose expected outcomes and then focus on the funded research project, but within that project, serendipity can play a large role. Having an expectation does not preclude finding that the expectation was wrong.

9. PT9, S2, Q19

universities should promote free flow and dissemination of ideas

+

universities with right to patent have incentive to suppress information

+

suppressing information is incompatible with obligation to promote free flow of ideas

 universities should not be entitled to patent inventions by faculty

Based on these premises, we can conclude that universities shouldn't suppress ideas, but we can't say they should not patent inventions. Patents give an incentive to suppress ideas, but we don't know whether that incentive is strong enough to be acted upon. If universities are able to resist the temptation so that there are patents *and* a free flow of ideas, there's no reason not to allow them to patent faculty members' inventions.

Be careful of the language shift here. An incentive or motivation is not the same as a definitive cause-and-effect relationship.

10. PT7, S1, Q7

system gives incentive to shift costs to others solutions for reducing costs cannot be found in current system

The author has spotted what he believes to be a problem with the system, but he never establishes that it is an insurmountable problem. Is it possible to remove those incentives while still keeping the system? Is it possible to reduce costs despite the incentives? We can't tell, so the author goes too far in saying that the system itself makes it impossible to reduce costs.

Conclusion

The topics and steps we introduced here play an important role in the majority of Logical Reasoning questions. Let's review:

1. **Identify the argument core.** Most logical reasoning questions require you to identify the conclusion of an argument and the supporting premise or premises. This is the argument core.

2. **Understand the other elements of an argument.** You should also be able to identify other elements of an argument, such as background information and intermediate conclusions.

3. **Read like a lawyer.** Most Logical Reasoning questions involve arguments that are not valid, meaning the arguments will have gaps or flaws. Once you've identified the argument core, your success will depend on being able to quickly identify the gaps or flaws in the argument.

4. **Become good friends with conditional logic.** Many Logical Reasoning questions involve conditional logic (it also plays an important role in many logic games). Learn the basics now, and be ready to explore some more advanced features of conditional logic later in this book.

Sneak Preview: The Assumption Family

Now that we've developed a lawyer-like eye for spotting weaknesses in arguments, we're ready to use this skill on an entire family of Logical Reasoning questions: the Assumption Family. Any question that requires us to identify missing assumptions in the argument is part of the Assumption Family. Just like a lawyer or law student, we'll be asked to do different things with a spotty argument—attack it, defend it, or simply analyze its weaknesses. We'll be exploring these question types one at a time in the upcoming chapters, but for a moment, let's return to a familiar argument so that you can see how these question types relate to each other:

> *PT7, S1, Q20*
>
> According to sources who can be expected to know, Dr. Maria Esposito is going to run in the mayoral election. But if Dr. Esposito runs, Jerome Krasman will certainly not run against her. Therefore Dr. Esposito will be the only candidate in the election.

We've already found the major flaw in this argument. We know that Esposito will run, and we can infer from this that Krasman won't run, but what about everybody else? Is Krasman the *only* possible candidate other than Esposito? Let's take a look at how our reasoning would play out for a few different Assumption Family question types:

Assumption: Which one of the following is an assumption on which the argument relies?

> No one other than Esposito and Krasman will run in the mayoral election.

Here, we're just stating the missing assumption, as we did in the previous drill. In the next chapter, we'll explore the nuances of Assumption questions.

Flaw: The argument above is most vulnerable to which of the following criticisms?

We already know what's wrong with the argument; we just need to express it in a slightly different way. One way would be to simply *point out* that the argument is making an assumption:

> It takes for granted that Dr. Maria Esposito and Jerome Krasman are the only possible candidates for the upcoming mayoral election.

We might also point out that it's neglecting another possibility:

> It overlooks the possibility that a candidate other than Esposito or Krasman might run for mayor.

We could even address a very specific possibility:

> It overlooks the possibility that Kermit the Frog might run for mayor.

What? There's a flaw in this argument that concerns a lovable nerdy amphibian? Well, yes. If the argument takes for granted that *no one else* will run for mayor, then any other candidate we can imagine represents a possibility that the argument is overlooking. If Kermit *were* planning to run, then we couldn't conclude that Dr. Esposito would be the only candidate.

Weaken: Which one of the following, if true, casts the most doubt on the argument above?

Here, we're looking for something that would weaken the argument, so we'll want to take one of the possibilities from above and say that it *is* happening or that at least it could happen:

> Several other qualified candidates have expressed an interest in running for mayor.

> Kermit the Frog is planning to run for mayor.

> Many citizens other than Esposito and Krasman are well-positioned to run for mayor.

Notice that none of these directly attack the conclusion by saying "Dr. Esposito will not be the only candidate in the election." Certainly, if this were a choice on a Weaken question, it would be the correct answer. However, this kind of answer is simply not going to show up. To weaken an argument, we want to attack the logic (the connection between the premises and the conclusion), not simply say "Nuh-uh!" to the conclusion.

Strengthen: Which one of the following, if true, provides the most support to the argument above?

MANHATTAN
PREP

We're back to supporting the argument, but Strengthen answers can look a bit different from assumptions. For one thing, a Strengthen answer can go further than we might expect from an Assumption answer:

> Only Dr. Maria Esposito and Jerome Krasman are eligible to run for mayor.

We didn't identify this as an assumption because it isn't one! At least, it isn't something that *needs* to be true for the argument to work. Even if others are *eligible,* they might choose not to run for mayor:

> Kermit the Frog will not run for mayor.

> Jerome Krasman is the only other person who is believed to be considering a run for mayor.

These statements certainly leave plenty of room for doubt about the conclusion—maybe Miss Piggy will run for mayor or maybe someone who is not currently believed to be considering a run will end up doing so. However, either of these statements would make the conclusion more likely, if even by just a small amount.

With this frame of mind at the ready, let's get to our topic for the first half of this book: the Assumption Family.

Chapter 3

Assumption Questions

In This Chapter...

Sufficient and Necessary Assumptions

Identifying Assumptions

As we saw briefly at the end of the last chapter, identifying assumptions is a crucial skill in Logical Reasoning. In fact, the majority of LR questions fall into the Assumption Family. With that in mind, let's dive a bit deeper into what assumptions are and how they work. What's the missing assumption in this argument?

it's raining outside it's cold outside

Remember that the argument core arrow means "therefore." It's raining outside. Therefore, it's cold outside. Is our "therefore" arrow justified in this case? No. There's a huge gap in this argument. Can you bridge it? Here's one version:

> If it's raining, then it's cold outside.

We've simply created a conditional (If/Then) statement connecting the premise and the conclusion. If this relationship is true and the premise is true, then the conclusion simply *must* follow! We could also phrase the same information in a different way, such as "It rains only when it's cold outside."

Let's try another:

the mouse is eating it must be hungry

Again, we can link the premise and conclusion with a conditional statement—"If the mouse is eating, it must be hungry"—or we can provide equivalent information, such as "The mouse would not eat if it were not hungry" or "The mouse eats only when it is hungry." (Do those seem equivalent to you? The first is just the contrapositive—remember those from Chapter 2? We'll revisit "only" later in the chapter, but "The mouse eats only when it is hungry" establishes the relationship *mouse eats → mouse is hungry*.)

Now, let's look at a few seriously unconvincing arguments:

> It's Monday. Therefore, it will snow.
>
> Gina will be promoted at work because she uses synthetic motor oil.
>
> Ramesh has two kids, so he must enjoy classical music.

How did you know right away that each argument was a bad one? These arguments probably seem especially bad to you because their conclusions don't have any real-world connection to their supporting premises. We know that there is at least *some* connection between rain and cold and between eating and hunger. But our first two conclusions could certainly be false (maybe there's a nice warm tropical storm and maybe the mouse is just stress-eating). Furthermore, any of these new conclusions could be true (Gina may well be promoted, regardless of her motor oil choices). The latter conclusions just *seem* worse because drawing these conclusions from their premises requires us to accept some very odd assumptions.

What's important here is that in logical terms, all five of the arguments above are equally invalid. We can provide assumptions for our latter arguments just as readily as for the earlier ones: "If it's Monday, it will snow," "Everyone with children likes classical music," etc. When we're reading like a lawyer, we must look for a disconnect between the premise and the conclusion, regardless of our personal opinion of the real-world scenario that the argument describes.

Sufficient and Necessary

The assumptions we've identified so far in this chapter might have struck you more as rewrites of the argument than as assumptions. Can an assumption simply tell us "If premise, then conclusion"? Yes! These are what we might call "perfect" assumptions, because they precisely and completely bridge the gap between premise and conclusion. We can also say that they are both sufficient and necessary. What does this mean?

A **sufficient** assumption is one that *guarantees* the conclusion. Add it to an argument and the conclusion must logically follow.

A **necessary** assumption is one that is *required* in order to reach the conclusion from the premise(s). Without it, the conclusion may be true, but the argument doesn't make sense. For instance, if it isn't necessarily cold outside when it's raining, why are we drawing the conclusion that it is cold?

We'll spend the rest of the chapter identifying assumptions and classifying them as sufficient, necessary, or both.

Necessary Assumptions

The LSAT will often ask you to identify a necessary assumption. You can tell by the way the question is asked:

> Which one of the following is **required** for the argument to hold?

> The argument **depends** on which one of the following assumptions?

> Which one of the following assumptions is **necessary** for the argument to hold?

In each of these cases, the correct answer will be an assumption that is required for the argument to work. However, since we are asked to identify a *necessary* assumption rather than a *sufficient* one, the answer does *not* need to be one that bridges the entire distance between the premise and the conclusion. If it happens to do so, that's fine, but we're not asked to find such an answer.

How can an assumption be necessary but not sufficient? Take a look at this argument core:

> Johnson is successful. Therefore, Johnson is both smart and funny.

The author is assuming that a successful person is also a smart and funny person. If we state this assumption explicitly, it's sufficient to fill the arrow and validate the conclusion. We'll illustrate this with a filled-in arrow between **premise** and conclusion:

MANHATTAN
PREP

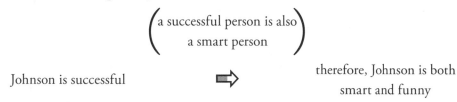

But what if we addressed only the smart part?

> Johnson is successful. (A successful person is also a smart person.) Therefore, Johnson is both smart and funny.

Notice that this assumption is no longer sufficient on its own to validate the conclusion. That is, by itself, this assumption does not provide enough information to justify the conclusion. (How do we know Johnson is funny?) However, it is an assumption that is *necessary* for this particular argument to hold. If this argument is going to make sense, we need to know that a successful person is also a smart person. This assumption fills in part of the gap in the argument. We'll illustrate this with a partially filled-in arrow:

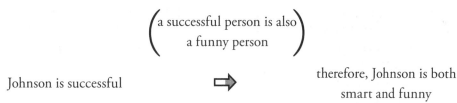

Likewise, if we had just the funny part on its own we'd get only partway to the conclusion (we'd fill the other half of the arrow):

(a successful person is also
a funny person)

Johnson is successful   ⟹   therefore, Johnson is both
                                              smart and funny

Both of these assumptions are *necessary* for the conclusion to follow logically from the premise. Together, they are sufficient to reach the conclusion, but neither one is sufficient on its own.

Premise Boosters

What about this one?

> Johnson runs several profitable businesses.

This certainly seems to support our general line of reasoning, but in what way? It lends credibility to our premise, right? However, if you remember our discussion of premises, you may remember that we always accept the premises as true. When evaluating an argument, the premises are simply taken for granted and so do not need any support. So the statement above represents neither a sufficient nor a necessary assumption. It merely supports a claim that we've already accepted as true—Johnson is successful. We call this type of statement a **premise booster,** and we can eliminate it if we see it in an answer choice.

The Negation Test

How do we tell if an assumption is necessary? Well, we know something is necessary if the argument can't get by without it. In other words, one way we can determine whether an assumption is necessary is to take it away and see how the argument holds up. We call this the **negation test.** Let's apply the negation test to each of the three assumptions we looked at above. Here's the argument one more time:

> Johnson is successful. Therefore, Johnson is both smart and funny.

And here are the three assumptions we considered, along with their negated forms:

Assumption	Negated Assumption
A successful person is also a smart person.	A successful person is NOT a smart person.
A successful person is also a funny person.	A successful person is NOT a funny person.
A successful person is also a smart and funny person.	A successful person is NOT a smart and funny person.

If we insert the first one into the argument core, we get this:

> Johnson is successful. (A successful person is NOT a smart person.) Therefore, Johnson is both smart and funny.

What do you think? Good argument? Of course not! The negated assumption completely destroys the argument—there is no bridge from the premises to the conclusion. When the original assumption is not true (when it's negated), the argument doesn't work. This means that the original assumption is required, or necessary, for the argument to hold.

In the same vein, the negated version of the second assumption would destroy the argument as well. Thus, the second assumption is also required. Let's try the negation of the third assumption:

> Johnson is successful. (A successful person is NOT a smart and funny person.) Therefore, Johnson is both smart and funny.

This one destroys the argument as well! So, that means the original version of the third assumption is required for the argument to hold. Remember, this assumption was also *sufficient* to bridge the entire distance between the premise and the conclusion. Thus, we can say that this assumption is both *necessary* for the argument to hold and *sufficient* on its own for the argument to hold. Here's a summary of what we've discovered:

Assumption	Necessary?	Sufficient?
A successful person is also a smart person.	Yes	No
A successful person is also a funny person.	Yes	No
A successful person is also a smart and funny person.	Yes	Yes

So, we can see that an assumption can be both sufficient and necessary or it can be necessary without being sufficient. (If you're wondering about assumptions that are sufficient but not necessary, we'll get to those soon.) The negation test tells us only whether a statement is necessary, but since that's such a common task, it's useful to practice a bit.

So far, we've negated statements by adding a big NOT to them. Sometimes that is all that is needed, but negating is often more complex than that. Remembering that our task is to state that the original proposition is not true, how would you negate this statement?

> Sasha always walks to the store.

You might try negating this by saying, "Sasha **never** walks to the store." Certainly, if this is right, then it's not true that she always walks to the store. But can you reason in the other direction? If you know it's not true that she always walks to the store, does that mean she *never* walks there? No, she might walk to the store most of the time but drive when she's in a hurry. Would that contradict the original statement that she always walks? Sure. You don't need to go all the way to "never" to negate the statement. There's a crucial difference between negating a statement and stating the opposite. So in this case, the negation would read as follows:

> Sasha DOES NOT always walk to the store.

Here, the "DOES NOT" applies to the word "always." It's not true that Sasha *always* walks.

Now try negating this:

> Some New Yorkers are very friendly.

You might respond to this with an opposing statement: "Some New Yorkers are not friendly at all." If you have had a hard time in the city, you might refute this with a bitter "No New Yorker is very friendly." Which serves as an accurate negation? Remember that our job is to negate, to provide a sentence that states the original to be untrue. If some New Yorkers are not friendly, does that mean it isn't true that some *are* friendly? Not necessarily. Some could be very friendly and some not at all. There's no contradiction there. Our job is to establish the statement as false, so we'll need to go all the way to "No New Yorker is very friendly."

For negating modifiers such as "some," it helps to get a strong technical sense of their meaning. "Some" doesn't give us a precise quantity—it basically just means "one or more" or "not none." So to negate "some," we substitute "no" or "none." In general, if we see a modifier such as "always" or "some," we look at what happens when that modifier is not correct. Try to fill in the rest of the table below:

Modifier	Logical Negation
always	not always
some	no/none
all	
never	

neither ... nor	
not always	
no/none	
not all	
sometimes	
either ... or	

Solutions

Modifier	Logical Negation
always	not always
some	no/none
all	not all
never	sometimes
neither ... nor	either ... or
not always	always
no/none	some
not all	all
sometimes	never
either ... or	neither ... nor

Notice any interesting patterns? First, negations work in both directions. The negation of "never" is "sometimes" and the negation of "sometimes" is "never." Also, it's useful to notice that extreme modifiers are generally negated with wishy-washy ones and vice versa. So, the negation of "always" is just "not always," but the negation of "sometimes" is "never." Let's practice statement negation.

Drill It: Negating Statements

Negate each of the following. For many of the statements, there are multiple correct answers. See if you can come up with more than one.

1. Our manager is a strong leader.

2. All of us are with you.

3. Some dogs are vicious.

4. Federico can't run far.

5. Most of these apples are rotten.

6. Not all of the pots are ready.

7. None of the actors is in the union.

8. John is probably the tallest.

9. It is unlikely that Simone will come.

10. Lisa never apologizes.

11. The prettiest houses are always painted white.

12. Harun sometimes eats pie.

13. Toni lives without water or electricity.

14. People who suffer from migraines sometimes feel better simply by drinking water.

15. There have been many instances in which the team has proven itself to be honorable.

16. Frank sometimes fails to clean up after his dog.

17. Alejandra is responsible and easy-going.

Solutions: Negating Statements

Note that there are often multiple ways to state a negation.

1. Our manager is a strong leader.

> Our manager is not a strong leader.

When no modifying terms are added, we can usually negate by simply adding (or removing) a "not."

2. All of us are with you.

> Not all of us are with you.
> Some of us are not with you.

3. Some dogs are vicious.

> No dog is vicious.
> All dogs are not vicious.

4. Federico can't run far.

> Federico can run far.

5. Most of these apples are rotten.

> Half or fewer of these apples are rotten.
> At least half of these apples are not rotten.

Where did this come from? Why didn't we just say, "Most of these apples are not rotten"? Well, "most" simply means "more than half." If we jump to "most are not," we're neglecting the possibility of a 50-50 split, so we have to interpret "not most" as half or less.

6. Not all of the pots are ready.

> All of the pots are ready.

7. None of the actors are in the union.

> Some of the actors are in the union.
> Not all of the actors are out of the union.

8. John is probably the tallest.

> It is not likely that John is the tallest.

"Probably" means that the chance is greater than 50%. What's the negation? 50% or less. We don't want to go all the way to "probably not," which means less than 50%.

9. It is unlikely that Simone will come.

> It is not unlikely that Simone will come.

As in the last one, we don't want to go all the way to the opposite: likely.

10. Lisa never apologizes.

> Lisa sometimes apologizes.

11. The prettiest houses are always painted white.

> The prettiest houses are not always painted white.
> Some of the prettiest houses are not painted white.

12. Harun sometimes eats pie.

> Harun never eats pie.
> Harun does not eat pie.

13. Toni lives with neither water nor electricity.

> Toni doesn't live with neither water nor electricity.

Aah! Too many negatives!

> Toni lives with either water or electricity, or both.

She may have both, but we know that if she doesn't live without them both, she has at least one.

14. People who suffer from migraines sometimes feel better simply by drinking water.

    People who suffer from migraines never feel better simply by drinking water.

15. There have been many instances in which the team has proven itself to be honorable.

    There have not been many instances in which the team has proven itself to be honorable.

16. Frank sometimes fails to clean up after his dog.

    Frank never fails to clean up after his dog.
    Frank always cleans up after his dog.

The first one is a double negative. If he never fails, then he always cleans up.

17. Alejandra is both responsible and easy-going.

    Alejandra isn't both responsible and easy-going.
    Alejandra is either irresponsible, not easy-going, or not both.

We don't want to say that she is neither *responsible nor easy-going. We just want to say that she's not* both. *She certainly could be neither, but we don't need that for the negation.*

Bridge and Defender Assumptions

Consider the following argument:

> Tea is known to be high in antioxidant compounds called polyphenols. Therefore, drinking tea on a daily basis can help to prevent illness.

The conclusion introduces several new concepts that we know nothing about. (Drinking? Daily? Prevent illness?) How can we identify the assumptions that underlie these concepts? It might help to notice that necessary assumptions tend to fall into two broad categories: **bridge assumptions** and **defender assumptions.** A bridge assumption helps the argument by connecting the premise to the new information in the conclusion. A defender assumption helps the argument by eliminating a potential objection to the conclusion. Let's see what these look like in action:

Bridge:

1. Polyphenols help to prevent illness.

2. Polyphenols work effectively when consumed daily.

Defender:

1. Tea is still high in polyphenols when prepared as a beverage.

2. The polyphenols in tea are not destroyed in the digestive process.

3. Drinking tea on a daily basis does not have any effects that make one more likely to become ill.

Bridge assumptions will typically be fairly predictable—they simply help us to see how something in the premise connects to the conclusion. These are usually the first assumptions we think of, and in a simple argument, a bridge assumption may be both sufficient and necessary, as we saw at the beginning of the chapter. However, more often, one assumption will not be sufficient to get us all the way to the conclusion on its own, since an argument can have multiple holes in its reasoning. For instance, if we know that polyphenols work effectively when consumed daily, it helps bridge the gap to the conclusion that tea helps to prevent illness, but this information by itself doesn't fill the arrow all the way. We still don't know anything about the connection between polyphenols and illness. If we add the other bridging assumption we listed—"polyphenols help to prevent illness"—the argument starts looking better, but even with both of these bridges in place, it's not perfect. One way to see that is to look at our defender assumptions.

The defender assumptions we've listed work to cover an important gap in the argument that we have not yet filled. We can't simply equate drinking tea, which contains polyphenols, with having those polyphenols in the body. While these assumptions are a bit less predictable, they also answer potential objections: "What if all the polyphenols are left behind in the tea leaves?" "What if tea has other ingredients that make you *more* likely to get sick?" Addressing these issues—defending the argument against them—is almost never going to lead us to a sufficient assumption, but ensuring that these objections aren't valid is *necessary* in order to reach the conclusion.

It's important to note that there may be significant overlap between bridge and defender assumptions, and even our instructors don't always agree on the categorization of a particular assumption. In fact, one can often be rewritten in the other form. For instance, we can change bridge 2 to a defender: "Polyphenols don't need to be consumed hourly to work effectively." We could also phrase our bridge assumptions strongly enough to counter many potential objections. For instance, if we said, "Any substance high in polyphenols helps to prevent illness when consumed," most of our objections would fly out the window, although we'd still need defender 1.

The point, in the end, is not to correctly categorize every assumption as a bridge or a defender. Some assumptions may look like both, depending on your perspective. We're presenting you with these categories to enrich your thinking about assumptions. In some cases, we'll definitely expect one of the two types of assumptions in the answer choices. For instance, in a very abstract argument, we are more likely to expect a bridge assumption. Take a look:

> Some legal marketing strategies are highly deceptive. Thus, we cannot expect to be protected from all forms of harmful behavior by the government.

In this case, we can find assumptions simply by looking at the switches in terminology. Are highly deceptive strategies a form of harmful behavior? If something is legal, does that mean the government won't protect us from it? We can turn these questions directly into bridge assumptions:

> Highly deceptive marketing strategies are harmful to consumers.

> The government can protect citizens from harm only by outlawing harmful forms of behavior.

We *could* still see a defender assumption. For instance, we might imagine some other way the government could protect us and negate that:

> The government cannot protect citizens from harmful but legal behavior through programs of character education.

Character education? That's certainly a new idea to defend the argument against. Defender assumptions often introduce a new idea that may seem unrelated to the argument if we're not thinking about that idea's *implications* for the argument.

Let's take a look at a different argument:

> Kai loves pizza. Therefore, he is sure to accept our invitation to take him out for pizza tomorrow at lunch.

Here, we can brainstorm plenty of reasons for Kai to decline our invitation. Maybe he's busy tomorrow at lunch. Maybe he doesn't like us. Maybe he's very picky about his pizza and only eats at certain restaurants that meet his standards. Maybe he loves pizza only for breakfast, after it's had a chance to refrigerate overnight.

What will be less likely here is a bridge assumption, especially for a Necessary Assumption question. We can get a sufficient assumption with a simple If/Then, but there aren't a lot of tricky issues to bridge. The right answer is more likely to be a defender, perhaps using an objection that we'd be unlikely to think of. Would you say this is a necessary assumption?

> Kai won't decline our invitation out of fear of the laser-toting aliens that own all the pizza restaurants in our city.

Is this assumption really necessary? Well, try negating it. If Kai *will* decline our invitation—for this reason or any other—then our argument falls apart. The LSAT sometimes generates necessary assumptions simply by saying that some unexpected obstacle *won't* happen. With that in mind, some of us think of defender assumptions as "alien" assumptions.

Conditional Logic: Part 2

Recap

So far, we've seen how to translate If/Then statements into conditional logic. We've looked at the one logical inference we can draw from a conditional (the contrapositive), as well as two common wrong moves to watch out for.

Example:

> If Awad is busy, he will not go to the concert.

Original Statement	$B \rightarrow -C$	
Illegal Negation	$-B \rightarrow C$	Invalid Inference
Illegal Reversal	$-C \rightarrow B$	Invalid Inference
Contrapositive	$C \rightarrow -B$	Valid Inference

Let's get a little more conditional logic practice while adding an important word to our conditional toolkit. As we progress through the book, we'll start using these conditional logic skills to work through the reasoning in tricky problems.

MANHATTAN
PREP

Only If

From "If" to "Only If"

The word "only" could be the single most important word on the LSAT. It shows up all over the place. In the Logical Reasoning section of the exam, "only" is often a conditional logic trigger. To see how it comes into play, consider the following conditional statement:

>   Marcus wears a jacket if it is raining outside.

This is a pretty simple conditional relationship:

>   raining → Marcus wears a jacket

In other words, the rain is enough, or *sufficient,* to trigger Marcus wearing a jacket. Anytime it rains, Marcus wears a jacket. We know by now that the reverse is *not* necessarily true: If Marcus wears a jacket, that doesn't necessarily mean that it is raining. Maybe he's wearing a jacket because it's cold out. Or, maybe he's wearing a jacket because he's trying it on for size.

Now, let's consider a slightly different statement:

>   Marcus wears a jacket *only if* it is raining outside.

Which one of the following is a correct interpretation of this new statement?

>   (A) If Marcus wears a Jacket, then it is raining outside. (J → R)
>   (B) If it is raining outside, then Marcus wears a jacket. (R → J)

(A) is correct.

We know that Marcus wears a jacket *only* when it rains outside, so he can't wear a jacket under any other circumstance. Thus, *if* he is wearing a jacket, *then* we know for certain it must be raining! (J → R)

(B) is incorrect.

Yes, Marcus wears a jacket *only when* it is raining (and no other time), but not necessarily *every* time it rains. R does not guarantee J.

Let's review:

Marcus wears a jacket *if* it is raining outside. (R → J)
Marcus wears a jacket *only if* it is raining outside. (J → R)

So, "only if" establishes the reverse relationship of "if." Note that replacing the word "if" with "when" establishes the same relationship:

Marcus wears a jacket *when* it is raining outside. (R → J)
Marcus wears a jacket *only when* it is raining outside. (J → R)

MANHATTAN
PREP

Drill It: Only If

Choose all of the answer choices that are logically equivalent to the given statement. Keep in mind that there may be more than one correct answer for each question (or no correct answer at all!). Check your answers after each exercise.

Example (bold answers are correct):

If B, then A.

(A)   B only if A.

(B)   If A, then B.

(C)   If not B, then not A.

(D)   If not A, then not B. (The contrapositive!)

1. If Janet goes to the party, then Bill goes to the party.

  (A)   If Janet does not go to the party, then Bill does not go.

  (B)   Janet goes to the party only if Bill goes.

  (C)   Bill goes to the party only if Janet goes.

  (D)   If Bill does not go to the party, then Janet does not go.

2. The play is popular if ticket sales exceed 100.

  (A)   Ticket sales for the play exceed 100 only if the play is popular.

  (B)   Only if the play is popular do ticket sales for the play exceed 100.

  (C)   If ticket sales exceed 100, then the play is popular.

  (D)   If the play is not popular, then ticket sales do not exceed 100.

3. Only if the car is new is it in good shape.

  (A)   The car is in good shape if, and only if, it is new.

  (B)   The car is new if, and only if, it is in good shape.

  (C)   If the car is in good shape, then it is new.

  (D)   If the car is new, then it is in good shape.

4. Only the good die young.

  (A)   good → die young

  (B)   –good → –die young

  (C)   One who dies young is good.

  (D)   One who is not good never dies young.

Solutions: Only If

1. If Janet goes to the party, then Bill goes to the party.

    (A) If Janet does not go to the party, then Bill does not go.
    (B) Janet goes to the party only if Bill goes.
    (C) Bill goes to the party only if Janet goes.
    (D) If Bill does not go to the party, then Janet does not go.

2. The play is popular if ticket sales exceed 100.

    (A) Ticket sales for the play exceed 100 only if the play is popular.
    (B) Only if the play is popular do ticket sales for the play exceed 100.
    (C) If ticket sales exceed 100, then the play is popular.
    (D) If the play is not popular, then ticket sales do not exceed 100.

3. Only if the car is new is it in good shape.

    (A) The car is in good shape if, and only if, it is new.
    (B) The car is new if, and only if, it is in good shape.
    (C) If the car is in good shape, then it is new.
    (D) If the car is new, then it is in good shape.

4. Only the good die young. (There's no "if" here, but we can read this the same way: Only if we are good do we die young.)

    (A) good → die young (Be careful. Only the good die young, but that doesn't mean ALL good people die young.)
    (B) –good → –die young
    (C) One who dies young is good.
    (D) One who is not good never dies young.

Sufficient? Necessary?

You now have the background needed to understand the nuances of difficult Assumption questions. You know that a sufficient assumption bridges the entire distance between the premise and the conclusion. A sufficient assumption is *enough,* on its own, to validate the conclusion. It fills the entire arrow. You know that a necessary assumption is *required* for the argument to hold, but may not be sufficient on its own for the argument to hold. A necessary assumption generally fills only part of the arrow.

Here's another example:

> The sweater costs $40. Thus, Ramon has enough money in his wallet to buy the sweater.

In concluding that Ramon has enough money in his wallet to buy the sweater, we are certainly making some assumptions. Take a second and think about this argument. Before reading on, see if you can do the following:

1. Write a sufficient assumption for this argument—one that would fill the entire arrow and allow the conclusion to be logically drawn:

2. Write a necessary assumption for this argument—one that is required for the argument to hold but does not necessarily bridge the entire distance:

Okay, now that you've thought about it and come up with your own ideas, let's discuss a sufficient assumption.

A sufficient assumption is anything that puts at least $40 in Ramon's wallet:

$$\left(\begin{array}{c} \text{Ramon has \$50 in} \\ \text{his wallet} \end{array} \right)$$

the sweater costs $40   ➡   Ramon has enough money in his wallet to buy the sweater

Seems logical, right? This assumption is sufficient to arrive at the conclusion. But is it necessary? No. How do we know? Negate it. Ramon does NOT have $50 in his wallet. The negated assumption does not destroy the argument (maybe he has $45 in his wallet), so the assumption is not necessary for the conclusion to hold. This assumption is sufficient but not necessary. Now, let's come up with an assumption that isn't sufficient but is necessary:

Ramon has at least $20 in his wallet.

In order to afford the sweater, Ramon *must* have at least $20 in his wallet. How do we know that this is necessary? Negate it. Ramon does NOT have at least $20 in his wallet. In that case, there's no way he has $40, so the argument is destroyed. This assumption is necessary, or required, for the argument to hold. That said, it's certainly not *sufficient* on its own to validate the conclusion. Knowing that he has at least $20 doesn't guarantee that he can buy the $40 sweater.

Let's look at a couple more variations. What do you think of the assumption we've added below? Is it necessary? Is it sufficient?

Ramon has at least $40 in his wallet.

If you said it's sufficient, you're right. Knowing that he has at least $40 is *enough* to guarantee that he has enough in his wallet to buy the $40 sweater. But is this assumption necessary for the conclusion to hold? Yes, it is necessary as well! How do we know? Negate it:

The sweater costs $40. (Ramon does NOT have at least $40 in his wallet.) Ramon has enough money in his wallet to buy the sweater.

The negated assumption destroys the argument, which means it's necessary. Let's try one last one. Consider this assumption:

Ramon has exactly $40 in his wallet.

This assumption is clearly sufficient, but is it necessary? You should know what to do at this point—go ahead and negate it. If Ramon does NOT have exactly $40, does this destroy the conclusion that he has enough to buy the sweater? No! He could have $41 or $49 or $120 in his wallet. He also might have only $27, but since we don't know what he has, we can't say that the negated assumption *destroys* the argument, so this assumption is not required. We don't need to know that Ramon has *exactly* $40. So, this assumption is sufficient to guarantee the conclusion, but it's not necessary to arrive at the conclusion.

When an LSAT question asks for a sufficient assumption, often the answer will provide enough information to arrive at the conclusion, but more information than is necessary to arrive at the conclusion. In a sense, the assumption is more than sufficient. We can think of the arrow as being overfilled:

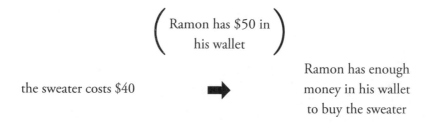

the sweater costs $40   ➡   Ramon has enough
                                           money in his wallet
                                           to buy the sweater

We'll try putting all this together on a full question after a brief procedural interlude…

MANHATTAN
PREP

Wrong-to-Right

If you've taken even one practice LSAT, you already know how easy it is to fall for trap answers. The LSAT writers are great at creating answer choices that include some version of what we expect, but are twisted in a way that makes them wrong. That is why better test-takers work wrong-to-right. This is essentially the process of elimination, but we prefer the term wrong-to-right because it emphasizes that we're actively deferring judgment on any answer that looks plausible until we've knocked off the answers that must be wrong.

When making your first pass through the answers, if you see an answer that could be correct, do not spend time proving its correctness. Instead, defer judgment, moving on quickly to examine the other answers. Spending time on a correct-seeming answer during your first pass might cause you to develop a bias against the other answer choices. You will have a tendency to want to prove to yourself that other answers are wrong rather than give each a fair shake. You need to think critically about every answer choice and focus first on eliminating ones that are definitely incorrect.

If you defer on one answer choice and confidently eliminate the other four, you don't need to make a deep examination of the remaining choice. Select it as the correct answer and move on. If you're left with two appealing choices, that's the time to slow down and compare the answers to the core (not to each other).

Also, remember that you can always come back to a tricky question at the end of the section if you have time. On the digital LSAT interface, you can use the "flag" feature to mark questions you hope to return to. When practicing in this book or with a paper test, you can draw a flag or put a star next to a question. In either case, be sure to select an answer the first time you attempt the question, just in case you don't have time to come back to it.

With that in mind, tackle this next question, working wrong-to-right.

3

Newspaper editor:　Law enforcement experts, as well as most citizens, have finally come to recognize that legal prohibitions against gambling all share a common flaw: no matter how diligent the effort, the laws are impossible to enforce. Ethical qualms notwithstanding, when a law fails to be effective, it should not be a law. That is why there should be no legal prohibition against gambling.

Which one of the following, if assumed, allows the argument's conclusion to be properly drawn?

(A)　No effective law is unenforceable.

(B)　All enforceable laws are effective.

(C)　No legal prohibitions against gambling are enforceable.

(D)　Most citizens must agree with a law for the law to be effective.

(E)　Most citizens must agree with a law for the law to be enforceable.

The language in the question stem ("allows the argument's conclusion to be properly drawn") indicates that this question is asking for a sufficient assumption. Our answer, on its own, needs to be enough to validate the conclusion. As with any Assumption Family question, we need to start by finding the argument core. If you didn't find the core the first time, go back now and be sure to do so before reading on.

The argument starts by citing an apparently widely held opinion: Prohibitions on gambling are impossible to enforce. Since the author seems to accept this widely held opinion, let's grant it as a premise. In other words, it's not an *assumption* that the popular view—gambling laws are unenforceable—is correct. That's an initial premise of the argument. This is followed up with a conditional premise: If a law is not effective, it should not be a law. From this, the author concludes that there should be no legal prohibition against gambling. Notice that the two premises are complementary—together, they are meant to lead to the conclusion:

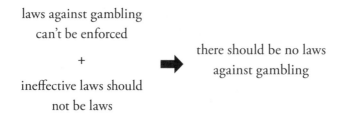

So, how well do they work together? If laws against gambling can't be enforced, and if ineffective laws should not be laws, does this mean there should be no gambling laws? Hopefully, you see the term shift here. Who says that laws that can't be enforced are ineffective laws? It might seem sensible to assume this, but it is nonetheless an assumption.

So, is this assumption sufficient? Does it fill the entire gap?

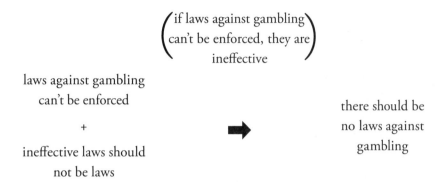

This looks like a winner! We can now link from the first premise all the way to the conclusion with conditional logic:

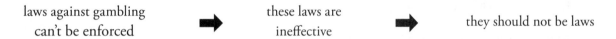

Let's see if we can find something similar to this assumption in our answer choices

    (A)   No effective law is unenforceable.

This isn't what we anticipated, but it does seem to link effectiveness with enforceability. In cases like this, it's best to defer and take another look once we've swept through all the answer choices.

    (B)   All enforceable laws are effective.

Again, keep it for now.

    (C)   No legal prohibitions against gambling are enforceable.

This restates the premise. We already granted that legal prohibitions against gambling can't be enforced. This is a premise booster. Eliminate it! (Notice that even if we didn't realize that this was already a premise, it would be a necessary assumption only. The argument would fail without it, but it doesn't fill the gap between enforceability and effectiveness.)

    (D)   Most citizens must agree with a law for the law to be effective.

The argument core isn't about whether citizen agreement makes laws effective, but rather if unenforceability makes a law ineffective. Out of scope. Eliminate it.

(E)   Most citizens must agree with a law for the law to be enforceable.

This has a similar problem to (D). Besides, we already know the laws are unenforceable, so this doesn't do anything for us.

So we're down to (A) and (B), but neither looks like our anticipated assumption. Remember, our anticipated assumption looked like this:

> If laws against gambling can't be enforced, they are ineffective.

We can think of our assumption in conditional terms:

> gambling laws unenforceable → gambling laws ineffective

Let's look at (A) again:

(A)   No effective law is unenforceable.

We can write this in conditional form as well. It's basically saying that if a law is effective, then it must be enforceable:

> effective law → enforceable law

We know from Chapter 2 that we can take the contrapositive of this by reversing and negating the terms:

> unenforceable law → ineffective law

This looks a lot like our initial assumption! Note that this assumption is sufficient, and then some. It's certainly enough to guarantee the conclusion, but we don't *need* to know that every single unenforceable law in the universe is ineffective. Simply knowing that unenforceable *gambling* laws in particular are ineffective would have been enough. It's the difference between saying that Ramon has at least $40 in his wallet and saying that Ramon has $50 in his wallet. The first is sufficient and necessary; the second is certainly sufficient, but is more than necessary. Since we're simply looking for a sufficient assumption, either flavor of sufficient assumption will do. Thus, (A) is the correct answer.

Let's look at the other attractive answer choice:

(B)   All enforceable laws are effective.

This can be translated to:

> enforceable law → effective law

This is an illegal negation of the assumption we're looking for. If we take the contrapositive, we'll get this:

> ineffective law → unenforceable law

This doesn't take us from our premise to our conclusion. Don't fall for it!

MANHATTAN
PREP

So this was a good example of a Sufficient Assumption question on which the answer is *more* than we need to bridge the gap. The correct answer is sufficient but not necessary. Let's work this territory with one more question:

<u>PT22, S4, Q22</u>

Dinosaur expert: Some paleontologists have claimed that birds are descendants of a group of dinosaurs called dromeosaurs. They appeal to the fossil record, which indicates that dromeosaurs have characteristics more similar to birds than do most dinosaurs. But there is a fatal flaw in their argument; the earliest bird fossils that have been discovered date back tens of millions of years farther than the oldest known dromeosaur fossils. Thus, the paleontologists' claim is false.

The expert's argument depends on assuming which one of the following?

(A)   Having similar characteristics is not a sign that types of animals are evolutionarily related.

(B)   Dromeosaurs and birds could have common ancestors.

(C)   Knowledge of dromeosaur fossils and the earliest bird fossils is complete.

(D)   Known fossils indicate the relative dates of origin of birds and dromeosaurs.

(E)   Dromeosaurs are dissimilar to birds in many significant ways.

When we see "depends on," what are we looking for? A necessary assumption. Let's break down the core.

We start with "Some paleontologists have claimed," which is a good indicator of an opposing point. If the dinosaur expert is attributing a view to some other group, the expert's view is going to be something else. The opposing point is even followed by support (an opposing premise). Then we get to "But"—a sign that we're now going to move in the other direction! The expert gives a premise that seems to spell trouble for the opposing argument and finally lands on the conclusion: The paleontologists' claim is false! When we think of the core, we can use the negated version of that claim as our conclusion. What's false? The idea that birds are descended from dromeosaurs.

the earliest known bird fossils date
back to tens of millions of years further
than the oldest known dromeosaur
fossils

birds did *not* descend from
dromeosaurs

Do you see any issues with this argument core? It doesn't seem *too* bad, right? If birds came before dromeosaurs, they might have had a common ancestor, but birds couldn't have *descended* from dromeosaurs. However, we have the advantage of knowing that there *has* to be a hole in this argument, so we can look again. Is this really what the argument says? No. The premise tells us only about the *earliest known* fossils. We don't actually know how long birds and dromeosaurs have been around. Maybe there are earlier dromeosaur fossils that we haven't yet discovered.

So how would we phrase this as a necessary assumption? *The expert is assuming that dromeosaurs didn't exist significantly earlier than the earliest known dromeosaur fossils.* Let's see if we can find something like that in the answer choices:

   (A)   Having similar characteristics is not a sign that types of animals are evolutionarily related.

This is interesting, in that it seems to support the conclusion that birds did not descend from dromeosaurs. But is it a necessary assumption? No, because it doesn't work with the argument core at all—it just attacks the evidence used by some paleontologists. The expert isn't disputing this, so (A) is not needed here. If we weren't sure, we could apply the negation test: *Having similar characteristics IS a sign that types of animals are evolutionarily related.* Can the argument hold up with this in place? Sure, because this doesn't address whether birds are actually descended from dromeosaurs. If the argument were that dromeosaurs and birds had no relationship, this might qualify as a necessary assumption, but for this argument we can eliminate (A).

   (B)   Dromeosaurs and birds could have common ancestors.

Again, the expert isn't making any larger points about the family tree—just that birds didn't descend from dromeosaurs. Eliminate it.

   (C)   Knowledge of dromeosaur fossils and the earliest bird fossils is complete.

Interesting. If knowledge of dromeosaur fossils and bird fossils is complete, then we know that the current fossil record is accurate and that birds could not have descended from dromeosaurs. This is very similar to what we anticipated. Keep it for now.

   (D)   Known fossils indicate the relative dates of origin of birds and dromeosaurs.

This seems to help as well. If known fossils indicate the relative dates of origin of birds and dromeosaurs, then we'd know that birds could not have descended from dromeosaurs, and we could conclude that the paleontologists are wrong. Keep it for now.

   (E)   Dromeosaurs are dissimilar to birds in many significant ways.

We don't need this, because it doesn't help us to bridge the gap between the fossil evidence and the conclusion that birds did not descend from dinosaurs. The negated form of (E) doesn't destroy the argument—so what if birds and dinosaurs *didn't* have lots of significant differences? Or, going all the way to the opposite: So what if they were similar? They still could be unrelated. Eliminate it.

So we're left with two answers, (C) and (D). Let's take a closer look, and let's be sure to keep in mind what our task is: Find a *necessary* assumption!

> (C) Knowledge of dromeosaur fossils and the earliest bird fossils is complete.

This choice is very helpful, but is it *necessary?* If knowledge of these fossils were complete, we'd know that birds came first and the author's conclusion would have to be correct. But what if knowledge of the fossils wasn't complete? Couldn't it be okay for the argument if there were a few fossils that we haven't found, as long as they would all tell us the same thing? This assumption is not necessary. (We just applied the negation test? Did you notice? Over time, you may start to do it unconsciously!)

In fact, as we saw above, this answer would be sufficient to guarantee the conclusion. In terms of our earlier example, it's like knowing Ramon has $100 in his wallet. We know he can buy the sweater, but it's more than we need. Sufficient but not necessary? It's out. Let's take another look at (D).

> (D) Known fossils indicate the relative dates of origin of birds and dromeosaurs.

This is really what we were trying to get at up front. The fossil record already tells us what we need to know—that birds were around before dromeosaurs. If we negate this—known fossils do NOT indicate the relative dates of origin of birds and dromeosaurs—it means we don't have the dates of origin correct, and therefore the conclusion comes into doubt. That means (D) is a necessary assumption. We have our answer.

To review, we've just looked at a question that seemed to have two perfectly good answer choices. The thing is, answer (C) would be the correct answer to a *Sufficient* Assumption question, not a Necessary Assumption question. Knowing your task is crucial.

Drill It: Sufficient? Necessary?

For each of the following exercises, you will be presented with an argument, two question prompts (numbered 1 and 2), and a series of answer choices. Next to each answer choice, write a "1" if the answer is a correct answer for question prompt 1, write a "2" if the answer is a correct answer for question prompt 2, write a "1" and a "2" if it's a correct answer for both prompts, and write an "X" if it is not a correct answer for either. This drill is tough, so think carefully!

Example:

The sweater costs $40. Thus, Ramon has enough money in his wallet to buy the sweater.

(1) The argument above depends on assuming which one of the following?

(2) Which of the following assumptions allows the conclusion above to be properly drawn?

___X___ Ramon has enough money in his wallet to buy a pair of jeans.

___1___ Ramon has at least $10 in his wallet.

___1, 2___ Ramon has at least $40 in his wallet.

___2___ Ramon has $50 in his wallet.

___X___ Ramon has less than $35 in his wallet.

___2___ Ramon has exactly $40 in his wallet.

1. Studies have shown that private tutoring is an effective approach for learning a second language. Thus, private tutoring is a fun way to learn a second language.

(1) Which of the following is an assumption that is required in order for the argument to hold?
(2) The conclusion follows logically if which of the following is assumed?

_____ Anything that is an effective approach for accomplishing a goal is also a fun approach for accomplishing that goal.

_____ The studies mentioned were conducted by a team of reputable linguists.

_____ Some activities that are effective are also fun.

2. Of the 25 movies released this year, only the three highest rated movies ("first" being the highest rating) of the year will be eligible for the award. Therefore, the movie *Darkness* will not be eligible for the award.

(1) Which of the following is an assumption upon which the argument relies?
(2) The conclusion can be properly drawn if which of the following is assumed?

_____ Of the 25 movies released this year, *Darkness* was the lowest rated movie.

_____ Of the 25 movies released this year, *Darkness* was rated fourth or worse.

_____ Many of the people who saw *Darkness* did not enjoy it.

_____ Of the 25 movies released this year, *Darkness* was not rated second.

MANHATTAN
PREP

3. The monthly revenue for Chad's Burger Shack was higher in July than it was in April. Thus, Chad's Burger Shack must have sold more burgers in July than in April.

(1) Which of the following is an assumption upon which the argument depends?
(2) The conclusion follows logically if which of the following is assumed?

____ Chad's Burger Shack is gaining popularity.

____ In the summer months, people tend to dine out more frequently than they do at other times of the year.

____ The difference in revenue between April and July was not due solely to an increase in beverage sales.

____ A third-party audit verified that the monthly revenue for Chad's Burger Shack was higher in July than it was in April.

____ The difference in revenue between April and July was due solely to an increase in the sales price of a Chad's Burger Shack burger.

____ Total costs for Chad's Burger Shack were not lower in July than they were in April.

____ For any restaurant, any difference in revenue from month to month can be explained by a difference in the number of burgers sold.

4. Maria must be a person who values faith because she attends church every Sunday.

(1) Which of the following is an assumption upon which the argument relies?
(2) The conclusion can be properly drawn if which of the following is assumed?

____ Anyone who attends church every Sunday is a person who values faith, family, and community.

____ There are no Sundays on which Maria is unable to attend church.

____ Maria never gets bored when she is attending church services.

____ If Maria attends church every Sunday, then she is a person who values faith.

5. An automatic bell above the front door rings whenever a customer enters the front door of the Town Convenience Store. Therefore, one can accurately determine the number of customers who enter Town Convenience on any given day simply by counting the number of rings from the front door bell.

(1) The argument depends on which of the following assumptions?
(2) The conclusion follows logically if which of the following is assumed?

____ The bell rings each time a customer leaves the store through the front door.

____ The bell does not ring when employees enter the store.

____ The bell never fails to ring when a customer enters the front door of the store.

____ On any given day, there are customers who visit the Town Convenience Store.

Solutions: Sufficient? Necessary?

1. Studies have shown that private tutoring is an effective approach for learning a second language. Thus, private tutoring is a fun way to learn a second language.

(1) Which of the following is an assumption that is required in order for the argument to hold?
(2) The conclusion follows logically if which of the following is assumed?

___2___ Anything that is an effective approach for accomplishing a goal is also a fun approach for accomplishing that goal.

This is enough to validate the conclusion, and more. We don't need to assume that *anything* that is effective is also fun. This is sufficient, but not necessary.

___X___ The studies mentioned were conducted by a team of reputable linguists.

This is a premise booster! We already know that studies have shown that private tutoring is an effective way to learn a second language. We don't need to support the premise, and we certainly don't need to assume that the study was conducted by linguists. Wouldn't it be okay if the study were conducted by social scientists?

___1___ Some activities that are effective are also fun.

This answer might seem too weak to be relevant, but try negating it. *No activity that is effective is also fun.* If that were the case, how could one conclude that tutoring is fun?

2. Of the 25 movies released this year, only the three highest rated movies ("first" being the highest rating) of the year will be eligible for the award. Therefore, the movie *Darkness* will not be eligible for the award.

(1) Which of the following is an assumption upon which the argument relies?
(2) The conclusion can be properly drawn if which of the following is assumed?

___2___ Of the 25 movies released this year, *Darkness* was the lowest rated movie.

If it's the lowest rated, we know for sure that it's not getting an award. Sufficient. But do we *need* it to be the *lowest* rated? No. Anywhere from 4th to 25th would suffice.

___1, 2___ Of the 25 movies released this year, *Darkness* was rated fourth or worse.

This has to be true for the conclusion to hold, so this is necessary. It's also sufficient to know that *Darkness* is not getting an award.

___X___ Many of the people who saw *Darkness* did not enjoy it.

Who cares if many people didn't enjoy it? This tells us nothing about the rating.

___1___ Of the 25 movies released this year, *Darkness* was not rated second.

We need this to be true in order for the conclusion to hold. We can tell by negating it: *Darkness* WAS rated second. This negation would destroy the argument, which means the original assumption is required. Is this assumption sufficient? No. Knowing that it was not rated second doesn't eliminate the possibility that it was rated first or third.

MANHATTAN
PREP

3. The monthly revenue for Chad's Burger Shack was higher in July than it was in April. Thus, Chad's Burger Shack must have sold more burgers in July than in April.

(1) Which of the following is an assumption upon which the argument depends?
(2) The conclusion follows logically if which of the following is assumed?

__X__ Chad's Burger Shack is gaining popularity.

This might help us explain why the shack had higher revenues in July, but it doesn't help us determine if more burgers were sold.

__X__ In the summer months, people tend to dine out more frequently than they do at other times of the year.

Again, this might help us explain why the shack had higher revenues in July, but we're not interested in explaining the premise, except to determine whether the increase was due to an increase in burger sales. This doesn't help.

__1__ The difference in revenue between April and July was not due solely to an increase in beverage sales.

This is a necessary assumption. Try negating it: The increase WAS due solely to an increase in beverage sales. If this is the case, then the increase was NOT due to an increase in burger sales! The negated assumption destroys the argument. Note that this assumption on its own is not enough to guarantee the conclusion. Perhaps there's still another explanation for the increased revenue, such as higher prices or an increase in t-shirt sales, or both.

__X__ A third-party audit verified that the monthly revenue for Chad's Burger Shack was higher in July than it was in April.

We certainly don't need to boost the premise in this way.

__X__ The difference in revenue between April and July was due solely to an increase in the sales price of a Chad's Burger Shack burger.

Careful! This says the increase WAS due solely to an increase in the sales price of the burgers. If this were the case, then we would know that the *number* of burgers sold was NOT the cause of the increase in revenue. By providing an alternate explanation for the increase, this assumption does the exact opposite of what we want. It weakens the argument.

__X__ Total costs for Chad's Burger shack were not lower in July than they were in April.

This is irrelevant. Costs have nothing to do with revenue.

__2__ For any restaurant, any difference in revenue from month to month can be explained by a difference in the number of burgers sold.

This may be far-fetched, but it's certainly enough to guarantee that the increase at Chad's was due to the number of burgers sold. While it's sufficient to guarantee the conclusion, it's certainly not necessary to assume that this is the case for *any* restaurant.

4. Maria must be a person who values faith because she attends church every Sunday.

(1) Which of the following is an assumption upon which the argument relies?
(2) The conclusion can be properly drawn if which of the following is assumed?

___2___ Anyone who attends church every Sunday is a person who values faith, family, and community.

Sufficient! If anyone who attends church every Sunday values faith, family, and community, then Maria attending church every Sunday guarantees that she values faith. We don't *need* to assume that this is the case for *anyone,* or that anyone who attends church every Sunday values family and community in addition to faith, but it's certainly enough.

___X___ There are no Sundays on which Maria is unable to attend church.

We already know this to be true. She attends church every Sunday. No need to boost the premise.

___X___ Maria never gets bored when she is attending church services.

Irrelevant. We don't know that those who are faithful don't get bored.

__1, 2__ If Maria attends church every Sunday, then she is a person who values faith.

This is both necessary and sufficient. It allows us to draw the conclusion, but if we negate the answer, the argument falls apart.

5. An automatic bell above the front door rings whenever a customer enters the front door of the Town Convenience Store. Therefore, one can accurately determine the number of customers who enter Town Convenience on any given day simply by counting the number of rings from the front door bell.

(1) The argument depends on which of the following assumptions?
(2) The conclusion follows logically if which of the following is assumed?

___X___ The bell rings each time a customer leaves the store through the front door.

This hurts the argument! If the bell rings when customers leave, then our counting would get messed up. We need to assume that the bell does NOT ring when customers leave. This assumption does the exact opposite of what we want.

___1___ The bell does not ring when employees enter the store.

We need this to be true. We can negate it to be sure: The bell DOES ring when employees enter. This would mess up our counting of customers, right? The negation destroys the argument, so the assumption is necessary.

___X___ The bell never fails to ring when a customer enters the front door of the store.

Premise booster! We already know this to be true. The passage tells us, "An automatic bell above the front door rings whenever a customer enters the front door of the Town Convenience Store."

___X___ On any given day, there are customers who visit the Town Convenience Store.

We don't need to assume that customers visit the store. All we care about is counting them when they do come.

Conclusion

We've examined two types of assumptions that appear in Logical Reasoning questions: sufficient assumptions and necessary assumptions. Here are important points to remember:

1. **Recognize the difference between sufficient assumptions and necessary assumptions.** Some questions will require you to specifically identify one type or the other.

2. **Practice using the negation test.** This test will allow you to determine whether an assumption is necessary.

3. **Understand how assumptions can act as bridges or defenders in arguments.** While the LSAT will not specifically ask you to identify an assumption as a bridge or defender, understanding these concepts can help you spot the assumptions in an argument and anticipate the correct answer choice.

4. **Work from wrong-to-right.** When you first look at answer choices, you aren't trying to spot the correct answer. Your goal is to eliminate clearly incorrect answers. Defer judgment on any answers that do not immediately seem wrong. Then, go back and evaluate the remaining answers.

Drill It: Assumption Questions

Let's practice with a set of Assumption questions. For this drill, and in most every other one in this book, we don't recommend that you time yourself. The pressure of a timed set is not useful when you're trying to implement something you've just learned. Apply timing pressure with the sets you should be doing in addition to reading this book.

1. PT22, S2, Q1

Braille is a method of producing text by means of raised dots that can be read by touch. A recent development in technology will allow flat computer screens to be made of a material that can be heated in patterns that replicate the patterns used in braille. Since the thermal device will utilize the same symbol system as braille, it follows that anyone who is accustomed to reading braille can easily adapt to the use of this electronic system.

Which one of the following is an assumption on which the conclusion depends?

(A)   Braille is the only symbol system that can be readily adapted for use with the new thermal screen.

(B)   Only people who currently use braille as their sole medium for reading text will have the capacity to adapt to the use of the thermal screen.

(C)   People with the tactile ability to discriminate symbols in braille have an ability to discriminate similar patterns on a flat heated surface.

(D)   Some symbol systems encode a piece of text by using dots that replicate the shape of letters of the alphabet.

(E)   Eventually it will be possible to train people to read braille by first training them in the use of the thermal screen.

2. PT33, S1, Q13

Ethicist: Studies have documented the capacity of placebos to reduce pain in patients who believe that they are receiving beneficial drugs. Some doctors say that they administer placebos because medically effective treatment reinforced by the placebo effect sometimes helps patients recover faster than good treatment alone. But administering placebos is nonetheless ethically questionable, for even if a placebo benefits a patient, a doctor might, for example, have prescribed it just to give the patient satisfaction that something was being done.

The ethicist's argument depends on which one of the following assumptions?

(A)   A patient's psychological satisfaction is not a consideration in administering medical treatment.

(B)   The motivation for administering a placebo can be relevant to the ethical justification for doing so.

(C)   Medical treatment that relies on the placebo effect alone is ethically indefensible.

(D)   The pain relief produced by the placebo effect justifies the deception involved in administering a placebo.

(E)   Administering a placebo is not ethically justified if that treatment is not prescribed by a doctor.

_3. PT11, S2, Q22_

Oil company representative: We spent more money on cleaning the otters affected by our recent oil spill than has been spent on any previous marine mammal rescue project. This shows our concern for the environment.

Environmentalist: You have no such concern. Your real concern is evident in your admission to the press that news photographs of oil-covered otters would be particularly damaging to your public image, which plays an important role in your level of sales.

The environmentalist's conclusion would be properly drawn if it were true that the

(A)   oil company cannot have more than one motive for cleaning the otters affected by the oil spill

(B)   otter population in the area of the oil spill could not have survived without the cleaning project

(C)   oil company has always shown a high regard for its profits in choosing its courses of action

(D)   government would have spent the money to clean the otters if the oil company had not agreed to do it

(E)   oil company's efforts toward cleaning the affected otters have been more successful than have such efforts in previous projects to clean up oil spills

_4. PT17, S3, Q14_

Many artists claim that art critics find it is easier to write about art that they dislike than to write about art that they like. Whether or not this hypothesis is correct, most art criticism is devoted to art works that fail to satisfy the critic. Hence it follows that most art criticism is devoted to works other than the greatest works of art.

The conclusion above is properly drawn if which one of the following is assumed?

(A)   No art critic enjoys writing about art works that he or she dislikes intensely.

(B)   All art critics find it difficult to discover art works that truly satisfy them.

(C)   A work of art that receives extensive critical attention can thereby become more widely known than it otherwise would have been.

(D)   The greatest works of art are never recognized as such until long after the time of their creation.

(E)   The greatest works of art are works that inevitably satisfy all critics.

3

_5. PT30, S2, Q11_

Teacher to a student: You agree that it is bad to
    break promises. But when we speak to each
    other we all make an implicit promise to tell
    the truth, and lying is the breaking of that
    promise. So even if you promised Jeanne that
    you would tell me she is home sick, you should
    not tell me that, if you know that she is well.

Which one of the following is an assumption on
which the teacher's argument depends?

(A)   Most people always tell the truth.

(B)   It is sometimes better to act in a friend's best
        interests than to keep a promise to that
        friend.

(C)   Breaking a promise leads to worse
        consequences than does telling a lie.

(D)   Some implicit promises are worse to break
        than some explicit ones.

(E)   One should never break a promise.

_6. PT33, S3, Q21_

Some government economists view their home
countries as immune to outside influence. But
economies are always open systems; international
trade significantly affects prices and wages. Just as
physicists learned the shortcomings of a mechanics
based on idealizations such as the postulation of
perfectly frictionless bodies, government economists
must look beyond national borders if their nations'
economies are to prosper.

The argument's conclusion follows logically if which
one of the following is assumed?

(A)   A national economy cannot prosper unless
        every significant influence on it has been
        examined by that nation's government
        economists.

(B)   Economics is weakly analogous to the
        physical sciences.

(C)   Economic theories relying on idealizations are
        generally less accurate than economic
        theories that do not rely on idealizations.

(D)   International trade is the primary significant
        variable influencing prices and wages.

(E)   Some government economists have been
        ignoring the effects of international trade on
        prices and wages.

MANHATTAN
PREP

7. PT30, S2, Q15

During the recent economic downturn, banks contributed to the decline by loaning less money. Prior to the downturn, regulatory standards for loanmaking by banks were tightened. Clearly, therefore, banks will lend more money if those standards are relaxed.

The argument assumes that

(A)   the downturn did not cause a significant decrease in the total amount of money on deposit with banks which is the source of funds for banks to lend

(B)   the imposition of the tighter regulatory standards was not a cause of the economic downturn

(C)   the reason for tightening the regulatory standards was not arbitrary

(D)   no economic downturn is accompanied by a significant decrease in the amount of money loaned out by banks to individual borrowers and to businesses

(E)   no relaxation of standards for loanmaking by banks would compensate for the effects of the downturn

8. PT29, S1, Q20

The price of a full-fare coach ticket from Toronto to Dallas on Breezeway Airlines is the same today as it was a year ago, if inflation is taken into account by calculating prices in constant dollars. However, today 90 percent of the Toronto-to-Dallas coach tickets that Breezeway sells are discount tickets and only 10 percent are full-fare tickets, whereas a year ago half were discount tickets and half were full-fare tickets. Therefore, on average, people pay less today in constant dollars for a Breezeway Toronto-to-Dallas coach ticket than they did a year ago.

Which one of the following, if assumed, would allow the conclusion above to be properly drawn?

(A)   A Toronto-to-Dallas full-fare coach ticket on Breezeway Airlines provides ticket-holders with a lower level of service today than such a ticket provided a year ago.

(B)   A Toronto-to-Dallas discount coach ticket on Breezeway Airlines costs about the same amount in constant dollars today as it did a year ago.

(C)   All full-fare coach tickets on Breezeway Airlines cost the same in constant dollars as they did a year ago.

(D)   The average number of coach passengers per flight that Breezeway Airlines carries from Toronto to Dallas today is higher than the average number per flight a year ago.

(E)   The criteria that Breezeway Airlines uses for permitting passengers to buy discount coach tickets on the Toronto-to-Dallas route are different today than they were a year ago.

3

Some people have been promoting a new herbal mixture as a remedy for the common cold. The mixture contains, among other things, extracts of the plants purple coneflower and goldenseal. A cold sufferer, skeptical of the claim that the mixture is an effective cold remedy, argued, "Suppose that the mixture were an effective cold remedy. Since most people with colds wish to recover quickly, it follows that almost everybody with a cold would be using it. Therefore, since there are many people who have colds but do not use the mixture, it is obviously not effective."

Each of the following is an assumption required by the skeptical cold sufferer's argument EXCEPT:

(A)   Enough of the mixture is produced to provide the required doses to almost everybody with a cold.

(B)   The mixture does not have side effects severe enough to make many people who have colds avoid using it.

(C)   The mixture is powerful enough to prevent almost everybody who uses it from contracting any further colds.

(D)   The mixture is widely enough known that almost everybody with a cold is aware of it.

(E)   There are no effective cold remedies available that many people who have colds prefer to the mixture.

MANHATTAN
PREP

_10. PT33, S1, Q19_

Historian: The spread of literacy informs more people of injustices and, in the right circumstances, leads to increased capacity to distinguish true reformers from mere opportunists. However, widespread literacy invariably emerges before any comprehensive system of general education; thus, in the interim, the populace is vulnerable to clever demagogues calling for change. Consequently, some relatively benign regimes may ironically be toppled by their own "enlightened" move to increase literacy.

Which one of the following is an assumption on which the historian's argument depends?

(A)   A demagogue can never enlist the public support necessary to topple an existing regime unless a comprehensive system of general education is in place.

(B)   Without literacy there can be no general awareness of the injustice in a society.

(C)   Any comprehensive system of general education will tend to preserve the authority of benign regimes.

(D)   A lack of general education affects the ability to differentiate between legitimate and illegitimate calls for reform.

(E)   Any benign regime that fails to provide comprehensive general education will be toppled by a clever demagogue.

Solutions: Assumption Questions

Answer Key

1. C   6. A
2. B   7. A
3. A   8. B
4. E   9. C
5. D   10. D

1. PT22, S2, Q1

Braille is a method of producing text by means of raised dots that can be read by touch. A recent development in technology will allow flat computer screens to be made of a material that can be heated in patterns that replicate the patterns used in braille. Since the thermal device will utilize the same symbol system as braille, it follows that anyone who is accustomed to reading braille can easily adapt to the use of this electronic system.

Which one of the following is an assumption on which the conclusion depends?

(A)   Braille is the only symbol system that can be readily adapted for use with the new thermal screen.

(B)   Only people who currently use braille as their sole medium for reading text will have the capacity to adapt to the use of the thermal screen.

(C)   People with the tactile ability to discriminate symbols in braille have an ability to discriminate similar patterns on a flat heated surface.

(D)   Some symbol systems encode a piece of text by using dots that replicate the shape of letters of the alphabet.

(E)   Eventually it will be possible to train people to read braille by first training them in the use of the thermal screen.

Answer choice (C) is correct.

heated dot braille uses same patterns as raised dot braille those who can read braille will easily adapt to reading heated dots

There are many possible objections to defend against here, and while you may not have predicted the one in (C), it makes sense to expect a defender assumption here. Unless something goes wrong, the conclusion seems fairly well connected to the premise. So what could go wrong? Maybe our fingers can't distinguish small heated areas as precisely as small raised areas. (Maybe the whole area would just feel hot.) Or maybe learning to read heated flat dots is just a lot different from learning to read traditional braille. Maybe our brains are much better at translating raised dots into language than translating heated dots. Perhaps learning to read in one manner even "blocks" our ability to learn in another. As we can see, there are plenty of situations that would make this transfer a problem, so we can expect that the answer will eliminate one of these possibilities—our answer is likely to be a defender.

(A) has a problem. There is no need for braille to be the *only* system that can be adapted in order for *this* particular adaptation to work. (If we negate this—braille is NOT the only system that can be adapted—it does nothing to hurt the argument.) Another way of thinking about this is that it's unclear how braille being the only possible system would help defend the argument against attack. Even if no other system can be adapted, this particular adaption might be hard for braille users to adjust to.

(B) actually places limitations on the usefulness of the new system by saying that only certain people will be able to adapt, so it certainly isn't necessary for the argument to work. If we negate this, it helps the argument! Notice that both this and (A) used the word "only" to limit the possibilities of the technology described. The word "only" is a red flag here, as in most

MANHATTAN
PREP

arguments in which we are proposing that something *will* work. The word "only" is better for showing that something will *not* work, because it places limitations on what is possible.

(D) is out of scope. We're not concerned with what other systems do. The argument is entirely about braille.

(E) is interesting, and it does seem to support the effectiveness of the new system. After all, if it will be usable for training, it must work! However, while this answer choice (unlike all the other incorrect choices) does at least help our argument, it isn't necessary. The argument is that people who can already read braille will be able to adapt easily to the heated dots. If we negate this answer—it's NOT possible to learn braille this way—it doesn't hurt the argument that people who already know braille will be able to adapt.

Bravo if you arrived at (C) without using the negation test and instead just eliminated the four rather sorry answer choices above; you're working from wrong-to-right. But it's good to practice the negation test during your review, as it's a great tool, especially when you are down to two attractive answers. Let's practice it: If we negate (C)—people with the tactile ability to discriminate symbols in braille do NOT have an ability to discriminate similar patterns on a flat heated surface—how can we conclude that these readers will be able to easily adapt? We can't. Negating (C) destroys the argument, and therefore we know that (C) is a necessary assumption for this argument.

2. PT33, S1, Q13

Ethicist: Studies have documented the capacity of placebos to reduce pain in patients who believe that they are receiving beneficial drugs. Some doctors say that they administer placebos because medically effective treatment reinforced by the placebo effect sometimes helps patients recover faster than good treatment alone. But administering placebos is nonetheless ethically questionable, for even if a placebo benefits a patient, a doctor might, for example, have prescribed it just to give the patient satisfaction that something was being done.

The ethicist's argument depends on which one of the following assumptions?

(A)   A patient's psychological satisfaction is not a consideration in administering medical treatment.

(B)   The motivation for administering a placebo can be relevant to the ethical justification for doing so.

(C)   Medical treatment that relies on the placebo effect alone is ethically indefensible.

(D)   The pain relief produced by the placebo effect justifies the deception involved in administering a placebo.

(E)   Administering a placebo is not ethically justified if that treatment is not prescribed by a doctor.

Answer choice (B) is correct.

We're asked to find a necessary assumption for this fairly long, and very detailed, argument. When it is a challenge to identify the core, it is generally helpful to start by identifying the conclusion. In this case, the LSAT has put the conclusion in its favorite hiding place—right in the middle of the argument! The conclusion takes the form of an opinion (administering placebos is ethically questionable) that is followed by support (a doctor might have prescribed the placebo just to give satisfaction). This might be a bit hard to spot, because the premise indicator "for" is actually followed by what looks like an opposing consideration ("even if a placebo benefits a patient"). Furthermore, *everything* that comes before the conclusion is an opposing point! The core is basically the last sentence of the argument:

> Doctors might prescribe placebos just to satisfy the patient that something is being done. So administering placebos is ethically questionable.

If you don't find this argument compelling, you have plenty of company! First, how do we know what is ethically questionable? Any time the conclusion introduces a new idea like this, we can spot a necessary assumption. Second, even if we know that this particular behavior (prescribing just for assurance) is bad, how do we know that it's a more important consideration than the potential benefits the argument describes? The author is assuming that the presence of one concern outweighs the benefits enough to make the practice ethically questionable.

Let's take a run through the answers:

(A) and (B) both seem worth considering. They both seem to be addressing what is worth looking at in deciding whether a treatment is justified. Let's defer on these and take a look at the rest.

(C) is tempting, but not necessary. We don't need to know anything about prescribing the placebo effect *alone*, especially since the argument specifically discusses the use of placebos in conjunction with "medically effective treatment." Further, this answer is too extreme. The author concludes that administering placebos is merely "questionable," not "indefensible." If we negate this—"Medical treatment that relies on the placebo effect alone *is ethically defensible*"—the conclusion can still hold. The treatment can be defensible, but still questionable. When looking for necessary assumptions, watch out for answer choices that go too far. These may

be helpful when we get to Strengthen questions, but "too much" is by definition not necessary.

(D) is the opposite of what we want—it might actually weaken the conclusion. If the deception is justified, why would the placebo be ethically questionable?

(E) tries, like (C), to take one specific case and say that it's definitely wrong. However, once again the answer steps out of scope (aren't we talking about prescriptions by doctors?) and goes too far (we just need "ethically questionable," not "not ethically justified").

Back to (A). On second thought, "considerations" is pretty vague. We're interested in ethics! Let's apply the negation test and get rid of the "not": A patient's psychological satisfaction IS a consideration in administering medical treatment. Does this disrupt the argument and its conclusion that administering a placebo may be ethically questionable? No! This actually boosts the author's premise that a doctor might prescribe a placebo just to provide assurance, and it definitely doesn't tell us whether the practice is ethically questionable. Besides, even if the patient's feelings are an ethical consideration, other considerations may be more important.

(B) gives us the ethical connection we need. If we negate it—the motivation for administering a placebo is NOT relevant to the ethical justification for doing so—the argument falls apart. The only supporting premise the author provides has to do with doctors' possible motivation for prescribing placebos. If that's not ethically relevant, then we have zero connection between premise and conclusion.

MANHATTAN
PREP

3. PT11, S2, Q22

Oil company representative: We spent more money on cleaning the otters affected by our recent oil spill than has been spent on any previous marine mammal rescue project. This shows our concern for the environment.

Environmentalist: You have no such concern. Your real concern is evident in your admission to the press that news photographs of oil-covered otters would be particularly damaging to your public image, which plays an important role in your level of sales.

The environmentalist's conclusion would be properly drawn if it were true that the

(A)   oil company cannot have more than one motive for cleaning the otters affected by the oil spill

(B)   otter population in the area of the oil spill could not have survived without the cleaning project

(C)   oil company has always shown a high regard for its profits in choosing its courses of action

(D)   government would have spent the money to clean the otters if the oil company had not agreed to do it

(E)   oil company's efforts toward cleaning the affected otters have been more successful than have such efforts in previous projects to clean up oil spills

Answer choice (A) is correct.

Did you recognize this as a Sufficient Assumption question? The words "properly drawn" help, but not by themselves. Here, we have "would be properly drawn if," which tells us that granting the answer choice should make the argument valid. (If the question had been phrased, "The environmentalist's conclusion would be properly drawn only if it were true that the," we'd be looking at a Necessary Assumption question.) First, let's take a look at the argument core and see if we can find the gap.

| oil co. concerned about bad publicity from oil-covered otters | ➡ | oil co. does not have concern for environment |

This argument would be valid if we added one more word to the premise: "oil co. concerned *only* about bad publicity from oil-covered otters." If we knew that, then we could logically infer that the company is not concerned about anything else—the environment, politics, the meaning of life, or even good old profits. This would be a very extreme statement! So what are we looking for in an answer choice? Something that assures us that if the company cares about bad publicity, then that's the *only* reason it has for helping the otters. We'd like an answer choice that lets us add that "*only*" to the premise. (A) gives us just what we want by saying that the company cannot have more than one motive. This means that if publicity is the motive, the company can't also be motivated by a concern for the environment. We have a winner right away, but let's confirm that the other choices are *not* sufficient.

(B) is out of scope. It doesn't tell us anything about the company's concerns.

(C) might go along with what the environmentalist is saying. If the company is usually focused on profits, then maybe it isn't acting out of concern for the environment. But at best, this is a premise booster. We already know that the company is motivated by something other than concern; the question is whether it can have more than one motive. This seems to say that it can. Even if we assume that publicity is valued because of its impact on profits (we don't actually know this!), this simply replaces the existing premise (the company is concerned with publicity) with a new one (the company is concerned with profits). We still have no idea whether the company cares about the environment.

(D) and (E) are out of scope. Knowing that the company didn't *need* to spend the money, or that the project went well, tells us nothing about the company's concerns or motivations in funding the cleanup.

Looking back, we can see that only (A) and (C) tell us anything about the company's motivations, and only (A) tells us something *exclusive* about those motivations. In other words, only (A) allows us to use knowledge of one motivation to rule out another.

4. PT17, S3, Q14

Many artists claim that art critics find it is easier to write about art that they dislike than to write about art that they like. Whether or not this hypothesis is correct, most art criticism is devoted to art works that fail to satisfy the critic. Hence it follows that most art criticism is devoted to works other than the greatest works of art.

The conclusion above is properly drawn if which one of the following is assumed?

(A)   No art critic enjoys writing about art works that he or she dislikes intensely.

(B)   All art critics find it difficult to discover art works that truly satisfy them.

(C)   A work of art that receives extensive critical attention can thereby become more widely known than it otherwise would have been.

(D)   The greatest works of art are never recognized as such until long after the time of their creation.

(E)   The greatest works of art are works that inevitably satisfy all critics.

Answer choice (E) is correct.

This problem is a great example of how narrowing our focus to an argument's core makes it much easier to evaluate answer choices. In this case, the author starts with an opposing point ("Many artists claim…") and then blatantly tells us that it doesn't matter whether this claim is correct. What does that tell us? The actual argument core must be elsewhere, and there's not much

room left! The author immediately presents a premise ("Most art criticism is devoted to art works that fail to satisfy the critic") and draws a conclusion, indicated by the nice keyword "Hence." So, ignoring the first half, which deals only with the opposing point, we have this core:

most art criticism is about art that fails to satisfy the critic	➡	most art criticism is about works that are not the greatest

At this point, we have a nice clean mismatch between the premise and conclusion. The premise is about satisfying the critic and the conclusion is about "the greatest." So what's the author assuming? That works that don't satisfy the critic are not the greatest. Since this is a Sufficient Assumption question, we need to find an answer that *guarantees* the conclusion. In conditional terms, it needs to tell us *not satisfy the critic* → *not the greatest*. Let's do a quick scan of the answers and eliminate anything that doesn't make this connection.

(A) through (C) don't mention the greatest works of art at all, so there is no way they can be sufficient to guarantee the conclusion.

(D) mentions great works of art, but it fails to link to the premise! *When* the greatest works of art are recognized as such is not relevant to the reasoning in this argument.

We're left with (E), the sufficient assumption we've been looking for all our lives! The words may not be in the same order, but the logic is the same. We can diagram the statement this way: *greatest work of art* → *satisfy all critics*. What's the contrapositive? ***not satisfy all critics*** → ***not greatest work of art***. This is exactly what we anticipated. In a Necessary Assumption question, we might have worried that the word "inevitably" was too extreme, but here that's exactly what we want. Conditionals need to hold true 100% of the time, so extreme language is just what we want in this case.

MANHATTAN
PREP

5. PT30, S2, Q11

Teacher to a student: You agree that it is bad to
    break promises. But when we speak to each
    other we all make an implicit promise to tell
    the truth, and lying is the breaking of that
    promise. So even if you promised Jeanne that
    you would tell me she is homesick, you should
    not tell me that, if you know that she is well.

Which one of the following is an assumption on
which the teacher's argument depends?

(A)   Most people always tell the truth.

(B)   It is sometimes better to act in a friend's best
       interests than to keep a promise to that
       friend.

(C)   Breaking a promise leads to worse
       consequences than does telling a lie.

(D)   Some implicit promises are worse to break
       than some explicit ones.

(E)   One should never break a promise.

Answer choice (D) is correct.

there is an implicit promise to tell the truth when speaking to another + it is bad to break a promise	→	you should not lie about J being home sick, even if you promised to do so

This argument is a mess of conditionals and abstract
generalizations! Perhaps you found yourself rereading
it several times in frustration. Where should we begin?
With the conclusion! It might be helpful to notice
here that the conclusion makes a recommendation—
you should not tell this particular lie. Whenever an
argument starts saying what *should* be done, we can
start reading like a lawyer! What support does the
teacher have for the idea that the student shouldn't lie?
Apparently, lying involves breaking an implicit promise.
But hold on—didn't the student promise Jeanne to

tell this lie? Why is one promise more important than
another? We need an assumption that helps us to
establish that this implicit promise to the teacher takes
precedence. Maybe it's more important to keep promises
to adults or authority figures, or maybe if you promise
to lie or to break some other promise, you don't need to
follow through.

At this point, we might make a quick sweep over the
answer choices to see which ones help us to value one
promise over the other. However, since these choices
provide such a great negation workout, let's run the
negation test on all five. Try it on your own before you
read on.

(A) **Half or fewer** of people always tell the truth.

We're not concerned about this. We want to know what
we *should* do, not what everyone else does. ("If everyone
else jumped off a cliff, would you do it, too?")

(B) It is **never** better to act in a friend's best interests
than to keep a promise to that friend.

We don't know what is in Jeanne's best interests, so this
is out of scope.

(C) Breaking a promise **does not** lead to worse
consequences than does telling a lie.

(We don't want to say that it leads to **better**
consequences. That would be the opposite, not a
negation.) If anything, this negation would seem to help
the argument, since it shows that it's not worse to break
a promise. However, we're not concerned with how bad
the consequences are; we just want to know what we
should do.

(D) **No** implicit promises are worse to break than
explicit ones.

Hmm, it's not worse to break implicit promises than
explicit promises? Does that matter? Defer.

(E) One should **sometimes** break a promise.

Well, we had no choice about that. The teacher is asking us to break one promise in order to keep another one. So this *negation* actually seems like a necessary assumption, which would make this choice the opposite of what we want.

So what's going on with (D)? Looking at it again in regular form, it doesn't really tell us what to do, but it does let us know that it *can* be worse to break an implicit promise (like the one to the teacher) than an explicit one (like the one to Jeanne). That certainly doesn't prove the conclusion, but remember that we are looking for a *necessary* assumption. This answer is necessary, because if it's never worse to break the implicit promise, then we have no basis for choosing the teacher's side rather than Jeanne's.

6. PT33, S3, Q21

Some government economists view their home countries as immune to outside influence. But economies are always open systems; international trade significantly affects prices and wages. Just as physicists learned the shortcomings of a mechanics based on idealizations such as the postulation of perfectly frictionless bodies, government economists must look beyond national borders if their nations' economies are to prosper.

The argument's conclusion follows logically if which one of the following is assumed?

(A)   A national economy cannot prosper unless every significant influence on it has been examined by that nation's government economists.

(B)   Economics is weakly analogous to the physical sciences.

(C)   Economic theories relying on idealizations are generally less accurate than economic theories that do not rely on idealizations.

(D)   International trade is the primary significant variable influencing prices and wages.

(E)   Some government economists have been ignoring the effects of international trade on prices and wages.

Answer choice (A) is correct.

This argument uses an analogy to support its point. What should we do with that? Is it a premise? No! The author simply compares the experience of physicists to the current situation for government economists without actually providing additional supporting premises, so we can toss this out! Since the first sentence states the opposing view ("Some economists" think this way, but the author directly contradicts this view), we can cut the whole argument down to one premise and a conclusion:

economies are open systems, affected by international influences		government economists need to look beyond their national borders for their economies to prosper

Interesting. The premise is about the *influences on economies* and the conclusion is about *economists.* Who says economists need to do anything at all? The author seems to think that just because a certain kind of influence exists, we need our government economists to look at it. What if we can prosper without noticing or studying that influence? Or what if someone other than government economists looked at it? Since this is a Sufficient Assumption question, the right answer must make it *absolutely essential* that government economists look at these outside influences. If there's any other way we could prosper, then the conclusion would not logically follow from the premise. Let's knock out the wrong answer choices at lightning speed!

(B) through (D) don't mention government economists. Strike them all!

(E) does mention government economists, but only to say what *some* of them have *not* been doing. This does nothing to establish what they *must* do. (A) had better be good!

MANHATTAN
PREP

(A) states that if a nation's economy is to prosper, the government economists of that nation must examine every significant influence affecting that economy. In other words, *economy prosper → economists examine all significant influences*. Since we learn that economies are affected by international influences, we can amend this to be *economy prosper → economists examine all significant influences including international influences*. This mirrors the argument's conclusion. Sufficient!

7. PT30, S2, Q15

During the recent economic downturn, banks contributed to the decline by loaning less money. Prior to the downturn, regulatory standards for loanmaking by banks were tightened. Clearly, therefore, banks will lend more money if those standards are relaxed.

The argument assumes that

(A)   the downturn did not cause a significant decrease in the total amount of money on deposit with banks which is the source of funds for banks to lend

(B)   the imposition of the tighter regulatory standards was not a cause of the economic downturn

(C)   the reason for tightening the regulatory standards was not arbitrary

(D)   no economic downturn is accompanied by a significant decrease in the amount of money loaned out by banks to individual borrowers and to businesses

(E)   no relaxation of standards for loanmaking by banks would compensate for the effects of the downturn

Answer choice (A) is correct.

The argument starts with what looks a lot like a conclusion: Banks contributed to the decline. How? By lending less money. But then the argument ends

with a conditional prediction that is preceded by *two* conclusion keywords ("Clearly, therefore"). Clearly, therefore, that conditional must be our conclusion: *standards relaxed → banks will lend more*. Why will banks lend more money if standards are relaxed? Because the standards were tightened and then the banks loaned less money. What looked like a conclusion at the beginning turned out to be a premise. Remember, premises can be facts or opinions, and we can only tell for sure what role a statement is playing when we look at the overall context. If the first statement were the conclusion, we'd need to see some support for the idea that banks contributed to the decline, and we don't get anything like that. If the author simply states something without support and uses it as support for a conclusion, it's a premise. So here's our core:

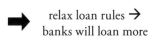

after loan rules tightened, banks loaned less ➡ relax loan rules → banks will loan more

We know that the rules were tightened and banks loaned less, but can we state this as a general rule? Will banks always loan less when the rules are tightened? The author seems to be assuming that one thing caused the other, or at least that the two consistently go together.

But okay, let's say this is a general rule: *tighten rules → less loan activity*. Can we now reach the same conclusion as the author? Well, no. This is a common logical error, one we've already seen in the conditional logic intro in Chapter 2. It's an illegal negation! If we know $A → B$, we can't conclude $-A → -B$. The correct contrapositive would be $-B → -A$. In other words, if we know that tightened rules lead to a decrease in loans, then we know that if loans don't decrease, the rules weren't tightened. We *don't* know that if those rules were relaxed the banks would loan more. To use a simpler analogy, if we know that winning the lottery makes you rich, we can't infer that *not* winning the lottery makes you poor.

So, long story short, we want an answer that helps us to conclude that because we saw one thing follow another (rules were tightened, banks loaned less money), reversing the first thing will reverse the second (relaxing rules will make banks loan more money). Okay, but what should our answer choice actually look like? It's unlikely that it will just give us permission to reverse the laws of logic! If we take a look over the answer choices, they all have something in common: They are negative statements that defend the argument against some possible objection. In other words, they're all defender assumptions. We know that relaxing the rules doesn't guarantee increased lending, so what could go wrong? To defend the conclusion, the right answer should eliminate some source of trouble that might prevent the increase in lending. This is unlikely to be *sufficient* to reach the conclusion, but it will be *necessary*. (Question stems that do not clearly ask for a sufficient or necessary assumption should be treated as Necessary Assumption questions by default.)

Looking through the answers, only (A) and (D) address lending by banks at all. Let's apply the negation test to see which one causes trouble in negated form.

(A) the downturn **did** cause a significant decrease in the total amount of money on deposit with banks which is the source of funds for banks to lend

If banks have less money to lend, they might not be able to increase lending even if the rules are relaxed. This would spell trouble for our argument!

(D) **some** economic downturns are accompanied by a significant decrease in the amount of money loaned out by banks to individual borrowers and to businesses

(Remember that the negation of "none" is "some.") In negated form, this choice appears to support our premise. Since it's not our job to strengthen or weaken the premise, this looks bad already. We might pick on the difference in wording here: The argument is about lending overall, and this is about individuals and businesses. Is there another category of borrower?

Perhaps, but we certainly don't need to know which groups actually experienced the drop in lending. This is an unnecessary comparison. Answer choice (A) is the last answer standing.

8. PT29, S1, Q20

The price of a full-fare coach ticket from Toronto to Dallas on Breezeway Airlines is the same today as it was a year ago, if inflation is taken into account by calculating prices in constant dollars. However, today 90 percent of the Toronto-to-Dallas coach tickets that Breezeway sells are discount tickets and only 10 percent are full-fare tickets, whereas a year ago half were discount tickets and half were full-fare tickets. Therefore, on average, people pay less today in constant dollars for a Breezeway Toronto-to-Dallas coach ticket than they did a year ago.

Which one of the following, if assumed, would allow the conclusion above to be properly drawn?

(A)   A Toronto-to-Dallas full-fare coach ticket on Breezeway Airlines provides ticket-holders with a lower level of service today than such a ticket provided a year ago.

(B)   A Toronto-to-Dallas discount coach ticket on Breezeway Airlines costs about the same amount in constant dollars today as it did a year ago.

(C)   All full-fare coach tickets on Breezeway Airlines cost the same in constant dollars as they did a year ago.

(D)   The average number of coach passengers per flight that Breezeway Airlines carries from Toronto to Dallas today is higher than the average number per flight a year ago.

(E)   The criteria that Breezeway Airlines uses for permitting passengers to buy discount coach tickets on the Toronto-to-Dallas route are different today than they were a year ago.

Answer choice (B) is correct.

This is a tricky argument to follow! We first learn that the "real" (inflation-adjusted) price of a specific airline ticket has stayed constant over the course of the year. For example, if inflation were 5%, then the ticket price would have risen 5% as well, leaving the "real" price unchanged.

Now, 90% of the tickets sold for this trip are discounted. A year ago only 50% were. The conclusion is that people are paying less on average for these tickets than a year ago, which would seem to make sense if more tickets today are sold at a discount. Here's the core of this argument:

the price of a regular T-D ticket is the same today as one year ago

+

the percent of tickets sold at discount prices increased from 50% to 90%

→ on average, people now pay less per T-D ticket

The math seems to work out, but this is an Assumption Family question, so we know there must be something wrong with this reasoning. Since this is a number-based argument, let's play with the numbers. How is it possible that even though there are more discounted tickets sold, people are *not* paying less on average? We know the full-fare tickets have remained the same price, so only the price of discount tickets is unknown. What if the discount has gone down? For example, imagine that a discount ticket used to be 99% off, and now it's just 5% off. Then, even if more people are buying discount tickets, the *average* price will have gone up. Roughly, we could say that last year the average price was about half the full price (since half the passengers were traveling for only 1% of full price), whereas this year the average price would scarcely be lower than the full price (since the discount passengers are paying nearly as much as the full-price passengers). We're looking for a sufficient assumption, so we need to fill this gap entirely. We can't leave *any* doubt about average prices, so we can

specifically predict that our answer should keep discount prices the same as (or higher than) before.

You certainly don't have to bust out crazy math during the exam. Instead, consider where we have *room for uncertainty.* Since we know full-fare tickets have kept up with inflation, the only hole in the argument is in the discount category. With that in mind, we can quickly eliminate most of the answer choices simply because they don't address the cost of discount tickets.

(A) Level of service? This is wildly out of scope.

(C) is out of scope. The argument is about the average cost of Toronto-to-Dallas coach tickets. The cost of tickets for other routes that Breezeway Airlines might offer is irrelevant to the average cost of Toronto-to-Dallas coach tickets.

(E) This seems to explain *why* more people are getting discount tickets. Our job is not to figure out why the premises are true, but to fill the gap between the premises and the conclusion!

(D) This is kind of interesting, because it talks about the total number of passengers. If the total has gone up, maybe airlines are collecting more money despite the increase in discount ticket sales. Did this tempt you? If so, take a look back at the argument core right now. Can you see why this answer choice is actually out of scope?

The conclusion is about what people pay *on average* for one ticket, not what the airline is collecting in total. Sales may be higher, but that doesn't tell us anything about the average price.

That leaves (B), which looks exactly like our prediction. If both full-fare *and* discount prices have stayed the same, then a higher percent of discount sales necessarily means a lower average price.

9. PT20, S1, Q20

Some people have been promoting a new herbal mixture as a remedy for the common cold. The mixture contains, among other things, extracts of the plants purple coneflower and goldenseal. A cold sufferer, skeptical of the claim that the mixture is an effective cold remedy, argued, "Suppose that the mixture were an effective cold remedy. Since most people with colds wish to recover quickly, it follows that almost everybody with a cold would be using it. Therefore, since there are many people who have colds but do not use the mixture, it is obviously not effective."

Each of the following is an assumption required by the skeptical cold sufferer's argument EXCEPT:

(A)　Enough of the mixture is produced to provide the required doses to almost everybody with a cold.

(B)　The mixture does not have side effects severe enough to make many people who have colds avoid using it.

(C)　The mixture is powerful enough to prevent almost everybody who uses it from contracting any further colds.

(D)　The mixture is widely enough known that almost everybody with a cold is aware of it.

(E)　There are no effective cold remedies available that many people who have colds prefer to the mixture.

Answer choice (C) is correct.

Here's a nice twist. Four of these answer choices are necessary assumptions, so the right answer will be something that is *not* necessary. If one of the answers were about the best reggae bands or the age of the universe, we'd want to jump right on it!

Oh, and there's another twist. The author describes two different views: "Some people" think the mixture is an effective remedy, but the cold sufferer does not. However, the author never comes to a conclusion of her own. We're actually asked to assess the cold sufferer's reasoning. Okay, let's look at just that core:

if a remedy were effective, most cold sufferers would use it

+

there are many cold sufferers not using this mixture

➡ the new herbal mixture must not be an effective cold remedy

Wait, isn't this argument valid? It establishes a rule: *remedy effective* ➔ *most people use* and then uses the next premise to trigger the contrapositive: **not** *most people use* ➔ *remedy* **not** *effective*. The use of a contrapositive is logically valid, so is there no assumption here?

Well, hold on. First, let's look at the negation of *most*. We saw in the negation drill (and earlier in this drill) that the negation of *most* is *half or fewer*. All we have is the vague term *many*. Maybe there are a million cold sufferers and 75% of them use the mixture. That would still leave 250,000 not using it. That would sure seem to qualify as *many*, but it wouldn't be *most*.

That's a useful point to catch, but we need to find four necessary assumptions this time. They can't all be about most vs. many. (In fact, none of them are!) So what's going on? The premises seem to work together, and we never question premises, right? If you find yourself stuck like this, take another look at the full argument. You may find that one of your "premises" is not a premise at all. In this case, one of the statements actually builds on an earlier premise and is therefore an intermediate conclusion. Can you tell which one?

Looking back, we missed some premise/conclusion cues: "*Since* most people with colds wish to recover quickly, *it follows that* almost everybody with a cold would be using it." It's a premise that most people with colds wish to recover quickly, but the part about most people using the mixture is actually an intermediate conclusion. Hooray! We get to question that part of the author's reasoning.

So why might it be that people would *not* use the mixture, even if it is effective? Maybe they don't know about it, or they don't know that it's effective. Maybe it's too expensive. Maybe it has unpleasant side effects. It could cure your cold but make you dream about scary clowns! We can't predict every possible reason, but we can expect that many (perhaps all) of the four necessary assumptions presented in the answer choices will defend the argument from one or more of these obstacles to the conclusion and establish that if the remedy were effective, most cold sufferers *would* use it.

Looking through the answer choices, four of these are definitely defenders. Let's eliminate them by considering the obstacle to using the herbal mixture that each of them eliminates.

(A) rules out the possibility of people not taking the mixture simply because there's not enough to go around.

(B) rules out side effects as the reason people aren't taking the herbal mixture.

(C) is complex. It's unclear how preventing future colds is relevant to this discussion. Perhaps it explains why a limited number of people use the mixture… Keep it.

(D) rules out the possibility that people aren't taking the mixture simply because they haven't heard of it.

(E) rules out the possibility that people are avoiding the mixture because they like something else better. (If that were the case, this mixture might still be effective, even if it were not widely consumed.)

That leaves (C). If anything, this praise of the mixture seems to go against the cold sufferer's argument. However, since the argument is about recovering from a cold (rather than preventing future colds), this answer is actually out of scope. Either way, it certainly isn't necessary to the argument. We have our winner!

10. PT33, S1, Q19

Historian: The spread of literacy informs more people of injustices and, in the right circumstances, leads to increased capacity to distinguish true reformers from mere opportunists. However, widespread literacy invariably emerges before any comprehensive system of general education; thus, in the interim, the populace is vulnerable to clever demagogues calling for change. Consequently, some relatively benign regimes may ironically be toppled by their own "enlightened" move to increase literacy.

Which one of the following is an assumption on which the historian's argument depends?

(A)   A demagogue can never enlist the public support necessary to topple an existing regime unless a comprehensive system of general education is in place.

(B)   Without literacy there can be no general awareness of the injustice in a society.

(C)   Any comprehensive system of general education will tend to preserve the authority of benign regimes.

(D)   A lack of general education affects the ability to differentiate between legitimate and illegitimate calls for reform.

(E)   Any benign regime that fails to provide comprehensive general education will be toppled by a clever demagogue.

Answer choice (D) is correct.

This is quite a tricky argument to follow! Did you notice the two conclusions right in a row? We have a "thus" statement followed by a "consequently." Since one conclusion follows from the other, the second is our main conclusion and the first is an intermediate conclusion. Here's what we have so far:

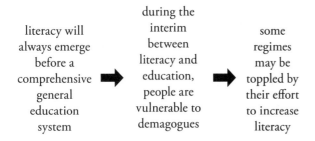

Now, where is the support for the intermediate conclusion? The first sentence tells us that literacy can help people tell the difference between true reformers and opportunists. This seems to contradict our main conclusion—that benign regimes may be toppled by efforts to increase literacy—which makes this first sentence an opposing point.

The next statement, after "however," gives us some support for the intermediate conclusion. It tells us that literacy always arrives ahead of comprehensive general education. This is what creates the "interim" period described in the intermediate conclusion. So here's our complete argument core:

```
literacy will          during the
always emerge          interim           some
before a        ➡      between     ➡     regimes
comprehensive          literacy and       may be
general                education,         toppled by
education              people are         their effort
system                 vulnerable to      to increase
                       demagogues         literacy
```

By the way, if you were thrown off by the word "demagogue," hopefully you used context ("become vulnerable to clever demagogues") to figure out that a demagogue is someone bad (and perhaps deceptive) who

could come into power. Specifically, the word refers to a political leader who gains popularity by playing on people's emotions and prejudices. So, in terms of this argument, a demagogue would be not a "true reformer" but rather an "opportunist."

Putting this all together, what can we make of the argument? The author thinks that because literacy arrives before comprehensive general education, there's a period in which people can't tell good reformers from bad. Because of this, the author concludes that a regime may bring about its own end by promoting literacy. When we have two conclusions like this, we can look for assumptions at either juncture: between the premises and the intermediate conclusion or between the intermediate and final conclusions. Let's look at both.

If we know that widespread literacy comes before comprehensive general education, can we conclude that the public is vulnerable to demagogues? This seems completely disconnected from the premise. The author is assuming that people who haven't had this comprehensive general education won't be able to tell the good reformers from the bad.

Now let's look at the second juncture. If we did know that this period of vulnerability came about when literacy improved, would it logically follow that regimes might be toppled by their own efforts to promote literacy? This would depend on whether these demagogues that the people fell prey to were actually capable of toppling the existing regime.

So we have two major assumptions:

1. General education is necessary for distinguishing true reformers from demagogues.
2. The demagogues that people fall for will sometimes be capable of toppling regimes.

(D) states the first assumption in somewhat milder terms. Since we're looking for a necessary assumption, a mild version is just fine. If we want to conclude that people are vulnerable before the education system kicks in, we need to know that a lack of education has at least some effect on people's ability to tell true reformers from phonies. Let's finish out this chapter by eliminating the four wrong answers:

(A) might look tempting, because it addresses the possibility that a demagogue might topple the existing regime. However, this choice is moving in the wrong direction. By telling us when a demagogue *cannot* take over, it tells us nothing about when they *can*. In fact, (A) weakens the argument by suggesting that a demagogue can't take over until the interim period is over and a general education system is in place.

(B) doesn't address either of the gaps we identified. Rather, it talks about what happens in the absence of literacy. Since the argument is about what happens when literacy increases, this is out of scope.

(C) links education to the preservation of the benign regimes, but it negates the argument's underlying logic. The argument concludes that a lack of education leads to some of those regimes being toppled, but this does not require that having a system of general education will protect those regimes. (We want **no education** → **some regimes toppled**, not **education** → **no regimes toppled**.) Another way to look at this choice is that, like (B), it addresses a situation outside the scope of the argument. The argument is about the period *before* general education is in place.

(E) may have been very tempting at first glance. If we're trying to support the argument *no education* → *some regimes toppled*, this seems to do just that. However, this answer choice represents a very common trap on Necessary Assumption questions: an answer that is more than what we need. Our conclusion is about *some* regimes; we don't need to know that this happens every time. While this answer may ensure the argument's conclusion, it is not needed to arrive at that conclusion. It's sufficient, but not necessary!

3

Chapter 4

Flaw Questions

In This Chapter...

Warm Up

Let's begin this chapter by evaluating a simple argument:

cats are friendlier than dog cats make the best pets

By now, you're getting pretty good at identifying the author's mismatched ideas, as well as generating objections relating to things that the author seems to have overlooked. Before reading on, take a second to jot down at least one assumption this argument makes and at least one objection you could make to its reasoning:

Assumptions:

Objections:

Now suppose you're asked to point out a fault in the author's reasoning. Which of these are valid responses?

> *The reasoning in the argument is flawed because the argument:*

1. Fails to consider that dogs are friendlier than cats

2. Takes for granted that cats and dogs are about as friendly as one another

3. Assumes that there is a way to accurately measure the friendliness of animals

4. Neglects the possibility that friendliness is not the primary consideration for what makes the best pet

5. Fails to specify why other characteristics, such as loyalty, are not relevant to determining the best pet

6. Presupposes the truth of the conclusion

7. Assumes, without warrant, that there are no pets other than cats and dogs that ought to be considered

8. Mistakes a condition required in order to be best pet for one that guarantees the status of best pet

Neither number 1 nor 2 happens in the argument. Since the author explicitly states that cats are friendlier than dogs, we can't accuse her of failing to consider relative friendliness or of assuming that dogs and cats are equally friendly. Beyond being false descriptions of the argument, these two choices also have the feel of fighting the truth of the premise, rather than the validity of the *reasoning* (the move from premise to conclusion). We find another premise challenge in number 3. The premise says that cats *are* friendlier than dogs. End of story. We know that our task is not to question premises. Accept the premise; challenge its connection to the conclusion!

Two answers, numbers 6 and 8, though failing to accurately describe the argument, do describe flaws that show up repeatedly on the LSAT (particularly in wrong answers to Flaw questions). Circular reasoning, number 6, occurs when the support offered for a conclusion is essentially just a restatement of the conclusion, such as "Cats are the best pet because no other pets are as good as cats." But the author of the argument comparing cats and dogs *did* have an actual premise. She didn't simply say that cats are the best because they're the best! Conditional Logic Flaws, as described in number 8, occur when the author misuses conditional logic. Of course, to have a misuse, we'd have to *see* some conditional logic, such as "If a pet is the best pet, it must be friendly. Since cats are friendly, they must be the best pet." (Can you spot the flaw? Illegal reversal!)

Only numbers 4, 5, and 7 accurately call into question the relationship between the premise and the conclusion. They speak directly to the questionable leap from establishing that cats are friendlier than one other type of animal to concluding that cats are therefore the best type of pet.

Are all your fault-finding faculties activated now? Good! Let's spend some time looking at what a Flaw question is asking us to do. Then we'll look at a number of specific reasoning flaws that you're likely to see not only in Flaw questions, but throughout the Logical Reasoning section.

Introduction to Flaw Questions

As the name implies, Flaw questions ask you to point out a flaw in the argument. In some respects, you need no introduction to this task—you've already been reading like a lawyer since Chapter 2, and Flaw questions are just another member of the Assumption Family.

The wording of a typical **Flaw** question looks like this:

> *Which one of the following most accurately expresses an error of reasoning in the mayor's argument?*
>
> *The reasoning above is most vulnerable to criticism because the argument…*

There are other wordings, but most Flaw question stems involve one of these keywords: flaw, vulnerable to criticism (most common), questionable reasoning, erroneous reasoning (rare).

As you can see, Flaw questions, like all Assumption Family questions, ask you to identify the gap in the argument. In fact, many answers to Flaw questions will describe the flaw as an assumption the argument takes for granted or an objection the argument has failed to consider:

> The argument *assumes* that athletes make only those decisions that they believe will improve their health.

> The argument *overlooks the possibility* that even athletes might sometimes make decisions that they believe will negatively impact their health.

Notice how the same idea can be expressed using either of the two forms. Keep this in mind as you learn to predict answer choices!

The Importance of Flaws

Flaw questions are one of the most common question types in Logical Reasoning. Of the roughly 50 Logical Reasoning questions on each LSAT, 5–9 of them will be Flaw questions (with a couple of others being a close cousin, Match the Flaw).

Beyond the fact that there are a good number of Flaw questions, working on these is one of the most effective ways to improve your performance on *all* Assumption Family questions. Not only will you practice reading like a lawyer—answer choices to Flaw questions literally sound like what a lawyer might say after yelling "Objection!"—but the arguments in Flaw questions can be some of the most complex you'll meet. Furthermore, the answer choices can be equally challenging. You'll have no choice but to up your game!

We're quickly going to see that Flaw questions tend to exhibit the same types of flaws over and over again. Some of them are specific to Flaw questions, but most are used throughout the Assumption Family and beyond! Thus, mastering these typical flaws will pay dividends beyond just one question type.

Flaws = Assumptions

Let's jump into a question! Remember that this is an Assumption Family question, so identify the core and find the gap in the argument's reasoning before you start working through the answer choices.

4

PT15, S3, Q2

Those who support the continued reading and performance of Shakespeare's plays maintain that in England appreciation for his work has always extended beyond educated elites and that ever since Shakespeare's own time his plays have always been known and loved by comparatively uneducated people. Skepticism about this claim is borne out by examining early eighteenth-century editions of the plays. These books, with their fine paper and good bindings, must have been far beyond the reach of people of ordinary means.

Which one of the following describes a reasoning error in the argument?

(A)   The argument uses the popularity of Shakespeare's plays as a measure of their literary quality.

(B)   The argument bases an aesthetic conclusion about Shakespeare's plays on purely economic evidence.

(C)   The argument anachronistically uses the standards of the twentieth century to judge events that occurred in the early eighteenth century.

(D)   The argument judges the literary quality of a book's text on the basis of the quality of the volume in which the text is printed.

(E)   The argument does not allow for the possibility that people might know Shakespeare's plays without having read them.

This argument actually follows a common form that you've seen in other Assumption Family questions: It begins with the opposing point, redirects to the conclusion, and provides evidence at the end. When the author tells us how the "skepticism … is borne out," that's another way of saying how the skepticism is *supported*. That makes skepticism of the first claim our conclusion. But this is still tricky! Some rephrasing is necessary. Whenever the conclusion of an argument is a statement that some other position is wrong, you should actually spell out that position in the conclusion, like this:

| in the 18th century, Shakespeare's plays were published in fancy books that were out of reach for common folks | | it is not true that since Shakespeare's time, common folks have always known and loved his plays |

Let's turn on our lawyer thinking: How can it be that the plays were indeed put out in expensive editions but poor folks still *did* know and love his plays? Well, after all, they were *plays*. Couldn't the poor people have *seen* them? This is what the correct answer, (E), points out. While some of the wrong answers are a bit tricky, if you thought of this objection, (E) most likely stood out to you as correct.

You can see that we were able to tackle this problem relying entirely on the Assumption Family skills we have already built up. Let's delve further by using this problem to examine the three main flavors of Flaw answer choices: **assumptions, objections,** and **bad moves.**

In this argument, the correct answer is worded as an *objection*. With a bit of imagination, you can picture yourself as an underpaid lawyer for the people whose opinions are cited in the first sentence of the argument. There you are, standing up in court, saying that "the opposing counsel does not allow for the possibility that people might know Shakespeare's plays without having read them."

Before reading on, take a moment to consider how the answer might have been stated as an *assumption*.

Here are some possibilities:

> The argument assumes that one must have access to a written version of a playwright's works in order to know and appreciate those works.

> The argument presumes, without justification, that reading a play is required in order to know and love that play.

But Flaw answer choices can get a bit nasty:

> The argument treats a certain medium as necessary for experiencing a certain phenomenon when it is in fact only sufficient.

The above phrasing is an example of both how Flaw answer choices can be phrased quite abstractly and how they can focus on describing a "bad move" in the argument—a logical misstep. This may seem like a far cry from "The argument does not allow for the possibility that people might know Shakespeare's plays without having read them," but both versions are actually referring to the same flaw.

Many answer choices that describe a bad move conform to one of the common flaws that we'll look at later in the chapter. For now, let's dig a bit deeper into the other flavors of Flaw answer choices: assumptions and objections.

When the answer to a Flaw question is phrased as an assumption, that answer choice is stating a necessary assumption of the argument and should be evaluated as such. That means, of course, that if the argument doesn't absolutely hinge on that thing being true, the answer is incorrect. That makes evaluation of these answer choices very straightforward. Does this need to be true in order for our argument to work? No? Then scrap it.

Because these are necessary assumptions, we can also use the negation test as a final check on an answer choice. For example, if we negate the assumption answers we wrote for the Shakespeare argument—*reading a play is NOT required in order to know and love that play*—the argument crumbles. It would make no sense to arrive at the conclusion from the given premise. You may not find yourself using the negation test as often with Flaw questions as you do with Necessary Assumption questions, but it's useful to know that it's available for any answer that is phrased as an assumption.

For objection answer choices, which are generally phrased as something the argument "overlooks" or "fails to consider," the answer choice is presenting a counterexample that would discredit the argument. These answers are, in a sense, pre-negated necessary assumption answers. Notice how the correct answer to the Shakespeare question renders the argument unworkable:

$$\left(\begin{array}{c}\text{people might know}\\\text{Shakespeare's plays without}\\\text{having read them}\end{array}\right)$$

in the 18th century, Shakespeare's plays were published in fancy books that were out of reach for common folks

it is not true that since Shakespeare's time, common folks have always known and loved his plays

Just like Necessary Assumption answers, objection answers to Flaw questions can feel out of scope when they introduce new information. But both types of answer introduce highly relevant, potentially argument-destroying information. Answers that represent necessary assumptions will serve as defenders, assuring us that a specific argument bomb is *not* true or possible, while objection answers to Flaw questions will drop that bomb right on the argument!

With the Shakespeare argument above, a correct objection answer could have mentioned a specific way that eighteenth-century commoners could have learned about Shakespeare's plays, such as attending them. Another, equally correct, objection might be that only manuscripts on fine paper with good bindings could have survived for so many years. This objection demonstrates that those surviving texts aren't necessarily representative of the texts actually circulating in the eighteenth century, opening up the possibility that cheaper versions may have been available to common people. Even though neither performances nor other texts were mentioned in the argument, they are both very much relevant to the argument and can appear in the correct answer.

With that in mind, let's consider another question:

_PT14, S2, Q22_

Gallery owner: Because this painting appears in no catalog of van Gogh's work, we cannot guarantee that he painted it. But consider: the subject is one he painted often, and experts agree that in his later paintings van Gogh invariably used just such broad brushstrokes and distinctive combinations of colors as we find here. Internal vidence, therefore, makes it virtually certain that this is a previously uncataloged, late van Gogh, and as such, a bargain at its price.

The reasoning used by the gallery owner is flawed because it

(A)   ignores the fact that there can be general agreement that something is the case without its being the case

(B)   neglects to cite expert authority to substantiate the claim about the subject matter of the painting

(C)   assumes without sufficient warrant that the only reason anyone would want to acquire a painting is to make a profit

(D)   provides no evidence that the painting is more likely to be an uncataloged van Gogh than to be a painting by someone else who painted that particular subject in van Gogh's style

(E)   attempts to establish a particular conclusion because doing so is in the reasoner's self-interest rather than because of any genuine concern for the truth of the matter

Did you spot how the argument fit in an intermediate conclusion *and* a final conclusion at the last minute?

subject matter, broad brushstrokes, and color combinations match van Gogh's work ➡ painting is almost certainly van Gogh ➡ painting is a bargain at its price

Reading like a lawyer, we want to attack the links between the pieces of this argument. How might it be that the subject, color, and brushstrokes are the same but the painting is *not* almost certain to be a van Gogh? And how might it be that a painting which is almost certainly a van Gogh is *not* a bargain at its price? We can predict that our correct answer will address one of these two gaps.

How about this?

> (D) provides no evidence that the painting is more likely to be an uncataloged van Gogh than to be a painting by someone else who painted that particular subject in van Gogh's style

Is "provides no evidence for something" equivalent to saying that the argument *assumes* that thing or *fails to consider* it? Consider that assumptions are logical leaps for which there is no justification, that is, no *evidence*. That means that when a Flaw answer choice begins with the phrase "provides no evidence for …," we can act as if it said "assumes" and check to see if it is indeed a necessary assumption. So, does our argument hinge on it being more likely that this painting is an uncataloged van Gogh than a painting by someone else who painted those subjects in that style? Absolutely—because what if that *wasn't* more likely? That would destroy the argument by ruining the intermediate conclusion! Answer choice (D) is correct.

One of the best things you can do during the course of your LSAT studies is to develop solid instincts about which answers are relevant and which are irrelevant, or "out of scope." In this case, (D) brings up other artists, and perhaps this made the answer less attractive to you at first. Many test-takers treat answers that introduce new information as though they are necessarily out of scope, but remember that defender assumptions often hinge on ideas that were not mentioned at all in the argument. On the flip side, incorrect answers will often make out-of-scope connections or comparisons between concepts that *were* mentioned in the argument. Thus, it is critical that you make a distinction between something being *unmentioned* and that thing being *out of scope*.

Now, let's turn to the incorrect answers. In Flaw questions, the majority of incorrect answers will have no direct connection to the premise–conclusion relationship. To illustrate this point, let's compare the answer choices to the core:

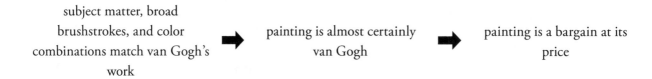

subject matter, broad brushstrokes, and color combinations match van Gogh's work ➡ painting is almost certainly van Gogh ➡ painting is a bargain at its price

(A) ignores the fact that there can be general
agreement that something is the case without its
being the case

"Ignores the fact that" is virtually the same as saying "overlooks the possibility that." Does the fact that people can agree about something without it actually being true mess up this argument? No, because the argument never says that everyone agrees that the painting was a van Gogh.

(B) neglects to cite expert authority to substantiate the
claim about the subject matter of the painting

Don't be tricked into thinking that we've got to justify the premise! True, the author cites experts about brushstrokes and color, and not about subject. But the part about the subject is still a premise, so it's not a flaw to rely on that information. Most arguments don't cite experts for *any* element of their premises.

(C) assumes without sufficient warrant that the only
reason anyone would want to acquire a painting
is to make a profit

In order to draw our conclusions that this is almost certainly a van Gogh and therefore a bargain, we don't need to assume anything about profit. This is an example of new information actually being out of scope—it is irrelevant to the argument. If it's true that people would only want to acquire a painting to make a profit, it doesn't help our argument, and if it is false, it doesn't discredit our argument.

(E) attempts to establish a particular conclusion
because doing so is in the reasoner's self-interest
rather than because of any genuine concern for
the truth of the matter

If you are the suspicious type, this answer might be attractive to you. It certainly seems like the owner just wants to turn a buck! Plus, it seems to address the relationship between the intermediate and final conclusions. But the fact that someone has a vested interest in the outcome of the argument isn't by itself a problem with their argument. Granted, in real life, it's a good reason to look at an argument with skepticism, which is why the LSAT makes answers like this— to trick you into treating the LSAT like real life! But a person's interest in an argument's outcome doesn't actually address the argument's logic, and thus is not a flaw in the argument's reasoning. Even in real life, you would not tell your doctor that her argument that you need an appendectomy is flawed because she stands to profit from performing the surgery.

Now that you've had some exposure to questions where the flaw is best described as an assumption the argument makes or an objection the argument has failed to consider, it's time to get familiar with the common reasoning errors that occur on Flaw questions, starting with the two most common: Causation Flaws and Conditional Logic Flaws.

Causation Flaws

Did you notice that the last question we looked at was a type of explanation? The gallery owner pointed out similarities between this painting and van Gogh's, and then explained those similarities by concluding that this painting was a van Gogh as well. When you see an argument like this, you need to be lawyerly, asking yourself if that *one* explanation is *the only* explanation. The correct answer hinged on that concept, accusing the argument of assuming that no other explanations were as likely. This flaw is intimately related to some of the most common reasoning errors you'll see in Flaw questions (and, arguably, throughout Logical Reasoning)—those that involve cause and effect, aka *causation*. Any claim of one element having a direct impact on another can be considered a claim of causation, and you should read those with the same lawyerly approach with which you read explanations.

Here are a few examples of causation claims:

> The success of the research project was *due in part* to the amount of money invested.

> The dishwashing soap is what *removed* the stain.

> Eating blueberries *lowers* one's chances of developing heart disease.

To support its causal conclusion, a flawed causation argument usually provides a correlation as evidence. Two typical forms of correlation are statistical and temporal:

> Statistical: People who are A are more likely to be B than people who are not. Thus, A causes B.
> Temporal: A happened. Then B happened. Thus, A caused B.

Both correlation and causation can sometimes be tricky to spot. To spot correlation, keywords such as "tends to," "associated with," and "followed by" can help. But sometimes you won't notice the correlation in the premise until you see the causal conclusion. On Flaw questions, whenever there's a causal conclusion, check the premises for unnoticed correlation.

Causation claims like the three we just saw are relatively easy to spot because the impact of one thing on the other is stated directly. But on the LSAT, issues of causation will not always be stated explicitly in the conclusion; often they will be implied by the way a premise *connects* to the conclusion.

Let's use two simple arguments to clarify the difference:

Explicit	**Implicit**
Ted didn't sleep well the night before the exam and performed poorly. Therefore, it's clear that his lack of sleep had a direct impact on his performance.	Ted didn't sleep well the night before the exam and performed poorly. Annie wants to perform well on her test, so she should be sure to get a good night's sleep.

MANHATTAN
PREP

The arguments are very similar, and they both involve a claim about causation. Notice in the first example that the causation claim is stated explicitly: "His lack of sleep had a **direct impact.**"

In the second example, that causation claim is never explicitly stated. Rather, it is implied. The author is making an unstated assumption in using the evidence to validate the conclusion—he is assuming that lack of sleep must have had some impact on Ted's performance and is therefore recommending that Annie not make the same mistake.

In both cases, the author is assuming that because two things are associated, one must have caused the other. Whenever this happens, the argument exhibits a Causation Flaw, no matter how reasonable that assumption might seem. The fact is that while correlation can serve as useful evidence, **correlation never proves causation.** Sure, in real life, if you drop a glass on the ground and it breaks, it would seem reasonable to infer that the glass broke because you dropped it. But that's only because you know a good deal more about the situation than can be summed up in the premise "I dropped a glass." For instance, you know whether the glass was knocked out of your hand by a stray baseball or whether you dropped it because it had started to shatter. However, just seeing a temporal correlation— the glass fell and then it broke—may serve as useful evidence for a causal conclusion, but it doesn't *prove* the causal connection.

This is a very important point to remember because the writers of the LSAT will do their best to make these claims of causation seem valid. In fact, some of the toughest causation questions are challenging precisely because the argument seems so very reasonable. Therefore, go in knowing that you should be suspicious of causal claims!

Debating Causation

As with any explanation, we can respond to claims of causation by asking, "Could it be something else?" Consider the following example:

> Studies indicate that older antelope are, on average, more cautious than younger antelope. This proves that getting older causes antelope to become more cautious.

This argument seems pretty good, right? Older antelope are more cautious, so it would make sense that getting older is what *causes* these antelope to become more cautious. However, all we're actually told is that there is a *correlation* between getting older and being more cautious. Whenever a correlation between A and B is treated as proof that A *caused* B, you should ask yourself two questions:

1. Does the reverse make some sense, too? Could B have caused A?

Instead of age having some impact on caution, could it be that the caution has some impact on getting older? Hmm. Perhaps it seems unlikely, but see if you can imagine how this might be true. Consider a herd of antelope, and consider in particular the young in the group. Imagine that some of these young are cautious and some of them are not. We've all seen nature shows—what might happen to some of these less cautious antelope? Chances are, they are more likely to run into unpleasant circumstances. Instead of caution increasing with age, it's possible that caution is what *allows* the antelope to *reach* old age—it's possible that *B causes A.*

4

2. Could some third thing cause both A and B?

Could it be that some other factor contributes significantly to both cautiousness and age? Could it be that there is a critical part of the equation that is missing? Absolutely. For one, what about having a higher level of intelligence? Perhaps brain power is what makes an antelope cautious, and it just so happens that smarter antelope can find more food and thus live longer.

Perhaps a third question occurred to you: "Could it just be a coincidence?" Maybe scientists have been studying a particular population of older antelope that just happen to be very cautious. This is certainly a possibility, but it's not one that the LSAT uses often. Since the LR section is testing your reasoning skills, a question is much more likely to make you consider different causal alternatives than to provide an answer that basically says that the premise is useless. If you spot this answer, jump on it, but since that doesn't require any up-front analysis, we've limited our questions to two.

When considering these alternatives, keep in mind that your job is not to evaluate which mode of causation is more likely. Your job is simply to recognize that the argument is flawed in assuming one path of causation when multiple paths are possible. If you had trouble seeing the alternative paths, that's perfectly understandable. Getting in the habit of running through those questions whenever you encounter a causal claim should help you develop better instincts about the way causality is used in LR questions. Even when you can't imagine specific alternatives, you'll be in great shape to answer questions correctly as long as you can do two things:

1. Recognize the explicit claim or implicit assumption the author makes about causation.

2. Stay open to answer choices that suggest possible alternative modes of causation.

Let's look at an example to illustrate:

PT39, S4, Q20

Some people believe that good health is due to luck. However, studies from many countries indicate a strong correlation between good health and high educational levels. Thus research supports the view that good health is largely the result of making informed lifestyle choices.

The reasoning in the argument is most vulnerable to criticism on the grounds that the argument

(A)   presumes, without providing justification, that only highly educated people make informed lifestyle choices

(B)   overlooks the possibility that people who make informed lifestyle choices may nonetheless suffer from inherited diseases

(C)   presumes, without providing justification, that informed lifestyle choices are available to everyone

(D)   overlooks the possibility that the same thing may causally contribute both to education and to good health

(E)   does not acknowledge that some people who fail to make informed lifestyle choices are in good health

Note that the conclusion of the argument is an explicit claim of causation: "Thus research supports the view that good health is largely *the result* of making informed lifestyle choices." That is, making informed lifestyle choices has a direct impact on good health.

The evidence in this argument explicitly states a correlation between good health and high educational levels. What this means is that there is some statistical evidence that connects the people who happen to have good health and the people who happen to have high educational levels. Statistically speaking, having one changes the percentage chance that you have the other.

The first thing that might have jumped out at you about this argument is the conceptual shift that takes place between "high education levels" in the premise and "informed lifestyle choices" in the conclusion. Be aware that Flaw questions can contain multiple flaws. In fact, some of the hardest Flaw questions will use a clear problem like this conceptual shift as a decoy to distract us from the more subtle flaw that ends up in the correct answer. If you go into these answers looking for a choice addressing the gap between education and lifestyle choices, you will come up empty.

So what's the other flaw in the argument? Surprise, surprise: correlation vs. causation. Just because we know that there is a *correlation* between good health and high educational levels doesn't mean we know that good health is a part of the *reason* for high educational levels.

Let's think about our two questions:

1. Could it be the reverse?

2. Could something else cause both?

We know that the correct answer will typically address one of these issues:

1. Could having good health help someone get more education? It doesn't seem likely, but we want to stay open-minded to this possibility when we evaluate the answer choices. Perhaps a significant number of people miss out on education due to poor health.

2. Could something else cause people to be both educated and healthy? Living in a place with access to public higher education and first-rate public health care certainly could!

The correct answer, (D), addresses the second of the two concerns: "overlooks the possibility that the same thing may causally contribute both to education and to good health." Notice that in this case, the answer choice stays in the abstract—it doesn't tell us what the "something else" is that contributes to both education and health.

So what's wrong with the most tempting wrong answers?

> (A)   presumes, without providing justification, that
>   only highly educated people make informed
>   lifestyle choices

This is a very tempting answer because it addresses the jump from education levels to informed lifestyle decisions. However, the word "only" makes this answer choice too strong. (In conditional logic terms, this is *informed lifestyle choices → highly educated*.) The argument assumes that highly educated people *are more likely* to make informed lifestyle choices, but it does not assume that they are the *only* ones who do so. Does this argument absolutely require that only the highly educated make good lifestyle choices, or could one uneducated person make those good choices without blowing up the argument? When you're on the fence about a Necessary Assumption–style answer, the negation test can help you get off of it!

What about (E)? Isn't this a flaw in the argument?

> (E)   does not acknowledge that some people who
>   fail to make informed lifestyle choices are in
>   good health

The author does not conclude that all healthy people make informed lifestyle choices. Like (A), this choice is more extreme than the actual argument, which concludes that such choices are *the major factor* in good health. This leaves open the possibility that some good health is not caused by high levels of education. The conclusion leaves room for outliers, and this is typical for statements about correlations. Unless stated otherwise, a correlation just means that one thing *tends* to go along with the other: Older antelope are more likely to be more cautious, and healthy people are more likely to be highly educated. Individual exceptions are not a problem for the argument, but they are a very common source of trap answers.

Let's look at another question:

> ### PT20, S1, Q10
>
> Premiums for automobile accident insurance are often higher for red cars than for cars of other colors. To justify these higher charges, insurance companies claim that, overall, a greater percentage of red cars are involved in accidents than are cars of any other color. If this claim is true, then lives could undoubtedly be saved by banning red cars from the roads altogether.
>
> The reasoning in the argument is flawed because the argument
>
> (A) accepts without question that insurance companies have the right to charge higher premiums for higher-risk clients
>
> (B) fails to consider whether red cars cost the same to repair as cars of other colors
>
> (C) ignores the possibility that drivers who drive recklessly have a preference for red cars
>
> (D) does not specify precisely what percentage of red cars are involved in accidents
>
> (E) makes an unsupported assumption that every automobile accident results in some loss of life

The conclusion of this argument is a good example of an implicit claim of causation. While it doesn't explicitly say that driving a red car increases the likelihood of an accident, that is certainly implied by the conclusion that removing them from the roads would save lives. The premise in this case is another statistical correlation: A greater percentage of red cars are involved in accidents than cars of any other color.

Let's think again about debating claims of causation:

1. Could it be the reverse? Probably not. The cars were red at the time that they became involved in the accident. It doesn't seem likely that they turned red as a *result* of the accident. In general, when the temporal sequence is established (A occurred before B), reversed causality is unlikely to be an issue.

2. Could something else cause both? Potentially. There could be some other factor that increases a car's likelihood of being red *and* its likelihood of being in an accident.

Did you notice any other problems with this argument? It draws a conclusion about saving lives based only on information about the number of traffic accidents. Just because red cars are involved in more accidents doesn't necessarily mean that any of those accidents involved fatalities. The correct answer could address that gap in reasoning as well, but if that were the case, we wouldn't be discussing this one in the section covering causation!

> (C)   ignores the possibility that drivers who drive
>   recklessly have a preference for red cars

This matches our prediction that some third factor would be introduced to explain the correlation. (C) is the correct answer.

But what about (E)?

> (E)   makes an unsupported assumption that every
>   automobile accident results in some loss of life

This is the most tempting of the wrong answers because it addresses the other gap in reasoning—that accidents don't necessarily imply fatalities. However, once again, we have a trap answer in which the language is too strong. The argument doesn't assume that *every* accident is a fatality. It just assumes that *some* are. If you had trouble ruling out (E), remember that because it accuses the argument of making an assumption, you can submit it to the negation test to see if that assumption is really necessary. Answer choice (E), negated, says that NOT EVERY accident results in some loss of life, and this doesn't knock down the argument.

Answer choices (A) and (B) are completely out of scope. The argument has nothing to do with the rights of insurance companies or the cost of repairs.

Answer choice (D) demands a greater amount of specificity than is actually necessary. We are told that red cars are proportionally more likely to be in accidents than cars of any other color. It's not necessary to know the precise numbers in order to reach the conclusion that banning red cars would save lives.

This question, with its implicit causal conclusion, may have been hard to spot as causal at first, but the statistical correlation was explicit. Whenever you encounter either causation or correlation on a Flaw question, do a quick sweep for the other. If you find that correlation is presented as evidence for causation, read like a lawyer and debate the causal claim. This concept is tested frequently on the LSAT, so make sure you are comfortable with the language of causality and correlation, and get in the habit of asking our two questions when you see a causal conclusion.

Common Wording for Causation Answers

It mistakes an effect for a cause.

It fails to consider that an association between two things might be due to their common relationship to a third factor.

Conditional Logic Flaws

In Chapters 2 and 3, you were introduced to the formal notation of conditional statements. This approach can be really helpful when you're dealing with an argument chock-full of conditional statements. Let's look at a full argument:

If you study, you will improve. Therefore, studying will guarantee a successful outcome.

study → improve study → successful outcome

What do we need to add to make this a valid argument? We already know that studying guarantees improvement. If we add the claim that improvement guarantees a successful outcome, we're in business. The conditional statements would then link up perfectly:

study → improve → successful outcome

If you saw this argument core on a Flaw question, you could predict that the correct answer would describe that gap in reasoning using either the language of assumption or the language of objection:

(A)   The argument presumes that any improvement leads to a successful outcome.

(B)   The argument fails to consider that one might improve somewhat without the outcome being successful overall.

More commonly, however, when you encounter conditional arguments on Flaw questions, they will hinge on one of two illegal logic moves: an illegal reversal or an illegal negation.

Remember from your earlier practice with conditionals that when you're given a conditional statement, you can infer its contrapositive. **You reach the contrapositive by both reversing *and* negating the statement.** For example:

All dogs are mammals: dog → mammal

If something is not a
mammal, then it is not a   –mammal → –dog
dog:

You cannot, however, just reverse *or* negate the statement:

Illegal reversal:	mammal → dog
Illegal negation:	–dog → –mammal

We can use our real-world knowledge for a moment here to make sense of these. Our original statement is a true story. All dogs are indeed mammals. But the reversal and negation are not true statements. All mammals are not, in fact, dogs. Likewise, just because something isn't a dog doesn't guarantee that it's not a mammal. (Did you notice that an illegal negation is just the contrapositive of an illegal reversal? Bonus points for you!) The simplest conditional Flaw questions will make one of these two moves: They will offer a conditional statement as its premise and then conclude the statement's reversal or negation. Consider the following:

> Buster goes to the local movie theatre only when the tickets are half-priced. Thus, any time the local movie theatre offers tickets at a 50% discount, Buster will certainly attend a movie.

Let's diagram the argument:

> <u>Buster goes to movie → ½ price tickets</u>
> ½ price tickets → Buster goes to movie

(Notice that here we used a line to separate the premise from the conclusion. This is a helpful notation because it's quick to use and it avoids the potential confusion of using conditional arrows and the argument core arrow in a single diagram.)

Did you spot the flaw here? We've seen this reasoning error before—the conclusion is an illegal reversal of the premise.

But what about this argument?

> Buster goes to the local movie theatre only when the tickets are half-priced. Thus, he will be sure to attend tonight's showing of *The Birds* because tickets are being offered at 50% off.

How is this argument different than the one we previously looked at? Take a moment to notate the argument core.

Did you notice that this argument had two premises instead of one? The first conditional premise is the same in both arguments, but the second argument offers an additional premise after the word "because." That second premise tells us that one of the two conditions from the first premise is actually happening. Our conclusion is that the other condition from the first premise is going to happen, too. The appropriate diagram is:

> Buster goes to movie → ½ price tickets
> <u>½ price tickets</u>
>
> Buster goes to movie

MANHATTAN
PREP

This argument is also an example of reversed logic, but it's a little more complicated than the first one. Instead of simply *concluding* the reversal of the premise, this argument *assumes* the reversal of the premise by treating the fact that there are half-price tickets to *The Birds* as though it guarantees that Buster will attend the film.

This is how conditional logic often plays out in Flaw questions: We're given a conditional statement (or two), then told that one of the things from the conditional statement actually takes place. In logic-speak, this is called **fulfilling the condition.** From that, the argument concludes that another thing from the conditional statement actually takes place (another condition is fulfilled). Depending on which condition is fulfilled and which is concluded, these arguments can be valid or invalid. Take a look at the following. Can you tell which are valid and which are not?

1. A → B
   A
   _____
   B

2. F → G
   –G
   _____
   –F

3. P → Q
   Q
   _____
   P

4. X → Y
   –X
   _____
   –Y

Argument 1 is valid. The conditional statement tells us that A guarantees B, so when we fulfill A, we know we're going to get B as well. Argument 2 is also valid. If F guarantees G, whenever we don't have G, we can't have F. That's the contrapositive. Argument 3 is invalid. It's reversing the logic, just like the argument about Buster at the movies. We know P guarantees Q, but that doesn't mean Q guarantees P. Argument 4 negates the logic. Just because X guarantees Y doesn't mean that –X guarantees –Y.

These are tough concepts and the learning curve can be steep, so if that was challenging for you, you weren't alone. Take a look at the following drill to get some more practice diagramming and assessing conditional arguments.

Drill It: Conditional Logic Flaws

For the following sets, diagram the arguments contained within. Determine if each argument depends on an illegal reversal, an illegal negation, or a valid contrapositive of the conditional premise, and then circle the appropriate term. Check your work after the first set to make sure you're practicing correctly. We've completed the first one for you as an example.

Set 1

1. If Jon uses his boat, he is on a river. Jon is on a river, so he must be using his boat.

> boat → river   (or, if you prefer, B → R)
> river
> _____
> boat

           Valid Contrapositive   Illegal Negation   (Illegal Reversal)

2. If Jon uses his boat, he is on a river. So, if Jon isn't on a river, he can't be using his boat.

           Valid Contrapositive   Illegal Negation   Illegal Reversal

3. If Jon uses his boat, he is on a river. Jon is not on a boat, so he isn't on a river.

           Valid Contrapositive   Illegal Negation   Illegal Reversal

Don't forget to check your work before moving on to Set 2.

MANHATTAN
PREP

Set 2

1. Luz calls Rebecca only in the morning. Luz could not have called Rebecca just now, since it's 3pm.

        Valid Contrapositive   Illegal Negation   Illegal Reversal

2. Luz calls Rebecca only in the morning. Luz has not called Rebecca, so it must not be the morning.

        Valid Contrapositive   Illegal Negation   Illegal Reversal

3. Luz calls Rebecca only in the morning. Thus, Luz and Rebecca talk daily.

        Valid Contrapositive   Illegal Negation   Illegal Reversal

Solutions: Conditional Logic Flaws

Set 1

1. If Jon uses his boat, he is on a river. Jon is on a river, so he must be using his boat.

$$\frac{\text{boat} \rightarrow \text{river} \quad \text{(or, if you prefer, B} \rightarrow \text{R) river}}{\text{boat}}$$

Valid Contrapositive   Illegal Negation   (Illegal Reversal)

2. If Jon uses his boat, he is on a river. So, if Jon isn't on a river, he can't be using his boat.

$$\frac{\text{B} \rightarrow \text{R}}{-\text{R} \rightarrow -\text{B}}$$

(Valid Contrapositive)   Illegal Negation   Illegal Reversal

3. If Jon uses his boat, he is on a river. Jon is not on a boat, so he isn't on a river.

$$\frac{\begin{array}{c} \text{B} \rightarrow \text{R} \\ -\text{B} \end{array}}{-\text{R}}$$

Valid Contrapositive   (Illegal Negation)   Illegal Reversal

Set 2

1. Luz calls Rebecca only in the morning. Luz cannot have called Rebecca just now, since it's 3 pm.

> call → morning
> −morning
> ――――――――――
> −call

(Valid Contrapositive)   Illegal Negation   Illegal Reversal

2. Luz calls Rebecca only in the morning. Luz has not called Rebecca, so it must not be the morning.

> call → morning
> −call
> ――――――――――
> −morning

Valid Contrapositive   (Illegal Negation)   Illegal Reversal

3. Luz calls Rebecca only in the morning. Thus, Luz and Rebecca talk daily.

> call → morning
> ――――――――――
> talk daily

This argument is a little different. Its conclusion isn't conditional, but it also isn't one of the fulfilled conditions from the premise. However, in concluding that the two women speak daily, what does this argument assume? It assumes the reversal of the first premise: that Luz calls Rebecca *every* morning (morning → call).

Valid Contrapositive   Illegal Negation   (Illegal Reversal)

Conditional Logic Chains

With the basics of conditional logic in mind, find the flaw in this argument:

> *PT13, S2, Q26*
>
> If Blankenship Enterprises has to switch suppliers in the middle of a large production run, the company will not show a profit for the year. Therefore, if Blankenship Enterprises in fact turns out to show no profit for the year, it will also turn out to be true that the company had to switch suppliers during a large production run.

The fact that both the premise (the first sentence) and the conclusion (the second) are conditional statements is a strong indication that notation might help us tackle this question. To that end, go ahead and notate the argument if you haven't already.

You should have come up with something like this:

> switch suppliers → –profit
> _____
> –profit → switch suppliers

It's hard to imagine a clearer visual example of reversed logic than the diagram above. How could the LSAT have made things trickier? Find the flaw in this argument:

> If Blankenship Enterprises has to switch suppliers in the middle of a large production run, the company will not show a profit for the year. The company will have a holiday party only if it shows a profit. Therefore, since there will be no holiday party this year, the company must have switched suppliers.

In this case, we see two conditional premises:

> switch suppliers → –profit
>
> party → profit

Taking the contrapositive of either statement will allow us to chain the conditional logic. If we contrapose the first statement (profit → –switch suppliers), we can link the two statements together into a chain:

> party → profit → –switch suppliers

If we contrapose the second statement (–profit → –party), we get this chain:

> switch suppliers → –profit → –party

MANHATTAN
PREP

Do you notice anything about the two chains? They are contrapositives of one another! This means that when you are manipulating conditional statements to link them to each other, it doesn't matter which statement you choose to contrapose, because either way, the resulting chains are logically equivalent.

Now, back to the argument. Unlike the original version, which has only conditional premises, this argument includes a simple factual premise: There will be no party. The author seems to think that this fulfills a condition, but there's a problem. Let's look at our conditional chain in both forms:

switch suppliers → –profit → –party

party → profit → –switch suppliers

Looking at the first chain, using *–party* to conclude *switch suppliers* would be an illegal reversal. You can't travel backwards up the chain! Similarly, if you used the second chain, you'd be relying on negated logic. It turns out that we can't infer anything from the fact that there's no party, because that never appears as a sufficient condition for us to fulfill. We have *–party* as a necessary condition and *party* as the sufficient condition.

Depending on which premise you chose to contrapose to link the two conditional statements, this argument might look like reversed logic or it might look like negated logic. Even though the two flaws operate in different ways, they are one another's logical equivalent. When an LSAT argument requires that you contrapose one of several conditional statements in order to chain them together, the correct answer will not ask you to differentiate between negated and reversed logic.

Drill It: Conditional Logic Chaining Flaws

Before we look at a full LSAT question, let's do one more set of the drill we did earlier. As before, notate each argument and determine if it depends on an illegal reversal, an illegal negation, or a valid contrapositive of the conditional premise.

1. Whit watches football every Sunday. He wears his Broncos jersey every time he watches football. Therefore, when it is not Sunday, he doesn't wear his Broncos jersey.

Valid Contrapositive   Illegal Negation   Illegal Reversal

2. Whit watches football every Sunday. He wears his Broncos jersey every time he watches football. It's clearly Sunday: Whit has on his Broncos jersey.

Valid Contrapositive   Illegal Negation   Illegal Reversal

3. Whit watches football every Sunday. He wears his Broncos jersey every time he watches football. Whit didn't wear a Broncos jersey today, so today must not be Sunday.

Valid Contrapositive   Illegal Negation   Illegal Reversal

Solutions: Conditional Logic Chaining Flaws

1. Whit watches football every Sunday. He wears his Broncos jersey every time he watches football. Therefore, when it is not Sunday, he doesn't wear his Broncos jersey.

Sunday → football
football → jersey
─────────────────
−Sunday → −jersey

        Valid Contrapositive   (Illegal Negation)   Illegal Reversal

2. Whit watches football every Sunday. He wears his Broncos jersey every time he watches football. It's clearly Sunday: Whit has on his Broncos jersey.

Sunday → football
football → jersey
jersey
─────────────────
Sunday

        Valid Contrapositive   Illegal Negation   (Illegal Reversal)

3. Whit watches football every Sunday. He wears his Broncos jersey every time he watches football. Whit didn't wear a Broncos jersey today, so today must not be Sunday.

Sunday → football
football → jersey
−jersey
─────────────────
−Sunday

        (Valid Contrapositive)   Illegal Negation   Illegal Reversal

Conditional Logic Flaws: Finding the Assumption

Before we leave the topic of Conditional Logic Flaws, let's try a full question that commits one, but includes a slightly twisted question stem:

PT14, S4, Q9

Since anyone who supports the new tax plan has no chance of being elected, and anyone who truly understands economics would not support the tax plan, only someone who truly understands economics would have any chance of being elected.

The reasoning in the argument is flawed because the argument ignores the possibility that some people who

(A)   truly understand economics do not support the tax plan

(B)   truly understand economics have no chance of being elected

(C)   do not support the tax plan have no chance of being elected

(D)   do not support the tax plan do not truly understand economics

(E)   have no chance of being elected do not truly understand economics

Here, we are given two premises and a conditional conclusion. With so many conditional statements, you should have used a diagram to avoid trying to hold the entirety in your head. (Even if you *could* hold all of this in your head, why use up your mental stamina doing so?)

Diagram:

> support tax plan → –electable
> understand economics → –support tax plan
> _____
> electable → understand economics

Can we chain these premises together? In order to do so, we'd need the necessary condition of one to be the sufficient condition of another. We don't have that at the moment, so as on the last example, we'll need to check the contrapositives. Here are the contrapositives of both statements:

> electable → –support tax plan
> support tax plan → –understand economics

Even with the contrapositives, it looks like there is no way to chain the two statements together. However, the conclusion of the argument combines elements from both premises: *electable* → *understand economics.* Where did the author go wrong?

The contrapositive of our first premise makes it clear that if you are electable you won't support the tax plan. That's a guarantee. But this author concludes that if you are electable, you understand economics. That means she is assuming that not supporting the tax plan means you understand economics:

> –support tax plan → understand economics

This is a reversal of the second premise!

Next, we need to take a look at this question stem. It tells us that the argument is flawed because it has overlooked a possibility. This should be familiar language. As we saw at the beginning of the chapter, answer choices themselves will often begin with that language. Those choices, if they are to be correct, must introduce a possibility that blows up the argument. The same applies here. If the question states that the argument is flawed because it has overlooked a possibility listed in the answers, the correct answer will invalidate the argument and the incorrect answers will not.

So, how can we use the assumption we identified to predict the correct answer? If the author assumes that *everyone* who doesn't support the tax plan does understand economics, what possibility has our argument overlooked? The possibility that some people who don't support the plan also don't understand economics!

This is a useful pattern to memorize: **Whenever an argument assumes a conditional relationship (A → B), it overlooks the possibility that A could occur without B.**

So to recap, we can look at the flaw in this argument in two complementary ways:

> Assumption: Anyone who *does not* support the tax plan *does* understand economics.

> Flaw: The argument overlooks the possibility that someone could not support the tax plan *and* not understand economics.

Correct answer (D) matches that prediction exactly: "[The reasoning in the argument is flawed because the argument ignores the possibility that some people who] do not support the tax plan do not truly understand economics."

If you found yourself confused by that question, you're not alone. Try it again in a few days. Spiraling back on tough topics is often how we learn best.

Speaking of how to study, let's look at a question through a nonformal lens. It can be really helpful to review questions with Conditional Logic Flaws in this manner, in order to strengthen your intuitive grasp of the underlying issues.

Don't diagram this argument. Who are we failing to consider in our conclusion?

Anyone who opposes the war on Pandora has no chance of being our next president. Everyone who was involved with the previous administration supports the war on Pandora. Therefore, only people involved with the previous administration have a chance of being our next president.

We accept that Pandora pacifists are unelectable this time around. But who says that war *supporters* have to come from within the ranks of the previous administration? That's a reversal! Couldn't some outsider also support the war and thus still have a chance at being the next president?

While you are always free to diagram a conditional argument on your scratch paper on test day, you may find that once you are comfortable with conditional reasoning, some arguments don't need diagramming. On the other hand, some arguments will be too much to handle *without* diagramming. In any case, after you try a question and before you check your answer, make sure you have worked the problem both ways—diagram and lawyerly intuition—and made the connection between the two. Your logic skills will grow immensely as you do.

Speaking of growing your logic skills, let's take a moment to talk about one of the most helpful tools in your logic-growing arsenal: blind review.

Blind Review

If you want to get the most out of every question you attempt, blind review is a must. Be forewarned—it's a time-consuming process, and it may *feel* more productive to hurry on to more new questions. That feeling, however, has led many an ambitious student astray. Practice doesn't make perfect unless you keep adjusting your ways of thinking about the test. A careful process of blind review will help you make the necessary adjustments.

Step 1. Flag questions as you do them

The central tenet of blind review is that you are reviewing questions *before* you know whether you got them right or wrong. This means that you need to decide which questions to review *as you do them*. Totally stumped? Flag it for review. Eliminated some answers but had to "go with your gut" for your final pick? Flag it for review. Confident you got it right, but boy did that take a while? Flag it for review. That answer *feels* wrong but I don't know why? Flag it for review.

Step 2. Try the flagged questions again

Without checking to see whether you got the flagged questions right or wrong, try each a second time, untimed.

Step 3. Check the answers, but don't record them

Now that you've made your second attempt at each flagged question, it's time to see if you got them right or wrong. Try to notice only whether you got questions correct or incorrect. Try *not* to take note of the correct answer for questions that you missed, because you'll be trying them one last time. Just mark them as incorrect, then move on to Step 4. If you find it hard not to remember the correct answers once you've seen them, take some time between Steps 3 and 4.

Step 4. The third attempt

Attempt any question that you marked incorrect in Step 3 one last time.

Step 5. The final check

Check your answers again, this time recording the correct answer for each question.

Step 6. The deep dive

Now that you know which answers are right and wrong, take a deep dive into any question or answer that's still giving you trouble. If there's an explanation, read it actively. If a lightbulb goes off in your head and you have an "aha" moment, stop reading and go back to the question. Try to work it from there with your newfound knowledge before returning to the explanation.

If all this sounds like more than you bargained for, don't worry—that's natural. But the LSAT test writers put a lot of time and thought into writing tempting wrong answers. In order to sidestep their traps, you need to match their effort. Like all things LSAT, the more you do blind review, the more efficient you'll become. And if you are facing a big time crunch and can't do all 6 steps sometimes, don't scrap the process entirely. Instead, cut out Steps 3 and 4, but leave the rest of the process intact. Don't fall into the bad habit of checking answers first and reviewing only the questions you got wrong. This approach robs you of the opportunity to learn! Figuring out what led you to make the *right* call on a tough question is just as valuable as figuring out what led you to make the wrong call, and you won't ever explore those *right* calls if you only review questions that you miss.

Common Wording for Conditional Logic Answers

Conditional Logic Flaws are immensely important to understand. Not only do the flaws themselves show up throughout the Logical Reasoning section, but within Flaw question *answer choices*, they are one of the most commonly mentioned. Given how often they show up, it should be no surprise that we often see them mentioned in wrong answers. Thus, not only do we need to know how to identify these flaws when they *are* occurring, we need to know when they *are not*. If we can do so, those wrong answers become easy eliminations.

Here are typical forms for answer choices referring to Conditional Logic Flaws, with the indicator words emphasized:

> The author treats a condition that is **required** for a certain outcome as though that condition is **enough** to produce that outcome.

> The author assumes that a **guaranteed** means of achieving a result is the **only** means of achieving that result.

> Takes a **necessary** condition for a phenomenon to be a **sufficient** condition.

MANHATTAN
PREP

Because these answers are abstract, they can be hard to untangle and therefore tempting. Here are two handy rules of thumb to help you turn these otherwise tempting answers into easy eliminations:

1. If there is no conditional logic present in the argument, the answer choice is very likely wrong.

2. If there is conditional logic present in the argument, defer judgment. Working wrong-to-right on the other choices may make it easier to confirm or deny the answer choice.

Let's take a look at one more tricky turn of phrase:

> The author mistakes a condition under which a phenomenon occurs for the *only* condition under which that phenomenon occurs.

With this phrasing, it can be easy to get turned around. Is this saying that the condition is necessary and was mistaken for sufficient or vice versa? Consider this sentence:

> Lauren mistook her enemy for a friend.

Is this person actually Lauren's friend or her enemy? This wording means that the person is actually an enemy. Whatever characterization comes after the "mistook" is the real deal; the one that follows the "for" is the mistake. So in the previous example, the author is mistaking a sufficient condition ("a condition under which a phenomenon occurs") for a necessary condition ("the only condition under which that phenomenon occurs"). This thing is sufficient, but the author believes it is necessary.

Meet the Other Flaws

Now that the two most common logical flaws, those involving causation and conditional logic, have been covered in depth, it's time to explore the other types that we will encounter in Flaw questions (and beyond).

Keep in mind that the language we use to describe the flaws here won't always be the language used to describe the flaw in an answer choice. Sometimes, the answers will be very abstract. Other times, the flaws will be presented in terms of what the argument assumes or fails to consider.

That shouldn't deter you from mastering these types! Flaw questions are perhaps the most flash card–friendly question type in Logical Reasoning. During this section (and the entire chapter), if you encounter an argument that stumps you or that you can't easily categorize, write out the stimulus on one side of a flash card and describe the flaw on the other side. Later, we'll discuss more ideas for how to improve on Flaw questions.

Introduce Yourselves

Take a look at these arguments. Each of them is flawed in some way. Describe each argument's flaw in as few words as possible. At the end, try to arrange all of the arguments into groups representing ones that have similar flaws. Each argument below has at least one other argument that commits the same flaw!

Argument	**Flaw Descriptions**

1. LSAT students should never take full-length practice tests in the weeks leading up to taking an official LSAT. After all, taking an LSAT, like running a marathon, is a huge test of endurance, and marathon runners do not practice for their races by running full marathons in the weeks leading up to a race.

2. In a recent study, 50 pairs of overweight adults committed to each other to exercise daily. If both partners kept to a prescribed exercise regimen, a significant donation was made to a charity of the pair's choice. Compared to the average overweight adult, these participants exercised far more often and lost more weight. Thus, a sense of responsibility toward others is a strong motivating factor in achieving personal goals.

3. Dr. Tanning is the world's foremost heart surgeon. In a recent editorial, she opposed the new health care bill on the grounds that the increased taxes it introduces would not be offset by a corresponding decrease in health care costs for the average consumer. For this reason, it is important to reject the new bill.

4. If everyone participates in the fundraiser, it will guarantee Kirby's reelection. If no one participates, it will guarantee Kirby's defeat. Thus, this upcoming fundraiser will determine the outcome of our next election.

5. Traveling by bus and traveling by plane are two ways to get to Las Vegas. Since Lucien is going to Las Vegas and can't afford to take a plane, he will have to take a bus.

MANHATTAN
PREP

Argument	**Flaw Descriptions**

6. We should not accept the health inspector's findings. He is the husband of the leader of the council of restaurant owners and thus would benefit financially from certifying restaurants.

7. Many people have attempted to prove that time travel is impossible. Since they have always failed to do so, it must be that time travel really is possible.

8. The professional dancers at the American Ballet Theatre tend to have interests in other types of art, including those that do not involve performance. Thus, it is clear that concentrated effort in one art leads one to develop interests in other art forms.

9. Samspoke is finally passing jPhone in popularity among smartphones. As evidence, consider a recent poll conducted on Samspoke's corporate campus in Michigan: 80% of those surveyed expressed greater preference for Samspoke's latest product offerings than for jPhone's.

10. My husband assumed that Jamie Lee was from Louisiana, based on her accent. But later we learned that she was rehearsing an accent for a play. Thus, Jamie Lee must not be from Louisiana.

11. My opponent suggests that we should ban the sale of sugary drinks in public buildings, but he himself drinks three cans of sugary beverages every day. Thus, his opinion cannot be trusted and the ban he proposes should not be enacted.

12. It is widely believed among professors that every paragraph needs a strong topic sentence. Thus, any paragraph that lacks a strong topic sentence must be flawed.

13. Francine's pies are considerably sweeter than Darrell's. Therefore, her pies are not as nutritious as his.

Here is how we categorize the flawed arguments above:

> Sampling Flaw: 2, 8, 9
>
> Comparison Flaw: 1, 13
>
> Ad Hominem: 6, 11
>
> Appeal to Inappropriate Authority: 3, 12
>
> Unproven vs. Untrue: 7, 10
>
> False Choice: 4, 5

You almost surely used different words to describe these flaws—that's fine. We'll explain each of these terms, but what is important is whether you can see how the pairs (or triplet) have the same underlying flaw.

Now, let's take a look at each of these flaws in more depth.

Sampling Flaws

2. In a recent study, 50 pairs of overweight adults committed to each other to exercise daily. If both partners kept to a prescribed exercise regimen, a significant donation was made to a charity of the pair's choice. Compared to the average overweight adult, these participants exercised far more often and lost more weight. Thus, a sense of responsibility toward others is a strong motivating factor in achieving personal goals.

8. The professional dancers at the American Ballet Theatre tend to have interests in other types of art, including those that do not involve performance. Thus, it is clear that concentrated effort in one art leads one to develop interests in other art forms.

9. Samspoke is finally passing jPhone in popularity among smartphones. As evidence, consider a recent poll conducted on Samspoke's corporate campus in Michigan: 80% of those surveyed expressed greater preference for Samspoke's latest product offerings than for jPhone's.

The LSAT loves to cite some study or piece of evidence and then take it too far. When arguments are based on one lone premise—a study, survey, sample, or example—ask yourself three questions about whether it's prudent to conclude anything **broader** from it:

1. Is it a robust enough sample size to draw the conclusion?

2. Does the sample seem representative of the group that the conclusion is about?

3. Is there a concern about biased or pressured responses to the survey?

Consider argument 8. It takes evidence about professional dancers in one single company, and from that, draws a conclusion about all artists. The sample that's drawn on here is way too small too support the breadth of that conclusion. This type of flaw is typically referred to as an overgeneralization, and it occurs anytime a sample or example is too narrow to support a broad conclusion. (You may have noticed that this argument also contains a Causation Flaw: How do we know that one thing *leads* to the other? As we've seen before, one argument may have several different flaws.)

Another concern about samples is whether they are representative. Take argument 9, for example. Here, the people surveyed about their phone preference all work for one of the two companies being compared in the survey. Is it likely that these people are representative of the general population? No way! They all share a characteristic that the broader population doesn't—working for Samspoke. This seems likely to impact their preferences, for one phone over the other.

Whether a group self-selects into a sample also impacts the sample's representativeness. A study might attract certain individuals who are predisposed in a way that affects the data. In argument 2, for example, the pairs of overweight adults had to consent to be a part of this study. It's possible that people who were willing to sign up for this study were especially motivated or simply had an excess of free time. For that reason, they may not be representative of the average overweight adult.

Although it makes sense to suspect a Sampling Flaw whenever an argument relies on a sample, it is important to recognize that some samples on the LSAT will be used in a valid way. Suppose an argument said, "Some of the third graders I talked to said that they liked peas. So it's not true that all grade-schoolers hate peas."

Is this argument taking for granted that the third graders in question are representative of grade-schoolers in general?

No, actually. This argument is valid. If even one third grader likes peas (or simply doesn't hate them), our conclusion is true. To prove that not all dogs are nice, you only need one mean Chihuahua! Thus, the sample of third graders doesn't need to be representative of grade-schoolers to prove the conclusion, since the conclusion does not generalize about all grade-schoolers. To disprove an "all" statement, we just need one counterexample.

TIPS: Recognizing and reacting to Sampling Flaws:

- Notice that the basis for the conclusion is one example, testimonial, survey, or sample.

- Assess the sample size and representativeness of the sample.

- Verify that the author's conclusion extrapolates away from the evidence.

Common Wording for Sampling Flaw Answers

> *It generalizes too hastily from a potentially atypical sample.*
>
> *It bases a general conclusion on too few examples.*
>
> *It takes for granted that the observed students are representative of students in general.*

Comparison Flaws

1. LSAT students should never take full-length practice tests in the weeks leading up to taking an official LSAT. After all, taking an LSAT, like running a marathon, is a huge test of endurance, and marathon runners do not practice for their races by running full marathons in the weeks leading up to a race.

13. Francine's pies are considerably sweeter than Darrell's. Therefore, her pies are not as nutritious as his.

Comparison Flaws are committed when a comparison between two things (or phenomena, as the LSAT likes to call them) is used to draw an invalid conclusion.

There are many forms that comparisons can take, but it's useful to focus on two general forms:

1. X is similar to Y in one respect, so they must be similar in another respect.

2. X is dissimilar to Y in one respect, so we can conclude that they are dissimilar in some other respect.

The first form includes the use of a bad analogy. Typically, the analogy is bad when the two things are similar in one respect but dissimilar in another, making them not analogous. That is the problem with argument 1.

In argument 13, the two pies are dissimilar in their level of sweetness, and it is inferred that they are also dissimilar in their nutritional value. But one dissimilarity doesn't necessarily lead to the other—we aren't told what makes a pie nutritious, but there are probably other elements of nutrition to consider than sweetness. For that matter, it could be that a sweeter pie is actually *more* nutritious. Thus, the comparison is incomplete. This is the most common problem with comparative arguments on the LSAT, so every time a comparison is made, your intuitive question should be "Is something missing in this comparison?"

Consider the following comparative argument:

> *PT33, S3, Q15*
>
> Scientists hoping to understand and eventually reverse damage to the fragile ozone layer in the Earth's upper atmosphere used a spacecraft to conduct crucial experiments. These experiments drew criticism from a group of environmentalists who observed that a single trip by the spacecraft did as much harm to the ozone layer as a year's pollution by the average factory, and that since the latter was unjustifiable so must be the former.

MANHATTAN
PREP

Wow, that's a lot of pollution! But is it fair to condemn both equally? *Unlike* the factory, the spacecraft is ultimately concerned with protecting and healing the ozone layer. That aspect of the difference is what is missing in this comparison.

TIPS: Recognizing and reacting to Comparison Flaws:

- Notice that two things are held up as similar, dissimilar, or analogous.

- Consider what might be missing or faulty in the comparison.

Common Wording for Comparison Flaw Answers

While some answers noting a Comparison Flaw will be explicit (*treats as similar two cases that are different in a critical respect*), often the reference is implicit. For example, the answer could point out an assumed relationship: *takes for granted that sweeter foods are less nutritious.* Or the answer might point out a problem with applying a comparison: *the argument overlooks the possibility that factors other than sweetness influence the nutritional value of a food.*

Ad Hominem Flaws

6. We should not accept the health inspector's findings. He is the husband of the president of the council of restaurant owners and thus would benefit financially from certifying restaurants.

11. My opponent suggests that we should ban the sale of sugary drinks in public buildings, but he himself drinks three cans of sugary beverages every day. Thus, his opinion cannot be trusted and the ban he proposes should not be enacted.

An argument commits an Ad Hominem Flaw when it presents someone else's claim and then rejects the validity of the claim through some personal attack. Most commonly, these arguments will accuse the arguer either of hypocrisy, as in argument 11, or of having a vested interest in the outcome of the argument, as in argument 6. Ad Hominem arguments can be appealing, since it is wise to be wary of hypocrites and those with ulterior motives. However, we still need to attack the *logic* of their arguments—the extent to which the premises prove the conclusion. A salesperson may well say some questionable things to convince you that his product is the best, but the mere fact that he wants your money does not help us to determine that his product is *not* the best.

Consider this example:

4

PT14, S4, Q15

Magazine article: The Environmental
            Commissioner's new proposals are called
            "Fresh Thinking on the Environment," and a
            nationwide debate on them has been
            announced. Well, "fresh thinking" from such
            an unlikely source as the commissioner does
            deserve closer inspection. Unfortunately we
            discovered that these proposals are virtually
            identical to those issued three months ago by
            Tsarque Inc. under the heading "New
            Environmentalism" (Tsarque Inc.'s chief is a
            close friend of the commissioner). Since
            Tsarque Inc.'s polluting has marked it as an
            environmental nightmare, in our opinion the
            "nationwide debate" can end here.

As we can expect, the correct answer—"dismisses the proposals because of their source rather than because of their substance"—points out that the argument focuses on attacking *the commissioner* instead of the commissioner's *ideas*.

TIPS: Recognizing and reacting to Ad Hominem Flaws:

- These arguments all pit the author against someone else whose claim the author is criticizing.

- Notice any accusations, either stated or implied, of bad character, hypocrisy, or potential ulterior motive.

Common Wording for Ad Hominem Flaw Answers

The author rejects a claim because of its source rather than its content.

The argument attempts to discredit a theory by discrediting those who espouse that theory.

The argument is flawed in that it criticizes the specialist's motives for holding a position rather than the position itself.

Appeal to Inappropriate Authority

3.   Dr. Tanning is the world's foremost heart surgeon. In a recent editorial, she opposed the new
     health care bill on the grounds that the increased taxes it introduces would not be offset by
     a corresponding decrease in health care costs for the average consumer. For this reason, it is
     important to reject the new bill.

12.   It is widely believed among professors that every paragraph needs a strong topic sentence. Thus,
      any paragraph that lacks a strong topic sentence must be flawed.

On the opposite side of the Ad Hominem Flaw is a rarer type of flaw in which the author appeals to a source of authority to support the conclusion. Instead of *discrediting* a theory by *criticizing* its bad source, these flawed arguments *support* a theory by *introducing* a source that may not be reliable. Sometimes an argument will use the fact that experts agree about something to conclude that that thing is actually the case, as in argument 12. This might not seem like a flaw at all. If the experts all agree, isn't the conclusion likely to be correct? Quite possibly, but the author is still assuming that the experts aren't wrong in some way. We have to accept the author's premise (that the experts agree), but we don't have to accept the experts' opinion when we haven't been given any actual evidence. If the experts are wrong, the argument falls apart.

Other times, this flaw appears as an appeal to an authority speaking outside his or her realm of expertise. Argument 3 is an example of the latter flaw. Dr. Tanning might be the best heart surgeon—we accept the premise—but that doesn't make her an expert in the economics of health care. Even if she were an expert in this domain, too, the author would still be assuming that her opinion is correct. Maybe other experts disagree!

TIPS: Recognizing and reacting to Appeal to Inappropriate Authority Flaws:

- These arguments all cite an expert opinion to support the conclusion.

- Ask yourself if there is any evidence other than the expert opinion cited.

- Ask yourself whether it's clear that the expert cited actually has expertise in the area relevant to the conclusion.

Common Wording for Appeal to Inappropriate Authority Answers

It appeals to the fact that supposed experts have endorsed the argument's main conclusion rather than appealing to direct evidence for that conclusion.

The argument fails to recognize that expertise in one area of medicine does not imply expertise in all areas of medicine.

Unproven vs. Untrue

7. Many people have attempted to prove that time travel is impossible. Since they have always failed to do so, it must be that time travel really is possible.

10. My husband assumed that Jamie Lee was from Louisiana, based on her accent. But later we learned that she was rehearsing an accent for a play. Thus, Jamie Lee must not be from Louisiana.

The name of this category doesn't refer to the idea that the conclusion is unproven—that's true in every flawed argument. Rather, it refers to arguments that conclude that something is untrue based on evidence that says only that the thing hasn't been sufficiently proven. Here are three versions:

1. Concluding that something doesn't exist because we can't prove that it does

2. Concluding that something is incorrect because it lacks support or the support is flawed

3. Concluding that something is real or correct because we can't prove it false

Argument 7 falls into the third category. Argument 10 is a bit trickier, and it falls into the second category. The husband, hearing an accent, came up with a theory about where Jamie Lee was from. When it came to be known that she was working on an accent for a play, the evidence for his theory was compromised. It could now be possible that the Louisiana accent he heard was the one that she was rehearsing. However, just because the evidence no longer lines up as strongly with his theory, we cannot guarantee that his theory is false. She could be from Louisiana *and* rehearsing a Louisiana accent.

Here is an example of an argument with an Unproven vs. Untrue Flaw and a correct answer:

> ### PT11, S4, Q3
>
> A group of scientists who have done research on the health effects of food irradiation has discovered no evidence challenging its safety. Supporters of food irradiation have cited this research as certain proof that food irradiation is a safe practice.
>
> A flaw in the reasoning of the supporters of food irradiation is that they
>
> (E) use the lack of evidence contradicting a claim as conclusive evidence for that claim

TIPS: Recognizing and reacting to Unproven vs. Untrue Flaws:

- Look for discussions of compromised or insufficient evidence in the premises with phrases such as "failed to prove" or "disproven."

- Remember that a lack of evidence never *disproves* something. Without evidence, we can't say whether the conclusion is true or false.

Common Wording for Unproven vs. Untrue Answers

> *The author takes a failure to prove a certain claim as proof that the claim is false.*
>
> *The author fails to consider that a claim that was believed for questionable reasons is nonetheless true.*

False Choice

4. If everyone participates in the fundraiser, it will guarantee Kirby's reelection. If no one participates, it will guarantee Kirby's defeat. Thus, this upcoming fundraiser will determine the outcome of our next election.

5. Traveling by bus and traveling by plane are two ways to get to Las Vegas. Since Lucien is going to Las Vegas and can't afford to take a plane, he will have to take a bus.

In this flaw, the author considers only two options or two groups, mistakenly assuming them to be the only two possibilities. Remember the mayoral race problem in Chapter 2? The conclusion was based on a False Choice between Esposito and Krasman.

In cases such as argument 4, this plays out as the failure to consider a middle ground between two extremes: everyone participates and no one participates. It seems possible (even quite likely) that *some, but not all* of the people will participate, and we don't know what outcome that will have. In argument 5, we cannot be sure that Lucien is taking a bus, since he might travel in a myriad of other ways. (Car? Bicycle? Broomstick?)

Consider this argument containing a False Choice Flaw:

> *PT8, S4, Q8*
>
> The director of a secondary school where many students were having severe academic problems empanelled a committee to study the matter. The committee reported that these students were having academic problems because they spent large amounts of time on school sports and too little time studying. The director then prohibited all students who were having academic problems from taking part in sports in which they were active. He stated that this would ensure that such students would do well academically.

Here, the director has overlooked that high school students may spend their time pursuing other activities that interfere with schoolwork, even if banned from school sports. If his assumption is wrong, they will have choices other than returning to academic studies.

TIPS: Recognizing and reacting to False Choice Flaws:

• Be on the lookout for two groups or options.

• Sometimes, both options will appear in the premises. Other times, an argument will rule out one possibility in the premise and arrive at some other, previously unmentioned, possibility in the conclusion.

3. Whenever you see a binary relationship in a Flaw question, ask yourself, "Are there any other options here that are being overlooked?"

Common Wording for False Choice Answers

The author fails to consider that there may be other...

The author neglects to rule out competing options.

Challenges of Flaw Answers

Recognizing the flaw in an argument is only half the battle. While any LR question can include tricky answers, Flaw questions are especially fraught with tempting wrong answers and hard-to-spot correct answers.

Here are some common challenges:

- The answers, especially those describing logical bad moves, are worded very abstractly.

- The wrong answers temptingly name something that does take place in the argument but is not a flaw.

- Wrong answers temptingly name a flaw that is not in that argument.

- The correct answer describes the flaw that we saw in an unexpected way or identifies a flaw we did not notice. Sometimes an easy-to-spot "decoy" flaw will distract us from the trickier flaw that is actually referenced in the correct answer.

Standing our ground by knowing what actually happened in the argument and whether it's a flaw will be crucial to our success.

Let's lay out five tools and then apply them to some LSAT questions:

1. Learn to recognize abstract references to common LSAT flaws.

2. When an abstract answer is not easily recognizable, replace the abstract language with parts of the argument.

3. Declare, "That didn't happen!" when an answer choice refers to a flaw not in the argument. (This hinges on the first tool above, as well as knowing the argument's core.)

4. Declare, "So what?" when an answer choice refers to a part of the argument that is not a flaw. (This hinges on understanding the nature of flaws.)

5. As usual, defer judgment and work wrong-to-right on Flaw questions.

Let's dive in with a pair of questions.

PT23, S2, Q19

Even in ancient times, specialized farms (farms that grow a single type of crop or livestock) existed only where there were large commercial markets for farm products, and such markets presuppose urban populations. Therefore the extensive ruins in the archaeological site at Kadshim are probably the remains of a largely uninhabited ceremonial structure rather than of a densely populated city, since the land in the region of Kadshim could never have supported any farms except mixed farms, which grow a variety of crops and livestock.

Which one of the following is an error of reasoning in the argument?

(A)   taking the fact that something is true of one sample of a class of things as evidence that the same is true of the entire class of things

(B)   taking the nonexistence of something as evidence that a necessary precondition for that thing also did not exist

(C)   interpreting an ambiguous claim in one way in one part of the argument and in another way in another part of the argument

(D)   supposing that because two things usually occur in conjunction with one another, one of them must be the cause of the other

(E)   drawing a conclusion that is simply a restatement of one of the premises on which the argument is based

PT34, S2, Q9

A university study reported that between 1975 and 1983 the length of the average workweek in a certain country increased significantly. A governmental study, on the other hand, shows a significant decline in the length of the average workweek for the same period. Examination of the studies shows, however, that they used different methods of investigation; thus there is no need to look further for an explanation of the difference in the studies' results.

The argument's reasoning is flawed because the argument fails to

(A)   distinguish between a study produced for the purposes of the operation of government and a study produced as part of university research

(B)   distinguish between a method of investigation and the purpose of an investigation

(C)   recognize that only one of the studies has been properly conducted

(D)   recognize that two different methods of investigation can yield identical results

(E)   recognize that varying economic conditions result in the average workweek changing in length

Challenge 1: Abstract Language

A common way that test writers will try to challenge you is to write the answer choices using generalized, or abstract, language. This is the LSAT's way of directly testing your ability to get to the underlying logic of the argument—whether the argument is specifically about archaeological sites or workweeks is secondary to the test writer.

The great news is that reading for the core, and for structural flaws, in the manner that we've recommended up to this point is the ideal way to get prepared to evaluate an abstract or generalized answer choice.

The bad news is that many of the answers may seem attractive at first, especially if you have not noticed the flaw in the argument. Since most of the incorrect answers could be correct for other arguments, you may read them and think, "Yeah, that sounds like a problem." This makes it even more important for you to be strong at finding the core and recognizing common flaws. With practice, you can get much more efficient at spotting which of the many possible flaws is being tested in a particular case.

Let's look back at the first of our two examples to discuss this issue in depth:

> *PT23, S2, Q19*
>
> Even in ancient times, specialized farms (farms that grow a single type of crop or livestock) existed only where there were large commercial markets for farm products, and such markets presuppose urban populations. Therefore the extensive ruins in the archaeological site at Kadshim are probably the remains of a largely uninhabited ceremonial structure rather than of a densely populated city, since the land in the region of Kadshim could never have supported any farms except mixed farms, which grow a variety of crops and livestock.
>
> Which one of the following is an error of reasoning in the argument?

The core of this argument could be seen as follows:

single-crop farms require large
markets, which require urban
population (city)

+

Kadshim couldn't have single-crop
farms

➡ Kadshim was likely a religious
site, not a city

If you considered the argument this way, you might have noticed the conclusion's leap from the idea that the site at Kadshim was not a city to the conclusion that it must have been a *religious site*. Perhaps it was some third option—perhaps a sports arena. This is a False Choice Flaw.

We got the core, but with so many conditional logic indicators, diagramming this argument makes a lot of sense. If you didn't do so already, diagram it now before reading on.

You should have come up with something like this:

single-crop farms → big markets
big markets → urban population
–single-crop farms
_____

–urban population (likely religious site)

Looking at it this way, you should be able to quickly spot another flaw: illegal negation!

Take another pass through the answer choices before reading on to make sure you still agree with your answer and to see if you understand what all the other answers are saying:

> Which one of the following is an error of reasoning in the argument?
>
> (A)   taking the fact that something is true of one sample of a class of things as evidence that the same is true of the entire class of things
>
> (B)   taking the nonexistence of something as evidence that a necessary precondition for that thing also did not exist
>
> (C)   interpreting an ambiguous claim in one way in one part of the argument and in another way in another part of the argument
>
> (D)   supposing that because two things usually occur in conjunction with one another, one of them must be the cause of the other
>
> (E)   drawing a conclusion that is simply a restatement of one of the premises on which the argument is based

Answer choice (B) is correct, but it uses very challenging language to describe the illegal negation we predicted. Take a moment to practice matching up the abstract elements of this answer choice with the actual components of the argument. This is an exercise you should make part of your regular review of abstract Flaw answer choices. Replace the abstract terms with the real terms of the argument.

In this case, "taking the nonexistence of something" refers to the fact that there could not have been single-crop farms. Next, we have some logical descriptors: "As evidence" indicates that the first part was a premise and "a necessary precondition for that thing" means something that single-crop farms required—in this case, urban populations. The answer says that this "necessary precondition"—an urban population—"also did not exist." Fully translated, (B) says, "The argument jumps from the fact that there couldn't have been single-crop farms to the idea that urban populations, which are required to have those farms, must not have existed."

If (B) threw you, you'll want to make a flash card. Put "taking the nonexistence of something as evidence that a necessary precondition for that thing also did not exist" on one side, and then describe that flaw in simpler terms (e.g., "illegal negation") on the other side.

Let's decode the answer choices. We'll start with (A).

(A)   taking the fact that something is true of one
        sample of a class of things as evidence that
        the same is true of the entire class of things

This is referring to a Sampling Flaw in an argument, but this argument didn't draw on a sample for its evidence, so **that didn't happen!** Also, if it had played out as (A) describes, we still might have said **so what?** Valid arguments can draw conclusions about a population from a sample of that population, as long as the sample is big enough and representative of the whole.

(C)   interpreting an ambiguous claim in one way in
        one part of the argument and in another way
        in another part of the argument

This describes a flaw we'll meet shortly: Equivocation. It means that a term is used to mean two different things in one argument. We know **that didn't happen** since the terms all retain their initial meaning.

(D)   supposing that because two things usually
        occur in conjunction with one another, one of
        them must be the cause of the other

We've met this before—a Causation Flaw! Specifically, this is suggesting that a correlation is used to support a causal claim. **That didn't happen!**

(E)   drawing a conclusion that is simply a
        restatement of one of the premises on which
        the argument is based

This is a flaw that rarely occurs in arguments, but that shows up *a lot* as an incorrect answer choice: Circular Reasoning. We'll see examples of this flaw shortly.

The key to recognizing correct answers written in an abstract or generalized way is to read for the core and anticipate the reasoning flaw. When stuck between a couple of answer choices, do not simply compare them against one another—this will lead you nowhere! Instead, compare each one to the argument core. Figure out which one best applies to the situation in the argument and to your understanding of the core.

Many abstract answer choices involve descriptions of LSAT flaws that show up almost exclusively in wrong answers and are rarely the flaw you actually have to identify. Many others incorrectly describe the evidence or the conclusion. Match the answer against the argument!

We'll get more practice with understanding abstract answer choices shortly, but now, let's look at the second question and another challenge of Flaw questions.

Challenge 2: From Another Point of View

Sometimes you do everything correctly and come to understand the flaw or flaws perfectly, and you get to the answer choices and *still*…none of the answers fit what you are looking for! What could be wrong?

Perhaps that didn't happen to you with this next problem, but in any case, let's use it to illustrate the issue:

> *PT34, S2, Q9*
>
> A university study reported that between 1975 and 1983 the length of the average workweek in a certain country increased significantly. A governmental study, on the other hand, shows a significant decline in the length of the average workweek for the same period. Examination of the studies shows, however, that they used different methods of investigation; thus there is no need to look further for an explanation of the difference in the studies' results.
>
> The argument's reasoning is flawed because the argument fails to

Here is a simplified version of the core:

two studies used different methods   no need to look further for an explanation of the difference in results

Do you spot a flaw in reasoning here? It looks like a Causation Flaw. In this case, the author assumes that because two studies used different methods of investigation and got different results, the different methods were the *reason* for the difference in the studies' results. Couldn't it be that, though the methods of investigation were different, something else caused the difference in the results?

We go in anticipating an answer that addresses this issue. One way it could be worded is that *"the author fails to recognize that there could be other reasons for differences in the studies' results."* We could also be more specific and say that *"the author fails to consider that some other factor could be responsible for both the difference in methods and the difference in results."* For instance, maybe one study was conducted by people with greater expertise, leading them both to adopt different methods and to work with greater accuracy.

Unfortunately, we don't have either of those in the answer choices! Let's review what we've got:

The argument's reasoning is flawed because the argument fails to

(A)   distinguish between a study produced for the
           purposes of the operation of government and a
           study produced as part of university research

Hmm, does this happen? The author certainly doesn't tell us what the difference between these two kinds of study is, just that these two particular studies used different methods. However, is this a problem? Is it necessary that there be a clear difference between these kinds of study? No, because the conclusion is about a stated difference in the methods of investigation. Therefore, (A) is out of scope.

(B)   distinguish between a method of investigation
           and the purpose of an investigation

The argument doesn't involve the purpose of the investigation. Look back at the argument: There is no gap between method and purpose.

(C)   recognize that only one of the studies has been
           properly conducted

We've been given no claim or evidence that only one of the studies was properly or improperly conducted.

(D)   recognize that two different methods of
           investigation can yield identical results

This is in the ballpark of our core, but certainly isn't what we anticipated. Still, it's the best we've seen so far, so let's keep it.

(E)   recognize that varying economic conditions
           result in the average workweek changing in
           length

This doesn't have a direct impact on the reasoning in the argument. Perhaps it might be relevant if the two studies covered different periods of time, but they don't.

The only answer that looks at all viable is (D), but could it be correct? Let's look at it one more time:

MANHATTAN
PREP

(D)   [The argument fails to] recognize that two different methods of
         investigation can yield identical results

What does this mean, exactly? The author doesn't consider the fact that you can use two different methods of investigation and end up with the same result. This doesn't sound like a Causation Flaw. It seems more like a Comparison Flaw: The author assumes that if two studies are different in one way (methods), they *must* be different in another way (results).

However, this is really just a different perspective on the flaw that we saw initially. The author is mistakenly assuming a one-to-one connection between methods and results. Different methods, the argument assumes, will of course lead to different results—that's still causation. We can think of the flaw as failing to consider other ways that the different results could have happened (Causation Flaw), or we can think of the flaw as failing to consider that different methods can yield the same result (Comparison Flaw).

In order to avoid eliminating correct answers, train yourself to eliminate not because the answer fails to match your prediction, but because it is wrong. Work wrong-to-right by deferring judgment on any answer that isn't a clear dud.

Meet Some Rarer Flaws

There are still some flaws that we have not discussed and that show up in Flaw questions. Often, these rarer flaws are the basis of incorrect answer choices. However, all of them have shown up as correct answers on the test, so we can't just eliminate them on sight. It will help to be comfortable with each of them.

The goal is not to become a master categorizer, but it will pay off to develop your familiarity with these flaws and the sort of answer choice wording that describes them.

Introduce Yourselves

Let's start, as we did last time, by first describing the flaw in the argument, and then trying to match the arguments that commit similar flaws. You know the drill!

Argument	**Flaw Description**

1. The new task force committee is sure to be an efficient one, since each member assigned to the committee is an efficient worker.

2. At Ben's office, the employee with the most seniority gets the closest parking spot. Since Janice is the only senior citizen at Ben's office, she must have the closest parking spot.

3. In 2013, the legislative assembly voted to raise gasoline taxes by 6%. So clearly, Ms. Tompkins, who was a member of that assembly, is disingenuous when she says that she opposes all tax increases.

4. Two-thirds of college-educated people support a proposal to limit access to guns to only those who have passed a security check, while one-third of those without a college degree support it. Thus, more people support the proposal than reject it.

5. Police should be permitted to charge individuals with whatever offense will result in the most just outcome. We know this because the healthy functioning of a business market requires that different businesses charge different prices for services so that the proper pricing is established and maintained through a balance of supply and demand.

6. The idea that comic book collectors are especially likely to attend science fiction movies on opening weekend is wrong. A large-scale study found that comic book collectors make up only 15% of opening weekend audiences for science fiction movies.

MANHATTAN
PREP

4

This page is intentionally blank. Enjoy!

Here is how we categorize the flawed arguments above:

Part vs. Whole: 1, 3
Equivocation: 2, 5
Percent vs. Amount: 4, 6

Part vs. Whole

1. The new task force committee is sure to be an efficient one, since each member assigned to the committee is an efficient worker.

3. In 2013, the legislative assembly voted to raise gasoline taxes by 6%. So clearly, Ms. Tompkins, who was a member of that assembly, is disingenuous when she says that she opposes all tax increases.

As we see above, Part vs. Whole Flaws can either take the form of extending the characterization of a group to each member or vice versa. In argument 1, we're told that each member of the committee is efficient. That characterization is then projected onto the committee as a whole, but perhaps the team doesn't work well together, despite their individual efficiency. In argument 3, we're told that the assembly as a whole voted a particular way, and it is concluded that an individual member of the assembly must have voted that way, too. Perhaps Ms. Tompkins opposed the tax increase but was outvoted.

To spot Part vs. Whole Flaws, look out for references to membership and for broad characterization about a group or its members. This can look like a Sampling Flaw, but instead of drawing statistical conclusions, these arguments usually come to conclusions about the properties of *every* member of a group or of the group as a whole.

This flaw can be well disguised:

> ### PT31, S3, Q18
>
> It is impossible to do science without measuring. It is impossible to measure without having first selected units of measurement. Hence, science is arbitrary, since the selection of a unit of measurement—kilometer, mile, fathom, etc.—is always arbitrary.

Because this argument opens up with two conditional statements that chain together, one might predict a Conditional Logic Flaw. We can represent the chained premises in one of two ways. We can read the negated terms rather directly (without measuring, no science: *–measure → –science*) or read the structure as showing that measurement is *necessary* for science (*science → measure*). Either chain, when contraposed, will yield the other:

science → measure → select units

–select units → –measure → –science

However, the flaw in this argument is not a reversal or negation of the chain. The argument introduces a new characteristic (arbitrary) and concludes that because one of the terms has this characteristic, another must have it, too. This isn't a Conditional Logic Flaw at all, unless we figure that the author is interpreting the conditional arrows as equal signs. The attribution of characteristics alerts us to the fact that this is a Part vs. Whole Flaw.

Common Wording for Part vs. Whole Answers

The author takes for granted that a characteristic of each part of the event must also be true of the whole event.

The author infers that each part of a system has a certain property on the basis that the system itself has that property.

Equivocation

2.   At Ben's office, the employee with the most seniority gets the closest parking spot. Since Janice is the only senior citizen at Ben's office, she must have the closest parking spot.

5.   Police should be permitted to charge individuals with whatever offense will result in the most just outcome. We know this because the healthy functioning of a business market requires that different businesses charge different prices for services so that the proper pricing is established and maintained through a balance of supply and demand.

Equivocation occurs when the author uses the same word or concept in two very different ways. Comparing the first usage to the second usage, we should see that the terms of the discussion have greatly shifted.

In argument 2, "seniority" means how long you've worked there, while "senior" means old. The oldest person at an office isn't necessarily the person who has worked there longest. Argument 5 makes a similar move with the word "charge."

Here is one last example. See if you can spot the Equivocation Flaw:

> *PT10, S1, Q10*
>
> Broadcaster: Our radio station has a responsibility
> to serve the public interest. Hence, when our
> critics contend that our recent exposé of events
> in the private lives of local celebrities was
> excessively intrusive, we can only reply that the
> overwhelming public interest in these matters
> makes it our responsibility to publicize them.

In the first sentence, the phrase "public interest" is used to suggest the well-being of society. In the last sentence, the same phrase is used in reference to the topics about which people are curious. The correct answer abstractly explains this: "improperly exploiting an ambiguity in the phrase 'public interest.'"

The vast majority of answer choices referencing an Equivocation Flaw are wrong. Most often, arguments with these wrong answers will use a term twice, but use it consistently. When you see this type of answer choice, take a second look at any words or concepts used twice. If a term has indeed shifted in meaning from one use to the other, then you've found the flaw within the argument (e.g., "Okay, the first time we said 'maturity,' we were talking about it in the sense of civic responsibility. The second time we said 'maturity,' we were discussing physical development").

Common Wording for Equivocation Answers

It uses the term "_____" in two different ways.

It equivocates with regard to a central concept.

It trades on an ambiguity in the term "_____."

Percent vs. Amount

4. Two-thirds of college-educated people support a proposal to limit access to guns to only those who have passed a security check, while one-third of those without a college degree support it. Thus, more people support the proposal than reject it.

6. The idea that comic book collectors are especially likely to attend science fiction movies on opening weekend is wrong. A large-scale study found that comic book collectors make up only 15% of opening weekend audiences for science fiction movies.

Doesn't the LSAT know that we're going to law school to get *away* from math?

Don't worry—although the LSAT will test us on some mathematical ideas, they are fairly rare and not too advanced. In fact, we've already covered this territory in the Reading Like a Lawyer drill in Chapter 2. In both of the arguments above, the essential flaw is ignoring the total from which each percent (or fraction) is taken.

In argument 4, the number of college-educated people could be far smaller than the number of those without a college education. Thus, it's impossible to use the fractions to compare actual numbers.

In argument 6, the total number of comic book collectors could be (and, of course, actually is) much smaller than the number of non–comic book collectors. If, say, only 5% of the population collects comic books, then the fact that these collectors make up 15% of opening weekend audiences at sci-fi films suggests that they are three times more likely to attend than others. (If you were wondering if there is a Sampling Flaw in this argument, note that the premise cites a "large-scale study." The sample size is large, and the wording indicates that we should accept the finding.)

Try to make a mathematical objection to this argument:

MANHATTAN
PREP

PT13, S2, Q24

> A certain airport security scanner designed to detect explosives in luggage will alert the scanner's operator whenever the piece of luggage passing under the scanner contains an explosive. The scanner will erroneously alert the operator for only one percent of the pieces of luggage that contain no explosives. Thus in ninety-nine out of a hundred alerts explosives will actually be present.

Think about the real numbers of the groups being discussed. How many bags will have bombs? Let's say 10 per day, which is still horrifyingly high. How many bags will not have bombs in them? Let's say 1,000 per day. With these numbers, we'll get 10 alerts from actual bomb bags (100% of 10 = 10) and we'll get 10 false alerts (1% of 1,000 = 10). Thus, there will be 20 alerts, but a bomb will be present for only 10. That's 50% of alerts, not 99%.

The correct answer points out that the author "substitutes one group for a different group in the statement of a percentage." (If the argument had concluded that "99% of the time that there isn't a bomb, there will be no alert," that would be correct, as it would draw a conclusion within the same group—bags without explosives.)

Whenever a comparison between two percents (or fractions) is used to make a point, compare the totals from which those two percents are drawn.

Wrong Answer Flaws

We just met some flaws above that tend to show up as wrong answers. However, some flaws are *far* more often used for wrong answers. While the following two flaws have shown up as the correct answer on several occasions, the real benefit to being familiar with them is to be more confident when eliminating them.

Circular Reasoning

> Chocolate is the best flavor of ice cream because all other flavors are inferior.

> Some critics have claimed that Bertram is a man of poor character, pointing to allegations that he committed fraud and paid coworkers to maintain their silence. But they are clearly mistaken, for his high character would prevent him from committing these acts.

An argument with this flaw boils down to saying, "Believe X. Why? Because X is true." No logical reason is offered for why you should believe X. In a more involved version, as seen in the second example above, the author will consider but sweep away potentially disconfirming evidence because he is already convinced of the truth of the conclusion.

When you encounter this flaw in an argument, the argument core should be hard to establish because the premise and conclusion are the same! You could see these arguments as having *no* flaw, since we're supposed to accept the premise.

However, another interpretation is that there is no premise. The author draws a conclusion and says that it's correct... because it's correct.

Common Wording for Circular Reasoning Answers

It assumes what it sets out to prove.

It presupposes what it seeks to establish.

The conclusion is merely a restatement of the premise.

Self-Contradiction

Self-Contradiction has shown up a few times as the correct answer, but it appears over and over again as a wrong answer. Why is the LSAT so reluctant to pull out this flaw? It would sound too jarring and obvious:

Tony is clearly the best athlete in the squad. Compared to his teammates, his performance is consistently regarded as subpar.

Huh? Obviously, the LSAT wouldn't present us with something that obvious. If this flaw were present, it would be buried a bit:

High snowfall is a boon to the economy of our state. Snow removal, road repair, and lost productivity cost our state more than the entirety of the tax revenue it receives, consistently requiring that the state issue bonds and assume an ever-increasing amount of debt. At the same time, a large snowfall results in a staggering influx of dollars from out-of-state tourists, providing enough money in sales taxes to pay for all state services.

How can it be that snow puts the state into debt *and* pays for everything?

The writers of the LSAT seem to agree that self-contradictory arguments are too ridiculous to actually use, but they love to add the description to wrong answer choices!

Common Wording for Self-Contradiction Answers

It bases its conclusion on claims that are inconsistent with each other.

It contains premises that cannot all be true.

4

This page is intentionally blank. Enjoy!

Drill It: Abstract Flaw Answers

While not every wrong answer choice will be one of the common LSAT flaws, many will be. Sometimes, these common flaws will be presented clearly in the answer choices, but at other times, they will be buried within abstract language. Let's practice decoding Flaw answers and spotting common flaws in them. Label each answer choice in the "Answer" list by writing the letter that corresponds to the flaw that it describes. Circle any answer choices that you are unable to immediately categorize so that you can review them later.

Abstract Flaws

A. Ad Hominem

B. Appeal to Inappropriate
   Authority

C. Causation Flaw

D. Circular Reasoning

E. Comparison Flaw

F. Conditional Logic (Reversal)

G. Conditional Logic (Negation)

H. Equivocation

I. False Choice

J. Part vs. Whole

K. Sampling Flaw

L. Self-Contradiction

M. Unproven vs. Untrue

Answers

_____ 1. bases its conclusion on claims that are inconsistent with
         each other

_____ 2. takes for granted that a characteristic of each part of the
         event must also be true of the whole event

_____ 3. contains premises that cannot all be true

_____ 4. the conclusion is a restatement of the premise

_____ 5. generalizes too hastily from a potentially atypical sample

_____ 6. relies on an ambiguity in the term "trace"

_____ 7. assumes that the animals observed are representative of
         animals in general

_____ 8. mistakes an effect for a cause

_____ 9. assumes that a condition under which a phenomenon is said to occur is the only condition under which that phenomenon occurs

_____ 10. concludes that each part of a system has a certain property on the basis that the system itself has that property

_____ 11. attempts to discredit a theory by discrediting those who espouse that theory

_____ 12. equivocates in regards to a central concept

_____ 13. rejects a claim because of its source rather than its content

_____ 14. treats a failure to prove a certain claim as proof that the claim is false

_____ 15. bases a general conclusion on too few examples

_____ 16. fails to consider that a claim that was believed for questionable reasons is nonetheless true

_____ 17. makes an illegitimate appeal to the authority of an expert

_____ 18. neglects the possibility that the phenomenon is the result of both factors

_____ 19. fails to consider that an association between two things might be due to their common relationship to a third factor

_____ 20. presupposes what it seeks to establish

_____ 21. overlooks the possibility that the same thing may contribute to both phenomena

_____ 22. fails to consider that the end result may be caused by neither phenomenon

_____ 23. treats a condition that is required for a certain outcome as though that condition is enough to produce that outcome

_____ 24. treats a potential cause as an effect

_____ 25. relies on the use of an inappropriate analogy

Solutions: Abstract Flaw Answers

Answer Key

1. L

2. J

3. L

4. D

5. K

6. H

7. K

8. C

9. F or G

10. J

11. A

12. H

13. A

14. M

15. K

16. M

17. B

18. I

19. C

20. D

21. C or I

22. I

23. F

24. C

25. E

Drill It: Flawed Arguments & Answers

Now that we're familiar with the common flaws and how they're worded within answer choices, let's put the two skills together by matching arguments to answer choices. To keep you on your toes, we've included a flaw or two that we haven't yet met.

Abstract Answers

A. generalizes too readily from a potentially atypical sample

B. does not distinguish between opinion and fact

C. presumes the truth of its conclusion

D. infers, on the grounds that a claim has never been proven true, that the claim is therefore false

E. interprets a factor that is guaranteed to produce a certain result as one required to produce that result

F. fails to consider that a property shared by each part of something need not be shared by the whole

G. bases its conclusion in part on a claim that is inconsistent with the conclusion

H. presumes that two methods mentioned are the only two methods available

I. opposes someone's claim because the claim, if true, would be advantageous to that person

J. allows the meaning of a key term to shift

K. mistakes a cause for an effect

MANHATTAN
PREP

Flawed Arguments

_____ 1. Every word used in McCracken's latest novel has been used in previous novels. Since the words in her novel fail to be innovative, her novel must also fail to be innovative.

_____ 2. People who take an LSAT course always improve their ability to do Logic Games. Clearly, José took an LSAT course. After all, his ability to do Logic Games has improved tremendously.

_____ 3. Most scientists believe that there is no life on Venus. However, we have never been able to send a probe there to prove such a contention. Therefore, there actually is life on Venus.

_____ 4. People who regularly nap are more likely than others to have insomnia. So, it seems that getting more rest during the day makes one more restless at night.

_____ 5. Mayor Henderson argues that her recent initiative to improve the quality of water fountain drinking water has been a success. However, this claim should not be believed, since she would undoubtedly benefit politically if people believed that she had improved water quality.

_____ 6. Haley plans to attend graduate school, but she is not interested in law, so she must be going to business school.

_____ 7. Nirvana was clearly the best band in the '90s. After all, consider all the other bands from the '90s: None of them compare to Nirvana.

_____ 8. According to a recent poll conducted at the Republican National Convention, 80% of respondents said that they would vote for a Republican candidate over any of the Democratic candidates. It seems likely, therefore, that Republicans will win the upcoming election.

_____ 9. People accuse Victor and Marissa of not having a committed relationship. But apparently those people are wrong, for Marissa recently committed Victor to a mental hospital.

_____ 10. The quickest way to learn a new language is to read and translate a novel that is written in that language. Although this takes longer than simply traveling to a country where that language is spoken and immersing yourself in it, learning a language via a novel teaches you subtext, symbolism, and many other advanced usages of the language.

_____ 11. A recent poll found that 87% of respondents considered genetically modified vegetables to be less healthful than nonmodified vegetables. Public health would be well served, therefore, by a ban on genetically modified vegetables.

4

Solutions: Flawed Arguments & Answers

Answer Key

(Don't forget to use blind review! Retry the tough ones first before you use this answer key, then use the key to check what you got right and wrong *without* recording the right answer so you can take a final stab at the ones you got wrong on your second pass.)

1. F	5. I	9. J
2. E	6. H	10. G
3. D	7. C	11. B
4. K	8. A	

Each explanation here focuses on the language cues from the argument that should have led to you considering the correct flaw. However, be careful: These cues are a starting point, not an ending point. If you see any of the language cues, it's a hint to consider whether the argument is committing that flaw; it's not a guarantee that the associated flaw is being committed.

1. **(F)**

This has a Part vs. Whole Flaw. Any time you see an argument mention individual elements, be on the lookout for a reference to the group (and vice versa). In this case, "Every word" is the red flag. Other language cues for this flaw include *society, individual, citizen, element,* and *entire.*

2. **(E)**

As soon as you saw "always," you should have been ready for a Conditional Logic Flaw (in this case, an illegal reversal). Look for this flaw in any argument that features a conditional keyword.

3. **(D)**

Unproven vs. Untrue Flaws can be difficult to spot. However, a good indicator that an argument is committing this type of flaw is that the author reaches the exact opposite conclusion of someone else. Also, consider this flaw any time there's an assertion that there are failed attempts to prove or disprove something.

4. **(K)**

Correlation vs. Causation: chestnut classic! Any time we have a causal conclusion (*because, causes, incurs, makes, decreases,* etc.), we should check for this flaw. Also, correlative words in the premises should be a sign that the argument is heading in this direction (*tend to, associated with, more/less likely, also,* etc.).

MANHATTAN PREP

5. (I)

Ad Hominem Flaws tend to seem a little funny, depending on what name the person gets called. If you see someone's motives questioned, they face accusations of being a hypocrite, or their past misdeeds are brought up, there's a good chance it's this flaw that's occurring.

6. (H)

False Choice flaws tend to have a conclusion that, well, makes a choice. Any time you see a recommendation or a selection in the conclusion, consider this flaw. Also, "must have been/must be" or similar language suggests that we might be dealing with this flaw.

7. (C)

Circular Reasoning rarely shows up as a correct Flaw answer on the LSAT, but this is what it looks like. The two statements convey the very same idea—Nirvana is the best band of the '90s. The only time you can pick the Circular Reasoning Flaw answer is when you can underline two sentences that say literally the same thing.

8. (A)

Sampling Flaws, like this one, tend to live in arguments that feature surveys, studies, or polls. Whenever an argument features one of these, consider whether the group mentioned in the premise matches the one in the conclusion.

9. (J)

Equivocation Flaws require the author to use the same word twice, while relying on different definitions each time. If an argument relies on a word that shows up a couple times, always check to make sure that the author didn't switch the meanings. This is a rare flaw on the LSAT.

10. (G)

The Self-Contradiction Flaw has shown up only a few times on the exam. These arguments feature conclusions that are contradicted by the premises. If the author brings up a fact as a supporting premise (not as part of an opposing point) and the fact runs directly against the conclusion, consider this flaw. However, it's unlikely you'll see this flaw anywhere other than in a wrong answer.

11. (B)

Whenever an argument talks about what people *believe*, or *think*, or what their *opinions* are, we might have an Opinion vs. Fact Flaw. These usually come up in surveys. Imagine the world we'd live in if everything that a majority of people believed were true…another version of this flaw is the inverse—just because something is true doesn't mean people *know* or *believe* it.

How to Improve on Flaw Questions

As we stated at the start of this chapter, improving on Flaw questions can pay dividends. Not only do Flaw questions show up frequently, but improvements you make on this question type will translate to success on other types throughout Logical Reasoning. Thus, it's worth honing your study routine for this question type.

In addition to blind review of questions and answer choices (both correct and not), one great technique for this question type is to make flash cards for hard-to-categorize arguments and answer choices. Put the argument or answer choice on one side and a simple explanation of the flaw and/or the flaw name on the other.

Another idea is to cut Flaw questions out of every paper LSAT you complete—as part of your review, not during the practice test! Label each one with the type of flaw it exhibits (if it's one you can categorize) and group them together. See what similarities and differences those arguments have.

Conclusion

Let's review what is required for success on Flaw questions:

1. **Read for the core.** Like all Assumption Family questions, Flaw questions are designed to test your ability to evaluate the relationship between the supporting evidence and the conclusion. Make sure you zero in on the core.

2. **See a gap and anticipate the flaw.** You know that these arguments are going to be flawed, and you know the flaw will be stated as an assumption, an objection, or a bad move. If you don't see a typical flaw (e.g., Part vs. Whole), try to state the flaw in one of those ways.

3. **Beware of all explanations, claims of causation, and conditional logic.** Recognize when the author is explaining something. Ask yourself, "Are any other explanations possible?" When you see a claim of causation, ask yourself, "Could the reverse be true, or could a third thing have caused both?" When you see conditional logic indicators, start diagramming, and be on the lookout for reversed or negated logic.

4. **Master the common flaws.** They show up over and over again, both in the arguments and in incorrect answers. Make flash cards for those that you struggle to identify quickly. See page 533 for a complete list of common flaw types.

5. **Stand up to challenging answers.** Practice interpreting abstract language—make it concrete by filling in terms from the argument—and be ready for answers that present the flaw from a slightly different perspective. Stand your ground when an answer references something that didn't happen in the argument or something that did happen but is not a flaw!

Drill It: Flaw Questions

1. PT14, S4, Q20

Monroe, despite his generally poor appetite, thoroughly enjoyed the three meals he ate at the TipTop Restaurant, but, unfortunately, after each meal he became ill. The first time he ate an extra large sausage pizza with a side order of hot peppers; the second time, he took full advantage of the all-you-can-eat fried shrimp and hot peppers special; and the third time, he had two of TipTop's giant meatball sandwiches with hot peppers. Since the only food all three meals had in common was the hot peppers, Monroe concludes that it is solely due to TipTop's hot peppers that he became ill.

Monroe's reasoning is most vulnerable to which one of the following criticisms?

(A)   He draws his conclusion on the basis of too few meals that were consumed at TipTop and that included hot peppers.

(B)   He posits a causal relationship without ascertaining that the presumed cause preceded the presumed effect.

(C)   He allows his desire to continue dining at TipTop to bias his conclusion.

(D)   He fails to establish that everyone who ate TipTop's hot peppers became ill.

(E)   He overlooks the fact that at all three meals he consumed what was, for him, an unusually large quantity of food.

2. PT11, S2, Q9

Any announcement authorized by the head of the department is important. However, announcements are sometimes issued, without authorization, by people other than the head of the department, so some announcements will inevitably turn out not to be important.

The reasoning is flawed because the argument

(A)   does not specify exactly which communications are to be classified as announcements

(B)   overlooks the possibility that people other than the head of the department have the authority to authorize announcements

(C)   leaves open the possibility that the head of the department never, in fact, authorizes any announcements

(D)   assumes without warrant that just because satisfying a given condition is enough to ensure an announcement's importance, satisfying that condition is necessary for its importance

(E)   fails to distinguish between the importance of the position someone holds and the importance of what that person may actually be announcing on a particular occasion

4

3. PT14, S2, Q10

The government of Penglai, an isolated island, proposed eliminating outdoor advertising except for small signs of standard shape that identify places of business. Some island merchants protested that the law would reduce the overall volume of business in Penglai, pointing to a report done by the government indicating that in every industry the Penglai businesses that used outdoor advertising had a larger market share than those that did not.

Which one of the following describes an error of reasoning in the merchants' argument?

(A)   presupposing that there are no good reasons for restricting the use of outdoor advertising in Penglai

(B)   assuming without giving justification that the outdoor advertising increased market share by some means other than by diverting trade from competing businesses

(C)   ignoring the question of whether the government's survey of the island could be objective

(D)   failing to establish whether the market-share advantage enjoyed by businesses employing outdoor advertising was precisely proportionate to the amount of advertising

(E)   disregarding the possibility that the government's proposed restrictions are unconstitutional

4. PT19, S2, Q14

Herbalist: Many of my customers find that their physical coordination improves after drinking juice containing certain herbs. A few doctors assert that the herbs are potentially harmful, but doctors are always trying to maintain a monopoly over medical therapies. So there is no reason not to try my herb juice.

The reasoning in the herbalist's argument is flawed because the argument

(A)   attempts to force acceptance of a claim by inducing fear of the consequences of rejecting that claim

(B)   bases a conclusion on claims that are inconsistent with each other

(C)   rejects a claim by attacking the proponents of the claim rather than addressing the claim itself

(D)   relies on evidence presented in terms that presuppose the truth of the claim for which the evidence is offered

(E)   mistakes the observation that one thing happens after another for proof that the second thing is the result of the first

5. PT19, S4, Q6

Videocassette recorders (VCRs) enable people to watch movies at home on videotape. People who own VCRs go to movie theaters more often than do people who do not own VCRs. Contrary to popular belief, therefore, owning a VCR actually stimulates people to go to movie theaters more often than they otherwise would.

The argument is most vulnerable to criticism on the grounds that it

(A)   concludes that a claim must be false because of the mere absence of evidence in its favor

(B)   cites, in support of the conclusion, evidence that is inconsistent with other information that is provided

(C)   fails to establish that the phenomena interpreted as cause and effect are not both direct effects of some other factor

(D)   takes a condition that by itself guarantees the occurrence of a certain phenomenon to be a condition that therefore must be met for that phenomenon to occur

(E)   bases a broad claim about the behavior of people in general on a comparison between two groups of people that together include only a small proportion of people overall

6. PT19, S2, Q23

A museum director, in order to finance expensive new acquisitions, discreetly sold some paintings by major artists. All of them were paintings that the director privately considered inferior. Critics roundly condemned the sale, charging that the museum had lost first-rate pieces, thereby violating its duty as a trustee of art for future generations. A few months after being sold by the museum, those paintings were resold, in an otherwise stagnant art market, at two to three times the price paid to the museum. Clearly, these prices settle the issue, since they demonstrate the correctness of the critics' evaluation.

The reasoning in the argument is vulnerable to the criticism that the argument does which one of the following?

(A)   It concludes that a certain opinion is correct on the grounds that it is held by more people than hold the opposing view.

(B)   It rejects the judgment of the experts in an area in which there is no better guide to the truth than expert judgment.

(C)   It rejects a proven means of accomplishing an objective without offering any alternative means of accomplishing that objective.

(D)   It bases a firm conclusion about a state of affairs in the present on somewhat speculative claims about a future state of affairs.

(E)   It bases its conclusion on facts that could, in the given situation, have resulted from causes other than those presupposed by the argument.

4

7. PT11, S2, Q26

Why should the government, rather than industry or universities, provide the money to put a network of supercomputers in place? Because there is a range of problems that can be attacked only with the massive data-managing capacity of a supercomputer network. No business or university has the resources to purchase by itself enough machines for a whole network, and no business or university wants to invest in a part of a network if no mechanism exists for coordinating establishment of the network as a whole.

Which one of the following indicates a weakness in the argument?

(A)   It does not furnish a way in which the dilemma concerning the establishment of the network can be resolved.

(B)   It does not establish the impossibility of creating a supercomputer network as an international network.

(C)   It fails to address the question of who would maintain the network if the government, rather than industry or universities, provides the money for establishing it.

(D)   It takes for granted and without justification that it would enhance national preeminence in science for the government to provide the network.

(E)   It overlooks the possibility that businesses or universities, or both, could cooperate to build the network.

8. PT10, S1, Q8

Of 2,500 people who survived a first heart attack, those who did not smoke had their first heart attack at a median age of 62. However, of those 2,500, people who smoked two packs of cigarettes a day had their first heart attack at a median age of 51. On the basis of this information, it can be concluded that nonsmokers tend to have a first heart attack eleven years later than do people who smoke two packs of cigarettes a day.

The conclusion is incorrectly drawn from the information given because this information does not include

(A)   the relative severity of heart attacks suffered by smokers and nonsmokers

(B)   the nature of the different medical treatments that smokers and nonsmokers received after they had survived their first heart attack

(C)   how many of the 2,500 people studied suffered a second heart attack

(D)   the earliest age at which a person who smoked two packs a day had his or her first heart attack

(E)   data on people who did not survive a first heart attack

MANHATTAN
PREP

9. PT20, S4, Q14

Advertisement: A leading economist has determined that among people who used computers at their place of employment last year, those who also owned portable ("laptop") computers earned 25 percent more on average than those who did not. It is obvious from this that owning a laptop computer led to a higher-paying job.

Which one of the following identifies a reasoning error in the argument?

(A)   It attempts to support a sweeping generalization on the basis of information about only a small number of individuals.

(B)   Its conclusion merely restates a claim made earlier in the argument.

(C)   It concludes that one thing was caused by another although the evidence given is consistent with the first thing's having caused the second.

(D)   It offers information as support for a conclusion when that information actually shows that the conclusion is false.

(E)   It uncritically projects currently existing trends indefinitely into the future.

10. PT21, S2, Q5

Irrigation runoff from neighoring farms may well have increased the concentration of phosphorus in the local swamp above previous levels, but the claim that the increase in phosphorus is harming the swamp's native aquatic wildlife is false; the phosphorus concentration in the swamp is actually less than that found in certain kinds of bottled water that some people drink every day.

The argument is vulnerable to criticism on the ground that it

(A)   makes exaggerations in formulating the claim against which it argues

(B)   bases its conclusion on two contradictory claims

(C)   relies on evidence the relevance of which has not been established

(D)   concedes the very point that it argues against

(E)   makes a generalization that is unwarranted because the sources of the data on which it is based have not been specified

4

11. PT4, S1, Q8

Political theorist: The chief foundations of all governments are the legal system and the police force; and as there cannot be a good legal system where the police are not well paid, it follows that where the police are well paid there will be a good legal system.

The reasoning in the argument is not sound because it fails to establish that

(A)   many governments with bad legal systems have poorly paid police forces

(B)   bad governments with good legal systems must have poorly paid police forces

(C)   a well-paid police force cannot be effective without a good legal system

(D)   a well-paid police force is sufficient to guarantee a good legal system

(E)   some bad governments have good legal systems

12. PT36, S1, Q19

Although it has been suggested that Arton's plays have a strong patriotic flavor, we must recall that, at the time of their composition, her country was in anything but a patriotic mood. Unemployment was high, food was costly, and crime rates were soaring. As a result, the general morale of her nation was at an especially low point. Realizing this, we see clearly that any apparent patriotism in Arton's work must have been intended ironically.

The reasoning above is questionable because it

(A)   posits an unstated relationship between unemployment and crime

(B)   takes for granted that straightforward patriotism is not possible for a serious writer

(C)   takes for granted that Arton was attuned to the predominant national attitude of her time

(D)   overlooks the fact that some citizens prosper in times of high unemployment

(E)   confuses irony with a general decline in public morale

13. PT36, S3, Q13

While it was once believed that the sort of psychotherapy appropriate for the treatment of neuroses caused by environmental factors is also appropriate for schizophrenia and other psychoses, it is now known that these latter, more serious forms of mental disturbance are best treated by biochemical—that is, medicinal—means. This is conclusive evidence that psychoses, unlike neuroses, have nothing to do with environmental factors but rather are caused by some sort of purely organic condition, such as abnormal brain chemistry or brain malformations.

The argument is vulnerable to criticism because it ignores the possibility that

(A)   the organic conditions that result in psychoses can be caused or exacerbated by environmental factors

(B)   the symptoms of mental disturbance caused by purely organic factors can be alleviated with medicine

(C)   organic illnesses that are nonpsychological in nature may be treatable without using biochemical methods

(D)   the nature of any medical condition can be inferred from the nature of the treatment that cures that condition

(E)   organic factors having little to do with brain chemistry may be at least partially responsible for neuroses

MANHATTAN
PREP

14. PT16, S3, Q11

A controversial program rewards prison inmates who behave particularly well in prison by giving them the chance to receive free cosmetic plastic surgery performed by medical students. The program is obviously morally questionable, both in its assumptions about what inmates might want and in its use of the prison population to train future surgeons. Putting these moral issues aside, however, the surgery clearly has a powerful rehabilitative effect, as is shown by the fact that, among recipients of the surgery, the proportion who are convicted of new crimes committed after release is only half that for the prison population as a whole.

A flaw in the reasoning of the passage is that it

(A) allows moral issues to be a consideration in presenting evidence about matters of fact

(B) dismisses moral considerations on the grounds that only matters of fact are relevant

(C) labels the program as "controversial" instead of discussing the issues that give rise to controversy

(D) asserts that the rehabilitation of criminals is not a moral issue

(E) relies on evidence drawn from a sample that there is reason to believe is unrepresentative

15. PT36, S1, Q10

Cotrell is, at best, able to write magazine articles of average quality. The most compelling pieces of evidence for this are those few of the numerous articles submitted by Cotrell that are superior, since Cotrell, who is incapable of writing an article that is better than average, must obviously have plagiarized superior ones.

The argument is most vulnerable to criticism on which one of the following grounds?

(A) It simply ignores the existence of potential counterevidence.

(B) It generalizes from atypical occurrences.

(C) It presupposes what it seeks to establish.

(D) It relies on the judgment of experts in a matter to which their expertise is irrelevant.

(E) It infers limits on ability from a few isolated lapses in performance.

16. PT16, S2, Q22

Director of personnel: Ms. Tours has formally requested a salary adjustment on the grounds that she was denied merit raises to which she was entitled. Since such grounds provide a possible basis for adjustments, an official response is required. Ms. Tours presents compelling evidence that her job performance has been both excellent in itself and markedly superior to that of others in her department who were awarded merit raises. Her complaint that she was treated unfairly thus appears justified. Nevertheless, her request should be denied. To raise Ms. Tours's salary because of her complaint would jeopardize the integrity of the firm's merit-based reward system by sending the message that employees can get their salaries raised if they just complain enough.

The personnel director's reasoning is most vulnerable to criticism on the grounds that it

(A) fails to consider the possibility that Ms. Tours's complaint could be handled on an unofficial basis

(B) attempts to undermine the persuasiveness of Ms. Tours's evidence by characterizing it as "mere complaining"

(C) sidesteps the issue of whether superior job performance is a suitable basis for awarding salary increases

(D) ignores the possibility that some of the people who did receive merit increases were not entitled to them

(E) overlooks the implications for the integrity of the firm's merit-based reward system of denying Ms. Tours's request

4

Solutions: Flaw Questions

Answer Key

1. E	7. E	13. A
2. D	8. E	14. E
3. B	9. C	15. C
4. C	10. C	16. E
5. C	11. D	
6. E	12. C	

1. PT14, S4, Q20

Monroe, despite his generally poor appetite, thoroughly enjoyed the three meals he ate at the TipTop Restaurant, but, unfortunately, after each meal he became ill. The first time he ate an extra large sausage pizza with a side order of hot peppers; the second time, he took full advantage of the all-you-can-eat fried shrimp and hot peppers special; and the third time, he had two of TipTop's giant meatball sandwiches with hot peppers. Since the only food all three meals had in common was the hot peppers, Monroe concludes that it is solely due to TipTop's hot peppers that he became ill.

Monroe's reasoning is most vulnerable to which one of the following criticisms?

(A) He draws his conclusion on the basis of too few meals that were consumed at TipTop and that included hot peppers.

(B) He posits a causal relationship without ascertaining that the presumed cause preceded the presumed effect.

(C) He allows his desire to continue dining at TipTop to bias his conclusion.

(D) He fails to establish that everyone who ate TipTop's hot peppers became ill.

(E) He overlooks the fact that at all three meals he consumed what was, for him, an unusually large quantity of food.

Answer choice (E) is correct.

Monroe is proposing that one event is "due to" something else—in other words, the first event is caused by the second. Anytime we see a causation argument, we can think through our causation checklist:

1. Could it be the reverse? We know that he ate the peppers before he became ill, so this is a dead end unless it turns out that he ate the peppers because he could tell he was going to be ill. This doesn't seem very likely.

2. Could it be that something else impacts both A and B? Could some condition that predisposed him to order peppers also be responsible for making him ill? Again, this is possible, but unlikely.

The fact that neither of these options makes much sense means that there isn't a clear alternative explanation for why the two things occurred together. This is pretty rare. Most causal Flaw questions have causal conclusions that explain the correlation in their premises. This question, on the other hand, is more about explaining *one* of the two things that are correlated—his illness. In a case like this, we also need to ask ourselves, "What else could have caused this illness?"

(A) is tempting because it describes a Sampling Flaw and this *does* draw on a small sample. But so what? The conclusion is only about those three meals; there is no generalization made.

(B) didn't happen. Stand your ground! The author does posit ("put forth") a causal relationship, but we know that the presumed cause (eating peppers) happened *before* the presumed effect (getting sick).

(C) also didn't happen. We have no information about whether he wants to dine at TipTop in the future.

(D) begins with the phrase "fails to establish." That's the same thing as saying "assumes." Is it a necessary assumption of this argument that everyone became ill?

MANHATTAN
PREP

No! We don't care if *everyone* became ill; we just want to know the cause of Monroe's illness.

(E) says the argument has overlooked something that might have caused Monroe's illness other than the peppers. Perhaps he just ate too much. In other words, maybe the correlation between peppers and illness was just a coincidence. We mentioned earlier that this is another causal possibility, but it's not one that shows up often. In any case, we can't definitively establish one cause when alternative causes are possible. Thus, this is a flaw in the argument.

2. PT11, S2, Q9

Any announcement authorized by the head of the department is important. However, announcements are sometimes issued, without authorization, by people other than the head of the department, so some announcements will inevitably turn out not to be important.

The reasoning is flawed because the argument

(A)   does not specify exactly which communications are to be classified as announcements

(B)   overlooks the possibility that people other than the head of the department have the authority to authorize announcements

(C)   leaves open the possibility that the head of the department never, in fact, authorizes any announcements

(D)   assumes without warrant that just because satisfying a given condition is enough to ensure an announcement's importance, satisfying that condition is necessary for its importance

(E)   fails to distinguish between the importance of the position someone holds and the importance of what that person may actually be announcing on a particular occasion

Answer choice (D) is correct.

The argument begins with a conditional statement:

authorized announcement → important

We then learn that the negation of the sufficient condition is sometimes true, and we can already see where this is going! Indeed, the conclusion is the negation of the necessary condition. This is a typical illegal negation:

authorized announcement → important
−authorized announcement
─────────────────────────
−important

With this flaw in mind, let's examine the answer choices.

(A) is irrelevant. The argument is about whether announcements are important, not whether communications are announcements. It's common for wrong answers to demand greater specificity from the argument than the argument actually requires.

(B) is tempting. It's true that the argument never discusses who else could be authorized, but this is not a flaw. The argument is about those announcements that are *not* authorized.

(C) is true but not a flaw. It's certainly possible that the head of department never authorizes any announcements, but the conclusion is about unauthorized announcements, so this doesn't make any difference.

(E) seems to be attacking the initial premise. We accept the premise that any announcement authorized by the head of department is important, so the argument doesn't need to establish anything more general about the relationship between a person's position and the importance of their announcements.

(D) is abstract, but we can make it more concrete by inserting terms from the argument: The argument assumes that because a head-of-department authorization is *sufficient* to guarantee that an announcement is important, we can conclude that such an authorization is *necessary* for the announcement to be important. In short, this answer is describing an illegal reversal. While we identified the flaw as an illegal negation, remember that these two are logically equivalent. Take the contrapositive of one and you get the other. Therefore, this choice describes the flawed move that the argument makes.

3. PT14, S2, Q10

The government of Penglai, an isolated island, proposed eliminating outdoor advertising except for small signs of standard shape that identify places of business. Some island merchants protested that the law would reduce the overall volume of business in Penglai, pointing to a report done by the government indicating that in every industry the Penglai businesses that used outdoor advertising had a larger market share than those that did not.

Which one of the following describes an error of reasoning in the merchants' argument?

(A)   presupposing that there are no good reasons for restricting the use of outdoor advertising in Penglai

(B)   assuming without giving justification that the outdoor advertising increased market share by some means other than by diverting trade from competing businesses

(C)   ignoring the question of whether the government's survey of the island could be objective

(D)   failing to establish whether the market-share advantage enjoyed by businesses employing outdoor advertising was precisely proportionate to the amount of advertising

(E)   disregarding the possibility that the government's proposed restrictions are unconstitutional

Answer choice (B) is correct.

While causality is not explicitly mentioned here, the merchants' objection to the proposed law is based on what they perceive to be a causal link between outdoor advertising and business volume: We are given a correlation between outdoor advertising and bigger market share. The conclusion treats that correlation as though it implied a causal relationship. This means it's time to run through the checklist:

1. Could it be reversed? Perhaps companies with bigger market share are the only ones that can afford outdoor advertising.

2. Could some other factor cause both big market share and outdoor advertising? Maybe the overall health of the business.

Also, always look carefully at the wording of the conclusion: "the law would reduce the overall volume of business" on the island. Could there be a Percent vs. Amount Flaw here? "Market share" is a percentage of overall volume. In other words, a larger market share doesn't necessarily mean more overall business for the island; it just means a bigger piece of the existing pie. The correct answer could also address this conceptual shift.

Let's go to the answers.

(A) begins with "presupposing," meaning that what follows must be a necessary assumption for this choice to be correct. Does this argument hinge on assuming anything about the reasons behind the restrictions? Certainly not. The reasons, or lack thereof, are irrelevant.

(C) is tempting because the survey's objectivity is not, in fact, addressed. But there is not enough information about the study to say this is an error. Besides, the government survey is used to oppose the government's position, so this doesn't seem like an issue of basing a decision on a biased study.

(D) begins with "failing to establish," so we're looking at another assumption answer. Does this argument need to establish such precise proportionality to work? Not at all. This choice demands greater specificity from the argument than is actually required.

(E) accuses the argument of disregarding constitutionality. Does our argument do this? Technically, yes, but so what? Concerns of constitutionality aren't relevant to this argument, especially since the merchants are arguing *against* the restrictions, so disregarding such concerns isn't a problem.

At first glance, answer (B) may seem too specific to be our flaw, especially if we fixated on the Causation Flaw first. But upon closer inspection, answer (B) directly addresses the shift between the "overall volume" of island business and "market share." If outdoor advertising did in fact increase market share, but did so only by stealing business from other competitors on the island, then the overall volume of business on the island would have been unaffected. Therefore, the merchants' argument wouldn't hold water, regardless of how the causation worked: We would predict that any changes in business from advertising restrictions would simply result in a shifting of who on the island got what share of the island business, not an overall change in the amount of island business.

4. PT19, S2, Q14

Herbalist: Many of my customers find that their physical coordination improves after drinking juice containing certain herbs. A few doctors assert that the herbs are potentially harmful, but doctors are always trying to maintain a monopoly over medical therapies. So there is no reason not to try my herb juice.

The reasoning in the herbalist's argument is flawed because the argument

(A)   attempts to force acceptance of a claim by inducing fear of the consequences of rejecting that claim

(B)   bases a conclusion on claims that are inconsistent with each other

(C)   rejects a claim by attacking the proponents of the claim rather than addressing the claim itself

(D)   relies on evidence presented in terms that presuppose the truth of the claim for which the evidence is offered

(E)   mistakes the observation that one thing happens after another for proof that the second thing is the result of the first

Answer choice (C) is correct.

The conclusion uses very strong wording: "there is no reason not to try my herb juice." This is an absolute statement, so be suspicious—claims this strong must be backed up with equally strong evidence. Has the argument addressed *all* possible reasons not to try the herb juice? No way. In fact, only one reason is addressed at all. (Hint: Be careful when interpreting double negatives. The conclusion does not say "you should try my herb juice"—it only says there is no reason not to try it.)

There is also an Ad Hominem Flaw here. There is one reason given for not trying the juice (a few doctors claim that the herbs might be harmful), and this is shot down on the grounds that "doctors are always trying to maintain a monopoly on therapies." The herbalist doesn't actually present any evidence to suggest that the herbs are safe.

(A) describes an Appeal to Emotion, in which the argument relies on emotion in place of facts. This is a flaw that doesn't show up often in actual arguments, and this argument is no exception. This choice might be tempting because a monopoly on medical treatment could be a scary thing. However, we are not told that rejecting the herbalist's claim will make things any worse. There is no frightening consequence for us to fear.

(B) describes a Self-Contradiction Flaw, but none of the herbalist's statements contradict each other. The herbalist certainly opposes the doctors' assertion, but that's not a flaw. As is typical, Self-Contradiction showed up as an incorrect answer choice.

MANHATTAN
PREP

(D) describes Circular Reasoning. Do we have to accept the conclusion—that there is no reason not to try the herb juice—in order to accept the evidence that for many customers, their coordination improves after drinking the stuff? No. That premise could be true even if there are many good reasons *not* to try the juice that those customers are ignoring.

(E) describes a Causation Flaw. It does seem likely that the herbalist wants us to see causation in the story that people's coordination improved after drinking the herb juice. However, this causal claim is never made. In fact, the herbalist never argues for any benefit of the juice at all, but rather attacks the doctors who say that the juice may be harmful. In the end, the argument is about whether there is any reason *not* to try the juice, so any beliefs the herbalist may hold about causation are not relevant to the structure of the argument.

That leaves us with answer choice (C), which addresses the Ad Hominem attack that the herbalist employs. Doctors claim that the herb juice might be dangerous, and the author rebuts this claim by accusing the doctors of having an ulterior motive—wanting to maintain a monopoly. But the author never addresses the doctors' claim that the herb juice might be dangerous, which seems to be a very clear reason not to try his herb juice. (C) is our answer.

5. PT19, S4, Q6

Videocassette recorders (VCRs) enable people to watch movies at home on videotape. People who own VCRs go to movie theaters more often than do people who do not own VCRs. Contrary to popular belief, therefore, owning a VCR actually stimulates people to go to movie theaters more often than they otherwise would.

The argument is most vulnerable to criticism on the grounds that it

(A)   concludes that a claim must be false because of the mere absence of evidence in its favor

(B)   cites, in support of the conclusion, evidence that is inconsistent with other information that is provided

(C)   fails to establish that the phenomena interpreted as cause and effect are not both direct effects of some other factor

(D)   takes a condition that by itself guarantees the occurrence of a certain phenomenon to be a condition that therefore must be met for that phenomenon to occur

(E)   bases a broad claim about the behavior of people in general on a comparison between two groups of people that together include only a small proportion of people overall

Answer choice (C) is correct.

The words "enable" and "stimulate" clue us in to the fact that this is a causal question argument. The word "VCR," on the other hand, clues us in to the fact that this question is very, very old. But, though times may have changed, the LSAT has largely stayed the same, so on we go with this 1996 classic. The causal conclusion is that owning a VCR causes one to go see more movies. The evidence? VCR ownership is correlated with increased attendance at movie theaters. Running through our checklist, could the causation run in the other direction? Absolutely. Maybe the more movies one goes to, the more likely one is to want to purchase a VCR to watch those movies again at home. Could some third thing cause both VCR ownership and movie attendance? Maybe a love of movies! With these two predictions in hand, let's take a look at the answer choices.

(A) describes an Unproven vs. Untrue Flaw. There's no absence of evidence here. Eliminate.

(B) describes a Self-Contradiction Flaw, but the elements of the argument don't contradict each other.

(D) describes a Conditional Logic Flaw, specifically an illegal reversal. (Are you starting to recognize that kind of wording?) There's no conditional reasoning here, so we can eliminate.

(E) describes a Sampling Flaw. This might seem tempting because the premise compares two groups

MANHATTAN
PREP

of people. However, the premise tells us that this comparison is true of the groups as a whole—it doesn't present a survey or sample.

Answer choice (C) lays out our second prediction! Perhaps it's not that one causes the other, but that both are the product of some other factor.

6. PT19, S2, Q23

A museum director, in order to finance expensive new acquisitions, discreetly sold some paintings by major artists. All of them were paintings that the director privately considered inferior. Critics roundly condemned the sale, charging that the museum had lost first-rate pieces, thereby violating its duty as a trustee of art for future generations. A few months after being sold by the museum, those paintings were resold, in an otherwise stagnant art market, at two to three times the price paid to the museum. Clearly, these prices settle the issue, since they demonstrate the correctness of the critics' evaluation.

The reasoning in the argument is vulnerable to the criticism that the argument does which one of the following?

(A)   It concludes that a certain opinion is correct on the grounds that it is held by more people than hold the opposing view.

(B)   It rejects the judgment of the experts in an area in which there is no better guide to the truth than expert judgment.

(C)   It rejects a proven means of accomplishing an objective without offering any alternative means of accomplishing that objective.

(D)   It bases a firm conclusion about a state of affairs in the present on somewhat speculative claims about a future state of affairs.

(E)   It bases its conclusion on facts that could, in the given situation, have resulted from causes other than those presupposed by the argument.

Answer choice (E) is correct.

The author agrees with the critics that in selling the paintings the director didn't like, the museum violated its duty. Why? Well, the critics claim that these were first-rate paintings. How can we tell? Apparently, money settles it: The price that the paintings resold for was two to three times the price the museum sold them for. Here's the core:

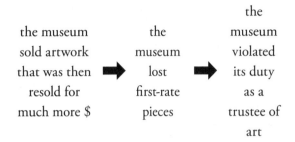

We can look for assumptions in two places: before or after the intermediate conclusion. If we accept the intermediate conclusion, we still need to assume that losing first-rate pieces is a violation of duty before we can reach the main conclusion. (Maybe it's actually fine to lose good pieces if it allows you to get something else that's good.)

However, there's also a big assumption leading up to the intermediate conclusion, namely, that price defines what a first-rate piece is. If it does, then why did the price change so quickly? The author may believe that the director undervalued these pieces, but we don't know anything about that. Perhaps, in the few months between the two sales, other factors caused the price of paintings in general, or of paintings by a particular artist, to jump in unexpected ways. Maybe whoever bought the paintings from the museum is just a really good negotiator. We can see this as a Causation Flaw: In presenting the sale price as evidence of the quality, the argument suggests that it was the quality of the paintings that caused the high sale price and neglects the other causal possibilities.

(A) didn't happen. The author never compares the number of people holding any of the views mentioned in the argument.

(B) didn't happen either. The author takes the side of a group of experts (the critics) against another expert (the director). We have no information to indicate that the director is a "better guide to the truth." Eliminate.

(C) is tempting because it sounds like something we might say in a real-world argument: "All you do is criticize! Why don't you offer some solutions for once?" However, the argument is not really about the larger objective of purchasing new works. The author may feel that there is a better way to achieve that objective or that it's not a worthy objective to begin with. However, this is not relevant to our task. We don't need to know whether there's a better way to finance new purchases to determine that the museum violated its duty in getting rid of old works. We also don't know whether this is a "proven means" of reaching the goal—perhaps the museum didn't raise enough money, or perhaps no desirable new works are available.

(D) didn't happen. There is no speculation about the future. Eliminate.

(E) is correct. It represents the Causation Flaw we discussed—maybe the paintings sold for a higher price for some other reason than quality.

7. PT11, S2, Q26

Why should the government, rather than industry or universities, provide the money to put a network of supercomputers in place? Because there is a range of problems that can be attacked only with the massive data-managing capacity of a supercomputer network. No business or university has the resources to purchase by itself enough machines for a whole network, and no business or university wants to invest in a part of a network if no mechanism exists for coordinating establishment of the network as a whole.

Which one of the following indicates a weakness in the argument?

(A)   It does not furnish a way in which the dilemma concerning the establishment of the network can be resolved.

(B)   It does not establish the impossibility of creating a supercomputer network as an international network.

(C)   It fails to address the question of who would maintain the network if the government, rather than industry or universities, provides the money for establishing it.

(D)   It takes for granted and without justification that it would enhance national preeminence in science for the government to provide the network.

(E)   It overlooks the possibility that businesses or universities, or both, could cooperate to build the network.

Answer choice (E) is correct.

Getting to the core of this argument can be tricky because the first sentence is phrased as a question. However, the rest of the stimulus is clearly explaining why businesses and universities cannot pay to build a supercomputer network. Thus, we know that the conclusion is that the government should provide the money to build such a network.

The wording that hints at the argument's flaw is "No business or university has the resources to purchase *by itself* enough machines…" We accept that no business or university could foot the bill on its own, but to jump to the conclusion that the government must pay for a network of supercomputers overlooks another possibility—a group of businesses/universities. This argument has set up a False Choice!

(A) didn't happen. The argument does suggest a solution: get the government to pay!

(B) is tempting since it introduces what seems like another possibility: Perhaps the network could be an international one. Indeed, the argument never suggests that this is impossible, but so what? We still don't know who will pay for the network of supercomputers.

MANHATTAN
PREP

(C) is about maintenance of the network. We're interested only in putting the network in place. Whether the proposal is executable once in place is irrelevant. This is out of scope.

(D) is out of scope. The issue is who will pay for the network of supercomputers, not what the outcome of completing a network of supercomputers will be.

(E) addresses the False Choice set up in the argument. Beyond the choices mentioned in the argument—the government or a single university/business pays for the network—there are other possibilities, such as a group of businesses/universities.

8. PT10, S1, Q8

Of 2,500 people who survived a first heart attack, those who did not smoke had their first heart attack at a median age of 62. However, of those 2,500, people who smoked two packs of cigarettes a day had their first heart attack at a median age of 51. On the basis of this information, it can be concluded that nonsmokers tend to have a first heart attack eleven years later than do people who smoke two packs of cigarettes a day.

The conclusion is incorrectly drawn from the information given because this information does not include

(A)   the relative severity of heart attacks suffered by smokers and nonsmokers

(B)   the nature of the different medical treatments that smokers and nonsmokers received after they had survived their first heart attack

(C)   how many of the 2,500 people studied suffered a second heart attack

(D)   the earliest age at which a person who smoked two packs a day had his or her first heart attack

(E)   data on people who did not survive a first heart attack

Answer choice (E) is correct.

The presence of numbers and a study should put us on the lookout for a Sampling Flaw. (Since there are no percentages within this argument, we know the argument does not equate a percent with an amount.) Let's review our survey questions:

1. Is it a robust enough sample size to draw the conclusion?
2. Does the sample seem representative of the group that the conclusion is about?
3. Is there a concern about biased or pressured responses to the survey?

The sample size does seem robust, except that we don't know how many of the people did not smoke and how many smoked two packs a day. If only a few of the 2,500 people were in one of those categories, that would be a problem, but we don't know for sure that there is such a flaw in the data. There's also nothing to indicate any concern about biasing or pressure, but there may be a representation problem. The study includes only those who survived a heart attack, but then extrapolates to people in general. The study is ignoring a statistically significant group: those who died when they had their first heart attack. At what age did they have their fatal first heart attacks? Perhaps in this group, smokers and nonsmokers had their first attacks closer together in age. If that were the case, we could not necessarily conclude that nonsmokers tend to have a first heart attack eleven years later than do people who smoke two packs of cigarettes a day.

(A) is about severity, which might be tempting if someone read superficially and assumed the argument was about fatalities or general risk. However, the argument is focused only on *when* heart attacks occur.

(B) seems to be addressing what might cause the difference between smokers and nonsmokers. However, this isn't necessary because the argument's conclusion is not a causal claim.

(C) is out of scope. We're looking only at first heart attacks.

(D) is irrelevant since the statistics we are given are about median ages and the conclusion is about tendencies.

(E) points out the flaw that we discussed: the limited scope of the study's sample.

9. PT20, S4, Q14

Advertisement: A leading economist has determined that among people who used computers at their place of employment last year, those who also owned portable ("laptop") computers earned 25 percent more on average than those who did not. It is obvious from this that owning a laptop computer led to a higher-paying job.

Which one of the following identifies a reasoning error in the argument?

(A)   It attempts to support a sweeping generalization on the basis of information about only a small number of individuals.

(B)   Its conclusion merely restates a claim made earlier in the argument.

(C)   It concludes that one thing was caused by another although the evidence given is consistent with the first thing's having caused the second.

(D)   It offers information as support for a conclusion when that information actually shows that the conclusion is false.

(E)   It uncritically projects currently existing trends indefinitely into the future.

Answer choice (C) is correct.

The phrase "led to" in the last line of this argument alerts us to the fact that this is a causal conclusion. The evidence is the correlation between owning the mysterious portable "laptop" computer and higher average earnings. Running through our checklist, the reverse of the causal relationship in the conclusion is certainly possible. Perhaps making more money is what allows one to own a luxury item like a portable computer. Or, a third option could cause both; for instance, perhaps college-educated people tend to have both laptops and higher paying jobs. If we sweep through the answers looking for causation, only (C) stands out. It describes the reverse causation possibility, so we have our answer! Let's look at the incorrect choices:

(A) describes a Sampling Flaw. This could be tempting because the argument does presumably hinge on a sample. It is extremely unlikely that the economist was able to survey every person who uses a computer at their job. However, we must accept the premise that the leading economist did in fact "determine" the correlation.

(B) describes a Circular Reasoning Flaw, but this isn't a circular argument. The conclusion does indeed look a lot like the premise, but it makes a causal connection, while the premise shows only correlation.

(D) describes a Self-Contradiction Flaw. Once again, this flaw shows up in an incorrect answer. While correlation doesn't *prove* causation, it certainly isn't evidence *against* causation.

(E) describes the Gambler's fallacy, a flaw in which the author holds that something which is true now will continue to be true in the future. In this argument, the phrase "led to" lets us know that the conclusion is about the past, so this answer choice is incorrect.

10. PT21, S2, Q5

Irrigation runoff from neighboring farms may well
have increased the concentration of phosphorus in
the local swamp above previous levels, but the claim
that the increase in phosphorus is harming the
swamp's native aquatic wildlife is false; the
phosphorus concentration in the swamp is actually
less than that found in certain kinds of bottled water
that some people drink every day.

The argument is vulnerable to criticism on the
ground that it

(A)   makes exaggerations in formulating the claim
         against which it argues

(B)   bases its conclusion on two contradictory claims

(C)   relies on evidence the relevance of which has
         not been established

(D)   concedes the very point that it argues against

(E)   makes a generalization that is unwarranted
         because the sources of the data on which it is
         based have not been specified

Answer choice (C) is correct.

If the author declares someone else's claim to be false
(or true), that declaration is almost invariably the
argument's main conclusion. What is the evidence used
to prove that the claim about phosphorus's harmfulness
to the swamp's native aquatic life is *false*? The fact that
there is less phosphorus in the swamp than in certain
common kinds of bottled water.

Do you see the Comparison Flaw? Whenever two
things are compared, ask, "What is missing in this
comparison?" Could water appropriate for human
consumption contain higher phosphorus than water
appropriate for a swamp's aquatic wildlife? Certainly!

Keeping this issue in mind, let's look at the answer choices:

(A) is unsupported. There is no reason to suspect that
the evidence was exaggerated in this argument.

(B) might seem accurate, since the author does
contradict a claim. However, this contradiction ("the

claim … is false") is the conclusion of the argument.
The author doesn't use contradictory claims as premises,
and in general the argument contradicts only that
opposing claim, not itself.

(D) also suggests a Self-Contradiction Flaw. Eliminate it.

(E) is mostly irrelevant. It's not clear that the author is
making a generalization. It's true that the sources of
the data are not disclosed. However, in evaluating an
argument, we accept the information presented in the
premises, so we're not concerned with the source of the
data. We can't say that a conclusion is unwarranted just
because we don't know where the data comes from or that
would be the answer on most LR questions!

That leaves answer choice (C), which addresses
the Comparison Flaw we discussed above. Maybe
mentioning phosphorus levels in human beverages is
irrelevant. Could the animals survive in a coffee swamp?
Unlike (E), which attacks the *truth* of the evidence, (C)
attacks the *relevance* of the evidence. This is our answer!

11. PT4, S1, Q8

Political theorist: The chief foundations of all
         governments are the legal system and the police
         force; and as there cannot be a good legal system
         where the police are not well paid, it follows that
         where the police are well paid there will be a
         good legal system.

The reasoning in the argument is not sound because
it fails to establish that

(A)   many governments with bad legal systems have
         poorly paid police forces

(B)   bad governments with good legal systems must
         have poorly paid police forces

(C)   a well-paid police force cannot be effective
         without a good legal system

(D)   a well-paid police force is sufficient to
         guarantee a good legal system

(E)   some bad governments have good legal
         systems

Answer choice (D) is correct.

Did you spot the Conditional Logic Flaw in the last sentence? The argument provides us with a conditional statement in the premise and then concludes the reversal:

$$\frac{\text{good legal system} \rightarrow \text{well paid police}}{\text{well paid police} \rightarrow \text{good legal system}}$$

(If you translated the premise as –*well paid police* → –*good legal system,* that's fine, too. Then the flaw is an illegal negation, but as we've seen, these are logically equivalent.)

So what does the argument fail to establish? The conclusion! We simply need to find the conclusion in the answer choices, and (D) translates to exactly that.

(A) is out of scope. While the contrapositive of the argument's conclusion is –*good legal system* → –*well paid police*, the argument is speaking hypothetically, and so whether there exist some governments with bad legal systems and a poorly paid police force does not speak to whether a well-paid police force will ensure a good legal system. A conditional can be true even if there aren't any (let alone "many") cases in which the sufficient condition is not satisfied. If we knew there were governments with bad legal systems, the author would need to establish that they had poorly paid police forces in order to save the conclusion, but we have no such data to go on.

(B) draws a connection between good legal systems and poorly paid police forces. But the argument suggests that bad legal systems require a poorly paid police force. The addition of "bad governments" is just there to confuse us—ignore it.

(C) is out of scope. The effectiveness of a police force is not an issue the argument discusses.

(E) is out of scope. Again, we don't need to establish anything about bad governments.

12. PT36, S1, Q19

Although it has been suggested that Arton's plays have a strong patriotic flavor, we must recall that, at the time of their composition, her country was in anything but a patriotic mood. Unemployment was high, food was costly, and crime rates were soaring. As a result, the general morale of her nation was at an especially low point. Realizing this, we see clearly that any apparent patriotism in Arton's work must have been intended ironically.

The reasoning above is questionable because it

(A) posits an unstated relationship between unemployment and crime

(B) takes for granted that straightforward patriotism is not possible for a serious writer

(C) takes for granted that Arton was attuned to the predominant national attitude of her time

(D) overlooks the fact that some citizens prosper in times of high unemployment

(E) confuses irony with a general decline in public morale

Answer choice (C) is correct.

Why does the author conclude that "any apparent patriotism in Arton's work must have been intended ironically"? She draws that conclusion from the fact that the *country's* morale was low, and that it was not in a patriotic mood. There is a Part vs. Whole Flaw here— does one citizen's writing necessarily reflect the overall mood of that country? Not necessarily. Let's look at the answers:

(A) didn't happen. The two things are both listed as happening during the time Arton's plays were written, but that is all. The argument doesn't draw on that correlation to posit any further relationship, causal or otherwise.

(B) also didn't happen. Because answers beginning with "takes for granted that" are functionally the same as Necessary Assumption answers, we should be careful when we see extreme language like this. The argument doesn't assume that patriotism is impossible for *any* serious writer, just for a writer in Arton's place and time. (Also, we have no idea whether Arton is a "serious" writer.)

(D) is tempting because it demonstrates that each part of the whole doesn't have to share its qualities. However, if some citizens still prosper in times of unemployment, so what? The author's assumption is that in a time when the national mood is low and unpatriotic, writers will not express sincere patriotism in their works. If some people were prospering, that wouldn't necessarily tell us anything about the national mood or its effect on writers.

(E) didn't happen. Both of these terms are mentioned, but they are not being confused. Low morale is used to explain why Arton was not likely to be patriotic. From this, the author concludes that any apparent patriotism in Arton's work was ironic.

Answer choice (C) properly addresses the Part vs. Whole Flaw regarding Arton's mood and the country's mood. Because it's a "takes for granted" answer, we can negate it to be sure it's correct. If Arton were *not* attuned to the predominant national attitude, she might have sincerely expressed patriotism, rather than ironically expressing it. This would destroy the argument's reasoning, and so (C) is correct.

13. PT36, S3, Q13

While it was once believed that the sort of psychotherapy appropriate for the treatment of neuroses caused by environmental factors is also appropriate for schizophrenia and other psychoses, it is now known that these latter, more serious forms of mental disturbance are best treated by biochemical—that is, medicinal—means. This is conclusive evidence that psychoses, unlike neuroses, have nothing to do with environmental factors but rather are caused by some sort of purely organic condition, such as abnormal brain chemistry or brain malformations.

The argument is vulnerable to criticism because it ignores the possibility that

(A)   the organic conditions that result in psychoses can be caused or exacerbated by environmental factors

(B)   the symptoms of mental disturbance caused by purely organic factors can be alleviated with medicine

(C)   organic illnesses that are nonpsychological in nature may be treatable without using biochemical methods

(D)   the nature of any medical condition can be inferred from the nature of the treatment that cures that condition

(E)   organic factors having little to do with brain chemistry may be at least partially responsible for neuroses

Answer choice (A) is correct.

What is the evidence for the conclusion's extreme claim of causation? The argument starts with an opposing point ("While it was once believed…"), then provides its star witness—an observation about the best treatment for schizophrenia and other psychoses. The core of the argument looks like this:

schizophrenia and other psychoses are best treated by biochemical/ medicinal means		psychoses have no environmental causes and only organic causes

Both the premise and the conclusion contain extreme language—"best" and "only," respectively—but these terms don't match up. Just because biochemical treatment is the *best* treatment, does that mean it's the *only* treatment? The alternative treatments may still work, but just not as well as biochemical treatments.

Further, just because a medicinal treatment is effective, that doesn't imply that the condition is caused only by biology. For instance, couldn't people take drugs to alleviate the effects of environmental stress? The author is making a flawed comparison: Psychoses have a different *best treatment* than neuroses, thus they must also have a different *cause*.

(B) didn't happen. The argument doesn't overlook this possibility; on the contrary, the argument establishes that psychoses are best treated medicinally and then concludes that they are caused by organic conditions.

(C) is out of scope. We are not concerned with nonpsychological illnesses.

(D) is tricky because it looks very much like an assumption of the argument. However, we're looking for a possibility that the argument *ignores*, so this is the opposite of what we want. Be careful not to lose track of the task at hand! Even if we did want an assumption, this wouldn't be quite right. The author does assume a connection between the type of treatment and the cause of a condition, but notice the extreme word "any." Does the author make an assumption about *any* condition? No, only about this particular subgroup.

(E) is out of scope. The author's claim is that organic factors are responsible for psychoses. Whether these factors are related to brain chemistry is irrelevant. The phrase "such as" in the conclusion introduces *examples* of organic causes, not the *only* types of organic causes.

Answer choice (A) addresses the alternative possibility that environmental factors may have an effect on psychoses (either by making conditions worse or by ultimately *causing* organic conditions that in turn cause psychoses). This is our answer!

14. PT16, S3, Q11

A controversial program rewards prison inmates who behave particularly well in prison by giving them the chance to receive free cosmetic plastic surgery performed by medical students. The program is obviously morally questionable, both in its assumptions about what inmates might want and in its use of the prison population to train future surgeons. Putting these moral issues aside, however, the surgery clearly has a powerful rehabilitative effect, as is shown by the fact that, among recipients of the surgery, the proportion who are convicted of new crimes committed after release is only half that for the prison population as a whole.

A flaw in the reasoning of the passage is that it

(A)   allows moral issues to be a consideration in presenting evidence about matters of fact

(B)   dismisses moral considerations on the grounds that only matters of fact are relevant

(C)   labels the program as "controversial" instead of discussing the issues that give rise to controversy

(D)   asserts that the rehabilitation of criminals is not a moral issue

(E)   relies on evidence drawn from a sample that there is reason to believe is unrepresentative

Answer choice (E) is correct.

The conclusion that the surgery has "a powerful rehabilitative effect" contains a word that lets us know the author is asserting a causal relationship—"effect." Does surgery truly cause lower rates of recidivism? Let's go to our checklist:

1. Does the reverse make some sense, too? Could B have a direct impact on A? No, because the temporal sequence is established, there's no way that committing fewer crimes after release could cause a prisoner to get the surgery.

MANHATTAN
PREP

2. Could it be that something else impacts both A and B? Prisoners were "awarded" surgery for good behavior—could this good behavior (or some underlying factor that caused the good behavior) also be responsible for fewer crimes committed after release? Absolutely.

Many of the answer choices address the morality of the surgery. However, it's important to note that the conclusion begins by putting the morality issue aside. This can help us eliminate some answers quickly.

(A) deals with the very issue our conclusion says to put aside! Eliminate.

(B) is tempting because it directly addresses the fact that the author sweeps morality aside. Should the author have done this? It's not our task to decide that. Our job is to assess the logic of the argument as written, and the conclusion excludes morality and focuses on the rehabilitative effect.

(C) didn't happen. The author did, in fact, discuss the issues that gave rise to the controversy.

(D) didn't happen. The author never states that rehabilitation is not a moral issue, but rather decides to set aside "these moral issues" (i.e., the concerns that some had expressed about the program).

This leaves us with answer (E), which seems to describe a Sampling Flaw rather than the Causation Flaw we found. But take a closer look. Why is the sample of prisoners unrepresentative? The group that receives surgery is selected based on good behavior—behavior that presumably surpasses that of the general prison population. That good behavior, or its underlying cause, is the same thing that we predicted might explain the correlation in a way that the conclusion overlooks. Answer choice (E) is correct.

15. PT36, S1, Q10

Cotrell is, at best, able to write magazine articles of average quality. The most compelling pieces of evidence for this are those few of the numerous articles submitted by Cotrell that are superior, since Cotrell, who is incapable of writing an article that is better than average, must obviously have plagiarized superior ones.

The argument is most vulnerable to criticism on which one of the following grounds?

(A)   It simply ignores the existence of potential counterevidence.

(B)   It generalizes from atypical occurrences.

(C)   It presupposes what it seeks to establish.

(D)   It relies on the judgment of experts in a matter to which their expertise is irrelevant.

(E)   It infers limits on ability from a few isolated lapses in performance.

Answer choice (C) is correct.

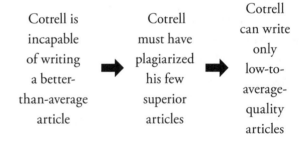

Once we break down the core, we can see that the conclusion merely restates the initial premise, without providing additional support—Circular Reasoning!

(A) didn't happen. The argument cites counterevidence (the few superior articles) but attempts to reframe that counterevidence to support the conclusion. Eliminate it.

(B) didn't happen. There are "atypical occurrences" mentioned (the superior articles), but rather than generalizing from these occurrences, the author attempts to prove the opposite of what they would imply.

(D) didn't happen either! There are no experts cited in this argument.

(E) is tempting because the first part of the answer ("infers limits on ability") is correct, but this conclusion is drawn from isolated superior performances, not from isolated lapses in performance. Eliminate it.

Answer choice (C) points out the Circular Reasoning Flaw.

16. PT16, S2, Q22

Director of personnel: Ms. Tours has formally requested a salary adjustment on the grounds that she was denied merit raises to which she was entitled. Since such grounds provide a possible basis for adjustments, an official response is required. Ms. Tours presents compelling evidence that her job performance has been both excellent in itself and markedly superior to that of others in her department who were awarded merit raises. Her complaint that she was treated unfairly thus appears justified. Nevertheless, her request should be denied. To raise Ms. Tours's salary because of her complaint would jeopardize the integrity of the firm's merit-based reward system by sending the message that employees can get their salaries raised if they just complain enough.

The personnel director's reasoning is most vulnerable to criticism on the grounds that it

(A) fails to consider the possibility that Ms. Tours's complaint could be handled on an unofficial basis

(B) attempts to undermine the persuasiveness of Ms. Tours's evidence by characterizing it as "mere complaining"

(C) sidesteps the issue of whether superior job performance is a suitable basis for awarding salary increases

(D) ignores the possibility that some of the people who did receive merit increases were not entitled to them

(E) overlooks the implications for the integrity of the firm's merit-based reward system of denying Ms. Tours's request

Answer choice (E) is correct.

There are different ways to envision this argument's core. Here is one way:

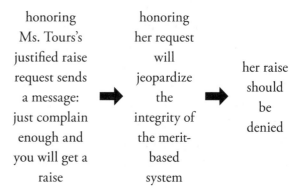

This is a pretty suspect argument. We'll accept the premise that giving Ms. Tours her deserved raise would send the message "just complain enough and you'll get a raise," but does that really mean that the integrity of the merit-based system would be compromised? She does deserve the raise, right? If the "integrity" of the merit-based system is the ultimate goal, wouldn't this goal be threatened by the unfair violation of merit-based rewards in Ms. Tours's case? Moving to the second relationship, even if we grant the intermediate conclusion—that the integrity of the system would be jeopardized—does that mean the company should deny her request? Does the system's overall integrity trump Ms. Tours's right to her raise?

Let's look at the choices and be sure not to work at that company.

(A) is out of scope. The author states that "an official response is required," so it is not necessary to consider an unofficial response.

MANHATTAN
PREP

(B) didn't happen. The director doesn't attempt to undermine the persuasiveness of Ms. Tours's evidence, but rather calls the evidence "compelling" and the claim "justified."

(C) is out of scope. The argument states that the company uses a merit-based reward system and cites Ms. Tours's superior performance as evidence that her claim was justified. The issue is not whether the company should offer performance-based salary increases, but whether the fair awarding of such an increase to Ms. Tours would undermine the system.

(D) is out of scope. We are concerned only with the effect of Ms. Tours's potential salary increase; we don't care about the salary increases of others.

Answer choice (E) addresses the first concern we identified. If integrity is what we are after, then choosing to uphold something that we know is unfair might undermine that same integrity.

4

Chapter 5

The Assumption
Family Process

In This Chapter...

Introduction

Assumption and Flaw are two of the most important question types that appear in the Logical Reasoning section. Now that you've had a chance to study both of them in depth, how do you feel?

Hopefully, you're excited about the fact that you now know more about the nature of these questions than you did before. However, this added knowledge can also be a burden. Perhaps these questions feel harder because you now realize just how much there is for you to think about!

Now is a good time to pause and consider your *process*. Your process is the strategy you use to arrive at an answer. Perhaps a more effective way to think about process is that it is the manner in which you choose to apply your understanding and judgment.

It's impossible to predict the key idea or spark of inspiration that will unlock any one particular Logical Reasoning problem. However, for all Logical Reasoning problems, the types of issues that need to be considered, and the ideal order in which you ought to consider them, are defined. That is, for every type of problem, there is a common set of decisions to be made and a logical order in which to make these decisions. Therefore, a process that helps you to think about the right issues at the right time can be a powerful tool.

For all Assumption Family questions—Assumption, Flaw, Strengthen, Weaken, and Principle (support) questions— the recommended process is the same. Let's take a look at that process in two parts:

1. Preparing to answer the question

2. Evaluating the answer choices

In future chapters, we'll discuss how this process can be adjusted for non–Assumption Family questions.

Preparing to Answer the Question

To get started, let's take a look at arguments and question stems for four Assumption and Flaw problems that appeared in one section of the October 2002 exam.

After you've read each one, please write down whatever you think is most important to know about the particular argument. See if you can correctly predict the key to identifying the correct answer.

<u>PT38, S4, Q8</u>

Politician: My opponent says our zoning laws too strongly promote suburban single-family dwellings and should be changed to encourage other forms of housing like apartment buildings. Yet he lives in a house in the country. His lifestyle contradicts his own argument, which should therefore not be taken seriously.

The politician's reasoning is most vulnerable to criticism on the grounds that

<u>PT38, S4, Q16</u>

People who do not believe that others distrust them are confident in their own abilities, so people who tend to trust others think of a difficult task as a challenge rather than a threat, since this is precisely how people who are confident in their own abilities regard such tasks.

The conclusion above follows logically if which one of the following is assumed?

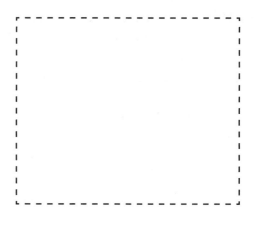

<u>PT38, S4, Q14</u>

Reducing speed limits neither saves lives nor protects the environment. This is because the more slowly a car is driven, the more time it spends on the road spewing exhaust into the air and running the risk of colliding with other vehicles.

The argument's reasoning is flawed because the argument

MANHATTAN
PREP

_PT38, S4, Q22_

In humans, ingested protein is broken down into amino acids, all of which must compete to enter the brain. Subsequent ingestion of sugars leads to the production of insulin, a hormone that breaks down the sugars and also rids the bloodstream of residual amino acids, except for tryptophan. Tryptophan then slips into the brain uncontested and is transformed into the chemical serotonin, increasing the brain's serotonin level. Thus, sugars can play a major role in mood elevation, helping one to feel relaxed and anxiety-free.

Which one of the following is an assumption on which the argument depends?

5

We'll take a look at the answer choices for these problems in just a bit. For now, let's use these arguments to break down and illustrate the first steps in your process.

A Series of Decisions

It's helpful to think about your process in terms of a series of decisions to be made. For _all_ Logical Reasoning problems, this will be your first one:

Decision 1: What is my task?

We recommend that you begin every Logical Reasoning question by reading the question stem.

Perhaps most important among the reasons for doing so is that the question stem can help you anticipate the _type_ of argument that you are about to read. For all Assumption Family questions, you know that the argument you are about to read will:

- Present a set of premises meant to support one main point
- Have gaps in its reasoning
- Have a correct answer that addresses these gaps in one way or another

Knowing all this can give you a tremendous head start on Assumption Family questions. Other question prompts will require a different mind-set, so it's important that you consider the question stem first.

Let's take a look at the two Assumption question prompts from the arguments you just evaluated:

1. "The conclusion above follows logically if which one of the following is assumed?"
2. "Which one of the following is an assumption on which the argument depends?"

MANHATTAN
PREP   203

Your understanding of the difference between the two will be most important when you evaluate the answer choices (more on this later), but it can also help you, in subtle ways, anticipate what you are about to read.

The first question stem requires us to find an answer that would make the conclusion *follow logically*. Remember, this means we need an answer that will make the argument airtight. The right answer will completely fill whatever gap exists, or, in some cases, give us even more than we need to fill that gap. Remember from Chapter 3, Assumptions Questions, that we call this a *sufficient assumption*.

A consequence of this is that you, the test-taker, know that there is going to be a clearly defined gap *to be filled*. You will not be presented with an argument that has an open-ended or vague gap, because one concise answer is going to have to make the argument airtight. Very often, this gap will be recognizable because of a term shift (a change of subject matter or attribute) between the premise and the conclusion. In arguments that involve a logical chain, there will be one clear link missing, and the right answer will supply this link. For these reasons, you should *expect* to know, before going into the answer choices, the exact gap that needs to be filled.

The second question stem asks for a different type of assumption—something that must be true in order for the conclusion to follow from the premises, but something that, in and of itself, doesn't have to make the argument "perfect." We're looking for something that at least partially fills the gap. Remember from the Assumptions question lesson that we call this a *necessary assumption*.

Consequently, you, the test-taker, have a smaller burden in terms of having to define the gap clearly. Perhaps the argument has a clearly definable gap, and, if so, of course it's to your advantage to understand it as such. But many of these arguments have multiple gaps or gaps that are less clearly definable. For these problems, your main goal is still to understand the core as well as you can, but you should not necessarily expect to know what function the right answer will play.

It's also helpful to know that the second type of assumption, the necessary assumption, is asked for far more often than the sufficient assumption. It's what you want to consider as your default, or standard, Assumption question.

It might be helpful now to compare some of the thoughts listed above to those you had as you read the question stems earlier. Did reading the question stems originally give you this type of head start? If so, fantastic! If not, make a conscious effort to devote extra focus to every question stem that you read, until defining your task is intuitively the first part of your process.

Finally, don't be afraid to revisit the question stem as you evaluate the answer choices. In fact, make a habit of it. Because you will primarily be focused on comparing answer choices against the argument itself, it's going to be very easy to forget whether you are looking for something that strengthens, weakens, fills a gap, or describes a flaw. It's true that all of these Assumption Family questions require us to think about the assumptions or gaps in an argument, but each question type presents us with a unique task. The last thing you want to do is pick the right answer for the wrong question.

Once you have decided what your task is, you're ready to move on to the argument itself. If you are reading an argument for an Assumption Family question, you must deal with this next issue before you deal with all the rest.

Decision 2: What is the conclusion?

This should be your primary focus as you read through an argument for the first time.

In previous chapters, we've stressed the importance of not just trying to understand the meaning of each sentence or clause in an argument but also the *function*—whether it supports or goes against the main point, is the main point, or serves as background information. It is impossible to assign these roles without first having an understanding of the author's main point, and so it makes sense that finding the conclusion should be your first priority.

Also in previous chapters, we've discussed the defining characteristics of conclusions. Conclusions are always opinions, not facts or truths. When an argument has multiple opinions or predictions, the conclusion is the primary opinion or prediction—the one that all others are meant to lead to. Conclusions are often signaled by words such as "thus" and "therefore," and conclusions also frequently come after a counterpoint and a pivot word, such as "however."

In some arguments, it's easy to see which part the conclusion is. In others, the test writers make your task far more difficult. It's important, in these situations, to take the time to get it right. Let's take a quick look at an example from earlier that illustrates some of the challenges:

5

> *PT38, S4, Q8*
>
> Politician: My opponent says our zoning laws too strongly promote suburban single-family dwellings and should be changed to encourage other forms of housing like apartment buildings. Yet he lives in a house in the country. His lifestyle contradicts his own argument, which should therefore not be taken seriously.

In this case, we have two opinions presented in the final sentence—the opponent's lifestyle contradicts his own argument, and the opponent's argument should not be taken seriously.

When dealing with two different opinions, you can identify the final conclusion based on order—which consequence comes last. One simple way to do this is to use the "Therefore Test."

Case 1: The opponent's argument should not be taken seriously. THEREFORE, the opponent's lifestyle contradicts his own argument.

This makes little sense. Let's try it the other way around.

Case 2: The opponent's lifestyle contradicts his own argument. THEREFORE, the opponent's argument should not be taken seriously.

Much better. So, "The opponent's argument should not be taken seriously" should be considered the final conclusion.

Another way that test writers will make it more difficult for you to identify the main conclusion is to borrow language from other parts of the argument. This is often done through the use of a pronoun, a pivot, or a clause that is meant to refer to a different part of the argument.

Notice the wording of the final conclusion: "The opponent's argument should not be taken seriously." In order to fully understand what this means, we have to know what the opponent's argument is, and it's stated earlier in the argument: "… our zoning laws … should be changed to encourage other forms of housing like apartment buildings."

Once you have a clear sense of the author's conclusion, you are ready to move on to the next decision point.

Decision 3: How is this conclusion supported?

Everything in the argument other than the conclusion is intended to support the conclusion, oppose the conclusion, or serve as background information. A clear understanding of the conclusion should clarify certain distinctions, such as that between supporting and opposing points, but other distinctions can remain vague and somewhat subjective. For example, it may be difficult to decide whether a certain clause is meant to support the conclusion or serve as background information, or do a little bit of both. Don't dwell on this. Generally, in these situations, identifying the answer will not require such distinctions.

What *is* essential is that you identify the *primary* premise(s) meant to support the conclusion. These are the premises that, combined with the conclusion, create the argument core. Simpler arguments will often have one premise, but others can have two or (rarely) three premises that complement each other or link together to lead to the final conclusion. For the vast majority of Assumption Family questions, the right answer will have something to do with the relationship between these supporting premises and the conclusion. A clear understanding of the core is essential for quickly recognizing correct answers and weeding out incorrect ones.

Sometimes, you will be able to see the argument core after just one read. The argument will be simple enough for you to keep all the pieces in mind at once, and you will understand it well enough that you can easily recognize the function of each component. Other times, you will have to go back and reread certain parts of the argument after you've identified the conclusion. Sometimes, you may even have to read an argument a third time in order to identify the core.

If you really get stuck on the occasional tough argument, it is wisest to guess and move on rather than use up your time on one question. Remember, every question is worth just one point! In general, though, time spent trying to identify the core is time well spent, so give yourself some slack when you need to. However, be mindful that you don't waste time trying to absorb details of parts of the argument that are *not* in the core. These details are far less likely to be relevant to the correct answer, and an incomplete understanding of these secondary details can distract you and tempt you toward incorrect answer choices. If you are still having trouble finding the argument core on a regular basis, it may help to revisit Chapter 2.

Often, you will find yourself (and us) identifying the conclusion and the premise at the same time. That's fine. In general, as arguments become more complex, it becomes more likely, however, that you will need to slow down and separate the steps.

Decision 4: What is the gap?

For every argument for every Assumption Family question, there will be a gap between the premises presented and the conclusion reached. That is, there will be some flaw in terms of how the author is trying to make his or her point. The correct answer will relate to an issue in this reasoning.

In your process, always pause after you identify the argument core to consider the gap. Compare the subject in the premise to the subject in the conclusion. How are they related? Does the relationship make sense? Compare an attribute in a premise to an attribute in the conclusion. How similar or different are they?

Look for strong words in the conclusion and use them to turn the conclusion into a question. If the conclusion is, "only cars equipped with brakes using the new technology should be considered safe," you should think, "Is it *only* those cars?" If the argument concludes that "it is because of our high-protein diet that more people generally have shorter lives," you should challenge that with "Does it have to be *because* of the high protein diet?" Remember, read like a debater! This will help you identify gaps.

If you correctly identify the gap or gaps in an argument, you'll put yourself in the perfect position to answer the question correctly. In fact, it'll often be true that you'll be able to predict the right answer. Unfortunately, no matter how much you prepare, there will be times when you don't see the gap clearly, even if you are at the 180 level. Still, even when you don't clearly see the gap, having searched for it will always be beneficial, because the action places your thinking firmly in the middle of the argument core, and that's where you want to be focused as you evaluate the answer choices.

Let's now deconstruct the four arguments we saw earlier to see how a consistent process can help prepare you to evaluate the answer choices:

> *PT38, S4, Q8*
>
> Politician: My opponent says our zoning laws too strongly promote suburban single-family dwellings and should be changed to encourage other forms of housing like apartment buildings. Yet he lives in a house in the country. His lifestyle contradicts his own argument, which should therefore not be taken seriously.
>
> The politician's reasoning is most vulnerable to criticism on the grounds that

Decision 1: What is my task?

This is an Assumption Family question: a Flaw question.

Decision 2: What is the conclusion?

The author's conclusion is that the opponent's argument should not be taken seriously. We know what the opponent's argument is—that zoning laws should be changed to encourage other forms of housing. We're ready to move on.

Decision 3: How is this conclusion supported?

The primary evidence presented is that the opponent's lifestyle contradicts his own argument—he lives in a house in the country.

We can see the argument core as follows:

lifestyle contradicts argument   argument shouldn't be taken
                                                             seriously

Decision 4: What is the gap?

While in real life, we often say "practice what you preach" as a form of criticism, there's no rule that says arguments shouldn't be taken seriously if the person making the argument acts in an inconsistent manner. That is, we have no reason at all to believe that there is any connection between where the opponent lives and the issue of whether his argument should be taken seriously. The gap here is an Ad Hominem Flaw. Since this is a Flaw question, we want to expose this gap.

> *PT38, S4, Q16*
>
> People who do not believe that others distrust them are confident in their own abilities, so people who tend to trust others think of a difficult task as a challenge rather than a threat, since this is precisely how people who are confident in their own abilities regard such tasks.
>
> The conclusion above follows logically if which one of the following is assumed?

Decision 1: What is my task?

This is an Assumption Family question. More specifically, it is asking for a sufficient assumption, so we will need to identify an answer that completely fills the gap and makes the argument valid. Therefore, we know we're going to see an argument that has a clearly defined gap.

Decision 2: What is the conclusion?

The conclusion is stated in the middle of the argument, with reasoning before and after:

> "So people who tend to trust others think of a difficult task as a challenge rather than a threat…"

Notice that the previous argument was far more grounded in reality, or at least a fictional version of reality. This is more of a philosophical conclusion—it's tempting to interpret it based on your real-life experiences, but you want to avoid thinking about the problem that way. Remember, it's not the truth of the conclusion that we are evaluating (maybe you disagree with this conclusion, but it doesn't matter). We're evaluating the connection between the premises and the conclusion.

Decision 3: How is this conclusion supported?

This is a short argument, and we can see that it's one where parts are meant to link with one another in a complementary fashion. The second premise also borrows from the conclusion. It says, "This is precisely how [confident people] regard such tasks." To understand this, we need to fill in language from elsewhere: "This [seeing a difficult task as a challenge and not a threat] is how confident people regard a [difficult] task."

With that work done, our two premises look like this:

1. People who do not believe that others distrust them are confident in their own abilities.

2. People who are confident in their own abilities think of a difficult task as a challenge rather than a threat.

These ideas are supposed to "link" to the conclusion, but we know there is going to be a gap here—a missing link.

Decision 4: What is the gap?

How do these two premises complement each other? Notice that the two statements have a common element (are confident in their own abilities), and we can use this common element to link these statements up:

> Since people who do not believe that others distrust them *are confident in their own abilities,* and *those who are confident in their own abilities* think of a difficult task as a challenge rather than a threat, we can say that…

> "People who do not believe others distrust them think of a difficult task as a challenge rather than a threat."

But that's not what the author's conclusion says. It says:

> "So people WHO TEND TO TRUST OTHERS think of a difficult task as a challenge rather than a threat."

What's the difference? It's between those who do not believe others distrust them and those who tend to trust others. These are similar ideas, but they are not the same.

In order for this argument to be valid, we need to show that people who do not believe others distrust them are people who tend to trust others. That's what the right answer will likely do.

While the terms of this argument are a bit unwieldy, if we use a diagram and keep the terms straight, the gap becomes quite clear:

–believe others distrust them	→	confident in own abilities
confident in own abilities	→	think of difficult tasks as a challenge

_____

trust others	→	see difficult tasks as a challenge

How does "trust others" link to the chain we're given in the premises?

trust others	→	–believe others trust them

Let's try another example:

> *PT38, S4, Q14*
>
> Reducing speed limits neither saves lives nor protects the environment. This is because the more slowly a car is driven, the more time it spends on the road spewing exhaust into the air and running the risk of colliding with other vehicles.
>
> The argument's reasoning is flawed because the argument

Decision 1: What is my task?

We can see that this is an Assumption Family question—a Flaw question to be more specific.

Decision 2: What is the conclusion?

The conclusion is twofold: Reducing speed limits neither saves lives nor protects the environment.

Decision 3: How is this conclusion supported?

The two parts of the conclusion are supported by separate premises.

MANHATTAN
PREP

"The more slowly a car is driven, the more time it spends on the road spewing exhaust into the air" is meant to support the idea that reducing speed limits doesn't protect the environment.

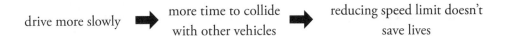

"…running the risk of colliding with other vehicles" is meant to support the idea that reducing speed limits doesn't save lives.

drive more slowly ➡ more time to collide with other vehicles ➡ reducing speed limit doesn't save lives

Decision 4: What is the gap?

There are some pretty wide gaps here between the premises presented and the two conclusions reached. For both conclusions, the support is too simple and limited to prove the larger generalization.

There are many reasons that would make the first argument core faulty (other ways that fast driving is bad for the environment, the relative amounts of exhaust that are produced at different speeds, etc.) and many considerations that could make the second core faulty (accidents at slower speeds are probably less dangerous, and perhaps driving at slower speeds helps one avoid accidents in general). The correct answer could point out any of these many reasons, so while we don't know exactly what to expect, we know the type of information we're looking for: something that makes slow speeds look safe or eco-friendly or that does the reverse for high speeds.

PT38, S4, Q22

In humans, ingested protein is broken down into amino acids, all of which must compete to enter the brain. Subsequent ingestion of sugars leads to the production of insulin, a hormone that breaks down the sugars and also rids the bloodstream of residual amino acids, except for tryptophan. Tryptophan then slips into the brain uncontested and is transformed into the chemical serotonin, increasing the brain's serotonin level. Thus, sugars can play a major role in mood elevation, helping one to feel relaxed and anxiety-free.

Which one of the following is an assumption on which the argument depends?

Decision 1: What is my task?

This is an Assumption Family question. Specifically, it's a Necessary Assumption question—we're looking for something that must be true for the conclusion to follow from the premises.

As we start reading, we're thinking about…

Decision 2: What is the conclusion?

Though the subject matter is challenging, the structure of the writing is not. We're given a series of incidents that lead to one another and eventually to the conclusion, which comes at the end of the paragraph:

> Thus, sugars can play a major role in mood elevation, helping one to feel
> relaxed and anxiety-free.

We're ready to move on.

Decision 3: How is the conclusion supported?

The argument describes a sequence of events that occur when sugars are ingested after protein. Here's the last event presented in the premises:

> Tryptophan then slips into the brain uncontested and is transformed into the
> chemical serotonin, increasing the brain's serotonin level.

sugars help tryptophan slip into brain, increasing serotonin level sugars can play a major role in mood elevation, helping one to feel relaxed and anxiety-free

Decision 4: What is the gap?

The premises end with tryptophan increasing the brain's serotonin level, but the conclusion is about mood elevation, specifically about one feeling relaxed and worry-free. Yet we've been told nothing about how serotonin affects mood! This is a huge gap, and it's more than likely that the right answer will address it.

Now is a good time to think about how you read the arguments originally. Take a look at the notes you wrote down. Did you put yourself in an ideal position to evaluate the answer choices? Consider now—are there any parts of this process that you routinely shortchange or overlook? On the flip side, are there other things that you focus on that now seem to be less important?

Here are the four arguments once again, this time with the answer choices. Evaluate each argument once more, then select the correct answer.

MANHATTAN
PREP

Politician: My opponent says our zoning laws too
strongly promote suburban single-family
dwellings and should be changed to encourage
other forms of housing like apartment
buildings. Yet he lives in a house in the
country. His lifestyle contradicts his own
argument, which should therefore not be taken
seriously.

The politician's reasoning is most vulnerable to
criticism on the grounds that

(A)   its characterization of the opponent's lifestyle
       reveals the politician's own prejudice against
       constructing apartment buildings

(B)   it neglects the fact that apartment buildings
       can be built in the suburbs just as easily as in
       the center of the city

(C)   it fails to mention the politician's own living
       situation

(D)   its discussion of the opponent's lifestyle is
       irrelevant to the merits of the opponent's
       argument

(E)   it ignores the possibility that the opponent
       may have previously lived in an apartment
       building

People who do not believe that others distrust them
are confident in their own abilities, so people who
tend to trust others think of a difficult task as a
challenge rather than a threat, since this is precisely
how people who are confident in their own abilities
regard such tasks.

The conclusion above follows logically if which one
of the following is assumed?

(A)   People who believe that others distrust them
       tend to trust others.

(B)   Confidence in one's own abilities gives one
       confidence in the trustworthiness of others.

(C)   People who tend to trust others do not believe
       that others distrust them.

(D)   People who are not threatened by difficult
       tasks tend to find such tasks challenging.

(E)   People tend to distrust those who they believe
       lack self-confidence.

5

PT38, S4, Q14

Reducing speed limits neither saves lives nor protects the environment. This is because the more slowly a car is driven, the more time it spends on the road spewing exhaust into the air and running the risk of colliding with other vehicles.

The argument's reasoning is flawed because the argument

(A)   neglects the fact that some motorists completely ignore speed limits

(B)   ignores the possibility of benefits from lowering speed limits other than environmental and safety benefits

(C)   fails to consider that if speed limits are reduced, increased driving times will increase the number of cars on the road at any given time

(D)   presumes, without providing justification, that total emissions for a given automobile trip are determined primarily by the amount of time the trip takes

(E)   presumes, without providing justification, that drivers run a significant risk of collision only if they spend a lot of time on the road

PT38, S4, Q22

In humans, ingested protein is broken down into amino acids, all of which must compete to enter the brain. Subsequent ingestion of sugars leads to the production of insulin, a hormone that breaks down the sugars and also rids the bloodstream of residual amino acids, except for tryptophan. Tryptophan then slips into the brain uncontested and is transformed into the chemical serotonin, increasing the brain's serotonin level. Thus, sugars can play a major role in mood elevation, helping one to feel relaxed and anxiety-free.

Which one of the following is an assumption on which the argument depends?

(A)   Elevation of mood and freedom from anxiety require increasing the level of serotonin in the brain.

(B)   Failure to consume foods rich in sugars results in anxiety and a lowering of mood.

(C)   Serotonin can be produced naturally only if tryptophan is present in the bloodstream.

(D)   Increasing the level of serotonin in the brain promotes relaxation and freedom from anxiety.

(E)   The consumption of protein-rich foods results in anxiety and a lowering of mood.

Evaluating the Answer Choices

Okay, we've read the argument. We've zeroed in on the most important components, and we've put ourselves in the right position to answer the question.

One more look at the question stem and…

Here we go. As we evaluate the answer choices for the first time, our primary consideration is going to be:

Decision 5: Which answer choices are clearly wrong?

It can be argued that being skilled at recognizing wrong answers is more important than being skilled at recognizing right answers. After all, 80% of the answers you evaluate are going to be wrong!

Many test-takers evaluate answer choices by looking for the right answer *and* eliminating wrong answers all at once. For most people, this is an inefficient strategy.

Certainly, there will be problems for which the right answer will jump out at you, and you'll be able to pick it and move on quickly. However, your general mind-set should not be "Which answer is correct and which are incorrect?" but rather "Which answer choices are clearly wrong?" We want to work wrong-to-right!

Though it may seem like a small difference, it is a significant one: If you are focused on finding reasons why answer choices are wrong, you will be able to spot problems far more efficiently. Furthermore, working from wrong-to-right will help ensure that you focus your attention appropriately and spend the majority of your time evaluating the most attractive answer choices.

The biggest payoff will be on the most challenging questions. For these problems, right answers are often written in an unpredictable fashion. Furthermore, tempting wrong answers are often variations on incorrect suppositions that the test-taker might have. Working in a disciplined fashion from wrong-to-right can significantly impact your accuracy rate on these most challenging questions.

In eliminating answer choices for Assumption Family questions, there are two main considerations that can help you weed out incorrect choices:

1. **Be suspicious of answer choices you cannot relate to the conclusion.** For Assumption Family questions, we are trying to relate an answer choice to a clearly defined argument core and, more specifically, to a gap we see. However, sometimes we see the argument core or gap incorrectly, and for some arguments this core is vague to begin with. For the first round of eliminations, it makes sense to be less rigid about the argument core.

Whether we see the core clearly or not, we should always be able to identify the correct conclusion. Furthermore, the test writers create many incorrect answers that have nothing to do with the conclusion (and, therefore, nothing to do with any version of the core).

The right answer must relate in some way to the main conclusion of the argument. If you see that an answer does not, or, as is commonly the case, you see that an answer choice relates to an incorrect interpretation of the conclusion, you can eliminate it.

Keep in mind that many incorrect answers are created through misinterpretations of secondary parts of an argument. Test-takers who try to read all parts of an argument with equal attention are more easily duped by these wrong choices. Focusing in on the argument core, and specifically the conclusion, will help you recognize these incorrect choices more easily.

2. **Recognize incorrect answers that may be relevant to a different question stem.** For Assumption questions, there will often be answers that would be correct for Flaw questions, and vice versa. It's the same with Strengthen and Weaken questions. Furthermore, the LSAT will throw in extra tricks, such as double negatives and contrasting perspectives, in order to increase the challenge. Don't lose sight of your task, and don't hesitate to revisit the question stem whenever necessary.

For your first round of eliminations, you want to make sure to defer judgment on answer choices that you cannot confidently eliminate. Once you eliminate an answer choice, you are not going to look at it again unless you mistakenly eliminate all five! (If you occasionally find yourself in this situation, don't worry. It happens to the best of us! It usually means we've missed or misinterpreted something and need to take another look. This takes time, which is why it's important to do our best to get it right on the first run.)

A good criterion for what you should eliminate and what you should not: For each wrong answer you eliminate in the first go-around, you should be able to pinpoint the exact reason why it is wrong. If it *seems* wrong but you don't know exactly why, keep it around. This is especially true if you are frequently tripped up by the wording used on the LSAT. Answers that feel this way can often be right answers in disguise.

Do you have trouble coming up with these exact reasons under time pressure? That's understandable, especially if you haven't thought about the answer choices in this way before. When doing your blind review of questions after timed practice, be as specific as possible about why answer choices are wrong. Find at least one definitive reason for every wrong answer you encounter. Soon enough, you will become much better at identifying the common ways in which the LSAT creates incorrect answer choices.

Once you have eliminated the clearly wrong choices, typically you will be left with just one, two, or three answers remaining. It's time to make the final decision!

Decision 6: What is the best available answer?

Left with answers that you can't confidently eliminate, you must now select the best available answer. Often, this decision will be less clear-cut than the first round of eliminations. You might find reasons why you like and dislike each of the remaining answer choices. Keep in mind that your job is not to find the *ideal* answer, but rather the best available answer. This doesn't mean that more than one answer is really correct, but rather that even the right answer might seem less than perfect. It just won't be *wrong*.

Of all the decisions that you have to make during the course of any one problem, this is the most subtle and difficult. More than ever, no single route can guarantee success. You want to stay as flexible and open-minded as you can, and be ready to consider both why answers might be wrong and why answers might be right. Still, there are some common issues that need considering. Here's a basic chain of reasoning you can lean on whenever you feel challenged in making the final call:

1. **Compare the answer choices to the argument core.** This may seem obvious, but we've seen many students who settle at this point for the answer that "sounds more like a right answer" or pick an answer by comparing the answer choices to one another. Remember that your task is to match the answer with the argument.

2. **Remember and utilize the exact question category.** If we are looking for an assumption that makes the argument vaild, or for the *most* significant flaw, we should lean toward answer choices that clearly have a *strong* impact on the conclusion.

If we are looking for a Necessary Assumption, we should look for an answer that is required. We want to be careful to avoid answers that are more creative or stronger than need be (answers that go beyond helping to fill the gap).

3. **Vet the right answer as much as possible.** While a strong wrong-to-right process can reduce the amount of correct-answer vetting you'll need to do, if you're stuck on two answers, spend some time proving that the right answer is right. Imagine the story that connects the answer choice to the conclusion. If you can't imagine it, it's a good sign the answer isn't correct.

For a Necessary Assumption, you can perform the negation test: If it's a Necessary Assumption, the negation of that assumption should invalidate the argument. The negation test is not typically effective for Sufficient Assumption questions.

4. **Consider each word of the answer.** If you can't justify why one answer is right, do your best to find one thing wrong with each potential wrong answer. Check every noun, verb, and modifier against the original argument. And check the orientation of the elements—often the most attractive incorrect answers are those that reverse cause and effect. Select the answer that is least wrong.

Let's go back to the four problems to discuss how this process might play out in real time:

_PT38, S4, Q8_

> Politician: My opponent says our zoning laws too strongly promote suburban single-family dwellings and should be changed to encourage other forms of housing like apartment buildings. Yet he lives in a house in the country. His lifestyle contradicts his own argument, which should therefore not be taken seriously.

The politician's reasoning is most vulnerable to criticism on the grounds that

(A)   its characterization of the opponent's lifestyle reveals the politician's own prejudice against constructing apartment buildings

(B)   it neglects the fact that apartment buildings can be built in the suburbs just as easily as in the center of the city

(C)   it fails to mention the politician's own living situation

(D)   its discussion of the opponent's lifestyle is irrelevant to the merits of the opponent's argument

(E)   it ignores the possibility that the opponent may have previously lived in an apartment building

Remember what we identified as the core:

lifestyle contradicts argument   argument shouldn't be taken seriously

Also remember that we had a pretty good sense of the role that the right answer would play: It should address the Ad Hominem Flaw.

Decision 5: Which answer choices are clearly wrong?

We want to quickly eliminate answers that are clearly wrong. On the first go-around, perhaps we quickly eliminate answers (B), (C), and (E). Answer choice (D) looks like the answer we predicted, but let's hold off on evaluating it fully for now.

(B) involves subjects (apartment buildings, suburbs, city center) that are in the argument, but it doesn't make a point that helps us judge whether the evidence presented should discourage us from taking the opponent's argument seriously.

(C) is tempting if we get creative, but has no direct bearing on the conclusion. The argument core involves the opponent's lifestyle, not the author's. It wouldn't fix the Ad Hominem Flaw to add this information.

(E) has no direct bearing on the conclusion. Again, in order to try to make it relevant, we would have to get creative. The opponent could have lived in an apartment in the past, but it's unclear how this would impact the author's point.

Decision 6: What is the best available answer?

Down to two choices, let's evaluate them more in depth:

(A) is somewhat tempting, but when we match up all the subjects and attributes, there's a problem with the end of this answer choice—prejudice against apartment buildings. It's unclear if the author is prejudiced against apartment buildings—we know only that he is against the opponent's opinion. This goes beyond the conclusion in question.

Answer choice (D) looked good from the beginning. Now let's verify it:

> (D)   its discussion of the opponent's lifestyle is
>   irrelevant to the merits of the opponent's
>   argument

This answer's subject matter matches that in the argument, and the relationship between lifestyle and argument is characterized as predicted. We can select answer (D) and move on.

PT38, S4, Q16

People who do not believe that others distrust them are confident in their own abilities, so people who tend to trust others think of a difficult task as a challenge rather than a threat, since this is precisely how people who are confident in their own abilities regard such tasks.

The conclusion above follows logically if which one of the following is assumed?

(A)   People who believe that others distrust them tend to trust others.

(B)   Confidence in one's own abilities gives one confidence in the trustworthiness of others.

(C)   People who tend to trust others do not believe that others distrust them.

(D)   People who are not threatened by difficult tasks tend to find such tasks challenging.

(E)   People tend to distrust those who they believe lack self-confidence.

Remember the gap we saw in the original argument? The premises link together so that we can infer, "People *who do not believe others distrust them* think of a difficult task as a challenge rather than a threat." But the author's conclusion states, "So people *who tend to trust others* think of a difficult task as a challenge rather than a threat."

We need to know that people who tend to trust others are people who don't believe that others distrust them.

Decision 5: Which answer choices are clearly wrong?

If we did not have a good sense of the core and its missing link, all the answer choices might have seemed attractive, because they all involve relationships between elements that are mentioned in the text. However, we know which specific pieces we need to link up in order to make the argument airtight: people who do not believe others distrust them and people who tend to trust others.

We can eliminate answers (B), (D), and (E), because none of them link the two ideas we need to connect in this argument.

Decision 6: What is the best available answer?

Answers (A) and (C) seem similar, but they're different in two crucial ways. Read answer choice (A) closely. It links those who *believe* that others distrust them and those who tend to trust others. We want to connect those who do NOT believe that others distrust them and those who tend to trust others. Also, (A) is a reversal of what we're looking for. We want "trust others" in the sufficient position leading to "don't believe others distrust them" in the necessary position.

Answer choice (C) provides the correct link and is therefore the correct answer.

PT38, S4, Q14

Reducing speed limits neither saves lives nor protects the environment. This is because the more slowly a car is driven, the more time it spends on the road spewing exhaust into the air and running the risk of colliding with other vehicles.

The argument's reasoning is flawed because the argument

(A)   neglects the fact that some motorists completely ignore speed limits

(B)   ignores the possibility of benefits from lowering speed limits other than environmental and safety benefits

(C)   fails to consider that if speed limits are reduced, increased driving times will increase the number of cars on the road at any given time

(D)   presumes, without providing justification, that total emissions for a given automobile trip are determined primarily by the amount of time the trip takes

(E)   presumes, without providing justification, that drivers run a significant risk of collision only if they spend a lot of time on the road

Remember that there were two related points made in this argument and that there were distinct premises meant to support each point:

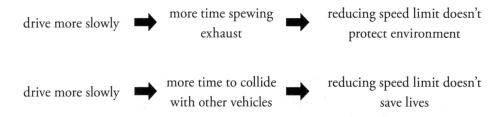

Since the gaps here are so wide, we weren't able to predict one likely answer. We just need anything that shows an environmental or safety benefit of driving slower.

Decision 5: Which answer choices are clearly wrong?

Perhaps the answers we eliminate first are (B), (C), and (E).

(B) could be tempting if we weren't zeroed in on the conclusion. If we keep in mind that the conclusion is only about environmental and safety benefits, this is clearly out of scope. The other benefits aren't relevant here.

(C) is out of scope because we don't know whether having more cars on the road is a bad thing. If it is indeed bad, this would actually strengthen the argument.

(E) might be attractive if you miss the word "only." However, if you catch it, it's a good tip-off that this answer is incorrect. Increased time on the road doesn't have to be the *only* reason for the increased risk of collision.

Decision 6: What is the best available answer?

(A) is not an answer we predicted, but it seems connected to both the premises and the conclusion. If some motorists ignore speed limits, this must make a difference in their effectiveness. But this doesn't tell us whether limiting speed in general would be good or not. Be wary of answer choices that object to a general statement by bringing up what *some* people would do.

(D) is not exactly the type of answer we expected because it doesn't do anything to defend slow driving or make fast driving look bad.

However, let's look at it one more time: "presumes, without providing justification, that total emissions for a given automobile trip are determined primarily by the amount of time the trip takes."

Notice that the author of the argument is making a generalization about the environmental impact just based on the amount of time spent driving. This answer choice points out that we don't really know whether we can judge emissions based on the length of the trip. As we considered earlier, maybe speed is a factor. Let's pick answer choice (D) and move on.

PT38, S4, Q22

In humans, ingested protein is broken down into amino acids, all of which must compete to enter the brain. Subsequent ingestion of sugars leads to the production of insulin, a hormone that breaks down the sugars and also rids the bloodstream of residual amino acids, except for tryptophan. Tryptophan then slips into the brain uncontested and is transformed into the chemical serotonin, increasing the brain's serotonin level. Thus, sugars can play a major role in mood elevation, helping one to feel relaxed and anxiety-free.

Which one of the following is an assumption on which the argument depends?

(A)   Elevation of mood and freedom from anxiety require increasing the level of serotonin in the brain.

(B)   Failure to consume foods rich in sugars results in anxiety and a lowering of mood.

(C)   Serotonin can be produced naturally only if tryptophan is present in the bloodstream.

(D)   Increasing the level of serotonin in the brain promotes relaxation and freedom from anxiety.

(E)   The consumption of protein-rich foods results in anxiety and a lowering of mood.

After the original read, the gap was pretty clear. The evidence ends with tryptophan increasing the brain's serotonin level, but the conclusion is about mood elevation, specifically about one feeling relaxed and worry-free:

sugars help tryptophan slip into brain, increasing serotonin level sugars can play a major role in mood elevation, helping one to feel relaxed and anxiety-free

We've been told nothing about how serotonin affects mood. We're ready to evaluate.

Decision 5: Which answer choices are clearly wrong?

Perhaps the answers to eliminate first are (B), (C), and (E).

(B) looks like an illegal negation of the conclusion. We don't need to assume that! In more specific terms, maybe there are other ways than sugar to relax and reduce anxiety. Some people enjoy a nice Logic Game!

(C) might be a more tempting trap answer if it weren't for the "only." In order for the argument to be valid, we don't need to know that this is the "only" way for serotonin to be produced. This is basically a reversal of the premise that tryptophan leads to serotonin. Furthermore, there's no connection to the issue of changing mood.

(E) states the complete opposite of the author's point. Protein and sugar work together to create the effect the author describes.

Decision 6: What is the best available answer?

We are down to answers (A) and (D). Can you see the difference between them?

Both choices link serotonin to the effects mentioned in the conclusion. However, (A) is a reversal! The word "require" puts serotonin in the necessary position and we want it in the sufficient.

Answer choice (D) is our winner. To verify, consider its negation: "Increasing the level of serotonin in the brain does NOT promote relaxation and freedom from anxiety." This would destroy the argument, and this proves that the original assumption was necessary.

Conclusion

In this chapter, we've broken down the general problem-solving process for all Assumption Family questions. The six decisions that need to be made correctly in order to solve an Assumption Family question are:

1. What is my task?

2. What is the conclusion?

3. How is that conclusion supported?

4. What is the gap?

5. Which answer choices are clearly wrong?

6. What is the best available answer?

Drill It: Assumption Family Questions

Here are the three remaining Assumption and Flaw questions from the fourth section of the October 2002 exam.

For the purposes of this exercise, don't worry about timing. Take as much time as you need. Consider each question carefully and deliberately. Use this exercise as a chance to reflect on your process. Make sure to make your six decisions in order, and, at each point along the way, do your best not to move on to the next step until you're completely ready. After each problem, compare the thoughts you had with those in the solution.

1. PT38, S4, Q6

In any field, experience is required for a proficient person to become an expert. Through experience, a proficient person gradually develops a repertory of model situations that allows an immediate, intuitive response to each new situation. This is the hallmark of expertise, and for this reason computerized "expert systems" cannot be as good as human experts. Although computers have the ability to store millions of bits of information, the knowledge of human experts, who benefit from the experience of thousands of situations, is not stored within their brains in the form of rules and facts.

The argument requires the assumption of which one of the following?

(A) Computers can show no more originality in responding to a situation than that built into them by their designers.

(B) The knowledge of human experts cannot be adequately rendered into the type of information that a computer can store.

(C) Human experts rely on information that can be expressed by rules and facts when they respond to new situations.

(D) Future advances in computer technology will not render computers capable of sorting through greater amounts of information.

(E) Human experts rely heavily on intuition while they are developing a repertory of model situations.

Decision 1: What is my task?

This is a Necessary Assumption question. We're looking for an assumption that must be true for the conclusion to follow from the premises.

Decision 2: What is the conclusion?

Computerized "expert systems" cannot be as good as human experts.

Decision 3: How is the conclusion supported?

The part before the conclusion is cited as the main reason. However, the information that follows the conclusion is also significant and adds to our understanding.

Taken together, we know the following...

human experts have a repertory
of model situations

\+   →   computerized "expert systems"
                                  cannot be as good as human experts

information is not stored as rules
and facts in human brain

Decision 4: What is the gap?

There are lots of gaps in this argument, both in terms of the way the premises are meant to connect to one another and in the way the premises are collectively meant to connect to the conclusion.

We're not actually told that human knowledge cannot be transferred to a computer; the author just seems to assume that computers can only store rules and facts. What if computers could build up the same repertory of model situations that human experts do? Furthermore, the author is assuming that since one type of expert (human) acquires expertise in one way (by developing this repertory), a computer can become an expert only in that same way.

It's fine if you didn't have these specific thoughts as you solved the question. As mentioned before, this is an argument that is flawed in numerous ways. What is most important is that you recognize the argument core and use it to evaluate the answer choices.

Decision 5: Which answer choices are clearly wrong?

(A) and (B) both seem attractive.

We can get rid of (C), (D), and (E) quickly.

(C) is certainly not necessary. The argument stresses that humans do not rely on rules and facts.

MANHATTAN
PREP

(D) is incorrect because the amount of information a computer can sort through is not in question, but rather the type of information. Also, the argument is about what can or can't be done now, not what will happen in the future.

(E) gives us more information about a premise, but bears no relation to the argument core.

Decision 6: What is the best available answer?

Let's review (A) and (B) carefully:

> (A)   Computers can show no more originality in responding to a situation than that built into them by their designers.

> (B)   The knowledge of human experts cannot be adequately rendered into the type of information that a computer can store.

The reason (A) is attractive is that if computers could show more originality, maybe they could become experts in an unexpected way. However, the limitation here is not clear. How much originality can designers build into a computer? In any case, must it be true that computers could not show more originality for this argument to be valid? Maybe computers could show a little originality, but not enough to become an expert. This doesn't seem like something that must be true.

(B) is pretty close to something we predicted.

Let's verify it. Since it's a Necessary Assumption question, we know that the negation of this assumption should really hurt the argument: "The knowledge of human experts CAN be adequately rendered into the type of information that a computer can store." We know this would hurt the author's argument.

(B) doesn't make the author's argument perfect, but it is something that must be true in order for the argument to be valid.

2. PT38, S4, Q20

Shy adolescents often devote themselves totally to a hobby to help distract them from the loneliness brought on by their shyness. Sometimes they are able to become friends with others who share their hobby. But if they lose interest in that hobby, their loneliness may be exacerbated. So developing an all-consuming hobby is not a successful strategy for overcoming adolescent loneliness.

Which one of the following assumptions does the argument depend on?

(A)   Eventually, shy adolescents are going to want a wider circle of friends than is provided by their hobby.

(B)   No successful strategy for overcoming adolescent loneliness ever intensifies that loneliness.

(C)   Shy adolescents will lose interest in their hobbies if they do not make friends through their engagement in those hobbies.

(D)   Some other strategy for overcoming adolescent loneliness is generally more successful than is developing an all-consuming hobby.

(E)   Shy adolescents devote themselves to hobbies mainly because they want to make friends.

Decision 1: What is my task?

We're looking for a necessary assumption.

Decision 2: What is the conclusion?

It comes right at the end: "Developing an all-consuming hobby is not a successful strategy for overcoming adolescent loneliness."

Decision 3: How is the conclusion supported?

The first two sentences describe a remedy for adolescent loneliness, but then the author introduces a potential problem with this remedy and so concludes that it is not a successful strategy. We've got a series of premises that link to one another:

MANHATTAN
PREP

if teens lose interest in their
hobby, their loneliness may   ➡️
be exacerbated

developing an all-consuming
hobby is not a successful
strategy for overcoming
adolescent loneliness

Decision 4: What is the gap?

The premises lead to negative consequences in only some instances (notice the "if" and the "may be"), and the conclusion is far more definitive ("is not a successful strategy"). Is the fact that there is sometimes a negative impact enough to conclude that developing an all-consuming hobby is never a successful strategy?

We should lean toward an answer choice that addresses this issue.

Decision 5: Which answers choices are clearly wrong?

(C) and (E) seem to have no direct relationship to the conclusion, so we can eliminate these quickly.

(C) is about what will lead adolescents to lose interest in their hobbies—that's not what the conclusion is about.

(E) is out of scope. We don't need to know why adolescents take up their hobbies. We are just trying to evaluate whether the hobbies help to overcome loneliness.

Decision 6: What is the best available answer?

(A) might seem attractive at first. If shy adolescents are going to want more friends, then perhaps developing this hobby is a bad idea.

But wait—we aren't just looking for problems with starting a hobby. We're looking for something that is needed to establish the conclusion that starting a hobby will not help with loneliness. If we negate answer choice (A), we get "Shy adolescents are NOT EVER going to want a wider circle of friends than is provided by their hobby." This doesn't seem absolutely necessary for the argument. In fact, it doesn't touch the author's reasoning, which is about what happens when the teen loses interest in the hobby and ends up lonelier than before.

(B) might work. Remember the gap we anticipated: "If it causes problems for some, it shouldn't be adopted." If we negate (B), we get something like this: "SOME successful strategies for overcoming adolescent loneliness intensify that loneliness." This would be a problem for the argument, which uses this intensifying of loneliness as its sole support. If a successful strategy can make loneliness worse in some cases, the argument falls apart. In fact, (B) looks a lot like our prediction. This is the correct answer.

(D) seems helpful because it tells us that there are more successful strategies than developing a hobby. But looking back at the conclusion, we can see that the author isn't trying to say which strategy is the best. The conclusion is just that the hobby approach is just not a successful approach at all. This comparative information is not needed. Even if there were no better strategies, it could still be true that this strategy was ineffective. We can eliminate (D).

3. PT38, S4, Q21

Political scientist: As a political system, democracy does not promote political freedom. There are historical examples of democracies that ultimately resulted in some of the most oppressive societies. Likewise, there have been enlightened despotisms and oligarchies that have provided a remarkable level of political freedom to their subjects.

The reasoning in the political scientist's argument is flawed because it

(A)   confuses the conditions necessary for political freedom with the conditions sufficient to bring it about

(B)   fails to consider that a substantial increase in the level of political freedom might cause a society to become more democratic

(C)   appeals to historical examples that are irrelevant to the causal claim being made

(D)   overlooks the possibility that democracy promotes political freedom without being necessary or sufficient by itself to produce it

(E)   bases its historical case on a personal point of view

Decision 1: What is my task?

This is an Assumption Family question. It's a Flaw question, to be more specific.

Decision 2: What is the conclusion?

This is given to us right at the beginning: "As a political system, democracy does not promote political freedom."

Decision 3: How is the conclusion supported?

The two premises that follow work in a complementary fashion:

> Some democracies have been oppressive.
> Some non-democracies have provided great freedom.

Together, they are meant to show that whether a country is democratic has no direct impact on the amount of freedom a country has.

MANHATTAN
PREP

Decision 4: What is the gap?

There's a statistical problem here. Take the following analogy:

> Some smokers do not get lung cancer.
> Some nonsmokers do get lung cancer.
> So, smoking does not affect the likelihood of getting lung cancer.

Of course, we know that smoking doesn't guarantee lung cancer, and of course we know that having lung cancer doesn't necessarily mean that you are a smoker, but does that mean that smoking doesn't impact your odds of getting lung cancer? In this analogous argument, the author fails to consider that smoking could indeed impact the odds of getting lung cancer even if smoking doesn't guarantee it, and even if smoking isn't necessary to get it.

The same sort of issue is present in the democracy example. Democracy may not guarantee freedom, and democracy may not be necessary for freedom, but does that mean that democracy doesn't improve the odds of having a free society?

By the way, we also could consider this an unusual type of Causation Flaw (because examples in which the purported cause and effect don't correlate are used to argue that there is no causal link) or a Sampling Flaw (because a few examples are used to draw a broad generalization). Time to dive into the choices.

Decision 5: Which answer choices are clearly wrong?

(A) involves conditional logic language that seems relevant. Too much to consider for now. Let's leave it.

We can eliminate answers (B), (C), and (E) quickly.

(B) matches some of the subjects in the argument, but moves in the wrong direction. We're interested in whether democracy promotes freedom, not whether increases in freedom promote democracy.

(C) is wrong because "irrelevant" is much too strong. The historical examples might not be enough to prove the point, but they are not irrelevant.

(E) is suggesting the argument contains a bias. Though the argument may be limited, it's tough to see a personal bias. We can't simply throw the premises out because the author is talking about potentially subjective concepts like freedom and oppression.

(D) also involves conditional language—let's leave it for now.

Decision 6: What is the best available answer?

Let's go back to answer (A) and reread it to check if it is indeed correct: "confuses the conditions necessary for political freedom with the conditions sufficient to bring it about."

Remember our previous analysis of the gap: Democracy may not guarantee (be sufficient for) freedom, and democracy may not be necessary for freedom, but that doesn't mean that democracy doesn't improve the odds of having a free society. So, it's not that the argument is "confusing" the necessary conditions and the sufficient conditions, but rather that the argument is taking the fact that democracy is NEITHER necessary NOR sufficient in order to show that democracy doesn't promote freedom.

Let's look at (D) one more time:

> overlooks the possibility that democracy
> promotes political freedom without being
> necessary or sufficient by itself to produce it

Ah, yes. The argument fails to consider ("overlooks the possibility") that democracy could affect freedom even if democracy is neither necessary nor sufficient to have freedom. (D) is the correct answer.

Again, these solutions are not meant to represent the exact thoughts you must have as you work through a question. There's no one way to think about a question; in fact, no two people are likely to think about a question in exactly the same way. However, these solutions can help you to evaluate your own process. Consider again—are there any parts to this process that you routinely shortchange or overlook? On the flip side, are there other things that you focus on that now seem less important? As you learn about the other question types in the chapters to come, keep mindful of the ideal process for each question type, and make sure your process helps you think about the right thing at the right time.

Time to Time

As you've been working to build a consistent process on untimed questions, you may have found yourself wondering how you'll execute that process under the pressure of a ticking timer. The answer? Clumsily! At least at first. That's why it's a good idea to start integrating timed practice now, even if you don't feel ready.

A good way to dip your toe into timed practice is to grab an official LSAT LR section and attempt the first six questions in eight minutes. That's a breakdown of one minute and twenty seconds per question to approximate the time you'd have on test day, if all the questions in a section took the same amount of time.

Of course, all the questions in a section *won't* take the same amount of time, and by test day, these earlier, easier questions will ideally be knocked out in a minute or less. But for now, give yourself a minute and twenty seconds per question and have at it. And if it hurts, don't worry. Painful though it may be, these are natural growing pains: necessary steps on the road to LSAT mastery.

Strengthen and Weaken Questions

In This Chapter...

One Extra Layer

Thus far, we've looked at two Assumption Family question types—Assumption and Flaw—and we've discussed the general process for attacking Assumption Family problems. Hopefully, you are feeling more and more comfortable with identifying the argument core and evaluating the issues that it might present.

We will continue to reinforce those skills in this chapter. Like Assumption and Flaw questions, Strengthen and Weaken questions test our ability to evaluate the reasoning in an argument—that is, the connection between the premises and the conclusion. However, Strengthen and Weaken questions present us with an additional challenge. Whereas Assumption and Flaw questions primarily require us to *identify* the argument core and *assess* it, Strengthen and Weaken questions require us to *identify, assess*, and then consider ways to *address* the issues in the argument core. For Assumption and Flaw questions, we select answers that directly represent our understanding of the reasoning within the argument. For Strengthen and Weaken questions, we must consider how different bits of *new* information might relate to that reasoning.

Let's use a simple example to illustrate the impact of this additional layer. Consider the following argument:

> Sally owns more cookbooks than Finn. Therefore, Sally is a better cook than Finn.

It's clear that the argument is flawed, but success on the LSAT requires that we understand this type of flaw in a specific way. The subjects, Sally and Finn, don't change from premise to conclusion, but what is discussed about these subjects does:

Sally **owns more cookbooks**   Sally **is a better cook**
than Finn   than Finn

What are the gaps or flaws?

For one, the argument is assuming that *owning* more cookbooks implies *being* a better cook. This is a pretty big assumption. One needs to do more than *own* cookbooks to be a good cook—at the least, one should probably *read* them. And learn from them. And incorporate what is learned into the cooking. Furthermore, the number of cookbooks is not indicative of the knowledge those books have to offer—it's likely that one great cookbook has more valuable information than 10 bad ones.

We can also say that the argument is assuming that owning more cookbooks is enough, by itself, to justify the conclusion—that is, that there are no other factors that significantly influence how well Sally and Finn cook. Again, that's a pretty big assumption. We know from our own lives that there are plenty of other factors that could be considered here: experience in the kitchen, teachers, parents, natural aptitude, taste, and even exposure to foods of various cultures.

We can generalize the flaws in the argument as follows:

- The author takes for granted that owning more cookbooks has a direct impact on being a better cook.

- The author fails to consider that other factors could be involved in determining who is the better cook.

Most commonly, correct answers to Strengthen questions help the argument by helping to plug a gap in the core. This gap can relate to how the elements of the premise and conclusion equate to one another or to the "What else?" the author should have considered but didn't. Correct answers to Weaken questions will most commonly expose these gaps.

With that in mind, take a look at some ways that we might strengthen or weaken the argument by helping to plug one of the two gaps we just discussed:

Assumption	Valid Strengthen Answers	Valid Weaken Answers
Owning more cookbooks is related to being a better cook.	The number of cookbooks one owns is an accurate gauge of how much one knows about cooking. Owning cookbooks inspires people to practice cooking, and, in turn, to become better cooks. In Sally's collection are some of the greatest cookbooks in the world, and she has read and learned from them.	Sally has not read any of her cookbooks. None of Sally's cookbooks describe anything aside from different ways of decorating gingerbread houses. People often misread cookbooks and end up becoming worse cooks after reading them.
There are no other significant factors involved in being a good cook.	A recent study found that owning cookbooks was the most significant factor in determining a person's understanding of cooking. Experience in the kitchen and exposure to foods of other cultures are not factors that significantly influence knowledge of cooking.	Finn is a cooking school instructor, and the books Sally owns were written by Finn. Finn has been apprenticed to a world-renowned chef for the past three years. Sally was born without taste buds and cannot accurately gauge the flavor of her cooking.

Keep in mind these three factors when thinking about the above samples:

1. **You do not have to consider whether the answer could be true in real life or not.** In fact, most question stems will explicitly ask that you treat the answers as if they are true.

MANHATTAN
PREP

So, even if you think it's not possible that reading cookbooks could make Sally a worse cook, it's not your job here to make that judgment. Even if you know that it's rare for people not to have taste buds, when evaluating an answer, you should work on the assumption that the statement is true.

2. **A Strengthen answer doesn't have to make the argument perfect and a Weaken answer doesn't have to destroy the argument entirely.** In fact, for some of the most challenging questions, a Strengthen answer will still leave the argument with significant gaps, and a Weaken answer may address the slightest of many issues in the core.

Consider this Weaken answer:

Finn is a cooking school instructor, and the books Sally owns were written by Finn.

Does this mean Sally isn't a better cook than Finn? Does this prove Finn is a better cook? No, certainly not if we are considering this with the strict reasoning eye the LSAT requires. Finn can be an instructor and a book writer—and a terrible cook! It's possible that Sally has never been to cooking school but is a phenomenal cook (we all know people like this in real life).

Furthermore, this answer has some characteristics that would, with good reason, cause us to shy away from it if it appeared on an Assumption or Flaw problem. If we think about one component of the answer—Finn teaches cooking—is this something that could play a critical role in an Assumption or Flaw answer? No. In making his argument, the author need not assume one thing or another about whether Finn teaches cooking, nor would any assumption about Finn teaching cooking be sufficient to make the argument valid.

So, why could this be the correct answer to a Weaken question? Because it dents an assumption the author is making. In thinking that the evidence is sufficient to prove the conclusion, the author is assuming that the relative number of cookbooks Sally and Finn respectively own is enough, by itself, to determine which of the two is the better cook—the author is assuming that there *must* be no other significant factors. An answer choice such as this one exposes the issue with that assumption simply by showing that there *could* be other factors.

This leads us to a third subtle but significant point:

3. **The answers to Strengthen and Weaken questions can address an assumption by bringing in new and unexpected information.** In this case, it could be the lack of taste buds or being a cooking instructor. Because answer choices can bring in new information, it is often true that correct answers to these questions will relate less obviously to the argument core than most Assumption and Flaw answers do. In a certain way, this is what we saw defender assumptions do; a necessary assumption can address an obvious gap in an unpredictable way, or it can address a gap that is itself unpredictable.

This freedom of scope is important on two fronts. First, you want to cast a wider net when it comes to thinking about what could be the right answer to a Strengthen or Weaken question. The answer's relation to the core can be less obvious than for other Assumption Family questions. We've also noticed that correct Strengthen and Weaken answers are more likely than correct Assumption and Flaw answers to address secondary, or perhaps less significant, gaps in the reasoning of the argument.

Second, you want to make sure that the skills you develop for connecting tangential answers do not take away from the sharp eye you've developed for spotting answers that are truly out of scope. Right answers to Assumption and Flaw questions tend to relate more directly to the core—and a lot of the work we've done has been designed to help you better separate the answers that relate to the core from the answers that don't. We'd hate for the work you do on Strengthen and Weaken questions to take away from the work you've done on Assumption and Flaw questions. Again, if you think of Strengthen and Weaken questions as questions that add an additional layer to the tasks required of you in Assumption and Flaw questions, you can keep these characteristics clear.

Consider this potential weakener of our argument about Sally owning more cookbooks than Finn and thus being a better cook than him:

> *Finn is a good cook.*

Why is this not a correct weakener? For one, it doesn't tell us if Finn is a *better* cook than Sally is. Also—and this is crucial—Finn being a good cook does not weaken the connection between the premises and the conclusion. Our job is not to weaken the conclusion but to weaken the *argument*. We'll look at some rare questions where we're specifically asked to weaken the conclusion, but for the overwhelming majority of Strengthen and Weaken questions, we're expected to focus on the *reasoning*.

Let's now practice our process on a real LSAT question. Remember to identify the premises and the conclusion, find one or more assumptions, and choose an answer that addresses an assumption.

PT36, S1, Q25

A 1991 calculation was made to determine what, if any, additional health-care costs beyond the ordinary are borne by society at large for people who live a sedentary life. The figure reached was a lifetime average of $1,650. Thus people's voluntary choice not to exercise places a significant burden on society.

Which one of the following, if true and not taken into account by the calculation, most seriously weakens the argument?

(A)   Many people whose employment requires physical exertion do not choose to engage in regular physical exercise when they are not at work.

(B)   Exercise is a topic that is often omitted from discussion between doctor and patient during a patient's visit.

(C)   Physical conditions that eventually require medical or nursing-home care often first predispose a person to adopt a sedentary life-style.

(D)   Individuals vary widely in the amount and kind of exercise they choose, when they do exercise regularly.

(E)   A regular program of moderate exercise tends to increase circulation, induce a feeling of well-being and energy, and decrease excess weight.

In the previous chapter, we deconstructed a thought process that aligns with, and works effectively for, almost all Assumption Family questions. Let's use it to break down this problem.

Decision 1: What is my task?

We're asked to find an answer that most weakens the argument. We know this is an Assumption Family question, and we're going to need to understand the argument core well in order to efficiently arrive at the correct answer.

Decision 2: What is the conclusion?

Let's model how this process might go in real time:

> A 1991 calculation was made to determine what, if any, additional health-care costs beyond the ordinary are borne by society at large for people who live a sedentary life.

This is background information. It gives us the context for the argument.

> The figure reached was a lifetime average of $1,650.

Is this still background? Unclear what role this plays.

> Thus people's voluntary choice not to exercise places a significant burden on society.

This is definitely the conclusion. It is the author's main point and, in fact, it's the only claim in the argument.

Decision 3: How is this conclusion supported?

Once we identify the conclusion, it's easier to see that the information in the previous sentence—that the figure reached was a lifetime average of $1,650—is being used to support that conclusion. Furthermore, the sentence before that tells us what "the figure" stands for: "additional health-care costs beyond the ordinary that are borne by society at large for people who live a sedentary life." Thus, we can think of the argument core as follows:

additional health-care costs beyond the ordinary borne by society at large for people who live a sedentary life average $1,650 people's voluntary choice not to exercise places a significant burden on society

Decision 4: What is the gap?

Perhaps you noticed the mismatch between the people who are discussed in the premises and those who are discussed in the conclusion. The premises are specifically about people who live a sedentary life, while the conclusion is specifically about people who voluntarily choose not to exercise.

Do we know that those who live a sedentary life do so because they *choose* not to exercise? Absolutely not! There may be other reasons why people *must* live a sedentary life. This is a significant mismatch, and it is very likely that the correct answer will have to address this discrepancy.

Furthermore, it's unclear whether an average of $1,650 represents a significant burden. We've been given no tools to decide. A correct Weaken answer could expose this gap by showing us why, for any of a variety of reasons, this would NOT be a significant burden.

With a clear understanding of these gaps, we are ready to evaluate the answer choices.

MANHATTAN
PREP

Decision 5: Which answer choices are clearly wrong?

> (A)   Many people whose employment requires
>   physical exertion do not choose to engage in
>   regular physical exercise when they are not at work.

This answer is about an apparently related subject. Let's keep it for now.

> (B)   Exercise is a topic that is often omitted from discussion between doctor
>   and patient during a patient's visit.

Interesting, but this is completely out of scope. It doesn't tell us whether people voluntarily choose not to exercise.

> (C)   Physical conditions that eventually require medical or nursing-home
>   care often first predispose a person to adopt a sedentary life-style.

This answer relates directly to a gap we saw initially in the argument—the idea that the sedentary life-style must be voluntary. This is evidence that shows that perhaps the sedentary life-style is not always voluntary. Let's keep it.

> (D)   Individuals vary widely in the amount and kind of exercise they
>   choose, when they do exercise regularly.

We're interested in people who do not exercise. We can eliminate this.

> (E)   A regular program of moderate exercise tends to increase circulation,
>   induce a feeling of well-being and energy, and decrease excess weight.

This is also about people who exercise. Eliminate.

Decision 6: What is the best available answer?

Keep in mind that even when a question asks for an answer that *most* weakens, there will typically only be one answer that actually weakens. This is the same for Strengthen questions as well. When you're down to two answers, your focus ought not to be on which one weakens more, but rather on which answer actually does weaken and which one does not. Let's evaluate the remaining choices one more time:

> (A)   Many people whose employment requires physical exertion do not
>   choose to engage in regular physical exercise when they are not at work.

Looking back at this one, it can be cut for the same reason as answers (D) and (E). It's about people who get exercise at work, while our argument is about people who live a sedentary life.

That leaves us with (C), the correct answer. Let's take one more look at it:

> (C)   Physical conditions that eventually require medical or nursing-home
>   care often first predispose a person to adopt a sedentary life-style.

Does this answer destroy the argument? No. Perhaps such physical conditions as those described in this answer choice are exceedingly rare, and perhaps the vast majority of people adopt a sedentary life-style voluntarily, in which case the argument could still be pretty strong (at least in respect to the "voluntary" aspect). However, this answer does weaken the reasoning within the argument. It shows that something the author is assuming to be true—that people choose to be sedentary—may in fact not be.

Let's take a look at another question. Try solving it and analyzing the answers you didn't choose before reading further:

PT36, S3, Q2

Several companies will soon offer personalized electronic news services, delivered via cable or telephone lines and displayed on a television. People using these services can view continually updated stories on those topics for which they subscribe. Since these services will provide people with the information they are looking for more quickly and efficiently than printed newspapers can, newspaper sales will decline drastically if these services become widely available.

Which one of the following, if true, most seriously weakens the argument?

(A) In reading newspapers, most people not only look for stories on specific topics but also like to idly browse through headlines or pictures for amusing stories on unfamiliar or unusual topics.

(B) Companies offering personalized electronic news services will differ greatly in what they charge for access to their services, depending on how wide a range of topics they cover.

(C) Approximately 30 percent of people have never relied on newspapers for information but instead have always relied on news programs broadcast on television and radio.

(D) The average monthly cost of subscribing to several channels on a personalized electronic news service will approximately equal the cost of a month's subscription to a newspaper.

(E)   Most people who subscribe to personalized
       electronic news services will not have to pay
       extra costs for installation since the services
       will use connections installed by cable and
       telephone companies.

Wow—apparently the decline of printed newspapers was big news in 2001! Anyway, the core of this argument comes at the end:

> these (electronic news) services will
> provide people with the information
> they are looking for more quickly and
> efficiently than printed newspapers can

> newspaper sales will decline
> drastically if these services
> become widely available

Perhaps, at least the first time through, this argument seems pretty solid! However, since it's an Assumption Family question, we know it's got to have some issues and, in this case, it's helpful to think about the conclusion in terms of "What else?" Why else do people buy and read papers? Do people primarily read newspapers searching for stuff they already know about?

No.

People often read with no idea of what's going to be in the paper (virtual or otherwise)—we read in part *to see* what's in the paper. People also buy newspapers for other reasons—for the crossword or for coupons, for example. The fact that people can identify information they are looking for faster through other forms is not the sole characteristic that needs to be considered in determining whether newspaper sales will drastically decrease.

Let's evaluate the answer choices:

(A)   In reading newspapers, most people not only
       look for stories on specific topics but also like
       to browse idly through headlines or pictures
       for amusing stories on unfamiliar or unusual
       topics.

Perhaps you predicted this, or perhaps you didn't. In either case, you ought to be able to recognize that this answer presents an alternative reason that needs to be considered when thinking about whether newspaper sales will drastically decline. If (A) is true, people may want to continue buying the paper.

(B)   Companies offering personalized electronic
       news services will differ greatly in what they
       charge for access to their services, depending
       on how wide a range of topics they cover.

A comparison among companies offering personalized electronic news services (as opposed to a comparison between such companies and newspapers) is of no relevance to this argument. We can quickly eliminate (B).

> (C)   Approximately 30 percent of people have never relied on newspapers for information but instead have always relied on news programs broadcast on television and radio.

It's unclear how this relates to the conclusion. We're concerned about the people who do currently buy newspapers. Will they switch to the new medium? Answer (C) is out of scope.

> (D)   The average monthly cost of subscribing to several channels on a personalized electronic news service will approximately equal the cost of a month's subscription to a newspaper.

Ah. This answer brings to light a gap in the argument. Perhaps newspaper sales won't decline because electronic services will be more costly. However, this answer choice states the opposite: that the costs are equal. This answer eliminates a potential gap we didn't see initially. In doing so, it *strengthens* the argument.

> (E)   Most people who subscribe to personalized electronic news services will not have to pay extra costs for installation since the services will use connections installed by cable and telephone companies.

This answer touches on the same issue as (D)—cost. But again, it doesn't weaken the argument because it's information about how people *won't* have to pay additional costs to switch away from the paper.

(A) is the correct answer.

Hopefully these two questions have helped place Strengthen and Weaken questions in context relative to the Assumption Family questions discussed in previous chapters. Keep in mind, though, that there is more variation in Strengthen and Weaken questions than there is in Assumption or Flaw questions. The arguments have gaps that are less absolute—often wider and often harder to clearly define—and the connection between argument and answer choice, for reasons discussed above, can be less obvious.

MANHATTAN
PREP

Let's look at one more challenging example:

PT38, S4, Q15

Loggerhead turtles live and breed in distinct groups, of which some are in the Pacific Ocean and some are in the Atlantic. New evidence suggests that juvenile Pacific loggerheads that feed near the Baja peninsula hatch in Japanese waters 10,000 kilometers away. Ninety-five percent of the DNA samples taken from the Baja turtles match those taken from turtles at the Japanese nesting sites.

Which one of the following, if true, most seriously weakens the reasoning above?

(A)   Nesting sites of loggerhead turtles have been found off the Pacific coast of North America several thousand kilometers north of the Baja peninsula.

(B)   The distance between nesting sites and feeding sites of Atlantic loggerhead turtles is less than 5,000 kilometers.

(C)   Loggerhead hatchlings in Japanese waters have been declining in number for the last decade while the number of nesting sites near the Baja peninsula has remained constant.

(D)   Ninety-five percent of the DNA samples taken from the Baja turtles match those taken from Atlantic loggerhead turtles.

(E)   Commercial aquariums have been successfully breeding Atlantic loggerheads with Pacific loggerheads for the last five years.

We can take what the new evidence *suggests* as the conclusion of the argument: "juvenile Pacific loggerheads that feed near the Baja peninsula hatch in Japanese waters 10,000 kilometers away." What is the reasoning given? DNA. Ninety-five percent of the DNA samples taken from the Baja turtles match those taken from turtles at the Japanese nesting sites.

We can think of the core as follows:

$$\boxed{\text{ninety-five percent of the DNA matches}} \Longrightarrow \boxed{\begin{array}{c}\text{pacific loggerhead turtles}\\\text{that feed near the Baja}\\\text{peninsula hatch in}\\\text{Japanese waters 10,000}\\\text{kilometers away}\end{array}}$$

What would we need to know in order for this argument to be valid? We would need to know that a 95% match is significant enough to prove the connection. Perhaps these loggerheads also have a 95% DNA match with cabbage (unlikely, we realize). We don't know the exact significance of 95%, not based on the information we are given. Therefore, we can say the author is assuming that 95% is enough of a match to prove a relation. It's likely an answer meant to weaken will exploit this assumption.

One of the things that makes this question more challenging is that several of the answer choices are very attractive. Let's look at them in depth:

(A)   Nesting sites of loggerhead turtles have been found off the Pacific coast of North America several thousand kilometers north of the Baja peninsula.

This answer choice doesn't address the exact gap we identified, but it does present an intriguing, alternative location from which these turtles in question could have come. Perhaps the turtles came from somewhere else…

However, there is no proof that these sites are more likely places for the turtles to have been born, and, more significantly, this answer does not address any gap in reasoning between the premise and conclusion. We're looking for something that shows us that the DNA evidence is perhaps not as significant as the author believes.

(B)   The distance between nesting sites and feeding sites of Atlantic loggerhead turtles is less than 5,000 kilometers.

This answer is related to an opposing point presented in the argument (the distance between the Baja peninsula and Japanese waters is over 10,000 kilometers). However, does this particular distance being 5,000 kilometers mean that 5,000 kilometers is a norm or a maximum? Not at all. Therefore, this doesn't help us evaluate the reasoning in the argument, and this answer has no direct bearing on the conclusion.

(C)   Loggerhead hatchlings in Japanese waters have been declining in number for the last decade while the number of nesting sites near the Baja peninsula has remained constant.

MANHATTAN
PREP

This is another somewhat tempting answer, but we haven't been told, or been given any indication, that all the hatchlings from Japanese waters come to the Baja peninsula. Therefore, it's unclear what relevance this decline would have for those particular turtles. Perhaps the decline in numbers is connected to turtles that end up going elsewhere. We can eliminate it.

> (D)   Ninety-five percent of the DNA samples taken
>   from the Baja turtles match those taken from
>   Atlantic loggerhead turtles.

It's unclear what this answer means in terms of where the Baja turtles came from.

The point of this answer is not that the turtles in question could have come from the Atlantic. We are told explicitly in the argument that Atlantic turtles and Pacific turtles are distinct.

However, this is a clever way to address the gap that we identified. If the turtles in the Baja peninsula have just as strong a DNA match with the Atlantic turtles—turtles that we know for certain are a distinct group—as they do with the Japanese hatchlings, this puts a big dent into the premise–conclusion relationship. This makes it seem that the DNA evidence is not strong enough to justify the conclusion. (D) seems like the correct answer.

> (E)   Commercial aquariums have been successfully
>   breeding Atlantic loggerheads with Pacific
>   loggerheads for the last five years.

This is out of scope. We can eliminate it quickly, leaving us with (D) as our answer.

Notice that the right answer is the one that is most directly relevant to the *gap* that we identified—specifically the author's assumption that a 95% DNA match is adequate proof that the Baja turtles hatched in Japanese waters. If we were just to look for an answer that matches keywords, we'd be in trouble here. Without a clear understanding of the argument core, and the gap therein, it's very difficult to see which answers can play a more significant role than others.

Rare Strengthen and Weaken Questions

Though most—in fact, almost all—Strengthen and Weaken questions will develop in a manner that is fairly consistent with other Assumption Family questions, as exampled by the problems above, there are certain Strengthen and Weaken questions that do not agree neatly with what we traditionally associate with Assumption Family questions. Again, these questions are fairly rare, but it's important that you are familiar with their characteristics.

Argument, Minus Core

Take a look at the following question. In addition to solving it, consider what makes this argument different from others we've been looking at:

PT 43, S2, Q8

Criminologist: Increasing the current prison term for robbery will result in no significant effect in discouraging people from committing robbery.

Each of the following, if true, supports the criminologist's claim EXCEPT:

(A)　Many people who rob are motivated primarily by thrill-seeking and risk-taking.

(B)　An increase in the prison term for embezzlement did not change the rate at which that crime was committed.

(C)　Prison terms for robbery have generally decreased in length recently.

(D)　Most people committing robbery believe that they will not get caught.

(E)　Most people committing robbery have no idea what the average sentence for robbery is.

This is an EXCEPT question. There is a specific way that we want you to approach EXCEPT Strengthen and Weaken questions, and we'll discuss this approach in greater detail later in the chapter.

For now, let's focus on the argument. Did you notice something unusual about it? We're given a conclusion, but nothing else!

There is no supporting premise and, therefore, no *reasoning* to evaluate, strengthen, or weaken. Notice that the question stem itself makes no mention of "author's reasoning" or "argument," but simply asks us to evaluate the answers relative to the conclusion. Again, this type of question is fairly rare, but it does show up once every few exams. So, if you see an argument on the exam that just doesn't seem to have a core, don't force it.

Let's finish considering this question.

This is really a conclusion about causation—the author is saying that a certain trigger (lengthening sentences) *won't* have a particular direct impact (discouragement) on a certain action (robbery).

How do we strengthen such an argument? In one of two ways:

1.　By showing that there is indeed little or no causal connection between lengthening term sentences and discouraging crime

2.　By showing that there are other factors that more strongly influence the rate of robbery (and in so doing, showing that the particular trigger in question is not primary, or significant, to the likelihood of the outcome)

MANHATTAN
PREP

Let's take a look at the answer choices:

(A)   Many people who rob are motivated primarily
      by thrill-seeking and risk-taking.

This addresses the second of our concerns. If this is the primary reason people are robbing, the increase in jail term is less likely to have an impact. This strengthens the claim.

(B)   An increase in the prison term for
      embezzlement did not change the rate at
      which that crime was committed.

This addresses the first of our concerns. In a similar scenario, we can see that a lengthening of the term didn't impact the rate of crime. This strengthens the claim.

(C)   Prison terms for robbery have generally
      decreased in length recently.

So what? Would an increase deter crime or not? The impact of this answer is unclear.

(D)   Most people committing robbery believe that
      they will not get caught.

If this is true, it's likely robbers are not thinking about prison term length. This would also strengthen the conclusion.

(E)   Most people committing robbery have no idea
      what the average sentence for robbery is.

This addresses the first of our issues. If people don't know how long the term is, it won't matter to them if it is lengthened. This strengthens the claim that increasing the term won't deter crime.

Four of the answers strengthen the conclusion. (C) has an uncertain impact on the conclusion, and is therefore the correct answer.

Beware of Claims within Premises

Another way in which Strengthen and Weaken questions can differ from other typical Assumption Family questions is that they can address the validity of a claim made within a premise. To illustrate, let's take a look at the following example:

my child says she ➡ therefore, my child
can see ghosts   can see ghosts

Notice, as with all other premises for Assumption Family questions, the truth of the *full* premise is not what needs evaluating—we should take it to be true that the child does indeed say this. Our job is not to evaluate whether the child says she can see ghosts.

What needs to be evaluated here is the claim *within* the premise—the child's claim that she can see ghosts. This is suspect. Perhaps she is seeing shadows. A strengthen answer might validate the fact that she does indeed see ghosts, and a weaken answer might give a reason to believe that she does not see ghosts.

Again, we want to be clear—it is not necessary for you to evaluate the truth of the vast majority of claims you see within premises—in fact, in general this will distract you from the far more important task, which is to evaluate the relationship *between* the premises and the conclusion. However, for certain rare Strengthen and Weaken questions, you may need to evaluate the truth of elements within a premise.

Let's take a look at another example:

> *PT29, S4, Q24*
>
> Medical researcher:　As expected, records covering the last four years of ten major hospitals indicate that babies born prematurely were more likely to have low birth weights and to suffer from health problems than were babies not born prematurely. These records also indicate that mothers who had received adequate prenatal care were less likely to have low birth weight babies than were mothers who had received inadequate prenatal care. Adequate prenatal care, therefore, significantly decreases the risk of low birth weight babies.
>
> Which one of the following, if true, most weakens the medical researcher's argument?
>
> (A)　The hospital records indicate that many babies that are born with normal birth weights are born to mothers who had inadequate prenatal care.
>
> (B)　Mothers giving birth prematurely are routinely classified by hospitals as having received inadequate prenatal care when the record of that care is not available.
>
> (C)　The hospital records indicate that low birth weight babies were routinely classified as having been born prematurely.
>
> (D)　Some babies not born prematurely, whose mothers received adequate prenatal care, have low birth weights.

(E)   Women who receive adequate prenatal care
       are less likely to give birth prematurely than
       are women who do not receive adequate
       prenatal care.

The medical researcher gives us a lot of information, then arrives at the conclusion at the end of the argument: "Adequate prenatal care significantly decreases the risk of low birth weight babies."

Like many long arguments, this one has its core at the end. The first sentence perhaps gives us more information about the subjects in the conclusion and the consequences of the conclusion, but it has no bearing on the reasoning used to reach the conclusion. The primary evidence comes in the sentence prior to the conclusion, and we can think of the argument core as follows:

records indicate mothers who received adequate prenatal   adequate prenatal care
care are less likely to give birth to low birth weight babies   significantly decreases risk of
than mothers who received inadequate prenatal care   low birth weight babies

Did you spot the Causation Flaw here? It could be true that there is a correlation between adequate prenatal care and the likelihood of giving birth to a low birth weight baby, but that the prenatal care has no direct impact on that outcome. Perhaps another element—such as mother's diet—is most important to birth weight, and those who are likely to follow the proper diet for a variety of indirect reasons, such as socioeconomic status, happen to be those who get adequate prenatal care. If that were the case, it would be incorrect to say that the prenatal care is what decreases risk.

Let's see if we can find an answer that addresses this Causation Flaw.

(A)   The hospital records indicate that many babies
       that are born with normal birth weights are
       born to mothers who had inadequate prenatal
       care.

The fact that "*many*" babies are born of normal weight to mothers who had inadequate prenatal care does not impact the *relative* likelihood of giving birth to low birth weight babies. This can be a tricky concept to understand, so let's take a look at a simpler example.

Suppose that at a certain ice cream shop, those who order the sundae are far more likely to request peanuts than those who order the banana split. This would not mean that all those who order the sundae request peanuts—just that ordering the sundae makes the request more likely. We can imagine the following results for 100 orders:

	Requested Peanuts	Didn't Request Peanuts
Ordered Sundae	40	10
Ordered Banana Split	10	40

In the above situation, it's true that *many* people who ordered the banana split requested peanuts, but it doesn't change the fact that those who ordered the sundae *were more likely* to request peanuts.

The same thing is happening with answer (A). Even if many of those who get inadequate care give birth to normal weight babies, it's unclear what impact this has on the conclusion, so we can eliminate it.

> (B)   Mothers giving birth prematurely are routinely
>   classified by hospitals as having received
>   inadequate prenatal care when the record of
>   that care is not available.

This doesn't address the flaw we discussed, but it does impact the premise—it provides an alternative reason for why the difference between likelihoods exists. Let's keep it for now.

> (C)   The hospital records indicate that low birth
>   weight babies were routinely classified as
>   having been born prematurely.

It's tough to see how this impacts the argument. This answer addresses the relationship between low birth weight and prematurity, but it does not address the relationship between prenatal care and birth weight. Let's eliminate it.

> (D)   Some babies not born prematurely, whose
>   mothers received adequate prenatal care, have
>   low birth weights.

This answer is similar to (A). "Some" is very vague, and so this gives us no insight into the relative likelihood for the different groups.

> (E)   Women who receive adequate prenatal care
>   are less likely to give birth prematurely than
>   are women who do not receive adequate
>   prenatal care.

If anything, answer (E) would strengthen the argument by connecting the factors in the premise and giving another reason why women who receive adequate prenatal care are going to be less likely to give birth to a low weight baby. We can eliminate this answer because it certainly doesn't weaken.

That leaves us only with answer choice (B). It certainly wasn't what we expected, but it does impact the conclusion. Let's review it one more time:

> (B)   Mothers giving birth prematurely are routinely
>   classified by hospitals as having received
>   inadequate prenatal care when the record of
>   that care is not available.

In what way does this impact our core? It's essentially telling us that the records themselves are not accurate. In other words, the support for the conclusion is not reliable! This answer choice weakens the reliability of a claim within a premise, and thus weakens the argument. Still, it's important to notice that we didn't go off the deep end: We didn't attack the validity of the premise itself. It's still true that the records indicate a correlation between inadequate care and low birth weight. It just turns out that the records aren't accurate. Usually, we expect an answer that more obviously attacks the connection between the premise and conclusion, but we should expect some curveballs in Strengthen and Weaken questions.

Here's another question with a similar issue. Try it completely before reading further:

PT44, S2, Q20

Scientist: My research indicates that children who engage in impulsive behavior similar to adult thrill-seeking behavior are twice as likely as other children to have a gene variant that increases sensitivity to dopamine. From this, I conclude that there is a causal relationship between this gene variant and an inclination toward thrill-seeking behavior.

Which one of the following, if true, most calls into question the scientist's argument?

(A)   Many impulsive adults are not unusually sensitive to dopamine.

(B)   It is not possible to reliably distinguish impulsive behavior from other behavior.

(C)   Children are often described by adults as engaging in thrill-seeking behavior simply because they act impulsively.

(D)   Many people exhibit behavioral tendencies as adults that they did not exhibit as children.

(E)   The gene variant studied by the scientist is correlated with other types of behavior in addition to thrill-seeking behavior.

Here's the argument core:

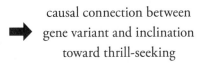

research indicates children who engage in impulsive behavior similar to adult thrill-seeking twice as likely to have gene variant ➡ causal connection between gene variant and inclination toward thrill-seeking

We've got ourselves another Causation Flaw. Will the answers address it this time?

> (A)   Many impulsive adults are not unusually
>   sensitive to dopamine.

This answer choice is very similar to a couple from the previous example—"many" does not, in any direct way, impact the likelihood of a characteristic in one group versus another. We can eliminate this quickly.

> (B)   It is not possible to reliably distinguish
>   impulsive behavior from other behavior.

Hmm. Interesting. Certainly doesn't have to do with any issue we saw, but, if this were true, it might weaken the argument. Let's keep it.

> (C)   Children are often described by adults as
>   engaging in thrill-seeking behavior simply
>   because they act impulsively.

This may be true, but we don't know if the researcher thought this way. In any case, the behavior was specifically labeled as impulsive, not thrill-seeking. We can eliminate it.

> (D)   Many people exhibit behavioral tendencies as
>   adults that they did not exhibit as children.

The research is about children—tendencies that develop later are irrelevant. Eliminate it.

> (E)   The gene variant studied by the scientist is
>   correlated with other types of behavior in
>   addition to thrill-seeking behavior.

This answer, if anything, would strengthen the connection between the genes and the behavior. We can eliminate it.

Once again, we're left with just one viable answer. Let's evaluate it again:

> (B)   It is not possible to reliably distinguish
>   impulsive behavior from other behavior.

What would the significance of this answer be? If it's not possible to reliably distinguish impulsive behavior, the research is far less likely to be accurate. If the research is not accurate, it doesn't provide compelling support for the conclusion.

(B) is correct.

This last problem is a perfect example of a difficult Strengthen and Weaken question. The right answer is tough to predict and is presented in a surprising manner. Once again, the argument presented a Causation Flaw that was not addressed in the answer choices. For this type of question, it is critical that you stay open-minded as you evaluate the answer choices. With that in mind, your elimination process becomes even more critical, so let's discuss it in more depth.

MANHATTAN
PREP

The Elimination Process for Strengthen and Weaken Questions

The characteristics of incorrect answers for Strengthen and Weaken questions are fairly consistent with the characteristics of incorrect answers for other Assumption Family questions. We've already discussed many incorrect answers in this chapter—let's try to organize our understanding of them. You can think of almost all wrong answers to Strengthen and Weaken questions as falling into one of three categories:

1. **The answer has no direct bearing on the conclusion.** Often, these answers are related to a vague, or slightly incorrect, understanding of the author's point. If you don't have a clear sense of the core, or if you've generalized beyond what the author is specifically discussing, you'll be in trouble with these. Typically, there is a subtle but significant shift (often a mismatch of terms) between the argument and the answer.

If you have a clear understanding of the core and, most importantly, the conclusion, these answers can be the simplest to eliminate. They also happen to be the most common wrong choices.

2. **The answer has an unclear bearing on the conclusion.** A slightly more tempting wrong answer is one that is related to the elements of the conclusion, but has an unclear impact on the author's point. We'll discuss these types of answers in more depth in the "EXCEPT" section. These answers may discuss the same subject matter as the argument, but in a manner that doesn't relate directly to the point that the author is making or to the reasoning that the author is using to reach that conclusion. If you can't see how the answer impacts the author's point, or if you can see the answer either strengthening or weakening the argument, depending on how you interpret the answer choice or on what assumptions you make, that's a good sign it neither strengthens nor weakens.

3. **The answer plays the opposite role relative to the argument.** Let's imagine you are given a Strengthen question. You read through the argument, immediately see one significant flaw, and move to the answer choices. Answers (A) through (C) have no direct impact on the author's point. You get to answer (D)—it is an example that accurately and absolutely proves the flaw you saw in the argument, and so you pick it...

But wait—wouldn't that mean answer choice (D) weakens the argument? We're supposed to strengthen!

As we've said before, answers that express an assumption when we should be looking for an objection, or answers that weaken an argument when we're looking for something that strengthens—answers that play the opposite role of what we're looking for—can often be the most tempting and most attractive. This is particularly true for EXCEPT questions!

Let's take a look at a real LSAT question. For each wrong choice, take the extra time to try to determine exactly why it is incorrect:

PT36, S3, Q7

Medical doctor: Sleep deprivation is the cause of
many social ills, ranging from irritability to
potentially dangerous instances of impaired
decision making. Most people today suffer from
sleep deprivation to some degree. Therefore we
should restructure the workday to allow people
flexibility in scheduling their work hours.

Which one of the following, if true, would most
strengthen the medical doctor's argument?

(A)   The primary cause of sleep deprivation is
overwork.

(B)   Employees would get more sleep if they had
greater latitude in scheduling their work hours.

(C)   Individuals vary widely in the amount of sleep
they require.

(D)   More people would suffer from sleep
deprivation today than did in the past if the
average number of hours worked per week
had not decreased.

(E)   The extent of one's sleep deprivation is
proportional to the length of one's workday.

The argument begins with a general statement about the consequences of sleep deprivation. The second sentence shows how widespread the issue is, and the author's conclusion comes at the end.

We can think of the core of the doctor's argument as follows:

most people today suffer
from sleep deprivation   we should restructure
                                            workday to allow more
+   ➡   flexibility in scheduling
                                            work hours
sleep deprivation is the
cause of many social ills

There is a fairly big gap in this argument. It's unclear what the relationship is between sleep deprivation and flexibility in scheduling work hours.

It's easy to misinterpret, or generalize, this argument to mean that workdays should be set up in such a way as to prevent people from overworking and not getting enough sleep. Notice though that that's not what this argument says.

If you thought of the conclusion in this way, many of the answer choices could have seemed a lot more attractive than they should have.

Let's go through them now:

> (A)   The primary cause of sleep deprivation is
>   overwork.

This may be true, but it's unclear what overwork has to do with flexibility in the schedule. This answer is not relevant to the conclusion.

> (B)   Employees would get more sleep if they had
>   greater latitude in scheduling their work hours.

This answer seems to help bridge the gap between elements in the premises (amount of sleep) and the conclusion (flexibility). Let's keep it for now.

> (C)   Individuals vary widely in the amount of sleep
>   they require.

Like many incorrect answers, this introduces an element of variation that doesn't matter. If some people need more sleep than others, that still doesn't tell us whether flexibility in work hours would help them to get the sleep they need.

> (D)   More people would suffer from sleep
>   deprivation today than did in the past if the
>   average number of hours worked per week
>   had not decreased.

Again, if you had generalized the conclusion to be about a workload that allowed for more sleep, this answer would seem tempting. However, it's unclear what connection there is between a decrease in work hours and the flexibility in hours discussed in the conclusion. You can have flexible work hours and still work a lot!

> (E)   The extent of one's sleep deprivation is
>   proportional to the length of one's workday.

Again, it's unclear what impact this has on an argument that has to do with flexibility.

That leaves us with (B), the correct answer. Let's review it one more time:

> (B)   Employees would get more sleep if they had
>   greater latitude in scheduling their work hours.

How does this strengthen the argument, exactly? If (B) is true, then giving more flexibility would allow employees to not be as sleep deprived. This is a good thing, since we're told that sleep deprivation is the cause of many social ills. This answer connects the premises to the conclusion, and it helps the premises justify that conclusion.

Note that in this case, there was only one answer that had any direct bearing at all on the conclusion. A careful understanding of the core should have helped you knock off the incorrect choices fairly quickly.

Here's another challenging problem for which many incorrect choices will have no relation to the core. Try to eliminate these answers first, before moving on to decide which answer choice is correct:

PT16, S3, Q18

Because dinosaurs were reptiles, scientists once assumed that, like all reptiles alive today, dinosaurs were cold-blooded. The recent discovery of dinosaur fossils in the northern arctic, however, has led a number of researchers to conclude that at least some dinosaurs might have been warm-blooded. These researchers point out that only warm-blooded animals could have withstood the frigid temperatures that are characteristic of arctic winters, whereas cold-blooded animals would have frozen to death in the extreme cold.

Which one of the following, if true, weakens the researchers' argument?

(A)   Today's reptiles are generally confined to regions of temperate or even tropical climates.

(B)   The fossils show the arctic dinosaurs to have been substantially smaller than other known species of dinosaurs.

(C)   The arctic dinosaur fossils were found alongside fossils of plants known for their ability to withstand extremely cold temperatures.

(D)   The number of fossils found together indicates herds of dinosaurs so large that they would need to migrate to find a continual food supply.

(E)   Experts on prehistoric climatic conditions believe that winter temperatures in the prehistoric northern arctic were not significantly different from what they are today.

Before reading the explanation, please think again about the answer choices that do not relate to the argument core and notate them in some way.

We can think of the core of this argument as follows:

dinosaur fossils discovered in
northern arctic

+   ➡   some dinosaurs may have
been warm-blooded

only warm-blooded animals
can withstand frigid arctic
winters

What are the gaps in this argument?

For one, perhaps the winters may have been different when the dinosaurs were around. Perhaps arctic winters weren't as cold back then as they are now and cold-blooded dinosaurs could have survived. For another, perhaps the dinosaurs migrated north in the warmer summer and migrated to warmer areas in the south for the winter. In this case, they wouldn't need to survive arctic winters.

It may not be tough to see the issues once the argument is dissected, but for many, this is a difficult argument to understand the first time through. We can do ourselves a big favor by first getting rid of answers that do not impact the reasoning in any way.

Here are two answer choices that simply have no relationship to the reasoning in the argument:

(A)   Today's reptiles are generally confined to
        regions of temperate or even tropical
        climates.

Does this generalization have any impact on our conclusion? No. The fact that reptiles generally live in temperate or tropical climates has no impact on our argument—this doesn't mean that reptiles don't ever live in cold climates. Furthermore, we don't have any information to connect the behavior of reptiles today with the behavior of dinosaurs.

(B)   The fossils show the arctic dinosaurs to have
        been substantially smaller than other known
        species of dinosaurs.

It's unclear what relevance the size of the dinosaurs has for this argument. So what if they were small? Perhaps you can imagine some relationship between size and heat retention. However, that requires assumptions that go too far beyond the text.

The other answer choices are a bit more tempting. Let's evaluate them in depth:

(C)   The arctic dinosaur fossils were found
        alongside fossils of plants known for their
        ability to withstand extremely cold
        temperatures.

Hmm. If this is true, it would seem the dinosaurs died during times of very cold temperatures. It supports the idea, perhaps, that the dinosaurs died in the winter. Let's leave it for now.

But wait a minute! That would make it so the author's argument sounds better, and we're looking to weaken. We can eliminate this answer because it plays a reverse role.

By the way, we can also eliminate this answer because it doesn't actually indicate whether these plants (and thus the dinosaurs) actually died in extremely cold temperatures; we simply know that these plants were capable of *withstanding* cold temperatures. If you noticed this, perhaps you also noticed that this answer has no direct bearing on the conclusion—that some dinosaurs may have been warm-blooded. It's often true that answers are wrong for multiple reasons.

> (D)   The number of fossils found together indicates herds of dinosaurs so large that they would need to migrate to find a continual food supply.

The first part of (D), about the size of the herds, makes this answer seem out of scope, but the second part is relevant—these herds migrated. If they migrated, perhaps they were in the north only during the summer months. Notice how this answer seems out of scope, but actually helps to break the bond between premise and conclusion. Thus, this answer weakens the author's argument by deflecting the impact of evidence the author uses to prove that there were warm-blooded dinosaurs. (D) is correct.

Let's finish this off by looking at (E):

> (E)   Experts on prehistoric climatic conditions believe that winter temperatures in the prehistoric northern arctic were not significantly different from what they are today.

This is a very tempting answer. Of all the choices, this one addresses a gap in the argument most directly. However, notice that this is an answer that would *strengthen* the argument. It's another answer that's the opposite of what we're looking for.

Clearly, this is a difficult question, especially if you didn't anticipate the gap about migration when you initially read the argument. However, it would make sense to hold on to (D) in any case, because it presents an alternative explanation of how bones could be found in an area where dinosaurs seemingly shouldn't be able to survive the winter: *The dinosaurs migrated.* In so doing, it directly addresses a gap in the core. Does it make it so that the argument is 100% wrong? Absolutely not. Is it an answer we'd be likely to predict? Absolutely not. Again, having the ability to quickly eliminate answers that don't directly relate to the core will give you a better chance of zeroing in on such an unlikely correct answer.

Here's one more question. Take the time to solve it and to classify the wrong answer choices before moving forward.

PT36, S1, Q8

It has been claimed that television networks should provide equal time for the presentation of opposing views whenever a television program concerns scientific issues—such as those raised by the claims of environmentalists—about which people disagree. However, although an obligation to provide equal time does arise in the case of any program concerning social issues, it does so because social issues almost always have important political implications and seldom can definitely be settled on the basis of available evidence. If a program concerns scientific issues, that program gives rise to no such equal time obligation.

Which one of the following, if true, most seriously weakens the argument?

(A)   No scientific issues raised by the claims of environmentalists have important political implications.

(B)   There are often more than two opposing views on an issue that cannot be definitely settled on the basis of available evidence.

(C)   Some social issues could be definitely settled on the basis of evidence if the opposing sides would give all the available evidence a fair hearing.

(D)   Many scientific issues have important political implications and cannot be definitely settled on the basis of the available evidence.

(E)   Some television networks refuse to broadcast programs on issues that have important political implications and that cannot be definitely settled by the available evidence.

It's very easy to get distracted in this argument, because it is long and because the author uses claims that we might have strong opinions about. It's great to read like a debater, but be sure to apply that to the entire core, not just to the premises or the conclusion.

Let's evaluate the argument core:

there is an obligation to provide
equal time for programs
involving social issues because
they almost always have
important political implications
and can rarely be solved with
available evidence

➡️

if program is about
scientific issues, there is no
such equal time obligation

This argument may leave us with many questions. Can't a program be both scientific and social? How do we know scientific problems don't have the characteristics the author describes? Who is to say an obligation doesn't exist to present equal sides for scientific issues *for other reasons*?

Because the gaps here run in so many different directions, we want to cast a wide net in terms of what could strengthen or what could weaken. Indeed, it will be far more effective to start by finding reasons that four of the answers don't work.

Let's review the answers one at a time:

(A)   No scientific issues raised by the claims of
        environmentalists have important political
        implications.

This definitely addresses a gap in the argument. If these issues have political implications, then maybe there is an obligation to give them equal time. However, this is saying that the issues do not have important political implications. If this were true, the argument would be strengthened. We must be careful to be clear about our task. If we are, we can eliminate this answer.

(B)   There are often more than two opposing views
        on an issue that cannot be definitely settled
        on the basis of available evidence.

Why does it matter if the number of opposing views is two or more than two? We can eliminate this answer.

(C)   Some social issues could be definitely settled
        on the basis of evidence if the opposing sides
        would give all the available evidence a fair
        hearing.

This answer has no bearing on the author's conclusion about scientific issues. Eliminate it.

(D)   Many scientific issues have important political
        implications and cannot be definitely settled
        on the basis of the available evidence.

MANHATTAN
PREP

This answer directly addresses the gap, and, if this were true, then the author's point would be weakened. Scientific issues would have the same characteristics that obligate networks to provide equal time for opposing views on social issues.

> (E)   Some television networks refuse to broadcast
>   programs on issues that have important
>   political implications and that cannot be
>   definitely settled by the available evidence.

This argument is about whether networks have an obligation to provide equal time for opposing views on issues they do cover. Whether they refuse to cover some issues is out of scope.

Answer choice (D) is correct.

To be clear, we do not want you to spend precious time during the exam categorizing incorrect choices. However, we think it's very useful for you to go into the exam knowing, in as clear a way as possible, why wrong answer choices are wrong. In reviewing your work, even for problems that you confidently answered correctly, take the time to consider exactly why each wrong choice is incorrect. A strong sense of how wrong answers are built will allow you to go through Strengthen and Weaken questions more efficiently and effectively.

EXCEPT

EXCEPT questions can be some of the most challenging questions in a Logical Reasoning section. They are easily misunderstood, and they can cause us to get all twisted around, especially if our attention slips for a moment.

All this is understandable. EXCEPT questions require us to think in the reverse of what we've grown accustomed to doing on other types of problems. Answers that directly relate to the core, and clearly strengthen or weaken—answers that we typically ought to be attracted to—are going to be the ones we'll generally want to eliminate. Therefore, it's important that you develop a process that is specific to these questions.

Here are a few key points to remember:

1. **Make sure you clearly understand what you are looking for.** Let's take a look at a typical phrasing of an EXCEPT question:

> "Each of the following, if true, would weaken the argument EXCEPT:"

A common misconception is that the answer choices for such a question will break down as follows: four answer choices that weaken and one answer choice that strengthens.

It's critical to remember that the right answer to this type of question need not, and often will not, strengthen the conclusion. The right answer will simply be the only one that *does not weaken*. It may strengthen or it may have no direct bearing on the conclusion. For the most challenging questions, the tendency will be that the right answer has no clearly discernible impact on the conclusion. So, remember that there are three categories of answers:

Weaken   **No clear bearing**   **Strengthen**

For a question such as "Each of the following, if true, would strengthen the argument EXCEPT," four answers will strengthen and the right answer will either weaken or, more commonly, have no clearly discernible impact on the conclusion.

How can this be? How can the LSAT outsmart you with answers that don't have an impact on the conclusion, and how can it do so to such a degree that these can be some of the most challenging questions on the exam? The key to these well-cloaked answers is that they will relate directly to some other part of the argument, often the primary premise, but not in a way that impacts the author's point. Remember, your job in most Strengthen and Weaken questions is to strengthen or weaken the *argument*, not the premises or conclusion alone. Your ability to recognize and focus in on the argument core is critical.

To illustrate, let's go back to the sample argument that started the chapter:

Sally **owns more**   Sally **is a better cook**
cookbooks than Finn   than Finn

Here are a few examples of answers that, if true, would strengthen the argument:

"The number of cookbooks one owns is an accurate gauge of how much one knows about cooking."

"Owning cookbooks inspires people to practice cooking, and, in turn, to become better cooks."

"Experience in the kitchen and exposure to foods of other cultures are not factors that significantly influence knowledge of cooking."

Here are a few examples of answers that would, if true, weaken the argument:

"Sally has not read any of her cookbooks."

"Sally often misreads cookbooks and ends up becoming a worse cook after reading them."

"Sally was born without taste buds and cannot accurately gauge the flavor of her cooking."

Each of these answers has a direct impact on the conclusion either because it supports the reasoning used in connecting the premise to the conclusion or because it exposes gaps in this reasoning. We can see how each of these answers would have a direct impact on our judgment of whether Sally is a better cook than Finn.

Here is an answer that *seems* related to the argument, but neither strengthens nor weakens the author's reasoning:

"Sally unexpectedly got all the cookbooks from her mother when her mother moved into a smaller house."

Note that this answer relates directly to our premise—in fact, it gives us a reason *why* our premise is true.

But does this answer impact the author's conclusion? Does it impact the reasoning used? Not in a clear, direct way.

The fact that Sally inherited the books could mean she didn't have any interest in owning them or it could mean she wanted the books. If we try to connect this answer to the argument in a way that impacts whether Sally is a better cook than Finn, we could only do so by adding significant conjectures, or assumptions. Therefore, we can say that this answer does not have a clearly definable impact on our argument.

Let's try a full EXCEPT question:

> *PT37, S2, Q20*
>
> Antarctic seals dive to great depths and stay submerged for hours. They do not rely solely on oxygen held in their lungs, but also store extra oxygen in their blood. Indeed, some researchers hypothesize that for long dives these seals also store oxygenated blood in their spleens.
>
> Each of the following, if true, provides some support for the researchers' hypothesis EXCEPT:
>
> (A)   Horses are known to store oxygenated blood in their spleens for use during exertion.
>
> (B)   Many species of seal can store oxygen directly in their muscle tissue.
>
> (C)   The oxygen contained in the seals' lungs and bloodstream alone would be inadequate to support the seals during their dives.
>
> (D)   The spleen is much larger in the Antarctic seal than in aquatic mammals that do not make long dives.
>
> (E)   The spleens of Antarctic seals contain greater concentrations of blood vessels than are contained in most of their other organs.

We discussed earlier that arguments for Strengthen and Weaken questions can stray farther from the norm than arguments for Assumption and Flaw questions. This isn't very common, but here's an example of an argument that doesn't fit the argument core model.

We could think of the core in this way:

seals stay submerged for
hours

+

don't rely solely on oxygen
in lungs   ➡   store oxygenated blood
in spleens

+

store oxygen in blood

However, a *more* accurate representation of this argument is that the first two sentences present background for a hypothesis that doesn't have a supporting premise. Here we have another argument without a core:

Seals store oxygenated blood in their spleens.

Again, we want to stress that being asked to strengthen or weaken an argument without a premise–conclusion core is fairly unusual—something you should expect to see no more than once, if that, on any given exam. By the way, it's no coincidence that both "core-free" arguments we've discussed in this chapter have come in the form of EXCEPT questions. Also, note that we were given a subtle clue in the way the question is asked:

"Each of the following, if true, **provides some support for the researchers' hypothesis** EXCEPT:"

The words in bold are of note because of what is *missing*—typically we are asked to evaluate what would strengthen or weaken *reasoning,* or an *argument.* In this case, we're asked to identify answers that simply support the *hypothesis,* or conclusion. We know we just need to compare the answers to the conclusion.

Now, it's time to look at the answer choices. Your frame of mind is critical to your success and efficiency. Here's our second tip:

2. **Eliminate the four that go in the same direction!** This may seem like obvious advice. However, the reason we make a point of stating this is that by the time you are done practicing all the Strengthen and Weaken questions that we hope you will practice, your default mind-set is going to be to look for the one answer that weakens or the one answer that strengthens. If you are not careful, this habit will slow you down or distract you on EXCEPT questions.

It is important that you change your mind-set for EXCEPT questions. What you know going in to the answer choices is that almost all of the answers, 80%, in fact, will go in one direction, either strengthening or weakening.

Let's focus in on the hypothesis one more time before going into the answer choices:

Seals store oxygenated blood in their spleens.

We know almost all the answers will support this idea, so we want to cast a wide net. Let's evaluate each in depth:

(A)   Horses are known to store oxygenated blood in
        their spleens for use during exertion.

This strengthens the argument because it shows that such a thing—an animal storing oxygenated blood in its spleen—is possible.

It's important to note that this would be out of scope for an Assumption or Flaw question. The author doesn't need to assume anything about horses to make her claim about seals, nor is it a flaw that she didn't. This is another example of how answers that strengthen or weaken can feel a bit further separated from the text than answers that represent assumptions or flaws.

(B)   Many species of seal can store oxygen directly
        in their muscle tissue.

How does this impact the conclusion? It's unclear. Let's leave (B) for now.

(C)   The oxygen contained in the seals' lungs and
        bloodstream alone would be inadequate to
        support the seals during their dives.

This strengthens the conclusion. It means that they need to store oxygen someplace else, and that supports the idea that they store it in the spleen.

(D)   The spleen is much larger in the Antarctic seal
        than in aquatic mammals that do not make
        long dives.

This also strengthens. If the spleen for these seals is larger, it's possible this difference is due to the use of the spleen for storing oxygenated blood.

(E)   The spleens of Antarctic seals contain greater
        concentrations of blood vessels than are
        contained in most of their other organs.

This also strengthens. This difference in the spleen is more evidence that it is used to store extra oxygen.

In the initial read, you may have felt that many of these answers did not strengthen the argument. If so, it's likely you were setting the bar too high. Remember that answers that strengthen need not make an argument perfect, or anywhere near that. Especially for an EXCEPT question, strengthen answers simply have to give you a stronger sense that the conclusion is true than you had before.

There is only one answer that doesn't have *any* discernible impact on the conclusion:

(B)   Many species of seal can store oxygen directly
        in their muscle tissue.

This is the correct answer. How does the fact that seals can store oxygen in their muscles support the idea that they also store it in their spleens? It doesn't. Notice that we could just as easily conclude that they store oxygen in their muscles *instead* of their spleens.

Let's try another challenging example:

PT33, S1, Q20

Recently discovered prehistoric rock paintings on small islands off the northern coast of Norway have archaeologists puzzled. The predominant theory about northern cave paintings was that they were largely a description of the current diets of the painters. This theory cannot be right, because the painters must have needed to eat the sea animals populating the waters north of Norway if they were to make the long journey to and from the islands, and there are no paintings that unambiguously depict such creatures.

Each of the following, if true, weakens the argument against the predominant theory about northern cave paintings EXCEPT:

(A) Once on these islands, the cave painters hunted and ate land animals.

(B) Parts of the cave paintings on the islands did not survive the centuries.

(C) The cave paintings that were discovered on the islands depicted many land animals.

(D) Those who did the cave paintings that were discovered on the islands had unusually advanced techniques of preserving meats.

(E) The cave paintings on the islands were done by the original inhabitants of the islands who ate the meat of land animals.

The author's conclusion is that the predominant theory cannot be right, and this predominant theory is that northern cave paintings were largely a description of the current diets of the painters. The premises are given in the sentence that follows in the argument, and we can think of the argument core as follows:

needed to eat sea animals
during journey to islands

+

no unambiguous paintings
of sea animals

➡ false that cave paintings
largely describe current
diets of painters

There are some significant gaps in the argument: We don't actually know anything about the diets of the painters once they are on the island, and we don't know if the paintings that have been discovered are representative of *all* the paintings on the island. It's certainly helpful to consider these gaps as we go into the answer choices.

We want to make sure to focus on eliminating answers that weaken this core. In this case—because we are asked specifically to weaken a claim that another claim is false—it's especially easy to get turned around. To keep focused, remember that the conclusion of the argument is that the paintings were not based on the diet.

Let's evaluate the answer choices carefully:

> (A)   Once on these islands, the cave painters
>   hunted and ate land animals.

This shows that the painters could have painted their current diet—that diet just didn't consist of seafood. Therefore, it weakens the author's claim. Let's eliminate it.

> (B)   Parts of the cave paintings on the islands did
>   not survive the centuries.

This shows that the evidence provided might be limited or unrepresentative, and therefore weakens the argument. Maybe they did paint sea animals, but those paintings have been lost. Let's eliminate it.

> (C)   The cave paintings that were discovered on the
>   islands depicted many land animals.

This answer seems less directly connected to the core than the first two. Let's leave it for now.

> (D)   Those who did the cave paintings that were
>   discovered on the islands had unusually
>   advanced techniques of preserving meats.

At first this seems out of scope, but (D) offers another explanation for how, perhaps, the food the painters were eating, and consequently painting, could have been something other than seafood. It calls into question the idea that the long journey required the eating of fish.

> (E)   The cave paintings on the islands were done by
>   the original inhabitants of the islands who ate
>   the meat of land animals.

MANHATTAN
PREP   269

If the paintings were done by people who didn't need to travel to get to the island, one of the premises is made irrelevant. This answer presents the possibility that even though the painters didn't paint seafood, they could have still painted the food they ate.

Once again, we're left with one answer that didn't get cut. Let's look at it one more time:

> (C)   The cave paintings that were discovered on the
>   islands depicted many land animals.

What does this answer choice do for the argument? It depends on what assumptions we make. We could see it as a premise booster, since we already know the paintings don't depict sea animals. But perhaps the painters ate river animals or birds, or perhaps they were vegans! If that were true, then the painting would not be an accurate representation of their current diet. On the other hand, if they ate land animals, then this match between paintings and diet would strengthen the predominant theory and weaken the argument. In other words, in order to determine whether this answer strengthens or weakens, we need a lot of conjecture. This is an answer that has an uncertain bearing on the conclusion, and it is therefore correct.

Conclusion

Strengthen and Weaken questions are still Assumption Family questions, and the skills you've developed for Assumption and Flaw questions should help you here. Here are some additional considerations specific to Strengthen and Weaken questions:

1. **One extra layer.** For Assumption and Flaw questions, we are expected to identify and assess the core. For Strengthen and Weaken questions, we also must *address* gaps in the core. The answers to Strengthen and Weaken questions may feel less directly connected to the argument than answers to Assumption and Flaw questions, and also less predictable.

2. **Unusual arguments.** Strengthen and Weaken arguments have more of a tendency to vary from the norm than other Assumption Family questions. It's critical to be flexible. Beware of arguments without cores and of claims within premises.

3. **The elimination process.** Because the right answers are less predictable, your elimination process is crucial. Eliminate answers that don't relate to the core, have an indeterminate relationship to the core, or—and this one can be tricky to spot—play an opposite role.

4. **EXCEPT questions.** Make sure to change your process for EXCEPT questions. Eliminate the four answer choices that all go in the same direction. The right answer will often relate to the elements in the argument, but it will have no clearly discernible bearing on the author's point.

MANHATTAN
PREP

Drill It: Strengthen and Weaken Questions

1. PT29, S1, Q3

There should be a greater use of gasohol. Gasohol is a mixture of alcohol and gasoline, and has a higher octane rating and fewer carbon monoxide emissions than straight gasoline. Burning gasohol adds no more carbon dioxide to the atmosphere than plants remove by photosynthesis.

Each of the following, if true, strengthens the argument above EXCEPT:

(A) Cars run less well on gasoline than they do on gasohol.

(B) Since less gasoline is needed with the use of gasohol, an energy shortage is less likely.

(C) Cars burn on the average slightly more gasohol per kilometer than they do gasoline.

(D) Gasohol is cheaper to produce and hence costs less at the pump than gasoline.

(E) Burning gasoline adds more carbon dioxide to the atmosphere than plants can remove.

2. PT29, S1, Q16

We can learn about the living conditions of a vanished culture by examining its language. Thus, it is likely that the people who spoke Proto-Indo-European, the language from which all Indo-European languages descended, lived in a cold climate, isolated from ocean or sea, because Proto-Indo-European lacks a word for "sea," yet contains words for "winter," "snow," and "wolf."

Which one of the following, if true, most seriously weakens the argument?

(A) A word meaning "fish" was used by the people who spoke Proto-Indo-European.

(B) Some languages lack words for prominent elements of the environments of their speakers.

(C) There are no known languages today that lack a word for "sea."

(D) Proto-Indo-European possesses words for "heat."

(E) The people who spoke Proto-Indo-European were nomadic.

6

3. PT29, S4, Q20

Amphibian populations are declining in numbers worldwide. Not coincidentally, the earth's ozone layer has been continuously depleted throughout the last 50 years. Atmospheric ozone blocks UV-B, a type of ultraviolet radiation that is continuously produced by the sun, and which can damage genes. Because amphibians lack hair, hide, or feathers to shield them, they are particularly vulnerable to UV-B radiation. In addition, their gelatinous eggs lack the protection of leathery or hard shells. Thus, the primary cause of the declining amphibian population is the depletion of the ozone layer.

Each of the following, if true, would strengthen the argument EXCEPT:

(A) Of the various types of radiation blocked by atmospheric ozone, UV-B is the only type that can damage genes.

(B) Amphibian populations are declining far more rapidly than are the populations of nonamphibian species whose tissues and eggs have more natural protection from UV-B.

(C) Atmospheric ozone has been significantly depleted above all the areas of the world in which amphibian populations are declining.

(D) The natural habitat of amphibians has not become smaller over the past century.

(E) Amphibian populations have declined continuously for the last 50 years.

4. PT30, S4, Q20

Consumer advocate: The introduction of a new drug into the marketplace should be contingent upon our having a good understanding of its social impact. However, the social impact of the newly marketed antihistamine is far from clear. It is obvious, then, that there should be a general reduction in the pace of bringing to the marketplace new drugs that are now being tested.

Which one of the following, if true, most strengthens the argument?

(A) The social impact of the new antihistamine is much better understood than that of most new drugs being tested.

(B) The social impact of some of the new drugs being tested is poorly understood.

(C) The economic success of some drugs is inversely proportional to how well we understand their social impact.

(D) The new antihistamine is chemically similar to some of the new drugs being tested.

(E) The new antihistamine should be on the market only if most new drugs being tested should be on the market also.

MANHATTAN
PREP

5. PT30, S4, Q11

High school students who feel that they are not succeeding in school often drop out before graduating and go to work. Last year, however, the city's high school dropout rate was significantly lower than the previous year's rate. This is encouraging evidence that the program instituted two years ago to improve the morale of high school students has begun to take effect to reduce dropouts.

Which one of the following, if true about the last year, most seriously weakens the argument?

(A)   There was a recession that caused a high level of unemployment in the city.

(B)   The morale of students who dropped out of high school had been low even before they reached high school.

(C)   As in the preceding year, more high school students remained in school than dropped out.

(D)   High schools in the city established placement offices to assist their graduates in obtaining employment.

(E)   The anti-dropout program was primarily aimed at improving students' morale in those high schools with the highest dropout rates.

6. PT30, S4, Q18

People who have political power tend to see new technologies as a means of extending or protecting their power, whereas they generally see new ethical arguments and ideas as a threat to it. Therefore, technical ingenuity usually brings benefits to those who have this ingenuity, whereas ethical inventiveness brings only pain to those who have this inventiveness.

Which one of the following statements, if true, most strengthens the argument?

(A)   Those who offer new ways of justifying current political power often reap the benefits of their own innovations.

(B)   Politically powerful people tend to reward those who they believe are useful to them and to punish those who they believe are a threat.

(C)   Ethical inventiveness and technical ingenuity are never possessed by the same individuals.

(D)   New technologies are often used by people who strive to defeat those who currently have political power.

(E)   Many people who possess ethical inventiveness conceal their novel ethical arguments for fear of retribution by the politically powerful.

6

7. PT30, S4, Q12

The television show *Henry* was not widely watched until it was scheduled for Tuesday evenings immediately after *That's Life*, the most popular show on television. During the year after the move, *Henry* was consistently one of the ten most-watched shows on television. Since *Henry's* recent move to Wednesday evenings, however, it has been watched by far fewer people. We must conclude that *Henry* was widely watched before the move to Wednesday evenings because it followed *That's Life* and not because people especially liked it.

Which one of the following, if true, most strengthens the argument?

(A)   *Henry* has been on the air for three years, but *That's Life* has been on the air for only two years.

(B)   The show that replaced *Henry* on Tuesdays has persistently had a low number of viewers in the Tuesday time slot.

(C)   The show that now follows *That's Life* on Tuesdays has double the number of viewers it had before being moved.

(D)   After its recent move to Wednesday, *Henry* was aired at the same time as the second most popular show on television.

(E)   *That's Life* was not widely watched during the first year it was aired.

8. PT32, S1, Q12

Navigation in animals is defined as the animal's ability to find its way from unfamiliar territory to points familiar to the animal but beyond the immediate range of the animal's senses. Some naturalists claim that polar bears can navigate over considerable distances. As evidence, they cite an instance of a polar bear that returned to its home territory after being released over 500 kilometers (300 miles) away.

Which one of the following, if true, casts the most doubt on the validity of the evidence offered in support of the naturalists' claim?

(A)   The polar bear stopped and changed course several times as it moved toward its home territory.

(B)   The site at which the polar bear was released was on the bear's annual migration route.

(C)   The route along which the polar bear traveled consisted primarily of snow and drifting ice.

(D)   Polar bears are only one of many species of mammal whose members have been known to find their way home from considerable distances.

(E)   Polar bears often rely on their extreme sensitivity to smell in order to scent out familiar territory.

9. PT32, S1, Q17

Detective: Because the embezzler must have had specialized knowledge and access to internal financial records, we can presume that the embezzler worked for XYZ Corporation as either an accountant or an actuary. But an accountant would probably not make the kind of mistakes in ledger entries that led to the discovery of the embezzlement. Thus it is likely that the embezzler is one of the actuaries.

Each of the following weakens the detective's argument EXCEPT:

(A)   The actuaries' activities while working for XYZ Corporation were more closely scrutinized by supervisors than were the activities of the accountants.

(B)   There is evidence of breaches in computer security at the time of the embezzlement that could have given persons outside XYZ Corporation access to internal financial records.

(C)   XYZ Corporation employs eight accountants, whereas it has only two actuaries on its staff.

(D)   An independent report released before the crime took place concluded that XYZ Corporation was vulnerable to embezzlement.

(E)   Certain security measures at XYZ Corporation made it more difficult for the actuaries to have access to internal financial records than for the accountants.

10. PT37, S4, Q2

The vomeronasal organ (VNO) is found inside the noses of various animals. While its structural development and function are clearer in other animals, most humans have a VNO that is detectable, though only microscopically. When researchers have been able to stimulate VNO cells in humans, the subjects have reported experiencing subtle smell sensations. It seems, then, that the VNO, though not completely understood, is a functioning sensory organ in most humans.

Which one of the following, if true, most weakens the argument?

(A)   It is not known whether the researchers succeeded in stimulating only VNO cells in the human subjects' noses.

(B)   Relative to its occurrence in certain other animals, the human VNO appears to be anatomically rudimentary and underdeveloped.

(C)   Certain chemicals that play a leading role in the way the VNO functions in animals in which it is highly developed do not appear to play a role in its functioning in humans.

(D)   Secondary anatomical structures associated with the VNO in other animals seem to be absent in humans.

(E)   For many animal species, the VNO is thought to subtly enhance the sense of smell.

6

Solutions: Strengthen and Weaken Questions

Answer Key

(Here's your friendly reminder to use blind review! Retry the tough ones first before you use this answer key, then use the key to check what you got right and wrong *without* recording the right answer so you can take a final stab at the ones you got wrong on your second pass.)

1. C	6. B
2. B	7. C
3. A	8. B
4. A	9. D
5. A	10. A

1. PT29, S1, Q3

There should be a greater use of gasohol. Gasohol is a mixture of alcohol and gasoline, and has a higher octane rating and fewer carbon monoxide emissions than straight gasoline. Burning gasohol adds no more carbon dioxide to the atmosphere than plants remove by photosynthesis.

Each of the following, if true, strengthens the argument above EXCEPT:

(A)　Cars run less well on gasoline than they do on gasohol.

(B)　Since less gasoline is needed with the use of gasohol, an energy shortage is less likely.

(C)　Cars burn on the average slightly more gasohol per kilometer than they do gasoline.

(D)　Gasohol is cheaper to produce and hence costs less at the pump than gasoline.

(E)　Burning gasoline adds more carbon dioxide to the atmosphere than plants can remove.

Answer choice (C) is correct.

Here, the author's conclusion is that there should be a greater use of gasohol. The support given is that gasohol is higher in octane and has fewer emissions than gasoline. Also, burning gasohol adds no more carbon to the atmosphere than plants remove.

This is a simple argument with a wide range of potential "strengtheners" (there might be a thousand additional reasons to use more gasohol), so we should keep our minds open and focus on eliminating choices that strengthen the conclusion.

(A) adds a reason that gasohol is superior to gasoline. This strengthens.

(B) tells us that gasohol use reduces the likelihood of an energy shortage. It doesn't take much outside knowledge to grant that energy shortages are undesirable, so this is a good thing for gasohol and therefore strengthens the argument.

(C) weakens the argument by saying that gasohol is a less efficient fuel than gasoline. This is definitely our answer, but let's rule out the other two just to be sure.

(D) says gasohol is cheaper. This strengthens.

(E) is a tempting choice. At first glance, it doesn't seem to say anything about gasohol. However, if we combine this answer with the last sentence of the argument, we get a clear comparison between the emissions of gasoline and gasohol. Gasoline adds more carbon dioxide to the atmosphere than plants can remove, and gasohol does not. This comparison strengthens the argument.

_2. PT29, S1, Q16_

We can learn about the living conditions of a vanished culture by examining its language. Thus, it is likely that the people who spoke Proto-Indo-European, the language from which all Indo-European languages descended, lived in a cold climate, isolated from ocean or sea, because Proto-Indo-European lacks a word for "sea," yet contains words for "winter," "snow," and "wolf."

Which one of the following, if true, most seriously weakens the argument?

(A)   A word meaning "fish" was used by the people who spoke Proto-Indo-European.

(B)   Some languages lack words for prominent elements of the environments of their speakers.

(C)   There are no known languages today that lack a word for "sea."

(D)   Proto-Indo-European possesses words for "heat."

(E)   The people who spoke Proto-Indo-European were nomadic.

Answer choice (B) is correct.

The author's conclusion is that the people who spoke Proto-Indo-European lived in a cold climate, isolated from the ocean. The only reasons given are the presence of the words "winter," "snow," and "wolf" in that language, and the absence of the word "sea."

The gap here is fairly clear: What exactly is the connection between the presence or absence of certain words in a language and the presence or absence of the features that those words represent? Since our task is to weaken the argument, we essentially want to select an answer choice that makes it possible for a culture to lack words for some of the features of its environment or living conditions.

Let's look at the choices:

(A) is a trap designed to make us associate "fish" with the "sea." Fish can live in rivers, lakes, and ponds, however, and the Proto-Indo-Europeans might have had those words.

(B) weakens. If some languages lack words for prominent features of the speakers' environment, then it is possible that the Proto-Indo-Europeans _did_ live by the sea and yet did not have a word for it.

(C) does not affect the argument about the environment in which the Proto-Indo-Europeans lived. If anything, this answer choice seems to be attacking the idea that a language could lack a word for "sea," but our job is to weaken the argument, not the premise.

(D) has no bearing whatsoever.

(E) is a trap. Even if they were nomadic, they may still have lived in a cold climate isolated from the ocean. Therefore, this choice neither strengthens nor weakens.

_3. PT29, S4, Q20_

Amphibian populations are declining in numbers worldwide. Not coincidentally, the earth's ozone layer has been continuously depleted throughout the last 50 years. Atmospheric ozone blocks UV-B, a type of ultraviolet radiation that is continuously produced by the sun, and which can damage genes. Because amphibians lack hair, hide, or feathers to shield them, they are particularly vulnerable to UV-B radiation. In addition, their gelatinous eggs lack the protection of leathery or hard shells. Thus, the primary cause of the declining amphibian population is the depletion of the ozone layer.

Each of the following, if true, would strengthen the argument EXCEPT:

(A)   Of the various types of radiation blocked by atmospheric ozone, UV-B is the only type that can damage genes.

(B)   Amphibian populations are declining far more rapidly than are the populations of nonamphibian species whose tissues and eggs have more natural protection from UV-B.

(C)   Atmospheric ozone has been significantly depleted above all the areas of the world in which amphibian populations are declining.

(D)   The natural habitat of amphibians has not become smaller over the past century.

(E)   Amphibian populations have declined continuously for the last 50 years.

Answer choice (A) is correct.

"Primary" is a very important word on the LSAT, and one we should notice immediately. The author's conclusion is not just that the depletion of the ozone layer is the cause of the decline in amphibian populations, but that it is the *primary* cause. The reasons given are that 1) depleted atmosphere blocks less UV-B radiation, which is dangerous to amphibians, and 2) amphibian eggs have less protection from radiation than others.

We should focus on eliminating the four choices that strengthen the argument. All four of them will in one way or another strengthen the correlation between UV-B exposure and population decline or rule out other causal possibilities.

(A) does not seem to strengthen. Does it matter how many kinds of radiation damage genes? No! We know that UV-B does, and amphibians are vulnerable to it, and the atmosphere blocks it. To say that UV-B is the *only* kind of radiation that damages genes does not support that reasoning.

(B) strengthens the idea that UV-B is killing the amphibians. Eliminate it.

(C) strengthens by directly correlating depleted ozone with the locations of declining amphibian populations. Eliminate it.

(D) strengthens by ruling out an alternative cause. A decline in habitat size could very well be the primary cause for the demise of the amphibians. By ruling out that possibility, we strengthen the idea that depleted ozone *is* the cause. Eliminate it.

(E) strengthens by matching up the timelines of the ozone depletion and the amphibian decline. Eliminate it.

4. PT30, S4, Q20

Consumer advocate: The introduction of a new drug into the marketplace should be contingent upon our having a good understanding of its social impact. However, the social impact of the newly marketed antihistamine is far from clear. It is obvious, then, that there should be a general reduction in the pace of bringing to the marketplace new drugs that are now being tested.

Which one of the following, if true, most strengthens the argument?

(A)   The social impact of the new antihistamine is much better understood than that of most new drugs being tested.

(B)   The social impact of some of the new drugs being tested is poorly understood.

(C)   The economic success of some drugs is inversely proportional to how well we understand their social impact.

(D)   The new antihistamine is chemically similar to some of the new drugs being tested.

(E)   The new antihistamine should be on the market only if most new drugs being tested should be on the market also.

Answer choice (A) is correct.

Here's the core:

the introduction of drugs to the marketplace should be contingent on understanding social impact

+

the social impact of a certain antihistamine (one already on the market) is unclear

➡ there should be a general reduction in the pace of bringing to market new drugs now being tested

The word "general" in the conclusion immediately jumps out. Our task is to strengthen, most likely

MANHATTAN
PREP

by supporting the connection of this particular antihistamine to the other drugs.

(A) does exactly what we want. If the social impact of the other drugs is understood even less than that of the antihistamine, then according to the argument, these other drugs should certainly not be brought to market soon. This is a good choice, so let's keep it.

(B) does not impact the argument in a clear way. It does not relate the antihistamine to the more general conclusion. Furthermore, the word "some" has a weak impact. Without knowing how prevalent the "some" is, it's tough to prescribe a general slowdown.

(C) is irrelevant—economic success does not play a role in the logic.

(D) may seem to strengthen if we read too quickly, but chemical similarity may or may not have anything to do with social impact. Eliminate it.

(E) is an error of reversed logic. Watch out for "only if"!

5. PT30, S4, Q11

High school students who feel that they are not succeeding in school often drop out before graduating and go to work. Last year, however, the city's high school dropout rate was significantly lower than the previous year's rate. This is encouraging evidence that the program instituted two years ago to improve the morale of high school students has begun to take effect to reduce dropouts.

Which one of the following, if true about the last year, most seriously weakens the argument?

(A)   There was a recession that caused a high level of unemployment in the city.

(B)   The morale of students who dropped out of high school had been low even before they reached high school.

(C)   As in the preceding year, more high school students remained in school than dropped out.

(D)   High schools in the city established placement offices to assist their graduates in obtaining employment.

(E)   The anti-dropout program was primarily aimed at improving students' morale in those high schools with the highest dropout rates.

Answer choice (A) is correct.

Let's take a look at the core:

some high school students drop out and go to work

+

last year the dropout rate was lower than the previous year

➡ the morale program is reducing the number of dropouts

There is definitely a Percent vs. Amount Flaw at work here, but it turns out that none of the choices address that issue. If we went in looking for that, we might have to start over with (A) and reconsider things with an open mind. So what else is there? Another Causation Flaw! What if something else was responsible for reducing the number of dropouts? That would be a clear way to weaken this argument.

(A) provides an alternative cause. If unemployment was especially high, then students would not have been able to drop out and find jobs. Therefore, they might have been more likely to stay in school. *This* might explain the reduced number of dropouts.

(B) does not relate to the argument. Was the program effective at reducing dropouts or not?

(C) does not directly relate to the argument, either. It simply says that in both years, the dropout rate was less than 50%.

(D) might seem to provide an alternative cause for the reduction in dropouts. However, there are a couple of problems here. First, if students were dropping out in order to go to work, we have no reason to believe that an employment program would be an important incentive for them. (It would be a big assumption to figure that the jobs available to graduates are more enticing.) Second, the argument is about students who feel that they are not succeeding in school. It's hard to say that any incentive targeted to graduates would help them to feel successful enough to stay in school. They would have no reason to believe that an employment program would be of any benefit to them.

(E) is irrelevant. Knowing where the program was targeted does not help us to know whether it was successful.

6. PT30, S4, Q18

People who have political power tend to see new technologies as a means of extending or protecting their power, whereas they generally see new ethical arguments and ideas as a threat to it. Therefore, technical ingenuity usually brings benefits to those who have this ingenuity, whereas ethical inventiveness brings only pain to those who have this inventiveness.

Which one of the following statements, if true, most strengthens the argument?

(A) Those who offer new ways of justifying current political power often reap the benefits of their own innovations.

(B) Politically powerful people tend to reward those who they believe are useful to them and to punish those who they believe are a threat.

(C) Ethical inventiveness and technical ingenuity are never possessed by the same individuals.

(D) New technologies are often used by people who strive to defeat those who currently have political power.

(E) Many people who possess ethical inventiveness conceal their novel ethical arguments for fear of retribution by the politically powerful.

Answer choice (B) is correct.

Once again, we should consider the core as simply as possible before going to the choices:

the politically powerful see new tech as good and new ethics as threatening		new tech brings benefits to those who invent it, and new ethics bring pain to those who invent them

There's a fairly large gap here: The author is assuming that the politically powerful are the primary determinants of benefit and pain and that they will dole these things out to those who they find helpful or threatening.

As we evaluate the answers, let's remember that our job is to strengthen the argument:

(A) sounds appealing, but actually does not apply to the case at hand. "New *technologies* as a means of *extending or protecting*" is not quite the same as "new *ways of justifying.*" And even if those terms were equivalent, the fact that this "often" benefits the creators does not add much support to the conclusion. How much is often? Ten percent of the time might be "often," but the conclusion is about what "usually" happens. "Usually," like "most of the time," means more than half the time.

(B) provides the second half of what we were looking for: that politically powerful people dole out benefits and pain in response to help or threats. It is reasonable to infer that people who invent new tech that can be used as a means to extend power are "useful" to those with power. And we can reasonably infer that "punishment" is roughly equivalent to "pain." This is the winner.

(C) might seem like a necessary assumption of the argument, but it isn't. Someone who had both traits might get benefits from one and pain from the other. The fact that no individual possesses both traits does not tell us anything about the results of possessing those traits.

MANHATTAN
PREP

(D) seems to weaken, but actually says nothing about the individuals who *invent* the new technology, which is who the argument concerns. Perhaps those who invent the new tech still receive benefits from the powerful, while other people use the new tech to defeat the powerful. These kinds of group/subgroup distinctions are important on the LSAT. In any case, notice that this answer choice tells us nothing about whether these people are successful in defeating the powerful. Maybe they suffer pain, too!

(E) weakens the argument slightly by suggesting that ethically inventive people can find ways to avoid pain. Eliminate it.

7. PT30, S4, Q12

The television show *Henry* was not widely watched until it was scheduled for Tuesday evenings immediately after *That's Life*, the most popular show on television. During the year after the move, *Henry* was consistently one of the ten most-watched shows on television. Since *Henry*'s recent move to Wednesday evenings, however, it has been watched by far fewer people. We must conclude that *Henry* was widely watched before the move to Wednesday evenings because it followed *That's Life* and not because people especially liked it.

Which one of the following, if true, most strengthens the argument?

(A)   *Henry* has been on the air for three years, but *That's Life* has been on the air for only two years.

(B)   The show that replaced *Henry* on Tuesdays has persistently had a low number of viewers in the Tuesday time slot.

(C)   The show that now follows *That's Life* on Tuesdays has double the number of viewers it had before being moved.

(D)   After its recent move to Wednesday, *Henry* was aired at the same time as the second most popular show on television.

(E)   *That's Life* was not widely watched during the first year it was aired.

Answer choice (C) is correct.

We are asked to strengthen the conclusion that the show *Henry* was widely watched because it followed *That's Life* rather than because people liked it. The evidence is that when *Henry* followed *That's Life*, it was widely watched, and since it was moved, it is watched by far fewer people.

We should anticipate that a correct answer will most likely give us additional evidence that *Henry*'s placement after *That's Life* was essential to its success. A correct answer might also give us reason to believe that *Henry* was *not* watched because people especially liked it.

(A) does not tell us anything about *why* the show was popular when it followed *That's Life* or why it declined in popularity after the move.

(B) tells us that the show now occupying *Henry*'s old slot is not popular. This hints at the fact that following *That's Life* does not guarantee success, and therefore weakens the argument.

(C) adds direct support to our conclusion. If another show has *doubled* its audience since being placed after *That's Life*, we have an additional reason to believe that *That's Life* contributed to *Henry*'s popularity as well.

(D) offers an alternate explanation of why fewer people watched *Henry* after its move. This is another weakener.

(E) is a premise booster. We already know the show was not popular right away.

6

8. PT32, S1, Q12

Navigation in animals is defined as the animal's ability to find its way from unfamiliar territory to points familiar to the animal but beyond the immediate range of the animal's senses. Some naturalists claim that polar bears can navigate over considerable distances. As evidence, they cite an instance of a polar bear that returned to its home territory after being released over 500 kilometers (300 miles) away.

Which one of the following, if true, casts the most doubt on the validity of the evidence offered in support of the naturalists' claim?

(A)   The polar bear stopped and changed course several times as it moved toward its home territory.

(B)   The site at which the polar bear was released was on the bear's annual migration route.

(C)   The route along which the polar bear traveled consisted primarily of snow and drifting ice.

(D)   Polar bears are only one of many species of mammal whose members have been known to find their way home from considerable distances.

(E)   Polar bears often rely on their extreme sensitivity to smell in order to scent out familiar territory.

Answer choice (B) is correct.

This is a slight twist on a Weaken question. Our task is to challenge the validity of the evidence itself, so in this case, we will emphasize the evidence in our analysis.

First, to meet the definition of navigation, an animal must find its way from *unfamiliar* territory to *familiar* territory *beyond* the range of its senses. Next, a polar bear returned home after being released 300 miles away.

If we're going to undermine this evidence, we're probably going to need some additional information about the polar bear's trip. Remember that we accept

the premises as given, so we need something that shows that the polar bear's trip did not actually fit the supplied definition of navigation.

(A) This tells us the polar bear changed course. So what? Nothing in the given definition of navigation says that changing direction is not allowed.

(B) Aha! If the place where the bear was released was on its annual migration route, then it was not unfamiliar territory. This is definitely our answer, but we'll check the others.

(C) This is irrelevant. Are we supposed to assume that polar bears are too wimpy for this route?

(D) If anything, this strengthens the claim being used as evidence. Apparently this polar bear is not the only navigator out there.

(E) So what? In order for this to weaken, we would need to know that the bear actually used its sense of smell in *this* case. If this choice said something like "the bear could smell its home from where it was released," it would be a good answer, because one of the conditions that must be met is "beyond the range of the senses."

9. PT32, S1, Q17

Detective: Because the embezzler must have had specialized knowledge and access to internal financial records, we can presume that the embezzler worked for XYZ Corporation as either an accountant or an actuary. But an accountant would probably not make the kind of mistakes in ledger entries that led to the discovery of the embezzlement. Thus it is likely that the embezzler is one of the actuaries.

Each of the following weakens the detective's argument EXCEPT:

(A)   The actuaries' activities while working for XYZ Corporation were more closely scrutinized by supervisors than were the activities of the accountants.

MANHATTAN
PREP

(B)   There is evidence of breaches in computer security at the time of the embezzlement that could have given persons outside XYZ Corporation access to internal financial records.

(C)   XYZ Corporation employs eight accountants, whereas it has only two actuaries on its staff.

(D)   An independent report released before the crime took place concluded that XYZ Corporation was vulnerable to embezzlement.

(E)   Certain security measures at XYZ Corporation made it more difficult for the actuaries to have access to internal financial records than for the accountants.

Answer choice (D) is correct.

In order to get this one right, we must stick to a disciplined process of elimination. Here's how that process might look:

First, the core:

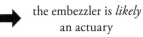

the embezzler was either an actuary or an accountant

+

an accountant would *probably* not make the kind of mistakes that were made

➡ the embezzler is *likely* an actuary

Since this is an EXCEPT question, we should try to eliminate the answer choices that weaken.

(A) weakens. If the actuaries were more closely scrutinized, it is reasonable to think that they were less likely to embezzle. Eliminate it.

(B) seems to contradict a premise. Didn't we establish that the embezzlement was done by an accountant or an actuary? If someone from outside took the money, that's not even embezzlement, right? But wait—let's look

back at the structure of the first sentence: "Because … we can presume …" The first premise supports the claim that the embezzler was an accountant or actuary. This makes that claim an intermediate conclusion, which means we can attack it all we like. With that in mind, we can say that this definitely weakens the argument by suggesting that the embezzler may not have worked for the company at all. Eliminate it.

(C) is unclear. Does it matter how many of each kind they were? Leave it for now.

(D) does not weaken. Of course the company was vulnerable to embezzlement—embezzlement happened! The fact that a report was released does not weaken the idea that an actuary did the embezzling. Leave it for now.

(E) definitely weakens by suggesting that an actuary may not have been able to obtain the kind of inside knowledge that the author says was necessary for the crime. Eliminate it.

Now, we're down to (C) and (D). It is unclear how (C) applies, and we know that (D) does not weaken. In a situation like this, which we will encounter many times in our LSAT adventures, we should choose (D) and move on.

To confidently eliminate (C), we must, as always, take another careful look at the wording of the argument's conclusion. It all comes down to simple math. If the embezzler is presumably either an accountant or an actuary, and there are eight accountants and only two actuaries, it seems to go against the idea that the embezzler was likely an actuary.

6

10. PT37, S4, Q2

The vomeronasal organ (VNO) is found inside the noses of various animals. While its structural development and function are clearer in other animals, most humans have a VNO that is detectable, though only microscopically. When researchers have been able to stimulate VNO cells in humans, the subjects have reported experiencing subtle smell sensations. It seems, then, that the VNO, though not completely understood, is a functioning sensory organ in most humans.

Which one of the following, if true, most weakens the argument?

(A)   It is not known whether the researchers succeeded in stimulating only VNO cells in the human subjects' noses.

(B)   Relative to its occurrence in certain other animals, the human VNO appears to be anatomically rudimentary and underdeveloped.

(C)   Certain chemicals that play a leading role in the way the VNO functions in animals in which it is highly developed do not appear to play a role in its functioning in humans.

(D)   Secondary anatomical structures associated with the VNO in other animals seem to be absent in humans.

(E)   For many animal species, the VNO is thought to subtly enhance the sense of smell.

Answer choice (A) is correct.

Let's start with the core:

when researchers have stimulated the VNO in humans, those humans have reported smell sensations ➡ the VNO is a functioning sensory organ in most humans

The word "most" really jumps out of the conclusion, and as this question is very early in the section, we might

expect the answer choice to relate to this "obvious" issue. Let's go to the choices and see.

(A) is a bit unclear. "Only" is certainly an important word on the LSAT, and this choice definitely relates to the argument's evidence. Let's leave it for now.

(B) does not directly relate to the conclusion. It doesn't matter if human VNOs are less developed than animal VNOs. We might say that human ears are less developed than the ears of deer, but human ears are still functioning organs! Eliminate it.

(C) makes the same "comparison" mistake that (B) makes. The question at hand is whether the human VNO functions at all—not whether it functions as well as an animal VNO. Eliminate it.

(D) says nothing about whether the human VNO *functions*. It is entirely possible that it functions without those secondary structures, as we have no evidence that those secondary structures are required for functioning.

(E), if anything, strengthens the argument by making clearer the connection between the VNO and smell, and thus, in a small way, validating the argument's evidence.

This leaves us with (A). Really? Absolutely. This is an example of a "claim in the premise" problem. Remember the "premature babies/adequate care" argument? While we must always accept the premises themselves as fact— the researchers definitely stimulated the VNO—we occasionally see a question that brings our attention to little assumptions hidden in those premises. Think about (A). What if the researchers did *not* stimulate *only* the VNO when they did their research? What if they also stimulated the subjects' ordinary scent receptors? Well, this would make us much less certain that the VNO was responsible for the smell sensations, and suddenly we have a bad experiment on our hands. Therefore, since (A) introduces the possibility that the research was imperfect, and the research is the only leg the conclusion has to stand on, (A) weakens the conclusion.

MANHATTAN
PREP

Time and Time Again

It's that time again! Take a deep breath, crack your knuckles, do a couple of neck rolls, and get ready for the humbling experience that is timed mixed practice.

At this point, we've covered a significant amount of ground. The question types we've covered so far will frequently constitute half of an LR section or more. That's why it's a good idea to start trying complete sections now.

After the last chapter, we asked you to dip your toe in by doing the first six questions of a section in eight minutes. That's a great exercise, and you can do it as frequently as you like. You can also add in the next six questions, either in the same exercise, undertaken in sixteen minutes, or as a separate six-questions-in-eight-minutes endeavor.

But in addition to those drills, it's a good idea to start attempting full, timed 35-minute sections. Let's be clear—these are not meant to be *evaluative*. Do not think of these as a measure of your progress. What they are meant to be is *productive*. What do we mean by that? Let us explain.

Full sections force you to practice switching gears 25 times in 35 minutes. The act of having to identify questions by type, retrieve the ideal process, and then execute that process over and over again is a skill unto itself and one that warrants practice early and often.

Full sections give you a chance to practice adaptability. In these sections, you will face question types we haven't covered yet. How can you adapt the processes you know to tackle the question types you don't? Answering that question will ready you for whatever the LSAT throws at you come test day.

Full sections give you the chance to hone your efficiency. Not overthinking, making quick eliminations, analyzing the relevant features of remaining answers, and sometimes picking an answer before you *feel* ready to leave the problem—these are the things great LSAT scores are made of. These are *not* the skills of intellectual mastery—the skills you've been building as you've worked through the pages of this book—but they *are* the skills of masterful execution, and you need both skill sets on test day.

Full sections help you get comfortable with discomfort. It's a fact: Nobody likes taking the LSAT. Even those of us who love to teach, write about, and think about this test do not look forward to our periodic retakes. Taking the LSAT is uncomfortable. The stakes are high. The room is unfamiliar. The test is long. And no matter how good you are—no matter how many years of your life you've dedicated to thinking about this test—the test is hard. Forcing yourself to take full sections at this stage will help you get used to the experience of discomfort. Getting used to discomfort, dare we say *comfortable* with discomfort, will neutralize the impact that discomfort can have on you. Think of it this way: If you showed up at work and somebody punched you in the face, you'd probably be pretty shaken up. But not if you're a boxer, because boxers are *comfortable* with the discomfort that their job entails.

So go ahead—punch yourself in the face with the LSAT (figuratively, of course). Take a full timed section. Then take another next week. Make this a regular part of your LSAT regimen from here on out. Focus on executing the process you've learned for each question type we've covered. And if you discover through this practice that you don't remember the process for a given type, go back and review it, then practice with it before attempting another section.

Chapter 7

Principle Support Questions

In This Chapter...

Principle Support Questions and the Assumption Family

At this point, we have covered just about all of the Assumption Family question types. Principle Support questions will round out our discussion of the Assumption Family.

It's important to know that there are actually two types of Principle questions on the LSAT. Principle Support questions, the topic of this chapter, require you to choose a principle that helps to justify, or support, the argument. Principle Example questions, the subject of Chapter 9, ask you to select an example that matches a *given* principle. Principle Example questions are NOT Assumption Family questions.

Principle Support questions, on the other hand, function just like any other Assumption Family question. Thus, our process should be the same. It will be driven by the following six questions:

1. What is my task?

2. What is the author's conclusion?

3. How is that conclusion supported?

4. What is the gap?

5. Which answer choices are clearly wrong?

6. What is the best available answer?

In a sense, Principle Support questions are Assumption questions in disguise. Here's a quick example:

> Dr. Singh is the best professor at Doug's college. Therefore, Doug should sign up for Dr. Singh's course.

This may seem like a great argument. It seems only natural to conclude that Doug should take a course with Dr. Singh, since she is the best. In fact, it's *so* reasonable that it may cause us to overlook a key assumption: that Doug should make his decision about which classes to take based on the quality of the professor. What if Dr. Singh teaches anthropology and Doug is a literature major? In order for the argument to be valid, we must assume that professor quality should be the deciding factor. Here's the argument core with the assumption inserted:

> Dr. Singh is the best professor at Doug's college. (*When making decisions about which courses to take, one should consider only professor quality.*) Therefore, Doug should sign up for Dr. Singh's course.

Notice that the assumption in this case can also be thought of as a general principle. Let's examine the concept of "principle" a bit more thoroughly.

Should We or Shouldn't We?

According to the Oxford American Dictionary, a principle is a fundamental proposition that serves as the foundation for a belief or behavior. In other words, principles are propositions that guide what we should and shouldn't think or do.

Let's look back again at the assumption, or principle, from the previous example: "When making decisions about which courses to take, one should consider only professor quality." It's a proposition that guides how we should behave in a particular situation. It tells us what we should do.

On the LSAT, Principle Support questions will often have conclusions that dictate how a person should or shouldn't act or behave. The correct answer will be a principle that strengthens, or supports, the opinion given in the conclusion. Here's a little exercise to illustrate the point. We'll give you an argument core. Take a second to think about what the assumption is, and then write a principle that bridges the gap. Here's the first one:

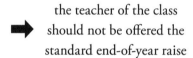

many students in the class
failed the final exam
→
the teacher of the class
should not be offered the
standard end-of-year raise

So, what's the principle that would support this argument? Take a second to think before reading on.

Here's the core with the principle inserted:

> Many students in the class failed the final exam. (Teachers should not be offered the standard end-of-year raise if many of their students failed the final exam.) The teacher of the class should not be offered the standard end-of-year raise.

Is the principle more obvious than you had anticipated? Let's try another one:

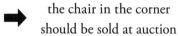

the chair in the corner is
an antique
→
the chair in the corner
should be sold at auction

And here it is with the principle inserted:

> The chair in the corner is an antique. (Antiques should be sold at auction.) The chair in the corner should be sold at auction.

Okay, hopefully you've got the hang of it now. It's really not that hard, right? Well, we all know that it's never this easy on the LSAT. Let's put all this thinking to work on an actual LSAT question. We'll begin by looking only at the argument and the question stem itself. Remember, this is an Assumption Family question, so we'll want to use the following questions to guide our process:

1. What is my task?

2. What is the author's conclusion?

3. How is that conclusion supported?

4. What is the gap?

5. Which answer choices are clearly wrong?

6. What is the best available answer?

> ### *PT20, S1, Q5*
>
> Archaeologist: A large corporation has recently offered to provide funding to restore an archaeological site and to construct facilities to make the site readily accessible to the general public. The restoration will conform to the best current theories about how the site appeared at the height of the ancient civilization that occupied it. This offer should be rejected, however, because many parts of the site contain unexamined evidence.
>
> Which one of the following principles, if valid, justifies the archaeologist's argument?

Decision 1: What is my task?

In this case, the question asks us to choose a principle that justifies, or supports, the argument. Thus, this is a Principle Support question. We'll need to start by identifying the argument core.

Decision 2: What is the author's conclusion?

Decision 3: How is that conclusion supported?

Let's look at the components of the argument one more time with the above questions in mind:

> A large corporation has recently offered to provide funding to restore an archaeological site and to construct facilities to make the site readily accessible to the general public.

Seems like background information so far.

> The restoration will conform to the best current theories about how the site appeared at the height of the ancient civilization that occupied it.

More background. Where's the argument?

> This offer should be rejected, however,

Aha. A clear conclusion—an expression of something we should do. But what exactly is the "offer" in question? Which "offer" should be rejected? We'll need to revisit the background information to find out: "A large corporation offered to use the best current theories about how an archaeological site once appeared in order to restore the site and make it available to the public for viewing." Following the "however," we have:

> because many parts of the site contain unexamined evidence.

The word "because" is a clear indication that this portion of the argument is the support for the conclusion. So, the argument core is:

many parts of the site contain unexamined evidence the offer to restore the site according to current theories of how it once appeared and then open it up to the public should be rejected

Decision 4: What is the gap?

Another way of asking this is, "What's the principle that would support this argument?" Think about it before reading on.

Why does the fact that there is unexamined evidence on-site make it inadvisable to open the site up to the public? There are two ways to think about the answer to this question:

1. Maybe presenting the archaeological site according to theories that are based on evidence that hasn't been fully examined could compromise the accuracy and integrity of the display.

2. Maybe presenting the site to the public while there is unexamined evidence inside will put that evidence in jeopardy (people might destroy or steal the evidence).

It's hard to know which of the two issues the author has in mind, but we can anticipate both. If the author has the first point in mind, we can close that gap with the following principle:

> Many parts of the site contain unexamined evidence. (We shouldn't open up sites for public viewing if the presentation of the site is based on an incomplete examination of evidence.) The offer to restore the site according to current theories of how it once appeared and then open it up to the public should be rejected.

If the author has the second point in mind, we can close that gap as follows:

> Many parts of the site contain unexamined evidence. (We shouldn't open up sites for public viewing if doing so could jeopardize the unexamined evidence.) The offer to restore the site according to current theories of how it once appeared and then open it up to the public should be rejected.

MANHATTAN
PREP

Now, all of this is simply preparation for the answer choices. We don't know for certain that either of these principles will appear—perhaps the correct answer is something we haven't yet thought of. At this point, there's no need to fret over anticipating every single possible correct answer. We just want to be focused on the argument core and note any possible gaps that pop into our minds. And, of course, we want to be *thinking* all of this, not writing it out as we've done here.

Decision 5: Which answer choices are clearly wrong?

The quickest eliminations will be answers that aren't related to the argument core. Here's our core again:

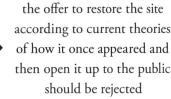

many parts of the site contain unexamined evidence ⬛➡ the offer to restore the site according to current theories of how it once appeared and then open it up to the public should be rejected

    (A)   The ownership of archaeological sites should not be under the control of business interests.

This has nothing to do with whether the site should be opened up to the public before all evidence is examined. Eliminate it.

    (B)   Any restoration of an archaeological site should represent only the most ancient period of that site's history.

Great. But this answer mentions nothing about unexamined evidence (which could be from any time period) and its impact on whether the site should be restored and opened to the public. Get rid of it.

    (C)   No one should make judgments about what constitutes the height of another civilization.

Again, should it be restored and opened to the public? This answer fails to address the central issue of the core argument. Eliminate it.

    (D)   Only those with a true concern for an archaeological site's history should be involved in the restoration of that site.

Out of scope again. Eliminate it.

Decision 6: What is the best available answer?

Well, we only have one answer left! We should check it quickly to be sure it's relevant:

(E)   The risk of losing evidence relevant to possible
       future theories should outweigh any
       advantages of displaying the results of
       theories already developed.

This looks like our second prediction. It mentions unexamined evidence ("evidence relevant to possible future theories") and how the potential of losing this evidence is more important ("should outweigh") than any advantage that could be gained by opening to the public now ("displaying results of theories already developed"). It's basically saying that the risk of losing the unexamined evidence is more important than displaying the stuff that's currently available. This is the only answer that addresses the core. Choose it and move on.

Answer choice (E) might have felt too broad to you—why is it not discussing theories about the archeological site? The correct answers to Principle questions often establish a rule about a general category that includes the topic of the argument. In some ways, this might remind you of Sufficient Assumptions questions in that the correct answer might go beyond what you need but still do the trick.

Now that you've got the hang of it, let's look at a few more questions. Each one is progressively more difficult than the next. We'll work our way up.

Take a shot at this first one before we discuss. Pay close attention to your process. Are you making the right decisions at the right time?

PT20, S4, Q24

Marianne is a professional chess player who hums audibly while playing her matches, thereby distracting her opponents. When ordered by chess officials to cease humming or else be disqualified from professional chess, Marianne protested the order. She argued that since she was unaware of her humming, her humming was involuntary and that therefore she should not be held responsible for it.

Which one of the following principles, if valid, most helps to support Marianne's argument against the order?

(A)   Chess players who hum audibly while playing their matches should not protest if their opponents also hum.

(B)   Of a player's actions, only those that are voluntary should be used as justification for disqualifying that player from professional chess.

(C)   A person should be held responsible for those involuntary actions that serve that person's interests.

(D)   Types of behavior that are not considered voluntary in everyday circumstances should be considered voluntary if they occur in the context of a professional chess match.

(E)   Chess players should be disqualified from professional chess matches if they regularly attempt to distract their opponents.

Decision 1: What is my task?

This question asks us to choose a principle to support the argument. Thus, this is a Principle Support question. This is an Assumption Family question.

Decision 2: What is the author's conclusion?

Decision 3: How is that conclusion supported?

The argument starts by describing a situation, but we only get to the core in the last sentence:

> She argued that since she was unaware of her humming, her humming was involuntary and that therefore she should not be held responsible for it.

This sentence gives us all the information we need to know. The word "since" is a language cue indicating support for something, and the word "therefore" clearly leads to the conclusion. Technically, we have an intermediate conclusion in the middle. Because she isn't aware of her humming, Marianne concludes that it is involuntary. From here, she goes on to the main conclusion that she should not be held responsible for her humming. While there is a gap here—if we're not aware of something, do we know it's involuntary?—this shift is so small that we might choose to see this all as one premise:

Marianne's humming is
involuntary (she's unaware of it)   Marianne should not be held
responsible for her humming

Decision 4: What is the gap?

This argument assumes that one should not be held responsible for actions that are involuntary. If you have a nervous, involuntary twitch that knocks a $25,000 vase off your friend's coffee table, does that mean you shouldn't be held responsible for the cost of that vase? Not necessarily, right? We've spotted the gap. Now let's eliminate some answers.

Decision 5: Which answer choices are clearly wrong?

> (A)   Chess players who hum audibly while playing their matches should not protest if their opponents also hum.

Is the humming involuntary? Should they be held responsible for the humming? Even if we could answer these questions, we don't know that anyone other than Marianne is humming. This answer has nothing to do with the argument core. Eliminate it.

> (B)   Of a player's actions, only those that are voluntary should be used as justification for disqualifying that player from professional chess.

Hmm. This one feels a bit closer. It mentions "voluntary," and this idea of disqualification is related to holding someone responsible. Keep it for now.

> (C)   A person should be held responsible for those involuntary actions that serve that person's interests.

This mentions "involuntary," and it also mentions holding someone responsible. Keep it for now.

>   (D)   Types of behavior that are not considered
>   voluntary in everyday circumstances should
>   be considered voluntary if they occur in the
>   context of a professional chess match.

But should someone be held responsible for these behaviors? Eliminate it.

>   (E)   Chess players should be disqualified from
>   professional chess matches if they regularly
>   attempt to distract their opponents.

This answer mentions nothing about involuntary or voluntary behaviors. If Marianne doesn't know she's humming, is she really attempting to distract her opponents? Even more importantly, this choice is going the wrong way. We want to support Marianne, not disqualify her! Get rid of it.

Decision 6: What is the best available answer?

We're down to two answers: (B) and (C). If we simply bounce back and forth between the two remaining choices, they'll start to look more and more alike. That won't help us. A better strategy is to compare each choice to the argument core. Let's remind ourselves of the core quickly:

Marianne's humming is
involuntary (she's unaware of it)   Marianne should not be held
responsible for her humming

Remember, we decided that the argument assumes that a person should not be held responsible for actions that are involuntary. Notice that (C) gives us the exact opposite!

>   (C)   A person *should* be held responsible for those
>   involuntary actions that serve that person's
>   interests.

We might reason that if Marianne's humming distracts her opponents, then her involuntary behavior is certainly serving her interests. However, since this would weaken Marianne's argument, we don't want to waste any time considering this. If we are trying to establish that something *should not* happen, we can quickly ignore any choice about what *should* happen unless it is restricted by something like "only if."

>   (B)   Of a player's actions, only those that are
>   voluntary should be used as justification for
>   disqualifying that player from professional
>   chess.

Ah. Much better. Only voluntary actions (not involuntary actions) should be used to disqualify a chess player. In other words, a person shouldn't be held responsible for involuntary actions. This is our answer.

Notice that this choice says "should," but uses "only" to restrict that recommendation with a necessary condition. This translates to "used as justification → voluntary," but without the word "only," it would translate to "voluntary → used as justification." Also notice that the correct answer doesn't focus simply on humming but instead establishes a rule about the broader category of "behavior," which includes humming.

Let's do another one. Again, pay attention to your process, even if that means taking a bit more time than you normally would:

> ### PT21, S3, Q17
>
> An editorial in the *Grandburg Daily Herald* claims that Grandburg's voters would generally welcome the defeat of the political party now in control of the Grandburg City Council. The editorial bases its claim on a recent survey that found that 59 percent of Grandburg's registered voters think that the party will definitely be out of power after next year's city council elections.
>
> Which one of the following is a principle that, if established, would provide the strongest justification for the editorial's conclusion?
>
> (A)   The way voters feel about a political party at a given time can reasonably be considered a reliable indicator of the way they will continue to feel about that party, barring unforeseeable political developments.
>
> (B)   The results of surveys that gauge current voter sentiment toward a given political party can legitimately be used as the basis for making claims about the likely future prospects of that political party.
>
> (C)   An increase in ill-feeling toward a political party that is in power can reasonably be expected to result in a corresponding increase in support for rival political parties.
>
> (D)   The proportion of voters who expect a given political possibility to be realized can legitimately be assumed to approximate the proportion of voters who are in favor of that possibility being realized.

(E)   It can reasonably be assumed that registered
        voters who respond to a survey regarding the
        outcome of a future election will exercise their
        right to vote in that election.

Decision 1: What is my task?

This question asks us to choose a principle to provide justification for the argument. Thus, this is a Principle Support question. This is an Assumption Family question.

Decision 2: What is the author's conclusion?

Decision 3: How is that conclusion supported?

We'll go line by line through the argument in order to identify the argument core:

> An editorial in the *Grandburg Daily Herald* claims that Grandburg's voters
> would generally welcome the defeat of the political party now in control of
> the Grandburg City Council.

This is a claim. Perhaps it's an opposing claim that the author will disagree with?

> The editorial bases its claim on a recent survey that found that 59 percent of
> Grandburg's registered voters think that the party will definitely be out of
> power after next year's city council elections.

Oh—"The editorial bases its claim…" This is support for the editorial's claim. That's the end of the argument, so the editorial's claim is our conclusion!

59% of Grandburg's registered
voters think that the party in
power will lose power in next
year's election

Grandburg's voters would
generally welcome the defeat
of the party now in control of
the city council

Decision 4: What is the gap?

This argument assumes that if a majority of people *think* something will happen, then a majority of people *welcome* that thing happening. We can think of a number of examples for which this sort of an argument doesn't hold. A majority of people might think that the world will become overpopulated at some point in the future, but does this necessarily mean that a majority of people would *welcome* an overpopulated world? Of course not! I think we see the problem with this argument. Let's move to the answer choices:

Decision 5: Which answer choices are clearly wrong?

(A)   The way voters feel about a political party at a
        given time can reasonably be considered a
        reliable indicator of the way they will
        continue to feel about that party, barring
        unforeseeable political developments.

Not sure about this one. It seems relevant. Keep it for now.

(B)   The results of surveys that gauge current voter
        sentiment toward a given political party can
        legitimately be used as the basis for making
        claims about the likely future prospects of
        that political party.

This is a reversal of the logic in the argument. The author is using information about what voters think will happen to determine how they feel. Answer (B) says that we can use information about how voters feel to determine what is likely to happen. Eliminate it.

(C)   An increase in ill-feeling toward a political
        party that is in power can reasonably be
        expected to result in a corresponding increase
        in support for rival political parties.

This is completely out of scope. This argument is not about increasing support for rival parties. It's about whether thinking something will happen translates to wanting that thing to happen. Get rid of this.

(D)   The proportion of voters who expect a given
        political possibility to be realized can
        legitimately be assumed to approximate the
        proportion of voters who are in favor of that
        possibility being realized.

Let's defer on this. It talks about one proportion approximating another, which doesn't look familiar, but it also relates expecting something to happen with being in favor of it happening. Let's keep this for now.

(E)   It can reasonably be assumed that registered
        voters who respond to a survey regarding the
        outcome of a future election will exercise their
        right to vote in that election.

Since the author isn't predicting what will actually happen, whether the survey respondents will vote is beside the point. This issue is whether thinking something will happen translates to wanting that thing to happen. Eliminate it.

Decision 6: What is the best available answer?

We're down to two answers: (A) and (D). Remember, we want to compare each choice against the argument core. Let's remind ourselves of the core quickly:

59% of Grandburg's registered voters think that the party in power will lose power in next year's election Grandburg's voters would generally welcome the defeat of the party now in control of the city council

Again, the argument assumes that a majority of people *believing* something will happen suggests that a majority of people *welcome* that thing happening.

(A)   The way voters feel about a political party at a given time can reasonably be considered a reliable indicator of the way they will continue to feel about that party, barring unforeseeable political developments.

This answer feels less attractive the second time through. It's nice to know that the way voters feel about a party is unlikely to change, but the way they feel about a political party tells us nothing about what they think will happen to that political party.

(D)   The proportion of voters who expect a given political possibility to be realized can legitimately be assumed to approximate the proportion of voters who are in favor of that possibility being realized.

This one is correct. It connects the voters' expectations (what they think will happen) with what they want to happen.

Looking again at the language about proportions, it's just saying that the percent of voters who expect something will be roughly the same as the percent of voters who want that thing to happen. Here's the core again, now with the principle inserted:

59% of Grandburg's registered voters think that the party in power will lose power in next year's election. (The proportion of voters who *expect* a given political possibility to be realized can legitimately be assumed to approximate the proportion of voters who are *in favor* of that possibility being realized.) Grandburg's voters would generally welcome the defeat of the party now in control of the city council.

Now, some of you may be thinking that the correct answer choice is way too general for this argument. After all, the argument discusses voters in *Grandburg specifically*, not any or all voters in general as answer (D) might suggest. Also, the argument discusses *the party in power losing power*, not just any old political possibility, as answer (D) indicates.

But consider the fact that when we talk about "voters" generally, this includes Grandburg's voters. And when we talk about a "political possibility" in general, that includes this specific possibility: the party in power losing power in Grandburg. Here's an analogous situation:

> The Blasters soccer team won two straight Riverville League Championships. Thus, the Blasters soccer team should be considered an exceptional team.

We could insert a very specific principle to support this argument:

> The Blasters soccer team won two straight Riverville League Championships. (If the Blasters soccer team won two straight Riverville League Championships, then the Blasters soccer team should be considered an exceptional team.) Thus, the Blasters soccer team should be considered an exceptional team.

That's a pretty straightforward, specific principle. But can we make it a bit more general?

> The Blasters soccer team won two straight Riverville League Championships. (If a team wins two straight championships, then that team should be considered exceptional.) Thus, the Blasters soccer team should be considered an exceptional team.

This principle is much more general, but it still helps the argument, doesn't it? After all, "team" in general would include the Blasters soccer team, and "championships" in general would include the Riverville League Championships. We can take it even one step farther:

> The Blasters soccer team won two straight Riverville League Championships. (An entity that accomplishes something two times in a row should be considered exceptional.) Thus, the Blasters soccer team should be considered an exceptional team.

This is an extremely general principle, but it still helps the argument. A general "entity" would include a soccer team, and "accomplishing something two times in a row" would certainly include winning two straight Riverville League Championships.

Let's go back to our original question. Here's the core one more time. Try to write the most general principle you possibly can to support this argument:

59% of Grandburg's registered voters think that the party in power will lose power in next year's election   Grandburg's voters would generally welcome the defeat of the party now in control of the city council

How'd you do? Don't read on until you've given it a try! Here's how we would write it:

59% of Grandburg's registered voters think that the party in power will lose power in next year's election. (If more than half of a group of people believe something will occur, then that group of people in general is in favor of that something occurring.) Grandburg's voters would generally welcome the defeat of the party now in control of the city council.

This answer would have been just as correct as answer (D) above. So, keep in mind that for Principle questions, general or broad answer choices are often correct.

Let's look at one more question. Remember, each of these questions is meant to be progressively more difficult than the last. Give yourself a minute and a half to complete this next one, and really pay attention to your process. Here we go!

PT37, S2, Q22

Political theorist: Many people believe that the punishment of those who commit even the most heinous crimes should be mitigated to some extent if the crime was motivated by a sincere desire to achieve some larger good. Granted, some criminals with admirable motives deserve mitigated punishments. Nonetheless, judges should never mitigate punishment on the basis of motives, since motives are essentially a matter of conjecture and even vicious motives can easily be presented as altruistic.

Which one of the following principles, if valid, most helps to justify the political theorist's reasoning?

(A)   Laws that prohibit or permit actions solely on the basis of psychological states should not be part of a legal system.

(B)   It is better to err on the side of overly severe punishment than to err on the side of overly lenient punishment.

(C)   The legal permissibility of actions should depend on the perceivable consequences of those actions.

(D)   No law that cannot be enforced should be enacted.

(E)   A legal system that, if adopted, would have disastrous consequences ought not be adopted.

Decision 1: What is my task?

This question asks us to choose a principle to provide justification for the theorist's reasoning. Thus, this is a Principle Support question. This is an Assumption Family question.

Decision 2: What is the author's conclusion?

Decision 3: How is that conclusion supported?

Again, we'll go line by line through the argument in order to identify the argument core:

> Political theorist: Many people believe that the punishment of those who commit even the most heinous crimes should be mitigated to some extent if the crime was motivated by a sincere desire to achieve some larger good.

"Many people believe…" sounds very much like an opposing point. So, many people believe that punishments should be lessened if there was some desire to achieve good. The author will likely disagree.

> Granted, some criminals with admirable motives deserve mitigated punishments.

"Granted…" The author is granting a point to the opposition, but she would do this only if there were a counter on the way!

> Nonetheless, judges should never mitigate punishment on the basis of motives,

"Nonetheless" is our pivot word, and we get the conclusion immediately following. The author believes judges should *never* mitigate punishments on the basis of motive. Why does the author believe this?

> since motives are essentially a matter of conjecture and even vicious motives can easily be presented as altruistic.

The word "since" is an indication that this will be support for the conclusion. Judges should never mitigate punishments based on motive because motives are a matter of conjecture (we can only guess at people's true motives).

motives are a matter of conjecture   judges should never mitigate punishments based on motives

Decision 4: What is the gap?

Hmm. This core is tricky. It seems to make sense, right? We can only guess at people's motives for committing heinous crimes, so judges should never weaken punishments based on motives. It's hard to see any major flaws in this reasoning, but we can always say that the author is assuming that the premise leads to the conclusion. We need a

principle that tells us that if we can only guess at someone's motives, we shouldn't mitigate that person's punishment based on those motives. Let's give it a try.

Decision 5: Which answer choices are clearly wrong?

> (A)   Laws that prohibit or permit actions solely on
>   the basis of psychological states should not be
>   part of a legal system.

This answer connects laws and psychological states, but we want to connect punishment and motives. This doesn't match our core. Eliminate it.

> (B)   It is better to err on the side of overly severe
>   punishment than to err on the side of overly
>   lenient punishment.

This doesn't seem right, but it does comment on varying degrees of punishment. Let's keep it for now.

> (C)   The legal permissibility of actions should
>   depend on the perceivable consequences of
>   those actions.

Uhh…not sure. This seems related as well. "The perceivable consequences of actions…" This means things we don't have to guess at, the opposite of conjecture. Better keep it for now.

> (D)   No law that cannot be enforced should be
>   enacted.

Okay, we can get rid of this one. This passage has nothing to do with whether laws should be enacted—that is, made into law in the first place—but rather whether punishments should be mitigated. Those are two different things. Eliminate it.

> (E)   A legal system that, if adopted, would have
>   disastrous consequences ought not be
>   adopted.

Adopting a legal system? Way out of scope. We need something related to whether punishments should be mitigated. Get rid of this.

Decision 6: What is the best available answer?

We're down to two answers: (B) and (C). Remember, we want to compare each choice to the argument core. Let's remind ourselves of the core quickly:

motives are a matter of conjecture   judges should never mitigate
punishments based on motives

We hadn't anticipated a certain answer, but having a strong sense for the core has helped us eliminate three answers, and it will help us decide between the final two.

(C)   The legal permissibility of actions should
depend on the perceivable consequences of
those actions.

Oh. This discusses the legal permissibility of actions—whether actions are legal or not. After reviewing the core one more time, we're reminded that we're interested in the severity of punishments, not the legal permissibility of actions. We also aren't interested in the consequences of people's actions, perceivable or not. This one doesn't seem to work.

(B)   It is better to err on the side of overly severe
punishment than to err on the side of overly
lenient punishment.

But this doesn't seem right, either! Okay, let's break this down by going back to the argument. Essentially, the argument is saying that if we're not sure of the motivation for the crime (maybe the motivation was to do something good, but we can only guess), we should keep punishments severe. Someone more merciful might argue that it makes more sense to be cautious when doling out punishment, to be more lenient in the face of uncertainty just in case we got it all wrong. However, the conclusion goes in the other direction—the punishment should *not* be mitigated, even in the face of uncertainty.

In order to justify this conclusion, we need some principle that states that it's better to be overly severe than too lenient. In other words, we should err on the side of being too harsh. If that's an underlying principle, then it would make sense to conclude that we shouldn't mitigate the punishment, even in the face of uncertainty. Let's look at the core with the principle inserted:

Motives are a matter of conjecture. (It is better to err on the side of overly severe punishment than to err on the side of overly lenient punishment.) Judges should never mitigate punishments based on motives.

(B) is correct! Wow. Tough question! We can see now that this answer choice would be very difficult to anticipate in advance, but we can make a lot of progress by identifying the core and then eliminating answers that stray from the core.

Conclusion

Principle Support questions are Assumption Family questions. We must treat them as such. The same six-step process that we covered a few chapters ago applies:

1. What is my task?

2. What is the author's conclusion?

3. How is that conclusion supported?

4. What is the gap?

5. Which answer choices are clearly wrong?

6. What is the best available answer?

If this process is taking longer than you'd like, that's understandable. However, keep in mind that these are all *necessary* steps—that is, if we were to shortchange any part of this process, we would have to answer questions with an incomplete understanding. So, we encourage you to keep at it. We're confident that it is through this process that you can best develop an effective approach that will lead to greater speed and accuracy in your LR work.

7

Drill It: Principle Support Questions

1. PT11, S2, Q10

The labeling of otherwise high-calorie foods as "sugarfree," based on the replacement of all sugar by artificial sweeteners, should be prohibited by law. Such a prohibition is indicated because many consumers who need to lose weight will interpret the label "sugarfree" as synonymous with "low in calories" and harm themselves by building weight-loss diets around foods labeled "sugar-free." Manufacturers of sugarfree foods are well aware of this tendency on the part of consumers.

Which one of the following principles, if established, most helps to justify the conclusion in the passage?

(A)   Product labels that are literally incorrect should be prohibited by law, even if reliance on those labels is not likely to cause harm to consumers.

(B)   Product labels that are literally incorrect, but in such an obvious manner that no rational consumer would rely on them, should nevertheless be prohibited by law.

(C)   Product labels that are literally correct but cannot be interpreted by the average buyer of the product without expert help should be prohibited by law.

(D)   Product labels that are literally correct but will predictably be misinterpreted by some buyers of the product to their own harm should be prohibited by law.

(E)   Product labels that are literally correct, but only on one of two equally accurate interpretations, should be prohibited by law if buyers tend to interpret the label in the way that does not match the product's actual properties.

2. PT11, S2, Q6

Cigarette smoking has been shown to be a health hazard; therefore, governments should ban all advertisements that promote smoking.

Which one of the following principles, if established, most strongly supports the argument?

(A)   Advertisements should not be allowed to show people doing things that endanger their health.

(B)   Advertisers should not make misleading claims about the healthfulness of their products.

(C)   Advertisements should disclose the health hazards associated with the products they promote.

(D)   All products should conform to strict government health and safety standards.

(E)   Advertisements should promote only healthful products.

3. PT33, S3, Q6

The recent cleaning of frescoes in the Sistine Chapel has raised important aesthetic issues. Art historians are now acutely aware that the colors of the works they study may differ from the works' original colors. Art historians have concluded from this that interpretations of the frescoes that seemed appropriate before the frescoes' restoration may no longer be appropriate.

Which one of the following principles, if valid, most helps to justify the art historians' reasoning?

(A)   The appropriateness of an interpretation of an artwork is relative to the general history of the period in which the interpretation is made.

(B)   The restoration of an artwork may alter it such that it will have colors that the artist did not intend for it to have.

(C)   The colors of an artwork are relevant to an appropriate interpretation of that work.

(D)   Art historians are the best judges of the value of an artwork.

(E)   Interpretations of an artwork are appropriate if they originated during the period when the work was created.

4. PT28, S1, Q4

Dental researcher: Filling a cavity in a tooth is not a harmless procedure: it inevitably damages some of the healthy parts of the tooth. Cavities are harmful only if the decay reaches the nerves inside the tooth, and many cavities, if left untreated, never progress to that point. Therefore, dentists should not fill a cavity unless the nerves inside the tooth are in imminent danger from that cavity.

Which one of the following principles, if valid, most strongly supports the researcher's reasoning?

(A)   Dentists should perform any procedure that is likely to be beneficial in the long term, but only if the procedure does not cause immediate damage.

(B)   Dentists should help their patients to prevent cavities rather than waiting until cavities are present to begin treatment.

(C)   A condition that is only potentially harmful should not be treated using a method that is definitely harmful.

(D)   A condition that is typically progressive should not be treated using methods that provide only temporary relief.

(E)   A condition that is potentially harmful should not be left untreated unless it can be kept under constant surveillance.

5. PT29, S1, Q19

Arbitrator: The shipping manager admits that he decided to close the old facility on October 14 and to schedule the new facility's opening for October 17, the following Monday. But he also claims that he is not responsible for the business that was lost due to the new facility's failing to open as scheduled. He blames the contractor for not finishing on time, but he too, is to blame, for he was aware of the contractor's typical delays and should have planned for this contingency.

Which one of the following principles underlies the arbitrator's argument?

(A)   A manager should take foreseeable problems into account when making decisions.

(B)   A manager should be able to depend on contractors to do their jobs promptly.

(C)   A manager should see to it that contractors do their jobs promptly.

(D)   A manager should be held responsible for mistakes made by those whom the manager directly supervises.

(E)   A manager, and only a manager, should be held responsible for a project's failure.

6. PT29, S1, Q22

Editorial: The government claims that the country's nuclear power plants are entirely safe and hence that the public's fear of nuclear accidents at these plants is groundless. The government also contends that its recent action to limit the nuclear industry's financial liability in the case of nuclear accidents at power plants is justified by the need to protect the nuclear industry from the threat of bankruptcy. But even the government says that unlimited liability poses such a threat only if injury claims can be sustained against the industry; and the government admits that for such claims to be sustained, injury must result from a nuclear accident. The public's fear, therefore, is well founded.

Which one of the following principles, if valid, most helps to justify the editorial's argumentation?

(A)   If the government claims that something is unsafe then, in the absence of overwhelming evidence to the contrary, that thing should be assumed to be unsafe.

(B)   Fear that a certain kind of event will occur is well founded if those who have control over the occurrence of events of that kind stand to benefit financially from such an occurrence.

(C)   If a potentially dangerous thing is safe only because the financial security of those responsible for its operation depends on its being safe, then eliminating that dependence is not in the best interests of the public.

(D)   The government sometimes makes unsupported claims about what situations will arise, but it does not act to prevent a certain kind of situation from arising unless there is a real danger that such a situation will arise.

(E)   If a real financial threat to a major industry exists, then government action to limit that threat is justified.

MANHATTAN
PREP

7. PT28, S3, Q18

The human brain and its associated mental capacities evolved to assist self-preservation. Thus, the capacity to make aesthetic judgments is an adaptation to past environments in which humans lived. So an individual's aesthetic judgments must be evaluated in terms of the extent to which they promote the survival of that individual.

Which one of the following is a principle that would, if valid, provide the strongest justification for the reasoning above?

(A)   All human adaptations to past environments were based on the human brain and its associated mental capacities.

(B)   Human capacities that do not contribute to the biological success of the human species cannot be evaluated.

(C)   If something develops to serve a given function, the standard by which it must be judged is how well it serves that function.

(D)   Judgments that depend on individual preference or taste cannot be evaluated as true or false.

(E)   Anything that enhances the proliferation of a species is to be valued highly.

7

Solutions: Principle Support Questions

Answer Key

(Pssst...don't forget about blind review! Okay, we're going to stop reminding you now.)

1. D	5. A
2. E	6. D
3. C	7. C
4. C	

1. PT11, S2, Q10

The labeling of otherwise high-calorie foods as "sugarfree," based on the replacement of all sugar by artificial sweeteners, should be prohibited by law. Such a prohibition is indicated because many consumers who need to lose weight will interpret the label "sugarfree" as synonymous with "low in calories" and harm themselves by building weight-loss diets around foods labeled "sugar-free." Manufacturers of sugarfree foods are well aware of this tendency on the part of consumers.

Which one of the following principles, if established, most helps to justify the conclusion in the passage?

(A) Product labels that are literally incorrect should be prohibited by law, even if reliance on those labels is not likely to cause harm to consumers.

(B) Product labels that are literally incorrect, but in such an obvious manner that no rational consumer would rely on them, should nevertheless be prohibited by law.

(C) Product labels that are literally correct but cannot be interpreted by the average buyer of the product without expert help should be prohibited by law.

(D) Product labels that are literally correct but will predictably be misinterpreted by some buyers of the product to their own harm should be prohibited by law.

(E) Product labels that are literally correct, but only on one of two equally accurate interpretations, should be prohibited by law if buyers tend to interpret the label in the way that does not match the product's actual properties.

Answer choice (D) is correct.

many consumers will harm themselves by mistakenly building diets around sugarfree foods

+

manufacturers of sugarfree foods are well aware of this tendency

the labeling of otherwise high-calorie foods as "sugarfree" should be prohibited

Wow, a product that truly has no sugar shouldn't be allowed to call itself "sugarfree," just because people will misinterpret that label? The author is making a pretty big assumption here: Even if a label is true, it should be prohibited if consumers tend to harm themselves by misinterpreting it. We're looking for a principle that expresses that assumption.

(A) is about labels that are literally *incorrect*; the argument is about labels that are literally *correct*. Eliminate it.

(B) is also about literally incorrect answers. Eliminate it.

(C) looks better, as it deals with the prohibition of literally correct labels. However, this argument is about labels that consumers will misinterpret *to their own harm,* not about whether consumers can interpret the labels without expert help.

(E) comes out of left field with its mention of "two equally accurate interpretations." That has nothing to do with this argument!

We're left with answer (D). This looks like a winner! It covers all our bases: These sugarfree labels make a true claim, so they are "literally correct," but the

MANHATTAN
PREP

7

manufacturers are well aware that "some buyers" (this matches with "many consumers") will misinterpret them "to their own harm." Therefore, they should be prohibited.

Therefore, (D) is correct.

2. PT11, S2, Q6

Cigarette smoking has been shown to be a health hazard; therefore, governments should ban all advertisements that promote smoking.

Which one of the following principles, if established, most strongly supports the argument?

(A)   Advertisements should not be allowed to show people doing things that endanger their health.

(B)   Advertisers should not make misleading claims about the healthfulness of their products.

(C)   Advertisements should disclose the health hazards associated with the products they promote.

(D)   All products should conform to strict government health and safety standards.

(E)   Advertisements should promote only healthful products.

Answer choice (E) is correct.

This is a very straightforward argument—all core, no clutter:

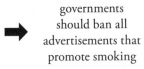

cigarette smoking has been shown to be a health hazard → governments should ban all advertisements that promote smoking

The logical gap here is likewise not too difficult to spot. The author of this argument assumes that if something is a health hazard, governments should ban advertisements that promote it. We can be confident that the correct answer will be a principle that expresses that assumption.

(A) is very tempting and may have made it through your first pass through the answer choices. It seems to suggest that advertisements shouldn't promote unhealthy acts, but it doesn't. Take a look at the subtle shift: from "promote" in the argument to "show people doing things" in the answer choice. This difference leaves large gaps in the argument: For instance, advertisers could still legally create ads that promote smoking simply by not including any images of people smoking.

(B) has nothing to do with whether the advertisements should be banned, and the argument never says anything about misleading claims, so we can eliminate it easily.

(C) is incorrect for the same reason: The argument is about whether governments should ban cigarette advertisements, not about what kinds of claims those advertisements should make.

(D) doesn't even address the issue of advertisements, so it's even further out of scope! Get rid of it.

So we're down to (E). This answer presents a broad rule that is more than we need to fill the argument's gap—and that's just fine on Principle Support questions. Notice that once again the LSAT uses the combination of "should" and "only" to create a restriction: promote → healthful. The contrapositive is just what we want: –healthful → –promote.

Therefore, (E) is the correct answer.

3. PT33, S3, Q6

The recent cleaning of frescoes in the Sistine Chapel has raised important aesthetic issues. Art historians are now acutely aware that the colors of the works they study may differ from the works' original colors. Art historians have concluded from this that interpretations of the frescoes that seemed appropriate before the frescoes' restoration may no longer be appropriate.

Which one of the following principles, if valid, most helps to justify the art historians' reasoning?

(A)   The appropriateness of an interpretation of an artwork is relative to the general history of the period in which the interpretation is made.

(B)   The restoration of an artwork may alter it such that it will have colors that the artist did not intend for it to have.

(C)   The colors of an artwork are relevant to an appropriate interpretation of that work.

(D)   Art historians are the best judges of the value of an artwork.

(E)   Interpretations of an artwork are appropriate if they originated during the period when the work was created.

(C) is correct.

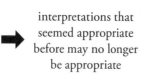

restoration of frescoes revealed that the colors of works may differ from the original colors ➡ interpretations that seemed appropriate before may no longer be appropriate

Why would the art historians conclude that the old interpretations may no longer be appropriate? They must be assuming that an appropriate interpretation of a work of art has something to do with the colors in that work. If the colors have changed, maybe what qualifies as an appropriate interpretation has also changed.

(A) is way out of scope. It doesn't address the color issue, and the argument has nothing to do with "the general history of the period."

(B) seems to attack the argument by suggesting that a restoration may actually misrepresent the original colors. That's not what we want to do, and in any case, this doesn't tell us anything about whether a change in our awareness of color affects the appropriateness of our interpretation.

(D) is out of scope. The argument is about whether the old interpretations are appropriate, not at all about the value of a work or who the best judges are.

(E) at least deals with the appropriateness of interpretations, but it doesn't help us get from the color-difference issue to the conclusion that the pre-restoration interpretations may no longer be appropriate. We don't know if the interpretations at issue actually date back to the period when the work was created. In any case, this answer choice doesn't allow us to deem any interpretations inappropriate, because it only identifies interpretations that *are* appropriate. (Notice that "only" doesn't show up to limit the statement.)

That leaves answer (C). Boring, but it gets the job done! If the colors of an artwork are relevant to interpreting it appropriately, then the fact that the pre-restoration interpretations were based on different colors could mean that those interpretations are no longer appropriate, given the newly revealed original colors.

Therefore, (C) is correct.

4. PT28, S1, Q4

Dental researcher: Filling a cavity in a tooth is not
    a harmless procedure: it inevitably damages
    some of the healthy parts of the tooth.
    Cavities are harmful only if the decay reaches
    the nerves inside the tooth, and many cavities,
    if left untreated, never progress to that point.
    Therefore, dentists should not fill a cavity
    unless the nerves inside the tooth are in
    imminent danger from that cavity.

Which one of the following principles, if valid, most
strongly supports the researcher's reasoning?

(A)   Dentists should perform any procedure that is
        likely to be beneficial in the long term, but
        only if the procedure does not cause
        immediate damage.

(B)   Dentists should help their patients to prevent
        cavities rather than waiting until cavities are
        present to begin treatment.

(C)   A condition that is only potentially harmful
        should not be treated using a method that is
        definitely harmful.

(D)   A condition that is typically progressive should
        not be treated using methods that provide
        only temporary relief.

(E)   A condition that is potentially harmful should
        not be left untreated unless it can be kept
        under constant surveillance.

Answer choice (C) is correct.

filling cavities does some
        harm to the tooth
                                        dentists shouldn't
            +   ➡   fill a cavity unless
                                        nerves are in
many cavities, if left   imminent danger
alone, never become
        harmful

This may seem like a pretty solid argument. After all,
why go to the trouble of filling in a cavity if it may not
even end up hurting you? But on the other hand, isn't
it possible that the potential damage from cavities is

so great, and the actual damage from filling them is
so negligible, that it makes sense to adopt a policy of
preemptive filling? So this argument actually depends
on the assumption that if something isn't guaranteed to
cause harm, and treating it *is* guaranteed to cause some
harm, then it shouldn't be treated.

(A) introduces a comparison between short-term and
long-term effects that the argument does not make, so
we can eliminate it.

(B) introduces another out-of-scope distinction, this
time between preventing cavities and treating them.
Prevention never comes up in the argument!

(D) refers to treatment methods that provide only
temporary relief, but the argument never says whether
filling in cavities is only a temporary solution. We also
don't know if cavities are "typically progressive." In fact,
the argument says that many cavities never progress
enough to reach the nerve.

(E) goes in the wrong direction by saying we should
err in the direction of treatment. (There's a tricky triple
negative here: "not … untreated … unless.") In any
case, what does constant surveillance have to do with
anything?

So, how about answer (C)?

The terminology in this one might look a little funky,
but it actually matches up well with the stimulus:
We're told that cavities may never get to the point of
harmfulness, so cavities that don't pose an imminent
danger are "only potentially harmful." On the other
hand, we know that filling cavities does inflict some
harm, so that qualifies as "a method that is definitely
harmful." So if we accept this principle, then the
researcher's conclusion absolutely follows from the
premises.

Therefore, answer choice (C) is correct.

5. PT29, S1, Q19

Arbitrator: The shipping manager admits that he decided to close the old facility on October 14 and to schedule the new facility's opening for October 17, the following Monday. But he also claims that he is not responsible for the business that was lost due to the new facility's failing to open as scheduled. He blames the contractor for not finishing on time, but he, too, is to blame, for he was aware of the contractor's typical delays and should have planned for this contingency.

Which one of the following principles underlies the arbitrator's argument?

(A) A manager should take foreseeable problems into account when making decisions.

(B) A manager should be able to depend on contractors to do their jobs promptly.

(C) A manager should see to it that contractors do their jobs promptly.

(D) A manager should be held responsible for mistakes made by those whom the manager directly supervises.

(E) A manager, and only a manager, should be held responsible for a project's failure.

Answer choice (A) is correct.

Here's a tricky problem, though its complexity may not be apparent at first. Notice that the argument is completely contained within the last sentence; the first two are background and an opposing point, respectively. The arbitrator concludes that the shipping manager is to blame along with the contractor, because the manager was aware of the contractor's delays and should have planned accordingly. So it looks like the core is as follows:

shipping manager was aware of contractor's typical delays and should have planned for them he shares blame with contractor

This argument assumes that if you know someone is likely to mess up and you don't plan for that possibility, then you're also to blame. So let's look for a principle that expresses this assumption:

(B) is out of scope. We aren't concerned with whether we should be able to rely on contractors, but whether we should be prepared if we know they are likely to run behind. Besides, if anything, this would weaken the argument.

(C) might be good advice, but this argument is about how the manager should take the contractor's tardiness into account, not about the manager trying to prevent that tardiness.

(D) is really tempting! This argument does depend on the assumption that the manager should be held responsible for the contractor's mistakes. However, there is zero indication in the stimulus that the manager directly supervises the contractor. So this principle wouldn't make the argument work, because it doesn't apply to the facts we're given.

(E) is incorrect because the argument isn't trying to limit blame. In fact, the conclusion implies that both parties are responsible by saying that "he, too, is to blame."

All right, so we're down to (A). This looks pretty good, since the arbitrator does say that the manager "should have planned for this contingency." But wasn't that just a premise? Aren't we looking for a principle that gets us to the conclusion that the manager is to blame?

Hmm…actually, if we look more closely, the point that the manager should have planned for this problem does seem to be based on the fact that "he was aware of the contractor's typical delays." (In other words, the manager saw it coming, so he should have planned ahead.) So we can refine our core to include an intermediate conclusion:

MANHATTAN
PREP

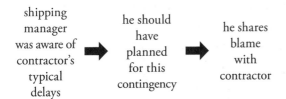

This is a very difficult intermediate conclusion to spot at first glance. There's no "thus" or "therefore" to signal an intermediate logical step. Notice, though, that by working from wrong to right, we were able to rule out four incorrect answers decisively. Once we narrowed our focus to the remaining choice, it became easier to spot the presence of this intermediate conclusion.

Now (A) makes more sense; it strengthens the arrow between the first premise and the intermediate conclusion. If this principle is valid, then the manager really should have planned for the possibility of the contractor being late, since he was aware of that tendency; that is, the problem was *foreseeable* to him.

Therefore, answer choice (A) is correct.

6. PT29, S1, Q22

Editorial: The government claims that the country's nuclear power plants are entirely safe and hence that the public's fear of nuclear accidents at these plants is groundless. The government also contends that its recent action to limit the nuclear industry's financial liability in the case of nuclear accidents at power plants is justified by the need to protect the nuclear industry from the threat of bankruptcy. But even the government says that unlimited liability poses such a threat only if injury claims can be sustained against the industry; and the government admits that for such claims to be sustained, injury must result from a nuclear accident. The public's fear, therefore, is well founded.

Which one of the following principles, if valid, most helps to justify the editorial's argumentation?

(A)   If the government claims that something is unsafe then, in the absence of overwhelming evidence to the contrary, that thing should be assumed to be unsafe.

(B)   Fear that a certain kind of event will occur is well founded if those who have control over the occurrence of events of that kind stand to benefit financially from such an occurrence.

(C)   If a potentially dangerous thing is safe only because the financial security of those responsible for its operation depends on its being safe, then eliminating that dependence is not in the best interests of the public.

(D)   The government sometimes makes unsupported claims about what situations will arise, but it does not act to prevent a certain kind of situation from arising unless there is a real danger that such a situation will arise.

(E)   If a real financial threat to a major industry exists, then government action to limit that threat is justified.

Answer choice (D) is correct.

This one is a real mouthful! As always, we should start by finding the conclusion. In this case, thankfully, it's clearly signaled at the end: "The public's fear of nuclear accidents is well founded." Now, what is that conclusion based on? Well, we're told that the government has limited the nuclear industry's financial ability in order to protect it from bankruptcy. Then we're told that, by the government's own admission, bankruptcy is only a threat if injury claims can be sustained and that injury claims can only be sustained in the event of a nuclear accident. If we condense that second statement, we end up with a two-premise core that looks like this:

the government has limited the nuclear industry's financial liability to protect it from bankruptcy

+

the government admits that bankruptcy is only a threat if nuclear accidents occur

➡️ the public's fear of nuclear accidents is well founded

So, even though the government claims that the nuclear power plants are safe, it has taken actions to protect those plants from a situation that could only occur as a result of a nuclear accident. From this, the argument concludes that the public is right to be afraid of nuclear accidents. The basic assumption, then, is that the government wouldn't make efforts to limit the consequences of a situation unless there was actually a chance of that situation occurring.

Now, even in condensed form, that's still a lot to keep track of. So, as we consider the answer choices, let's remember to make things easier by really focusing on how they relate to the core. The correct answer *must* help us conclude that the public's fear is well founded.

(A) can be eliminated because the government doesn't claim that anything is unsafe; it does the exact opposite!

(B) addresses the issue of whether the fear is well founded, but nowhere does the argument suggest that those who have control over nuclear accidents (who would that be, anyway?) stand to benefit from them. Limiting your financial liability just means there's a limit to how much money you *lose*; it doesn't mean you're profiting.

(C) is out of scope; the argument is about whether the public's fear is justified, not about the best interests of the public.

(E) is similarly out of scope. The question is not whether the government's action is justified, but rather should we be afraid of nuclear accidents?

That leaves (D). This looks a lot like the assumption we identified earlier. The government does not act to prevent *bankruptcy* from arising unless there is a real danger that it will arise. And, according to the argument, bankruptcy is only a danger if a nuclear accident occurs. If this principle is true, then the public would have good reason to fear nuclear accidents, despite the government's "unsupported claims" to the contrary.

Therefore, answer choice (D) is correct.

7. PT28, S3, Q18

The human brain and its associated mental capacities evolved to assist self-preservation. Thus, the capacity to make aesthetic judgments is an adaptation to past environments in which humans lived. So an individual's aesthetic judgments must be evaluated in terms of the extent to which they promote the survival of that individual.

Which one of the following is a principle that would, if valid, provide the strongest justification for the reasoning above?

(A) All human adaptations to past environments were based on the human brain and its associated mental capacities.

(B) Human capacities that do not contribute to the biological success of the human species cannot be evaluated.

(C) If something develops to serve a given function, the standard by which it must be judged is how well it serves that function.

(D) Judgments that depend on individual preference or taste cannot be evaluated as true or false.

(E) Anything that enhances the proliferation of a species is to be valued highly.

Answer choice (C) is correct.

MANHATTAN
PREP

This argument does us the favor of making its logical structure fairly clear through the use of the keywords "thus" and "so," which we know mean "therefore." Since there are *two* "therefore" moments, we know we're dealing with an intermediate conclusion, and we can map the core like this:

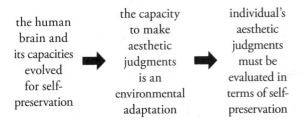

It's always important that we recognize the presence of an intermediate conclusion, because as we saw two problems ago, it's possible for the correct answer to fit between the premise and the intermediate conclusion. In this case, though, there doesn't appear to be a gap there; since the capacity to make aesthetic judgments is clearly a mental capacity, the first half of the argument is actually logically valid.

So let's turn our attention to the second half of the argument. Does it really make sense to evaluate aesthetic judgments in terms of their contribution to a person's survival? The Post-it® Note was originally invented to mark pages in a hymn book; must we evaluate them as bookmarks every time we leave a note on the refrigerator? ("PLEASE wash the dishes!") Only if we assume that things should be evaluated in terms of their original reason for being. We're looking for a principle that establishes this assumption.

(A) doesn't help the argument. Whether *all* adaptations were based on the human brain is irrelevant to the question of evaluating aesthetic judgments.

(B) is about what *cannot* be evaluated, but the argument is about how something *should* be evaluated.

(D) is out of scope because the argument has nothing to do with evaluating judgments as true or false.

(E) is also out of scope. The argument never says we should value aesthetic judgments (or anything else, for that matter) highly. For all we know, the author thinks evolutionary adaptations stink!

That leaves answer (C).

Ah, this looks better. If we accept this principle, then the standard by which aesthetic judgments must be evaluated is indeed the extent to which they promote an individual's survival, because the capacity to make these judgments originally developed for that purpose.

Therefore, answer choice (C) is correct.

Time to Mix It Up

At this point, you've learned about each question type within the Assumption Family—it's time to put all of that knowledge to work! So far, each of the practice sets you've seen have been of one question type only (e.g., Flaw questions, Strengthen/Weaken questions, etc.). Sets of individual question types are very important for working through question-specific strategies. However, on the LSAT, question types are mixed and it's important to become comfortable shifting from one type of task to another during the test. We recommend that you read the question stem before the stimulus to ensure you know your task before diving into the argument. To practice these important skills, it's time you strike out on your own. Instead of being told which questions to do, you need to make the call. It's time to try a homemade mixed practice set.

First, grab a real LSAT. For this exercise, an old paper test will do just fine, but if you have a bunch of digital tests at your disposal, you could use one of those as well. Next, find one of the test's two LR sections. Your mission, should you choose to accept it, is to go through that section, read every question stem, and complete all (and only!) the Assumption Family questions.

Make sure that you're still sticking to your standard Assumption Family process: Find the core, consider the gap, work wrong-to-right.

And be sure to use the blind review process to thoroughly review your work. Avoid the trap of reviewing only the questions you got wrong by flagging any question that gave you trouble on your first pass. After you complete your practice set, go back and retry those challenging questions before checking whether you got them right. And for any question, regardless of whether you ultimately conquered it, dig into any answer that you didn't have a concrete reason for eliminating.

Chapter 8

Conditional Logic

In This Chapter...

Introduction to Conditional Logic

Conditional logic. The phrase itself has been known to induce the sweats for many an LSAT test-taker. Yes, knowing and understanding conditional logic is important for your success on the LSAT, but it doesn't have to cause you undue anxiety. We got you started with the basics in Chapters 2 through 4, and we'll give you an opportunity to see if you should flip back and review those sections. Then, we'll take you through the tough stuff. By the end of this chapter, you'll be able to use your conditional logic skills to fight off some of the toughest Logical Reasoning questions out there. Let's get started.

Drill It: Conditional Logic Basics Review

Here's your chance to check if you really did grasp the basics. Diagram each of the conditional statements below, then diagram the contrapositive relationship by reversing and negating the components of the original. Finally, decide whether the conclusion on the bottom of each set is a valid inference or not (note that you sometimes will find an additional premise there). You'll likely want to diagram to figure that out. Be sure to check your responses against the solutions after each one.

Example: GIVEN: If X is not selected, then Y is selected.
               GIVEN DIAGRAM: $-X \rightarrow Y$
               CONTRAPOSITIVE DIAGRAM: $-Y \rightarrow X$
               If Y is selected, then X is not selected. VALID (INVALID) $(Y \rightarrow -X)$

1. GIVEN: If Sid is on the committee, then Jana is on the committee.

GIVEN DIAGRAM:

CONTRAPOSITIVE DIAGRAM:

When Sid is not on the committee, Jana is not either.   VALID / INVALID

2. GIVEN: If Raul is invited to the party, then Shaina is not invited to the party.

GIVEN DIAGRAM:

CONTRAPOSITIVE DIAGRAM:

If Shaina was invited to the party, then Raul was not invited.   VALID / INVALID

3. GIVEN: If Brooks is not on the bus, then Traiger is not on the bus.

GIVEN DIAGRAM:

CONTRAPOSITIVE DIAGRAM:

If Traiger is not on the bus, neither is Brooks.   VALID / INVALID

4. GIVEN: The tiger is not in the cage, only if the lion is in the cage.

GIVEN DIAGRAM:

CONTRAPOSITIVE DIAGRAM:

The tiger is not in the cage. Therefore, the lion must be in the cage.　VALID / INVALID

5. GIVEN: I will not go jogging if it is raining outside.

GIVEN DIAGRAM:

CONTRAPOSITIVE DIAGRAM:

It is not raining outside. Thus, I am jogging.　VALID / INVALID

6.　GIVEN: Juan plays drums only if Yohei plays guitar.

GIVEN DIAGRAM:

CONTRAPOSITIVE DIAGRAM:

Yohei did not play guitar. That is why I know that Juan did not play drums.　VALID / INVALID

7. GIVEN: If T is not chosen for the team, then N is not chosen for the team.

GIVEN DIAGRAM:

CONTRAPOSITIVE DIAGRAM:

N is chosen for the team only if T is chosen.　VALID / INVALID

8. GIVEN: G is not selected for the club if F is selected for the club.

GIVEN DIAGRAM:

CONTRAPOSITIVE DIAGRAM:

G was not selected, thus F wasn't either.　VALID / INVALID

9. GIVEN: Beethoven is played only when Mozart is also played.

GIVEN DIAGRAM:

CONTRAPOSITIVE DIAGRAM:

Beethoven is not played when Mozart is not played.　VALID / INVALID

10. GIVEN: Dmitry might play volleyball or squash, but he definitely can't play both.

GIVEN DIAGRAM:

CONTRAPOSITIVE DIAGRAM:

Dmitry is not playing volleyball, so he must be playing squash.　VALID / INVALID

Solutions: Conditional Logic Basics Review

1. GIVEN: If Sid is on the committee, then Jana is on the committee.

GIVEN DIAGRAM: S → J

CONTRAPOSITIVE DIAGRAM: –J → –S

When Sid is not on the committee, Jana is not either.   VALID (INVALID)   (–S → –J)

2. GIVEN: If Raul is invited to the party, then Shaina is not invited to the party.

GIVEN DIAGRAM: R → –S

CONTRAPOSITIVE DIAGRAM: S → –R

If Shaina was invited to the party, then Raul was not invited. (VALID) INVALID   (S → –R)

3. GIVEN: If Brooks is not on the bus, then Traiger is not on the bus.

GIVEN DIAGRAM: –B → –T

CONTRAPOSITIVE DIAGRAM: T → B

If Traiger is not on the bus, neither is Brooks.   VALID (INVALID)   (–T → –B)

4. GIVEN: The tiger is not in the cage, only if the lion is in the cage.

GIVEN DIAGRAM: –T → L

CONTRAPOSITIVE DIAGRAM: –L → T

The tiger is not in the cage. Therefore, the lion must be in the cage. (VALID) INVALID

$$
\begin{array}{l}
-T \to L \\
\underline{-T} \\
L
\end{array}
$$

Notice that this last question is asking you to *apply* the given conditional, a somewhat different task than the earlier examples, which required *finding a match* to the given or its contrapositive.

5. GIVEN: I will not go jogging if it is raining outside.

GIVEN DIAGRAM: R → –J

CONTRAPOSITIVE DIAGRAM: J → –R

It is not raining outside. Thus, I am jogging. VALID (INVALID)

$$R \rightarrow -J$$
$$-R$$
$$\overline{}$$
$$J$$

The fact that it is not raining outside would require you to (illegally) use the negation of the given.

6. GIVEN: Juan plays drums only if Yohei plays guitar.

GIVEN DIAGRAM: JD → YG

CONTRAPOSITIVE DIAGRAM: –YG → –JD

Yohei did not play guitar. That is why I know that Juan did not play drums. (VALID) INVALID

$$-YG \rightarrow -JD$$
$$-YG$$
$$\overline{}$$
$$-JD$$

This is a valid application of the contrapositive.

7. GIVEN: If T is not chosen for the team, then N is not chosen for the team.

GIVEN DIAGRAM: –T → –N

CONTRAPOSITIVE DIAGRAM: N → T

N is chosen for the team only if T is chosen. (VALID) INVALID   (N → T)

8. GIVEN: G is not selected for the club if F is selected for the club.

GIVEN DIAGRAM: F → –G

CONTRAPOSITIVE DIAGRAM: G → –F

G was not selected, thus F wasn't either.   VALID (INVALID)

$$G \rightarrow -F$$
$$-G$$
$$\overline{}$$
$$-F$$

This argument is invalid since –G is not a sufficient condition in either the given or the contrapositive.

9. GIVEN: Beethoven is played only when Mozart is also played.

GIVEN DIAGRAM: B → M

CONTRAPOSITIVE DIAGRAM: –M → –B

Beethoven is not played when Mozart is not played. (VALID) INVALID   (–M → –B)

10. GIVEN: Dmitry might play volleyball or squash, but he definitely can't play both.

GIVEN DIAGRAM: V → –S   or   S → –V

CONTRAPOSITIVE DIAGRAM: S → –V   or   V → –S

Dmitry is not playing volleyball, so he must be playing squash. VALID (INVALID)

$$\begin{array}{l} V \rightarrow -S \\ \underline{-V} \\ S \end{array}$$

This argument is invalid since –V is not a sufficient condition in either the given or the contrapositive. Dmitry might not play either sport.

"If and Only If"?

If you struggled with the previous drill, please flip back to pages 37, 66, and 125 to review diagramming conditional statements and contrapositives. If, however, you are comfortable with the diagramming in the previous drill, let's take diagramming one step farther:

Marcus wears a jacket *if, and only if,* it is raining outside.

This is an LSAT favorite. It's a conditional construction that throws many test-takers for a serious loop. However, with a bit of thinking, we can make sense of this construction without much trouble. In fact, you already know all you need to know in order to properly interpret this statement. This statement is the combination of two simpler statements:

Marcus wears a jacket *if* it is raining outside (R → J)	+	Marcus wears a jacket *only if* it is raining outside (J → R)	=	Marcus wears a jacket *if, and only if,* it is raining outside (R → J, J → R)

As you can see, the "if and only if" construction actually gives us two conditional statements, the second of which is simply the reverse of the first. Remember that each of these will yield a contrapositive. In the end, we get four relationships:

R → J and the contrapositive –J → –R

J → R and the contrapositive –R → –J

Another way to express the sum of these relationships is:

R ↔ J

–J ↔ –R

For "if and only if" statements, the arrows work in both directions. Here are some other terms that indicate this biconditional relationship:

A if, but only if, B.   A when, and only when, B.

A when B, and only then.   All A, and only A, are B.

Conditional Logic 1: The Basics in Arguments

Now that you've got the basics under your belt, let's review how standard conditional statements and contrapositives relate to a typical argument core.

> *PT36, S1, Q26*
>
> In the paintings by seventeenth-century Dutch artist Vermeer, we find several recurrent items: a satin jacket, a certain Turkish carpet, and wooden chairs with lion's-head finials. These reappearing objects might seem to evince a dearth of props. Yet we know that many of the props Vermeer used were expensive. Thus, while we might speculate about exactly why Vermeer worked with a small number of familiar objects, it was clearly not for lack of props that the recurrent items were used.
>
> The conclusion follows logically if which one of the following is assumed?
>
> (A)   Vermeer often borrowed the expensive props he represented in his paintings.
>
> (B)   The props that recur in Vermeer's paintings were always available to him.
>
> (C)   The satin jacket and wooden chairs that recur in the paintings were owned by Vermeer's sister.
>
> (D)   The several recurrent items that appeared in Vermeer's paintings had special sentimental importance for him.
>
> (E)   If a dearth of props accounted for the recurrent objects in Vermeer's paintings, we would not see expensive props in any of them.

By now, you should be comfortable recognizing this as an Assumption Family question, specifically a Sufficient Assumption question, and you should be familiar with the optimal approach for attacking such questions. Let's run through it.

Decision 1: What is my task?

This question is asking us to select an assumption that would allow the conclusion to follow logically. In other words, we need a *sufficient* assumption.

MANHATTAN
PREP

(NOTE: Remember, we use the word *sufficient* in two different contexts: *sufficient* assumption and *sufficient* condition. Just as a reminder, a *sufficient* assumption is an assumption that is *enough* on its own to get to the conclusion. A *sufficient* condition is a condition that is *enough* on its own to guarantee an outcome. While the term *sufficient* is used in two different contexts, the implication is the same in both: One thing is *sufficient*, or enough, on its own to lead to, guarantee, or require something else.)

Decision 2: What is the author's conclusion?

Decision 3: How is that conclusion supported?

Let's read the argument again with the above questions in mind:

> In the paintings by seventeenth-century Dutch artist Vermeer, we find several recurrent items: a satin jacket, a certain Turkish carpet, and wooden chairs with lion's-head finials.

Background information so far.

> These reappearing objects might seem to evince a dearth of props.

The phrase "… might seem …" sounds like the author is about to counter this viewpoint.

> Yet we know that many of the props Vermeer used were expensive.

Yes. The word "yet" is a pivot word. So, some might say that Vermeer used the same props over and over again because he was lacking in props, but the author is countering this viewpoint.

> Thus, while we might speculate about exactly why Vermeer worked with a small number of familiar objects, it was clearly not for lack of props that the recurrent items were used.

Okay, this is the conclusion. Vermeer did not reuse these items because of a lack of props. We know this because his props were expensive. So the argument core is:

Vermeer used expensive props ➡️ Vermeer did not reuse due to a lack of props

It's important that we really understand the logic behind this argument. Think about it. If your friend drove the same Porsche around for 10 years, would you conclude that she hadn't bought a new car because she was lacking in means? Probably not. She drives an expensive Porsche! You would likely conclude that she has plenty of money to get a different car if she wanted to. She's sticking with her Porsche, but it's probably not because she's lacking the means to get something else.

The same sort of logic is used here. Because Vermeer's props were expensive, the author concludes that Vermeer could have had access to other props if he wished. The question is, does this make a valid argument?

Decision 4: What is the gap?

The author assumes that because the props were expensive, Vermeer must have had access to many more props. So, in attempting to explain why Vermeer would use the same props repeatedly, the author rules out the possibility that he didn't have access to other props. This doesn't necessarily need to be the case. Maybe the expensive props were gifted to Vermeer and those were the only ones he had access to. Maybe he didn't have the money to buy new props because he spent all his money on those few expensive ones. Maybe he had borrowed those props.

Okay, at this point, we have a sense of what might come up in the answer choices.

Decision 5: Which answer choices are clearly wrong?

The easiest eliminations will be answers that aren't related to the argument core. Here's our core again:

Vermeer used   ➡   Vermeer did not
expensive props   reuse due to a lack
                               of props

    (A)   Vermeer often borrowed the expensive props
            he represented in his paintings.

Ooh, this is attractive! Be careful though. This actually weakens the argument. If he had borrowed the expensive props (likely because he couldn't purchase them on his own), it wouldn't make sense to conclude that he had the means to access many props. It would actually suggest that he *was* lacking in props. Eliminate it.

    (B)   The props that recur in Vermeer's paintings
            were always available to him.

This seems related to the conclusion. If they were always available to him, then he wasn't lacking in props. Keep it for now.

    (C)   The satin jacket and wooden chairs that recur
            in the paintings were owned by Vermeer's
            sister.

Again, this actually weakens the argument. If he had borrowed the expensive props, there would be reason to believe that he WAS lacking in props. Remember, correct assumption answers ought to strengthen the argument, not weaken it. Eliminate this answer.

    (D)   The several recurrent items that appeared in
            Vermeer's paintings had special sentimental
            importance for him.

MANHATTAN
PREP

This is attractive. Maybe he used these props repeatedly because he was emotionally attached to them and *not* because he was lacking in props. This seems to help. Keep it for now.

> (E)   If a dearth of props accounted for the
>   recurrent objects in Vermeer's paintings, we
>   would not see expensive props in any of them.

This is the only answer choice that mentions both the expensive props and the lack of props ("dearth of props"). There seems to be a connection made between the two in this answer choice. Keep it.

Decision 6: What is the best available answer?

We are down to three answer choices. When making a final decision, it's critical that we revisit the core. The correct answer will be the one that most clearly addresses the relationship between the premise and the conclusion:

> (B)   The props that recur in Vermeer's paintings
>   were always available to him.

On second glance, (B) seems unrelated. The conclusion that Vermeer was not lacking in props refers to other props aside from the ones he used regularly. The fact that his recurring props were always available to him doesn't make it any more likely that he was not lacking in other props. Furthermore, what does this have to do with the cost of the props?

> (D)   The several recurrent items that appeared in
>   Vermeer's paintings had special sentimental
>   importance for him.

This might explain why he used those props over and over again, but it doesn't give us any more reason to argue that since the props he used were pricey he was not lacking in props. Maybe he used the same props over and over because he was sentimental about them, but maybe he was also lacking in other props! This answer is not enough to ensure that the conclusion follows logically from the premise.

Down to answer (E). Let's look at the core one more time:

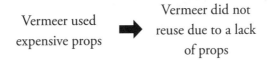

We can think of this argument as having the structure "A. Therefore, B." The simplest sufficient assumption to any argument of this form is: "If A, then B." For the above argument, that would look like this: "If Vermeer used expensive props, then Vermeer did not reuse due to a lack of props."

Let's imagine what this would look like inserted this into our argument:

> Vermeer used expensive props. (If Vermeer used expensive props, then Vermeer did not reuse due to a lack of props.) Thus, Vermeer did not reuse due to a lack of props.

Notice that the simple conditional statement would make the argument valid by connecting premise to conclusion.

Let's take a look at (E) one more time:

> (E)   If a dearth of props accounted for the
> recurrent objects in Vermeer's paintings, we
> would not see expensive props in any of them.

Let's try to think about this answer choice in simple If/Then terms:

> "If a lack of props did account for recurring objects, then we would not see
> expensive props."

Is this answer what we were looking for? Not exactly. But it seems related. Let's compare the conditional in this answer choice with the conditional we originally determined would be sufficient.

Sufficient Conditional: If Vermeer used expensive props, then Vermeer did not reuse due to a lack of props. EP → –LP.

Conditional in (E): If a lack of props did account for recurring objects, then we would not see expensive props. LP → –EP.

Do you notice the relationship between the two? This answer is the contrapositive of what we need! If we reverse and negate it, we can infer the assumption that bridges the gap between the premise and conclusion. EP → –LP.

Perhaps (E) seemed somewhat relevant but a bit confusing on your first read. When examined through the conditional logic lens, (E) is clearly correct.

The assumption in the above argument has a logical structure that we've seen before. It's the "perfect" assumption we encountered in Chapter 3. Although the structure is simple, it is worth noting, since many Sufficient Assumption questions play on this form. Here it is again:

> Original argument: A. Therefore, B.
> Sufficient assumption: If A, then B.

The correct answer could be "If A, then B" or its contrapositive, "If not B, then not A."

MANHATTAN
PREP

Compound Conditional Statements

Compound conditional statements are statements that have a two-part *sufficient* condition (a two-part trigger such as "If X and Y, then…") and/or a two-part *necessary* condition (a two part outcome such as "…then Y or Z"). The following example has a two-part outcome:

> If M is selected, then both G and H must be selected.

What do we know? If M is selected, then G must be selected. Also, if M is selected, then H must be selected. We can deal with this by splitting the statement into two separate conditionals:

> If M is selected, then G is selected. (M → G)
> If M is selected, then H is selected. (M → H)

While this is the most common type of compound statement that you'll see, it's not the only type. Let's take a moment to define the four types of compound statements that are fair game on the LSAT, starting with the type discussed above.

1. **AND in the outcome:** If M is selected, then both G and H must be selected.

In this case, M, the sufficient condition, is enough to trigger *both* G and H. In other words, M alone is enough to trigger G, and M alone is enough to trigger H. Thus, we can split the compound statement into two simple statements:

> If M is selected, then G is selected. (M → G)
> If M is selected, then H is selected. (M → H)

Of course, from these two simple statements, we can derive two contrapositives:

> If G is not selected, then M is not selected. (–G → –M)
> If H is not selected, then M is not selected. (–H → –M)

It's important to note that this type of compound statement won't always have the word "and" explicitly written in the outcome. For example:

> If M is selected, then G is selected but H is not.

This is the same type of compound statement in disguise! Selecting M triggers two outcomes: G is selected AND H is *not* selected. We can split this up as follows:

> M → G
> M → –H

2. **OR in the trigger:** If M or G is selected, then H must be selected.

In this case, M on its own is enough to trigger H. We can say the same for G. *Either one* is enough to trigger the outcome, H. Thus, we can split this compound statement into two simple statements:

> If M is selected, then H is selected. (M → H)
> If G is selected, then H is selected. (G → H)

Again, we can generate contrapositives:

> If H is not selected, then M is not selected. (–H → –M)
> If H is not selected, then G is not selected. (–H → –G)

3. **AND in the trigger:** If M and G are selected, then H is selected.

Here, *both* M and G *together* are enough to trigger H, but we're not sure if either one *alone* is enough. Thus, we CANNOT split this statement into two parts. We must keep it together:

> M + G → H

Oh boy. So how on earth can we take the contrapositive of a statement like this? Well, let's think about it. M and G together give us H. If we don't have H, then we couldn't have had M and G together. In other words, if we don't have H, either M is missing or G is missing (or both): –H means –M or –G. To find the contrapositive of a statement like this, reverse and negate the elements and **SWAP "AND" for "OR":**

> –H → –M or –G

Note: It's important to know that "–M or –G" leaves open the possibility that neither is selected. It's not necessarily one or the other. For example, if you're told "Either Tamara or Igor will be invited," you know for certain that at least one of them must be invited, but it's possible that both will be invited. Similarly, if you're told "Either M or G is not selected," you know that at least one of them is left out, but it's possible that both are left out. Does this seem counterintuitive? It's a small example of the difference between our everyday language and the legalistic language used by the LSAT—and law students!

4. **OR in the outcome:** If M is selected, then G or H is selected.

Notice that M is enough to trigger G or H, but not necessarily both. Thus, we CANNOT split this statement into two parts. We must keep it together:

> M → G or H

Again, to find the contrapositive, reverse, negate, and SWAP "OR" for "AND" or vice versa:

> –G + –H → –M

MANHATTAN
PREP

The last three compound statement types are quite rare on the LSAT, but you need to be prepared to deal with them if they do show up. Let's summarize the four types:

Type	Example	Strategy	Notation	Contrapositive	Frequency
AND as an outcome	If J, then K and L.	Split it up	J → K J → L	–K → –J –L → –J	Common
OR as a trigger	If M or N, then P.	Split it up	M → P N → P	–P → –M –P → –N	Rare
AND as a trigger	If R and S, then X.	Together	R + S → X	–X → –R or –S	Rare
OR as an outcome	If Q, then T or V.	Together	Q → T or V	–T + –V → –Q	Rare

Time to practice.

Drill It: Compound Conditional Statements

Convert each of the statements into conditional diagrams, and then derive contrapositive inferences. Be sure to check your responses against the solutions **after each exercise.**

Example: If X is selected, then both Y and Z are selected.

	Conversions:	Contrapositives:
	$X \rightarrow Y$	$-Y \rightarrow -X$
	$X \rightarrow Z$	$-Z \rightarrow -X$

1. If H is selected, then J is selected but G is not.

2. K is selected, only if neither M nor N is selected.

3. If both P and Q are on the team, then R is on the team.

4. Paulson is selected, only if Oster is selected but Vicenza is not.

5. If both X and Y are chosen, Z is chosen.

6. If the car is red or green, then it is a used car.

7. A good parent is both empathetic and sympathetic.

8. A country has both a skilled labor force and a competent government only if it is economically healthy.

9. If one lives with both peace and love, then happiness is attainable.

8

10. Climate change can be minimized if, and only if, we can reduce the growth in the use of gas-powered cars.

Solutions: Compound Conditional Statements

1. If H is selected, then J is selected but G is not.

Conversions:	Contrapositives:
H → J	–J → –H
H → –G	G → –H

2. K is selected, only if neither M nor N is selected.

Be careful! "Neither/nor" is NOT the same as "or." "Neither/nor" means neither one! We can translate "neither M nor N" to "not M *and* not N."

Conversions:	Contrapositives:
K → –M	M → –K
K → –N	N → –K

3. If both P and Q are on the team, then R is on the team.

Conversion:	Contrapositive:
P + Q → R	–R → –P or –Q

4. Paulson is selected, only if Oster is selected but Vicenza is not.

Conversions:	Contrapositives:
P → O	–O → –P
P → –V	V → –P

5. If both X and Y are chosen, Z is chosen.

Conversion:	Contrapositive:
X + Y → Z	–Z → –X or –Y

6. If the car is red or green, then it is a used car.

Conversions: Contrapositives:

R → U   –U → –R

G → U   –U → –G

7. A good parent is both empathetic and sympathetic.

Conversions: Contrapositives:

GP → E   –E → –GP

GP → S   –S → –GP

8. A country has both a skilled labor force and a competent government only if it is economically healthy.

Conversion: Contrapositive:

SLF + CG → EH   –EH → –SLF or –CG

9. If one lives with both peace and love, then happiness is attainable.

Conversion: Contrapositive:

P + L → HA   –HA → –P or –L

10. Climate change can be minimized if, and only if, we can reduce the growth in the use of gas-powered cars.

Did you fall for the trap? This is not a compound conditional but a biconditional! As we learned earlier, this translates into two statements:

Conversions: Contrapositives:

Min. CC → Red. GPC   –Red. GPC → –Min. CC
Red. GPC → Min. CC   –Min. CC → –Red. GPC

We can also write this as one biconditional statement:

Conversion: Contrapositive:

Min. CC ←→ Red. GPC   –Red. GPC ←→ –Min. CC

Conditional Logic 2: Compound Conditional Statements

Let's apply these skills to a real LSAT question:

> *PT22, S2, Q18*
>
> To classify a work of art as truly great, it is necessary that the work have both originality and far reaching influence upon the artistic community.
>
> The principle above, if valid, most strongly supports which one of the following arguments?
>
> (A)   By breaking down traditional schemes of representation, Picasso redefined painting. It is this extreme originality that warrants his work being considered truly great.
>
> (B)   Some of the most original art being produced today is found in isolated communities, but because of this isolation these works have only minor influence, and hence cannot be considered truly great.
>
> (C)   Certain examples of the drumming practiced in parts of Africa's west coast employ a musical vocabulary that resists representation in Western notational schemes. This tremendous originality coupled with the profound impact these pieces are having on musicians everywhere, is enough to consider these works to be truly great.
>
> (D)   The piece of art in the lobby is clearly not classified as truly great, so it follows that it fails to be original.
>
> (E)   Since Bach's music is truly great, it not only has both originality and a major influence on musicians, it has broad popular appeal as well.

This question is a Principle question that requires us to find an answer that illustrates the given principle. This is a Principle Example question. We'll study these in the next chapter. Note that this is *not* the same as a Principle Support question (the kind we studied in the last chapter).

Did you recognize the given principle as a conditional statement? It's not written in traditional If/Then form, but it is a conditional statement nonetheless. A bit later, we'll discuss disguised conditionals in greater detail. For now, just know that the word "necessary" is a conditional trigger. It makes sense, right? Every conditional statement has a *necessary* component, or outcome. So, if one thing makes something else *necessary,* you've got a conditional situation on your hands. In this case, to be an example of truly great art (TGA), two things are necessary: 1) originality (O) and 2) far reaching influence on the artistic community (FRI). In other words:

> If TGA, then both O and FRI.

> TGA → O + FRI

Look! A compound conditional statement! Now, we're looking for an answer choice that conforms to this principle. What would a correct answer look like? Well, a correct answer might give us a work of TGA and then describe how it is both O and FRI. Or, and this is the more likely scenario, a correct answer might play off of the contrapositive of this principle:

> –O or –FRI → –TGA

Since either –O or –FRI by itself guarantees –TGA, we can split this conditional statement into two parts:

> –O → –TGA
> –FRI → –TGA

Maybe the answer will describe how a particular art is either not O, or not FRI, and then conclude that the art is not truly great. Let's look at the choices, but before we do, we'll revisit the principle one last time:

> TGA → O + FRI
>   –O → –TGA
> –FRI → –TGA

Any answer choice that conforms to any one of the three statements above will be a correct answer.

(A)   By breaking down traditional schemes of representation, Picasso redefined painting. It is this extreme originality that warrants his work being considered truly great.

This says the work is O ("redefined painting"), so it must be TGA (O → TGA). Does this fit the principle? No, it does not. Eliminate it.

(B)   Some of the most original art being produced today is found in isolated communities, but because of this isolation these works have only minor influence, and hence cannot be considered truly great.

This says the work is O, but also that it is –FRI (not far reaching). Because it is –FRI, it is –TGA. Does this match the principle? Indeed it does: –FRI → –TGA.

>   (C)   Certain examples of the drumming practiced
> in parts of Africa's west coast employ a
> musical vocabulary that resists representation
> in Western notational schemes. This
> tremendous originality coupled with the
> profound impact these pieces are having on
> musicians everywhere, is enough to consider
> these works to be truly great.

This is very tempting. The work is both O and has FRI. Thus, the answer states, it must be TGA: O + FRI → TGA.

Be careful. This is an illegal reversal of the original principle! While great art must be original and have a "far reaching influence," those characteristics are not sufficient to guarantee that a work of art is truly great.

>   (D)   The piece of art in the lobby is clearly not
> classified as truly great, so it follows that it
> fails to be original.

This translates to –TGA → –O. This is a reversal of what we've got as well. Eliminate it.

>   (E)   Since Bach's music is truly great, it not only has
> both originality and a major influence on
> musicians, it has broad popular appeal as well.

This is saying TGA → O + FRI + BPA. This is very tempting. We seem to get the TGA → O + FRI that we need, but we have to be very careful here. This answer choice adds in a third necessary element that is not mentioned in the original principle.

Therefore, (B) is correct.

Beyond If/Then Triggers

We discussed the fact that If/Then phrasing indicates we're dealing with a conditional statement, but we also mentioned that disguised conditional statements won't contain the If/Then structure. For you to get the most out of your conditional logic knowledge on the LSAT, you'll need to learn to work with disguised conditionals. The key is the guarantee.

Looking for Guarantees

Have a look at this standard conditional statement:

> If one is young, then one is happy.

According to this statement, being young guarantees happiness. Always. Without exception. Every time. We can express this exact idea in many different ways:

> All young people are happy.
> Being young assures happiness.
> A young person is a happy person.

Each of these three statements conveys the exact same meaning as the original If/Then statement. Being young guarantees happiness. Always. Without exception. Every time. Thus, we can say these three statements are conditional statements, even though they may not look like it. When the LSAT gives us a conditional statement on a Logical Reasoning question, it will often be disguised like this. How can we learn to recognize these disguised conditionals? We need to learn to recognize *words that imply a guarantee*. There are three main categories of such words. Here they are with examples for each. Notice that every disguised conditional statement can be translated to If/Then form:

1. Absolute modifiers (all, any, every, always, none, never)

All engineers enjoy math. (If one is an engineer, then one enjoys math.)

Any hamburger is worth $2. (If it is a hamburger, then it is worth $2.)

Every good movie has a star actor. (If it is a good movie, then it has a star actor.)

A new car **always** smells good. (If it is a new car, then it smells good.)

None of the pies at the party had blueberry filling. (If it was a pie at the party, then it did not have blueberry filling.)

Good soccer players are **never** good football players. (If one is a good soccer player, then one is not a good football player.)

2. Words of necessity (necessary, require, depend, assure, guarantee, must, is essential for)

A large vocabulary is **necessary** to be a great writer. (If one is a great writer, one has a large vocabulary.)

Success **requires** patience. (If a person is successful, then that person is patient.)

Being happy **depends on** being healthy. (If a person is happy, then that person is healthy.)

Repeated practice **assures** an error-free performance. (If one practices repeatedly, then one will have an error-free performance.)

Buying a ticket online **guarantees** a seat on the bus. (If one buys a ticket online, then one will have a seat on the bus.)

A good pizza **must** be hot. (If a pizza is good, then it is hot.)

Experience **is essential for** humility. (If one is humble, then one has experience.)

8

3. Verbs of certainty (is, are, will be, do, do not, has/have)

A long story **is** a boring story. (If a story is long, then it is boring.)

Oranges **are** fruits. (If it is an orange, then it is a fruit.)

Mixing yellow and blue **does not** make red. (If yellow and blue are mixed, then red is not the result.)

Dogs **have** fleas. (If it is a dog, then it has fleas.)

This is certainly not an exhaustive list of words that imply a guarantee, but it is a start, and it should put you in the right mind-set for recognizing the clues when they are present.

Conditional Logic 3: Only, Must, and No

Here's an LSAT question that requires a strong understanding of what we just discussed:

> *PT34, S2, Q10*
>
> Although the charter of Westside School states that the student body must include some students with special educational needs, no students with learning disabilities have yet enrolled in the school. Therefore, the school is currently in violation of its charter.
>
> The conclusion of the argument follows logically if which one of the following is assumed?
>
> (A)   All students with learning disabilities have special educational needs.
> (B)   The school currently has no student with learning disabilities.
> (C)   The school should enroll students with special educational needs.
> (D)   The only students with special educational needs are students with learning disabilities.
> (E)   The school's charter cannot be modified in order to avoid its being violated.

Again, we're dealing with an Assumption question. Let's apply our approach:

Decision 1: What is my task?

This question is asking us to select an assumption that would allow the conclusion to "follow logically." In other words, we need a *sufficient* assumption.

Decision 2: What is the author's conclusion?

Decision 3: How is that conclusion supported?

Let's read the argument again with the above questions in mind:

> Although the charter of Westside School states that the student body must include some students with special educational needs,

"Although" is a sign that we're about to get some contrary information.

> no students with learning disabilities have yet enrolled in the school.

And here it is. The charter states that the student body must include some special needs students, but as of yet the school does not have any students with learning disabilities. Hmm. Notice the difference between the two concepts: "special needs students" and "students with learning disabilities." Are these groups necessarily the same? We'll keep this in mind.

> Therefore, the school is currently in violation of its charter.

This is obviously the conclusion. So the argument core is:

charter requires SN students

+   ➡   school is in violation of its charter

no students with LD enrolled

However, the presence of two conditional logic indicators—"must" and "no"—suggests that a more formal approach might be useful here. Let's diagram what we're given:

charter → SN

–LD _____

–charter

Decision 4: What is the gap?

We've already noticed the potential difference between special needs (SN) and learning disabilities (LD). If the school needs to have SN students to comply with its charter, and it doesn't have LD students, does that mean the school is in violation of the charter? There's something going on here with the connection between SN and LD. Looking at our diagram, if we're to reach "no charter" from "no LD," we need a way to connect that to the conditional statement we've been given. Our answer needs to connect LD and SN, and in the right way.

Decision 5: Which answer choices are clearly wrong?

The easiest eliminations will be answers that aren't related to the argument core. Here's our core again:

charter requires SN students

\+   ➡   school is in violation of its charter

no students with LD enrolled

    (A)   All students with learning disabilities have
             special educational needs.

This looks attractive. It makes a direct connection between LD and SN. Keep it for now.

    (B)   The school currently has no student with
             learning disabilities.

This is a premise booster. In fact, it simply repeats information from one of our premises! Eliminate it.

    (C)   The school should enroll students with special
             educational needs.

This is tempting. It seems logical that they should enroll some special needs students. However, this isn't an assumption that would allow us to conclude that the school is currently in violation of the charter. Since the conclusion is not normative, we should be wary of answers that express "shoulds" or "should nots." Eliminate it.

    (D)   The only students with special educational
             needs are students with learning disabilities.

Here's another one that seems to connect SN with LD. Better keep it for now.

    (E)   The school's charter cannot be modified in
             order to avoid its being violated.

This is out of scope. We're looking for an assumption that would allow us to conclude that the school is currently in violation of the charter. Whether the charter could be modified is irrelevant.

Decision 6: What is the best available answer?

Okay, so we're down to two answers, (A) and (D), and they both look very good. When we're down to two, we always want to revisit the core before making a final decision. Since we're also able to represent this argument with a diagram, let's use that:

charter → SN
– LD
––––––––––
– charter

MANHATTAN
PREP

Since there are two answers that connect SN and LD, let's focus in on the specific connection we need. If we start at –LD and are to conclude with –charter, then we're going to want to use the contrapositive of the first premise: –SN → –charter. We *almost* have a chain:

–LD → _____ –SN → –charter

It's now clear that the argument assumes that if –LD, then there are –SN. We can express this in conditional form:

–LD → –SN

Look at (A) one more time, and try to translate it into a conditional statement:

(A) All students with learning disabilities have special educational needs.

Don't read on until you've given it a shot. Does it match the assumption we've written above?

This translates to "If LD, then SN" (LD → SN).

What do you think of (A) now? It's the exact negation of what we need! We need: –LD → –SN. Back to (D):

(D) The only students with special educational needs are students with learning disabilities.

Don't continue on until you've tried to translate this statement. It's an "only" statement, so be careful. To review the use of "only," let's look at a simpler, more intuitive statement that uses the same structure:

The only people who water ski are those who can swim.

We've got two choices, right? It's either W → S or S → W. Which one is it? Well, consider it from the perspective of guarantees. Which one guarantees the other?

If you water ski, does that guarantee that you can swim? Yes, it does, because the only people who water ski are those who can swim.

If you can swim, does that guarantee that you water ski? No, it doesn't. A five-year-old might be able to swim but not water ski. So, we have W → S.

Back to (D) again.

(D) The only students with special educational needs are students with learning disabilities.

This is saying that the only students with SN are those who also have LD. In other words, if you have SN, then it is a guarantee that you also have LD:

SN → LD

This doesn't match our predicted assumption directly, –LD → –SN, but it's the contrapositive! Therefore, (D) is our answer.

Unless

It's time to discuss one of the most disguised conditional structures you'll see on the LSAT: "unless" statements. Take a look:

> Javier arrives to work on time unless there is traffic.

We've learned that conditional statements are guarantees. This doesn't look much like a guarantee, does it? Well, think about it again. What do you know if there is NOT traffic? You got it. Javier arrives to work on time, guaranteed. So, if there is no traffic, Javier arrives to work on time.

> NO traffic → Javier arrives on time

This is what we call an "unless" statement. Something, call it the normal state of affairs, always happens unless something else intrudes on the situation (call it the intruder). If the intruder does not occur, then we're guaranteed to have the normal state of affairs. If there is no traffic, then Javier arrives on time. Here's another example:

> Gloria reads before bed unless there is something good on TV.

> Normal state of affairs: Gloria reads before bed.
> Intruder: Something good on TV.

If the intruder does not intrude, then we're assured to get the normal state of affairs:

> NOT something good on TV → Gloria reads before bed

Now, it's important that you don't fall into the "unless trap." The trap is to assume that if the intruder *does* intrude, you *won't* get the normal state. Here's how this would be written:

> something good on TV → Gloria does NOT read before bed

Note that this is an illegal negation of what we got earlier. It's wrong. Yes, the intruder is the only thing that can disrupt the normal state of affairs, but it doesn't *necessarily* disrupt the normal state. Say there was something good on TV. *Perhaps* Gloria would watch TV instead of reading, but the operative word is *perhaps*. You can't represent *perhaps* with a conditional relationship, because *perhaps* isn't a guarantee. Be careful!

So, here's a formula for interpreting "unless" statements:

1. Identify the normal state of affairs.

2. Identify the intruder.

3. Think: If the intruder does NOT intrude, we must get the normal state.

4. Write your conditional statement accordingly (NOT intruder → normal state).

MANHATTAN
PREP

Try this one. Make sure you give it your best shot before reading on:

Unless Kevin Durant gets injured, his team will win the championship.

Normal state of affairs: Kevin Durant's team will win the championship.
Intruder: Kevin Durant gets injured.
Think: If Kevin Durant does NOT get injured, we must get the normal state of affairs.
Conditional statement: Kevin Durant does NOT get injured → Kevin Durant's team will win the championship.

This one might have felt a little different because "unless" was at the beginning of the sentence instead of in the middle of it. But in fact, the process is still the same. "Unless" will always introduce the intruder, no matter where it is in the sentence. And don't fall for the "unless trap"! Even if Kevin Durant *does* get injured, this doesn't *necessarily* mean his team will lose. Maybe the rest of the team will lead them to a win.

Time to practice.

8

Drill It: Unless Statements

Translate the following statements into conditional notation. Be sure to check your answer after each exercise.

Example:　　Ronaldo cannot be chosen for the position unless he prepares for the interview.

$$\textbf{(–preparation} \rightarrow \textbf{–chosen)}$$

1. Tommy cannot win the marathon unless Eugene drops out.

2. The carnival cannot proceed unless the clown gets better.

3. The car won't start unless we fill it with gas.

4. Jill does not drive unless her sister gets tired.

5. Unless the field dries, the game cannot be played.

Solutions: Unless Statements

1. Tommy cannot win the marathon unless Eugene drops out.

   –Eugene drops out → –Tommy wins

2. The carnival cannot proceed unless the clown gets better

   –clown better → –carnival proceed

3. The car won't start unless we fill it with gas.

   –fill with gas → –car start

4. Jill does not drive unless her sister gets tired.

   –sister tired → –Jill drive

5. Unless the field dries, the game cannot be played.

   –dries → –game played

Conditional Logic 4: Unless Statements

It's time to test your knowledge. Note that this question is not an Assumption Family question; instead it is asking you to choose an inference, an answer that must be true:

> *PT15, S3, Q7*
>
> Politician: Unless our nation redistributes wealth, we will be unable to alleviate economic injustice and our current system will lead inevitably to intolerable economic inequities. If the inequities become intolerable, those who suffer from the injustice will resort to violence to coerce social reform. It is our nation's responsibility to do whatever is necessary to alleviate conditions that would otherwise give rise to violent attempts at social reform.
>
> The statements above logically commit the politician to which one of the following conclusions?
>
> (A)   The need for political reform never justifies a resort to violent remedies.
>
> (B)   It is our nation's responsibility to redistribute wealth.
>
> (C)   Politicians must base decisions on political expediency rather than on abstract moral principles.
>
> (D)   Economic injustice need not be remedied unless it leads to intolerable social conditions.
>
> (E)   All that is required to create conditions of economic justice is the redistribution of wealth.

This is an Inference question. We'll discuss Inference questions in Chapter 11, but for now, just know that an Inference question requires us to choose an answer that we can prove from the given information in the passage. Note that this is *not* an Assumption Family question. We do not need to identify gaps or holes in the argument. Rather, we need to consider the information given, synthesize it, and then choose an answer that follows logically.

Many of you likely got this question correct without using any formal conditional logic. If the argument made sense to you, and you were able to anticipate the logical outcome, great! The conditional logic thought process we're about to demonstrate will give you a slightly different perspective on the question. If you weren't able to see the logical outcome, the conditional logic angle should help. Let's give it a shot. We'll start with the first sentence:

Politician: Unless our nation redistributes wealth, we
will be unable to alleviate economic injustice
and our current system will lead inevitably to
intolerable economic inequities.

An "unless" statement! Let's break it down using the steps we outlined above:

Normal state of affairs: We will be unable to alleviate economic injustice and our current system will lead inevitably to intolerable economic injustice.
Intruder: Our nation redistributes wealth.
Think: If our nation does NOT redistribute wealth, then the normal state will occur.

Conditional statement: –redistribute → economic injustice + intolerable economic inequities

If the inequities become intolerable, those who suffer from the injustice will resort to violence to coerce social reform.

Another conditional statement! This one is in standard If/Then form:

intolerable economic inequities → violence

Notice that this conditional statement can be chained onto the first one:

–redistribute → economic injustice + intolerable economic inequities → violence

In other words, if we don't redistribute, we'll end up with violence (follow the chain!):

–redistribute → violence

It is our nation's responsibility to do whatever is necessary to alleviate conditions that would otherwise give rise to violent attempts at social reform.

So, we must do whatever we can to avoid violence. Well, if we don't want violence, we need to redistribute wealth. The contrapositive tells us as much:

–violence → redistribute

Answer choice (B) is the correct answer that follows logically from the information given:

(B)   It is our nation's responsibility to redistribute
wealth.

Again, you may have arrived at (B) without resorting to conditional diagramming. That's okay. In fact, that's good. You only need to diagram statements when you're not able to make sense of the information in your head. It's kind of like asking someone for directions. We all resist writing them down, especially if they're easy to remember (like "drive to the river and make a left"), but as soon as they get complicated, we reach for a pen. Trying unsuccessfully to keep it all in your head can be disastrous, and there's no excuse for a disaster when a few simple notes could have saved the day. That's the way you should think about conditional logic diagramming: You won't always need it, but if you do, you better use it. And if you're going to use it effectively and efficiently come test day, you need to devote some serious time to practice.

Chaining Conditional Statements

This last question provides a good transition into the next section of the chapter. In our solution to the last question, we linked two conditional statements that shared a common element (intolerable economic inequities). Linking conditionals into a longer chain is crucial to getting the most out of your conditional logic knowledge on the LSAT. You've already done a bit of linking when we looked at Flaw questions, but now let's look at the issue in more depth. There are two basic types of linkages that you'll want to master:

1. The direct link

> Given: A → B
> Given: B → C
> The direct link: A → B → C
> We can infer: A → C

2. The contrapositive link

> Given: A → B
> Given: C → –B
> Take the contrapositive to get a like term: B → –C
> The link: A → B → –C
> We can infer: A → –C

Now, there's one type of *invalid* link that you will be tempted to make. Let's exorcise these temptations right here and now:

> Given: A → B
> Given: A → C
> Temptation: B → C

No, no, no! This is the equivalent of saying:

> All apples are fruits. (A → F)
> All apples are red. (A → R)
> So, all fruits are red. (F → R)

This doesn't work. In fact, there is no way to create a chain from this information, even after we try taking the contrapositives of the statements.

Let's practice making links.

Drill It: Conditional Chains

For each exercise, connect the pair of conditional statements into a chain. Some won't connect. Don't be tempted to jam them together! Be sure to check your answer after each exercise.

Example: If you invite Aaron, Brian must be invited as well. If Chuck isn't invited, neither is Brian.
            A → B → C

1. If Sam eats a piece of cake, he will not be hungry for dinner. If Jeremy bakes a cake, Sam will eat a piece of it.

2. If it's raining out, the picnic will be canceled. Simone will be sad if the picnic is canceled.

3. Every pianist knows the music of Bach. No one in my family knows the music of Bach.

4. A good apple is a ripe apple, and an apple will not be picked unless it is ripe.

5. Carrie is anxious when her dog misbehaves, and if Carrie is anxious, then her boyfriend is anxious as well.

6. Only troublemakers stay after school. All students who arrive late will stay after school.

7. Sarah apologizes only when she means it, and she always wears her purple sweater when she apologizes.

8. Being a good parent requires understanding and empathy. Those without experience cannot be empathetic.

9. Almost all flowers are pretty, and anything that is pretty is worth displaying in the home.

10. A wise person is never a talkative person, but every talkative person has something interesting to say.

11. Unless the street is dark, Jeffrey will walk home. The street is dark only on the weekends.

12. Tall trees require sunlight to survive. Tall trees get sunlight only when they are not blocked by other trees.

Solutions: Conditional Chains

1. If Sam eats a piece of cake, he will not be hungry for dinner. If Jeremy bakes a cake, Sam will eat a piece of it.

   Jeremy bakes a cake → Sam eats a piece of cake → –Sam hungry for dinner

2. If it's raining out, the picnic will be canceled. Simone will be sad if the picnic is canceled.

   raining → picnic cancelled → Simone sad

3. Every pianist knows the music of Bach. No one in my family knows the music of Bach.

   in my family → –know Bach → –pianist

   Or, perhaps you came up with a chain of contrapositives of the above:

   pianist → know Bach → –in my family

   Note that for each of these exercises, the contrapositives of the relationships are also correct.

4. A good apple is a ripe apple, and an apple will not be picked unless it is ripe.

   good → ripe
   –ripe → –picked

   These can't be chained up, but we can say this:

   –ripe → –good + –picked

5. Carrie is anxious when her dog misbehaves, and if Carrie is anxious, then her boyfriend is anxious as well.

   dog misbehaves → Carrie anxious → boyfriend anxious

6. Only troublemakers stay after school. All students who arrive late will stay after school.

   arrive late → stay after school → troublemaker

MANHATTAN
PREP

7. Sarah apologizes only when she means it, and she always wears her purple sweater when she apologizes.

   Sarah apologizes → Sarah means it

   Sarah apologizes → wears purple sweater

   These can't be chained! However, we could notate this as: **Sarah apologizes → Sarah means it + wears a purple sweater.**

8. Being a good parent requires understanding and empathy. Those without experience cannot be empathetic.

   –experience → –empathy → –good parent

   Note that we didn't include "understanding" in the chain because it doesn't link with the second conditional.

9. Almost all flowers are pretty, and anything that is pretty is worth displaying in the home.

   "Almost all" is not a guarantee!

   pretty → worth displaying

   Don't worry, we'll talk about how to handle "almost," "some," and related terms later on.

10. A wise person is never a talkative person, but every talkative person has something interesting to say.

    wise → –talkative

    talkative → has something interesting to say

    These cannot be chained.

11. Unless the street is dark, Jeffrey walks home from work. The street is dark only on the weekends.

    –Jeffrey walks home → street dark → weekend

12. Tall trees require sunlight to survive. Tall trees get sunlight only when they are not blocked by other trees.

    tall trees survive → sunlight → –blocked by other trees

Conditional Logic 5: Conditional Chains

Let's give it a try on a real one. Take your time and try approaching it using formal logic. Note that this is another Inference question:

PT13, S2, Q10

Every political philosopher of the early twentieth century who was either a socialist or a communist was influenced by Rosa Luxemburg. No one who was influenced by Rosa Luxemburg advocated a totalitarian state.

If the statements above are true, which one of the following must on the basis of them also be true?

(A)   No early twentieth-century socialist political philosopher advocated a totalitarian state.

(B)   Every early twentieth-century political philosopher who did not advocate a totalitarian state was influenced by Rosa Luxemburg.

(C)   Rosa Luxemburg was the only person to influence every early twentieth-century political philosopher who was either socialist or communist.

(D)   Every early twentieth-century political philosopher who was influenced by Rosa Luxemburg and was not a socialist was a communist.

(E)   Every early twentieth-century political philosopher who did not advocate a totalitarian state was either socialist or communist.

Notice that the two statements given in the original "argument" are facts. There is no conclusion. In fact, this is not an argument at all. This is another Inference question (again, we'll cover these in more detail later on). For now, remember that this question is asking us to choose an answer that must be true based on the information in the text.

The first word is "Every," a common conditional trigger. The start of the second sentence is "No one," another absolute term that expresses a guarantee. So, both sentences in the passage are conditional statements. Most likely, we're going to need to connect the conditionals in order to draw an inference. Let's take it one step at a time. Take a minute to translate the first sentence into conditional terms:

Every political philosopher of the early twentieth century who was either a socialist or a communist was influenced by Rosa Luxemburg.

How would you convert this into standard If/Then form? Well, *every* socialist political philosopher (SPP) and every communist political philosopher (CPP) of the twentieth century was influenced by Rosa Luxemburg (IRL). So, if you were a SPP, then you were IRL. Furthermore, if you were a CPP, then you were IRL. Given the complex nature of this particular statement, it would be a good idea to get this down on scratch paper:

SPP or CPP → IRL

No one who was influenced by Rosa Luxemburg advocated a totalitarian state.

What about this one? Translate before reading on.

If you were IRL, then you did not advocate a totalitarian state (ATS):

IRL → –ATS

Taking both of these together, the link should be clear!

SPP or CPP → IRL → –ATS

By making this connection, we can infer a number of things:

SPP → –ATS (and contrapositive: ATS → –SPP)
CPP → –ATS (and contrapositive: ATS → –CPP)

We just need to be sure we can trace our abbreviations back to their actual meanings! Let's look at the answers:

(A)   No early twentieth-century socialist political
       philosopher advocated a totalitarian state.

If no SPP advocated a totalitarian state (ATS), then if you were an SPP, you did not ATS.

SPP → –ATS

This is exactly one of the inferences we made by connecting the two conditionals. This is the correct answer.

(B)   Every early twentieth-century political
       philosopher who did not advocate a totalitarian
       state was influenced by Rosa Luxemburg.

We know that IRL → –ATS. This was given to us. Answer (B) says –ATS → IRL. An illegal reversal! While it might be true, we can't infer that it is true for certain. Eliminate it.

(C)   Rosa Luxemburg was the only person to
         influence every early twentieth-century
         political philosopher who was either socialist
         or communist.

We can't know if she was the only person. This is way too extreme. Eliminate it.

(D)   Every early twentieth-century political
         philosopher who was influenced by Rosa
         Luxemburg and was not a socialist was a
         communist.

We don't know this to be true from the information given. There could have been people who were influenced by Luxemburg but were not socialist *or* communist.

(E)   Every early twentieth-century political
         philosopher who did not advocate a totalitarian
         state was either socialist or communist.

Perhaps there were political philosophers who did not advocate a totalitarian state but were, say, anarchists or libertarians rather than socialists or communists. From the stimulus, we didn't learn anything we can infer about –ATS.

Let's try another one:

PT22, S4, Q25

Essayist: Every contract negotiator has been lied to by
                someone or other, and whoever lies to
                anyone is practicing deception. But, of course,
                anyone who has been lied to has also lied to
                someone or other.

If the essayist's statements are true, which one of the
following must also be true?

(A)   Every contract negotiator has practiced
         deception.
(B)   Not everyone who practices deception is lying
         to someone.
(C)   Not everyone who lies to someone is practicing
         deception.
(D)   Whoever lies to a contract negotiator has been
         lied to by a contract negotiator.
(E)   Whoever lies to anyone is lied to by someone.

MANHATTAN
PREP

This question asks us to find an answer choice that "must be true" based on the information given in the passage. Again, this is what we call an Inference question (to be discussed in greater detail later on).

Take a second and read through the paragraph again. Make a list of all the conditional triggers that you encounter. Don't read on until you've given it a shot.

Did you spot the following triggers?

> Every
> Whoever (meaning every person)
> Anyone

Every piece of this paragraph contains conditional logic. Thus, we pretty much know that we can infer the correct answer from a conditional chain. We'll start by translating the conditional statements into arrow diagrams. (Again, if you were able to track the conditionals in your head, that's great. Seeing it written out should strengthen your understanding. If you weren't able to track the pieces mentally, then the diagram will certainly help.)

Every contract negotiator has been lied to by someone or other:

> contract negotiator → has been lied to

And whoever lies to anyone is practicing deception:

> lie → deception

But, of course, anyone who has been lied to has also lied to someone or other:

> has been lied to → lied

Now take a second and see if you can make a chain. Remember, if you're given multiple conditionals, chances are you'll be able to connect them.

> contract negotiator → has been lied to → lied → deception

So, this is saying that every contract negotiator has been lied to, which means every contract negotiator has lied to someone else, which means every contract negotiator has practiced deception!

> contract negotiator → deception

Let's look at the answer choices:

> (A)   Every contract negotiator has practiced
>   deception.

This is exactly the inference that we were able to draw above. This must be true, and so this is the correct answer.

> (B)   Not everyone who practices deception is lying
>   to someone.

8

"Not everyone" cannot be written as a conditional. This is saying that if you practice deception, you *may not* be lying. We know that if you lie to someone, you are practicing deception: lie → deception. But, we don't know if the reverse is true: deception → lie. Since we don't know anything about the truth of this, we can't say for sure whether there are any people who practice deception without lying. We can't infer (B).

> (C)   Not everyone who lies to someone is practicing
>   deception.

We know this is false. We know: lie → deception. If you lie, you are practicing deception. Every time.

> (D)   Whoever lies to a contract negotiator has been
>   lied to by a contract negotiator.

There's no way we can know this from our conditional chain.

> (E)   Whoever lies to anyone is lied to by someone.

We know: have been lied to → lied, but we don't know the reverse!

Linking Assumptions

Conditional logic is often used on Assumption questions. We've already seen an example. Here was the diagram for an earlier question:

> charter → SN
> –LD
> –charter

And the correct answer boiled down to SN → LD, which we could use (in its contrapositive form) to create this chain:

> –LD → –SN → –charter

In this case, we identified the assumption that could link the premise to the conclusion.

There's another type of linking that we will have to do. Here's a simple example:

> Every child likes ice cream. Everyone who likes ice cream buys ice cream. Thus, every child is rich.

Hmm. Bad argument, right? Where did the "rich" come from?

There's obviously a problem here.

Let's translate the conditionals into arrow notation. We'll start with the premises:

> child → likes ice cream
> likes ice cream → buys ice cream

And now the conclusion, which is a conditional statement (unlike the argument above, in which the conclusion was simply "no charter"):

child → rich

When the conclusion of an argument is a conditional statement, keep in mind what you have to prove: the *relationship*. You are not proving "rich"; you are proving "child → rich," or, in plain terms, that every child is rich. Of course, to prove "child → rich," we're going to have to use our premises, along with the assumption provided in an answer choice. Let's start by "spreading out" the conclusion on our scratch paper:

child ⋯>   ⋯> rich

Now, let's see how we can use the premises to bridge the gap.

Just as we practiced, we can link the premises together. Look for the shared term and use that as the middle of your link. In this case, the shared term is "likes ice cream":

child → likes ice cream → buys ice cream ⋯> rich

We're almost there! We're missing just that last link (and that is usually the case). We need to know the following:

buys ice cream → rich

In other words, we need to assume:

Anyone who buys ice cream is rich.

8

If we put this back into the argument we'll see that this is exactly the missing link that we needed:

child → likes ice cream → buys ice cream → rich

Meaning, we can now say that every child is rich, or "child → rich."

Let's review the steps we took:

1. We recognized the conditional triggers. Since there were three conditional statements in the original argument, we knew we could attack this question by linking conditionals.

2. We translated the conditionals into arrow notation.

3. Because the conclusion was a conditional statement, we "spread it out." We used the premises to try to fill in the gap (the space between the sufficient and necessary parts of the conclusion).

4. We identified the assumption by considering what we needed to complete the chain.

5. Spreading out the conclusion is a great tool—but it works only when the conclusion is a conditional statement. Don't overapply this idea! Some arguments that involve conditional logic have conclusions that are *not* conditional relationships; they are simply a fulfilled condition, the last element in a conditional chain, as we saw in the Westside school question earlier.

Conditional Logic 6: Conditional Conclusions

Let's try it on a real question. Push yourself to use a formal approach:

> ### PT35, S1, Q14
>
> Novelists cannot become great as long as they remain in academia. Powers of observation and analysis, which schools successfully hone, are useful to the novelist, but an intuitive grasp of the emotions of everyday life can be obtained only by the kind of immersion in everyday life that is precluded by being an academic.
>
> Which one of the following is an assumption on which the argument depends?
>
> (A)   Novelists require some impartiality to get an intuitive grasp of the emotions of everyday life.
>
> (B)   No great novelist lacks powers of observation and analysis.
>
> (C)   Participation in life, interspersed with impartial observation of life, makes novelists great.
>
> (D)   Novelists cannot be great without an intuitive grasp of the emotions of everyday life.
>
> (E)   Knowledge of the emotions of everyday life cannot be acquired by merely observing and analyzing life.

Of course, this question can be tackled without diagramming the conditional logic. However, since that is the focus of this chapter, let's work the problem through that lens. If you did not use a diagram, try the question one more time.

Let's look at each sentence in isolation to see if we can express it in conditional terms:

> Novelists cannot become great as long as they remain in academia.

Believe it or not, this is a conditional statement. The big clue is the verb of certainty, *cannot*. Think about it in terms of guarantees. Does being or doing one thing guarantee another? Indeed. Being an academic novelist guarantees that you will NOT be, or *cannot* be, a great novelist. In other words, if you are an academic novelist, then you are NOT a great novelist:

> academic novelist → –great novelist

MANHATTAN
PREP

Powers of observation and analysis, which schools successfully hone, are useful to the novelist,

This statement has no conditional structure, so let's leave it for now.

> but an intuitive grasp of the emotions of everyday life can be obtained only by the kind of immersion in everyday life that is precluded by being an academic.

Did you spot the "only" trigger? "An intuitive grasp of the emotions of everyday life can be obtained *only* by immersion in everyday life." Thus, if you are to have an intuitive grasp of everyday emotions, then you must immerse yourself in everyday life:

> intuitive grasp of emotions → immerse in everyday life

This sentence also contains a second conditional. Immersion in everyday life is precluded by being an academic. In other words, if you are an academic, you cannot immerse yourself in everyday life:

> academic → –immerse in everyday life

So, now we have the following conditionals:

> intuitive grasp of emotions → immerse in everyday life
> academic → –immerse in everyday life

And these premises lead to the following conclusion:

> academic novelist → –great novelist

This is the relationship that we have to prove! Let's spread out the conclusion on our scratch paper:

> academic novelist ⋯>   ⋯> –great novelist

Next step, use the premises to fill in as much as we can. Given that an academic novelist is an academic, and that an intuitive grasp of emotions requires an immersion in everyday life, we can fill in quite a bit:

> academic novelist → –immerse in everyday life → –intuitive grasp of emotions

But we can't get all the way to *–great novelist*. We're missing the final link from *–intuitive grasp of emotions* to *–great novelist,* and thus we still cannot conclude that *academic novelist* → *–great novelist*.

We need to assume this:

> –intuitive grasp of emotions → –great novelist

In other words, if you don't have an intuitive grasp of emotions, you can't be a great novelist. This is exactly what answer (D) says:

> (D)   Novelists cannot be great without an intuitive
>   grasp of the emotions of everyday life.

Therefore, (D) is correct. When we approach a question like this using conditional logic and formal notation, we can predict the answer almost to a T. Here, we didn't analyze each answer choice, but instead simply compared it to our prediction. If you practice conditional logic enough, you can get to the correct answer very quickly in a question like this!

Some and Most

Okay, we've spent the entire chapter harping on the idea that conditional statements express guarantees. We include a discussion of "some" and "most" here because "some" and "most" statements do *not* express guarantees, but they are often confused with conditional statements. Here's an example illustrating the difference:

> All movies have a message. (movie → message)

This means every movie. Every time. Always. No exceptions. Guaranteed.

> Most movies have a message.

We might be tempted to write *movie → message*, but "most" means "most," *not* "all"! In other words, for any given movie, there's a good chance (more than half) that it will have a message, but it's *not* guaranteed.

> Some movies have a message.

This is even less certain. "Some" simply means more than zero—at least one. "Some" is definitely not a guarantee.

If we can't treat "some" and "most" statements in the same way that we treat conditional statements, what do we do with them?

First, it's important to understand the context of "some" and "most" on the LSAT. Generally speaking, "some" and "most" statements are used most often on Inference questions. So, when learning how to deal with these statements, it's very important to think about these statements in terms of inferences. In other words, given a set of "some" and "most" statements, what can we infer? What do we know *for sure*? Let's develop a set of rules that will come in handy in drawing valid inferences from "some" and "most" statements.

"Some" and "Most" Equivalents

The first step is to be able to recognize and understand the words and phrases that are synonyms of "some" and "most." Here's a list of the most common:

Words and Phrases	Definition
some	**one or more**
most	**more than half**
a few	= some
majority	= most
nearly all	= most
many	= some

Single Statement Inferences

Next, we need to understand what sorts of inferences we can draw from a single "some" or "most" statement. Look at this:

> Some teachers are musicians.

Can we reverse this statement? Indeed we can. If some teachers are musicians, then it must be true that some musicians are teachers (maybe not most or all, but definitely some). So, we have our first inference:

Original Statement	Inference
Some A's are B's.	Some B's are A's.

What about this one?

> Most ice cream is delicious.

Can we reverse this one? We've purposely chosen a real-life statement to make it easier to consider. Think about it. Most ice cream is delicious. Are most delicious things ice cream? Of course not. There are zillions of delicious foods that are not ice cream. This statement cannot necessarily be reversed. The only thing we know for sure is that *some* delicious things (even if just a tiny fraction) are ice cream. This leads to our second inference:

Original Statement	Inference
Some A's are B's.	Some B's are A's.
Most A's are B's.	Some B's are A's.

Now, let's look at this one:

> All apples are fruits.

This sort of statement should be familiar—it's a conditional statement, a guarantee. All apples, every apple, every single one, is a fruit. We already know that we *cannot* reverse this one, but we also know from this statement that some fruits must be apples:

Original Statement	Inference
Some A's are B's.	Some B's are A's.
Most A's are B's.	Some B's are A's.
All A's are B's.	Some B's are A's.

Not too bad, right? Now, let's see what happens when we get more than one statement.

Multiple Statement Inferences

Suppose we had the following two statements:

> Some people are happy.
> Some people are old.

What can you infer? Can you infer that some happy people are old? Or that most happy people are old? Or maybe that all happy people are old? Let's use a diagram to figure this out. Assume that the box below represents all people:

All people

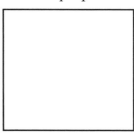

We know that *some* of these people are happy. Remember "some" means one or more. So, if we were going to shade part of the box to represent the happy people, how much would we shade? Well, it's unclear. It could be less than half, but it could also be more than half. We'll start with this—the stars will represent the happy people:

All people

We also know that *some* people are old. "Some" means one or more. Let's use circles to represent the old people:

All people

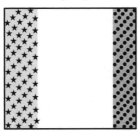

This is a valid representation of our statements, isn't it? Some are happy and some are old. So what can we conclude? It seems from the picture that we would conclude that no happy people are old. In other words, the patterns don't overlap. Be careful though. Couldn't we have represented our statements like this?

All people

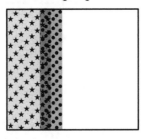

Or maybe even like this?

All people

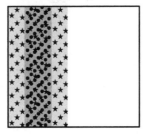

The answer is yes. All three of these representations are accurate. Each one of them *could* be an actual representation of the statements. However, we don't know *for sure* that any of them represent the actual scenario, so we can't really conclude anything. Maybe none of them overlap (no old people are happy), maybe some of them overlap (some old people are happy), or maybe all of them overlap (all old people are happy). Without more information, we can't know for sure. This leads to our first overlap inference:

Original Statement	Overlap Type	Overlap Inference
Some A's are B's. Some A's are C's.	Some + Some	Can't infer anything about overlap between B and C. (They may or may not overlap.)

Let's look at two more statements:

> Most people are happy.
>
> Some people are old.

We can analyze this using the same thought process. "Most" means more than half, and "some" means one or more. We'll start by filling in "most" of the box with happy people:

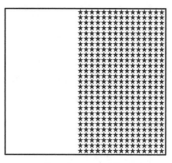

Since we're dealing with a "most" statement, we need to be sure that more than half of the box is filled.

Take a second and think about how you could shade the box with old people. Remember, "some" people are old. There are actually a number of possibilities, aren't there? Here are three such possibilities:

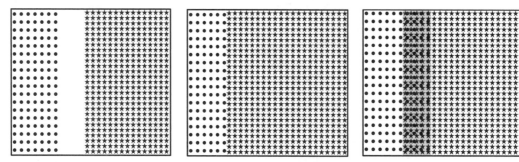

Most people are happy (stars), and some people are old (circles). Do we know if they overlap? Well, they might (the right picture), but they might not (the left picture and the center picture). Perhaps all the old people are happy! We don't know for sure, so we can't infer anything about the overlap.

Original Statement	Overlap Type	Overlap Inference
Some A's are B's. Some A's are C's.	Some + Some	Can't infer anything about overlap between B and C. (They may or may not overlap.)
Most A's are B's. Some A's are C's.	Most + Some	Can't infer anything about overlap between B and C. (They may or may not overlap.)

One more combination:

> Most people are happy.
>
> Most people are old.

Now, set your timer for 2 minutes. Use this time to really think about what you can or cannot infer about the overlap of happy and old in this case. Use a box diagram if need be, and don't read on until you have an answer.

Again, we'll start by filling "most" of the box with happies:

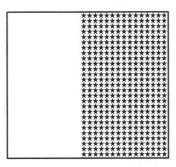

"Most" people are also old. We'll need to fill "most" of the box with old people as well. There are a few ways we can do this:

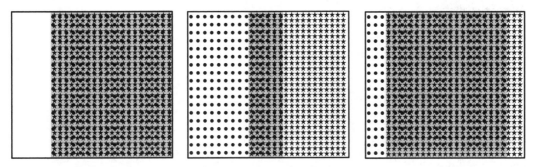

All of these are valid, aren't they? In all three cases, more than half the box are stars, and more than half are circles. And, in every case, there is at least *some* overlap. Try to come up with a shaded scenario for which there is no overlap. You can't do it. (If you're having trouble seeing that, imagine there are only ten people in the world; you'll need at least six happies and six oldies. Can you avoid an overlap?) When we combine two "most" statements, at least *some* will always overlap:

Original Statement	Overlap Type	Overlap Inference
Some A's are B's. Some A's are C's.	Some + Some	Can't infer anything about overlap between B and C. (They may or may not overlap.)
Most A's are B's. Some A's are C's.	Most + Some	Can't infer anything about overlap between B and C. (They may or may not overlap.)
Most A's are B's. Most A's are C's.	Most + Most	Some B's are C's.

Got it? Time to practice.

Drill It: Some and Most

Choose the answer that must be true from the information given.

1. Some cars are sedans and some cars are red.

    (A)   Most cars that are sedans are red.

    (B)   Some things that are red are cars.

    (C)   None of the above.

2. Most people are patient and most people are sympathetic.

    (A)   Some sympathetic people are patient.

    (B)   Most patient people are sympathetic.

    (C)   None of the above.

3. Most children play sports and some children play instruments.

    (A)   Some children who play instruments play sports.

    (B)   Some people who play sports are children.

    (C)   None of the above.

4. Many dogs weigh more than 20 pounds and many dogs are difficult to train.

    (A)   Most dogs that weigh more than 20 pounds are difficult to train.

    (B)   Some dogs that are difficult to train weigh more than 20 pounds.

    (C)   None of the above.

5. The majority of flights arrive late and few flights have empty seats.

    (A)   Some flights with empty seats arrive late.

    (B)   Most flights that arrive late have empty seats.

    (C)   None of the above.

6. Every ethical person succeeds and some Americans are ethical.

    (A)   Some people who succeed are Americans.

    (B)   Most Americans succeed.

    (C)   None of the above.

7. Nearly all of Jason's books are fiction books and all of Jason's books are written in Spanish.

    (A)   Most of Jason's books are fiction books written in Spanish.

    (B)   Most of Jason's books are not fiction books.

    (C)   None of the above.

8. Some children are happy, some children are healthy, and some children are smart.

    (A)   Some children are both happy and healthy.

    (B)   Some children are at once happy, healthy, and smart.

    (C)   None of the above.

| Want more practice? |
| Try playing "Ah-hah" in our LSAT Arcade. |
| (www.manhattanprep.com/lsat/arcade) |

Solutions: Some and Most

Choose the answer that must be true from the information given.

1. Some cars are sedans and some cars are red.

    (A) Most cars that are sedans are red.

    (B) Some things that are red are cars.

    (C) None of the above.

2. Most people are patient and most people are sympathetic.

    (A) Some sympathetic people are patient.

    (B) Most patient people are sympathetic.

    (C) None of the above.

3. Most children play sports and some children play instruments.

    (A) Some children who play instruments play sports.

    (B) Some people who play sports are children.

    (C) None of the above.

4. Many dogs weigh more than 20 pounds and many dogs are difficult to train.

    (A) Most dogs that weigh more than 20 pounds are difficult to train.

    (B) Some dogs that are difficult to train weigh more than 20 pounds.

    (C) None of the above.

5. The majority of flights arrive late and few flights have empty seats.

    (A) Some flights with empty seats arrive late.

    (B) Most flights that arrive late have empty seats.

    (C) None of the above.

6. Every ethical person succeeds and some Americans are ethical.

    (A) Some people who succeed are Americans.

    (B) Most Americans succeed.

    (C) None of the above.

7. Nearly all of Jason's books are fiction books and all of Jason's books are written in Spanish.

    (A) Most of Jason's books are fiction books written in Spanish.

    (B) Most of Jason's books are not fiction books.

    (C) None of the above.

8. Some children are happy, some children are healthy, and some children are smart.

    (A) Some children are both happy and healthy.

    (B) Some children are at once happy, healthy, and smart.

    (C) None of the above.

Conclusion

We've covered a lot of ground in conditional logic! Here's a summary of the main points:

1. A standard conditional statement is expressed in If/Then form:

    IF one is happy, THEN one is smiling.

2. The "If" part of the statement is called the *sufficient* condition, because it is *sufficient* on its own to guarantee the "Then" part of the statement. The "Then" part of the statement is called the *necessary* condition, because it must be true when the sufficient condition is satisfied.

3. We can express conditional statements using arrow notation:

    happy → smiling

4. For any conditional statement, the *contrapositive* can be inferred. The *contrapositive* is found by reversing and negating the original statement:

    –smiling → –happy

5. There are four types of compound conditionals. Some can be split into two separate statements; others cannot:

    AND in the Outcome (split):

    If one is happy, then one is smiling AND cheerful.

    happy → smiling

    happy → cheerful

    OR in the Trigger (split):

    If one is happy OR cheerful, then one is smiling.

    happy → smiling

    cheerful → smiling

    AND in the Trigger (can't split):

    If one is happy AND cheerful, then one is smiling.

    happy + cheerful → smiling

    OR in the Outcome (can't split):

    If one is happy, then one is smiling OR cheerful.

    happy → smiling or cheerful

6. To take the contrapositive of a compound conditional statement, reverse and negate the terms and swap AND for OR (or vice versa):

> happy + cheerful → smiling
>> –smiling → –happy or –cheerful

>> party → birthday or graduation
> –birthday + –graduation → –party

7. "Only" is one of the most important words on the LSAT. Watch out for "only if" and "if and only if" language:

> Jenny smiles only if she is happy.
> smiles → happy

> Jenny smiles if, and only if, she is happy.
> smiles ⟷ happy

8. Be on the lookout for words that express a guarantee. Words like "always," "never," "every," "anyone," "everyone," etc., are generally used on the LSAT to express conditional relationships:

> Every child likes chocolate.
> child → likes chocolate

9. "Unless" is used to express a conditional statement:

> The picnic will be canceled unless the sun comes out.
> –sun comes out → canceled picnic

10. Learn to link conditional statements to form a conditional chain:

> A → B
> B → C
> So, A → B → C

11. "Some" and "most" are not "all"! Don't confuse "some" and "most" with conditional logic. Know your "some" and "most" rules—you'll need them on some Inference questions.

Drill It: Conditional Logic Questions

The following questions represent a mix of question types, some of which you have not yet studied. The common thread is that each question contains conditional logic. You will be forced to use your understanding of conditional logic in flexible ways, so don't get too mechanical!

1. PT13, S2, Q9

In a mature tourist market such as Bellaria there are only two ways hotel owners can increase profits: by building more rooms or by improving what is already there. Rigid land-use laws in Bellaria rule out construction of new hotels or, indeed, any expansion of hotel capacity. It follows that hotel owners cannot increase their profits in Bellaria since Bellarian hotels

_____.

Which one of the following logically completes the argument?

(A)   are already operating at an occupancy rate approaching 100 percent year-round

(B)   could not have been sited any more attractively than they are even in the absence of land-use laws

(C)   have to contend with upward pressures on the cost of labor which stem from an incipient shortage of trained personnel

(D)   already provide a level of luxury that is at the limits of what even wealthy patrons are prepared to pay for

(E)   have shifted from serving mainly Bellarian tourists to serving foreign tourists traveling in organized tour groups

2. PT23, S2, Q9

Every action has consequences, and among the consequences of any action are other actions. And knowing whether an action is good requires knowing whether its consequences are good, but we cannot know the future, so good actions are impossible.

Which one of the following is an assumption on which the argument depends?

(A)   Some actions have only other actions as consequences.

(B)   We can know that past actions were good.

(C)   To know that an action is good requires knowing that refraining from performing it is bad.

(D)   Only actions can be the consequences of other actions.

(E)   For an action to be good we must be able to know that it is good.

3. PT23, S3, Q14

If the proposed tax reduction package is adopted this year, the library will be forced to discontinue its daily story hours for children. But if the daily story hours are discontinued, many parents will be greatly inconvenienced. So the proposed tax reduction package will not be adopted this year.

Which one of the following, if assumed, allows the argument's conclusion to be properly drawn?

(A)   Any tax reduction package that will not force the library to discontinue daily story hours will be adopted this year.

(B)   Every tax reduction package that would force the library to discontinue daily story hours would greatly inconvenience parents.

(C)   No tax reduction package that would greatly inconvenience parents would fail to force the library to discontinue daily story hours.

(D)   No tax reduction package that would greatly inconvenience parents will be adopted this year.

(E)   Any tax reduction package that will not greatly inconvenience parents will be adopted this year.

4. PT24, S2, Q24

No mathematical proposition can be proven true by observation. It follows that it is impossible to know any mathematical proposition to be true.

The conclusion follows logically if which one of the following is assumed?

(A)   Only propositions that can be proven true can be known to be true.

(B)   Observation alone cannot be used to prove the truth of any proposition.

(C)   If a proposition can be proven true by observation, then it can be known to be true.

(D)   Knowing a proposition to be true is impossible only if it cannot be proven true by observation.

(E)   Knowing a proposition to be true requires proving it true by observation.

MANHATTAN
PREP

5. PT18, S2, Q23

Teachers are effective only when they help their students become independent learners. Yet not until teachers have the power to make decisions in their own classrooms can they enable their students to make their own decisions. Students' capability to make their own decisions is essential to their becoming independent learners. Therefore, if teachers are to be effective, they must have the power to make decisions in their own classrooms.

According to the argument, each of the following could be true of teachers who have enabled their students to make their own decisions EXCEPT:

(A)   Their students have not become independent learners.

(B)   They are not effective teachers.

(C)   They are effective teachers.

(D)   They have the power to make decisions in their own classrooms.

(E)   They do not have the power to make decisions in their own classrooms.

6. PT24, S3, Q10

All material bodies are divisible into parts, and everything divisible is imperfect. It follows that all material bodies are imperfect. It likewise follows that the spirit is not a material body.

The final conclusion above follows logically if which one of the following is assumed?

(A)   Everything divisible is a material body.

(B)   Nothing imperfect is indivisible.

(C)   The spirit is divisible.

(D)   The spirit is perfect.

(E)   The spirit is either indivisible or imperfect.

8

Solutions: Conditional Logic Questions

Answer Key

1. D   4. E

2. E   5. E

3. D   6. D

1. PT13, S2, Q9

In a mature tourist market such as Bellaria there are only two ways hotel owners can increase profits: by building more rooms or by improving what is already there. Rigid land-use laws in Bellaria rule out construction of new hotels or, indeed, any expansion of hotel capacity. It follows that hotel owners cannot increase their profits in Bellaria since Bellarian hotels _____.

Which one of the following logically completes the argument?

(A)   are already operating at an occupancy rate approaching 100 percent year-round

(B)   could not have been sited any more attractively than they are even in the absence of land-use laws

(C)   have to contend with upward pressures on the cost of labor which stem from an incipient shortage of trained personnel

(D)   already provide a level of luxury that is at the limits of what even wealthy patrons are prepared to pay for

(E)   have shifted from serving mainly Bellarian tourists to serving foreign tourists traveling in organized tour groups

Answer choice (D) is correct.

We're facing an Inference question, which is not in the Assumption Family, so there's no core to find. This type of question will be covered in Chapter 11. Instead of a core, we're given a rule and asked to apply it. The rule is:

$$\text{more hotel profits} \rightarrow \text{more rooms or improving}$$

The contrapositive is:

$$\text{NOT more rooms and NOT improving} \rightarrow \text{NOT more hotel profits}$$

Then we're told that it's impossible to build more rooms, and thus hotel owners cannot increase their profits since _____.

We're looking for something that completes this argument. If the conclusion is NOT more hotel profits, we can arrive at that by "triggering" the sufficient side of the contrapositive shown above. We already know that the hotels cannot build more rooms, so the argument will be valid if improvements to the hotels are also impossible.

(D) provides the other part of the sufficient condition. If hotels are already providing the highest level of luxury possible (or at least what even the wealthy customers are willing to pay for), then the hotels cannot improve upon what already exists. Because of how it's phrased, this isn't an obvious answer, so understanding why the wrong answers are wrong comes in handy.

(A) is irrelevant to the argument. Full occupancy does not lead to "NOT more hotel profits." Perhaps in the real world this would be relevant, but we're asked to complete the argument provided.

(B) is out of scope. Where the hotel is sited is irrelevant as far as the argument is concerned.

(C) is out of scope—the cost of labor is relevant in the real world, but it's not discussed in the argument.

MANHATTAN
PREP

Furthermore, how much will the cost of labor rise? Will it become a problem?

(E) is completely irrelevant.

2. PT23, S2, Q9

Every action has consequences, and among the consequences of any action are other actions. And knowing whether an action is good requires knowing whether its consequences are good, but we cannot know the future, so good actions are impossible.

Which one of the following is an assumption on which the argument depends?

(A)   Some actions have only other actions as consequences.

(B)   We can know that past actions were good.

(C)   To know that an action is good requires knowing that refraining from performing it is bad.

(D)   Only actions can be the consequences of other actions.

(E)   For an action to be good we must be able to know that it is good.

Answer choice (E) is correct.

Let's look at this question using an approach based on formal notation and then again using one based on the argument core.

> Every action has consequences:
>
> action   →   consequences
>
> And among the consequences of any action are other actions:
>
> consequences   →   actions

Hmm, where is this going? So far we just get from one action to others.

> And knowing whether an action is good requires knowing whether its consequences are good:

> know action   →   know consequences
>   good   good

But we cannot know the future:

> −know consequences good

Note: Since the consequences happen after the action, it's clear that the argument is suggesting that we cannot know whether the consequences will be good.

> So good actions are impossible:
>
> −action good

Going back over the argument, it looks like that first sentence was really just background introducing the idea that actions have consequences. Here are the key elements of the argument core:

> know action good → know consequences good
> −know consequences good
> ———————————————————
> −action good

In this sort of argument structure, our goal is to get from the premise *−know consequences good* to the conclusion *−action good,* using the given relationships. The final premise, *−know consequences good,* triggers the contrapositive of the relationship *know action good → know consequences good.*

Rewriting the argument yields this:

> −know consequences good → −know action good
> −know consequences good
> ———————————————————
> −action good

We're missing this connection:

> −know action good   →   −action good

Looking for an answer that might be a match, none of (A) through (D) talk about both actions *being* good and us *knowing* that actions are good. Let's check (E):

(E) For an action to be good we must
be able to know that it is good.

This can be notated:

action good　　→　　know action good

And the contrapositive matches the missing link that we identified:

−know action good　　→　　−action good

Core Approach

The conclusion of this argument is that good actions are impossible. How sad. Support for this is provided in the beginning of that sentence: "… we cannot know the future and thus whether consequences are good." But why is that relevant? The first sentence provides the other premise: Knowing whether an action is good requires knowing whether its consequences are good.

The core can be represented like this:

we have to know if
consequences are good to
know if an action is good　　➡　　good
　　　　　　　+　　　　　　　　　actions are
we cannot know future　　　　　impossible
(consequences)

With a bit of thinking, the two premises can be combined into one premise, leaving us with this core:

we cannot know if　　➡　　good actions
an action is good　　　　　are impossible

Did you notice the term shift? The premises are focused on whether an action or its consequences can be known to be good, while the conclusion is about whether a good action is possible.

Scanning the answer choices, only (E) connects knowing whether an action is good and that action being good. If we negate (E)—this is a Necessary

Assumption question, so the negation test applies here—we get something like this: "An action can be good even if we don't know that it is good." If that were true, the argument would not make sense, since good actions would be possible.

The wrong answers all fail to connect the premises to the conclusion.

(A) does not discuss actions being possible.

(B) does not address whether any actions actually were good. Besides, if we did know that some past actions were good, this would actually weaken the argument!

(C) is out of scope—the argument is not about whether one refrains from an action or what one knows if one refrains.

(D) does not discuss an action being good. This looks like a confused version of the first sentence. We know that consequences *lead to* actions, not that they *are* actions.

Which approach is easier or faster? It's important to be judicious in using your formal logic notations. Sometimes fancier isn't faster.

3. PT23, S3, Q14

If the proposed tax reduction package is adopted this year, the library will be forced to discontinue its daily story hours for children. But if the daily story hours are discontinued, many parents will be greatly inconvenienced. So the proposed tax reduction package will not be adopted this year.

Which one of the following, if assumed, allows the argument's conclusion to be properly drawn?

(A)　Any tax reduction package that will not force the library to discontinue daily story hours will be adopted this year

MANHATTAN
PREP

(B)   Every tax reduction package that would force the library to discontinue daily story hours would greatly inconvenience parents.

(C)   No tax reduction package that would greatly inconvenience parents would fail to force the library to discontinue daily story hours.

(D)   No tax reduction package that would greatly inconvenience parents will be adopted this year.

(E)   Any tax reduction package that will not greatly inconvenience parents will be adopted this year.

Answer choice (D) is correct.

This argument can be approached formally:

$$\text{tax adopted} \rightarrow -\text{story hour} \rightarrow \text{many parents inconvenienced}$$

Therefore, tax NOT adopted.

How can this argument chain lead to the tax package NOT being adopted? The contrapositive of the chain leads to that:

$$-\text{many parents inconvenienced} \rightarrow \text{story hour} \rightarrow -\text{tax adopted}$$

To trigger this chain, we'd need to know that parents will not accept being inconvenienced. More specifically, as (D) states, no legislation that will inconvenience parents will be adopted. In other words, parents will not accept the original chain being triggered as they refuse to endure its final result.

(A) is out of scope since it is about tax reductions that do not discontinue story hours. Answer choice (A)'s logic, story hour → adopted, is not helpful to the argument.

(B) is an extreme premise booster. We already know that –story hour → inconvenience. It's irrelevant whether this is true for all tax reduction packages.

(C) is a bit confusing. When a statement is filled with negatives, try to restate it in the positive. We can rephrase answer (C) as: "Every tax reduction package that would inconvenience parents will force the end of story hours." This is similar to (B). We already know what would happen if the proposed tax reduction package were to pass.

(E) is similar to answer (A). We aren't interested in tax reductions that do not inconvenience parents.

4. PT24, S2, Q24

No mathematical proposition can be proven true by observation. It follows that it is impossible to know any mathematical proposition to be true.

The conclusion follows logically if which one of the following is assumed?

(A)   Only propositions that can be proven true can be known to be true.

(B)   Observation alone cannot be used to prove the truth of any proposition.

(C)   If a proposition can be proven true by observation, then it can be known to be true.

(D)   Knowing a proposition to be true is impossible only if it cannot be proven true by observation.

(E)   Knowing a proposition to be true requires proving it true by observation.

Answer choice (E) is correct.

With this problem, the core approach and a more formal approach feel quite similar. Here's the core:

$$\text{mathematical propositions can't be proven true by observation} \implies \text{mathematical propositions can't be known to be true}$$

The key is to notice the term shift. The premise is about proving something true by observation, while the conclusion is about something being known to be true. If you were reading like a debater, you may have

8

thought, "Perhaps some things are known to be true even though they cannot be proven true by observation. For example, they may be provable through deduction."

More formally, the premise tells us that if something is a math proposition, then it can't be proven by observation:

$$\text{proposition} \rightarrow \text{not provable by observation}$$

It concludes with another relationship:

$$\text{proposition} \rightarrow \text{not possible to know it's true}$$

The premise tell us we can get from proposition to not provable by observation, but we don't know the missing link between that and not possible to know it's true.

(E) fills this gap: know that proposition is true → proving true by observation. Its contrapositive is: can't be proven true by observation → can't know proposition to be true.

There are some very tempting wrong answers here:

(A) provides us this: propositions known to be true → propositions proven true. The contrapositive is: propositions not proven true → propositions not known to be true. This seems like what we need—it definitely has terms we saw in the argument and the necessary condition is a perfect match. However, (A) is not specific about proving true "by observation." Answer choice (A) may seem like a sufficient assumption since it is broader than what we need. However, the fact that something can't be proven true by observation does not mean that it cannot be proven true by some other means. Thus, the assumption might not apply.

Consider this analogous flaw:

If you don't own some sort of vehicle, you can't move heavy furniture. So,

if Peter doesn't have an SUV, he can't move the couch.

Perhaps Peter has a truck!

(B) connects observation and proving the truth of something. This is a premise booster. We already know that observation can't prove a mathematical proposition. Where's the connection to knowing something to be true?

(C) tells us: proposition proven true → known to be true. This is the negation of what we need.

(D) is tempting since it references proving by observation. But the logic is the reverse of what we need. The conditional logic in (D) is: NOT knowing a proposition to be true → NOT proven by observation. We need: NOT proven true by observation → NOT know proposition to be true.

5. PT18, S2, Q23

Teachers are effective only when they help their students become independent learners. Yet not until teachers have the power to make decisions in their own classrooms can they enable their students to make their own decisions. Students' capability to make their own decisions is essential to their becoming independent learners. Therefore, if teachers are to be effective, they must have the power to make decisions in their own classrooms.

According to the argument, each of the following could be true of teachers who have enabled their students to make their own decisions EXCEPT:

(A)   Their students have not become independent learners.

(B)   They are not effective teachers.

(C)   They are effective teachers.

(D)   They have the power to make decisions in their own classrooms.

(E)   They do not have the power to make decisions in their own classrooms.

Answer choice (E) is correct.

MANHATTAN
PREP

What a hairy-looking question! But, when taken apart carefully, this one actually folds quite easily. First, let's notice that this is not an Assumption Family question. This is a "could be true EXCEPT" question, so what will the correct answer be? It will be something that we can infer (prove) to be false. There's no flaw or assumption to uncover in the argument. Thus, we're not reading like a debater; we're reading to grasp the rules. We can translate each sentence as follows:

Sentence 1: t. effective → s. ind. learners

Sentence 2: (t. enables) s. decisions → t. decisions

Sentence 3: s. ind. learning → s. decisions

Conclusion: t. effective → t. decisions

Notice that we've taken some liberty in paraphrasing, and that's both crucial and dangerous. In order to quickly boil down an argument to simple statements, we often have to reduce ideas like "the power to make decisions in their own classrooms" to "t. decisions," but it's important to know that we may have lost some crucial details and that we may need to reconsider those details if we find multiple tempting answer choices.

Let's link up our statements. From the conclusion, we know that we can link all the way from t. effective to t. decisions. Indeed, it is possible:

t. effective → s. ind. learners → s. decisions → t. decisions

The question asks us what cannot be possible if (t. enables) s. decisions. Looking at our chain, that's triggering our third element, requiring (i.e., triggering) all the elements that are down the chain. In this case, all that is required is t. make decisions, and so we know that (E) cannot be true.

Three of the wrong answers are not on the chain or require us to read the chain in reverse. For that reason, they could be true or false. We don't know one way or another.

(A) offers something not even on the chain: s. NOT ind. learners.

(B) is similar: t. NOT effective.

(C) is tempting, since t. effective is on the chain. However, we cannot go backwards along a logic chain. That would be an illegal reversal!

(D) is t. make decisions, something that we can infer! But don't forget your mission—we need to find what *cannot* be true.

6. PT24, S3, Q10

All material bodies are divisible into parts, and everything divisible is imperfect. It follows that all material bodies are imperfect. It likewise follows that the spirit is not a material body.

The final conclusion above follows logically if which one of the following is assumed?

(A)   Everything divisible is a material body.

(B)   Nothing imperfect is indivisible.

(C)   The spirit is divisible.

(D)   The spirit is perfect.

(E)   The spirit is either indivisible or imperfect.

Answer choice (D) is correct.

Core Approach

$$\text{material bodies NOT perfect} \implies \text{spirit is NOT material body}$$

The gap here is that if something is imperfect, it can't be the spirit. Or, as (D) states, the spirit is perfect.

Formal Approach

material bodies → (material bodies) divisible → (material bodies) NOT perfect
_____
(material bodies) NOT spirit

We're asked to find a sufficient assumption. (D) provides us the link between the last two elements of the chain, specifically the contrapositive: spirit → perfect (e.g., NOT imperfect).

Which is easier? It depends on you. The approaches were not very different because, as is often the case, the gap that the answer hinges upon is found in the final connection, which is essentially the core of the argument. In short, if you can get to the core of an argument, it's often faster than a more formal approach.

Looking at the wrong answers, none of them provide the right connection:

(A) provides a reversal of a relationship in the premise: divisible → material.

(B) also provides a reversal of a relationship in the premise: imperfect → divisible.

(C) tells us that spirit → divisible. If that's true, then spirit is imperfect. This doesn't help the argument; it actually negates it!

(E) offers a choice: spirit → NOT divisible or NOT perfect. If we knew that spirit is definitely NOT divisible, then we could conclude that spirit is not material (by applying the contrapositive of "All material bodies are divisible …"). However, we don't know that spirit is definitely NOT divisible, since it might be NOT perfect (it's an either/or statement!). If spirit were NOT perfect, we could not infer that spirit is immaterial; actually, we would be unable to infer anything about that using the given premises.

Time after Time

Now that you've covered the entire Assumption Family of questions *and* the type of reasoning that's most central to the LSAT (conditional logic!), you're more ready than ever to tackle a complete section. That's why, instead of doing just one complete section, you're going to do five! That's right, a full, five-section practice LSAT. If you don't have access to an LSAT with five sections, you can cannibalize a second PrepTest and allot one of its four sections to each of your next four practice exams. Heads up, if you are a student taking one of our courses, your syllabus will assign you plenty of PrepTests and complete sections. Do that work in accordance with your syllabus. The timed practice assignments contained herein are specifically for folks who are using our books but are *not* enrolled in one of our courses.

MANHATTAN
PREP

Chapter 9

Principle Example Questions

In This Chapter...

Beyond Assumption Family Questions

Up until now, we've focused almost exclusively on Assumption Family questions. We've looked at Assumption questions, Flaw questions, Strengthen questions, Weaken questions, and Principle Support questions. All of these require that we find the argument core and then choose an answer to address that core.

Now it's time to move beyond Assumption Family questions. The first Non-Assumption Family question type we'll look at is called Principle Example. This type is not to be confused with the Principle Support questions that we studied earlier.

Assumption Family	Non-Assumption Family
Assumption questions	
Flaw questions	
Strengthen questions	
Weaken questions	
you are here	
Principle Support ------------●------------▶	**Principle** Example
	Analyze Argument
	Inference questions
	Matching questions

Principle Support Review

Remember that Principle Support questions are Assumption Family questions. They require us to find the core in a given argument and then choose a principle that supports that core by bridging the gap between the premise and the conclusion. Here's a very simple example to jog your memory:

> The bag of cash that Sanjay found was not claimed by anyone. Thus, Sanjay should keep the bag of cash for himself.

This argument has a premise and conclusion, and a pretty significant gap between the two. If this were a Principle Support question, we would want to choose a principle to bridge the gap. Perhaps the correct answer would be something like this:

9

One should keep for oneself anything one finds that is not claimed by anyone else.

If we insert the principle into the core, we get:

The bag of cash that Sanjay found was not claimed by anyone. (One should keep for oneself anything one finds that is not claimed by anyone else.) Thus, Sanjay should keep the bag of cash for himself.

In short, we're given an argument and we're asked to choose a principle to support the argument. We know we're dealing with a Principle Support question when we get language such as this:

Which one of the following PRINCIPLES most helps to JUSTIFY the reasoning above?

Which one of the following PRINCIPLES provides the most SUPPORT for the argument?

Principle Example questions are different. For Principle Example questions, we're *given* a principle and then asked to choose an example that conforms to that principle.

The Principle Example Mind-Set: Conform to the Conditions

Have a look at this. You'll notice that this is the same principle from above:

One should keep for oneself anything one finds that is not claimed by anyone else.

Which one of the following judgments most closely CONFORMS to the PRINCIPLE above?

This time, the principle is given to us and we're asked to choose an answer that conforms to the principle. Did you notice that the principle can be expressed in conditional terms? The word "anything" should have been a clue.

one found something

+   ➡   should keep for oneself

no one else claimed it

Here's an answer choice that would work:

The bag of cash that Sanjay found was not claimed by anyone. Thus, Sanjay should keep the bag of cash for himself.

Notice that the statement above satisfies the criteria in the sufficient condition (found something + no one claimed it), which means the necessary condition is triggered (he should keep it).

Much of the time (not always), this is how these questions work. We're given a general principle that can be expressed in conditional form, and then we're asked to choose an answer that conforms to the conditional statement.

Simple enough, right? Let's try it on a real LSAT question. Focus on getting a good translation of the principle. If you want to try this under timed conditions, give yourself 1:20.

PT23, S3, Q24

A person's failure to keep a promise is wrong only if, first, doing so harms the one to whom the promise is made and, second, all of those who discover the failure to keep the promise lose confidence in the person's ability to keep promises.

Which one of the following judgments most closely conforms to the principle above?

(A)   Ann kept her promise to repay Felicia the money she owed her. Further, this convinced everyone who knew Ann that she is trustworthy. Thus, Ann's keeping her promise was not wrong.

(B)   Jonathan took an oath of secrecy concerning the corporation's technical secrets, but he sold them to a competitor. His action was wrong even though the corporation intended that he leak these secrets to its competitors.

(C)   George promised to repay Reiko the money he owed her. However, George was unable to keep his promise to Reiko and as a result, Reiko suffered a serious financial loss. Thus, George's failure to keep his promise was wrong.

(D)   Because he lost his job, Carlo was unable to repay the money he promised to Miriam. However, Miriam did not need this money nor did she lose confidence in Carlo's ability to keep promises. So, Carlo's failure to keep his promise to Miriam was not wrong.

(E)   Elizabeth promised to return the book she borrowed from Steven within a week, but she was unable to do so because she became acutely ill. Not knowing this, Steven lost confidence in her ability to keep a promise. So, Elizabeth's failure to return the book to Steven was wrong.

Were you able to translate the original principle into a conditional statement? If you had trouble, go back and start with the "only if" conditional trigger. Try it again before reading on.

Here's how the principle breaks down into conditional form:

$$\text{failure to keep promise is wrong} \quad \rightarrow \quad \begin{array}{c} \text{harm} \\ + \\ \text{lost confidence} \end{array}$$

We can split this into two conditionals:

$$\text{failure to keep promise is wrong} \quad \rightarrow \quad \text{harm}$$

$$\text{failure to keep promise is wrong} \quad \rightarrow \quad \text{lost confidence}$$

Now, we're looking for an answer choice that conforms to one or both of these conditional statements. So what are the wrong answers going to do? You got it. The wrong answers are likely to reverse or negate the logic. Let's look at the answer choices:

> (A)　Ann kept her promise to repay Felicia the money she owed her. Further, this convinced everyone who knew Ann that she is trustworthy. Thus, Ann's keeping her promise was not wrong.

We know what happens when failing to keep a promise is wrong (there are two outcomes), but do we know anything about what happens when a promise is kept? We don't. This answer does not conform to the principle, so we can eliminate it.

> (B)　Jonathan took an oath of secrecy concerning the corporation's technical secrets, but he sold them to a competitor. His action was wrong even though the corporation intended that he leak these secrets to its competitors.

Jonathan failed to keep a promise, and this was apparently wrong, but this answer gives no indication of whether this led to harm or lost confidence. In other words, we get no necessary condition with this answer choice. This does not conform to the principle.

(C)   George promised to repay Reiko the money he
      owed her. However, George was unable to
      keep his promise to Reiko and as a result,
      Reiko suffered a serious financial loss. Thus,
      George's failure to keep his promise was wrong.

Harm was done to Reiko, so George's failure to keep his promise was wrong.

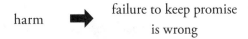

harm ➡ failure to keep promise
          is wrong

This is reversed logic! This answer looks attractive because it contains many of the component parts of the conditional statement, but it does not conform.

(D)   Because he lost his job, Carlo was unable to
      repay the money he promised to Miriam.
      However, Miriam did not need this money
      nor did she lose confidence in Carlo's ability
      to keep promises. So, Carlo's failure to keep
      his promise to Miriam was not wrong.

Miriam was NOT harmed, nor did she lose confidence in Carlo's ability to keep promises. Thus, Carlo's failure to keep his promise was not wrong.

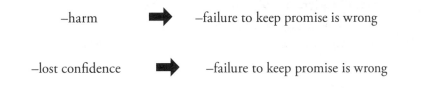

–harm ➡ –failure to keep promise is wrong

–lost confidence ➡ –failure to keep promise is wrong

Does this conform? Indeed it does. This answer choice represents the contrapositive of the original principle. This is the correct answer.

(E)   Elizabeth promised to return the book she
      borrowed from Steven within a week, but she
      was unable to do so because she became
      acutely ill. Not knowing this, Steven lost
      confidence in her ability to keep a promise.
      So, Elizabeth's failure to return the book to
      Steven was wrong.

Steven lost confidence in Elizabeth's ability to keep a promise, so Elizabeth's failure to return the book (or, Elizabeth's failure to keep her promise) was wrong.

lost confidence   failure to keep promise is wrong

This is another answer choice with reversed logic. This does not conform.

Let's try another one. If you want to try this under timed conditions, give yourself 1:20.

_PT28, S1, Q10_

It is a principle of economics that a nation can experience economic growth only when consumer confidence is balanced with a small amount of consumer skepticism.

Which one of the following is an application of the economic principle above?

(A)   Any nation in which consumer confidence is balanced with a small amount of consumer skepticism will experience economic growth.

(B)   Any nation in which the prevailing attitude of consumers is not skepticism will experience economic growth.

(C)   Any nation in which the prevailing attitude of consumers is either exclusively confidence or exclusively skepticism will experience economic growth.

(D)   Any nation in which the prevailing attitude of consumers is exclusively confidence will not experience economic growth.

(E)   Any nation in which consumer skepticism is balanced with a small amount of consumer confidence will experience economic growth.

We're looking for an answer choice that is an "application" of the economic principle given. In other words, we're looking for an answer that conforms to the principle (in either its original form or its contrapositive). The "only when" in the principle is a clue that we should translate the principle into a conditional statement. If you didn't do this the first time through, take a second to try it now.

"Only when" functions exactly the same way as "only if." So, we can translate as follows:

economic growth   consumer confidence balanced with small amount of consumer skepticism

MANHATTAN
PREP

Let's evaluate the choices. Watch out for common conditional traps!

> (A)   Any nation in which consumer confidence is
>   balanced with a small amount of consumer
>   skepticism will experience economic growth.

> consumer confidence balanced with small
> amount of consumer skepticism economic growth

Reversed logic! This does not conform. Eliminate it.

> (B)   Any nation in which the prevailing attitude of
>   consumers is not skepticism will experience
>   economic growth.

This says nothing about having a "balance" of confidence and skepticism. Besides, this logic moves in the wrong direction as well. It can be eliminated.

> (C)   Any nation in which the prevailing attitude of
>   consumers is either exclusively confidence or
>   exclusively skepticism will experience
>   economic growth.

If the consumer attitude is either exclusively confidence or exclusively skepticism, then there is NO balance. So, this is saying NO balance leads to economic growth.

> –consumer confidence balanced with small
> amount of consumer skepticism economic growth

This does not conform to the original principle. Eliminate it.

> (D)   Any nation in which the prevailing attitude of
>   consumers is exclusively confidence will not
>   experience economic growth.

Again, if the attitude is exclusively confidence, then there is NO balance. In this case, this leads to NO economic growth. In other words, this is the reversed and negated form of the original:

> –consumer confidence balanced with small
> amount of consumer skepticism –economic growth

This is the contrapositive! This does conform, so this is the correct answer.

(E)   Any nation in which consumer skepticism is
       balanced with a small amount of consumer
       confidence will experience economic growth.

This looks a lot like answer (A), reversed logic, but it has another problem as well. The modifier "small amount of" is attached to "consumer confidence." In the original, this modifier is attached to "consumer skepticism."

The Implied Principle

In the above questions, the principle was given to us directly. Sometimes, however, the LSAT will give us the principle indirectly by using a scenario to *illustrate* a principle. For example, imagine we had the following:

> Professional athletes should donate a portion of their salary to projects that improve the local community, since most professional athletes make more money than they need.

In this case, our job involves an extra dimension: We need to extract the principle from an example before we match it to the answer choices. Remember, principles can be thought of in much the same way as assumptions—they complete the connection between the premises and conclusion. The argument above can be said to be an illustration of the following principle:

> If one makes more money than one needs, then one should donate a portion of that money to the local community.

So, from the scenario we generate a principle, and, in this case, we can think of the principle in conditional terms:

make more money than needed   →   should donate some to community

Then, we would look for an answer choice that conforms.

So, how do you know when to evaluate the argument (as you would for an Assumption Family question) and how do you know when to generate a principle from the argument? It all comes down to the question stem. If the question asks you to choose an answer that conforms to the principle illustrated, you simply want to generate a principle from the given information. Let's see an example:

MANHATTAN
PREP

PT29, S4, Q10

Parents should not necessarily raise their children in the ways experts recommend, even if some of those experts are themselves parents. After all, parents are the ones who directly experience which methods are successful in raising their own children.

Which one of the following most closely conforms to the principle that the passage above illustrates?

(A) Although music theory is intrinsically interesting and may be helpful to certain musicians, it does not distinguish good music from bad: that is a matter of taste and not of theory.

(B) One need not pay much attention to the advice of automotive experts when buying a car if those experts are not interested in the mundane factors that concern the average consumer.

(C) In deciding the best way to proceed, a climber familiar with a mountain might do well to ignore the advice of mountain climbing experts unfamiliar with that mountain.

(D) A typical farmer is less likely to know what types of soil are most productive than is someone with an advanced degree in agricultural science.

(E) Unlike society, one's own conscience speaks with a single voice; it is better to follow the advice of one's own conscience than the advice of society.

The given information is clearly an argument. The premise is that parents directly experience which methods are successful and which ones are not. The conclusion is that parents shouldn't necessarily listen to experts. So, because parents have direct experience, they shouldn't always listen to experts. There are gaps in this argument, but this question asks us to choose an answer that conforms to the principle. We need to use the argument to generate a principle:

If one has direct experience, one should not necessarily act on the advice of experts.

$$\text{direct experience} \quad \rightarrow \quad -\text{act on advice of experts}$$

Let's look at the answer choices:

> (A)   Although music theory is intrinsically
>   interesting and may be helpful to certain
>   musicians, it does not distinguish good music
>   from bad: that is a matter of taste and not of
>   theory.

This has nothing to do with having experience or listening to experts. Eliminate it.

> (B)   One need not pay much attention to the advice
>   of automotive experts when buying a car if
>   those experts are not interested in the mundane
>   factors that concern the average consumer.

This does say that the advice of experts need not be heeded, but this answer choice is wrong. The advice of experts should not be heeded when "those experts are not interested." This has nothing to do with the car buyer having direct experience. Eliminate it.

> (C)   In deciding the best way to proceed, a climber
>   familiar with a mountain might do well to
>   ignore the advice of mountain climbing
>   experts unfamiliar with that mountain.

Ah, yes. The climber has direct experience, so she should ignore the advice of experts who are less familiar. This conforms to the principle, so this is the correct answer.

> (D)   A typical farmer is less likely to know what types
>   of soil are most productive than is someone
>   with an advanced degree in agricultural science.

So, should the farmer ignore the advice of experts? This isn't even close.

> (E)   Unlike society, one's own conscience speaks with
>   a single voice; it is better to follow the advice of
>   one's own conscience than the advice of society.

What about experts? What about experience? This answer is clearly wrong.

MANHATTAN
PREP

Conclusion

You're ready to try some on your own. First, let's review:

1. **Don't confuse Principle Support with Principle Example!** Principle Support questions ask you to support the argument by bridging the gap between the premise and the conclusion. The principle is the answer choice. Principle Example questions ask you to choose an answer that conforms to a *given* principle. No need to evaluate the logic of the argument.

2. **Conform to the conditions.** Many Principle Example questions will give you a principle that can be translated directly into conditional form. Your job is to choose the answer that conforms to the conditional statement.

3. **Generate a principle when the principle is implied.** Sometimes a scenario will be presented in argument form (with a premise and conclusion). Use this argument to generate a principle, and then choose an answer that conforms.

Now, let's practice.

Drill It: Principle Example Questions

1. PT43, S3, Q5

Art critic: The aesthetic value of a work of art lies in its ability to impart a stimulating character to the audience's experience of the work.

Which one of the following judgments most closely conforms with the principle cited above?

(A) This painting is aesthetically deficient because it is an exact copy of a painting done 30 years ago.

(B) This symphony is beautiful because, even though it does not excite the audience, it is competently performed.

(C) This sculpted four-inch cube is beautiful because it is carved from material which, although much like marble, is very rare.

(D) This painting is aesthetically valuable because it was painted by a highly controversial artist.

(E) This poem is aesthetically deficient because it has little impact on its audience.

2. PT35, S1, Q7

Due to wider commercial availability of audio recordings of authors reading their own books, sales of printed books have dropped significantly.

Which one of the following conforms most closely to the principle illustrated above?

(A) Because of the rising cost of farm labor, farmers began to make more extensive use of machines.

(B) Because of the wide variety of new computer games on the market, sales of high-quality computer video screens have improved.

(C) Because a new brand of soft drink entered the market, consumers reduced their consumption of an established brand of soft drink.

(D) Because a child was forbidden to play until homework was completed, that child did much less daydreaming and focused on homework.

(E) Because neither of the two leading word processing programs has all of the features consumers want, neither has been able to dominate the market.

9

3. PT39, S2, Q11

A gift is not generous unless it is intended to benefit the recipient and is worth more than what is expected or customary in the situation; a gift is selfish if it is given to benefit the giver or is less valuable than is customary.

Which one of the following judgments most closely conforms to the principle above?

(A) Charles, who hates opera, was given two expensive tickets to the opera. He in turn gave them to his cousin, who loves opera, as a birthday gift. Charles's gift was selfish because he paid nothing for the tickets.

(B) Emily gives her brother a year's membership in a health club. She thinks that this will allow her brother to get the exercise he needs. However, the gift is selfish because Emily's brother is hurt and offended by it.

(C) Amanda gives each of her clients an expensive bottle of wine every year. Amanda's gifts are generous, since they cause the clients to continue giving Amanda business.

(D) Olga gives her daughter a computer as a graduation gift. Since this is the gift that all children in Olga's family receive for graduation, it is not generous.

(E) Michael gave his nephew $50 as a birthday gift, more than he had ever given before. Michael's nephew, however, lost the money. Therefore, Michael's gift was not generous because it did not benefit the recipient.

4. PT39, S4, Q24

A park's user fees are employed to maintain the park. When fewer people use the park, it suffers less wear. Thus raising user fees improves park maintenance even if the number of people who stop using the park because of higher fees is great enough to reduce the revenues devoted to maintenance.

Which one of the following conforms most closely to the principle illustrated by the statements above?

(A) To increase its market share, a car company improves the service warranty it provides to those who purchase a new car. Making good on the warranties proves expensive enough that the company's profits decrease even though its market share increases.

(B) A grocery store's overall revenues increase even though it no longer remains open 24 hours daily. The manager theorizes that customers find the store more pleasant because it can be cleaned well during the hours it is closed.

(C) Road taxes are raised to encourage more people to use mass transit. But since the fee paid by each commuter does not equal the cost of providing transit for that commuter, a mass transit service will deteriorate even as it takes in more money.

(D) By spending more on zoo maintenance, a city increases the number of zoo patrons. The extra revenue generated by the sale of memorabilia more than makes up for the extra costs of maintenance.

(E) Library fees have been increased to raise money for book repair. Since the library now has fewer patrons, the books are in better repair even though the number of library patrons has decreased to such an extent that the money available for book repair has decreased.

9

5. PT52, S1, Q22

Moralist: A statement is wholly truthful only if it is true and made without intended deception. A statement is a lie if it is intended to deceive or its speaker, upon learning that the statement was misinterpreted, refrains from clarifying it.

Which one of the following judgments most closely conforms to the principles stated above by the moralist?

(A)   Ted's statement to the investigator that he had been abducted by extraterrestrial beings was wholly truthful even though no one has ever been abducted by extraterrestrial beings. After all, Ted was not trying to deceive the investigator.

(B)   Tony was not lying when he told his granddaughter that he did not wear dentures, for even though Tony meant to deceive his granddaughter, she made it clear to Tony that she did not believe him.

(C)   Siobhan did not tell a lie when she told her supervisor that she was ill and hence would not be able to come to work for an important presentation. However, even though her statement was true, it was not wholly truthful.

(D)   Walter's claim to a potential employer that he had done volunteer work was a lie. Even though Walter had worked without pay in his father's factory, he used the phrase "volunteer work" in an attempt to deceive the interviewer into thinking he had worked for a socially beneficial cause.

(E)   The tour guide intended to deceive the tourists when he told them that the cabin they were looking at was centuries old. Still, his statement about the cabin's age was not a lie, for if he thought that this statement had been misinterpreted, he would have tried to clarify it.

6. PT42, S2, Q9

Challenge can be an important source of self-knowledge, since those who pay attention to how they react, both emotionally and physically, to challenge can gain useful insights into their own weaknesses.

Which one of the following most closely conforms to the principle above?

(A)   A concert pianist should not have an entirely negative view of a memory lapse during a difficult performance. By understanding why the memory lapse occurred, the pianist can better prepare for future performances.

(B)   A salesperson should understand that the commission earned is not the only reward of making a sale. Salespeople should also take satisfaction from the fact that successful sales reflect well on their personalities.

(C)   Compassion is valuable not only for the wonderful feelings it brings, but also for the opportunities it affords to enrich the lives of other people.

(D)   While some of the value of competition comes from the pleasure of winning, the primary reward of competition is competition itself.

(E)   Even people who dread public speaking should accept invitations to speak before large groups. People will admire their courage and they will experience the fulfillment of having attempted something that is difficult for them.

9

_7. PT42, S2, Q21_

If one has evidence that an act will benefit other people and performs that act to benefit them, then one will generally succeed in benefiting them.

Which one of the following best illustrates the proposition above?

(A) A country's leaders realized that fostering diplomatic ties with antagonistic nations reduces the chances of war with those nations. Because those leaders worried that war would harm their chances of being reelected, they engaged in diplomatic discussions with a hostile country, and the two countries avoided a confrontation.

(B) A government study concluded that a proposed bureaucratic procedure would allow people to register their cars without waiting in line. The government adopted the procedure for this reason, and, as with most bureaucratic procedures, it was not successful.

(C) Betsy overheard a heating contractor say that regularly changing the filter in a furnace helps to keep the furnace efficient. So Betsy has regularly changed the furnace filter in her daughter's house. As a result, the furnace has never required maintenance due to becoming clogged with dust or dirt.

(D) Sejal learned in a psychology class that the best way to help someone overcome an addiction is to confront that person. So she confronted her friend Bob, who was struggling with a chemical dependency.

(E) Zachary hoped that psychotherapy could help his parents overcome their marital difficulties. He persuaded his parents to call a psychotherapist, and eventually their problems were resolved.

_8. PT42, S4, Q8_

When presented with the evidence against him, Ellison freely admitted to engaging in illegal transactions using company facilities. However, the company obtained the evidence by illegally recording Ellison's conversations. Therefore, although the company may demand that he immediately cease, it cannot justifiably take any punitive measures against him.

Which one of the following judgments best illustrates the principle illustrated by the argument above?

(A) After Price confessed to having stolen money from Long over a period of several years, Long began stealing from Price. Despite Price's guilt, Long was not justified in taking illegal action against him.

(B) Shakila's secretary has admitted that he is illegally receiving cable television without paying for it. Shakila would not be justified in reporting him, though, since she once did the same thing.

(C) After Takashi told Sarah's parents that he had seen her at the movies on Tuesday, Sarah confessed to sneaking out that day. On Monday, however, Takashi had violated the local curfew for minors. Hence Sarah's parents cannot justifiably punish her in this case.

(D) After a conservation officer discovered them, Kuttner admitted that he had set the illegal animal traps on his land. But, because she was trespassing at the time, the conservation officer cannot justifiably punish Kuttner in this case.

(E) Ramirez was forced by the discovery of new evidence to admit that she lied about her role in managing the chief of staff's financial affairs. Nevertheless, the board of directors cannot justifiably take action against Ramirez, because in past instances it has pardoned others guilty of similar improprieties.

9

Solutions: Principle Example Questions

Answer Key

1. E   5. D
2. C   6. A
3. D   7. C
4. E   8. D

1. PT43, S3, Q5

Art critic: The aesthetic value of a work of art lies in
its ability to impart a stimulating character to the
audience's experience of the work.

Which one of the following judgments most
closely conforms with the principle cited
above?

(A)   This painting is aesthetically deficient because
it is an exact copy of a painting done 30 years
ago.

(B)   This symphony is beautiful because, even
though it does not excite the audience, it is
competently performed.

(C)   This sculpted four-inch cube is beautiful
because it is carved from material which,
although much like marble, is very rare.

(D)   This painting is aesthetically valuable because
it was painted by a highly controversial artist.

(E)   This poem is aesthetically deficient because it
has little impact on its audience.

Answer choice (E) is correct.

We're given a principle that, though not obviously a
conditional statement, can be translated into conditional
form:

has aesthetic value   →   imparts a stimulating
                          character to audience's
                          experience

Now, we just need to find an example that conforms to
this conditional statement:

(A) is out of scope. We need to know whether the
work is stimulating. Whether it's a copy doesn't tell us
anything with respect to our principle.

(B) clearly violates the principle; if a work does not
excite the audience, it doesn't have aesthetic value.

(C) is out of scope. Rareness is irrelevant.

(D) is similarly out of scope. Controversial artist?

That leaves answer (E).

Let's try to match this to the language of the argument:

–stimulating   –aesthetic value

That's the contrapositive of our original conditional
statement, so it conforms to the principle. Therefore,
answer choice (E) is correct.

2. PT35, S1, Q7

Due to wider commercial availability of audio
recordings of authors reading their own books, sales
of printed books have dropped significantly.

Which one of the following conforms most closely to
the principle illustrated above?

(A)   Because of the rising cost of farm labor, farmers
began to make more extensive use of machines.

(B)   Because of the wide variety of new computer
games on the market, sales of high-quality
computer video screens have improved.

(C)   Because a new brand of soft drink entered the
market, consumers reduced their consumption
of an established brand of soft drink.

(D)   Because a child was forbidden to play until
homework was completed, that child did
much less daydreaming and focused on
homework.

MANHATTAN
PREP

(E)   Because neither of the two leading word processing programs has all of the features consumers want, neither has been able to dominate the market.

Answer choice (C) is correct.

Here, we're not explicitly given a principle; we need to derive one from the example, something like:

wider availability of newer, competing product → decline in sales of older existing product

Now, let's find an answer choice that conforms to our principle.

(A) is about rising cost, not availability, and it doesn't mention anything declining. Get rid of it.

(B) has wider availability of a new product leading to an increase in sales of a related product, so it's not a match.

(D) is just from outer space. No part of it comes close to our principle.

(E) makes no mention of a more widely available product driving down sales of another, so it's no good.

We're down to answer (C).

This looks pretty good:

 new product available → decline in consumption (i.e., sales) of established product

This is definitely the closest fit, so answer (C) is correct.

3. PT39, S2, Q11

A gift is not generous unless it is intended to benefit the recipient and is worth more than what is expected or customary in the situation; a gift is selfish if it is given to benefit the giver or is less valuable than is customary.

Which one of the following judgments most closely conforms to the principle above?

(A)   Charles, who hates opera, was given two expensive tickets to the opera. He in turn gave them to his cousin, who loves opera, as a birthday gift. Charles's gift was selfish because he paid nothing for the tickets.

(B)   Emily gives her brother a year's membership in a health club. She thinks that this will allow her brother to get the exercise he needs. However, the gift is selfish because Emily's brother is hurt and offended by it.

(C)   Amanda gives each of her clients an expensive bottle of wine every year. Amanda's gifts are generous, since they cause the clients to continue giving Amanda business.

(D)   Olga gives her daughter a computer as a graduation gift. Since this is the gift that all children in Olga's family receive for graduation, it is not generous.

(E)   Michael gave his nephew $50 as a birthday gift, more than he had ever given before. Michael's nephew, however, lost the money. Therefore, Michael's gift was not generous because it did not benefit the recipient.

Answer choice (D) is correct.

This principle can be broken down into four conditional statements if we split up the "and" and "or," which can help avoid confusion:

generous → intended to benefit the recipient

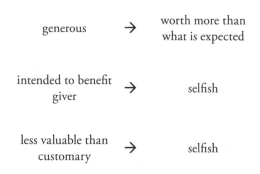

That's the contrapositive of the second conditional statement, so it conforms!

Therefore, answer (D) is correct.

4. PT39, S4, Q24

A park's user fees are employed to maintain the park. When fewer people use the park, it suffers less wear. Thus raising user fees improves park maintenance even if the number of people who stop using the park because of higher fees is great enough to reduce the revenues devoted to maintenance.

Which one of the following conforms most closely to the principle illustrated by the statements above?

(A)   To increase its market share, a car company improves the service warranty it provides to those who purchase a new car. Making good on the warranties proves expensive enough that the company's profits decrease even though its market share increases.

(B)   A grocery store's overall revenues increase even though it no longer remains open 24 hours daily. The manager theorizes that customers find the store more pleasant because it can be cleaned well during the hours it is closed.

(C)   Road taxes are raised to encourage more people to use mass transit. But since the fee paid by each commuter does not equal the cost of providing transit for that commuter, a mass transit service will deteriorate even as it takes in more money.

(D)   By spending more on zoo maintenance, a city increases the number of zoo patrons. The extra revenue generated by the sale of memorabilia more than makes up for the extra costs of maintenance.

We're looking for an example that conforms to some or all of these rules, and we can expect some of the wrong answers to try to entice us with reversed or negated logic. Let's look at the choices:

(A) concludes that a gift is selfish because it doesn't cost the giver any money. But according to our principle, the cost of the gift doesn't tell us anything; we would need to know the giver's intent or the *value* of the gift, which is different from its cost, to know whether it was selfish.

(B) concludes that a gift is selfish, but like (A), it doesn't base that conclusion on either of the sufficient conditions. We don't know anything about the gift's value, and we only know that it was intended to benefit the *recipient*. That certainly doesn't make it selfish!

(C) concludes that a gift is generous. But looking back at our conditional statements, "generous" only appears in the sufficient condition, so we have no way of concluding whether something is generous.

(E) is tempting. It concludes that a gift is not generous because it doesn't benefit the recipient. But notice that the first necessary condition of a generous gift is that it is *intended* to benefit the recipient. Whether it *actually* benefits the recipient is irrelevant to the principle.

We're left with one answer: (D).

This one concludes that Olga's gift is not generous. Why? Because it's the gift that all the children in the family receive in that context—in other words, it's worth no more than what's expected. In terms of our principle, that gives us this:

(E)   Library fees have been increased to raise money for book repair. Since the library now has fewer patrons, the books are in better repair even though the number of library patrons has decreased to such an extent that the money available for book repair has decreased.

Answer choice (E) is correct.

This one is a little trickier. Again, we need to derive a principle from the given statements. Since the statements are in argument form, isolating the premise and conclusion should allow us to generate the principle we need.

The argument concludes that raising user fees improves park maintenance, even if the higher fees dissuade enough people from coming that the maintenance revenues go down. That *whole thing* is the conclusion. It's based on the premise that when fewer people use the park, the park suffers less wear. So our argument core, abstracted away from the park example, looks like this:

fewer users means less wear → raising fees improves maintenance, even if this leads to fewer users and lower revenues

So that's our principle, more or less. Now, let's see if we can find the example that fits this principle most closely.

(A) talks about market share vs. profits, improving the service warranty, etc., which has nothing to do with fewer users, raising fees, maintenance, or anything we're interested in. It's way out of scope; eliminate it.

(B) is a bit more tempting, but we have no idea whether there are fewer users. Further, our principle is about revenues *decreasing*, not increasing.

(C) concludes that the mass transit service will deteriorate. Our principle is about maintenance being improved. Get rid of it.

(D) doesn't mention the zoo raising any fees, and it has the number of patrons *increasing* when we're looking for a decrease. (If you found (B) and (D) tempting, watch out that you're not responding to the subject matter rather than the logic. The original argument is about maintenance, but the correct answer may not specifically mention maintenance or cleaning. We'll see a lot of this kind of trap in Chapter 12, Matching Questions.)

So, how about the last answer, (E)?

Let's see: Raising fees has decreased the number of patrons to the extent that there's less book-repair money available, but because there are fewer patrons, the books are in better shape. This is a direct match!

Therefore, answer (E) is correct.

_5. PT52, S1, Q22_

Moralist: A statement is wholly truthful only if it is true and made without intended deception. A statement is a lie if it is intended to deceive or its speaker, upon learning that the statement was misinterpreted, refrains from clarifying it.

Which one of the following judgments most closely conforms to the principles stated above by the moralist?

(A)   Ted's statement to the investigator that he had been abducted by extraterrestrial beings was wholly truthful even though no one has ever been abducted by extraterrestrial beings. After all, Ted was not trying to deceive the investigator.

(B)   Tony was not lying when he told his granddaughter that he did not wear dentures, for even though Tony meant to deceive his granddaughter, she made it clear to Tony that she did not believe him.

(C)   Siobhan did not tell a lie when she told her supervisor that she was ill and hence would not be able to come to work for an important presentation. However, even though her statement was true, it was not wholly truthful.

(D)   Walter's claim to a potential employer that he had done volunteer work was a lie. Even though Walter had worked without pay in his father's factory, he used the phrase "volunteer work" in an attempt to deceive the interviewer into thinking he had worked for a socially beneficial cause.

(E)   The tour guide intended to deceive the tourists when he told them that the cabin they were looking at was centuries old. Still, his statement about the cabin's age was not a lie, for if he thought that this statement had been misinterpreted, he would have tried to clarify it.

Answer choice (D) is correct.

Here we're given a series of conditional statements. We're told of two necessary conditions for a statement to be wholly truthful (it must be true and made without intended deception) and two sufficient conditions that make a statement a lie (if it's intended to deceive or the speaker doesn't clarify a misinterpretation, it's a lie). We can express the conditionals like this:

wholly truthful	→	true
wholly truthful	→	not intended to deceive
intended to deceive	→	lie
speaker doesn't clarify misinterpretation	→	lie

Now, we just need to find a statement that conforms with these conditionals, keeping an eye out for illegal negations and reversals:

(A) is reversed. Not intending to deceive is a necessary, not sufficient, condition of a wholly truthful statement.

(B) violates the principle, according to which Tony definitely *was* lying if he intended to deceive his granddaughter. Whether she believed him or not is irrelevant.

(C) says that a statement is not a lie and not wholly truthful, but doesn't base those judgments on any sufficient conditions.

(E) violates the principle in the same way as (B): The tour guide intended to deceive the tourists, so his statement was absolutely a lie—end of story!

That leaves answer (D).

Walter attempted to deceive the interviewer, so his statement was a lie. This directly conforms to our third conditional statement.

Therefore, answer (D) is correct.

6. PT42, S2, Q9

Challenge can be an important source of self-knowledge, since those who pay attention to how they react, both emotionally and physically, to challenge can gain useful insights into their own weaknesses.

Which one of the following most closely conforms to the principle above?

(A)   A concert pianist should not have an entirely negative view of a memory lapse during a difficult performance. By understanding why the memory lapse occurred, the pianist can better prepare for future performances.

(B)   A salesperson should understand that the commission earned is not the only reward of making a sale. Salespeople should also take satisfaction from the fact that successful sales reflect well on their personalities.

(C)   Compassion is valuable not only for the wonderful feelings it brings, but also for the opportunities it affords to enrich the lives of other people.

MANHATTAN
PREP

(D)   While some of the value of competition comes from the pleasure of winning, the primary reward of competition is competition itself.

(E)   Even people who dread public speaking should accept invitations to speak before large groups. People will admire their courage and they will experience the fulfillment of having attempted something that is difficult for them.

Answer choice (A) is correct.

This principle is stated as an argument. The premise is that those who pay attention to their reactions to challenge can gain useful insights into their weaknesses. The conclusion is that challenge can therefore be an important source of self-knowledge. From this, we generate the principle:

paying attention to reactions to challenge leads to useful insights	→	challenge can be an important source of self-knowledge.

Now, let's compare the answer choices to this principle:

(B) has nothing to do with challenge, insight, or self-knowledge. It's way out of scope; get rid of it.

(C) tells us two ways in which compassion is valuable, neither of which has anything to do with our principle.

(D) is incorrect in basically the same way: We get two ways in which competition is valuable, but this has nothing to do with challenge as a source of insights or self-knowledge. This also compares the two benefits to each other, something that our original principle does not do.

(E) doesn't fit. Our principle is about challenge being useful because it leads to useful insights, not because people admire your courage or because you experience fulfillment.

So we're down to answer (A).

This may have seemed suspect since it has a normative element that does not appear in our original: Because understanding the cause of a memory lapse during a difficult performance can help the pianist better prepare, the pianist shouldn't have an entirely negative view of this lapse. Does this match? Well, "a difficult performance" is certainly a challenge, and the memory lapse is a reaction to it; understanding that reaction leads to better preparation, which sounds like a useful insight. So far, we've got our premise. Now, does the conclusion match? Well, it's not exactly the same, since it doesn't talk about self-knowledge, but it does say that the pianist shouldn't have an entirely negative view, which does jibe somewhat: If it's a source of self-knowledge, we can reasonably say it's not entirely a bad thing. So this is a pretty good match. This is another case where working wrong-to-right can pay off!

Therefore, answer (A) is correct.

7. PT42, S2, Q21

If one has evidence that an act will benefit other people and performs that act to benefit them, then one will generally succeed in benefiting them.

Which one of the following best illustrates the proposition above?

(A)   A country's leaders realized that fostering diplomatic ties with antagonistic nations reduces the chances of war with those nations. Because those leaders worried that war would harm their chances of being reelected, they engaged in diplomatic discussions with a hostile country, and the two countries avoided a confrontation.

(B)   A government study concluded that a proposed bureaucratic procedure would allow people to register their cars without waiting in line. The government adopted the procedure for this reason, and, as with most bureaucratic procedures, it was not successful.

9

(C)　Betsy overheard a heating contractor say that regularly changing the filter in a furnace helps to keep the furnace efficient. So Betsy has regularly changed the furnace filter in her daughter's house. As a result, the furnace has never required maintenance due to becoming clogged with dust or dirt.

(D)　Sejal learned in a psychology class that the best way to help someone overcome an addiction is to confront that person. So she confronted her friend Bob, who was struggling with a chemical dependency.

(E)　Zachary hoped that psychotherapy could help his parents overcome their marital difficulties. He persuaded his parents to call a psychotherapist, and eventually their problems were resolved.

Answer choice (C) is correct.

This principle is given as a straightforward conditional statement:

$$
\begin{array}{c}
\text{evidence that act} \\
\text{will benefit others} \\
+ \\
\text{performs act to} \\
\text{benefit them}
\end{array}
\quad \rightarrow \quad
\begin{array}{c}
\text{generally succeed} \\
\text{in benefiting them}
\end{array}
$$

So, we need to find an example that illustrates this conditional relationship.

(A) has people succeeding at something, but if we look closely, we see that the leaders engage in diplomacy in order to protect their own chances of being reelected, so they're performing the act to benefit *themselves*. We have the necessary condition, but not the sufficient. This doesn't conform. You might reasonably figure that avoiding war benefits others, too, but this example doesn't do anything to establish that the leaders knew of this benefit or took action for that purpose.

(B) starts strong: The government has evidence (a study) that a procedure will help people, and it adopts this

procedure in order to help them. But according to our principle, this should generally lead to success; instead, we're told that "as with most bureaucratic procedures, it was not successful." This is the opposite of our desired outcome.

(D) gives us the sufficient conditions—Sejal has evidence that confrontation will help, and she confronts Bob with that goal, but we never find out the necessary—that is, whether she's successful.

(E) tells us that Zachary has hope, but not evidence, that psychotherapy will help his parents. Further, if psychotherapy is the act in question, Zachary doesn't actually perform it himself. So we have neither of the sufficient conditions.

That leaves answer (C).

Betsy overhears a contractor describing the benefit of changing the filter in a furnace. That may not be conclusive proof, but it is a form of evidence. Then she changes the filter in her daughter's house. Although we aren't told explicitly that she takes the action to benefit her daughter, we can reasonably infer that she does from the use of the word "so": "So Betsy has regularly changed the furnace filter." This means we have our two sufficient conditions. As a result, we're told, the furnace has never required maintenance—so Betsy is successful in her goal of keeping her daughter's furnace efficient.

Even though this isn't a 100% match—it would be nice to have Betsy's reason for changing the filter spelled out more explicitly—it comes by far the closest to giving us our sufficient and necessary conditions.

Therefore, answer (C) is correct.

8. PT42, S4, Q8

When presented with the evidence against him, Ellison freely admitted to engaging in illegal transactions using company facilities. However, the company obtained the evidence by illegally recording Ellison's conversations. Therefore, although the company may demand that he immediately cease, it cannot justifiably take any punitive measures against him.

Which one of the following judgments best illustrates the principle illustrated by the argument above?

(A)   After Price confessed to having stolen money from Long over a period of several years, Long began stealing from Price. Despite Price's guilt, Long was not justified in taking illegal action against him.

(B)   Shakila's secretary has admitted that he is illegally receiving cable television without paying for it. Shakila would not be justified in reporting him, though, since she once did the same thing.

(C)   After Takashi told Sarah's parents that he had seen her at the movies on Tuesday, Sarah confessed to sneaking out that day. On Monday, however, Takashi had violated the local curfew for minors. Hence Sarah's parents cannot justifiably punish her in this case.

(D)   After a conservation officer discovered them, Kuttner admitted that he had set the illegal animal traps on his land. But, because she was trespassing at the time, the conservation officer cannot justifiably punish Kuttner in this case.

(E)   Ramirez was forced by the discovery of new evidence to admit that she lied about her role in managing the chief of staff's financial affairs. Nevertheless, the board of directors cannot justifiably take action against Ramirez, because in past instances it has pardoned others guilty of similar improprieties.

Answer choice (D) is correct.

Here, we have to generate a principle from the given argument, which concludes that the company cannot justifiably punish Ellison for his illegal activity. Why? Because although he confessed when presented with the evidence against him, that evidence was obtained illegally. So the argument core, and therefore our principle, looks like this:

$$\text{evidence obtained illegally} \rightarrow \begin{array}{c}\text{illegal activity cannot}\\ \text{justifiably be punished}\\ \text{(even if confessed)}\end{array}$$

There are a couple of major assumptions there, but our job here is not to evaluate the argument, it's to find an example that most closely conforms to it. Let's look.

(A) has someone confessing to a crime and concludes that the response is not justified, but doesn't tell us anything about where the evidence comes from, so it doesn't conform.

(B) concludes that Shakila can't report her secretary, but bases that conclusion not on her obtaining the evidence illegally, but on her having once done the same thing. This has nothing to do with our principle. It looks more like an Ad Hominem.

(C) is very tempting. The conclusion looks right: Sarah's parents can't justifiably punish her. And we have Sarah confessing to her misdeed after the evidence is presented. There's only one problem: Although Takashi violated the curfew, that was on Monday, and he saw Sarah on Tuesday. So his violation was not the source of the evidence against Sarah. In any case, it's not clear that Sarah's parents are obtaining information illegally just because their informant was out past curfew. Since we don't know whether the evidence was obtained illegally, we can't conclude whether Sarah's parents are justified in punishing her.

(E) is also tempting, but as in (B), the conclusion that punishment is unjustified is based on the wrong premise. We care about the source of the evidence, not about past pardons.

9

We're down to answer (D).

The core breaks down to this:

| officer trespassed at time of discovery of crime | → | can't justifiably punish Kuttner for illegal traps (even though he confessed) |

That's a match! Because the evidence was obtained illegally, the admitted perpetrator cannot be punished justifiably.

Therefore, answer (D) is correct.

Time for Some More!

Some more timed practice, that is. This time, it's dealer's choice. If you want to do a full PrepTest as you did after Chapter 8, go for it. If you'd prefer to practice with only LR sections, now's your chance. You can do them solo, or you can do them back-to-back. Consider that every LSAT has two scored LR sections and an experimental section. If that experimental section is LR, too, you might find yourself facing three back-to-back LR sections on test day. Are you ready for that much logic? Only one way to find out…

Analyze the Argument Questions

In This Chapter...

Analyze Argument Structure Questions on the LSAT

The ability to think about an argument in terms of structure is a necessary tool for all test-takers who want to get a top score. Approximately 15% of all Logical Reasoning questions will directly test your ability to analyze the structure of an argument.

Fortunately for us, we've been thinking about argument structure from the beginning of the book. Argument structure can simply be thought of as the organization of background information, supporting premises, and opposing points relative to a main conclusion, and we've needed to consider this structure for all Assumption Family questions.

Analyze Argument Structure questions do differ just a bit from Assumption Family questions, and we'll review these differences later. For now, let's use the following example to review the different components that make up the structure of an argument:

> The Law School Admissions Test (LSAT) is an exam that tests certain logical instincts and processing abilities. The LSAT is a useful and necessary tool for the law school admissions process. Some critics disagree with the use of the LSAT in admissions decisions. They argue that the exam is culturally biased and bears no direct relation to the process of being a lawyer. Though the test is imperfect, as all standardized tests are, it is necessary and useful because, without it, admissions officers would have no objective way to compare applicants from different backgrounds. After all, grading standards vary from university to university, and placing value on life or work experience is a highly subjective enterprise.

The Law School Admissions Test (LSAT) is an exam that tests certain logical instincts and processing abilities.	**BACKGROUND INFORMATION** Background information helps the reader become more familiar with the subject matter of the argument. Background information is often necessary for the reader to understand and contextualize the argument being made.
The LSAT is a useful and necessary tool for the law school admissions process.	**THE CONCLUSION** The conclusion is the main point of an argument. It is always a claim of some sort, and therefore it is always subjective. If there are multiple claims made in an argument, the conclusion is always the ultimate, or final, claim. Another way to think about the conclusion is that it is always last in the chain of logic. Identifying the correct conclusion is the most important step involved in correctly understanding argument structure.

Some critics disagree with the use of the LSAT in admissions decisions. They argue that the exam is culturally biased and bears no direct relation to the process of being a lawyer. Though the test is imperfect…	**OPPOSING POINT** An opposing point is an opinion, or support for an opinion, that runs counter to the main conclusion of the argument.
…without it, admissions officers would have no objective way to compare applicants from different backgrounds.	**INTERMEDIATE CONCLUSION** Intermediate conclusions are conclusions that are used to support the main conclusion. Note that this conclusion is *not* the main point of the argument.
After all, grading standards vary from university to university, and placing value on life or work experience is a highly subjective enterprise.	**SUPPORTING PREMISE** Supporting premises present information that supports, in a direct or indirect way, the main conclusion of an argument.

Intermediate Conclusions, Supporting Premises, and Main Conclusions

Differentiating between intermediate conclusions and supporting premises can be messy, and it is generally unnecessary. There is great overlap between those two roles—after all, intermediate conclusions always support the main conclusion. You can think of an intermediate conclusion as any supporting premise that has two characteristics—it is a claim of some sort and it is supported by other premises in the argument.

It *is* imperative that you correctly differentiate between intermediate conclusions and the main conclusion of an argument. Remember, the main conclusion will always be last in the chain of logic.

Let's look at a visual representation of the relationship between the supporting evidence, the intermediate conclusion, and the main conclusion of our argument:

Supporting Premises		Intermediate Conclusion		Conclusion
Grading standards vary from university to university.	➡	Without the LSAT, admissions officers would have no objective way to compare applicants from different backgrounds.	➡	The LSAT is a useful and necessary part of the admissions process.
Placing value on life or work experience is highly subjective.	➡			

MANHATTAN
PREP

10

On your LSAT exam, you'll see four different question types that will require you to understand the structure of an argument: 1) Identify the Conclusion of an argument, 2) Determine the Function of a component of an argument, 3) Identify the Disagreement between two people in a conversation, and 4) summarize the Procedure used by the author of an argument. Let's discuss each in depth.

Identify the Conclusion Questions

Identify the Conclusion questions ask you to identify the main point, or final conclusion, of an argument. These questions can be made easier if you keep these five key points in mind:

1. **Always identify the conclusion first!** This may seem like an obvious step, but some test-takers might be tempted to read the argument and then jump directly into the answer choices. Remember to take a moment after you finish the argument to make sure that you've correctly identified its conclusion *before* you look at the answer choices.

2. **Watch for conclusions that are "stuck in the middle."** We mentioned earlier in the book that the conclusion of the argument can appear at the start of the argument, in the middle, or at the end. Typically, it's much easier to spot a conclusion when it appears at the beginning or at the end of an argument. For this reason, when the LSAT asks you to identify a conclusion, that conclusion is typically buried somewhere in the middle of the argument, just to make things a bit more difficult on you. Let's look at two versions of the same argument to illustrate:

Premise–Premise–Conclusion:
My electricity bill was $45 last month. I will be out of town more this month than I was last month. Thus, my electricity bill will be less than $45 this month.

Premise–Conclusion–Premise:
My electricity bill was $45 last month. My electricity bill will be less than $45 this month since I will be out of town more this month than I was last month.

In each case, we have two premises that support a conclusion: "My bill will be less than $45 this month." The *logical* structure is identical and the conclusion comes last in the *logical* chain each time (each of the premises leads up to, or supports, the conclusion). What is different is the *organizational* structure. In the second case, the conclusion is buried in the middle of the passage. For Identify the Conclusion questions, you can expect the second structure more often than the first.

3. **Find the author's conclusion, not yours.** In the next chapter, we'll look at Inference questions, which require you to *infer* from information given in the text—that is, to uncover a truth beyond what is literally stated. When a question asks you to *identify* the main conclusion of an argument, however, you must not infer anything at all. Remember, you're looking for the author's conclusion, not yours, and the conclusion of an argument will always be stated explicitly. Here's an example:

> **Legislator:** We are joining a nationwide campaign to reduce the number of car accidents. In our state, the majority of serious car accidents occur between the hours of 11pm and 4am. Thus, most serious car accidents are the result of drivers being overly tired while they drive.

10

Imagine you were asked to choose an answer that best represents the conclusion made in the argument. You might be tempted by an answer choice such as, "People shouldn't drive if they are overly tired." It makes sense to draw this conclusion based on the argument and your outside knowledge, but this is not what the legislator has concluded! The legislator's conclusion is that most serious car accidents are the result of drivers being overly tired. The legislator may very well believe that people shouldn't drive when they are tired, but this is not stated. Don't be tempted to draw your own conclusion!

4. **Main conclusions are last in the chain of logic.** If you have trouble identifying the final conclusion, it's probably because the argument contains an intermediate conclusion that seems like it could be the final conclusion. Earlier in the book, we learned to use the Therefore Test to help determine which point actually comes last in the chain of logic. Here's the example we used previously:

> A new lemonade stand has just opened for business in the town square. The stand will surely fail. A popular juice store already sells lemonade in the town square, so the new lemonade stand will not be able to attract customers.

This argument seems to have two possible conclusions: 1) the stand will surely fail, and 2) the new lemonade stand will not be able to attract customers. There can only be one final conclusion. Again, we can use the Therefore Test to identify the final conclusion:

> **Case 1:** The stand will surely fail. THEREFORE, the new lemonade stand will not be able to attract customers.

> **Case 2:** The new lemonade stand will not be able to attract customers. THEREFORE, the stand will surely fail.

We've proposed two different logical statements by changing the order of the two possible conclusions. The first case doesn't make a whole lot of sense. In the second case, however, the first part of the statement clearly supports, or leads into, the second part of the statement. Because the stand will not be able to attract customers, it will surely fail. Thus, the final conclusion is, "The stand will surely fail." Don't get fooled by intermediate conclusions!

5. **Don't be fooled by rewordings of the conclusion.** The LSAT will often attempt to disguise the correct answer by rewording the conclusion in the correct answer choice. You should not expect the correct answer to be an exact replica of the conclusion as it is presented in the argument. Consider this example:

MANHATTAN
PREP

10

Many people who work for nonprofit companies claim that they are not motivated at all by personal gain. This just isn't true. The executive director of Bright Lives, a local nonprofit, makes over $100,000 per year.

This argument has the form Opposing Point–Conclusion–Premise. If we were to identify the conclusion in this argument, we would point to "This just isn't true." However, we can be sure that the correct answer will be written much differently. After you've identified the conclusion in the argument, you may need to clarify in your own mind what the different pieces actually mean. For example, what does "this" refer to? What isn't true? "This" refers to the claim that "the employees are not motivated at all by personal gain." So, the conclusion is really this:

[The claim made by many nonprofit employees that they are not motivated at all by personal gain] just isn't true.

Furthermore, we can probably expect the correct answer choice to be one that rephrases even more. For example:

Many employees of nonprofit companies are motivated by personal gain.

Notice that this rewording takes a double negative ("It ISN'T true that they are NOT motivated by personal gain") and turns it into a positive ("They ARE motivated by personal gain"). This isn't an inference since we haven't drawn any new conclusions from the given premises. It's simply another way of expressing the author's point. Expect that the correct answer will be disguised by a rewording!

Let's apply these concepts to a full LSAT question:

PT29, S1, Q11

It is well known that many species adapt to their environment, but it is usually assumed that only the most highly evolved species alter their environment in ways that aid their own survival. However, this characteristic is actually quite common. Certain species of plankton, for example, generate a gas that is converted in the atmosphere into particles of sulfate. These particles cause water vapor to condense, thus forming clouds. Indeed, the formation of clouds over the ocean largely depends on the presence of these particles. More cloud cover means more sunlight is reflected, and so the Earth absorbs less heat. Thus plankton cause the surface of the Earth to be cooler and this benefits the plankton.

Of the following, which one most accurately expresses the main point of the argument?

(A) The Earth would be far warmer than it is now if certain species of plankton became extinct.

(B) By altering their environment in ways that improve their chances of survival, certain species of plankton benefit the Earth as a whole.

(C) Improving their own chances of survival by altering the environment is not limited to the most highly evolved species.

(D) The extent of the cloud cover over the oceans is largely determined by the quantity of plankton in those oceans.

(E) Species such as plankton alter the environment in ways that are less detrimental to the well-being of other species than are the alterations to the environment made by more highly evolved species.

Last in the chain of logic. Did you start by identifying the conclusion in the argument before looking at the answer choices? If so, did you identify the last sentence of the argument as the conclusion? Be careful! This is an understandable choice, since it begins with the word "thus," but what about the statement that "this characteristic is actually quite common"? This statement feels like a claim as well. How do we decide which is the final conclusion? We'll use the Therefore Test:

Possibility 1: This characteristic [species altering their own environment] is actually quite common. THEREFORE, plankton cause the surface of the Earth to be cooler and this benefits the plankton.

Possibility 2: Plankton cause the surface of the Earth to be cooler and this benefits the plankton. THEREFORE, this characteristic [species altering their own environment] is actually quite common.

The second possibility gives us the correct ordering. The fact that even lowly life forms such as plankton alter their environment supports the claim that the characteristic (species altering their environment) is actually quite common and not just a characteristic of the most highly evolved species.

So the conclusion of the argument is "However, this characteristic is actually quite common."

Stuck in the middle. Did you notice that the final conclusion is "stuck in the middle" of the argument? This argument has the form Opposing Point–Conclusion–Supporting Premises–Intermediate Conclusion, a common argument form for Identify the Conclusion questions. When in doubt, look for the conclusion in the middle of the passage.

The author's conclusion, not yours. Now that we've identified our conclusion, we'll search for an answer choice that best expresses this conclusion. Notice that some of the incorrect answer choices are tempting because they seem like conclusions that a reasonable person might make. Take answer (A) as an example:

> (A)   The Earth would be far warmer than it is now
>   if certain species of plankton became extinct.

Given the information in the passage, answer (A) seems right, doesn't it? Remember, though, that we're looking for the conclusion made by the *author,* not a conclusion that we might infer ourselves.

Don't be fooled by rewordings. We want an answer choice that basically rewords the conclusion we've identified. Answer (C) does just that. Let's compare the conclusion as stated in the argument with the language used in the correct answer:

> **Conclusion:** However, this characteristic is actually quite common.

> **Correct answer (C):** Improving their own chances of survival by altering the environment is not limited to the most highly evolved species.

Notice the difference in wording. In order to see that these actually say the same thing, we need to do some translating.

The conclusion contains some tricky language. The "characteristic" referred to is the tendency for species to alter their environment in order to aid their own survival. Let's rewrite the original conclusion to make this clear:

> **Conclusion rewritten:** The tendency for species to alter their environment in order to aid their own survival is actually quite common.

The wording of the correct answer (C) presents its own challenges. The answer uses the negatively phrased "not limited to the most highly evolved species" (echoing the wording of the opposing point) to stand in for "common." If the characteristic is "not limited to" certain species, then this characteristic is "common." Let's rewrite it:

> **Correct answer (C) rewritten:** Improving their own chances of survival by altering the environment is common.

Now, let's compare our rewritten sentences:

> **Conclusion rewritten:** The tendency for species to alter their environment in order to aid their own survival is actually quite common.

> **Correct answer (C) rewritten:** Improving their own chances of survival by altering the environment is common among species.

The initial differences boil down to simple rewordings. While the correct answer uses different words from the conclusion, they mean the same thing. (Note: You wouldn't want to spend the time on the exam to *write out* these rewordings, but you do want to compare and contrast the phrasing used to see if they say the same things using different words.)

Okay, now let's try it out on another one. If you want to time yourself, give yourself 1:20.

> *PT29, S4, Q6*
>
> Some judges complain about statutes that specify mandatory minimum sentences for criminal offenses. These legal restrictions, they complain, are too mechanical and prevent judges from deciding when a given individual can or cannot be rehabilitated. But that is precisely why mandatory minimum sentences are necessary. History amply demonstrates that when people are free to use their own judgment they invariably believe themselves to act wisely when in fact they are often arbitrary and irrational. There is no reason to think that judges are an exception to this rule.
>
> Which one of the following sentences most accurately expresses the main point of the passage?

MANHATTAN
PREP

(A)   People believe that they have good judgment
          but never do.

(B)   Mandatory minimum sentences are too
          mechanical and reduce judicial discretion.

(C)   Judges should be free to exercise their own
          judgment.

(D)   Judges are often arbitrary and irrational.

(E)   Mandatory minimum sentences are needed to
          help prevent judicial arbitrariness.

Once again, we want to remember to identify the conclusion in the argument before we evaluate the answer choices. Once again, we have multiple claims we have to choose between:

Claim 1: Mandatory minimum sentences are necessary to prevent judges from deciding…

Claim 2: When free to use their own judgment, people often act in an arbitrary and irrational
          manner.

Which of these is a consequence of the other? Are judges acting arbitrarily because mandatory minimum sentences are necessary? No, that doesn't make sense. Are mandatory minimum sentences necessary because judges are acting arbitrarily? That makes a lot more sense, and so we want to take claim 1 as our conclusion. Notice, once again, that the conclusion comes in the middle of the argument.

Let's next evaluate each of the answer choices relative to our conclusion.

Conclusion: Mandatory minimum sentences are necessary to prevent judges from deciding when a given individual can or cannot be rehabilitated.

(A)   People believe that they have good judgment
          but never do.

This is not the final conclusion. Furthermore, the "never" is stronger than what the argument presents. The argument says that people "invariably" (translation: always) believe they are acting wisely, but it only says that they *often* act in an arbitrary and irrational manner.

(B)   Mandatory minimum sentences are too
          mechanical and reduce judicial discretion.

This is given as an opposing point; it is not the main point.

(C)   Judges should be free to exercise their own
          judgment.

This answer is actually the opposite of what the author seems to feel.

MANHATTAN
PREP   425

(D)   Judges are often arbitrary and irrational.

This is a nice representation of the second claim and, as such, probably the most attractive wrong answer. However, as we've discussed, this is not the author's main, or final, point.

(E)   Mandatory minimum sentences are needed to
       help prevent judicial arbitrariness.

This is the correct answer. It's a very close match to the conclusion in the argument.

As we discussed earlier, it is common for the test writers to try to challenge us by using relative pronouns ("this," "that," etc.) in the actual conclusion. In the above example, we had "that" in the place of judges deciding when a given individual can or cannot be rehabilitated. On the exam, once we've found an answer we like, we want to make sure to check any "this" or "that" from the conclusion of the argument against that answer to make sure there hasn't been any significant change in what the pronoun represents.

Determine the Function Questions

Determine the Function questions require you to correctly identify the role a specific part of the argument plays. Keep the following in mind as you work to determine the function of an argument component:

1. **Identify the conclusion first.** Without knowing the conclusion, it's virtually impossible to assign a function to any other part of the argument. Thus, we always start by identifying the conclusion.

2. **Relate the element in question to the conclusion.** Does it support the conclusion or does it oppose it? Is it the conclusion?

Let's take a look at an example:

> PT36, S3, Q6
>
> Government official: A satisfactory way of
>   eliminating chronic food shortages in our
>   country is not easily achievable. Direct aid
>   from other countries in the form of food
>   shipments tends to undermine our prospects
>   for long-term agricultural self-sufficiency. If
>   external sources of food are delivered
>   effectively by external institutions, local food
>   producers and suppliers are forced out of
>   business. On the other hand, foreign capital
>   funneled to long-term development projects
>   would inject so much cash into our economy
>   that inflation would drive the price of food
>   beyond the reach of most of our citizens.
>
> The claim that foreign capital funneled into the
> economy would cause inflation plays which one of the
> following roles in the government official's argument?
>
> (A)   It supports the claim that the official's country
>   must someday be agriculturally self-sufficient.
>
> (B)   It supports the claim that there is no easy
>   solution to the problem of chronic food
>   shortages in the official's country.
>
> (C)   It is supported by the claim that the official's
>   country must someday be agriculturally self-
>   sufficient.
>
> (D)   It supports the claim that donations of food
>   from other countries will not end the chronic
>   food shortages in the official's country.
>
> (E)   It is supported by the claim that food
>   producers and suppliers in the official's
>   country may be forced out of business by
>   donations of food from other countries.

10

Did you find it challenging to read the question first in this case? It's hard to make much of such an involved question before we've read the argument. It's still worth skimming over the question to determine our task, but it's okay to go back and look for the specific statement after we've had a chance to read and understand the argument. In any case, in order to understand the role played by any part of the argument, we must first identify the conclusion. In this argument, there are multiple claims being made. Let's review them here:

1. A satisfactory way of eliminating chronic food shortages in our country is not easily achievable.

2. Direct aid from other countries in the form of food shipments tends to undermine our prospects for long-term agricultural self-sufficiency.

3. If external sources of food are delivered effectively by external institutions, local food producers and suppliers are forced out of business.

4. Foreign capital funneled to long-term development projects would inject so much cash into our economy that inflation would drive the price of food beyond the reach of most of our citizens.

Which one of these is the ultimate conclusion? We are typically looking for something that generalizes, and we are always looking for something that comes last in a chain of reasoning. In this case, the first claim has both of those characteristics.

Let's imagine you saw the above argument on the exam and weren't certain about the conclusion. Perhaps you think another claim could be the final claim in the chain of reasoning. How can you verify? Remember, the Therefore Test can be a great tool. Let's use it to compare the first claim with the one mentioned in the question stem.

Which relationship makes more sense?

Scenario 1: Eliminating chronic food shortages in our country is not easily achievable.
THEREFORE, foreign capital would drive the price of food beyond the reach of most of our citizens.

Scenario 2: Foreign capital would drive the price of food beyond the reach of most of our citizens.
THEREFORE, eliminating chronic food shortages in our country is not easily achievable.

In terms of an order of reasoning, the second scenario makes a lot more sense, and we can see, therefore, that the part of the argument that's in question is meant to *support* the conclusion that a satisfactory way of eliminating chronic food shortages in our country is not easily achievable.

Let's evaluate the answer choices:

> (A)   It supports the claim that the official's country must someday be agriculturally self-sufficient.

This answer correctly identifies the role—"supports"—but incorrectly identifies the actual conclusion. The conclusion in this answer extrapolates well beyond what the argument discusses.

> (B)   It supports the claim that there is no easy solution to the problem of chronic food shortages in the official's country.

This answer choice matches what we predicted and is correct.

> (C)   It is supported by the claim that the official's country must someday be agriculturally self-sufficient.

MANHATTAN
PREP

Like (A), this answer choice brings in an idea—the country must someday be agriculturally self-sufficient—that is not discussed in the argument and assigns this idea to an incorrect role relative to the part of the argument in question.

> (D)   It supports the claim that donations of food
>   from other countries will not end the chronic
>   food shortages in the official's country.

This answer represents a misunderstanding of the author's main conclusion. The claim about the donations of food is not the main conclusion of the argument, and it is not what the element in question is meant to support.

> (E)   It is supported by the claim that food
>   producers and suppliers in the official's
>   country may be forced out of business by
>   donations of food from other countries.

The claim mentioned in the question plays a parallel role to the claim mentioned in this answer—both support the general conclusion. They do not directly support one another.

Here's one more:

> ### PT29, S4, Q15
>
> Ambiguity inspires interpretation. The saying, "We are the measure of all things," for instance, has been interpreted by some people to imply that humans are centrally important in the universe, while others have interpreted it to mean simply that, since all knowledge is human knowledge, humans must rely on themselves to find the truth.
>
> The claim that ambiguity inspires interpretation figures in the argument in which one of the following ways?
>
> (A)   It is used to support the argument's
>   conclusion.
> (B)   It is an illustration of the claim that we are the
>   measure of all things.
> (C)   It is compatible with either accepting or
>   rejecting the argument's conclusion.
> (D)   It is a view that other statements in the
>   argument are intended to support.
> (E)   It sets out a difficulty the argument is intended
>   to solve.

10

Once again, our first task is to identify the conclusion. In this case, our job is made a bit easier for us because there is only one opinion, or claim, in the argument: Ambiguity inspires interpretation. What follows—information about how different people interpret a particular statement—is fact, and therefore cannot be the author's main point.

Fortunately for us, the conclusion is the element of the argument that the question is asking about. Armed with this understanding, we can evaluate each of the answer choices:

    (A)   It is used to support the argument's
                conclusion.

It doesn't *support* the conclusion; it *is* the conclusion.

    (B)   It is an illustration of the claim that we are the
                measure of all things.

The varying interpretations of the statement "We are the measure of all things" are used as examples to support the conclusion. This answer states a reverse relationship.

    (C)   It is compatible with either accepting or
                rejecting the argument's conclusion.

This answer would be tempting if we misunderstood what the conclusion of the argument was. Otherwise, it can be easily eliminated. The part in question is the argument's conclusion.

    (D)   It is a view that other statements in the
                argument are intended to support.

This is another way of saying that the part of the argument in the question stem is the conclusion of the argument. This is the correct answer.

    (E)   It sets out a difficulty the argument is intended
                to solve.

It is not a difficulty, and there is nothing the argument is intended to solve.

Identify the Disagreement Questions

Identify the Disagreement questions present you with two perspectives on an argument (in the form of a conversation between two people) and then ask you to find their specific point of disagreement. The two opinions can be directly opposing sides of one argument, or they can be indirectly related to a common argument.

Success on Identify the Disagreement questions depends on your ability to analyze the relationship between two perspectives. Keep the following in mind:

MANHATTAN
PREP

1. **Don't assume anything.** There may be hints that the authors have different opinions, or different definitions of a particular phrase, or different ways of seeing evidence, but an answer choice is unlikely to be correct unless it contains elements that are *specifically*, rather than indirectly, mentioned in the text. This leads to the next point…

2. **Identify the overlap!** Two people can only disagree about something they each have an opinion about. Most of the time, there is only one point of overlap, and recognizing this overlap will point you toward the right answer.

Take the following simple example to illustrate these two concepts:

> Yasmine: It's really raining hard outside. The school should cancel the football game.

> Alfredo: It's not really raining very much at all. Look! None of the people outside are using umbrellas.

We know that Yasmine thinks the school should cancel the game because of the rain. It would be very tempting to *assume* that Alfredo thinks the school should go ahead with the game. After all, he doesn't think it's really raining at all! If we were to make this assumption, we might choose an answer such as "Yasmine and Alfredo disagree over whether the school should cancel the football game." However, this would be a big mistake on our part. Alfredo mentions nothing about the game at all, which makes it very difficult to *infer* his opinion on canceling the game.

Consider the following diagram that is designed to identify the specific point of disagreement:

	Yasmine	**Alfredo**
How much it's raining	Raining hard	Not really raining at all
Canceling the game	Cancel it!	
People outside		Not using umbrellas

While you wouldn't take the time to draw this out during the test, this diagram does a good job of keeping you focused. Of all the topics discussed (listed along the left side), only one is common between them. The only point of overlap is in regard to the degree to which it is raining. Since this is the only point of overlap, it is the *only* possible point of disagreement. They disagree over how hard it is raining, and the correct answer would represent this.

3. **Anticipate the point of disagreement.** The two participants in a conversation will likely express their disagreement over 1) the main conclusion, or 2) a supporting premise. In the previous example, Scott takes issue with Julie's *supporting premise* (the degree to which it is raining). He mentions nothing of her conclusion (cancel the game).

ID the Agreement

While the majority of the Identify the Disagreement questions you will see will indeed ask you to identify the disagreement, we've seen some lately that ask you to identify the agreement. The strategy is still the same, just switch the target!

Let's try this out on a full question:

> *PT38, S1, Q5*
>
> Naima: The proposed new computer system, once
> we fully implemented it, would operate more
> smoothly and efficiently than the current
> system. So we should devote the resources
> necessary to accomplish the conversion as
> soon as possible.
>
> Nakai: We should keep the current system for as
> long as we can. The cost in time and money of
> converting to the new system would be greater
> than any predicted benefits.
>
> Naima and Nakai disagree with each other over
> whether
>
> (A) the predicted benefits of the new computer
>   system will be realized
>
> (B) it is essential to have the best computer system
>   available
>
> (C) accomplishing the conversion is technically
>   impossible
>
> (D) the current computer system does not work
>   well enough to do what it is supposed to do
>
> (E) the conversion to a new computer system
>   should be delayed

While this question is pretty straightforward, it does illustrate the idea of overlap. The best way to consider the overlapping and nonoverlapping parts of Naima's and Nakai's arguments is to create a visual representation, as we did before. Again, while you probably wouldn't want to take the time during your actual exam to draw out the following diagram, you would want to keep this representation in your mind's eye:

	Naima	**Nakai**
Current vs. new system	New will operate more smoothly and efficiently	
When to convert	As soon as possible	Wait as long as we can
Cost of conversion		Would outweigh any predicted benefits

MANHATTAN
PREP

In this diagram, we have represented every point made by either of the two conversation participants. While it may have initially seemed as if their arguments were related in many ways, there is actually only one point of intersection, or overlap, between the two: when to convert to the new system. Both participants support their claims with a supporting premise, but these premises do not overlap. Naima uses a comparison of *system quality* to justify her point, while Nakai cites the *cost* of making the conversion to justify his point. So in the end, they disagree over the main conclusion.

Thus, the only point of overlap, and therefore the only possible point of disagreement, is when to convert to the new system. Answer (E) is the correct answer.

Notice that some of the other answer choices are tempting because they *seem* related, and they *seem* like points of disagreement. Take (B), for example. It seems like Naima would believe that "it is essential to have the best computer system available" and that Nakai wouldn't necessarily agree with this (especially if it's too expensive). But neither of them ever really addresses this point directly. Don't assume!

Here's another one. It's tough! Remember to find the overlap and don't go beyond what is stated directly:

> ## PT33, S3, Q19
>
> Raphaela: Forcing people to help others is morally wrong. Therefore, no government has the right to redistribute resources via taxation. Anyone who wants can help others voluntarily.
>
> Edward: Governments do have that right, insofar as they give people the freedom to leave and hence not to live under their authority.
>
> Raphaela and Edward disagree about the truth of which one of the following?
>
> (A)   Any government that does not permit emigration would be morally wrong to redistribute resources via taxation.
>
> (B)   Any government that permits emigration has the right to redistribute resources via taxation.
>
> (C)   Every government should allow people to help others voluntarily.
>
> (D)   Any government that redistributes resources via taxation forces people to help others.
>
> (E)   Any government that forces people to help others should permit emigration.

This question presents us with a higher level of challenge. Each of the five answer choices seems to be related to points made by the conversation participants. We can make our job much easier by identifying the overlap (in our mind if not on paper):

	Raphaela	**Edward**
Forcing people to help others	Morally wrong; should be done voluntarily	
Government rights	No right to redistribute resources through taxation	Governments do have this right
Emigration		Governments give people the freedom to leave

Notice that there is just one point of intersection: the main conclusion (governments' rights to redistribute resources through taxation). This shouldn't be surprising. Remember, the overlap will generally occur on 1) the main conclusion, or 2) a supporting premise. Raphaela argues that governments do NOT have this right, while Edward argues that they DO have this right. Each participant uses a supporting premise to support his or her argument, but there is no overlap between these premises.

Thus, there is just one possible point of disagreement. Let's look at the answer choices:

(A)   Any government that does not permit emigration would be morally wrong to redistribute resources via taxation.

This does not address the issue of government rights. Eliminate it.

(B)   Any government that permits emigration has the right to redistribute resources via taxation.

This addresses a government's right to redistribute resources (the point of overlap), but it also mentions emigration, which is a topic unique to Edward's argument. Let's put this one on hold for now.

(C)   Every government should allow people to help others voluntarily.

Answer (C) discusses the concept of people helping others (unique to Raphaela's argument) and fails to mention anything about the right of governments. Eliminate it.

(D)   Any government that redistributes resources via taxation forces people to help others.

Answer (D) mentions forcing people to help others (unique to Raphaela's argument) and fails to mention anything about the right of governments. Eliminate it.

(E)   Any government that forces people to help others should permit emigration.

This mentions forcing people to help others (unique to Raphaela) and emigration (unique to Edward) and fails to mention anything about the right of governments. Eliminate it.

MANHATTAN
PREP

Therefore, (B) is the correct answer as it addresses the one point of overlap. It does mention emigration (unique to Edward's argument), but this is appropriate. After all, Raphaela argues that NO government has the right to redistribute resources through taxation. Edward argues that governments do have this right, as long as they allow emigration. In other words, the two disagree only if emigration is allowed. Thus, this qualification must be part of the answer.

Procedure Questions

Procedure questions are fairly rare, but they come up frequently enough to warrant a short discussion. Procedure questions ask you to identify the "procedure," or strategy, used in presenting an argument or responding to an argument. Just as all Analyze Argument Structure questions do, these questions require a strong understanding of how arguments are formed.

Let's try a Procedure question:

PT35, S1, Q11

Linguist: Some people have understood certain
        studies as showing that bilingual children have a
        reduced "conceptual map" because bilingualism
        overstresses the child's linguistic capacities.
        Vocabulary tests taken by bilingual children
        appear to show that these children tend to have a
        smaller vocabulary than do most children of the
        same age group. But these studies are deeply
        flawed since the tests were given in only one
        language. Dual-language tests revealed that the
        children often expressed a given concept with a
        word from only one of their two languages.

The linguist's argument proceeds by

(A)   offering evidence for the advantages of
        bilingualism over monolingualism

(B)   pointing out an inconsistency in the view that
        bilingualism overstresses a child's linguistic
        capacities

(C)   offering evidence that undermines the use of
        any vocabulary test to provide information
        about a child's conceptual map

(D)   providing a different explanation for the
        apparent advantages of bilingualism from the
        explanation suggested by the results of certain
        studies

(E)   pointing out a methodological error in the
        technique used to obtain the purported
        evidence of a problem with bilingualism

For this problem, our job is to understand the author's method of reasoning, or the manner in which he attempts to prove his point. This problem is asking us to describe something we've become very familiar with: the argument core.

What is the author's conclusion? It comes in the middle of the argument:

    But these studies are deeply flawed

Why are these studies deeply flawed?

    … since the tests were given in only one language.

Of course, we need to reference other parts of the argument in order to know what the studies are, and we need to reference other parts of the argument to understand why it might be an issue that the tests were only given in one language, and in real time during the exam we want our understanding to be rounded out in this way, but we can also essentialize the core as follows:

tests were given in only one language ➡ studies are deeply flawed

The question asks us to find an answer that represents how the argument plays out. Let's evaluate the answer choices against our core:

(A)   offering evidence for the advantages of
          bilingualism over monolingualism

Close, but no cigar. There is comparison of the two, but the author does not present evidence for the advantages of bilingualism. This answer can be eliminated quickly.

(B)   pointing out an inconsistency in the view that
          bilingualism overstresses a child's linguistic
          capacities

The author is not pointing out an inconsistency in the view, but rather a flaw in the method of testing.

(C)   offering evidence that undermines the use of
          any vocabulary test to provide information
          about a child's conceptual map

Sure, these answers can all sound alike, but by this point you should be hypersensitive to words like "any"—is the author talking about one specific test or all vocabulary tests? This answer is far too broad.

(D)   providing a different explanation for the
          apparent advantages of bilingualism from the
          explanation suggested by the results of certain
          studies

The author does not provide a different explanation.

(E)   pointing out a methodological error in the
          technique used to obtain the purported
          evidence of a problem with bilingualism

This is what the author does. He points out an error in the methods used to gather evidence—the error being that the children were tested in only one language. This is the correct answer.

Like the majority of LR questions, Procedure questions are much easier to solve if you have a strong and simple understanding of the core.

Oftentimes, as evidenced by the question above, these questions come with longer arguments, and the test writer tends to make it tougher than normal to identify the core. If you can't see the core completely, that's fine—make sure you focus in on the conclusion of the argument, and use this as a way to eliminate wrong answers and identify the right one.

In our example above, simply knowing that the author's point was that the study was flawed would have made several answer choices—such as (A), (B), and (D)—seem very unlikely to be correct (and in real time, you would check each of these against the rest of the argument to confirm that they are indeed incorrect). Plus, knowing the conclusion would have made (E) the clear favorite because it is the only answer that speaks directly to a flaw in the study. It is often true of Procedure questions that an understanding of the author's conclusion can, in and of itself, help you eliminate several of the answer choices.

The second type of Procedure question asks that we consider how a certain author proceeds in rebutting another argument. Let's take a look:

PT30, S2, Q7

Opponent of offshore oil drilling: The projected benefits of drilling new oil wells in certain areas in the outer continental shelf are not worth the risk of environmental disaster. The oil already being extracted from these areas currently provides only 4 percent of our country's daily oil requirement, and the new wells would only add one-half of 1 percent.

Proponent of offshore oil drilling: Don't be ridiculous! You might just as well argue that new farms should not be allowed, since no new farm could supply the total food needs of our country for more than a few minutes.

The drilling proponent's reply to the drilling opponent proceeds by

(A)   offering evidence in support of drilling that is more decisive than is the evidence offered by the drilling opponent

(B)   claiming that the statistics cited as evidence by the drilling opponent are factually inaccurate

(C)   pointing out that the drilling opponent's argument is a misapplication of a frequently legitimate way of arguing

(D)   citing as parallel to the argument made by the drilling opponent an argument in which the conclusion is strikingly unsupported

(E)   proposing a conclusion that is more strongly supported by the drilling opponent's evidence than is the conclusion offered by the drilling opponent

In order to be successful on questions such as the above, it is essential to have a clear and *simple* understanding of an argument's structure. We can organize the opponent's argument as follows:

Conclusion: The projected benefits of drilling new oil wells in certain areas in the outer continental shelf are not worth the risk of environmental disaster.

Supporting Premises: The oil already being extracted from these areas currently provides only 4 percent of our country's daily oil requirement, and the new wells would only add one-half of 1 percent.

Now, let's consider the proponent's rebuttal relative to the structure of the original argument:

> *"Don't be ridiculous!*
> **This doesn't give us very much that is specific.**
>
> *"You might just as well argue that new farms should not be allowed ..."*
> **This is a conclusion that is analogous to the conclusion the opponent reached.**
>
> *"... since no new farm could supply the total food needs of our country for more than a few minutes."*
> **This part is analogous to the premises in the original argument.**

So, what do we have in the proponent's response? We have an argument with the same structure as the original—but one that isn't reasonable. Just because one farm can't feed the country doesn't mean, of course, that no new farms should be allowed. The proponent proceeds by presenting an analogous argument that is obviously flawed.

Answer choice (D) represents this, and is therefore the correct answer.

Let's review the other answer choices quickly:

> (A)   offering evidence in support of drilling that is
>   more decisive than is the evidence offered by
>   the drilling opponent

The proponent could have done this, but did not. In fact, she did not offer any direct evidence, one way or the other, that related to drilling.

> (B)   claiming that the statistics cited as evidence by
>   the drilling opponent are factually inaccurate

This is incorrect. The proponent is questioning the use of the stats, not their accuracy.

> (C)   pointing out that the drilling opponent's
>   argument is a misapplication of a frequently
>   legitimate way of arguing

The proponent does try to point out flaws in the reasoning structure of the opponent's argument, but we have no direct indication that the drilling opponent's way of arguing is usually legitimate. Perhaps it's always illegitimate!

> (E)   proposing a conclusion that is more strongly
>   supported by the drilling opponent's evidence
>   than is the conclusion offered by the drilling
>   opponent

The proponent does not present a conclusion that can be related to the evidence presented by the opponent, and therefore this answer cannot represent the correct procedure.

Conclusion

There are four types of questions that require you to analyze the argument structure in one way or another. Here they are again with a list of takeaways for each:

Identify the Conclusion

1. **Always identify the conclusion first!** This may seem like an obvious step, but some test-takers might be tempted to read the argument and then jump directly into the answer choices. Remember to take a moment after you finish an argument to make sure that you've correctly identified its conclusion *before* you look at the answer choices.

2. **Watch for conclusions that are "stuck in the middle."** We mentioned earlier that the conclusion of the argument can appear at the start of the argument, in the middle, or at the end. Typically, it's much easier to spot a conclusion when it appears at the beginning or at the end of an argument. For this reason, when the LSAT asks you to identify a conclusion, that conclusion will typically be buried somewhere in the middle of the argument, just to make things a bit more difficult on you.

3. **Find the author's conclusion, not yours.** When a question asks you to *find* the main conclusion of an argument, you must not infer anything at all. Remember, you're looking for the author's conclusion. Don't be tempted to draw your own conclusion.

4. **Main conclusions are last in the chain of logic.** If you have trouble identifying the final conclusion, it's probably because the argument contains an intermediate conclusion that seems like it could be the final conclusion. Use the Therefore Test to help determine which point actually comes last in the chain of logic.

5. **Don't be fooled by rewordings of the conclusion.** The LSAT will often attempt to disguise the correct answer by rewording the conclusion in the correct answer choice. You should not expect the correct answer to be an exact replica of the conclusion as it is worded in the argument.

Determine the Function

1. **Identify the conclusion first.** Without knowing the conclusion, it's virtually impossible to assign a function to any other part of the argument. Thus, always start by identifying the conclusion.

2. **Keep the sides straight.** Your ability to avoid trap answers on Determine the Function questions will often depend on how well you can separate the sides of the argument. Make sure to separate supporting premises from opposing points.

10

Identify the Disagreement

1. **Don't assume anything!** There may be hints that the authors have different opinions, or different definitions of a particular phrase, or different ways of seeing evidence, but an answer choice is unlikely to be correct unless it contains elements that are specifically, rather than indirectly, mentioned in the text. This leads us to...

2. **Identify the overlap!** Two people can only disagree about something they each have an opinion about. Most of the time, there is only one point of overlap, and recognizing this overlap will point you toward the right answer.

3. **Anticipate the point of disagreement.** Generally speaking, the two participants in a conversation will likely express their disagreement through opposing conclusions. However, the participants will sometimes disagree over a piece of supporting evidence instead. If you know that disagreements will most often occur 1) over the conclusion, or 2) over a piece of supporting evidence, you'll have a better shot at identifying the correct answer.

Procedure

1. **Know your argument components and how they work to form an argument!** You know the drill: Find the core.

2. **When in doubt, find the conclusion.** Even if you don't see all the components, you can often eliminate multiple answers that misrepresent the conclusion.

Drill It: Analyze Argument Structure Questions

1. PT29, S4, Q2

Economist: To the extent that homelessness arises from a lack of available housing, it should not be assumed that the profit motive is at fault. Private investors will, in general, provide housing if the market allows them to make a profit; it is unrealistic to expect investors to take risks with their property unless they get some benefit in return.

Which one of the following most accurately describes the role played in the economist's argument by the phrase "To the extent that homelessness arises from a lack of available housing"?

(A)   It limits the application of the argument to a part of the problem.

(B)   It suggests that the primary cause of homelessness is lack of available housing.

(C)   It is offered as evidence crucial to the conclusion.

(D)   It expresses the conclusion to be argued for.

(E)   It suggests a possible solution to the problem of homelessness.

2. PT36, S1, Q7

It is widely believed that eating chocolate can cause acne. Indeed, many people who are susceptible to acne report that, in their own experience, eating large amounts of chocolate is invariably followed by an outbreak of that skin condition. However, it is likely that common wisdom has mistaken an effect for a cause. Several recent scientific studies indicate that hormonal changes associated with stress can cause acne and there is good evidence that people who are fond of chocolate tend to eat more chocolate when they are under stress.

The argument employs which one of the following argumentative strategies?

(A)   It cites counterevidence that calls into question the accuracy of the evidence advanced in support of the position being challenged.

(B)   It provides additional evidence that points to an alternative interpretation of the evidence offered in support of the position being challenged.

(C)   It invokes the superior authority of science over common opinion in order to dismiss out of hand the relevance of evidence based on everyday experience.

(D)   It demonstrates that the position being challenged is inconsistent with certain well-established facts.

(E)   It provides counterexamples to show that, contrary to the assumption on which the commonly held position rests, causes do not always precede their effects.

3. PT18, S4, Q2

Zoo director: The city is in a financial crisis and must reduce its spending. Nevertheless, at least one reduction measure in next year's budget, cutting City Zoo's funding in half, is false economy. The zoo's current budget equals less than 1 percent of the city's deficit, so withdrawing support from the zoo does little to help the city's financial situation. Furthermore, the zoo, which must close if its budget is cut, attracts tourists and tax dollars to the city. Finally, the zoo adds immeasurably to the city's cultural climate and thus makes the city an attractive place for business to locate.

Which one of the following is the main conclusion of the zoo director's argument?

(A)   Reducing spending is the only means the city has of responding to the current financial crisis.

(B)   It would be false economy for the city to cut the zoo's budget in half.

(C)   City Zoo's budget is only a very small portion of the city's entire budget.

(D)   The zoo will be forced to close if its budget is cut.

(E)   The city's educational and cultural climate will be irreparably damaged if the zoo is forced to close.

4. PT16, S2, Q13

Alexander: The chemical waste dump outside our town should be cleaned up immediately. Admittedly, it will be very costly to convert that site into woodland, but we have a pressing obligation to redress the harm we have done to local forests and wildlife.

Teresa: But our town's first priority is the health of its people. So even if putting the dump there was environmentally disastrous, we should not spend our resources on correcting it unless it presents a significant health hazard to people. If it does, then we only need to remove that hazard.

Which one of the following is the point at issue between Alexander and Teresa?

(A)   whether the maintenance of a chemical waste dump inflicts significant damage on forests and wildlife

(B)   whether it is extremely costly to clean up a chemical waste dump in order to replace it by a woodland

(C)   whether the public should be consulted in determining the public health risk posed by a chemical waste dump

(D)   whether the town has an obligation to redress damage to local forests and wildlife if that damage poses no significant health hazard to people

(E)   whether destroying forests and wildlife in order to establish a chemical waste dump amounts to an environmental disaster

5. PT33, S1, Q5

A recent national study of the trash discarded in several representative areas confirmed that plastics constitute a smaller proportion of all trash than paper products do, whether the trash is measured by weight or by volume. The damage that a given weight or volume of trash does to the environment is roughly the same whether the trash consists of plastics or paper products. Contrary to popular opinion, therefore, the current use of plastics actually does less harm to the environment nationwide than that of paper products.

The main conclusion of the argument is that

(A)   plastics constitute a smaller proportion of the nation's total trash than do paper products

(B)   the ratio of weight to volume is the same for plastic trash as it is for paper trash

(C)   popular opinion regards the use of paper products as less harmful to the environment than the use of products made from plastic

(D)   contrary to popular opinion, a shift away from the use of paper products to the use of plastics would benefit the environment nationwide

(E)   at this time more harm is being done to the environment nationwide by the use of paper than by the use of plastics

6. PT16, S3, Q4

Bart: A mathematical problem that defied solution for hundreds of years has finally yielded to a supercomputer. The process by which the supercomputer derived the result is so complex, however, that no one can fully comprehend it. Consequently, the result is unacceptable.

Anne: In scientific research, if the results of a test can be replicated in other tests, the results are acceptable even though the way they were derived might not be fully understood. Therefore, if a mathematical result derived by a supercomputer can be reproduced by other supercomputers following the same procedure, it is acceptable.

The exchange between Bart and Anne most strongly supports the view that they disagree as to

(A)   whether a scientific result that has not been replicated can properly be accepted

(B)   whether the result that a supercomputer derives for a mathematical problem must be replicated on another supercomputer before it can be accepted

(C)   the criterion to be used for accepting a mathematical result derived by a supercomputer

(D)   the level of complexity of the process to which Bart refers in his statements

(E)   the relative complexity of mathematical problems as compared to scientific problems

7. PT34, S3, Q14

People's political behavior frequently does not match their rhetoric. Although many complain about government intervention in their lives, they tend not to reelect inactive politicians. But a politician's activity consists largely in the passage of laws whose enforcement affects voters' lives. Thus, voters often reelect politicians whose behavior they resent.

Which one of the following most accurately describes the role played in the argument by the claim that people tend not to reelect inactive politicians?

(A)   It describes a phenomenon for which the argument's conclusion is offered as an explanation.

(B)   It is a premise offered in support of the conclusion that voters often reelect politicians whose behavior they resent.

(C)   It is offered as an example of how a politician's activity consists largely in the passage of laws whose enforcement interferes with voters' lives.

(D)   It is a generalization based on the claim that people complain about government intervention in their lives.

(E)   It is cited as evidence that people's behavior never matches their political beliefs.

8. PT32, S4, Q20

Dana: It is wrong to think that the same educational methods should be used with all children. Many children have been raised in more communal environments than others and would therefore learn better through group, rather than individual, activities. A child's accustomed style of learning should always dictate what method is used.

Pat: No, not always. The flexibility of being able to work either on one's own or in a group is invaluable in a world where both skills are in demand.

The conversation lends the most support to the claim that Dana and Pat disagree on which one of the following?

(A)   All children can learn valuable skills from individual activities.

(B)   All children should learn to adapt to various educational methods.

(C)   Many children would learn better through group, rather than individual, activities.

(D)   The main purpose of education is to prepare children to meet the demands of the job market as adults.

(E)   It is sometimes desirable to tailor educational methods to the way a child learns best.

<u>9. PT33, S1, Q3</u>

Juan: Unlike the ancient Olympic games on which they are based, the modern Olympics include professional as well as amateur athletes. But since amateurs rarely have the financial or material resources available to professionals, it is unlikely that the amateurs will ever offer a serious challenge to professionals in those Olympic events in which amateurs compete against professionals. Hence, the presence of professional athletes violates the spirit of fairness essential to the games.

Michiko: But the idea of the modern Olympics is to showcase the world's finest athletes, regardless of their backgrounds or resources. Hence, professionals should be allowed to compete.

Which one the following most accurately expresses the point at issue between Juan and Michiko?

(A)   whether the participation of both amateur and professional athletes is in accord with the ideals of the modern Olympics

(B)   whether both amateur and professional athletes competed in the ancient Olympic games upon which the modern Olympics are based

(C)   whether the athletes who compete in the modern Olympics are the world's finest

(D)   whether any amateur athletes have the financial or material resources that are available to professional athletes

(E)   whether governments sponsor professional as well as amateur athletes in the modern Olympics

<u>10. PT37, S2, Q13</u>

Adam: Marking rod edges with reflecting posts gives drivers a clear view of the edges, thereby enabling them to drive more safely. Therefore, marking road edges with reflecting posts will decrease the annual number of road accidents.

Aiesha: You seem to forget that drivers exceed the speed limit more frequently and drive close to the road edge more frequently on roads that are marked with reflecting posts than on similar roads without posts, and those are driving behaviors that cause road accidents.

Aiesha responds to Adam's argument by

(A)   questioning Adam's assertion that reflecting posts give drivers a clear view of road edges

(B)   presenting a possible alternative method for decreasing road accidents

(C)   raising a consideration that challenges the argument's assumption that facilitating safe driving will result in safer driving

(D)   denying that the drivers' view of the road is relevant to the number of road accidents

(E)   providing additional evidence to undermine the claim that safer driving does not necessarily reduce the number of road accidents

10

Solutions: Analyze the Argument Questions

Answer Key

1. A	6. C
2. B	7. B
3. B	8. B
4. D	9. A
5. E	10. C

1. PT29, S4, Q2

Economist: To the extent that homelessness arises
       from a lack of available housing, it should not
       be assumed that the profit motive is at fault.
       Private investors will, in general, provide
       housing if the market allows them to make a
       profit; it is unrealistic to expect investors to
       take risks with their property unless they get
       some benefit in return.

Which one of the following most accurately describes
the role played in the economist's argument by the
phrase "To the extent that homelessness arises from a
lack of available housing"?

(A)   It limits the application of the argument to a
       part of the problem.

(B)   It suggests that the primary cause of
       homelessness is lack of available housing.

(C)   It is offered as evidence crucial to the conclusion.

(D)   It expresses the conclusion to be argued for.

(E)   It suggests a possible solution to the problem
       of homelessness.

Answer choice (A) is correct.

The first sentence is the conclusion of the argument. The
following sentences provide support for that conclusion.
What's interesting about this particular problem is that
we are asked to define the role of *one phrase* within the
conclusion. So what does that phrase actually do? By

saying "To the extent that," the author is qualifying, or
setting boundaries on, the conclusion. Let's look for a
choice that reflects this.

(A) is the one! The author is limiting the argument to
one part of the larger problem of homelessness.

(B) is certainly incorrect—this particular phrase does
not say anything about the primacy of the cause.

(C) is not quite right. While the phrase certainly relates
to the conclusion in an intimate way, it is not a fact (it's
not even a complete grammatical sentence) and thus
cannot be called "evidence."

(D) is very close. It is a *part* of the conclusion, but
certainly does not represent the conclusion itself. It
just sets a limit on the larger conclusion that the profit
motive is not at fault.

(E) is not even close.

2. PT36, S1, Q7

       It is widely believed that eating chocolate can cause
acne. Indeed, many people who are susceptible to acne
report that, in their own experience, eating large amounts
of chocolate is invariably followed by an outbreak of that
skin condition. However, it is likely that common wisdom
has mistaken an effect for a cause. Several recent scientific
studies indicate that hormonal changes associated with
stress can cause acne and there is good evidence that
people who are fond of chocolate tend to eat more
chocolate when they are under stress.

The argument employs which one of the following
argumentative strategies?

(A)   It cites counterevidence that calls into question
       the accuracy of the evidence advanced in
       support of the position being challenged.

(B)   It provides additional evidence that points to
       an alternative interpretation of the evidence
       offered in support of the position being
       challenged.

MANHATTAN
PREP

10

(C)   It invokes the superior authority of science over common opinion in order to dismiss out of hand the relevance of evidence based on everyday experience.

(D)   It demonstrates that the position being challenged is inconsistent with certain well-established facts.

(E)   It provides counterexamples to show that, contrary to the assumption on which the commonly held position rests, causes do not always precede their effects.

Answer choice (B) is correct.

This is clearly a very challenging question, and we want to begin by understanding the core as carefully as we can.

The author's main point, "However, it is likely that common wisdom has mistaken an effect for a cause" is not terribly difficult to find, but it takes some diligence to understand what it means specifically. The cause in question is discussed in the first sentence: Eating chocolate can cause acne (notice the close relationship between "common wisdom" and "widely believed"). The author is stating that eating chocolate is an *effect* that has been mistaken for a *cause*.

How does the author try to prove this? By saying that studies show that both eating chocolate and getting acne may be caused by something else: stress. We can think of the reasoning in the core as follows:

studies show that stress can cause chocolate eating and acne ➡ likely that common wisdom has mistaken effect for cause

Okay, the author is pointing out a potential Causation flaw. You should be quite familiar with those by now! However, it's important to note here that our job is not to evaluate the *validity* of this particular argument's

reasoning. Rather, it's simply to understand the argument's structure. We want to spend time being careful thinking about the structure laid out above, and we don't want to distract ourselves by worrying about whether the author's argument is a valid one.

We need to keep our focus in order to successfully evaluate what turn out to be some very challenging answer choices:

(A) This answer is certainly tempting, but the counter-evidence presented does not call into question the *accuracy* of the other evidence—more specifically, it does not call into question whether people actually get acne after eating chocolate, nor does it call into question the fact that they report this to be the case. Rather, the counterevidence is used to call into question the causal connection between chocolate and acne—that is, it calls into the question the *interpretation* of that evidence.

(B) Though this answer choice is worded in a somewhat challenging fashion, this is the answer we ought to expect, and this is the correct answer. The additional evidence gives us another reason, or *an alternative interpretation*, for the fact that eating chocolate and getting acne are correlated—they have a common cause: stress. Thus, the argument does exactly what this answer choice claims.

(C) This could be a tempting answer, but in order for an answer like this to be correct on the LSAT, the argument would have to literally state something that is very close to "scientific authority is superior to common opinion." Without a statement like that actually in the argument, this answer requires too much speculation on our part. Furthermore, the author does not dismiss the *relevance* of the other evidence. Rather, she gives an alternative explanation for it.

(D) This is another very attractive answer! However, the very big shift from "well-established facts" in the answer choice to "recent scientific studies" (i.e., not well-established) and "good evidence" (i.e., not facts) in

10

the argument should make it clear that this answer is not representative of the given argument. Furthermore, the conventional wisdom the author is challenging isn't actually inconsistent with the new data. It could still be true that chocolate causes acne; this new evidence just allows us to consider another possibility.

(E) This answer choice is about a general idea that causes always come before their effects. The original argument did not depend on the idea that causes always happen before their effects, and the counterexample was not given to show that causes don't always happen before their effects.

3. PT18, S4, Q2

Zoo director: The city is in a financial crisis and must reduce its spending. Nevertheless, at least one reduction measure in next year's budget, cutting City Zoo's funding in half, is false economy. The zoo's current budget equals less than 1 percent of the city's deficit, so withdrawing support from the zoo does little to help the city's financial situation. Furthermore, the zoo, which must close if its budget is cut, attracts tourists and tax dollars to the city. Finally, the zoo adds immeasurably to the city's cultural climate and thus makes the city an attractive place for business to locate.

10

Which one of the following is the main conclusion of the zoo director's argument?

(A)   Reducing spending is the only means the city has of responding to the current financial crisis.

(B)   It would be false economy for the city to cut the zoo's budget in half.

(C)   City Zoo's budget is only a very small portion of the city's entire budget.

(D)   The zoo will be forced to close if its budget is cut.

(E)   The city's educational and cultural climate will be irreparably damaged if the zoo is forced to close.

Answer choice (B) is correct.

This argument is a great example of the "conclusion in the middle" structure that we've emphasized. It goes a bit further, in fact, adding Premise–Premise–Premise to the tail end! The keyword "nevertheless" is a telltale signal that the argument is turning away from the first statement and into conclusion territory.

(A) is the trap answer for test-takers who believe the first sentence is the conclusion. But notice how the rest of the argument simply takes it as known fact that the city must reduce its budget. In order to be a true conclusion, a claim must have support in the argument. All of the support in this argument, however, is designed to add logical weight to the second sentence, which is the true conclusion.

(B) is definitely the conclusion, supported by the final three sentences of the argument. A quick Therefore Test would settle any lingering doubts about this one.

(C) is true, but is not a claim, so it's not a viable candidate for the conclusion. It is a simple fact.

(D) functions the same as answer (C).

(E) goes beyond the scope of the argument and therefore cannot be the main conclusion.

MANHATTAN
PREP

4. PT16, S2, Q13

Alexander: The chemical waste dump outside our town should be cleaned up immediately. Admittedly, it will be very costly to convert that site into woodland, but we have a pressing obligation to redress the harm we have done to local forests and wildlife.

Teresa: But our town's first priority is the health of its people. So even if putting the dump there was environmentally disastrous, we should not spend our resources on correcting it unless it presents a significant health hazard to people. If it does, then we only need to remove that hazard.

Which one of the following is the point at issue between Alexander and Teresa?

(A)   whether the maintenance of a chemical waste dump inflicts significant damage on forests and wildlife

(B)   whether it is extremely costly to clean up a chemical waste dump in order to replace it by a woodland

(C)   whether the public should be consulted in determining the public health risk posed by a chemical waste dump

(D)   whether the town has an obligation to redress damage to local forests and wildlife if that damage poses no significant health hazard to people

(E)   whether destroying forests and wildlife in order to establish a chemical waste dump amounts to an environmental disaster

Answer choice (D) is correct.

Notice that it's left unclear whether Teresa actually agrees or disagrees about the need to clean up the waste dump. She only states that if it were to be done, it should be done for particular reasons and within certain parameters.

So what is the point of disagreement? Is it Alexander's second sentence, that it would be very costly to convert to woodland? No. Teresa doesn't comment on that.

What about Alexander's final point, that we have a pressing obligation to redress the harm we have done to local forests and wildlife? Yes, Teresa does disagree with this, albeit in a somewhat indirect fashion. She says that the only consideration is whether there is a risk to people's health.

Let's evaluate the answers:

(A) is something Alexander would agree with, but Teresa may or may not. We don't actually know.

(B) is something Alexander would agree with, while Teresa may or may not.

(C) is not mentioned by either person.

(D) would be quite acceptable to Alexander—his position is that the town has an obligation to redress the harm done to the environment. Teresa would definitely disagree, so this must be the right answer.

(E) is interesting in that Alexander definitely thinks harm has been done, but he never mentions the word "disaster." Furthermore, Teresa does not reveal her own opinion about this matter, so we can eliminate the choice for that reason. Her argument simply says "even if" it is a disaster—we don't know whether she believes it is.

5. PT33, S1, Q5

A recent national study of the trash discarded in several representative areas confirmed that plastics constitute a smaller proportion of all trash than paper products do, whether the trash is measured by weight or by volume. The damage that a given weight or volume of trash does to the environment is roughly the same whether the trash consists of plastics or paper products. Contrary to popular opinion, therefore, the current use of plastics actually does less harm to the environment nationwide than that of paper products.

MANHATTAN
PREP

The main conclusion of the argument is that

(A)   plastics constitute a smaller proportion of the
       nation's total trash than do paper products

(B)   the ratio of weight to volume is the same for
       plastic trash as it is for paper trash

(C)   popular opinion regards the use of paper
       products as less harmful to the environment
       than the use of products made from plastic

(D)   contrary to popular opinion, a shift away from
       the use of paper products to the use of
       plastics would benefit the environment
       nationwide

(E)   at this time more harm is being done to the
       environment nationwide by the use of paper
       than by the use of plastics

Answer choice (E) is correct.

This problem is rather straightforward if you have
trained yourself effectively in identifying pivots that
lead to conclusions. Remember that "therefore" does not
always indicate the main conclusion, but most of the
time, as in this case, it does.

The first two sentences are facts that we must take to be
true, and the final sentence is a claim that synthesizes
these two facts, thus it is last in the chain of logic and
must be the conclusion. Though this conclusion may
look like another fact, it makes a subtle but important
leap in logic. Can you identify a big assumption that the
argument makes?

(A) is a fact, and therefore not the conclusion.

(B) is not stated in the argument.

(C) would be a great answer for an Inference question. It
is not, however, the author's conclusion.

(D) is not stated. In fact, this seems to go against the
argument, which states that plastic is doing less harm
than paper.

(E) is the conclusion! It has simply been reworded
from "plastics … less" to "paper … more." This kind of
rewording is quite common.

6. PT16, S3, Q4

Bart: A mathematical problem that defied solution for
        hundreds of years has finally yielded to a
        supercomputer. The process by which the
        supercomputer derived the result is so complex,
        however, that no one can fully comprehend it.
        Consequently, the result is unacceptable.

Anne: In scientific research, if the results of a test can
        be replicated in other tests, the results are acceptable
        even though the way they were derived might not be
        fully understood. Therefore, if a mathematical result
        derived by a supercomputer can be reproduced by
        other supercomputers following the same procedure,
        it is acceptable.

The exchange between Bart and Anne most strongly
supports the view that they disagree as to

(A)   whether a scientific result that has not been
       replicated can properly be accepted

(B)   whether the result that a supercomputer
       derives for a mathematical problem must be
       replicated on another supercomputer before
       it can be accepted

(C)   the criterion to be used for accepting a
       mathematical result derived by a
       supercomputer

(D)   the level of complexity of the process to which
       Bart refers in his statements

(E)   the relative complexity of mathematical
       problems as compared to scientific problems

Answer choice (C) is correct.

Bart says the result is unacceptable because the manner
in which it was derived cannot be comprehended by
humans. Anne says that the result is acceptable if it can

MANHATTAN
PREP

be reproduced by other supercomputers and that it isn't necessary that humans fully understand it.

(A) is a tempting choice. But do we actually know what Bart's opinion is about a process being verified via replication? No. And, while we know Anne believes that replication can make results acceptable, do we know whether she believes that replication is *required* for acceptance? No.

(B) is another tempting choice. Read carefully. Does Anne think that the result *must* be replicated in order to be accepted? Not quite. We simply know that Anne believes replication *allows* results to be accepted. This is a bit of conditional logic. While Anne says that replication would be sufficient for this result to be accepted, she does not say that it is necessary.

(C) is better. Bart believes that, since the *method* used for this result is incomprehensible, the result is unacceptable. Anne, on the other hand, believes that if this result can be *replicated*, it is acceptable. Bart focuses on understanding as his criterion, while Anne focuses on replication.

(D) is out because Anne does not offer an opinion on the complexity.

(E) is out because science vs. math is not mentioned by either Bart or Anne.

7. PT34, S3, Q14

People's political behavior frequently does not match their rhetoric. Although many complain about government intervention in their lives, they tend not to reelect inactive politicians. But a politician's activity consists largely in the passage of laws whose enforcement affects voters' lives. Thus, voters often reelect politicians whose behavior they resent.

Which one of the following most accurately describes the role played in the argument by the claim that people tend not to reelect inactive politicians?

(A) It describes a phenomenon for which the argument's conclusion is offered as an explanation.

(B) It is a premise offered in support of the conclusion that voters often reelect politicians whose behavior they resent.

(C) It is offered as an example of how a politician's activity consists largely in the passage of laws whose enforcement interferes with voters' lives.

(D) It is a generalization based on the claim that people complain about government intervention in their lives.

(E) It is cited as evidence that people's behavior never matches their political beliefs.

Answer choice (B) is correct.

This problem presents a good lesson in flexibility. Though the LSAT is filled with predictable patterns, it does pitch us a curveball every now and again. The first and last sentences both seem to state the conclusion, and the "But" does not really represent the same kind of logical pivot we've come to expect from it—here it's merely used to define "activity."

So let's try assembling the facts to see how they lead to the conclusion:

10

1. Many people complain about government intervention in their lives.
2. They tend not to reelect inactive politicians.
3. Active politicians pass laws that affect people's lives.

Therefore, voters often reelect politicians whose behavior they resent (political behavior does not match rhetoric). "Often" and "resent" are rather strong, but the flow of logic generally works. If people do not reelect inactive politicians, the author reasons, they must reelect active ones, and complaining about something is roughly equivalent to resenting it.

So how does the claim in question relate to the conclusion? It supports it! Fortunately, we don't have to evaluate the logic of this argument. We just need to identify the statement from the question stem as a premise. Let's look at our choices:

(A) is not quite right. The conclusion does not tell us *why* people do not reelect inactive politicians.

(B) is spot on.

(C) is not even close.

(D) is incorrect because the claim in question is not *based* on the claim about peoples' complaints simply because the two follow one another in a sentence—rather, they are both claims upon which the conclusion is based.

(E) might seem good at first glance. The statement is definitely evidence for the conclusion, but this answer choice misrepresents the author's position. The argument says that people's behavior *frequently does not* match their beliefs, not that it *never* matches.

Dana: It is wrong to think that the same educational methods should be used with all children. Many children have been raised in more communal environments than others and would therefore learn better through group, rather than individual, activities. A child's accustomed style of learning should always dictate what method is used.

Pat: No, not always. The flexibility of being able to work either on one's own or in a group is invaluable in a world where both skills are in demand.

The conversation lends the most support to the claim that Dana and Pat disagree on which one of the following?

(A) All children can learn valuable skills from individual activities.

(B) All children should learn to adapt to various educational methods.

(C) Many children would learn better through group, rather than individual, activities.

(D) The main purpose of education is to prepare children to meet the demands of the job market as adults.

(E) It is sometimes desirable to tailor educational methods to the way a child learns best.

Answer choice (B) is correct.

Dana makes the point that a child's accustomed style of learning should always dictate the method of education used, and Pat responds by saying, "No, not always." Why? Because she feels that the ability to work in different ways—on one's own or in a group—is an invaluable tool in today's world.

Answer choice (B) is the only one about which we know there are strong feelings on both sides. We know for sure that Dana disagrees with this statement, because she thinks the child's accustomed style should always dictate the educational method. We have a strong sense Pat agrees with this statement. We know she doesn't think the child's accustomed learning style should always dictate the educational method, and we know she feels this way *because* she thinks it's important for children to learn to work in a variety of ways.

(A) is not directly discussed by either person.

(C) is not discussed by Pat, nor is it insinuated that Pat would disagree with this.

(D) goes well beyond the scope of either statement.

(E) is tempting, but not necessarily something they would disagree about. It is something Dana would likely agree with, but not an answer Pat would definitely disagree with. She just says that it is not *always* desirable.

9. PT33, S1, Q3

Juan: Unlike the ancient Olympic games on which they are based, the modern Olympics include professional as well as amateur athletes. But since amateurs rarely have the financial or material resources available to professionals, it is unlikely that the amateurs will ever offer a serious challenge to professionals in those Olympic events in which amateurs compete against professionals. Hence, the presence of professional athletes violates the spirit of fairness essential to the games.

Michiko: But the idea of the modern Olympics is to showcase the world's finest athletes, regardless of their backgrounds or resources. Hence, professionals should be allowed to compete.

Which one the following most accurately expresses the point at issue between Juan and Michiko?

(A)   whether the participation of both amateur and professional athletes is in accord with the ideals of the modern Olympics

(B)   whether both amateur and professional athletes competed in the ancient Olympic games upon which the modern Olympics are based

(C)   whether the athletes who compete in the modern Olympics are the world's finest

(D)   whether any amateur athletes have the financial or material resources that are available to professional athletes

(E)   whether governments sponsor professional as well as amateur athletes in the modern Olympics

Answer choice (A) is correct.

Juan thinks that the presence of professional athletes violates the spirit of the Olympics, because amateurs do not have the financial resources to compete with them. Michiko thinks professionals should be allowed to compete because the Olympics are supposed to showcase the world's finest athletes. Technically, Juan never says that professionals should not be allowed to compete, but since Michiko says nothing about fairness, this is the closest we can get to expressing the point at issue between them.

(A) is the correct answer. Do not be fooled by the presence of "amateur." Juan would say "no" to professionals on the basis of fairness, Michiko would say "yes" on the basis of having the finest athletes.

(B) is addressed only by Juan.

(C) is not actually supported by either person. Michiko says the games *should* showcase the world's finest, but does not actually state whether they *do*.

(D) is not addressed by Michiko, and it goes beyond what is stated by Juan. He does not say that amateurs *never* have financial resources equal to pros; he just says they *rarely* do.

(E) is not addressed by either person.

10

10. PT37, S2, Q13

Adam: Marking road edges with reflecting posts gives drivers a clear view of the edges, thereby enabling them to drive more safely. Therefore, marking road edges with reflecting posts will decrease the annual number of road accidents.

Aiesha: You seem to forget that drivers exceed the speed limit more frequently and drive close to the road edge more frequently on roads that are marked with reflecting posts than on similar roads without posts, and those are driving behaviors that cause road accidents.

Aiesha responds to Adam's argument by

(A)   questioning Adam's assertion that reflecting posts give drivers a clear view of road edges

(B)   presenting a possible alternative method for decreasing road accidents

(C)   raising a consideration that challenges the argument's assumption that facilitating safe driving will result in safer driving

(D)   denying that the drivers' view of the road is relevant to the number of road accidents

(E)   providing additional evidence to undermine the claim that safer driving does not necessarily reduce the number of road accidents

10   Answer choice (C) is correct.

Adam says that marking road edges will allow drivers to drive safely and thus decrease accidents. Aiesha says that drivers actually drive *unsafely* on roads with marked edges. How does this relate to Adam's argument? It's evidence that points to the exact opposite conclusion! With this contradictory aspect in mind, we should go to the choices.

(A) is not quite right. She doesn't argue with the fact that the marked edges give a clear view.

(B) is totally incorrect—she does not present an alternative method.

(C) seems good at first glance—she's definitely raising a point that challenges Adam's view. Does he assume that "facilitating safe driving will result in safer driving"? Sure. He thinks that if we enable people to drive more safely, there will actually be fewer accidents. This is our answer.

(D) is kind of like (A). This is not quite right. In fact, Aiesha seems to believe the opposite. View of the road *is* relevant; it just increases, rather than decreases, accidents in this case.

(E) is a tempting choice. Read it carefully. Is that the claim that Aiesha is undermining? Not quite. First of all, she does not even think that the marked edges will, in fact, result in "safer driving," and we can eliminate the choice for this reason. Second, if we did not spot that error, we know that Aiesha's statements *support* rather than undermine the idea that *something* (marking edges) does not necessarily lead to fewer accidents.

MANHATTAN
PREP

Chapter 11

Inference Questions

In This Chapter...

Introduction

About one in every eight Logical Reasoning questions can be categorized as Inference questions. These questions require you to *derive* a conclusion (not to be confused with *identifying* a conclusion) from the information given.

Inference questions can be asked in a variety of ways:

1. **Support (the most common)**

   Example: The statements above, if true, most strongly *support* which one of the following?

2. **Must be true (occasionally "must be false")**

   Example: If the statements above are true, which one of the following *must be true*?

3. **Infer**

   Example: Which one of the following can be properly *inferred* from the statements above?

4. **Completes the argument (fill in the blank)**

   Example: Which one of the following most logically *completes the argument*?

5. **Follows logically**

   Example: Which one of the following claims *follows logically* from the statements?

There are some subtle differences in what these question stems are asking of us, but there is also great commonality. For Inference questions, our main task is to identify the most provable answer of the five available.

Let's start our discussion of Inference questions by first contrasting them with some of the other question types we've already reviewed.

What Inference Questions Are NOT

1. **Inference questions are *not* in the Assumption Family.** To be effective and efficient on the Logical Reasoning section, it is critical that you have a clear understanding of the specific processes required by the various question types.

For questions in the Assumption Family, we want to identify the conclusion and the supporting premises, and we want to evaluate the relationship between them. Our success on Assumption Family questions hinges on our ability to evaluate the reasoning within the argument core.

Inference questions do not require us to evaluate reasoning in the same way. Though some right answers for Inference questions will require that we put two or more statements from the argument together, these questions, in general, are not testing our ability to evaluate how premises lead to a conclusion. In fact, most Inference questions will involve a series of statements that are not meant to fit into an "argument core" sort of mold, so don't force it.

Why is this important? At best, evaluating the reasoning in an argument for an Inference question can be a waste of your precious time. At worst, it can distract you from the correct answer and make incorrect answers more tempting.

2. **Inference questions are *not* Strengthen questions.** The danger comes from how similar the question stems for the two can look.

Take a look at the following:

Example: The statements above, if true, most strongly support which one of the following?

Example: Which of the following, if true, most strongly supports the argument above?

The first is an example of an Inference question—we're asked to identify an answer that is most provable based on the information given. In other words, we're taking the information from the stimulus and seeing which answer choice is supported by it. We infer down, from the stimulus to the answers.

The second is an example of a Strengthen question—we're asked to identify an answer that helps support the given argument. In other words, we're adding the information from the answers to the argument to see which one supports the conclusion. We strengthen up, from the answers to the argument in the stimulus.

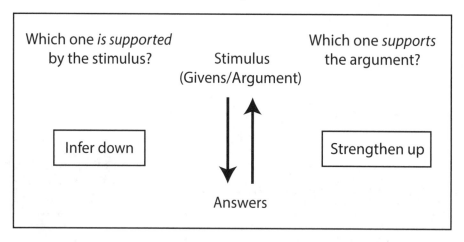

Again, be careful not to confuse one question type for the other.

3. **Inference questions are *not* Identify the Conclusion questions.** This is a common but dangerous misunderstanding. Perhaps part of the reason this is such an issue is that we spend so much time looking for the conclusion on other question types. However, an Inference question will ask us to draw a conclusion of our own, not to identify something that has already been said.

On an Identify the Conclusion question, the right answer will be something directly stated in the argument. The argument may have used different words, but if an answer contains a completely new idea, it will never be the correct answer. By contrast, an Inference question is asking for something that we can logically infer from the given information. None of the answers will simply repeat something from the argument; that would certainly be a correct inference, but it would be too easy! If an Inference answer appears to precisely repeat information from the argument, take a second look. You'll likely find that a key idea or term has been changed to make the answer incorrect.

Again, it is critical that you understand the specific task that each question presents. Now that we've discussed what Inference questions are not, let's talk about the characteristics that *do* define Inference questions.

Inference Questions Often Have Unpredictable Answers

To begin this discussion, take a look at the following argument. Take as much time as you'd like to take notes, underline, diagram, infer, and do whatever else you would like before moving further.

> Most voters prefer Candidate A to Candidate B. Of those who prefer Candidate A, some feel that budgeting for schools is the most important issue. All voters who prefer Candidate B feel that budgeting for schools is the most important issue.

Here are three potential answer choices. Do your best to identify which of these answer choices, if any, can be logically concluded and which, if any, cannot. Cover up the explanations that follow if you are tempted to peek!

> (A)   Some voters who feel budgeting for schools is the most
>   important issue prefer Candidate B.
>
> (B)   Budgeting for schools is the most important issue for at
>   least some of the voters.
>
> (C)   Some voters who prefer Candidate A are concerned about
>   at least one issue about which voters who prefer Candidate B
>   are concerned.

Now, let's evaluate the answer choices:

(A) is inferable. We know that all voters who prefer Candidate B feel that budgeting for schools is the most important issue, so that certainly allows us to infer the weaker statement that at least some of the people who find budgeting for schools to be the most important issue prefer Candidate B. Remember that "some" doesn't mean "not all." It means "at least one."

(B) is inferable. We're given ample evidence that budgeting for schools is the most important issue for at least some people. In fact, we know that at least some people who prefer Candidate A find it most important, and all people who prefer Candidate B do so.

(C) is inferable. We know that *some* people who prefer Candidate A are concerned about budgeting for schools. Since we also know that *all* people who prefer Candidate B have *the same concern,* we can say that some people who prefer Candidate A share a concern in common with those who prefer Candidate B.

If you were correct in assessing all of these answers, fantastic. You have a great knack for this! If you weren't, that's fine, too. We'll all get better and better as we go. For now, consider two issues for your own assessment:

1. Did you find yourself predicting certain answers and, as a consequence, being quick to reject some of the choices that were provided?

2. Did you diagram or draw out this information on your scratch paper, and, if so, was it helpful in evaluating all, or some, of the answers?

We anticipate that different readers will answer the above questions differently—that's understandable. In particular, some of you will find diagramming to be more useful than others will. However, one point we do want to make clear is that correct answers to Inference questions are often not predictable. Many scenarios will be able to yield multiple, equally valid answers.

Here are three more answer choices for you to evaluate. We've transferred the argument for your convenience—please transfer any notation you made previously. Once again, cover up the explanations if you'd like.

> Most voters prefer Candidate A to Candidate B. Of those who prefer Candidate A, some feel that budgeting for schools is the most important issue. All voters who prefer Candidate B feel that budgeting for schools is the most important issue.

(A)   A majority of voters feel that budgeting for schools is the most important issue.

(B)   At least some voters who prefer Candidate B do not share at least one common concern with at least one voter who prefers Candidate A.

(C)   Most voters who find budgeting for schools to be the most important issue prefer Candidate B.

(A) is *not* inferable. Like many other tempting wrong answers, this is a statement that could either be true or false based on the given information:

> Imagine that there are five voters.
> Let's say that three prefer A and two prefer B.
> Of those who prefer A, one finds school budgeting to be the most important issue.
> We already know that the two who prefer B find school budgeting to be most important.

Therefore, we would have three out of five people, a *majority*, who find school budgeting to be the most important issue. So we know that (A) is *possible*. But let's look at a counterexample:

> Now let's imagine that four voters prefer A and one prefers B.
> Of those who prefer A, one finds school budgeting to be the most important issue.
> We already know that the one who prefers B finds school budgeting to be most important.
> In this case, only two out of the five, a *minority*, would find school budgeting to be the most important issue.

Therefore, based on the information given, this statement can be true or false, and so it is not inferable.

(B) is *not* inferable. In fact, it is false. All voters who prefer Candidate B are concerned with school budgeting, and some voters who prefer Candidate A are as well, so it must be true that at least one voter who prefers Candidate A shares a concern in common with *all* of the voters who prefer Candidate B. Even if this were not the case, we've been given no information about what other concerns the voters have, so we could never infer that they have no concerns in common. If even one person in every group were concerned about a particular issue, such as civil rights or clean energy, then this choice would be invalidated.

(C) is *not* inferable. This is another statement that could either be true or false based on the given information:

> Once again, imagine five voters, three of those who prefer A and two who prefer B.
>
> Of those who prefer A, one finds school budgeting most important.
>
> We already know that the two who prefer B find school budgeting to be most important.
>
> In this case, a majority of voters who felt school budgeting was the most important issue could be said to prefer B.
>
> However, it could just as easily be that four of the five voters prefer A and that all of those voters find school budgeting to be the most important issue. In that case, the majority of those who feel that way would be in favor of A.

Keep in mind that the word "some" does *not* mean "less than half." (Please refer to the Conditional Logic chapter for more discussion on "some" issues.)

If you were drawn to any of those three answers, chances are you were tempted into making false inferences, perhaps linking information in an incorrect way. It's understandable. Consistently, we've found that some of the most tempting incorrect choices for challenging Inference questions involve such false connections.

Here's a full question for you. Focus on identifying the most provable answer:

PT31, S2, Q20

One of the most vexing problems in historiography is dating an event when the usual sources offer conflicting chronologies of the event. Historians should attempt to minimize the number of competing sources, perhaps by eliminating the less credible ones. Once this is achieved and several sources are left, as often happens, historians may try, though on occasion unsuccessfully, to determine independently of the usual sources which date is more likely to be right.

Which one of the following inferences is most strongly supported by the information above?

(A)   We have no plausible chronology of most of the events for which attempts have been made by historians to determine the right date.

(B)   Some of the events for which there are conflicting chronologies and for which attempts have been made by historians to determine the right date cannot be dated reliably by historians.

(C)   Attaching a reliable date to any event requires determining which of several conflicting chronologies is most likely to be true.

(D)   Determining independently of the usual sources which of several conflicting chronologies is more likely to be right is an ineffective way of dating events.

(E)   The soundest approach to dating an event for which the usual sources give conflicting chronologies is to undermine the credibility of as many of these sources as possible.

Again, for this type of argument, searching for a conclusion or a core is likely going to be an ineffective use of your time. We simply want to have a general sense of the discussion. If it seems to lead to an inescapable conclusion that has yet to be stated, it's important to note that. However, it's more likely that we will just want to move on quickly to the answer choices.

In this case, the argument begins by describing a problem in dating certain events in history and describes one method of trying to solve this problem. This doesn't seem to be building to a big "Aha!" moment.

MANHATTAN
PREP

(A)   We have no plausible chronology of most of
       the events for which attempts have been made
       by historians to determine the right date.

Is (A) provable?

No. The word that should jump out is "most"—we don't have nearly enough evidence to prove that the information is missing most of the time.

(B)   Some of the events for which there are
       conflicting chronologies and for which
       attempts have been made by historians to
       determine the right date cannot be dated
       reliably by historians.

Is (B) provable?

It seems so. We are told specifically that historians are sometimes unsuccessful in their attempts to date (no pun intended). Let's keep this for now.

(C)   Attaching a reliable date to any event requires
       determining which of several conflicting
       chronologies is most likely to be true.

Is (C) provable?

No. The word that perhaps tips us off right away is "any"—there are many events (what time you woke up this morning, for example) for which a time can be determined without examining conflicting chronologies.

(D)   Determining independently of the usual
       sources which of several conflicting
       chronologies is more likely to be right is an
       ineffective way of dating events.

Is (D) provable?

No. It might be tempting if we are looking for some bigger point to be extracted from this argument, but it is not a statement that we can say can be "proven" based on this argument. It hasn't discussed "effectiveness" directly, and it hasn't given us a way to gauge whether the success rate determined in the argument can be considered effective.

(E)   The soundest approach to dating an event for
       which the usual sources give conflicting
       chronologies is to undermine the credibility
       of as many of these sources as possible.

Is (E) provable?

Absolutely not! To eliminate less credible sources is not the same thing as undermining credibility. The author is not suggesting that undermining credibility is a sound approach.

Let's return to answer choice (B), the correct answer.

> (B)   Some of the events for which there are conflicting chronologies and for which attempts have been made by historians to determine the right date cannot be dated reliably by historians.

Down to one answer, you want to check each part of the argument. We know for sure that there are some events for which there are conflicting chronologies, and we know for sure that historians have made attempts to date these events. We're told they are sometimes unsuccessful. Nothing in this answer requires too great a leap from what we've been given.

Was this answer the author's main point? No, and, in fact, the information that most supports this answer—"though on occasion unsuccessfully"—could be thought of as playing a secondary role in the argument.

Is this answer 100% provable? The truth is, no. There are many reasons why this does not have to be 100% true. For one, perhaps at some point in the future a more accurate dating system for historians will emerge.

This leads us to the next part of our discussion…

Right Answers Will Have a Range of Provability

For some Inference questions, we are asked to identify one answer that *must* be true based on the information given. For these questions, the right answer is designed to be *perfectly provable*. For other Inference questions, we are asked to identify the *most* provable answer based on the information given. In these latter cases, right answers are typically not designed to be perfectly provable, but they will still be very well supported by the statements provided. Otherwise, the correct answer would be a matter of opinion, and that is never the case.

Let's take a look at an example of one of each.

Here's a MUST be true question:

> ### PT25, S2, Q21
>
> If this parking policy is unpopular with the faculty, then we should modify it. If it is unpopular among students, we should adopt a new policy. And, it is bound to be unpopular either with the faculty or among students.
>
> If the statements above are true, which one of the following must also be true?
>
> (A) We should attempt to popularize this parking policy among either the faculty or students.
>
> (B) We should modify this parking policy only if this will not reduce its popularity among students.
>
> (C) We should modify this parking policy if modification will not reduce its popularity with the faculty.
>
> (D) If the parking policy is popular among students, then we should adopt a new policy.
>
> (E) If this parking policy is popular with the faculty, then we should adopt a new policy.

We're told to assume that the statements in the argument are true, so we need not doubt, for example, whether the policy will indeed be unpopular either with the faculty or among students.

From our initial read, what we know is that the stimulus contains some suggestions of what to do if a parking policy is unpopular with either the faculty or the students, then states that the policy will indeed be unpopular with either the faculty or the students.

The correct answer is (E), and it is provable based on the text.

We are told that the policy is unpopular either with the faculty or the students. If it is popular with the faculty, therefore, it MUST BE TRUE that it is unpopular with the students. If it is unpopular with the students, we are told, we should adopt a new policy. Therefore, if it is popular with faculty, it must be true that we should adopt a new policy.

Let's take a look at the other answer choices:

11

(A)   We should attempt to popularize this parking
policy among either the faculty or students.

This is not provable. The author gives no indication that an attempt should be made to popularize the policy with one group or another.

(B)   We should modify this parking policy only if
this will not reduce its popularity among
students.

This is not provable. It links elements of the argument together in incorrect ways. Reducing popularity with students has no direct relation to when the policy should be modified.

(C)   We should modify this parking policy if
modification will not reduce its popularity
with the faculty.

This is not provable. We haven't been given information that can help us evaluate whether modifications will or won't result in reducing popularity with faculty.

(D)   If the parking policy is popular among
students, then we should adopt a new policy.

This is not provable. In fact, we're told we should adopt a new policy if it is unpopular with students.

This argument can also be more formally considered in terms of conditional logic, and it can be helpful to do so. To illustrate, let's break this argument down into a simpler form:

If this parking policy is unpopular with the faculty, then we should modify it.

We can notate this as follows: $-PF \rightarrow M$

If it is unpopular among students, we should adopt a new policy.

$-PS \rightarrow N$

And, it is bound to be unpopular either with the faculty or among students.

If this statement is true, we know that if it is popular with the faculty, it must be unpopular with the students, and if it is popular with students, it must be unpopular with the faculty.

We can represent these two relationships in this way:

$PF \rightarrow -PS$
$PS \rightarrow -PF$

MANHATTAN
PREP

Note that this statement is not a biconditional and does *not* mean that if the policy is unpopular with either group, it must be popular with the other. This would be an illegal reversal of the terms. (For more on this, please refer back to Chapter 3, Conditional Logic.)

The four relationships we know are as follows:

$-PF \rightarrow M$
$-PS \rightarrow N$
$PF \rightarrow -PS$
$PS \rightarrow -PF$

If you can see the links easily, go ahead and write them out quickly:

$PS \rightarrow -PF \rightarrow M$ (If it's popular with students, we should modify it.)
$PF \rightarrow -PS \rightarrow N$ (If it's popular with faculty, we should adopt a new policy.)

Now, let's see if any of our answers match one of the two chains above.

(A)   We should attempt to popularize this parking policy among either the faculty or students.

It's tough to match this answer up with the conditionals above, and that's with good reason: Whom we ought to popularize this policy with is not discussed.

(B)   We should modify this parking policy only if this will not reduce its popularity among students.

$M \rightarrow$ reduce PS

Reducing popularity also is not discussed. Notice that in no way can we manipulate any of the known conditionals so that M acts as a trigger that results in this particular consequence.

(C)   We should modify this parking policy if modification will not reduce its popularity with the faculty.

Again, reducing popularity is not in any of our conditionals.

(D)   If the parking policy is popular among students, then we should adopt a new policy.

$PS \rightarrow N$

This answer is a mix-up of the conditionals we laid out above. It's not inferable.

(E)   If this parking policy is popular with the
        faculty, then we should adopt a new policy.

    PF → N

This is indeed provable. It's the second of our two chains.

As you can see, being able to notate arguments in a formal fashion can be very helpful, especially for verifying the correct answer or choosing between two attractive answers to a Must be True Inference question.

Do always keep in mind that these notations are one tool, but not your only tool. When transferring from English to conditional notation, be careful that you don't forget about the nuances of the argument.

In the above example, it is critical to recognize the fact that the argument is about the consequences of *being* popular or unpopular, whereas several of the answer choices are about *becoming* more or less popular. This is the type of difference that can be obscured by notation.

Now let's take a look at a question that asks us to find the *most* provable answer:

> ## *PT36, S1, Q4*
>
> Most antidepressant drugs cause weight gain. While dieting can help reduce the amount of weight gained while taking such antidepressants, some weight gain is unlikely to be preventable.
>
> The information above most strongly supports which one of the following?
>
> (A)   A physician should not prescribe any
>   antidepressant drug for a patient if that
>   patient is overweight.
> (B)   People who are trying to lose weight should
>   not ask their doctors for an antidepressant
>   drug.
> (C)   At least some patients taking antidepressant
>   drugs gain weight as a result of taking them.
> (D)   The weight gain experienced by patients taking
>   antidepressant drugs should be attributed to
>   lack of dieting.
> (E)   All patients taking antidepressant drugs
>   should diet to maintain their weight.

What we know from the argument is that most antidepressant drugs cause weight gain and that some weight gain from such antidepressants is unlikely to be preventable. While we don't know exactly what the answer will be, we know that all of the information we have been given is about weight gain, so that is sure to show up in the answer. We can also expect that several of the answer choices will introduce reasonable seeming ideas that are beyond the scope of what we've been told.

Glancing down the list, we may be drawn to answer (C).

> (C)   At least some patients taking antidepressant
>   drugs gain weight as a result of taking them.

From what we've been told, it seems reasonable to conclude that at least some patients taking antidepressant drugs gain weight as a result of taking them.

Is this answer 100% provable? Not exactly. For one, "unlikely to be preventable" does not mean it won't be preventable. Furthermore, imagine a scenario where most antidepressant drugs cause weight gain, but everyone happens to take the one antidepressant drug that doesn't cause weight gain. In this case, answer choice (C) would not be true. However, we had to stretch a bit to come up with these cases, and (C) still seems pretty reasonable. Let's see what the other choices have to offer.

> (A)   A physician should not prescribe any
>   antidepressant drug for a patient if that
>   patient is overweight.

We don't know anything about what a physician should or should not do. Maybe depression is a more serious problem than being overweight.

> (B)   People who are trying to lose weight should
>   not ask their doctors for an antidepressant
>   drug.

This is identical to answer choice (A), except that it focuses on what patients should do. Again, we know nothing about this.

> (D)   The weight gain experienced by patients taking
>   antidepressant drugs should be attributed to
>   lack of dieting.

This answer is not provable based on the statements in the argument. While dieting is mentioned as something that can sometimes alleviate weight gain, lack of dieting is not mentioned as the cause of weight gain.

> (E)   All patients taking antidepressant drugs
>   should diet to maintain their weight.

Again, we don't know what anyone should do. Besides, maybe some patients would benefit from gaining weight.

11

Now that we've worked wrong-to-right, the problems with (C) are looking pretty minor. Can we definitively infer that some patients taking antidepressants will gain weight? No, but given the statements provided, it seems fairly likely. Meanwhile, all of the other answer choices make unsupported normative statements. We have no idea what doctors or patients should do. We need to work directly from the statements provided, without assuming, for instance, that people should avoid gaining weight. Note that there will be right answers to Must be True questions that seem less than perfect, and answers to Support questions that seem 100% provable. However, in general, it is helpful to look out for absolute terms, such as "must," versus relative terms, such as "most," to help get a sense of how strongly the right answer needs to be supported.

Let's look at one more problem:

PT27, S4, Q5

Ticks attach themselves to host animals to feed. Having fed to capacity, and not before then, the ticks drop off their host. Deer ticks feeding off white-footed mice invariably drop off their hosts between noon and sunset, regardless of time of attachment. White-footed mice are strictly nocturnal animals that spend all daytime hours in their underground nests.

Which one of the following conclusions can be properly drawn from the statements above?

(A)   Deer ticks all attach themselves to white-footed mice during the same part of the day, regardless of day of attachment.

(B)   Deer ticks sometimes drop off their hosts without having fed at all.

(C)   Deer ticks that feed off white-footed mice drop off their hosts in the hosts' nests.

(D)   White-footed mice to which deer ticks have attached themselves are not aware of the ticks.

(E)   White-footed mice are hosts to stable numbers of deer ticks, regardless of season of the year.

Notice that in this stimulus, we are given four absolute statements:

1. Ticks drop off host when fed to capacity, and not before.

2. Deer ticks feeding off white-footed mice always drop off between noon and sunset.

3. White-footed mice are strictly nocturnal.

4. White-footed mice spend all daytime hours in underground nests.

MANHATTAN
PREP

We might try to combine some of these statements, but they cover a lot of ground, and the correct answer could be anything that follows from any combination of them. Armed with all these truths, let's just see which answer can be properly drawn:

> (A)   Deer ticks all attach themselves to white-
>   footed mice during the same part of the day,
>   regardless of day of attachment.

We don't know what time of day ticks attach to the mice, and we don't have a clear way to define "same part" of day.

> (B)   Deer ticks sometimes drop off their hosts
>   without having fed at all.

This is not inferable. In fact, it's false. We know they don't fall off until fed to capacity.

> (C)   Deer ticks that feed off white-footed mice drop
>   off their hosts in the hosts' nests.

The deer ticks fall off during the day, and the mice are in underground nests during the day. Let's keep it.

> (D)   White-footed mice to which deer ticks have
>   attached themselves are not aware of the ticks.

We don't know anything about what the mice are aware of!

> (E)   White-footed mice are hosts to stable numbers
>   of deer ticks, regardless of season of the year.

Neither the number of ticks on any mouse nor the consistency of that number, is discussed in the argument. (E) is not inferable.

(C) is the only viable answer, and it is the correct answer.

At this point, we wouldn't recommend circling back to think about whether (C) is 100% provable (though it is). Instead, rely on your eliminations on answers that clearly weren't provable to drive you to the correct answer.

Again, one point we strongly want to emphasize is that while it might be helpful during your studies to develop a good sense of what is 95% provable versus 100% provable, this type of thinking can be a distraction during the exam. It is important for you to know that these questions are not designed for you to differentiate between that which is almost provable and that which is absolutely provable—almost all of these problems are designed for you to separate out one answer that could fall into *either* of those categories from the four that, upon careful review, clearly cannot be inferred at all.

Therefore, your ability to see that four answers are indeed *not* provable is what is most crucial to your success.

Get to the Right Inference by Eliminating Wrong Answers

Because there are so many potentially correct answers, and because the paths to these potential answers are fraught with danger, the best approach for Inference questions is to focus on eliminating those answers that are most certainly *not* provable based on the information given.

Here are some guiding principles to help you in your process:

1. **Look for term shifts between stimulus and answer choice.** Many answer choices to Inference questions are designed to test your ability to accurately discern differences in the meaning of words and phrases. A great way to spot these differences is to actively look for mismatches in subject matter or attribute between the answer choice and the stimulus. Once you get in this habit, you will see that these differences jump out at you more and more.

Let's use the following stimulus and chart of wrong answers to discuss some significant term shifts that you are likely to see in incorrect answers to Inference questions:

Most people with significant credit card debt will benefit from this bill. Many of these people may be able to eliminate interest payments altogether.

Invalid Inference	Why the Answer Would Be Incorrect
This bill will benefit **all** people with significant credit card debt.	This answer has a **degree** issue. We're told the bill can benefit most of these people, not all.
Very few people with significant credit card debt will benefit from this bill.	This answer has the **opposite meaning.** This is more common than you might think.
Most people who **pay large credit card bills** monthly will benefit from this bill.	This answer has a **detail creep,** or a subtle change in detail. Paying a large credit card bill is not the same as having a large credit card debt. For example, someone might pay the complete bill each month and have no debt.
This new bill is **popular** with most people with significant credit card debt.	This answer has **scope** issues. We have not been given any evidence to show that the bill is *popular* with one group or another.

2. **Be suspicious of answers with faulty reasoning.** Many answers are incorrect because they require inferences that go beyond what the given stimulus can reasonably support. Here are some examples that are representative of common reasoning issues:

Most people with significant credit card debt will benefit from this bill. Many of these people may be able to eliminate interest payments altogether.

Invalid Inference	Why the Answer Would Be Incorrect
If someone with significant credit card debt benefits, it will be due to this bill.	This answer **reverses the logic** of the argument. We're told the bill will benefit people, but that does not mean that if people benefit, it is due to the bill. They might benefit from something else.
This bill will benefit the debt situation of the country as a whole.	This answer incorrectly **generalizes** from the text. We don't have nearly enough evidence to show that the bill will impact the country as a whole.
All people with interest payments have significant credit card debt.	This answer hinges on **unjustified connections.** The argument discusses interest payments, and it discusses those with significant credit card debt, but this answer choice falsely connects those ideas, and it does so with the extreme word "all."

As we've stated in other chapters, there is great overlap in incorrect answer characteristics, and many answers are incorrect for multiple reasons. However, it's to your benefit to develop as specific a sense as you can of incorrect answer characteristics. This will help in both your timing and your accuracy.

Let's finish this lesson by taking a look at four final sample problems. We will use these to get a more complete understanding of incorrect answer characteristics, so consider carefully why you eliminated each incorrect choice before moving on to the explanation:

_PT30, S4, Q22_

In a recent study, a group of subjects had their normal daily caloric intake increased by 25 percent. This increase was entirely in the form of alcohol. Another group of similar subjects had alcohol replace nonalcoholic sources of 25 percent of their normal daily caloric intake. All subjects gained body fat over the course of the study, and the amount of body fat gained was the same for both groups.

Which one of the following is most strongly supported by the information above?

(A)   Alcohol is metabolized more quickly by the body than are other foods or drinks.

(B)   In the general population, alcohol is the primary cause of gains in body fat.

(C)   An increased amount of body fat does not necessarily imply a weight gain.

(D)   Body fat gain is not dependent solely on the number of calories one consumes.

(E)   The proportion of calories from alcohol in a diet is more significant for body fat gain than are the total calories from alcohol.

As you evaluate the answers, you should be focused on trying to identify the characteristics that indicate that a particular answer is _not_ provable based on the text. We've highlighted some of them here.

(A)   Alcohol is **metabolized more quickly** by the body than are other foods or drinks.

How fast alcohol and other food or drinks are metabolized is not discussed, and we can consider this answer out of scope.

(B)   In the **general population**, alcohol is the **primary** cause of gains in body fat.

This answer generalizes and has degree issues. We know nothing of the general population; this stimulus presents no evidence that proves that alcohol is a primary cause, let alone _the_ primary cause, of gains in body fat for this population.

11

(C)   An increased amount of body fat **does not
        necessarily imply a weight gain.**

We don't have enough information to infer any relationship between body fat and weight gain, and in fact, weight gain is never discussed.

(D)   Body fat gain is not dependent solely on the
        number of calories one consumes.

(D) is the correct answer. Notice that one group changed the total amount of calories it consumed, while the other group did not. Both groups gained the same amount of body fat. Since both groups attained the same result even though they consumed a different number of calories, it's reasonable to conclude there must be factors other than calories that are involved. This kind of mild-mannered answer shows up quite frequently on the LSAT. Rather than making a bold proclamation, it just says that something isn't the only factor. A statement like this is pretty easy to support, but it doesn't naturally grab our attention until we've racked up some experience.

(E)   The **proportion** of calories from alcohol in a
        diet is **more significant** for body fat gain than
        are the **total** calories from alcohol.

(E) is a tempting answer that brings together various elements of the argument, but it is not provable. In fact, the evidence seems to suggest that since the results were the same for both groups, total calories from alcohol may play a bigger role than proportion. Even if it wasn't a reversal of what the text implies, there would not be enough evidence from this argument to support a claim such as this one. This is an answer that relies on an incorrect linking of elements of the stimulus.

Here's another example. Again, be specific about why you feel the wrong answers are wrong before moving on to the explanation.

PT37, S4, Q8

Commentator: In the new century, only nations
with all the latest electronic technology will
experience great economic prosperity. The
people in these nations will be constantly
bombarded with images of how people in
other countries live. This will increase their
tendency to question their own customs and
traditions, leading to a dissolution of those
customs and traditions. Hence, in the new
century, the stability of a nation's cultural
identity will likely _____.

Which one of the following most logically completes the
commentator's argument?

(A)   depend on a just distribution of electronic
        technology among all nations

(B)   decrease if that nation comes to have a high
        level of economic wealth

(C)   be ensured by laws that protect the customs
        and traditions of that culture

(D)   be threatened only if the people of that culture
        fail to acquire the latest technical skills

(E)   be best maintained by ensuring gradual
        assimilation of new technical knowledge and
        skills

Of all the questions that are categorized as Inference, questions that ask us to complete the argument may have the
most predictable correct answers. Since we're asked to "logically complete" the argument, these questions tend to be
associated with arguments featuring clean, almost mathematical, structures.

In this problem, the first sentence gives us our first absolute statement: *only* nations with …" From there, there is a
simple order to the new ideas that are introduced, and we can see that these ideas are meant to link together:

only nations with all the latest
electronic technology will experience
great economic prosperity

+

the people in these nations will be
constantly bombarded with images of
how people in other countries live

➡

this will increase
their tendency
to question their
own customs
and traditions

➡

leading to a
dissolution of
those customs
and traditions

Remember, our job in an Inference question is *not* to question the validity of the reasoning, but rather to see it clearly and make a logical inference from the information.

Answers to questions that ask us to complete the argument are a bit more predictable for another reason that has to do with the structure of stimulus: We are given a portion of the statement we are meant to infer. This narrows the scope of what could be the right answer.

In this case, we are given the phrase, "Hence, in the new century, the stability of a nation's cultural identity will likely _____ ." In terms of the information we've already been presented with in the argument, "stability of a nation's cultural identity" is most directly related to the statement that immediately precedes the sentence: "a dissolution of those customs and traditions."

Let's discuss the exact wording of the question: "completes the commentator's argument." While on most Inference questions we are looking for anything that we can conclude from the given information, here we need to determine what the commentator is *likely* to conclude. What would be a reasonable conclusion to the argument that would actually follow from the given premises?

We know that those with the latest technology—the only ones who will experience economic prosperity—will experience a dissolution of customs and traditions. A dissolution of customs and traditions is something that typically goes very much against the idea of having stability in cultural identity: If customs and traditions are being dissolved, cultural identity is losing stability. If we know that he believes those with the latest technology—the only ones who will experience economic prosperity—will have a decrease in the stability of their cultural identity, we can predict that the author would conclude something like this:

> Hence, in the new century, the stability of a nation's cultural identity will likely decrease if that
> nation comes to have a high level of economic wealth.

This is what answer choice (B) states, and (B) is the correct answer.

If you were able to predict that answer, great. However, we want to stress that even if you are amazing at predicting the right answer, we strongly recommend that you confirm that right answer by eliminating wrong ones. In some questions that ask us to complete the argument, the answer is not what you would predict. In others, the right answer is written in such a convoluted way that it's very difficult to match up with what you predicted. Eliminating wrong choices first gives you the best chance at consistent success.

11

Whether you predicted (B) or not, you can get there by eliminating the other answers:

    (A)   depend on a just distribution of electronic
            technology among all nations

This answer is tempting, because a just distribution seems like it could pass for being the opposite of only wealthy nations having the latest technology, but we have no evidence at all that just distribution would lead in any way to stability. There is also a detail creep: Distribution of technology is different from the distribution of the latest technology. By this point, we can see that this answer is clearly not inferable based on the text.

    (C)   be ensured by laws that protect the customs
            and traditions of that culture

We are given no information about such laws, so this answer can be eliminated very quickly because it is out of scope.

    (D)   be threatened only if the people of that culture
            fail to acquire the latest technical skills

This is an answer that conflicts with the information we are given. Per the given argument, those who acquire the latest technology will feel a threat to their stability. There is also an unjustified shift from technology to technical skills.

    (E)   be best maintained by ensuring gradual
            assimilation of new technical knowledge and
            skills

Like (A), (E) poses as some sort of opposite or remedy of the situation the author describes. However, the author's argument is only about nations with the latest technology, and it's unlikely that those nations who "ensure" gradual assimilation will be relevant to this discussion. Furthermore, as mentioned before, technical knowledge and skills are not the same as technology itself. Finally, and perhaps most importantly, we do not have nearly enough information to conclude anything about what would be *best* for maintaining a stable social identity.

The four wrong choices have clearly defining characteristics. Once we eliminate these choices, we are left with (B), the correct choice.

Here's another one. Again, focus your attention on eliminating answers that are not provable.

PT27, S4, Q23

Much of today's literature is inferior: most of our authors are intellectually and emotionally inexperienced, and their works lack both the intricacy and the focus on the significant that characterize good literature. However, Hypatia's latest novel is promising; it shows a maturity, complexity, and grace that far exceeds that of her earlier works.

Which one of the following statements is most strongly supported by the information in the passage?

(A)   Much of today's literature focuses less on the significant than Hypatia's latest novel focuses on the significant.

(B)   Much of today's literature at least lacks the property of grace.

(C)   Hypatia's latest novel is good literature when judged by today's standards.

(D)   Hypatia's latest novel is clearly better than the majority of today's literature.

(E)   Hypatia's latest novel has at least one property of good literature to a greater degree than her earlier works.

In this argument, there is discussion of two distinct subjects: "much of today's literature" and the work of Hypatia. There is a temptation, built into the structure of the argument itself, to compare Hypatia's work to today's literature, but read though the argument again carefully and you should realize that there is very little direct comparison of these two subjects.

(A)   Much of today's literature **focuses less** on the significant **than** Hypatia's latest novel focuses on the significant.

This is a flawed comparison. We have no idea how much Hypatia's latest novel focuses on the significant and, in this regard, we have no idea how it relates to much of today's literature.

(B)   Much of **today's literature** at least lacks the property of **grace.**

This is another unsupported comparison. We're told that Hypatia's latest novel has a grace that was lacking from her earlier work, but, again, we have no idea how this relates to today's literature. The author does not connect the concept of grace with much of today's literature.

(C) **Hypatia's latest novel** is **good literature** when judged by today's standards.

This links elements from the text together incorrectly. We have no idea if Hypatia's novel is good enough to fall into the category of good literature. We only know that her novel is stronger, in certain ways, than her own previous work.

(D) Hypatia's latest novel is clearly **better than** the majority of today's literature.

Again, we have no idea how Hypatia's novel compares to much of today's literature.

(E) Hypatia's latest novel has at least one property of good literature to a greater degree than her earlier works.

This is the correct answer. We know that intricacy is a characteristic of good literature. Intricacy and complexity are very similar concepts, and we know that her current novel has more complexity than her previous work. Therefore, it's reasonable to conclude that Hypatia's latest novel has at least one property of good literature to a greater degree than her earlier works. Notice that once again, the right answer is fairly unambitious. It doesn't say that her work is great or that it's better than other literature. It just says that it exceeds her previous work in at least one way.

Here is one final challenging example for which it can be tempting to make false links. Remember to eliminate incorrect answers before verifying the correct one.

PT29, S1, Q18

Some planning committee members—those representing the construction industry—have significant financial interests in the committee's decisions. No one who is on the planning committee lives in the suburbs, although many of them work there.

If the statements above are true, which one of the following must also be true?

(A)   No persons with significant financial interests in the planning committee's decisions are not in the construction industry.

(B)   No person who has significant financial interest in the planning committee's decisions lives in the suburbs.

(C)   Some persons with significant financial interests in the planning committee's decisions work in the suburbs.

(D)   Some planning committee members who represent the construction industry do not work in the suburbs.

(E)   Some persons with significant financial interests in the planning committee's decisions do not live in the suburbs.

Each part of the argument taken by itself is simple enough. However, for those who are familiar with the LSAT, this is the type of argument that *screams* danger. There is various information that can be connected in a variety of ways, and there is also a great risk of combining information in an incorrect way—in fact, the four wrong answers will try to tempt you to do just that.

One way we can organize this information is to consider it in terms of larger groups and subgroups. Let's think about each sentence in those terms:

Some planning committee members—those representing the construction industry—have significant financial interests in the committee's decisions.

The larger group, in this case, are the members of the planning committee. Out of this larger group, a subgroup—those members representing the construction industry—have a significant financial interest in the committee's decisions. We can visualize this in the following manner:

Now, let's take a look at the second statement:

> No one who is on the planning committee lives in the suburbs, although many of them work there.

Notice the larger group in this case is also the planning committee. Of this group, we know none live in the suburbs, and many work there. We can represent that as follows:

These diagrams are just meant to be learning tools, and in general we do not feel it is necessary to draw the arguments out in this manner in order to get the questions correct. However, if you find these types of visual systems helpful, you may want to practice using such drawing tools on your scratch paper for test day. Let's put the images up one more time, side by side, and use them to knock off the four wrong choices:

(A)   No persons with significant financial interests
       in the planning committee's decisions are not
       in the construction industry.

Notice that we only know about people who are on the planning committee—we know nothing about people in general with financial interests. Some people with a financial interest in the committee's decisions may not be on the committee! Therefore, we don't have the information to evaluate this conclusion, and it cannot be proven.

(B)   No person who has significant financial
       interest in the planning committee's decisions
       lives in the suburbs.

For the same reason, (B) can't be proven. We have some information about people with a financial interest who happen to be on the committee, but without knowing more about others who have financial interests, we can't prove that this answer is true.

(C)   Some persons with significant financial
       interests in the planning committee's
       decisions work in the suburbs.

Again, since we don't know about all the people with financial interests, this answer could be true. We also know that many committee members work in the suburbs, and that makes this answer tempting. However, we have no direct proof that those with financial interests are the ones working in the suburbs (perhaps the "many" committee members who work in the suburbs don't have a financial interest).

(D)   Some planning committee members who
       represent the construction industry do not
       work in the suburbs.

This answer is similar to (C)—we know many members work in the suburbs, but we don't know which ones. It could be those in the construction industry, or it could not.

(E)   Some persons with significant financial
       interests in the planning committee's
       decisions do not live in the suburbs.

We know that those on the committee who are in the construction industry have a significant financial interest, and we know that *no one* on the committee lives in the suburbs. Therefore, we can prove that at least some people who have a financial interest do not live in the suburbs.

Answer choice (E) is correct.

Conclusion

1. **Understand what inference questions are NOT.** It is critical that you develop processes that are specific to each question type. Be careful not to let your understanding of Assumption Family questions hinder your process on Inference questions.

2. **Right answers are not predictable.** Again, some right answers will match up with your expectations and others will not. Therefore, in general, you should not expect to predict the right answer.

3. **Right answers have a range of provability.** Some questions require us to find the answer that must be true, others ask for something that is most provable, and finally others fall somewhere in between. It's dangerous to think that every answer must be 100% provable. No matter the question stem, you can never go wrong by trying to find the *most* provable of the five choices.

4. **Get to the right answer by eliminating wrong answers.** Incorrect answers for Inference questions are generally easier to identify than correct answers are. Many don't match up with the stimulus in terms of what is being discussed. Many contain unsupported connections or other faulty reasoning. Your success on Inference questions hinges on your ability to see what is not provable.

Drill It: Inference Questions

1. PT39, S2, Q6

Poor writers often express mundane ideas with elaborate syntax and esoteric vocabulary. Inattentive readers may be impressed but may well misunderstand the writing, while alert readers will easily see through the pretentiousness. Thus, a good principle for writers is: _____.

Which one of the following completes the passage most logically?

(A)   the simpler the style, the better the writing

(B)   inattentive readers are not worth writing for

(C)   only the most talented writers can successfully adopt a complex style

(D)   a writing style should not be more complex than the ideas expressed

(E)   alert readers are the only readers who are sensitive to writing style

2. PT30, S4, Q4

A certain gene can be stimulated by chemicals in cigarette smoke, causing lung cells to metabolize the chemicals in a way that makes the cells cancerous. Yet smokers in whom this gene is not stimulated have as high a risk of developing lung cancer from smoking as other smokers do.

If the statements above are true, it can be concluded on the basis of them that

(A)   stimulation of the gene by chemicals in cigarette smoke is not the only factor affecting the risk for smokers of developing lung cancer

(B)   nonsmokers have as high a risk of developing lung cancer as do smokers in whom the gene has not been stimulated

(C)   smokers in whom the gene has been stimulated are more likely to develop lung cancer than are other smokers

(D)   the gene is more likely to be stimulated by chemicals in cigarette smoke than by other chemicals

(E)   smokers are less likely to develop lung cancer if they do not have the gene

3. PT37, S2, Q2

The solidity of bridge piers built on pilings depends largely on how deep the pilings are driven. Prior to 1700, pilings were driven to "refusal," that is, to the point at which they refused to go any deeper. In a 1588 inquiry into the solidity of piers for Venice's Rialto Bridge, it was determined that the bridge's builder, Antonio Da Ponte, had met the contemporary standard for refusal: he had caused the pilings to be driven until additional penetration into the ground was no greater than two inches after twenty-four hammer blows.

Which one of the following can properly be inferred from the passage?

(A)   The Rialto Bridge was built on unsafe pilings.

(B)   The standard of refusal was not sufficient to ensure the safety of a bridge.

(C)   Da Ponte's standard of refusal was less strict than that of other bridge builders of his day.

(D)   After 1588, no bridges were built on pilings that were driven to the point of refusal.

(E)   It is possible that the pilings of the Rialto Bridge could have been driven deeper even after the standard of refusal had been met.

11

4. PT37, S4, Q3

An instructor presented two paintings to a class. She said that the first had hung in prestigious museums but the second was produced by an unknown amateur. Each student was asked which painting was better. Everyone selected the first. The instructor later presented the same two paintings in the same order to a different class. This time she said that the first was produced by an unknown amateur but the second had hung in prestigious museums. In this class, everyone said that the second painting was better.

The statements above, if true, most strongly support which one of the following?

(A) Most of the students would not like any work of art that they believed to have been produced by an unknown amateur.

(B) None of the claims that the instructor made about the paintings was true.

(C) Each of the students would like most of the paintings hanging in any prestigious museum.

(D) In judging the paintings, some of the students were affected by what they had been told about the history of the paintings.

(E) Had the instructor presented the paintings without telling the students anything about them, almost all of the students would have judged them to be roughly equal in artistic worth.

5. PT37, S4, Q1

Criminals often have an unusual self-image. Embezzlers often think of their actions as "only borrowing money." Many people convicted of violent crimes rationalize their actions by some sort of denial; either the victim "deserved it" and so the action was justified, or "it simply wasn't my fault." Thus, in many cases, by criminals' characterization of their situations, _____.

Which one of the following most logically completes the passage?

(A) they ought to be rewarded for their actions

(B) they are perceived to be the victim of some other criminal

(C) their actions are not truly criminal

(D) the criminal justice system is inherently unfair

(E) they deserve only a light sentence for their crimes

6. PT37, S4, Q6

In a study, infant monkeys given a choice between two surrogate mothers—a bare wire structure equipped with a milk bottle, or a soft, suede-covered wire structure equipped with a milk bottle—unhesitatingly chose the latter. When given a choice between a bare wire structure equipped with a milk bottle and a soft, suede-covered wire structure lacking a milk bottle, they unhesitatingly chose the former.

Which one of the following is most supported by the information above?

(A) Infant monkeys' desire for warmth and comfort is nearly as strong as their desire for food.

(B) For infant monkeys, suede is a less convincing substitute for their mother's touch than animal fur would be.

(C) For infant monkeys, a milk bottle is a less convincing substitute for their mother's teat than suede is for their mother's touch.

(D) For infant monkeys, a milk bottle is an equally convincing substitute for their mother's teat as suede is for their mother's touch.

(E) Infant monkeys' desire for food is stronger than their desire for warmth and comfort.

7. PT39, S4, Q6

A politician can neither be reelected nor avoid censure by his or her colleagues if that politician is known to be involved in any serious scandals. Several prominent politicians have just now been shown to be involved in a conspiracy that turned into a serious scandal. These politicians will therefore not be reelected.

If the statements above are all true, which one of the following statements must also be true?

(A) The prominent politicians cannot escape censure by their colleagues.

(B) If there had been no scandal, the prominent politicians would be reelected.

(C) No politician is censured unless he or she is known to be involved in a serious scandal.

(D) The prominent politicians initially benefited from the conspiracy that caused the scandal.

(E) Some politicians who are involved in scandalous conspiracies avoid detection and censure.

8. PT36, S3, Q17

The purpose of a general theory of art is to explain every aesthetic feature that is found in any of the arts. Premodern general theories of art, however, focused primarily on painting and sculpture. Every premodern general theory of art, even those that succeed as theories of painting and sculpture, fails to explain some aesthetic feature of music.

The statements above, if true, most strongly support which one of the following?

(A)   Any general theory of art that explains the aesthetic features of painting also explains those of sculpture.

(B)   A general theory of art that explains every aesthetic feature of music will achieve its purpose.

(C)   Any theory of art that focuses primarily on sculpture and painting cannot explain every aesthetic feature of music.

(D)   No premodern general theory of art achieves its purpose unless music is not art.

(E)   No premodern general theory of art explains any aesthetic features of music that are not shared with painting and sculpture.

9. PT30, S4, Q10

Twelve healthy volunteers with the Apo-A-IV-1 gene and twelve healthy volunteers who instead have the Apo-A-IV-2 gene each consumed a standard diet supplemented daily by a high-cholesterol food. A high level of cholesterol in the blood is associated with an increased risk of heart disease. After three weeks, the blood cholesterol levels of the subjects in the second group were unchanged, whereas the blood cholesterol levels of those with the Apo-A-IV-1 gene rose 20 percent.

Which one of the following is most strongly supported by the information above?

(A)   Approximately half the population carries a gene that lowers cholesterol levels.

(B)   Most of those at risk of heart disease may be able to reduce their risk by adopting a low-cholesterol diet.

(C)   The bodies of those who have the Apo-A-IV-2 gene excrete cholesterol when blood cholesterol reaches a certain level.

(D)   The presence of the Apo-A-IV-1 gene seems to indicate that a person has a lower risk of heart disease.

(E)   The presence of the Apo-A-IV-2 gene may inhibit the elevation of blood cholesterol.

10. PT33, S3, Q8

Most people invest in the stock market without doing any research of their own. Some of these people rely solely on their broker's advice, whereas some others make decisions based merely on hunches. Other people do some research of their own, but just as often rely only on their broker or on hunches. Only a few always do their own research before investing. Nonetheless, a majority of investors in the stock market make a profit.

If the statements in the passage are true, which one of the following must also be true?

(A)   Some people who make a profit on their investments in the stock market do so without doing any research of their own.

(B)   Most people who invest in the stock market either rely solely on their broker or make decisions based merely on hunches.

(C)   Some people who do investment research on their own, while just as often relying on their broker or on hunches, make a profit in the stock market.

(D)   Most people who invest in the stock market without doing any research of their own make a profit.

(E)   Most people who rely solely on their broker rather than on hunches make a profit in the stock market.

11

Solutions: Inference Questions

Answer Key

1. D	6. E
2. A	7. A
3. E	8. D
4. D	9. E
5. C	10. A

1. PT39, S2, Q6

Poor writers often express mundane ideas with elaborate syntax and esoteric vocabulary. Inattentive readers may be impressed but may well misunderstand the writing, while alert readers will easily see through the pretentiousness. Thus, a good principle for writers is: _____.

Which one of the following completes the passage most logically?

(A)   the simpler the style, the better the writing

(B)   inattentive readers are not worth writing for

(C)   only the most talented writers can successfully adopt a complex style

(D)   a writing style should not be more complex than the ideas expressed

(E)   alert readers are the only readers who are sensitive to writing style

Answer choice (D) is correct.

In the stimulus, we are told that poor writers often represent simple ideas in overly complex ways. Then we are told of two negative consequences of this: Poor readers, who may be falsely impressed, may misunderstand the writing, and alert readers will see easily see through the pretentiousness.

Let's consider what could follow logically:

(A) is very attractive. The author seems to be advocating for a simpler style. However, on closer inspection, (A) is not supportable based on the text. The stimulus is about a mismatch in the complexity levels of the subject matter and style of writing—not about simple writing in general. Besides, this statement is quite extreme. Even if the author prefers simple writing, she may not want it to be as simple as possible!

(B) expresses a very harsh opinion that is not supported by the statements. We are given no indication of who is or is not worth writing for.

(C) is not supported by the statements. We have almost no information about who can or cannot successfully adopt a complex style.

Answer choice (D) is most supported, and it is therefore correct. In the first sentence, we are told that a writing style that *is* more complex than the ideas expressed is representative of poor writing, and in the second sentence, we are given two negative consequences of a writing style more complex than the ideas expressed. Therefore, it is logical to conclude that a writing style should not have this characteristic.

(E) is not supported by the statements. In fact, we know that inattentive readers are sensitive to writing style, too: We are told they may be impressed by poor writing style.

2. PT30, S4, Q4

A certain gene can be stimulated by chemicals in cigarette smoke, causing lung cells to metabolize the chemicals in a way that makes the cells cancerous. Yet smokers in whom this gene is not stimulated have as high a risk of developing lung cancer from smoking as other smokers do.

If the statements above are true, it can be concluded on the basis of them that

(A)   stimulation of the gene by chemicals in cigarette smoke is not the only factor affecting the risk for smokers of developing lung cancer

MANHATTAN
PREP

(B)   nonsmokers have as high a risk of developing
        lung cancer as do smokers in whom the gene
        has not been stimulated

(C)   smokers in whom the gene has been stimulated
        are more likely to develop lung cancer than
        are other smokers

(D)   the gene is more likely to be stimulated by
        chemicals in cigarette smoke than by other
        chemicals

(E)   smokers are less likely to develop lung cancer if
        they do not have the gene

Answer choice (A) is correct.

The passage states that stimulating a certain gene via
smoke can cause cancer, but that smokers without
a stimulated gene have as high a risk of developing
smoking-related lung cancer as other smokers (who do
not have the stimulated gene). The words "it can be
concluded" signal that we are dealing with an Inference
question—there might be an inference that quickly
comes to mind (e.g., if people with the nonstimulated
gene still have a high risk of developing smoking-related
lung cancer, then there may be other factors at play)—
but remember that what you are expecting may not be
what the answers provide.

Choice (A), in this case, was exactly what we predicted:
Even though the stimulated gene can cause cancer,
people without the gene still have as high a risk of
developing lung cancer as those with the gene, so
something else must affect risk! If it were the *only*
factor, then we would see a higher risk for those with
the stimulated gene. This is our answer. Notice that
once again the right answer is a fairly weak statement. It
just says that something isn't the only factor. We could
probably approve this answer without even reading
the stimulus! Surely there are plenty of factors (such as
frequency of smoking) that affect risk. But of course,
we don't need to rely on common sense. The stimulus
proves this answer correct!

(B) is out of scope. We are not given any information
comparing nonsmokers and smokers at all! The passage
only compares smokers with the stimulated gene and
those without.

(C) is an unsupported comparison. The exact wording
of the statements is that smokers with the nonstimulated
gene "have as high a risk"—this does not necessarily
mean they are *more likely* to develop cancer.

(D) is an unsupported comparison. There is no
comparison of different chemicals—only the chemicals
in cigarette smoke are mentioned.

(E) is not supported by the statements. The passage
never distinguishes between those who *have* the gene
and those who *don't have* the gene—it only distinguishes
between groups that have the gene *stimulated* and those
who do not. Additionally, having the gene (and having
it stimulated) does not necessarily mean a lower risk of
lung cancer, since those without the stimulated gene had
"as high a risk" as other smokers.

3. PT37, S2, Q2

The solidity of bridge piers built on pilings depends
largely on how deep the pilings are driven. Prior to
1700, pilings were driven to "refusal," that is, to the
point at which they refused to go any deeper. In a
1588 inquiry into the solidity of piers for Venice's
Rialto Bridge, it was determined that the bridge's
builder, Antonio Da Ponte, had met the
contemporary standard for refusal: he had caused
the pilings to be driven until additional penetration
into the ground was no greater than two inches
after twenty-four hammer blows.

Which one of the following can properly be inferred
from the passage?

(A)   The Rialto Bridge was built on unsafe pilings.

(B)   The standard of refusal was not sufficient to
        ensure the safety of a bridge.

(C)   Da Ponte's standard of refusal was less strict
        than that of other bridge builders of his day.

11

(D)   After 1588, no bridges were built on pilings that were driven to the point of refusal.

(E)   It is possible that the pilings of the Rialto Bridge could have been driven deeper even after the standard of refusal had been met.

Answer choice (E) is correct.

When an Inference question contains this much information, the test writers hope that you will forget or confuse details due to the length of the statements. Be vigilant!

(A) is not supported by the passage. What would constitute "unsafe" bridges is never discussed.

(B) is not supported, for the exact same reason.

(C) is not supported by the passage. Da Ponte "met the contemporary standard for refusal," and we have no other information about others' standards.

(D) is not supported by the passage. The statements only say that building pilings were driven to refusal prior to 1700; we do not have information about any other bridges built between 1588 and 1700.

(E) uses the vague wording "it is possible," which makes this choice a bit easier to support. Could the pilings of the Rialto have been driven deeper? Da Ponte met the standard and drove the pilings "until additional penetration into the ground was not greater than 2 inches after twenty-four hammer blows." Basically, he drove the pilings in until they didn't move much with repeated strikes. It's possible that they were in as deep as they could go, but perhaps with another 24 blows, or another 240, the pilings could have gone in a bit further. It's hard to say; all we know is that it was getting difficult to drive them further. It's like stopping the popcorn after it slows down to a pop every three seconds. It's basically done, but there's always the possibility that another kernel or two could have popped.

4. PT37, S4, Q3

An instructor presented two paintings to a class. She said that the first had hung in prestigious museums but the second was produced by an unknown amateur. Each student was asked which painting was better. Everyone selected the first. The instructor later presented the same two paintings in the same order to a different class. This time she said that the first was produced by an unknown amateur but the second had hung in prestigious museums. In this class, everyone said that the second painting was better.

The statements above, if true, most strongly support which one of the following?

(A)   Most of the students would not like any work of art that they believed to have been produced by an unknown amateur.

(B)   None of the claims that the instructor made about the paintings was true.

(C)   Each of the students would like most of the paintings hanging in any prestigious museum.

(D)   In judging the paintings, some of the students were affected by what they had been told about the history of the paintings.

(E)   Had the instructor presented the paintings without telling the students anything about them, almost all of the students would have judged them to be roughly equal in artistic worth.

Answer choice (D) is correct.

All we know is that every single one of the students in each class preferred the museum painting (even though that painting was not preferred when presented as an unknown artist's painting). If we had heard this story in real life, we might jump to all kinds of conclusions about the reason for the discrepancy in the two different classes. However, be extra suspicious of what a "normal" person might think when confronted with LSAT information—the test writers will try to trip us up with those expectations! By now, hopefully you are growing wary of strongly worded answers that aren't fully supported and are paying careful attention to answers that don't seem to say that much.

(A) is not supported by the statements. The extreme wording "any" demands an extreme justification, as does "most." If choice (A) were true, then the situation we described might result—but we want to know what is most likely to be true given the situation, not the other way around. Technically, we don't know anything about *why* students said one painting was better than the other; we just know that under these two different circumstances, two different classes said they preferred different paintings. Eliminate it.

(B) is tempting, because the instructor switches the description of the paintings to the different classes, but we don't have proof that *none* of the claims were true. Perhaps one of the paintings really was by an unknown amateur! In fact, either set of claims (or both!) could be true. A painting produced by an unknown amateur could be sold and find its way into a prestigious museum. Eliminate it.

(C) is not supported by the statements. Notice the extreme wording here: "Each" (meaning every single one) of the students? "Most" of the paintings in "any" prestigious museum? Eliminate it.

(E) is not supported by the statements. This is an extreme claim in disguise. "Equal" artistic worth? That is a very specific claim to make about a hypothetical situation, and nothing in the statements is strong enough to give us that degree of specificity. Eliminate it.

Choice (D) is not something that absolutely *must* be true. It is possible that the students were not swayed by what they had been told. But the fact that everyone in each class preferred the "museum" painting (even when those paintings were different pieces) does make it seem very likely that there was something related to that information involved in the decision, even if we can't be certain about to what degree.

Notice that the word "some" is used here—a nice, vague term that could mean as few as one. Choice (D) is by no means provably true—in fact, there are many other possibilities that could have caused the discrepancy (the differences in students themselves, the instructor's nonverbal cues, etc.). But out of the five choices, this is the one that requires the smallest jump in logic to justify, because so many of the other answers make specific and more extreme claims. This is our answer.

5. PT37, S4, Q1

Criminals often have an unusual self-image. Embezzlers often think of their actions as "only borrowing money." Many people convicted of violent crimes rationalize their actions by some sort of denial; either the victim "deserved it" and so the action was justified, or "it simply wasn't my fault." Thus, in many cases, by criminals' characterization of their situations, _____.

Which one of the following most logically completes the passage?

(A)   they ought to be rewarded for their actions

(B)   they are perceived to be the victim of some
        other criminal

(C)   their actions are not truly criminal

(D)   the criminal justice system is inherently unfair

(E)   they deserve only a light sentence for their
        crimes

Answer choice (C) is correct.

The information in this paragraph can be boiled down to the following:

- Criminals have an unusual self-image.
- Embezzlers often think they are "only borrowing money."
- Many violent criminals rationalize or deny their crimes.

The question is asking us for criminals' characterization of their situations. What do we know about the criminals' perspective? Sadly, they don't seem to think they're doing anything wrong.

(A) is not supported by the statements. While the criminals may not accept blame for their actions, nowhere is it said that these people actually expect a reward. This generalization goes too far.

(B) is not supported by the statements. Nowhere are "other criminals" mentioned.

(D) fits very nicely with our prediction, but it's taking an extra step that is not supported by the statements. There is nothing mentioned about the criminal justice system; the passage only discusses how criminals perceive their own actions.

(E) is not supported by the statements. Like (D), it might well be true. Certainly these criminals (who take their own actions lightly) might think they deserved only a light sentence, but there is nothing mentioned about what types of sentences are deserved. Besides, since none of the criminals seem to think their actions were that bad, it's quite possible that they might think they don't deserve sentences at all.

(C) matches our prediction very well. We're never told exactly what "truly criminal" means, but if the criminals are rationalizing or denying their crimes, it's likely that their perceptions fall short of their own standard for being "truly criminal." The question asks which choice "most logically completes the passage," and the other choices contain more concrete and severe flaws, so (C) is our answer.

6. PT37, S4, Q6

In a study, infant monkeys given a choice between two surrogate mothers—a bare wire structure equipped with a milk bottle, or a soft, suede-covered wire structure equipped with a milk bottle—unhesitatingly chose the latter. When given a choice between a bare wire structure equipped with a milk bottle and a soft, suede-covered wire structure

lacking a milk bottle, they unhesitatingly chose the former.

Which one of the following is most supported by the information above?

(A) Infant monkeys' desire for warmth and comfort is nearly as strong as their desire for food.

(B) For infant monkeys, suede is a less convincing substitute for their mother's touch than animal fur would be.

(C) For infant monkeys, a milk bottle is a less convincing substitute for their mother's teat than suede is for their mother's touch.

(D) For infant monkeys, a milk bottle is an equally convincing substitute for their mother's teat as suede is for their mother's touch.

(E) Infant monkeys' desire for food is stronger than their desire for warmth and comfort.

Answer choice (E) is correct.

We know the following facts:

1. Baby monkeys preferred the soft/milk mother to the wire/milk mother.
2. Baby monkeys preferred the wire/milk mother to the soft/no-milk mother.

What is the difference between these two sets of circumstances? In the second, the softer suede mother no longer had milk, and the babies switched their previous preference. This suggests that this variable (milk/no milk) is somehow important.

(A) is tempting because it seems to address the underlying decision between warmth/food, but this choice is ultimately not supported by the statements. We know that the babies chose milk over no milk in the second experiment (and we can guess that this is a choice of food over warmth), but we have no way to compare that desire with the *level* of preference for the soft mother in the first experiment. What if they strongly preferred food, but only marginally cared about warmth/comfort? We have no way of knowing.

(B) is not supported by the statements. We cannot make a comparison to fur when this experiment only involves a distinction between suede and wire.

(C) is another flawed comparison. The only comparisons in this experiment are between soft/wire and milk/no milk. We cannot make any inferences about how comparable the experimental conditions were to "real" mother conditions.

(D) is wrong for the same reasons as (C).

Choice (E) contains many of the same words as choice (A), but with an important difference: Choice (E) only makes a statement about which of the two types of desire (for food/for warmth)—when in conflict with each other—wins out. If the monkeys preferred the soft mother with all other things being equal, but went with the wire/food mother when forced to choose between that and wire/no-food, this indicates that their previous preference was overpowered by the food/no food distinction. Could it be that there was some other factor than food that swayed their decision? (Maybe they liked the smell of the bottle or the location of the structure.) There are other possibilites, but this interpretation is certainly strongly supported by the evidence. This is our answer.

7. PT39, S4, Q6

A politician can neither be reelected nor avoid censure by his or her colleagues if that politician is known to be involved in any serious scandals. Several prominent politicians have just now been shown to be involved in a conspiracy that turned into a serious scandal. These politicians will therefore not be reelected.

If the statements above are all true, which one of the following statements must also be true?

(A)   The prominent politicians cannot escape
        censure by their colleagues.

(B)   If there had been no scandal, the prominent
        politicians would be reelected.

(C)   No politician is censured unless he or she is
        known to be involved in a serious scandal.

(D)   The prominent politicians initially benefited
        from the conspiracy that caused the scandal.

(E)   Some politicians who are involved in
        scandalous conspiracies avoid detection and
        censure.

Answer choice (A) is correct.

From the statements, we know the following truths:

* If politician is known to be involved in serious scandals, politician can't be reelected.
* If politician is known to be involved in serious scandals, politician can't avoid censure.
* Several prominent politicians known to be involved in conspiracy that is now serious scandal.
* These politicians will not be reelected.

(A) must be true. We are told these politicians are known to be involved in a serious scandal, and we know that an absolute consequence is that they cannot avoid censure. Notice that the conditional statements, which are by definition extreme, allow us to draw an absolute conclusion without worry.

(B) is an illegal negation of the first statement. The argument gives us no evidence that the politicians would be reelected otherwise. They might fail to be reelected for other reasons.

(C) is is another illegal negation (or reversal, depending on how you look at it). Just because being involved in scandal results in censure does not mean it is the only action that results in censure. Perhaps a politician can be censured for another reason.

(D) is not supported by any part of the text.

(E) is not supported by any part of the text.

_8. PT36, S3, Q17_

The purpose of a general theory of art is to explain every aesthetic feature that is found in any of the arts. Premodern general theories of art, however, focused primarily on painting and sculpture. Every premodern general theory of art, even those that succeed as theories of painting and sculpture, fails to explain some aesthetic feature of music.

The statements above, if true, most strongly support which one of the following?

(A) Any general theory of art that explains the aesthetic features of painting also explains those of sculpture.

(B) A general theory of art that explains every aesthetic feature of music will achieve its purpose.

(C) Any theory of art that focuses primarily on sculpture and painting cannot explain every aesthetic feature of music.

(D) No premodern general theory of art achieves its purpose unless music is not art.

(E) No premodern general theory of art explains any aesthetic features of music that are not shared with painting and sculpture.

Answer choice (D) is correct.

We know from the argument the following:

- The purpose of general theories of art (GTA) is to explain EVERY aesthetic feature of ANY art (notice the extreme wording).
- Premodern GTA focused on painting and sculpture.
- EVERY premodern GTA failed to explain SOME aesthetic feature of music.

(A) is not supported by the statements. We do not have enough information to make this claim about _any_ GTA. Would it be possible, given these statements, for GTA to explain painting but _not_ explain sculpture (or

vice versa)? Absolutely—the statements say only that premodern theories focused "primarily" on painting and sculpture and that "some" premodern theories succeeded for painting and sculpture. Eliminate it.

(B) is not supported by the statements. What if the theory explained every feature of music but did _not_ explain every feature of painting and sculpture (or other arts)? Eliminate it.

(C) is not supported by the statements. If the word "any" were replaced with "some," we would have our answer, but we do not have enough information to make this claim about "any" GTA. What about non-premodern GTA that focused on painting and sculpture? We don't know anything about them, and there's nothing that says _they_ couldn't fully explain music's aesthetic features. Eliminate it.

(D) combines what we know about premodern GTA (that they failed to fully explain some aesthetic feature of music) and the purpose of GTA—to explain fully all aesthetic features of the arts. If music is an art, then a premodern GTA cannot fulfill its purpose, so a premodern GTA cannot achieve its purpose unless we exclude music as a category. This is our answer.

By the way, if you objected to (D) because you're sure that music is an art, be careful. This choice just says that if the theories achieve their purpose, music is not an art. Maybe they don't achieve their purpose! In any case, when we prove a conditional, that says nothing about whether the conditions within it are true.

(E) is tempting because it combines many of the words from the passage, throwing in a "no" and a "not" to confuse us more. But look at exactly what this choice says. All we know about music/premodern GTA is that premodern GTA did not fully explain music—meaning there was at least one feature of music that couldn't be explained by those theories. Does that mean those theories did not explain _any_ parts of music that didn't overlap with painting and sculpture? Absolutely not.

9. PT30, S4, Q10

Twelve healthy volunteers with the Apo-A-IV-1 gene and twelve healthy volunteers who instead have the Apo-A-IV-2 gene each consumed a standard diet supplemented daily by a high-cholesterol food. A high level of cholesterol in the blood is associated with an increased risk of heart disease. After three weeks, the blood cholesterol levels of the subjects in the second group were unchanged, whereas the blood cholesterol levels of those with the Apo-A-IV-1 gene rose 20 percent.

Which one of the following is most strongly supported by the information above?

(A)   Approximately half the population carries a gene that lowers cholesterol levels.

(B)   Most of those at risk of heart disease may be able to reduce their risk by adopting a low-cholesterol diet.

(C)   The bodies of those who have the Apo-A-IV-2 gene excrete cholesterol when blood cholesterol reaches a certain level.

(D)   The presence of the Apo-A-IV-1 gene seems to indicate that a person has a lower risk of heart disease.

(E)   The presence of the Apo-A-IV-2 gene may inhibit the elevation of blood cholesterol.

Answer choice (E) is correct.

Two healthy groups with two different genes consumed standard diets plus a high-cholesterol food, but only one group had a 20% increase in blood cholesterol. We are also told that high blood cholesterol is associated with increased heart disease risk. What is most likely to be true given these facts? Well, correlation never proves causation, but we can say that this gene may have been a factor in the difference in cholesterol between the two groups.

(A) is not supported by the statements. We are not given any information about the relative frequency of Apo-A-IV-1 and -2 in the general population, just in this controlled experiment. Also, does the gene "lower" cholesterol levels? Causation Flaw aside, the statements say that the type 2 group was stable, while the type 1 group's levels increased—there is no lowering mentioned.

(B) is not supported by the statements. A low-cholesterol diet is never mentioned, so this answer choice is out of scope.

(C) may be a plausible explanation for the results, but the question does not ask for an explanation. It merely asks what is most strongly supported, and we have no information about this. Eliminate it.

(D) is tempting because there is a link between the two types of genes and high blood cholesterol, which in turn is linked to risk of heart disease. But be very careful! There is an important detail creep here—the type 1 gene group had *higher* blood cholesterol levels after the diet, and this choice implies the opposite. Even if we didn't spot this, we don't know anything about people's overall risk of heart disease, just their cholesterol levels when on a high-cholesterol diet. Eliminate it.

(E), like many "most strongly supported" answers, is not 100% provable. There could be other explanations for the results of this experiment. But the test writers use the vague word "may," and since the type 1 group had levels of cholesterol that rose, while the type 2 group had stable levels, this statement expresses a very strong possibility (and is certainly more strongly supported than answers (A) through (D), which have fatal flaws).

11

10. PT33, S3, Q8

Most people invest in the stock market without doing any research of their own. Some of these people rely solely on their broker's advice, whereas some others make decisions based merely on hunches. Other people do some research of their own, but just as often rely only on their broker or on hunches. Only a few always do their own research before investing. Nonetheless, a majority of investors in the stock market make a profit.

If the statements in the passage are true, which one of the following must also be true?

(A) Some people who make a profit on their investments in the stock market do so without doing any research of their own.

(B) Most people who invest in the stock market either rely solely on their broker or make decisions based merely on hunches.

(C) Some people who do investment research on their own, while just as often relying on their broker or on hunches, make a profit in the stock market.

(D) Most people who invest in the stock market without doing any research of their own make a profit.

(E) Most people who rely solely on their broker rather than on hunches make a profit in the stock market.

Answer choice (A) is correct.

This paragraph contains the same few terms—"invest," "research," "broker," and "hunches"—over and over again, so it may help to rewrite the claims in simpler terms:

- Most people invest without research (some rely only on brokers, some only on hunches).

- Others do research sometimes (but sometimes rely only on brokers or hunches).

- A few always do research.

- BUT a majority make a profit.

What "must also be true" given these facts? Be vigilant about the specific small words in each answer, and don't let the repetitive nature of the choices confuse you. Let's look at the wrong answer choices first:

(B) is not supported by the statements. What does the passage tell us about those who rely solely on their brokers or solely on hunches? Out of the group of people who invest without research, "some" rely only on brokers and "some others" on hunches. Are these the only possible groups? No, they could be just "some" of the people. What if the rest of the people (a potentially large proportion) rely both on their broker's advice *and* hunches, or neither? Eliminate it.

(C) is tempting because if most investors make a profit, this profit-making group may include people who do research *and* rely on their broker *and* rely on hunches. But is this *necessarily* true? Is it possible that this could be the one subgroup that *fails* to make a profit? Yes, so we can eliminate it.

(D) is tempting because most people invest in the stock market without research and a majority of investors make a profit. But what exactly constitutes a majority? Anything over 50%. Try testing the smallest possible majorities: If 51 out of 100 people make a profit, and 51 out of 100 people invest without doing research, does that mean that most of the 51 who invested without research made a profit? Is there a way this could be false? Absolutely—check out the Venn diagram below:

MANHATTAN
PREP

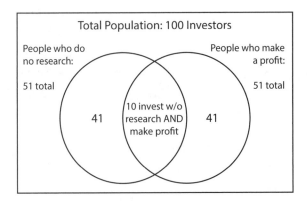

In this scenario, only 10 out of the 41 people who invested without research made a profit. Testing the "extremes" of the words "some," "most," etc. can often be a useful tactic. Or, to save time, memorize the rules in Chapter 8. Most + Most = Some! Eliminate it.

(E) is not supported by the statements. We don't know anything about the number of people who rely solely on their brokers rather than on hunches (except that it is "some" of the population), so we can't make a claim about what "most" of this group does.

The meaning of choice (A) is very similar to that of (D), but with the substitution of "some" for "most" to describe the overlap between these two groups. Does choice (A) *have* to be true? Is there any way it could *not* be? Imagine that none of the people who make a profit on their investments in the stock market do so

without doing research. Then the overlap of the two circles would be empty—0 people. This would leave 51 investors who make a profit (without research) and 51 people who do no research (without profit). That would mean we would have a minimum of 51 + 51 = 102 people—more people than our total population of 100! Let's diagram:

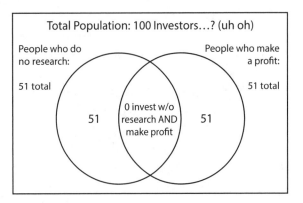

Of course, that's not possible. In order for our numbers to work out, we must have *some* overlap. Again, Most + Most = Some. (A) is our answer.

By the way, we're not suggesting you draw Venn diagrams—there are plenty of times when they will not work (e.g., when there are five categories). We just want to keep reinforcing the underlying reasoning about "some" and "most." Refer back to Chapter 8 if you need a refresher.

Time to Mix It Up Again

Just as you did after Chapter 7, it's time for you to strike out on your own once more. Ready for another homemade mixed practice set?

First, grab another real LSAT. For this exercise, an old paper test will do just fine, but if you have a bunch of digital tests at your disposal, you could use one of those as well. Next, find one of the test's two LR sections. Your mission this time is to go through that section, read every question stem, and complete all (and only!) the questions from the Inference Family (including Principle Example questions) and the Analyze the Argument Family. Set the Assumption Family questions aside to practice with the following day.

When that day comes, use your Assumption Family practice to review your approach to those question types and get ready to tackle a pair of complete LR sections.

Once you've thoroughly reviewed each of the question types covered, it's time to test! Don't worry about the question types you haven't covered yet: There won't be many of them! Instead, focus on switching gears 50 times in a row by doing two back-to-back LR sections with only a 1-minute break in between.

Go get 'em!

MANHATTAN
PREP

Chapter 12

Matching Questions

In This Chapter...

Introduction

Matching questions are the Logical Reasoning questions that LSAT takers love to hate, and it's no wonder—they're intimidating! These are the questions that ask you to match an argument in the answer choices to the argument in the stimulus. Since each answer choice is an entire argument unto itself, these questions are unusually long. To make matters worse, they tend to show up toward the end of the section, when time is in short supply.

There are usually two of these in a section. Because of their length, skipping them makes sense for many test-takers. However, matching questions can often be tackled easily if you have the right toolkit. In fact, you may be surprised by how quickly you can move through them.

First, you are going to learn to use each of these tools separately, as you might learn the separate skills of playing a great tennis game. But though you'll learn and practice the skills separately at first, by the end of this chapter, you'll be using them all together, seamlessly transitioning from one to the other as you move through the answer choices.

What are these mysterious tools? We'll call them mismatches. While your goal is to match the given argument, the majority of your energy will be spent figuring out which answers *don't* match. Each type of mismatch is a way to spot nonmatching elements in answer choices and thus eliminate your way to a correct answer.

Let's start with some of the easiest mismatches to spot: conclusion mismatches.

Conclusion Mismatches

The closely-guarded secret of Matching questions is that many answers can be quickly eliminated because they have conclusions that don't match the conclusion in the stimulus. We will go into a lot of detail on the various types of conclusion mismatches, but we bet you can figure out how to eliminate a lot of the answers in the question below with just that idea in mind. We'll keep you focused by covering up all but the conclusion in the stimulus:

12

PT22, S2, Q16

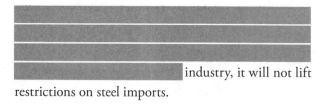 industry, it will not lift restrictions on steel imports.

The pattern of reasoning in the argument above is most similar to that in which one of the following?

(A) Building construction increases only when people are confident that the economy is doing well. Therefore, since people are now confident in the economy we can expect building construction to increase.

(B) Since workers are already guaranteed the right to a safe and healthful workplace by law, there is no need for the government to establish further costly health regulations for people who work all day at computer terminals.

(C) In countries that have deregulated their airline industry, many airlines have gone bankrupt. Since many companies in other transportation industries are in weaker economic condition than were those airlines, deregulating other transportation industries will probably result in bankruptcies as well.

(D) The chief executive officer of Silicon, Inc., will probably not accept stock in the company as a bonus next year, since next year's tax laws will require companies to pay a new tax on stock given to executives.

(E) The installation of bright floodlights on campus would render the astronomy department's telescope useless. The astronomy department will not support any proposal that would render its telescope useless; it will therefore not support proposals to install bright floodlights on campus.

Which answers could you eliminate? Surprisingly, you could have eliminated all four incorrect answers just by spotting conclusion mismatches! If you didn't knock out four answers, go back and try again before reading on.

PT22, S2, Q16

Allowing more steel imports would depress domestic steel prices and harm domestic steel manufacturers. Since the present government will not do anything that would harm the domestic steel industry, it will not lift restrictions on steel imports.

The conclusion is basically someone will not do Y. *Let's see how it matches up.*

The pattern of reasoning in the argument above is most similar to that in which one of the following?

(A)   Building construction increases only when people are confident that the economy is doing well. Therefore, since people are now confident in the economy (we can expect) building construction to increase.

Shifting from *will not* to *we can expect*. That's grounds for elimination!

(B)   Since workers are already guaranteed the right to a safe and healthful workplace by law, there (is no need) for the government to establish further costly health regulations for people who work all day at computer terminals.

Is no need? That's not a match for *will not.*

Goodbye, (B).

(C)   In countries that have deregulated their airline industry, many airlines have gone bankrupt. Since many companies in other transportation industries are in weaker economic condition than were those airlines, deregulating other transportation industries (will probably) result in bankruptcies as well.

Will probably? That's not a match for *will not.* Adios.

(D)   The chief executive officer of Silicon, Inc., (will probably) not accept stock in the company as a bonus next year, since next year's tax laws will require companies to pay a new tax on stock given to executives.

(E)   The installation of bright floodlights on campus would render the astronomy department's telescope useless. The astronomy department will not support any proposal that would render its telescope useless; it will therefore not support proposals to install bright floodlights on campus.

12

Choice (E) is the correct answer, and we think you'll agree that we didn't have to do too much thinking to spot it. Is every Matching question this easy? No, but some are! We'll get to fancier mismatches later, but let's start by learning the simpler ones; we want to use these conclusion mismatches as often as possible since they require the least amount of work on our part.

Conclusion Mismatch Types

Strength Mismatches

As we just saw, if the original conclusion states with certainty that something *will* or *will not* happen, we can confidently eliminate answers that make the milder suggestion that something *might* happen or will *probably* happen.

Now let's look at a more subtle, but related mismatch. Consider how these two conclusions differ:

> Jana is probably going to agree to sell that house.

> Jana tends to agree to sell houses like that.

The first is a *prediction* while the second states a *tendency*. This is a mismatch the LSAT loves to test.

Quantifier Mismatches

Related to strength mismatches are mismatches in quantity. If the original conclusion is about *all, most,* or *some,* the correct answer will be, too. Any answer that doesn't match in this regard can be eliminated.

Similarly, conclusions should match with regard to the use of an "and" or an "or."

Type Mismatches

One of the easiest conclusion mismatches to spot is when one conclusion is a conditional statement and the other is not. Here's an example:

> Martin is an avid photographer. Thus, he will surely agree to run the photo booth.

> Martin is an avid photographer, so he will surely agree to run the photo booth if he is free that night.

This mismatch is all about the presence or absence of conditional language triggers such as "if," "only," and "unless." In this case, the first conclusion is a simple prediction (Martin will surely agree), while the second is a conditional. (The argument doesn't predict whether Martin will actually agree; it just specifies the condition under which he would agree.)

Another type mismatch occurs when the conclusion is a normative (or prescriptive) statement. In simple terms, conclusions with a "should" must be matched with other "should" conclusions. The same goes, of course, for conclusions *without* a "should." These two conclusions, for instance, are very different:

MANHATTAN
PREP

My grandmother ought to be put in charge of our national budget.

My grandmother will be put in charge of our national budget.

Yellow Flag Mismatches

The mismatches you see above are your bread and butter ones because they consistently serve as grounds for elimination. You're also going to notice some other, lesser mismatches that alert you to the fact that an answer is *probably* wrong. We tend to see another mismatch accompanying these "yellow flag" ones, and sometimes, particularly in Match the Flaw questions, the LSAT will let one slip through *in the correct answer*. Thus, while it's good to know about these, they are not grounds for elimination in and of themselves.

Negative vs. Positive Mismatches: Conclusions that state something is not true or will not happen almost always match a similarly negatively phrased conclusion. We saw this in (A), (C), and (D) in the question we worked above, but each of those choices had a strength mismatch as well ("expect," "probably"). If the original argument says "will not" and one of the answer choices says "will," we should defer judgment and see what else we can eliminate before definitively scratching that answer choice.

Temporal Mismatches: The right answer will generally match the original conclusion in terms of time. In other words, if the original conclusion is about what *will* happen, what *did* happen, or what *is* happening, it's very likely that the correct answer will refer to the same time period.

12

Drill It: Conclusion Mismatches

In each set of arguments below, one of the three will have a conclusion that doesn't match the other two. Determine which is the mismatch. Bonus points if you can categorize the mismatch type!

Set 1:

(A) Professional football players, taken as a group, have the largest stature of any professional athletes. Thus, most professional football players are large people.

(B) Professional jockeys, taken as a group, have the smallest stature of any professional athletes. This proves that jockeys are small people.

(C) Professional soccer players, taken as a group, run more per game than any other professional team-sport athletes. Therefore, the majority of soccer players must excel at running.

Set 2:

(A) Brahm will go to the prom only if Lydia invites him. But Lydia has already invited Clyde, so Brahm is not likely to attend the prom.

(B) Jane will ride the bull only if Juanita rides it first. But Juanita has been experiencing back pain, so Jane probably won't ride the bull.

(C) Artie eats a hamburger for lunch only when Elan invites him out. But Elan doesn't invite Artie out very often. More often he invites Sanjay. So Artie tends not to eat hamburgers for lunch.

Set 3:

(A) Advertisement: Dotty's detergent is the best-performing detergent on the market. Unlike bargain brands, Dotty's will get your clothes sparkling clean every time. Every home should be a Dotty's home!

(B) Advertisement: Unlike the bargain brand dog food, Pop's Kibble is made from quality meats and heart-healthy grains. Every pup wants to be a Pop's pup!

(C) Advertisement: Every Valentine's Day should begin at DeeDee's Diamonds. The quality of our stones far surpasses that of the discount diamonds offered elsewhere, and Valentine's Day is no time to skimp on quality.

Set 4:

(A) Jamal lives in California and drives to work only on rainy days. In California, it rains only in the winter and the spring. So, Jamal drives to work only in the winter and the spring.

(B) Lonny eats breakfast only when he has time to cook. Lonny has time to cook only on days when he can carpool rather than take the bus. Today, Lonny carpooled, so he must have eaten breakfast.

(C) Esme wears goggles only when she is working in the lab. She works in the lab only when one of her assistants takes the day off. Esme is wearing goggles, so one of her assistants must have taken the day off.

12

Solutions: Conclusion Mismatches

Set 1: Choice (B) is a mismatch.

Conclusions:

> (A) *Most* professional football players are large people.
> (B) Jockeys are small people.
> (C) The *majority* of soccer players must excel at running.

Answer choices (A) and (C) both deal with explicit quantities—"most" and "the majority"—that translate to more than half. Choice (B), on the other hand, doesn't specify the quantity. It just says that jockeys are small. How many jockeys, you might ask? Since there's no quantifier here, it must mean all of them. Thus, (B) has a *quantifier* mismatch.

Set 2: Choice (C) is a mismatch.

Conclusions:

> (A) Brahm is not *likely* to attend prom.
> (B) Jane *probably* won't ride the bull.
> (C) Artie *tends* not to eat hamburgers for lunch.

Both answers (A) and (B) are predictive. They deal in likelihood and probability, which are essentially the same. But answer (C) is not predictive. Instead, it deals in tendency, which is about evaluating the past and the present—what *tends* to happen—rather than predicting the future. This is a *strength* mismatch. Beware of the subtle difference between tendency and probability!

Set 3: Choice (B) is a mismatch.

Start by isolating each conclusion:

> (A) Every home *should be* a Dotty's home.
> (B) Every pup *wants* to be a Pop's pup.
> (C) Every Valentine's Day *should* begin at DeeDee's Diamonds.

While answers (A) and (C) tell us about what *should* happen (these are normative statements), choice (B) is evaluative—it tells us what is or isn't true. Specifically, it tells us what every pup *wants*, not what it *should* want. This is a *type* mismatch.

You may have noticed that answer choice (A) is a three-part argument with a premise, an intermediate conclusion, and a main conclusion. If you had trouble determining which was the main conclusion, you should zero in on the word "should." If only one statement in an argument is normative, it is almost invariably the main conclusion.

You also might have noticed that in advertisement (A), the main conclusion is the last statement, whereas in advertisement (C), the main conclusion is first. That will *never* matter. The order of the statements has no relationship to their logic, and it's their *logical* structure, not their *grammatical* structure, that we're trying to match.

Set 4: Choice (A) is a mismatch.

Conclusions:

> (A) John drives to work *only* in the winter and the spring.
> (B) He *must have* eaten breakfast.
> (C) One of her assistants *must have* taken the day off.

(A)'s conclusion is a conditional statement. It's a rule: He drives to work only in the winter and spring. Answers (B) and (C) are not conditional, and they aren't rules that apply generally. Instead, they each establish what must have happened in one particular instance. This is another *type* mismatch.

It can be tough to notice a nonconditional conclusion in an otherwise conditional argument. Both choices (B) and (C) have two conditional premises, but in each argument, there is a third premise that fulfills one of the conditions. In answer (C), for example, we're given two rules about Amy: She wears goggles only when she is working in the lab (goggles → lab), and she works in the lab only when one of her assistants takes the day off (lab → asst. day off). These are our conditional premises. Then we're told that she is indeed wearing goggles. This triggers our conditional chain: goggles → lab → asst. day off. The conclusion that one of her assistants must have taken the day off is the end of the conditional chain, not a conditional statement of its own.

One thing that may have made this mismatch hard to spot was that a premise was in the same sentence as the conclusion. This structure can lead some test-takers to mistake the premise–conclusion relationship for a conditional relationship. To determine whether an argument conclusion is a conditional statement or just the end result of a conditional argument, zero in on the presence and location of language that indicates conditionality ("if," "only," "only if," "unless," etc.).

While (B) and (C) have matching conclusions, did you notice a different mismatch that is leaving you concerned? Good! We'll discuss that later…

Let's try one more full question to put our conclusion mismatches to work.

PT14, S4, Q8

The years 1917, 1937, 1956, 1968, 1979, and 1990 are all notable for the occurrence of both popular uprisings and near-maximum sunspot activity. During heavy sunspot activity, there is a sharp rise in positively charged ions in the air people breathe, and positively charged ions are known to make people anxious and irritable. Therefore, it is likely that sunspot activity has actually been a factor in triggering popular uprisings.

Which of the following exhibits a pattern of reasoning most similar to that in the passage?

(A)   The ancient Greeks sometimes attempted to predict the outcome of future events by watching the flight patterns of birds. Since the events themselves often matched the predictions, the birds were probably responding to some factor that also influenced the events.

(B)   Martha, Sidney, and Hilary are the city's three most powerful politicians, and all three graduated from Ridgeview High School. Although Ridgeview never had a reputation for excellence, it must have been a good school to have produced three such successful graduates.

(C)   Unusually cold weather last December coincided with a rise in fuel prices. When it is cold, people use more fuel to keep warm; and when more fuel is used, prices rise. Therefore if prices are high next winter, it will be the result of cold weather.

(D)   The thirty healthiest people in a long-term medical study turned out to be the same thirty whose regular diets included the most vegetables. Since specific substances in vegetables are known to help the body fight disease, vegetables should be part of everyone's diet.

(E)   Acme's most productive managers are
        consistently those who occupy the corner
        offices, which have more windows than other
        offices at Acme. Since people are more alert
        when they are exposed to abundant natural
        light, the greater productivity of these
        managers is probably at least in part a result
        of their working in corner offices.

If you haven't already, take a moment to describe the conclusion abstractly, and take notes on why each wrong answer is wrong—then compare your notes to the solution below.

The conclusion is a causal statement (X causes Y) that says a cause is *likely*. We can expect some mismatched conclusions based on type and strength. Let's move to the answer choices:

(A)   The ancient Greeks sometimes attempted to
        predict the outcome of future events by
        watching the flight patterns of birds. Since the
        events themselves often matched the
        predictions, the birds were probably
        responding to some factor that also
        influenced the events.

Is probability the same as likelihood? It sure is. How about language indicating cause and effect? "Responding to" and "influenced" are both causal terms, so this conclusion seems like a decent match. Defer judgment and move on.

(B)   Martha, Sidney, and Hilary are the city's three
        most powerful politicians, and all three
        graduated from Ridgeview High School.
        Although Ridgeview never had a reputation
        for excellence, it must have been a good
        school to have produced three such successful
        graduates.

Saying something "must have been" is not a causal statement. Although this argument makes a causal *assumption,* the actual conclusion is a factual claim. This is a type mismatch. The switch from "it is likely" to "must have been" also creates a strength mismatch. Eliminate.

(C)   Unusually cold weather last December
         coincided with a rise in fuel prices. When it is
         cold, people use more fuel to keep warm; and
         when more fuel is used, prices rise. Therefore
         if prices are high next winter, it will be the
         result of cold weather.

"Will be the result" is causal but 100% certain, so we're looking at a strength mismatch. We're also looking at a type mismatch because (C)'s conclusion is a conditional statement. True, it also deals in cause and effect, but that cause-and-effect relationship has to be triggered by high prices at the pump. Speaking of those high prices, when is it exactly that they'll trigger this relationship? Sometime in the future. This creates a temporal mismatch. The conclusion of the original argument is about a causal relationship in the past. (C)'s conclusion is a prediction of a causal relationship in the future.

(D)   The thirty healthiest people in a long-term
         medical study turned out to be the same
         thirty whose regular diets included the most
         vegetables. Since specific substances in
         vegetables are known to help the body fight
         disease, vegetables should be part of
         everyone's diet.

(D) contains a type mismatch: Its conclusion is normative (a "should" statement), whereas the original argument's is not.

(E)   Acme's most productive managers are
         consistently those who occupy the corner
         offices, which have more windows than other
         offices at Acme. Since people are more alert
         when they are exposed to abundant natural
         light, the greater productivity of these
         managers is probably at least in part a result
         of their working in corner offices.

The phrase "probably at least in part a result of" is an excellent match for our original argument. Conclusion mismatches, then, have gotten us down to two answer choices: (E) and (A). Before reading on, take another look at the original argument and the two remaining answer choices, paying attention to the entirety of each argument, not just the conclusions.

The original argument tells us that near-maximum sunspot activity and popular uprisings both occurred in all of the given years. Similarly, (E) tells us that the most productive managers are consistently in the corner offices. However, (A) tells us that the predictions *often* matched the events. This is a quantifier mismatch. However, there's another big difference between (A) and the matched pair of the original and (E). The original argument gave an explanation for how one event could cause the other: The charged ions make people anxious. We find a similar sort of additional premise in (E)—light exposure promotes alertness—but not in (A). This brings us to premise mismatches, the subject of our next section!

Premise Mismatches

This is going to be quick! The premises of the wrong answers will often display the same sorts of mismatches that we encountered with conclusions. Instead of restating those, let's revisit the first question we looked at. In the process, we'll see how applying a mismatch filter too strictly can eliminate the correct answer.

To get you started, let's examine the argument's premises:

> *PT22, S2, Q16*
>
> Allowing more steel imports would depress domestic
> steel prices and harm domestic steel manufacturers.
> Since the present government will not do anything
> that would harm the domestic steel industry, it will
> not lift restrictions on steel imports.

As we move through the answer choices, we don't want to hold "Allowing more steel imports would..." in our head because we are not matching content. Instead, we want to remember the *type* of premise and, since there can be multiple premises, the *number* of them. How would you describe the premise(s) above? Think about it before reading on.

In this case, one useful description to hold in your head is "There's a causal relationship and then a premise that says someone doesn't want what would be caused." Could this be more precise? Yes. It's not a some*one*, but a some*thing*—an organization. If you thought of this as conditional (i.e., more steel imports → lower dom. steel prices), that's fine, too. This is a case where the two reasoning structures are functionally interchangeable.

With only that description of the premises in mind, see how many answer choices you can eliminate.

12

PT22, S2, Q16

There's a causation relationship and then a premise that says someone doesn't want what would be caused.

The pattern of reasoning in the argument above is most similar to that in which one of the following?

(A)   Building construction increases only when people are confident that the economy is doing well. Therefore, since people are now confident in the economy we can expect building construction to increase.

(B)   Since workers are already guaranteed the right to a safe and healthful workplace by law, there is no need for the government to establish further costly health regulations for people who work all day at computer terminals.

(C)   In countries that have deregulated their airline industry, many airlines have gone bankrupt. Since many companies in other transportation industries are in weaker economic condition than were those airlines, deregulating other transportation industries will probably result in bankruptcies as well.

(D)   The chief executive officer of Silicon, Inc., will probably not accept stock in the company as a bonus next year, since next year's tax laws will require companies to pay a new tax on stock given to executives.

(E)   The installation of bright floodlights on campus would render the astronomy department's telescope useless. The astronomy department will not support any proposal that would render its telescope useless; it will therefore not support proposals to install bright floodlights on campus.

You should have been able to eliminate fours answers again! If you didn't, look again before reading on.

PT22, S2, Q16

Allowing more steel imports would depress domestic steel prices and harm domestic steel manufacturers. Since the present government will not do anything that would harm the domestic steel industry, it will not lift restrictions on steel imports.

There's a causation relationship and then a premise that says someone doesn't want what would be caused.

The pattern of reasoning in the argument above is most similar to that in which one of the following?

(A)   Building construction increases only when people are confident that the economy is doing well. Therefore, since people are now confident in the economy we can expect building construction to increase.

This is a conditional trigger, but we're looking for causation. *X would cause* something is different from *X requires* something.

(B)   Since workers are already guaranteed the right to a safe and healthful workplace by law, there is no need for the government to establish further costly health regulations for people who work all day at computer terminals.

No causation! You're out!

(C)   In countries that have deregulated their airline industry, many airlines have gone bankrupt. Since many companies in other transportation industries are in weaker economic condition than were those airlines, deregulating other transportation industries will probably result in bankruptcies as well.

No causation again! This is just correlation.

(D)   The chief executive officer of Silicon, Inc., will probably not accept stock in the company as a bonus next year, since next year's tax laws will require companies to pay a new tax on stock given to executives.

This requirement is not a great match for a premise about causation. But more importantly, *where is the second premise?*

(E)   The installation of bright floodlights on campus would render the astronomy department's telescope useless. The astronomy department will not support any proposal that would render its telescope useless; it will therefore not support proposals to install bright floodlights on campus.

We're missing the second result ("and harm domestic steel manufacturers"). Eliminate!

12

Whoa! We just eliminated the correct answer. What's up with that?

This is exactly the sort of thing you'll do as you first use these tools to identify mismatches. Whenever this happens, spend some time figuring out why the LSAT permitted that mismatch. Can you see the reason in choice (E)?

In this example, while we were originally given the compound premise *X causes Y and Z*, the argument hinged only on X causing Z (increasing steel imports would harm domestic manufacturers). Thus, answer choice (E) matches the overall *pattern* of reasoning even though it has a singular result in its premise, because the compound result in the original didn't impact the logic of the argument.

This is an important moment in your learning about mismatches:

We want to treat our lesser premise and conclusion mismatches forgivingly. When you come across a mismatch, decide if it's a clear answer-killer or not. If you're not sure, defer. The most devastating conclusion mismatches are strength and type. The most devastating premise mismatches are type and number (if the original has two premises the right answer better have the same number!). Compound vs. singular mismatches like we see in answer choice (E), and the aforementioned negative vs. positive and temporal mismatches are, especially in the premises, generally not fatal by themselves. Why not? Because these mismatches often fail to indicate a difference in the *logic*, which is what we're ultimately looking to match. Premise mismatches are fatal only if they demonstrate a difference in the way an argument's conclusion is supported. The stronger mismatches—strength, number, and type—are stronger because they generally represent definitive changes in logic.

Let's take a look at another question.

> *PT16, S2, Q19*
>
> The Volunteers for Literacy Program would benefit if Dolores takes Victor's place as director, since Dolores is far more skillful than Victor is at securing the kind of financial support the program needs and Dolores does not have Victor's propensity for alienating the program's most dedicated volunteers.
>
> The pattern of reasoning in the argument above is most closely paralleled in which one of the following?
>
> (A) It would be more convenient for Dominique to take a bus to school than to take the subway, since the bus stops closer to her house than does the subway and, unlike the subway, the bus goes directly to school.

(B)   Joshua's interest would be better served by taking the bus to get to his parent's house rather than by taking an airplane, since his primary concern is to travel as cheaply as possible and taking the bus is less expensive than going by airplane.

(C)   Belinda will get to the concert more quickly by subway than by taxi, since the concert takes place on a Friday evening and on Friday evenings traffic near the concert hall is exceptionally heavy.

(D)   Anita would benefit financially by taking the train to work rather than driving her car, since when she drives she has to pay parking fees and the daily fee for parking a car is higher than a round-trip train ticket.

(E)   It would be to Fred's advantage to exchange his bus tickets for train tickets, since he needs to arrive at his meeting before any of the other participants and if he goes by bus at least one of the other participants will arrive first.

Once again, before you read the solutions below, make sure you've thought about the form of the stimulus and the mismatches in each answer. This time, pay particular attention to the premises.

When assessing the premises of an argument, take stock of their number, type, strength, and relationship. This argument has two premises, both strong comparatives that assess Dolores favorably to Victor. Each of the premises independently supports the conclusion. The two do not build upon each other in any way.

(A)   It would be more convenient for Dominique to take a bus to school than to take the subway, since the bus stops closer to her house than does the subway and, unlike the subway, the bus goes directly to school.

In (A), the bus is compared favorably to the subway in each of the two premises. They are unrelated to one another, but both support the conclusion. These seem like matching premises. Defer judgment.

(B)   Joshua's interest would be better served by taking the bus to get to his parent's house rather than by taking an airplane, since his primary concern is to travel as cheaply as possible and taking the bus is less expensive than going by airplane.

In (B), the two premises build upon each other and one of them is not comparative. The first establishes a principle guiding Joshua's decision: travel cheaply. The second tells us that the bus is cheaper than the plane. Together, they support the conclusion that the bus is the better choice, but independently they offer no support at all.

> (C)   Belinda will get to the concert more quickly by
>   subway than by taxi, since the concert takes
>   place on a Friday evening and on Friday
>   evenings traffic near the concert hall is
>   exceptionally heavy.

(C)'s first premise is not comparative at all. Its second premise is comparative in that it says traffic is *exceptionally* heavy on Fridays, but it doesn't compare two specific entities like the premises in the original argument. Furthermore, these premises cannot function independently; in order to support the conclusion they have to operate together.

> (D)   Anita would benefit financially by taking the
>   train to work rather than driving her car,
>   since when she drives she has to pay parking
>   fees and the daily fee for parking a car is
>   higher than a round-trip train ticket.

(D)'s first premise is conditional, not comparative, and like the premises in (B) and (C), these premises build upon each other rather than functioning independently.

> (E)   It would be to Fred's advantage to exchange his
>   bus tickets for train tickets, since he needs to
>   arrive at his meeting before any of the other
>   participants and if he goes by bus at least one
>   of the other participants will arrive first.

(E)'s premises compare Fred to the other participants, but they don't address the comparison in the conclusion, which is about bus vs. train tickets. The first establishes a need and the second tells us that the bus won't meet that need. A comparison to the train, however, is nowhere to be found.

This leaves (A) as the only possible answer choice. The premise mismatches in the incorrect answers were so potent because they did exactly what a strong mismatch must do: They seriously impacted the logic of the argument. In fact, all the mismatches that we've talked about can eliminate answer choices only insofar as they indicate a difference in the argument's logic. This brings us to the most challenging and most important type of mismatch to identify: the logic mismatch.

12

Logic Mismatches

We already know that we'll often sniff out a logic mismatch through a mismatched conclusion or premise. However, sometimes those pieces match, or seem to, and we need to dig into how the pieces connect.

Let's consider these two familiar arguments:

> Esme wears goggles only when she is working in the lab. She works in the lab only when one of her assistants takes the day off. Esme is wearing goggles, so one of her assistants must have taken the day off.

> Lonny eats breakfast only when he has time to cook. Lonny has time to cook only on days when he can carpool rather than take the bus. Today, Lonny carpooled, so he must have eaten breakfast.

While these formed the matching pair in an earlier drill focused only on conclusions, these arguments don't actually match because of a fundamental difference in their logic. If you didn't spot the logic mismatch, take one more look.

The first argument is airtight. The conclusion is inferable from the premises. But the second argument has a classic flaw! While we could conclude that he carpooled if knew he ate breakfast, we can't reason in the other direction. That's an illegal reversal. Thus, these two arguments with matched premises and matched conclusions do not actually match.

Of course, validity mismatches work both ways: If we are given an invalid argument, the correct answer must also be invalid and for the same reasons. (This will be the engine of our Match the Flaw approach.)

Logic mismatches are all about the way that the argument pieces connect. Given that spotting such a mismatch isn't simply a matter of noticing a shift in what modifier is used (though such shifts can sometimes indicate a change in reasoning), we need tools for comparing arguments' underlying structures. The first tool to practice using is the same one we used to describe the premises in the last question: abstracting the argument. When we went to compare the steel imports argument with the answer choices, we boiled it down to "Doing X would lead to Y and Z. Z isn't wanted." The essential task here is to *strip out the content and preserve the structure.*

Since Matching questions are testing our ability to compare reasoning structure, not the specific content that overlays that structure, we need a way to hold the structure in our heads as we work through the answer choices. You may well be able to remember a simple abstracted structure without writing it down, but feel free to jot down an abbreviated form on your scratch paper if it helps.

The second, related, tool is formal diagramming. Some Matching questions involve enough conditional logic that the natural abstraction is formal notation. You've used formal notation to tackle questions of various types, so it should be no surprise that the signal to use it is always the same: the presence of multiple conditional triggers (e.g., "if," "only," "unless"). Putting the structure of the original argument onto scratch paper is a great, though somewhat counterintuitive, way to reduce the work involved with the question. While it can seem like a lot of work to write out the notation for the original argument and all five answer choices, never fear. Typically, you can eliminate a few answer choices that have clear premise or conclusion mismatches before diagramming them. As you diagram the remaining answer choices, you often will be able to eliminate a choice before you've finished diagramming it, because even the first stages of

12

diagramming the answer will expose mismatches that were hidden in the text. You may feel that you don't have time to diagram, but this fear is often misguided. Deployed strategically, diagramming will actually *save* you time because it will spare you the experience of trying to untangle and retain multiple similar arguments in your head.

Matching Traps

Part of the reason we want to create an abstract or formal version of the original argument is to sidestep two misconceptions that some test-takers consciously or unconsciously carry about this question type: that order and content matter.

To be clear, the order of the premises and conclusion in a correct answer does not have to follow the order of the original argument.

Similarly, as you have probably noticed, the correct answer's content is unimportant. In fact, be wary of an answer choice that has the same content as the original argument—it can be a trap!

Now, on to the practice!

Drill It: Abstracting Arguments

Practice stripping away the content of the following arguments to expose the underlying reasoning. Write down your abstracted version of each argument in the space provided. We've done the first one for you. Then, because this is the Matching chapter, identify any matching pairs before turning to the solutions (you can draw lines between the matching arguments). There are seven pairs and one lonely, unmatched argument.

1. The federal government should ban texting while driving because texting while driving is a factor in numerous fatal accidents annually.

   We should ban a thing because it's dangerous.

2. All salads at the diner come with ranch or bleu cheese dressing. Jim doesn't like ranch, so he will order bleu cheese on his side salad.

3. Every chef's special at Chez Vivienne is expertly crafted. But some menu items are not chef's specials. Therefore, some menu items at Chez Vivienne are not expertly crafted.

4. Not all exercise is good for you. Jogging, for example, is very high-impact, making it hard on the joints.

5. As a person's consumption of leafy green vegetables increases, so does the pH of that person's blood. Mia has recently been skipping her usual helping of leafy green vegetables in favor of fruiting vegetables. Thus, the pH of Mia's blood must have decreased.

6. The hotel shouldn't ban smoking in its rooms just because of the fire risk. The hotel has kitchenettes in each room, which also increases the risk of fire, but no one is suggesting removing them.

7. Kai is giving up his diesel car. He must be getting an electric.

8. Bikes-R-Us sells only two brands of bicycles: Windly and Carm. Pol bought a bike from Bikes-R-Us yesterday, and I know it wasn't a Windly, so it must have been a Carm.

9. The federal government shouldn't ban texting while driving just because of the inherent danger. After all, eating behind the wheel is dangerous, too, but we all agree that it should remain legal.

10. Smoking in hotel rooms significantly impacts the overall fire risk at a given hotel, so the hotel shouldn't allow it.

11. Assistant Coach Carter doesn't write all of the team's plays, but those that she does write emphasize fundamentals. It follows, then, that not all of the team's plays emphasize fundamentals.

12. Basketball requires that players run only in short bursts, so not all sports are endurance sports.

13. When children spend more time reading, their active vocabularies grow. Marvin has recently been spending less time reading and more time watching TV, so his active vocabulary must have shrunk.

14. All of Chef Dardine's specials are exceptionally delicious. The soup was not exceptionally delicious, so it must not have been one of Chef Dardine's specials.

15. So-called "cold turkey" quitting is an ineffective way to quit smoking, so the doctor will recommend a drug to help with cravings.

12

Solutions: Abstracting Arguments

Of course, not everyone will come up with the same way of describing each of these arguments. We've tried to model a variety of different ways to describe arguments abstractly. Some of these reduce the arguments to relationships between variables and others do not. You will probably have used different language than we did at least some of the time. As long as the *structure* you described was the same, count it as a win. A good indication of your proficiency is the number of arguments that you correctly matched!

Arguments 1 and 10

We should ban a thing because it is dangerous.

Arguments 2 and 8

Two options: A and B. A won't work, so B must be true.

The core logic of these arguments is the same, but there is a subtle mismatch. If you didn't notice it, take another look before reading on.

If you noticed a temporal mismatch in these conclusions, bravo! This difference between what will happen in the future and what must have happened in the past is a mismatch, but it is the lesser kind that might slide through in a correct answer choice if the argument's logic is otherwise the same.

Arguments 3 and 11

Everything in a category has a certain characteristic. Some things aren't in that category, so those things don't have that characteristic.

If you got tripped up on a quantifier mismatch in these conclusions, remember that "not all do" is equivalent to "some do not." Though the *terms* do not match, the *concepts* are the same.

Arguments 4 and 12

It's not true that all A's are B, because here's an example of A that is C.

Arguments 5 and 13

As thing one goes up, so does thing two. Thing one has been going down, so thing two must have, as well. (Sorry, Dr. Seuss.)

Arguments 6 and 9

We shouldn't ban A just because of characteristic B, since C is analogous and C is allowed.

Arguments 7 and 15

X is off the table, so it's going to be Y. (False choice!)

Argument 14 is the odd man out.

This argument just relies on a contrapositive: A → B; −B, therefore −A.

Diagramming Matches

Now that you've practiced abstracting arguments, let's delve into the particular kind of abstraction unique to conditional arguments—formal diagramming. You'll have to develop your own preference for when to use abstract language as shown above and when to break out the logic arrows. Make sure that you are comfortable with both approaches!

Drill It: Diagramming Matches

Match each diagrammed argument to the sentence or argument with the same logical structure. Keep in mind that it can be easy to overlook the difference between a conditional conclusion ("Thus, if there's a storm, the hike will not happen") and a conclusion that is simply the end result of applying a conditional argument ("Thus, the hike will not happen").

Diagram 1

B → A

Diagram 2

A → B

Diagram 3

A → B
–B
–A

Diagram 4

A → B
B
A

Diagram 5

A → B
B → C
A → C

Diagram 6

A → B
B → C
A
C

Diagram 7

A → B
–B → –A

i. All animals breathe.

ii. Only animals breathe.

iii. All animals breathe. That creature is breathing, which means that creature must be an animal.

iv. When Alicia goes to a party, she brings booze, and wherever there's booze, there are cocktails! Alicia is going to the party, so there will be cocktails at the party.

v. All animals breathe, so if something doesn't breathe, it isn't an animal.

vi. All animals breathe, but since my pet rock does not, my pet rock is not an animal.

vii. Any piece of art is at risk of being burgled, and wherever there is a risk of burglary, there is a risk of cat burglars. Therefore, all art is subject to being cat-burgled.

MANHATTAN
PREP

Solutions: Diagramming Matches

1. All animals breathe.

   Diagram 2:

   A → B

2. Only animals breathe.

   Diagram 1:

   B → A

3. All animals breathe. That creature is breathing, which means that creature must be an animal.

   Diagram 4:

   A → B
   <u>B   </u>
   A

4. When Alicia goes to a party, she brings booze, and wherever there's booze, there's cocktails! Alicia is going to the party, so there will be cocktails at the party.

   Diagram 6:

   A → B
   B → C
   <u>A   </u>
   C

5. All animals breathe, so if something doesn't breathe, it isn't an animal.

   Diagram 7:

   <u>A → B </u>
   –B → –A

6. All animals breathe, but since my pet rock does not, my pet rock is not an animal.

   Diagram 3:

   A → B
   <u>–B   </u>
   –A

7. Any piece of art is at risk of being burgled, and wherever there is a risk of burglary, there is a risk of cat burglars. Therefore, all art is subject to being cat-burgled.

   Diagram 5:

   A → B
   <u>B → C</u>
   A → C

Now that you've got some practice under your belt, test out your skills on the following questions:

PT11, S4, Q20

If the majority of the residents of the apartment complex complain that their apartments are infested with ants, then the management of the complex will have to engage the services of an exterminator. But the majority of the residents of the complex indicate that their apartments are virtually free of ants. Therefore, the management of the complex will not have to engage the services of an exterminator.

Which one of the following arguments contains a pattern of flawed reasoning parallel to that contained in the argument above?

(A)   A theater will be constructed in the fall if funds collected are at least sufficient to cover its cost. To date, the funds collected exceed the theater's cost, so the theater will be constructed in the fall.

(B)   The number of flights operated by the airlines cannot be reduced unless the airlines can collect higher airfares. But people will not pay higher airfares, so it is not the case that the number of flights will be reduced.

(C)   In order for the company to start the proposed building project, both the town council and the mayor must approve. Since the mayor has already approved, the building project will be started soon.

(D)   Most employees will attend the company picnic if the entertainment committee is successful in getting a certain band to play at the picnic. But that band will be out of the country on the day of the picnic, so it is not true that most employees will attend.

(E)   Either the school's principal or two-thirds of the parent council must approve a change in the school dress code in order for the code to be changed. Since the principal will not approve a change in the dress code, the code will not be changed.

PT18, S4, Q20

Last year the county park system failed to generate enough revenue to cover its costs. Any business should be closed if it is unprofitable, but county parks are not businesses. Therefore, the fact that county parks are unprofitable does not by itself justify closing them.

The pattern of reasoning in the argument above is most closely paralleled in which one of the following?

(A)   A prime-time television series should be canceled if it fails to attract a large audience, but the small audience attracted by the documentary series is not sufficient reason to cancel it, since it does not air during prime time.

(B)   Although companies that manufacture and market automobiles in the United States must meet stringent air-quality standards, the OKESA company should be exempt from these standards since it manufactures bicycles in addition to automobiles.

(C)   Although the province did not specifically intend to prohibit betting on horse races when it passed a law prohibiting gambling, such betting should be regarded as being prohibited because it is a form of gambling.

(D)   Even though cockatiels are not, strictly speaking, members of the parrot family, they should be fed the same diet as most parrots since the cockatiel's dietary needs are so similar to those of parrots.

(E)   Since minors are not subject to the same criminal laws as are adults, they should not be subject to the same sort of punishments as those that apply to adults.

PT11, S4, Q20

> If the majority of the residents of the apartment complex complain that their apartments are infested with ants, then the management of the complex will have to engage the services of an exterminator. But the majority of the residents of the complex indicate that their apartments are virtually free of ants. Therefore, the management of the complex will not have to engage the services of an exterminator.

First, did you notice that we slipped in a slightly different type of Matching question? This one asks you to match the flawed reasoning. We'll discuss these in more depth shortly, but we wanted to demonstrate how the tools you've already learned also help with this type.

This argument is purely conditional, so your first move should be to think through the mechanics of the conditional relationships. For most people, this will mean diagramming.

maj. complain → hire exterm.
—maj. complain
―――――――――――――――――
—hire exterm.

If you recognized this common conditional reasoning error, well done! This is an illegal negation. Any answer choice that doesn't contain this reasoning error has a logic mismatch.

>   (A)   A theater will be constructed in the fall if funds collected are at least sufficient to cover its cost. To date, the funds collected exceed the theater's cost, so the theater will be constructed in the fall.

This is a *valid* argument and thus contains a fatal logic mismatch:

funds cover cost → build theater
funds cover cost
―――――――――――――――――
build theater

>   (B)   The number of flights operated by the airlines cannot be reduced unless the airlines can collect higher airfares. But people will not pay higher airfares, so it is not the case that the number of flights will be reduced.

This is also a valid argument and therefore incorrect. Our diagram looks like this:

MANHATTAN
PREP   529

number of flights reduced → collect higher airfare

–collect higher airfare
_____

–number of flights reduced

> (C)   In order for the company to start the proposed
>   building project, both the town council and
>   the mayor must approve. Since the mayor has
>   already approved, the building project will be
>   started soon.

The first conditional premise here has a compound necessary condition. That's a mismatch, but maybe not a deal-breaker. The second premise—the mayor has already approved—fulfills one but not both of the necessary conditions. Fulfilling the necessary means we're looking at a reversal, not a negation, and the fact that we fulfilled only half of the compound makes it even more logically mismatched.

> (D)   Most employees will attend the company picnic
>   if the entertainment committee is successful
>   in getting a certain band to play at the picnic.
>   But that band will be out of the country on
>   the day of the picnic, so it is not true that
>   most employees will attend.

Right off the bat, (D) seems to have a premise mismatch because of the quantifier "most." But if we investigate further, the quantifier doesn't actually impact the *logic* of the argument. You could switch it out for "all" or "some" and the argument would still work in the same way. That means you can let it slide. Our diagram should look like this:

band → most attend

–band
_____

–most attend

This is a definite match for the original argument. That "most" was just a red herring! Answer (D) looks correct, but let's check answer (E) just to be sure.

> (E)   Either the school's principal or two-thirds of
>   the parent council must approve a change in
>   the school dress code in order for the code to
>   be changed. Since the principal will not
>   approve a change in the dress code, the code
>   will not be changed.

This argument begins with an either/or premise. That premise is still a conditional, but the either/or is denoting a compound necessary condition. This creates a mismatch:

dress code change → principal approve OR two-thirds of parent council approve

12

Another mismatch occurs when the next premise says the principal won't approve. That negates one of the necessary conditions, making it impossible for the argument to exhibit the same negated logic as the original argument (to match that, we would want to negate the sufficient condition—dress code change—and thus conclude the negation of the necessary condition). This argument is flawed—though differently than we want—because it discounts the parent council, treating the principal's disapproval as though it alone could prevent the dress code change.

> ### PT18, S4, Q20
>
> Last year the county park system failed to generate enough revenue to cover its costs. Any business should be closed if it is unprofitable, but county parks are not businesses. Therefore, the fact that county parks are unprofitable does not by itself justify closing them.

The second premise of this argument is a conditional with a normative necessary condition:

> unprofitable business → should be closed

The first premise establishes that the county parks were unprofitable, and the third establishes that they are not businesses. These are not clear conditionals, though they do establish that the county parks fail to fulfill the sufficient condition set forth in the second premise: Parks are not unprofitable businesses (because they're not businesses). The conclusion is that the necessary condition, closing the park, is not justified by the park's unprofitability. (Note that this is different than a conclusion suggesting the parks should not be closed.) While formal diagramming could help, it alone cannot account for all the pieces of this argument and so some informal abstraction is useful. Let's look at the answer choices:

> (A)   A prime-time television series should be canceled if it fails to attract a large audience, but the small audience attracted by the documentary series is not sufficient reason to cancel it, since it does not air during prime time.

This answer choice begins by establishing a normative conditional:

> prime-time TV doesn't get big audience → should be cancelled

It goes on to say that the documentary, although it didn't get the big audience, isn't on prime time. This tells us that the show doesn't fulfill the sufficient condition (it can't be a prime-time TV show that doesn't get a big audience since it's not a prime-time TV show), and (A) concludes that the lack of a big audience is therefore not reason enough to cancel the show. This seems like a darn good match for our original argument. Defer judgment—we've been fooled before!

12

(B)   Although companies that manufacture and
        market automobiles in the United States must
        meet stringent air-quality standards, the
        OKESA company should be exempt from
        these standards since it manufactures bicycles
        in addition to automobiles.

The conditional premise that begins answer choice (B) is not normative. The conclusion, on the other hand, is. These type mismatches are enough to eliminate (B). Also, the second premise doesn't demonstrate that OKESA doesn't fulfill the sufficient condition: OKESA *does* manufacture and market automobiles in the United States. It just *additionally* manufactures bicycles. This logic mismatch is also grounds for elimination.

(C)   Although the province did not specifically
        intend to prohibit betting on horse races
        when it passed a law prohibiting gambling,
        such betting should be regarded as being
        prohibited because it is a form of gambling.

This answer choice has every flavor of mismatch. Like (B), its conclusion, rather than its premise, is normative. There are no clear conditionals in (C) and no premises that say an entity fails to fulfill a sufficient condition.

(D)   Even though cockatiels are not, strictly
        speaking, members of the parrot family, they
        should be fed the same diet as most parrots
        since the cockatiel's dietary needs are so
        similar to those of parrots.

Once again, the normative statement here is in the conclusion, rather than the premise, and there are no premises establishing that something doesn't fulfill a sufficient condition of a conditional premise.

(E)   Since minors are not subject to the same
        criminal laws as are adults, they should not be
        subject to the same sort of punishments as
        those that apply to adults.

Not only does this have the same type of normative conclusion that has been ruling out so many other answers, it also has only one premise. This argument doesn't use conditionals to prove its conclusion: It uses an analogy.

We've eliminated answers (B) through (E). Therefore, choice (A) is correct.

Match the Flaw

As you likely already know, there is a subcategory of Matching questions that explicitly asks us to match flawed reasoning. However, did you notice that the arguments on pages 512 and 518 were flawed? The former had a Causation Flaw and the latter had a Comparison Flaw. It turns out that the LSAT doesn't always announce that the original argument is flawed. Regardless of the fact that we've already matched flawed arguments, it's worth spending a moment looking at this specific flavor of Matching question because there are some differences.

The obvious difference is that arguments in Match the Flaw questions are *always* flawed! More important to your success, however, is the fact that the LSAT permits more premise and conclusion mismatches with Match the Flaw questions. With a standard, valid Matching question, you can often get away with eliminating your way to a correct answer, but *with any flawed Matching question, you must confirm that the answer you select is flawed in the same way as the original argument.* That said, you will still use your other tools for locating mismatches, but locating *flaw* mismatches will typically drive your process. Incorrect answers either will be valid arguments or, more commonly, will exhibit a different flaw than the original argument. To that end, on Match the Flaw questions, your first order of business is to articulate the flaw in the original argument.

What flaws will you encounter? Actually, you have already met most of them! Take another look at the list of flawed arguments that you met in the Flaw chapter:

Classic Flaws

Ad Hominem	Comparison Flaw	Part vs. Whole	Self-Contradiction
Appeal to Inappropriate Authority	Conditional Logic Flaw	Percent vs. Amount	Unproven vs. Untrue
Causation Flaw	Equivocation	Sampling Flaw	
Circular Reasoning	False Choice		

The most commonly tested among these are Causation and Conditional Logic Flaws, but any of these flaws (and a few rare others) make regular appearances, and all of them are fair game!

As a quick review, let's practice identifying flaws in arguments.

Drill It: Name That Flaw Review

Figure out the flaw in each of the arguments below. It's fine to simply describe the flaw, but bonus points for remembering the names you learned in Chapter 4! Be aware that not every argument below is flawed. While you won't meet valid arguments in a Match the Flaw stimulus, you will meet them in some incorrect answer choices!

1. Jeremy is deciding whom to promote to manager. Maya has extensive experience, but Amir, who lacks experience, has more passion. Jeremy determines that experience is more important than passion for this position. Therefore, Jeremy will promote Maya.

   Flaw: _____

2. Studying math involves logical thinking. This is clearly true because any time someone studies math, he is thinking logically.

   Flaw: _____

3. The linguini, lasagna, and fettuccini produced by this Italian restaurant are the best in the city. This must be the best Italian restaurant in the city.

   Flaw: _____

4. Dara's work is significantly better than Ana's. Therefore, when choosing between the two, we can be confident that Dara will produce good work, while Ana may not.

   Flaw: _____

5. Due to the age of Elias's washing machine, it will no longer run at peak efficiency without one or more replacement parts. Since the machine is no longer running at peak efficiency, he must not have had any of its core components replaced.

   Flaw: _____

6. Extrasensory Perception (ESP) does not exist. Despite extensive research, no scientist has been able to find any reliable evidence that ESP actually exists.

   Flaw: _____

7. In order to reduce his weight, Floyd must either change his diet or start exercising. Floyd is committed to losing weight, but his schedule doesn't permit him to start exercising. Therefore, he must change his diet.

   Flaw: _____

8. Every time Anita was sad over the past four months, it had recently rained. She has concluded that the rain negatively affects her mood.

   Flaw: _____

9. The only way to consistently make three-point shots in basketball is to practice extensively. Jackson cannot consistently make three-point shots. He clearly has not practiced extensively.

   Flaw: _____

10. Josef claims that sales of board games in his store have been increasing over recent months. But Josef often makes broad claims about sales in his store that are actually untrue. Therefore, sales of board games in his store have not been increasing over recent months.

    Flaw: _____

11. By definition, every plant cell has cell walls. Roy
    is examining a cell from an unknown source. He
    determines that it does not have cell walls. He
    concludes that it must not be a plant cell.

    Flaw: _____

12. We can be confident that Neil will provide us with
    the best available investment advice because he works
    for Investments Unlimited, a company known to
    provide the best available investment advice.

    Flaw: _____

13. Jacob Sanders, a psychology professor at the
    University of Better Living, has stated that no one
    ever consistently makes money from the stock market.
    Based on Mr. Sanders's comments, we can conclude
    that it would be unwise to try to consistently make
    money by investing in the stock market.

    Flaw: _____

14. Numerous studies indicate that the only way to have
    peace is to find a balance between the obligations
    and pleasures of one's life. Yet, clearly, this is
    incorrect. Peace can be achieved by something as
    simple as a treaty between two countries.

    Flaw: _____

Solutions: Name That Flaw Review

1. False Choice

While it *might* be justified to say that Maya is preferred over Amir, it is a huge leap to say that Maya will be promoted. We are not necessarily choosing just between Maya and Amir. Maybe Tom, Dick, and Harold are also being considered for the promotion. Don't assume that just because we're only talking about two choices, we're limited to those two choices.

2. Circular Reasoning

What's the conclusion? Math goes hand-in-hand with logical thinking. What's the premise? Math goes hand-in-hand with logical thinking. Are you getting a sense of déjà vu? When the conclusion and premise are the same, the argument is circular.

3. Part vs. Whole

Sounds like you should go to this restaurant if you want great linguini. What if you want great manicotti? Hmm, we're not sure. Just because the restaurant is great in three ways doesn't mean it's the best overall. What's true of the part is not necessarily true of the whole.

4. Comparison Flaw

Did this sound like a good argument to you at first? For many people, this is a hard flaw to spot. Yet it is absolutely a flawed argument. The key here is the difference between relative and absolute. If the conclusion told us that Dara will likely produce better work than Ana, we would have a valid argument. Better, however, is not the same as good. Perhaps both produce bad work, but Dara is the best of the worst. We cannot conclude that Dara's work will be good or that Ana's work will be bad. Watch out for any switch from relative language to absolute or vice versa.

5. Conditional Logic Flaw

Since we're starting with a conditional, diagramming is a smart move:

> −replace parts → −run at p.e.
> −run at p.e.
> _____
> −replace parts

This conclusion is relying on reversed logic. We don't know why the machine is not running at peak efficiency. It could be because the core components need to be replaced or it could be there's something else that's problematic.

6. Unproven vs. Untrue

The fact that we have no evidence that something exists does not mean that that thing does not exist. Maybe we haven't found the evidence yet. Maybe we'll never find the evidence. All we know is that we don't have enough

information to conclude anything. This is true no matter how unlikely you may personally find the prospect of ESP. The flaw would remain the same if we replaced ESP with unicorns or Voldemort.

7. Valid

This argument is valid. There are two options presented, one of which is not possible. We're also told that Floyd is committed to completing one of the two options. We can therefore conclude that he must pursue the second option.

8. Causation Flaw

There is certainly a correlation between Anita's sadness and rain. But correlation does not imply causation. The correlation could be coincidence. What if rain is very common where Anita is, so it's likely to have just rained no matter what her mood is? Alternatively, there could be a causal relationship, but not the one the author predicts. Maybe cloudy days make her sad, and the clouds cause both the sadness and the rain. As we learned in the Flaw chapter, correlation does not prove causation!

9. Conditional Logic Flaw

Since this is a conditional argument, diagramming can expose its flawed structure:

> consistent 3-pt. → practice ext.
> −consistent 3-pt.
> _____
> −practice ext.

We can't simply negate both parts of a conditional statement! In everyday language, it might be that Jackson's inconsistent shots indicate a lack of practice or perhaps there is another reason. He may simply not be strong enough to consistently make a three-pointer. Extensive practicing is necessary, but it's not sufficient.

10. Ad Hominem

The author has made it clear that Josef is not reliable. However, in this case, Josef might have broken out of character and told the truth—perhaps by accident! Attacking the speaker isn't sufficient reason to conclude anything about the sales figures. We need facts, not attacks.

11. Valid

Let's diagram this out:

> plant cell → cell walls
> −cell walls
> _____
> −plant cell

This argument relies on a perfect contrapositive. If a cell doesn't have walls, it's impossible for it to be a plant cell. The conclusion is valid and the argument is not flawed.

12

12. Part vs. Whole

The whole (Investments Unlimited) provides the best advice. However, not every part will necessarily live up to that standard. Some people might be excellent while others might be subpar. Neil might be the best in his company or he might be the worst. We simply can't conclude anything about his advice based solely on the info about the company. What is true of the whole may not be true of the part.

13. Appeal to Inappropriate Authority

Mr. Sanders may very well be a psychology expert. However, nothing in the argument indicates that he knows anything about the stock market. Yes, he is an authority, but not in the field of economics. Even if he were an economist, the argument would still be flawed—what if he's simply wrong? But, in this case, we have an appeal to an inappropriate authority.

14. Equivocation

The word "peace" is being used in two different ways in this argument. Initially, "peace" refers to a personal inner peace. In the final premise, "peace" refers to the absence of war. The author is therefore equivocating with respect to the meaning of "peace."

Now, let's put all of this work into practice on an actual Match the Flaw question:

> ### PT12, S1, Q17
>
> On average, city bus drivers who are using the new computerized fare-collection system have a much better on-time record than do drivers using the old fare-collection system. Millicent Smith has the best on-time record for any bus driver in the city. Therefore, she must be using the computerized fare-collection system.
>
> Which of the following contains flawed reasoning most similar to that contained in the argument above?
>
> (A) All the city's solid-waste collection vehicles acquired after 1988 have a larger capacity than any of those acquired before 1988. This vehicle has the largest capacity of any the city owns, so it must have been acquired after 1988.

(B)   The soccer players on the blue team are
        generally taller than the players on the gold
        team. Since Henri is a member of the blue
        team, he is undoubtedly taller than most of
        the members of the gold team.

(C)   This tomato is the largest of this year's crop.
        Since the tomatoes in the experimental plot
        are on average larger than those grown in the
        regular plots, this tomato must have been
        grown in the experimental plot.

(D)   Last week's snowstorm in Toronto was
        probably an average storm for the area. It was
        certainly heavier than any snowstorm known
        to have occurred in Miami, but any average
        snowstorm in Toronto leaves more snow than
        ever falls in Miami.

(E)   Lawn mowers powered by electricity generally
        require less maintenance than do lawn
        mowers powered by gasoline. This lawn
        mower is powered by gasoline, so it will
        probably require a lot of maintenance.

First thing's first: We have to assess what's wrong with the argument in the stimulus. The first premise is a comparison, telling us that the average on-time record for drivers using the new system is better than the average on-time record for those using the old system. We should be on the lookout for a Comparison Flaw. The second premise introduces Millicent, the driver with the best on-time record. The conclusion tells us that Millicent must be using the new system, but that doesn't actually have to be true. Just because she's the best doesn't mean she must belong to the group that is the best *on average*. If she doesn't use the new system, she is certainly bringing up the average in her group, but the overall figure could still be lower than for those who use the new system. As an analogy, consider that some of the richest people in the world live in countries in which the *average* level of wealth is very low.

Formal diagramming may be a stretch here, but informal abstraction should work fine:

Group X is, on average, better than Group Y.
This person is the best.
She must be a member of Group X.

Let's look at the answer choices:

(A)   All the city's solid-waste collection vehicles
       acquired after 1988 have a larger capacity
       than any of those acquired before 1988. This
       vehicle has the largest capacity of any the city
       owns, so it must have been acquired after
       1988.

This is a great answer to scan and defer on—unless you noticed the mismatched quantity words. This argument establishes that *all* the post-1988 solid-waste collecting vehicles are bigger than *any* of the pre-1988's. The flaw in the original hinges on the concept of group *averages*. If we knew that the vehicle in question here was a solid-waste collecting vehicle, this actually would be a valid argument. But we don't know that, bringing us to the flaw that our original argument does not have: assuming the thing is actually subject to the rule set forth in the conditional premise. That would be like introducing Millicent and saying that she was the city's most punctual *person* rather than the city's most punctual *bus driver*. It's also worth noting that this choice also has a content trap. It's trying to look similar to the original argument by talking about similar content (changes to municipal vehicles) rather matching the logic. Unless all five choices are about the same thing, distrust such answers.

(B)   The soccer players on the blue team are
       generally taller than the players on the gold
       team. Since Henri is a member of the blue
       team, he is undoubtedly taller than most of
       the members of the gold team.

This flawed argument does hinge on the concept of averages, but the directionality doesn't match the original—the argument goes from "member of group X" to "high #." This move is a classic Part vs. Whole Flaw. Just because the blue team is taller *on the whole*, it doesn't mean *each part* of the blue team is taller than *each part* of the gold team. Compare this to the original argument that states that because Millicent has the best on-time record, she must use the new system; this assumes that because a person has the quality of a group, that person must be a member of that group. Answer choice (B) has it backwards.

(C)   This tomato is the largest of this year's crop.
       Since the tomatoes in the experimental plot
       are on average larger than those grown in the
       regular plots, this tomato must have been
       grown in the experimental plot.

The tomatoes in the experimental plot, on average, are bigger than the others. The biggest tomato, then, must be from that plot. This argument hinges on averages and states that because an individual has the characteristic of the group, it must be a member of the group. This seems like a match, but to be certain, we should check (D) and (E).

(D)   Last week's snow storm in Toronto was
            probably an average storm for the area. It was
            certainly heavier than any snowstorm known
            to have occurred in Miami, but any average
            snowstorm in Toronto leaves more snow than
            ever falls in Miami.

This oddball argument operates in a totally different way than the original because the fact that the storm in question was heavier than those in Miami provides no evidence that it was an average storm in Toronto. The premise offers no support for the conclusion at all—it just counters the opposing point.

(E)   Lawn mowers powered by electricity generally
            require less maintenance than do lawn
            mowers powered by gasoline. This lawn
            mower is powered by gasoline, so it will
            probably require a lot of maintenance.

This answer choice starts off strong with a comparison as the first premise. There are two groups of mowers, and one, on average, needs more maintenance. But then, instead of introducing a mower with that quality (amount of maintenance required) and concluding that the mower must be a member of one of the two groups, it introduces a mower in one of the groups and concludes the mower must have a particular quality. Like (B), this moves in the wrong direction. This choice has the additional flaw of confusing relative information for absolute. The premise tells us only how much maintenance the two groups require relative to one another. Just because one requires *more than the other* doesn't mean it requires *a lot* of maintenance.

Therefore, answer choice (C) is correct.

Your Matching Process

You now have all the tools you need to conquer any Matching question, flawed or not! As we mentioned at the beginning of the chapter, while we learned the tools separately, you should use whichever ones seem best suited to the question at hand, and in whatever order is most efficient. For all Matching questions, you'll begin by assessing the original argument. Notice if it has any flaws or unique elements that can help you sift through the answer choices. Abstract or diagram the argument, if appropriate. Once you get to the answer choices, things will be a little different every time. Your process may look something like this:

First, read and abstract. Notice any flaws or distinctive elements. Then…

Read through (A). It seems right, so defer.

Read through (B) and quickly notice a conclusion mismatch. Eliminate.

Read through (C) and defer.

Read through (D), and notice a premise mismatch. It's fishy, but not terrible, so keep it.

Read through (E), and notice a strong premise mismatch (or is it a logic mismatch?). Eliminate.

Return to the remaining answer choices, and look more closely at the underlying logic. Eliminate, choose, and move on!

We're not aiming for a rigid approach to these questions. Use all your tools and develop your instinct for what's worth a definite elimination and what is not. When in doubt, dig deeper into the logic.

Timing

While you should be able to move through Matching questions more quickly by targeting mismatches, you still might find these to be time-consuming questions. To get their best scores, many test-takers need to cut bait quickly on some tougher questions, perhaps even skipping them outright. If that's you, and if this question type is a particularly time-consuming one, go right ahead and save your time for questions you can tackle more quickly. However, try to do a quick pass through the question, looking only for easy conclusion and premise mismatches. Spending 30–45 seconds on such a pass can shift the odds significantly in your favor by allowing you to eliminate some answer choices before making your guess.

How to Practice

Practicing Matching questions is obviously a component of improving your performance with this question type, but it turns out that the skills tested here pay dividends with other question types as well. Success with Matching questions involves abstracting, diagramming, noticing flaws, and spotting subtle differences. It's pretty tough to think of a Logical Reasoning question that doesn't involve at least some of these skills! What's more, a Matching question presents you with six arguments instead of one, so you're even getting bonus practice with these essential skills.

When you review your work with Matching questions, try to do the following:

1. If you had a sloppy or rushed process, work through the question more thoroughly when reviewing. Abstract or diagram the argument and the answer choices.

2. Identify all mismatches.

3. Categorize any flaw or flaws in the original argument and in each answer choice, and notice when arguments are valid.

Speaking of practice, let's get to it!

MANHATTAN
PREP

Drill It: Matching Questions

1. PT15, S2, Q18

Everyone who is a gourmet cook enjoys a wide variety of foods and spices. Since no one who enjoys a wide variety of food and spices prefers bland foods to all other foods, it follows that anyone who prefers bland foods to all other foods is not a gourmet cook.

The pattern of reasoning displayed in the argument above is most similar to that displayed in which one of the following?

(A) All of the paintings in the Huang Collection will be put up for auction next week. Since the paintings to be auctioned next week are by a wide variety of artists, it follows that the paintings in the Huang Collection are by a wide variety of artists.

(B) All of the paintings in the Huang Collection are abstract. Since no abstract painting will be included in next week's art auction, nothing to be included in next week's art auction is a painting in the Huang Collection.

(C) All of the paintings in the Huang Collection are superb works of art. Since none of the paintings in the Huang Collection is by Roue, it stands to reason that no painting by Roue is a superb work of art.

(D) Every postimpressionist painting from the Huang Collection will be auctioned off next week. No pop art paintings from the Huang Collection will be auctioned off next week. Hence none of the pop art paintings to be auctioned off next week will be from the Huang Collection.

(E) Every painting from the Huang Collection that is to be auctioned off next week is a major work of art. No price can adequately reflect the true value of a major work of art. Hence the prices that will be paid at next week's auction will not adequately reflect the true value of the paintings sold.

2. PT11, S2, Q17

Of the two proposals for solving the traffic problems on Main Street, Chen's plan is better for the city as a whole, as is clear from the fact that the principal supporter of Ripley's plan is Smith Stores. Smith Stores, with its highly paid consultants, knows where its own interest lies and, moreover, has supported its own interests in the past, even to the detriment of the city as a whole.

The faulty reasoning in which one of the following is most parallel to that in the argument above?

(A) Surely Centreville should oppose adoption of the regional planning commission's new plan since it is not in Centreville's interest, even though it might be in the interest of some towns in the region.

(B) The school board should support the plan for the new high school since this plan was recommended by the well-qualified consultants whom the school board hired at great expense.

(C) Of the two budget proposals, the mayor's is clearly preferable to the city council's, since the mayor's budget addresses the needs of the city as a whole, whereas the city council is protecting special interests.

(D) Nomura is clearly a better candidate for college president than Miller, since Nomura has the support of the three deans who best understand the president's job and with whom the president will have to work most closely.

(E) The planned light-rail system will clearly serve suburban areas well, since its main opponent is the city government, which has always ignored the needs of the suburbs and sought only to protect the interests of the city.

3. PT11, S4, Q22

Paulsville and Longtown cannot both be included in the candidate's itinerary of campaign stops. The candidate will make a stop in Paulsville unless Salisbury is made part of the itinerary. Unfortunately, a stop in Salisbury is out of the question. Clearly, then, a stop in Longtown can be ruled out.

The reasoning in the argument above most closely parallels that in which one of the following arguments?

(A)　The chef never has both fresh radishes and fresh green peppers available for the chef's salad at the same time. If she uses fresh radishes, she also uses spinach. But currently there is no spinach to be had. It can be inferred, then, that she will not be using fresh green peppers.

(B)　Tom will definitely support Parker if Mendoza does not apply; and Tom will not support both Parker and Chung. Since, as it turns out, Mendoza will not apply, it follows that Chung will not get Tom's support.

(C)　The program committee never selects two plays by Shaw for a single season. But when they select a play by Coward, they do not select any play by Shaw at all. For this season, the committee has just selected a play by Shaw, so they will not select any play by Coward.

(D)　In agricultural pest control, either pesticides or the introduction of natural enemies of the pest, but not both, will work. Of course, neither will be needed if pest-resistant crops are planted. So if pesticides are in fact needed, it must be that there are no natural enemies of the pest.

(E)　The city cannot afford to build both a new stadium and the new road that would be needed to get there. But neither of the two projects is worth doing without the other. Since the city will not undertake any but worthwhile projects, the new stadium will not be constructed at this time.

4. PT11, S2, Q25

The fact that tobacco smoke inhaled by smokers harms the smokers does not prove that the much smaller amount of tobacco smoke inhaled by nonsmokers who share living space with smokers harms the nonsmokers to some degree. Many substances, such as vitamin A, are toxic in large quantities but beneficial in small quantities.

In which one of the following is the pattern of reasoning most similar to that in the argument above?

(A)　The fact that a large concentration of bleach will make fabric very white does not prove that a small concentration of bleach will make fabric somewhat white. The effect of a small concentration of bleach may be too slight to change the color of the fabric.

(B)　Although a healthful diet should include a certain amount of fiber, it does not follow that a diet that includes large amounts of fiber is more healthful than one that includes smaller amounts of fiber. Too much fiber can interfere with proper digestion.

(C)　The fact that large amounts of chemical fertilizers can kill plants does not prove that chemical fertilizers are generally harmful to plants. It proves only that the quantity of chemical fertilizer used should be adjusted according to the needs of the plants and the nutrients already in the soil.

(D)　From the fact that five professional taste testers found a new cereal product tasty, it does not follow that everyone will like it. Many people find broccoli a tasty food, but other people have a strong dislike for the taste of broccoli.

(E)　Although watching television for half of every day would be a waste of time, watching television briefly every day is not necessarily even a small waste of time. After all, it would be a waste to sleep half of every day, but some sleep every day is necessary.

12

MANHATTAN
PREP

5. PT14, S2, Q25

A letter submitted to the editor of a national newsmagazine was written and signed by a Dr. Shirley Marin who, in the text of the letter, mentions being a professor at a major North American medical school. Knowing that fewer than 5 percent of the professors at such schools are women, the editor reasons that the chances are better than 19 to 1 that the letter was written by a man.

Which one of the following involves flawed reasoning most like that used by the editor?

(A) Since 19 out of 20 home computers are purchased primarily for use with computer games, and the first computer sold today was purchased solely for word processing, the next 19 computers sold will almost certainly be used primarily for computer games.

(B) Fewer than 1 in 20 of the manuscripts submitted to Argon Publishing Co. are accepted for publication. Since only 15 manuscripts were submitted last week, there is almost no chance that any of them will be accepted for publication.

(C) Fewer than 5 percent of last year's graduating class took Latin in secondary school. Howard took Latin in secondary school, so if he had graduated last year, it is likely that one of the other Latin scholars would not have graduated.

(D) More than 95 percent of the planes built by UBC last year met government standards for large airliners. Since small planes account for just under 5 percent of UBC's output last year, it is almost certain that all their large planes met government standards.

(E) Since more than 19 out of every 20 animals in the wildlife preserve are mammals and fewer than 1 out of 20 are birds, there is a greater than 95 percent chance that the animal Emily saw flying between two trees in the wildlife refuge yesterday morning was a mammal.

6. PT12, S1, Q23

The capture of a wild animal is justified only as a last resort to save that animal's life. But many wild animals are captured not because their lives are in any danger but so that they can be bred in captivity. Hence, many animals that have been captured should not have been captured.

Which one of the following arguments is most similar in its pattern of reasoning to the argument above?

(A) Punishing a child is justified if it is the only way to reform poor behavior. But punishment is never the only way to reform poor behavior. Hence, punishing a child is never justified.

(B) Parents who never punish a child are not justified in complaining if the child regularly behaves in ways that disturb them. But many parents who prefer not to punish their children complain regularly about their children's behavior. Hence, many parents who complain about their children have no right to complain.

(C) Punishing a young child is justified only if it is done out of concern for the child's future welfare. But many young children are punished not in order to promote their welfare but to minimize sibling rivalry. Hence, many children who are punished should not have been punished.

(D) A teacher is entitled to punish a child only if the child's parents have explicitly given the teacher the permission to do so. But many parents never give their child's teacher the right to punish their child. Hence, many teachers should not punish their pupils.

(E) Society has no right to punish children for deeds that would be crimes if the children were adults. But society does have the right to protect itself from children who are known threats. Hence, confinement of such children does not constitute punishment.

7. PT14, S4, Q14

The commissioner has announced that Judge Khalid, who was on the seven-member panel appointed to resolve the Amlec labor dispute, will have sole responsibility for resolving the Simdon labor dispute. Since in its decision the Amlec panel showed itself both reasonable and fair, the two sides in the Simdon dispute are undoubtedly justified in the confidence they have expressed in the reasonableness and fairness of the arbitrator assigned to their case.

Which one of the following contains flawed reasoning most parallel to that contained in the passage?

(A)   Representing the school board, Marcia Barthes presented to the school's principal a list of recently elected school board members. Since only an elected member of the school board can act as its representative, Ms. Barthes's name undoubtedly appears on that list.

(B)   Alan Caldalf, who likes being around young children, has decided to become a pediatrician. Since the one characteristic common to all good pediatricians is that they like young children, Mr. Caldalf will undoubtedly be a very good pediatrician.

(C)   Jorge Diaz is a teacher at a music school nationally known for the excellence of its conducting faculty. Since Mr. Diaz has recently been commended for the excellence of his teaching, he is undoubtedly a member of the school's conducting faculty.

(D)   Ula Borg, who has sold real estate for Arcande Realty for many years, undoubtedly sold fewer houses last year than she had the year before since the number of houses sold last year by Arcande Realty is far lower than the number sold the previous year.

(E)   The members of the local historical society unanimously support designating the First National Bank building a historical landmark. Since Evelyn George is a member of that society, she undoubtedly favors according landmark status to the city hall as well.

8. PT10, S4, Q5

When girls are educated in single-sex secondary schools, they tend to do better academically than girls who attend mixed-sex schools. Since Alice achieved higher grades than any other woman in her first year at the university, she was probably educated at a single-sex school.

Which one of the following most closely parallels the flawed reasoning used in the argument above?

(A)   When students have individual tutoring in math, they usually get good grades on their final exams. Celia had individual tutoring in math so she will probably get a good grade.

(B)   When babies are taught to swim, they have more than the average number of ear infections as they grow up. Janice has more ear infections than any other person at the local swimming club, so she probably was taught to swim when she was a baby.

(C)   When children study music at an early age, they later tend to appreciate a wide variety of music, so the talent of future musicians is best fostered at an early age.

(D)   When children practice their piano scales for half an hour each day, they usually pass their piano exams. Sally practices scales for less than half an hour each day, so she will probably fail her piano exam.

(E)   When children have parents who help them with their homework, they usually do well in school. Therefore, having help with homework is probably the cause of high academic achievement.

9. PT10, S1, Q25

Large inequalities in wealth always threaten the viability of true democracy, since wealth is the basis of political power, and true democracy depends on the equal distribution of political power among all citizens.

The reasoning in which one of the following arguments most closely parallels the reasoning in the argument above?

(A)   Consumer culture and an emphasis on technological innovation are a dangerous combination, since together they are uncontrollable and lead to irrational excess.

(B)   If Sara went to the bookstore every time her pocket was full, Sara would never have enough money to cover her living expenses, since books are her love and they are getting very expensive.

(C)   It is very difficult to write a successful science fiction novel that is set in the past, since historical fiction depends on historical accuracy, whereas science fiction does not.

(D)   Honesty is important in maintaining friendships. But sometimes honesty can lead to arguments, so it is difficult to predict the effect a particular honest act will have on a friendship.

(E)   Repeated encroachments on one's leisure time by a demanding job interfere with the requirements of good health. The reason is that good health depends on regular moderate exercise, but adequate leisure time is essential to regular exercise.

10. PT12, S4, Q23

Insurance industry statistics demonstrate that cars with alarms or other antitheft devices are more likely to be stolen or broken into than cars without such devices or alarms. Therefore antitheft devices do not protect cars against thieves.

The pattern of flawed reasoning in the argument above is most similar to that in which one of the following?

(A)   Since surveys reveal that communities with flourishing public libraries have, on average, better-educated citizens, it follows that good schools are typically found in communities with public libraries.

(B)   Most public libraries are obviously intended to serve the interests of the casual reader, because most public libraries contain large collections of fiction and relatively small reference collections.

(C)   Studies reveal that people who are regular users of libraries purchase more books per year than do people who do not use libraries regularly. Hence using libraries regularly does not reduce the number of books that library patrons purchase.

(D)   Since youngsters who read voraciously are more likely to have defective vision than youngsters who do not read very much, it follows that children who do not like to read usually have perfect vision.

(E)   Societies that support free public libraries are more likely to support free public universities than are societies without free public libraries. Hence a society that wishes to establish a free public university should first establish a free public library.

12

Solutions: Matching Questions

It should be pretty clear by now that many of the wrong answers in Matching questions are wrong for a lot of reasons. We've explained all the mismatches we could find in the following solutions; the discussion is meant to be pretty darn close to exhaustive. We want to be certain that if you saw a mismatch and eliminated an answer because of it, you would see that mismatch explained in the solutions. This means you'll likely see mismatches that you didn't catch the first time around unless you go back now and deeply review all the wrong answers, including those in questions you're confident that you got right, *before* reading the solutions. That experience is invaluable and it models what you should be aiming for when you review Matching questions on your own: a souped-up blind review!

You'll also find some good information about strategy, common flaws, and how to weigh mismatches against one another. If you read the solutions only for the questions you got wrong, you're cheating yourself out of a learning opportunity! We recommend you first go back and rework any questions that you felt were tough, then check your answers, then do a review of the wrong answers, finding all the mismatches, and then, finally, compare what you found against our solutions. It's a lot of work, but it's brain-sharpening work the average LSAT test-taker won't have done.

Answer Key

1. B	6. C
2. E	7. D
3. B	8. B
4. E	9. E
5. E	10. C

1. PT15, S2, Q18

Everyone who is a gourmet cook enjoys a wide variety of foods and spices. Since no one who enjoys a wide variety of food and spices prefers bland foods to all other foods, it follows that anyone who prefers bland foods to all other foods is not a gourmet cook.

The pattern of reasoning displayed in the argument above is most similar to that displayed in which one of the following?

(A)   All of the paintings in the Huang Collection will be put up for auction next week. Since the paintings to be auctioned next week are by a wide variety of artists, it follows that the paintings in the Huang Collection are by a wide variety of artists.

(B)   All of the paintings in the Huang Collection are abstract. Since no abstract painting will be included in next week's art auction, nothing to be included in next week's art auction is a painting in the Huang Collection.

(C)   All of the paintings in the Huang Collection are superb works of art. Since none of the paintings in the Huang Collection is by Roue, it stands to reason that no painting by Roue is a superb work of art.

(D)   Every postimpressionist painting from the Huang Collection will be auctioned off next week. No pop art paintings from the Huang Collection will be auctioned off next week. Hence none of the pop art paintings to be auctioned off next week will be from the Huang Collection.

(E)   Every painting from the Huang Collection that is to be auctioned off next week is a major work of art. No price can adequately reflect the true value of a major work of art. Hence the prices that will be paid at next week's auction will not adequately reflect the true value of the paintings sold.

Answer choice (B) is correct.

This is a conditional argument, so diagramming is the first tool to use here:

GC → likes variety of F and S

likes variety of F and S → −prefers bland

prefers bland → −GC

This argument structure should be familiar: two statements that chain together (using the contrapositive of one) with a conditional conclusion. If you struggled to diagram the second premise, remember that the conditional indicator "no" introduces the sufficient condition and negates the necessary condition. It's a little counterintuitive, but a statement such as No A's are B's establishes that if you *are* A, you're *not* B:

A → −B

Answer choice (B) shares the contrapositive argument structure and is a perfect match.

HC → abstract

abstract → −included in the auction

included in the auction → −HC

There's actually a problem with diagramming (A)—we'll address that in a moment—but perhaps you saw it as follows:

HC → put up for auction

put up for auction → wide variety of artists

HC → wide variety of artists

Because (A) doesn't employ the contrapositive, we're looking at a potential logic mismatch. But since the contrapositive of a statement is logically equivalent (they may look different but represent the same logic), this is a yellow flag mismatch. More importantly, this is actually a flawed argument. It exhibits the Part vs. Whole fallacy. When we learn that the paintings put up for auction, *as a group,* are by a wide variety of artists, that doesn't mean that each *part* of the group is by a wide variety of artists. There might be more paintings in the auction than just those from the Huang Collection. Thus, the paintings in the Huang Collection might not have that feature, even though they are part of the auctioned group.

You might be wondering why we can't just chain together the two premises to reach the conclusion. We can't because the second premise *isn't really a conditional*. If we know a painting is being auctioned, we don't know it's from a wide variety of artists—that would be weird!—so we can't actually make that premise into a conditional and chain the two premises together.

Answer choice (C) starts off strong with an initial conditional premise, but the second premise is a mismatch:

HC → superb art

HC → –Roue

Both of these premises have the same sufficient condition, so this argument can't exhibit the same contrapositive structure as the original. The mismatched conclusion seals the deal when it invalidly concludes that none of Roue's paintings are superb works of art. We do know that Roue → –HC, but we would need to negate the first premise to make the chain that (C) suggests:

Roue → –HC → –superb art

That would be nice, but it requires an illegal negation. Although being in the Huang Collection would *guarantee* that a painting is a superb work of art, not being in the collection doesn't *prevent* it from being superb.

Answer (D) begins with two conditional premises, but they don't link up in the same way as the premises in the original argument:

post imp. from HC → auctioned

pop art from HC → –auctioned

However, if you contrapose either of the premises, they can be linked. Occasionally, the LSAT will present an original argument that *doesn't* require contraposition to establish a link and match it to a correct answer that *does*, or vice versa, so this isn't a fatal mismatch, but it is a yellow flag one. These premises also divide a category (Huang Collection) into two subcategories

(postimpressionist and pop art). By itself, this might not constitute a serious enough mismatch to eliminate, but, taken with the contraposition mismatch, it does. The logic here is also fatally mismatched since it relies on only one premise. (It's also suspect how the conclusion combines characteristics to form the sufficient condition—pop art and auctioned—while the original simply was a singular characteristic—prefers bland foods.)

Answer choice (E) is like (D) in that it begins with two conditional premises that must be contraposed to be linked:

auctioned HC paintings → major art works

price reflects true value → –major art works

Since this alone isn't grounds for elimination, we can turn to the conclusion. Choice (E) concludes that the prices paid at the auction will not reflect the true value of the paintings sold. This assumes that *all* paintings to be auctioned off will be major works of art, but we don't know this to be true. We know only about the Huang Collection paintings, not the rest of the paintings in the auction. Thus, we have two logic mismatches. First, we needed to use the contrapositive of a premise. Second, and more importantly, (E) isn't a valid argument.

2. PT11, S2, Q17

Of the two proposals for solving the traffic problems on Main Street, Chen's plan is better for the city as a whole, as is clear from the fact that the principal supporter of Ripley's plan is Smith Stores. Smith Stores, with its highly paid consultants, knows where its own interest lies and, moreover, has supported its own interests in the past, even to the detriment of the city as a whole.

The faulty reasoning in which one of the following is most parallel to that in the argument above?

(A)   Surely Centreville should oppose adoption of the regional planning commission's new plan since it is not in Centreville's interest, even though it might be in the interest of some towns in the region.

(B)   The school board should support the plan for
        the new high school since this plan was
        recommended by the well-qualified
        consultants whom the school board hired at
        great expense.

(C)   Of the two budget proposals, the mayor's is
        clearly preferable to the city council's, since
        the mayor's budget addresses the needs of the
        city as a whole, whereas the city council is
        protecting special interests.

(D)   Nomura is clearly a better candidate for college
        president than Miller, since Nomura has the
        support of the three deans who best
        understand the president's job and with
        whom the president will have to work most
        closely.

(E)   The planned light-rail system will clearly serve
        suburban areas well, since its main opponent
        is the city government, which has always
        ignored the needs of the suburbs and sought
        only to protect the interests of the city.

Answer choice (E) is correct.

Because this is a Match the Flaw question, the first order
of business is to articulate the flaw. The conclusion that
Chen's plan is better than Ripley's is drawn solely by
criticizing Ripley's principal supporter. This is an Ad
Hominem attack.

The argument also supports its conclusion by referring
to past behavior. While the past behavior of a person or
organization may be a clue to its future actions, we can't
rely on the past as a consistent predictor of behavior. It's
quite possible that Smith Stores will continue to pursue
its own interests to the city's detriment, but we don't
know this with any certainty.

Answer (E) concludes that the light-rail system will serve
suburban interests. The only support for this is that the
city government, which has historically ignored suburban
needs, opposes the light-rail system. Just as in the original
argument, choice (E) draws a conclusion about a proposal
based on a criticism of the past behavior of those on the
other side of the issue.

(A) begins with a mismatched normative conclusion
(the original is simply that the plan *is* better). However,
since this is a Match the Flaw question, we have to look
further. Remember, if the argument contains all the
fallacies of the original, a mismatch such as this one may
be allowable. This argument, however, neither contains
the Ad Hominem Flaw nor uses the past to predict the
future.

(B) also begins with a mismatched normative conclusion,
so that's one strike against it. Like the original, this
argument presents information about the supporters of a
proposal as evidence about the proposal itself, but in this
case the flaw looks more like an Appeal to Inappropriate
Authority. Also, unlike the original, there is no choice
between two options and no predictive flaw.

(C) starts out strong with its conclusion that one thing is
preferable to another. The rest of the argument, however,
fails to match. "Protecting special interests" is not a
match for the Ad Hominem attack because it is offered
as a fact about the plan, not the people behind the plan.
Finally, there's no predictive flaw.

(D) also starts out strong with a comparative conclusion,
and the evidence for a proposal is about the supporters of
that proposal. It does not, however, exhibit the fallacies of
the original. There is no prediction and the discussion of
the supporters is not about their character or motives but
about a relationship that is relevant to doing the job well.

3. PT11, S4, Q22

Paulsville and Longtown cannot both be included in
the candidate's itinerary of campaign stops. The
candidate will make a stop in Paulsville unless
Salisbury is made part of the itinerary. Unfortunately,
a stop in Salisbury is out of the question. Clearly,
then, a stop in Longtown can be ruled out.

The reasoning in the argument above most closely
parallels that in which one of the following arguments?

12

(A)   The chef never has both fresh radishes and
       fresh green peppers available for the chef's
       salad at the same time. If she uses fresh
       radishes, she also uses spinach. But currently
       there is no spinach to be had. It can be
       inferred, then, that she will not be using fresh
       green peppers.

(B)   Tom will definitely support Parker if Mendoza
       does not apply; and Tom will not support
       both Parker and Chung. Since, as it turns out,
       Mendoza will not apply, it follows that Chung
       will not get Tom's support.

(C)   The program committee never selects two
       plays by Shaw for a single season. But when
       they select a play by Coward, they do not
       select any play by Shaw at all. For this season,
       the committee has just selected a play by
       Shaw, so they will not select any play by
       Coward.

(D)   In agricultural pest control, either pesticides or
       the introduction of natural enemies of the
       pest, but not both, will work. Of course,
       neither will be needed if pest-resistant crops
       are planted. So if pesticides are in fact needed,
       it must be that there are no natural enemies
       of the pest.

(E)   The city cannot afford to build both a new
       stadium and the new road that would be
       needed to get there. But neither of the two
       projects is worth doing without the other.
       Since the city will not undertake any but
       worthwhile projects, the new stadium will not
       be constructed at this time.

Answer choice (B) is correct.

The words "cannot both" and "unless" alert us to the fact
that this is a conditional argument, so diagramming is
the first order of business.

There are various ways to represent the conditional logic
in the first sentence. You could have written P $\rightarrow$ –L and
L $\rightarrow$ –P, though some people find just one of those
enough to remember both of the relationships. If you

had trouble with the first premise because you didn't
recognize "cannot both" as a conditional indicator, think
through what that statement actually means: It tells
us that you can't stop in both towns. Logically, then,
stopping in one means you can't stop in the other. If you
stop in P, you can't stop in L and vice versa.

The argument diagram looks like this:

$$P \rightarrow -L$$
$$-S \rightarrow P$$
$$\underline{-S}$$
$$-L$$

Depending on which approach you take to diagramming
"unless" statements, your diagram for that premise may
have looked like this: –P $\rightarrow$ S. If it did, that's totally fine.
Both are equally valid approaches, and the diagrams they
yield, because they are contrapositives of one another, are
logically equivalent.

Linking the premises together gives us this:

$$-S \rightarrow P \rightarrow -L$$
$$\underline{-S}$$
$$-L$$

This is a valid argument. When your original argument
is a valid conditional argument, you should be on the
lookout for answer choices that contain illegal reversals or
negations.

(B) presents the premises in a different order, but
remember that order doesn't impact logical structure, so
there's no problem there.

$$-M \rightarrow P$$
$$P \rightarrow -C$$
$$\underline{-M}$$
$$-C$$

Depending on how you diagrammed the "unless"
statement in the stimulus, (B) may or may not seem to
be a perfect match. If it appeared to you that the original
argument utilizes the contrapositive while answer (B) did
not, you should defer judgment. Remember, the LSAT
will sometimes allow this type of mismatch, especially
because it depends as much on how you diagram as on

MANHATTAN
PREP

what the argument actually says.

Choice (A) is very tempting. The diagram is almost identical to the original argument's:

$$R \rightarrow -P$$
$$R \rightarrow S$$
$$\underline{-S}$$
$$-P$$

However, here, both of our conditionals have the same sufficient condition, so we can't connect them. This argument is flawed.

(C) is a little tougher to diagram because the first premise deals with two plays by the same author without providing names to distinguish them. We'll number them to keep them straight:

$$\text{Shaw 1} \rightarrow -\text{Shaw 2}$$
$$\text{Coward} \rightarrow -\text{Shaw}$$
$$\underline{\text{Shaw}}$$
$$-\text{Coward}$$

But wait—this argument doesn't even utilize the first "premise" to draw the conclusion. The conclusion, while valid, is drawn from the second and third statements alone. The logic doesn't match the stimulus, which relies on chained conditionals.

(D) begins with an "either/or but not both" statement. Although this contains the mutual exclusivity of the original argument's premise, the "either/or" is suspect. This tells us that one of the items alone is definitely effective, and there's no match for this in the original. The next premise contains a fatal mismatch: It introduces a condition that rules out both options presented in the first premise. The conclusion is also fatally mismatched because it is a conditional statement, not a fulfilled condition. There is also a logic mismatch: Like (C), this choice only uses one of its premises. The conclusion doesn't build on the second premise at all. Finally, it doesn't help that (D) is invalid. It conflates *no introduction of natural enemies* with the complete absence of natural enemies.

(E) has a serious premise mismatch. Did you recognize the biconditionals in the second premise? This statement chains its two conditionals to reach the conclusion that neither of the options is possible:

$$S \rightarrow -R$$
$$-R \leftrightarrow -S$$

Do you see what happens when we chain these together? S leads to –S, or if we connect them the other way, R leads to –R. Hmm, actually, looking back at the second premise, there's a shift in the meaning of our terms. We aren't just talking about whether R and S will be built, but whether they are worth building. So what we really know is that if S is built, it isn't worth building, and the same for R! The final premise tells us that the city will only take on worthwhile projects, so we know that neither project will be built and the conclusion is valid. This is all very interesting, but it's much more complicated than the argument in the stimulus.

4. PT11, S2, Q25

The fact that tobacco smoke inhaled by smokers harms the smokers does not prove that the much smaller amount of tobacco smoke inhaled by nonsmokers who share living space with smokers harms the nonsmokers to some degree. Many substances, such as vitamin A, are toxic in large quantities but beneficial in small quantities.

In which one of the following is the pattern of reasoning most similar to that in the argument above?

(A)   The fact that a large concentration of bleach will make fabric very white does not prove that a small concentration of bleach will make fabric somewhat white. The effect of a small concentration of bleach may be too slight to change the color of the fabric.

(B)   Although a healthful diet should include a certain amount of fiber, it does not follow that a diet that includes large amounts of fiber is more healthful than one that includes smaller amounts of fiber. Too much fiber can interfere with proper digestion.

12

(C)   The fact that large amounts of chemical fertilizers can kill plants does not prove that chemical fertilizers are generally harmful to plants. It proves only that the quantity of chemical fertilizer used should be adjusted according to the needs of the plants and the nutrients already in the soil.

(D)   From the fact that five professional taste testers found a new cereal product tasty, it does not follow that everyone will like it. Many people find broccoli a tasty food, but other people have a strong dislike for the taste of broccoli.

(E)   Although watching television for half of every day would be a waste of time, watching television briefly every day is not necessarily even a small waste of time. After all, it would be a waste to sleep half of every day, but some sleep every day is necessary.

Answer choice (E) is correct.

This argument concludes that although smoking hurts the smoker, this doesn't prove that smoking hurts the people nearby, who inhale much less smoke. The only evidence this rests on is the analogy of smoking to vitamin A. We might see this as a Comparison Flaw, since it isn't clear that smoke and vitamins are similar enough with respect to how they impact health, but the author merely concludes that one kind of harm doesn't prove the other. As we've seen in Inference questions, this kind of reasoning is hard to deny. It's certainly possible that cigarette smoke could be sensitive in this way, but the analogy offered as premise does not make this an airtight argument. Fortunately, since this is a Match the Reasoning question, we don't really have to worry about whether the reasoning is perfect. We just need to make sure that the answer we choose uses the same kind of reasoning by analogy. In fact, this distinctive feature may even override lesser mismatches, as in a Match the Flaw question.

Like the original, (E) concludes that one thing being true doesn't prove a lesser, related thing to be true. The only evidence is the analogy of TV watching to sleep, which

again might strike us as a bad analogy. The analogy itself is slightly different than the original argument's, in that it establishes that small quantities of sleep are *necessary*, whereas the original establishes that small quantities of vitamin A are *beneficial*. But because the primary concern here is matching the use of this odd analogy, this minor mismatch is allowable.

(A) has a matching conclusion, but no analogy.

(B)'s conclusion suspiciously discusses whether more of something has more of an effect than less of that thing (vs. the original argument's discussion of whether something that has an effect when in large quantities has *any of that effect at all* when in smaller quantities). But the clearer mismatch is that there is no analogy. Instead, this argument provides an actual reason to suspect that a very high-fiber diet is unhealthful.

(C) begins with a statement that has the same structure as the original argument's conclusion. But it then goes on to argue that while one thing was not proven, another thing was. That makes the second sentence the conclusion, which creates conclusion and logic mismatches. There is also no analogy, which is an equally potent logic mismatch.

(D) has an analogy, and a much closer one: Both cases are about the taste of food. However, we don't have to consider the relative appropriateness of the analogy to eliminate (D), because there is a significant logic mismatch here. (D) is pointing out a Sampling Flaw in the opposing argument, while the original is making an argument about quantity.

5. PT14, S2, Q25

A letter submitted to the editor of a national newsmagazine was written and signed by a Dr. Shirley Marin who, in the text of the letter, mentions being a professor at a major North American medical school. Knowing that fewer than 5 percent of the professors at such schools are women, the editor reasons that the chances are better than 19 to 1 that the letter was written by a man.

Which one of the following involves flawed reasoning most like that used by the editor?

(A)   Since 19 out of 20 home computers are purchased primarily for use with computer games, and the first computer sold today was purchased solely for word processing, the next 19 computers sold will almost certainly be used primarily for computer games.

(B)   Fewer than 1 in 20 of the manuscripts submitted to Argon Publishing Co. are accepted for publication. Since only 15 manuscripts were submitted last week, there is almost no chance that any of them will be accepted for publication.

(C)   Fewer than 5 percent of last year's graduating class took Latin in secondary school. Howard took Latin in secondary school, so if he had graduated last year, it is likely that one of the other Latin scholars would not have graduated.

(D)   More than 95 percent of the planes built by UBC last year met government standards for large airliners. Since small planes account for just under 5 percent of UBC's output last year, it is almost certain that all their large planes met government standards.

(E)   Since more than 19 out of every 20 animals in the wildlife preserve are mammals and fewer than 1 out of 20 are birds, there is a greater than 95 percent chance that the animal Emily saw flying between two trees in the wildlife refuge yesterday morning was a mammal.

Answer choice (E) is correct.

This argument concludes that a person named Shirley is almost definitely a man because that person is a professor at a major school and almost all such professors are men. While this might be a good argument if the person in question were unnamed, the fact that the person has a traditionally female name means this argument is ignoring relevant evidence.

(E) has the same flaw. It states that almost all animals in the wildlife preserve are mammals and concludes that the animal Emily saw flying around at the preserve was almost definitely a mammal. This would all be well and good if the animal Emily saw was sitting on the ground, but the fact that it was flying is relevant evidence that should be considered when assessing the likelihood of the animal being a mammal vs. a bird.

(A) contains a reasoning error that is fairly rare on the LSAT but very common in casinos: the Gambler's Fallacy. Odds are not impacted by previous outcomes. If you flip a coin and it lands on heads, it is no less likely to land on heads the second time you flip it. The odds are 50/50, and they remain so for each subsequent flip no matter how many times it has landed consecutively on heads. Similarly, if 19 out of 20 computers are purchased for gaming, and the first one sold today was bought for word processing, the odds of the subsequent purchases being used for word processing are not changed.

(B) also contains a slightly different flavor of the Gambler's Fallacy. For each of the 15 manuscripts submitted, the odds are 1 in 20 that it will be accepted. The fact that there are fewer than 20 submissions does not change the odds that any one will be accepted.

(C) is flawed, but not in the same way as the original argument. The flaw here is Percent vs. Amount. Since we don't know how many graduates there were, we don't know if it's reasonable for more than one Latin scholar to have graduated. Further, there is no overlooked information like the feminine name in the original argument or the fact that the animal flies in the correct answer.

(D) is flawed in that it presumes near exclusivity of two things that we have no reason to believe are exclusive. For all we know, it is entirely possible for any small plane to be capable of meeting the standards for large airliners. Thus, the fact that 95% of UBC's planes met those standards doesn't make it almost certain that all their large planes did. If all the small planes did meet the standards for large airliners, a corresponding number of large airliners would have to have failed to make the numbers work.

6. PT12, S1, Q23

The capture of a wild animal is justified only as a last resort to save that animal's life. But many wild animals are captured not because their lives are in any danger but so that they can be bred in captivity. Hence, many animals that have been captured should not have been captured.

Which one of the following arguments is most similar in its pattern of reasoning to the argument above?

(A)   Punishing a child is justified if it is the only way to reform poor behavior. But punishment is never the only way to reform poor behavior. Hence, punishing a child is never justified.

(B)   Parents who never punish a child are not justified in complaining if the child regularly behaves in ways that disturb them. But many parents who prefer not to punish their children complain regularly about their children's behavior. Hence, many parents who complain about their children have no right to complain.

(C)   Punishing a young child is justified only if it is done out of concern for the child's future welfare. But many young children are punished not in order to promote their welfare but to minimize sibling rivalry. Hence, many children who are punished should not have been punished.

(D)   A teacher is entitled to punish a child only if the child's parents have explicitly given the teacher the permission to do so. But many parents never give their child's teacher the right to punish their child. Hence, many teachers should not punish their pupils.

(E)   Society has no right to punish children for deeds that would be crimes if the children were adults. But society does have the right to protect itself from children who are known threats. Hence, confinement of such children does not constitute punishment.

Answer choice (C) is correct.

This argument begins with a conditional statement, so your first impulse may have been to diagram. But because the next statement is quantified (many) and the last statement is normative (should), you may need to mix in a looser style of abstraction with your formal diagramming:

capture justified → last resort to save life
many captures aren't to save life
many animals should not have been captured

This is a subtly flawed argument. The premises would prove that many captures were not *justified,* but they don't prove that any animals *should not have been captured.* Consider that spending some money on extravagant shoes might not be justified—there's not a good reason to do it—but we could still agree that it is acceptable to do it. This argument assumes that if a capture is unjustified, it should not have taken place.

However, this isn't a Match the Flaw question, so if you didn't see this argument as flawed, you may have done fine. You could have focused on the idea that the argument basically relied on triggering the contrapositive of the premise:

X → Y
many cases of –Y
many cases of –X

(C) starts off with the same kind of conditional rule about justification, and goes on to say that many instances don't fulfill the necessary condition that would make them justified. It concludes that many children *should not* have been punished, just as the original argument concludes that many animals should not have been captured. Therefore, it is the correct answer.

(A)'s second premise has a quantifier mismatch (*never* instead of *many*). The conclusion is also mismatched because it is not normative. Also, because the argument is valid, there is a logic mismatch there as well.

(B)'s opening premise uses justification in the negative. Because of this, it might be hard to see whether this can match or not. Diagramming or abstracting it may be helpful:

never punish → –justified in complaining
many complaining parents prefer not to punish their children.

Since contraposition creates a logically equivalent statement, the first premise isn't fatally mismatched. Its contrapositive is a good match:

justified in complaining → sometimes punish

The mismatch occurs when the second premise is not the negation of the first statement's necessary condition. Just because many parents *prefer* not to punish *regularly* doesn't mean that they *never* punish. The conclusion is also mismatched, in that it is not normative.

(D) may seem fairly similar to the stimulus on the surface. However, the premises don't match up. Like (C), the original addresses the *purpose* behind an action as a basis for justifying that action. Both the original and (C) also specify the actual purpose that often exists in place of the desired one. (Animals are captured to be bred, and children are punished to minimize sibling rivalry.) But choice (D) simply says that teachers need permission and that they often haven't received that permission. There is no other factor and no mention of justification.

There is also a subtle conclusion mismatch there. Our original argument concludes that many animals that have been captured should not have been captured. Answer (D) concludes that many teachers should not punish their pupils. So while the matched arguments address whether something should have been done to members of a certain group (children or animals) in the past, choice (D) focuses on whether a party should take a certain action in the future ("teachers should not punish their pupils").

(E)'s second premise provides an additional general principle with all new concepts, creating a definite mismatch. Because (E)'s conclusion is not normative, there is also a conclusion mismatch.

If you found this question tough, don't worry—you have plenty of company. The subtle differences between choices (C) and (D) make this one of the more challenging LR problems you'll see.

_7. PT14, S4, Q14_

The commissioner has announced that Judge Khalid, who was on the seven-member panel appointed to resolve the Amlec labor dispute, will have sole responsibility for resolving the Simdon labor dispute. Since in its decision the Amlec panel showed itself both reasonable and fair, the two sides in the Simdon dispute are undoubtedly justified in the confidence they have expressed in the reasonableness and fairness of the arbitrator assigned to their case.

Which one of the following contains flawed reasoning most parallel to that contained in the passage?

(A)   Representing the school board, Marcia Barthes presented to the school's principal a list of recently elected school board members. Since only an elected member of the school board can act as its representative, Ms. Barthes's name undoubtedly appears on that list.

(B)   Alan Caldalf, who likes being around young children, has decided to become a pediatrician. Since the one characteristic common to all good pediatricians is that they like young children, Mr. Caldalf will undoubtedly be a very good pediatrician.

(C)   Jorge Diaz is a teacher at a music school nationally known for the excellence of its conducting faculty. Since Mr. Diaz has recently been commended for the excellence of his teaching, he is undoubtedly a member of the school's conducting faculty.

(D)   Ula Borg, who has sold real estate for Arcande Realty for many years, undoubtedly sold fewer houses last year than she had the year before since the number of houses sold last year by Arcande Realty is far lower than the number sold the previous year.

(E)   The members of the local historical society unanimously support designating the First National Bank building a historical landmark. Since Evelyn George is a member of that society, she undoubtedly favors according landmark status to the city hall as well.

Answer choice (D) is correct.

The premise is that Judge Khalid was one of seven panel members on a case that was decided fairly. From this, the author concludes that the confidence in Khalid as an arbitrator is justified. This is a Part vs. Whole Flaw: The panel as a whole might have been reasonable and fair even if Judge Khalid was not. (This argument is also reasoning from past performance—perhaps Judge Khalid is fairer in some cases than in others—but none of the answer choices actually repeat that flaw.)

(D) exhibits the same Part vs. Whole Flaw when it concludes that one member of the realty group had lower sales last year than the year before because the company as a whole had lower sales last year than the year before.

(A) does contain a whole—the list of recently elected school board members. It concludes that an individual must be a part of that whole. That's not the same thing as concluding that a part of the whole has the qualities of the whole, and so there is a logic mismatch here. The flaw in choice (A) arises from the fact that we don't know if Ms. Barthes is a _recently_ elected member, so we don't know if she's on the list. This flaw doesn't appear in the original argument.

(B) is a conditional argument. It presents a characteristic common to a group and concludes that because an individual has that characteristic, he will undoubtedly be a good fit for the group. This is reversed logic. Just because all good pediatricians like kids doesn't mean that anyone who likes kids will make a good pediatrician.

(C), like choice (A), concludes that an individual _is a part_ of a whole, not that an individual _has the characteristics_ of the whole.

(E) begins with a premise stating that the members of a society _unanimously_ support a proposal. This establishes that the whole society supports it _and_ that each individual member supports it. Therefore, there is no Part vs. Whole Flaw here. Furthermore, (E) concludes that a member will support something entirely separate from the first premise's proposal, so both the conclusion and the logic are mismatched.

MANHATTAN
PREP

_8. PT10, S4, Q5_

When girls are educated in single-sex secondary schools, they tend to do better academically than girls who attend mixed-sex schools. Since Alice achieved higher grades than any other woman in her first year at the university, she was probably educated at a single-sex school.

Which one of the following most closely parallels the flawed reasoning used in the argument above?

(A)   When students have individual tutoring in math, they usually get good grades on their final exams. Celia had individual tutoring in math so she will probably get a good grade.

(B)   When babies are taught to swim, they have more than the average number of ear infections as they grow up. Janice has more ear infections than any other person at the local swimming club, so she probably was taught to swim when she was a baby.

(C)   When children study music at an early age, they later tend to appreciate a wide variety of music, so the talent of future musicians is best fostered at an early age.

(D)   When children practice their piano scales for half an hour each day, they usually pass their piano exams. Sally practices scales for less than half an hour each day, so she will probably fail her piano exam.

(E)   When children have parents who help them with their homework, they usually do well in school. Therefore, having help with homework is probably the cause of high academic achievement.

Answer choice (B) is correct.

We've seen this particular Part vs. Whole Flaw a few times now. We just saw it in answer choice (C) of the previous problem, and we saw it earlier in the chapter in the argument about Millicent Smith the fare collector (PT12, S1, Q17, page 538). Just because one group outperforms another group _overall_ does not mean that

any high-performing individual we find must be a member of that group. We can find a high-performing individual in a group with low average performance. It also helps to notice that we don't even know how significant the difference is between the two groups. Perhaps single-sex education only brings people's grades up by 2%.

This argument also has a Sampling Flaw. We don't know how well Alice's entering class represents the general population, so we don't know how high her grades really are.

One other notable thing about this argument that is likely to generate mismatches is the _probably_ in the conclusion. While it's most important that we match the flaws in the argument, we can expect the conclusion in the correct answer to be about something probable rather than certain.

(B) matches both of the flaws we identified. It concludes that someone is _probably_ in a particular group (those taught to swim as babies) because that person is high in a measure of something (ear infections) that members of that group are higher in. Like the original, this argument relies on what may not be a representative sample: We have no idea if members of the swimming club are more likely than the average person to get ear infections, so we don't really know if Janice gets a lot of ear infections compared to the average.

(A) doesn't actually contain a comparison—maybe people who _don't_ have tutoring also usually get good grades. In any case, there's no flaw here. We have a conditional that is then fulfilled, so the argument works.

(C) uses the premise to make a recommendation, rather than to place an individual in a group.

(D) features a good old-fashioned illegal negation. There are no Part vs. Whole or Sampling Flaws here.

(E) relies on a Causation Flaw, but it sticks to generalizations, so there's no chance for Part vs. Whole or Sampling Flaws.

9. PT10, S1, Q25

Large inequalities in wealth always threaten the
viability of true democracy, since wealth is the basis
of political power, and true democracy depends on
the equal distribution of political power among all
citizens.

The reasoning in which one of the following
arguments most closely parallels the reasoning in the
argument above?

(A)   Consumer culture and an emphasis on
      technological innovation are a dangerous
      combination, since together they are
      uncontrollable and lead to irrational excess.

(B)   If Sara went to the bookstore every time her
      pocket was full, Sara would never have
      enough money to cover her living expenses,
      since books are her love and they are getting
      very expensive.

(C)   It is very difficult to write a successful science
      fiction novel that is set in the past, since
      historical fiction depends on historical
      accuracy, whereas science fiction does not.

(D)   Honesty is important in maintaining
      friendships. But sometimes honesty can lead
      to arguments, so it is difficult to predict the
      effect a particular honest act will have on a
      friendship.

(E)   Repeated encroachments on one's leisure time
      by a demanding job interfere with the
      requirements of good health. The reason is
      that good health depends on regular
      moderate exercise, but adequate leisure time
      is essential to regular exercise.

Answer choice (E) is correct.

This is a tricky argument to grasp. However, most of
the answer choices can be eliminated because of rather
straightforward mismatches. The original argument has
two conditional premises and a conclusion stating that
lack of one element threatens another:

power → wealth

true democracy → equal power

unequal wealth threatens true democracy

If you didn't read the first premise as conditional,
you're not alone. However, X being *the basis* for Y
establishes that X *is necessary* for Y. Now, how do these
conditionals combine to support the conclusion? Can
we chain them together? Not quite, but that's what the
argument seems to do. The reasoning looks something
like this:

true democracy → equal power → equal wealth

so unequal wealth → unequal power → threat to true
democracy

This doesn't quite follow from the premises, but it's how
the argument proceeds. The author chains together two
conditionals, one of which needs a bit of adjusting to
make this happen, and then draws a conclusion from the
contrapositive.

(A) has only one premise.

(B) draws a conclusion that doesn't really follow from the
premises. First, the two premises don't chain together
at all; they just tell us two different things about books.
Second, the conclusion introduces new ideas, such as
going to the bookstore and covering living expenses. We
have no idea how much she would spend if she went to
the bookstore when her pocket was full, and we have
no idea how this spending would relate to her living
expenses. Maybe Sara can afford all the books she wants!

(C) provides only one conditional premise. The other
premise states that something is *not* necessary. We *cannot*
translate that to S → –A. "Does not depend on A" is not
the same thing as "depends on not A." Some science
fiction could be historically accurate even if it doesn't
depend on this accuracy.

In any case, (C) does not match the logic of the original
argument. It jumps from a premise about relying on
accuracy to an unsupported conclusion about the
difficulty of writing.

(D)'s argument is based on two contrasting premises about honesty: It can help maintain friendships, but it can also lead to arguments. The premises in our original argument don't present this type of contrast, and the original argument's conclusion isn't about the difficulty of making a certain prediction.

Through these eliminations, we can arrive at (E), but taking a moment to confirm is a smart move. Like our original argument, (E) has two conditional premises and a conclusion that relies on chaining the premises and taking the contrapositive:

GH → RE
RE → AL
―――――――――
−AL → −GH

These two conditionals actually chain, whereas in the original they needed a little adjusting, but the difference is not stark enough to disqualify (E), especially given that there are no other near matches. Remember, we're asked to find the answer that *most closely* matches the original argument's reasoning.

10. PT12, S4, Q23

Insurance industry statistics demonstrate that cars with alarms or other antitheft devices are more likely to be stolen or broken into than cars without such devices or alarms. Therefore antitheft devices do not protect cars against thieves.

The pattern of flawed reasoning in the argument above is most similar to that in which one of the following?

(A)   Since surveys reveal that communities with flourishing public libraries have, on average, better-educated citizens, it follows that good schools are typically found in communities with public libraries.

(B)   Most public libraries are obviously intended to serve the interests of the casual reader, because most public libraries contain large collections of fiction and relatively small reference collections.

(C)   Studies reveal that people who are regular users of libraries purchase more books per year than do people who do not use libraries regularly. Hence using libraries regularly does not reduce the number of books that library patrons purchase.

(D)   Since youngsters who read voraciously are more likely to have defective vision than youngsters who do not read very much, it follows that children who do not like to read usually have perfect vision.

(E)   Societies that support free public libraries are more likely to support free public universities than are societies without free public libraries. Hence a society that wishes to establish a free public university should first establish a free public library.

Answer choice (C) is correct.

Two things are correlated: antitheft devices and likelihood of theft. From this, the argument draws a negative causal conclusion: Antitheft devices *don't* protect cars against thieves. This is a slight twist on the usual Causation Flaw. As with all Causation Flaws, it overlooks a potential alternative explanation. In this case, the cars worth stealing may be more likely to have antitheft devices. Perhaps even more of these cars would be stolen if they didn't have antitheft devices. Just because something doesn't prevent *all* theft doesn't mean that it isn't a theft deterrent.

(C) is a match. People who use the library regularly buy more books than people who don't. This correlation is used to reach the negative causal conclusion that using the library doesn't reduce the number of books people buy. This overlooks the possibility that book-lovers tend to both buy a lot of books and frequent libraries. Perhaps if they didn't frequent libraries, they'd buy more books.

(A) tries to explain a particular correlation (flourishing libraries and better-educated citizens) by introducing a new cause in the conclusion: good schools. This may be a Causation Flaw, but it looks nothing like the original argument.

12

(B) has neither a correlation premise nor a negative causal conclusion.

(D) doesn't deal with causation, but features a Comparison Flaw. It draws the extreme conclusion that children who aren't in the group that is likely to have a trait (defective vision) usually don't have that trait at all (they must have perfect vision!).

(E) exhibits a more standard Causation Flaw: It establishes a positive correlation between two things (support for free libraries and for free universities) and concludes that if you want the second, you ought to get the first. This isn't quite the same as the causal reasoning in the stimulus.

More importantly, the causal reasoning here is in the *assumption,* while in the original argument, the conclusion is explicitly about causation. The actual conclusion in (E) is normative (we *should establish* a free public library), so we have a definite conclusion mismatch.

Time to Turn Up the Heat

Want to hit your Matching questions with plenty of time to show off your shiny new process? Then you may need to turn up the heat on the first questions of the section. Way back in Chapter 6, we told you that the early questions should ideally be knocked out in a minute a piece on test day. Now's the time to start working toward that goal. Grab the first 5 questions of a section, set your timer for 5 minutes, and have at it. If that's a breeze, do 10 questions in 10 minutes next time. If *that's* a breeze, try 15 in 15. No matter how many questions you're attempting, the goal of these sets should always be 100% accuracy. If you can't execute that level of accuracy at a minute per question, try adding an extra minute until you can. Work at that pace for a while, then start whittling it down.

Chapter 13

Explain a Result
Questions

In This Chapter...

Explain a Result Questions on the LSAT

Questions that ask you to explain a result make up about 6% of all Logical Reasoning questions on the LSAT. While these questions tend to fall on the lower end of the difficulty spectrum, certain ones can be tricky.

Recognizing Explain a Result Questions

An Explain a Result question typically presents a scenario that ends in some unexpected result. Here's a very basic example:

> The Crab Leg, a local seafood restaurant on Main Street, expected to see a decrease in sales after a popular seafood restaurant chain opened a new restaurant just two blocks away. However, The Crab Leg has actually experienced a 50 percent increase in business since the opening of the new restaurant.

You will be asked to choose an explanation for this unexpected result. The LSAT phrases these questions in a few different ways. Here are the most common phrasings:

Which one of the following, if true, most effectively resolves the paradox presented above?

Which one of the following, if true, most helps to reconcile the apparent discrepancy presented above?

Which one of the following, if true, most helps to explain the apparent paradox presented above?

As you work to recognize these questions, also note that the "argument" is not really an argument at all. There is no conclusion or opinion stated. For Explain a Result questions, the text will be a list of objective facts. It's your job to choose an answer that reconciles these facts.

Let's discuss this task in more detail.

How to Explain a Result

Expected vs. Unexpected

The first step in explaining a result is to identify, and make explicit in your mind, the "paradox" or "discrepancy" presented in the text. Thus, you will start by identifying 1) that which might be **expected** given the scenario at hand and 2) that which is presented as the **unexpected** result. Let's look back at the seafood restaurant example:

> The Crab Leg, a local seafood restaurant on Main Street, expected to see a decrease in sales after a popular seafood restaurant chain opened a new restaurant just two blocks away. However, The Crab Leg has actually experienced a 50 percent increase in business since the opening of the new restaurant.

13

What Would Be Expected: The Crab Leg loses business after the other restaurant opens.

The Unexpected Result: The Crab Leg actually increases its business by 50% after the other restaurant opens.

In this case, the expected and the unexpected results are fairly easy to identify. Keep in mind that this won't always be the case. Sometimes, you'll have to think a bit harder to separate the two. Regardless, it's always the place to start, since your job will be to explain the UNEXPECTED result.

Should You Anticipate the Explanation?

Sometimes you'll be able to see the explanation coming. In this case, for example, we can perhaps already imagine at least one scenario that would help explain why The Crab Leg has experienced growth: Maybe the new restaurant is so popular that it continuously has an overflow crowd that dines at The Crab Leg when tables aren't available at the new restaurant.

Who knows? Maybe this explanation will show up among the answer choices, maybe not. It's certainly okay to anticipate the answer, but remember that you need to be flexible. Often, the correct answer will be an explanation that you haven't thought of.

The Three Answer Buckets

It's helpful to think about the answers to these questions as falling into one of three buckets:

Bucket 1	Bucket 2	Bucket 3
further evidence for the EXPECTED result	explains the UNEXPECTED result	irrelevant to the discrepancy presented

Of course, you want to choose the one answer that falls into Bucket 2: explains the UNEXPECTED result. The LSAT will try to tempt you with answers that provide further evidence for the EXPECTED result (Bucket 1) and with answers that seem related to the subject matter but are actually irrelevant in terms of explaining the paradox or discrepancy. Knowing this ahead of time will help you to avoid the traps. Let's examine some answer choices for the seafood example:

Bucket 1	Bucket 2	Bucket 3
further evidence for the EXPECTED result	explains the UNEXPECTED result	irrelevant to the discrepancy presented
Wrong!	Right!	Wrong!

MANHATTAN
PREP

The Crab Leg, a local seafood restaurant on Main Street, expected to see a decrease in sales after a popular seafood restaurant chain opened a new restaurant just two blocks away. However, The Crab Leg has actually experienced a 50 percent increase in business since the opening of the new restaurant.

Which one of the following, if true, most helps to explain the result above?

(A)   Some of The Crab Leg's previous patrons have begun dining regularly at the new restaurant.

(B)   In anticipation of the opening of the new restaurant, the owner of The Crab Leg significantly increased spending on advertising and marketing.

(C)   The food at the new restaurant is better and cheaper than the food at The Crab Leg.

(D)   Some of the servers hired to work at the new restaurant had previously worked at The Crab Leg.

(E)   Other than The Crab Leg and the new restaurant, there are no other seafood restaurants in town.

EXPECTED: The Crab Leg experiences a decrease in sales after the new restaurant opens.

UNEXPECTED: The Crab Leg actually increases business by 50 percent.

Our job is to choose an answer that explains this **UNEXPECTED** result.

(A) Bucket 1: This provides further support for the expected result—decreased sales.

(B) Bucket 2: Correct answer! This provides an explanation for the unexpected result. If the owner spent more on advertising and marketing, the increase in business makes sense.

(C) Bucket 1: This would seem to pull people away from The Crab Leg. This provides further support for the expected result: decreased sales.

(D) Bucket 3: This neither supports the expected result nor explains the unexpected result. It's irrelevant!

(E) Bucket 3: Again, irrelevant!

Let's try two more questions. We'll again consider the answer choices through the three-bucket lens:

Bucket 1	**Bucket 2**	**Bucket 3**
further evidence for the EXPECTED result Wrong!	explains the UNEXPECTED result Right!	irrelevant to the discrepancy presented Wrong!

13

PT37, S4, Q5

After 1950, in response to record growth in worldwide food demand, farmers worldwide sharply increased fertilizer use. As a result, the productivity of farmland more than doubled by 1985. Since 1985, farmers have sought to increase farmland productivity even further. Nevertheless, worldwide fertilizer use has declined by 6 percent between 1985 and the present.

Which one of the following, if true, most helps to resolve the apparent discrepancy in the information above?

(A)   Since 1985 the rate at which the world's population has increased has exceeded the rate at which new arable land has been created through irrigation and other methods.

(B)   Several varieties of crop plants that have become popular recently, such as soybeans, are as responsive to fertilizer as are traditional grain crops.

(C)   Between 1950 and 1985 farmers were able to increase the yield of many varieties of crop plants.

(D)   After fertilizer has been added to soil for several years, adding fertilizer to the soil in subsequent years does not significantly improve crop production.

(E)   Between 1975 and 1980 fertilizer prices temporarily increased because of labor disputes in several fertilizer-exporting nations, and these disputes disrupted worldwide fertilizer production.

PT29, S1, Q4

Cats spend much of their time sleeping; they seem to awaken only to stretch and yawn. Yet they have a strong, agile musculature that most animals would have to exercise strenuously to acquire.

Which one of the following, if true, most helps to resolve the apparent paradox described above?

(A)   Cats have a greater physiological need for sleep than other animals.

(B)   Many other animals also spend much of their time sleeping yet have a strong, agile musculature.

(C)   Cats are able to sleep in apparently uncomfortable positions.

(D)   Cats derive ample exercise from frequent stretching.

(E)   Cats require strength and agility in order to be effective predators.

PT37, S4, Q5

After 1950, in response to record growth in worldwide food demand, farmers worldwide sharply increased fertilizer use. As a result, the productivity of farmland more than doubled by 1985. Since 1985, farmers have sought to increase farmland productivity even further. Nevertheless, worldwide fertilizer use has declined by 6 percent between 1985 and the present.

Which one of the following, if true, most helps to resolve the apparent discrepancy in the information above?

(A) Since 1985 the rate at which the world's population has increased has exceeded the rate at which new arable land has been created through irrigation and other methods.

(B) Several varieties of crop plants that have become popular recently, such as soybeans, are as responsive to fertilizer as are traditional grain crops.

(C) Between 1950 and 1985 farmers were able to increase the yield of many varieties of crop plants.

(D) After fertilizer has been added to soil for several years, adding fertilizer to the soil in subsequent years does not significantly improve crop production.

(E) Between 1975 and 1980 fertilizer prices temporarily increased because of labor disputes in several fertilizer-exporting nations, and these disputes disrupted worldwide fertilizer production.

EXPECTED: To further increase productivity, farmers would use even more fertilizer.

UNEXPECTED: Fertilizer use has declined by 6 percent since 1985.

Our job is to choose an answer that explains this UNEXPECTED result.

(A) Bucket #1: This gives us even more reason to expect that farmers would want to use more fertilizer (as they did last time in response to similar demand). Don't be fooled!

(B) Bucket #1: This would seem to support the expected result. If soybeans respond to fertilizer, use more fertilizer!

(C) Bucket #1: Perhaps they increased the yield through the use of fertilizer; it'd be natural to expect them to use more of it now.

(D) Bucket #2: Aha! This explains why they would *stop* using as much fertilizer. This is the correct answer.

(E) Bucket #3: A temporary increase in prices between 1975 and 1980 is irrelevant to fertilizer use after 1985. Don't be tempted by this!

Bucket 1	Bucket 2	Bucket 3
further evidence for the EXPECTED result Wrong!	explains the UNEXPECTED result Right!	irrelevant to the discrepancy presented Wrong!

PT29, S1, Q4

Cats spend much of their time sleeping; they seem to awaken only to stretch and yawn. Yet they have a strong, agile musculature that most animals would have to exercise strenuously to acquire.

Which one of the following, if true, most helps to resolve the apparent paradox described above?

(A)   Cats have a greater physiological need for sleep than other animals.

(B)   Many other animals also spend much of their time sleeping yet have a strong, agile musculature.

(C)   Cats are able to sleep in apparently uncomfortable positions.

(D)   Cats derive ample exercise from frequent stretching.

(E)   Cats require strength and agility in order to be effective predators.

EXPECTED: Cats should be out of shape.

UNEXPECTED: Cats have strong, agile musculature.

Our job is to choose an answer that explains this UNEXPECTED result.

(A) Bucket 3: This gives an explanation for why cats are more inactive, but we already know that they sleep all day. Like a premise booster, this answer doesn't change our understanding of the situation.

(B) Bucket 1: This doesn't exactly make the expected result more likely, but we put it in Bucket #1 because it actually heightens the mystery. How are all these animals staying in shape if they sleep all the time? (If you put this in Bucket 3, that's fine, but it's definitely not Bucket 2 because it doesn't explain why this is happening!)

(C) Bucket 3: What does this have to do with the argument?

(D) Bucket 2: This explains it! Now we understand how cats can sleep so much yet stay so muscular. Who knew stretching was so effective? This is the correct answer.

(E) Bucket 3: Tempting, but irrelevant. This may explain why they need the muscles, but not how they become muscular.

EXCEPT Questions

EXCEPT questions are a common subcategory of Explain a Result questions. While the orientation is slightly different, the process should be the same. The difference is just that now, four of the five answer choices will be explanations for the *unexpected* result (Bucket 2) and one will not. We're looking for this outlier.

MANHATTAN
PREP

PT29, S1, Q25

The indigenous people of Tasmania are clearly related to the indigenous people of Australia, but were separated from them when the land bridge between Australia and Tasmania disappeared approximately 10,000 years ago. Two thousand years after the disappearance of the land bridge, however, there were major differences between the culture and technology of the indigenous Tasmanians and those of the indigenous Australians. The indigenous Tasmanians, unlike their Australian relatives, had no domesticated dogs, fishing nets, polished stone tools, or hunting implements like the boomerang and the spear-thrower.

Each of the following, if true, would contribute to an explanation of differences described above EXCEPT:

(A)   After the disappearance of the land bridge the indigenous Tasmanians simply abandoned certain practices and technologies that they had originally shared with their Australian relatives.

(B)   Devices such as the spear-thrower and the boomerang were developed by the indigenous Tasmanians more than 10,000 years ago.

(C)   Technological innovations such as fishing nets, polished stone tools, and so on, were imported to Australia by Polynesian explorers more recently than 10,000 years ago.

(D)   Indigenous people of Australia developed hunting implements like the boomerang and the spear-thrower after the disappearance of the land bridge.

(E)   Although the technological and cultural innovations were developed in Australia more than 10,000 years ago, they were developed by groups in northern Australia with whom the indigenous Tasmanians had no contact prior to the disappearance of the land bridge.

13

PT29, S1, Q25

The indigenous people of Tasmania are clearly related to the indigenous people of Australia, but were separated from them when the land bridge between Australia and Tasmania disappeared approximately 10,000 years ago. Two thousand years after the disappearance of the land bridge, however, there were major differences between the culture and technology of the indigenous Tasmanians and those of the indigenous Australians. The indigenous Tasmanians, unlike their Australian relatives, had no domesticated dogs, fishing nets, polished stone tools, or hunting implements like the boomerang and the spear-thrower.

Each of the following, if true, would contribute to an explanation of differences described above EXCEPT:

(A)   After the disappearance of the land bridge the indigenous Tasmanians simply abandoned certain practices and technologies that they had originally shared with their Australian relatives.

(B)   Devices such as the spear-thrower and the boomerang were developed by the indigenous Tasmanians more than 10,000 years ago.

(C)   Technological innovations such as fishing nets, polished stone tools, and so on, were imported to Australia by Polynesian explorers more recently than 10,000 years ago.

(D)   Indigenous people of Australia developed hunting implements like the boomerang and the spear-thrower after the disappearance of the land bridge.

(E)   Although the technological and cultural innovations were developed in Australia more than 10,000 years ago, they were developed by groups in northern Australia with whom the indigenous Tasmanians had no contact prior to the disappearance of the land bridge.

EXPECTED: Indigenous Australians and Tasmanians ought to be similar 2,000 years after the land bridge disappeared.

UNEXPECTED: Tasmanians lacked many of the advances that Australians had.

Our job is to choose an answer that *fails* to explain this UNEXPECTED result.

(A) Bucket 2: This is one of several possible explanations for the unexpected result, so it's *not* the answer.

(B) Bucket 3: Hmm. This answer seems to open up more questions. If these things were developed by the Tasmanians, why did they stop using them? This answer doesn't help explain our discrepancy, and it is therefore correct.

(C) Bucket 2: This provides a potential explanation for the unexpected result.

(D) Bucket 2: This also provides a potential explanation for the unexpected result.

(E) Bucket 2: Again, another reason why the Tasmanians didn't have particular advancements that the Australians had.

Conclusion

Before you try some of these questions on your own, reconsider the following:

1. **Expected result vs. unexpected result.** The discrepancy, or paradox, presented in these questions lies in the space between what we might EXPECT from a given scenario and what is actually presented as the UNEXPECTED result. To effectively consider an explanation for the discrepancy, you must start by explicitly identifying and separating what is the EXPECTED vs. the UNEXPECTED result.

2. **Three answer buckets.** The LSAT will try to get you to confuse the world of expected things with the world of unexpected things. Wrong answers will often provide further evidence for the EXPECTED outcome or otherwise heighten the discrepancy. Don't be tempted by these. Additionally, some wrong answers will be irrelevant with regard to explaining the discrepancy.

Bucket 1	Bucket 2	Bucket 3
further evidence for the EXPECTED result Wrong!	explains the UNEXPECTED result Right!	irrelevant to the discrepancy presented Wrong!

3. **EXCEPT questions.** Slightly different orientation, same approach! Four of the answers will be Bucket 2 answers; they'll effectively provide an explanation for the UNEXPECTED result. Your job is to find the one answer that falls outside of Bucket 2.

Drill It: Explain a Result Questions

1. PT30, S4, Q5

In a poll of eligible voters conducted on the eve of a mayoral election, more of those polled stated that they favored Panitch than stated that they favored any other candidate. Despite this result, another candidate, Yeung, defeated Panitch by a comfortable margin.

Each of the following, if true, contributes to a resolution of the discrepancy described above EXCEPT:

(A) Of Yeung's supporters, a smaller percentage were eligible to vote than the percentage of Panitch's supporters who were eligible to vote.

(B) A third candidate, Mulhern, conducted a press conference on the morning of the election and withdrew from the race.

(C) The poll's questions were designed by staff members of Panitch's campaign.

(D) Of the poll respondents supporting Yeung, 70 percent described the election as "important" or "very important," while 30 percent of respondents supporting Panitch did the same.

(E) The poll, conducted on a Monday, surveyed persons in the downtown area, and the percentage of Yeung's supporters who work downtown is lower than that of Panitch's supporters.

2. PT31, S2, Q11

Several thousand years ago, people in what is now North America began to grow corn, which grows faster and produces more food per unit of land than do the grains these people had grown previously. Corn is less nutritious than those other grains, however, and soon after these people established corn as their staple grain crop, they began having nutrition-related health problems. Yet the people continued to grow corn as their staple grain, although they could have returned to growing the more nutritious grains.

Which one of the following, if true, most helps to explain why the people mentioned continued to grow corn as their staple grain crop?

(A) The variety of corn that the people relied on as their staple grain produced more food than did the ancestors of that variety.

(B) Modern varieties of corn are more nutritious than were the varieties grown by people in North America several thousand years ago.

(C) The people did not domesticate large animals for meat or milk, either of which could supply nutrients not provided by corn.

(D) Some grain crops that could have been planted instead of corn required less fertile soil in order to flourish than corn required.

(E) The people discovered some years after adopting corn as their staple grain that a diet that supplemented corn with certain readily available nongrain foods significantly improved their health.

3. PT31, S3, Q2

One way kidney stones can form is when urine produced in the kidneys is overly concentrated with calcium or oxalate. Reducing dietary calcium has been thought, therefore, to decrease the likelihood that calcium will concentrate and form additional stones. Oddly enough, for many people the chances of recurrence are decreased by increasing calcium intake.

Which one of the following, if true, most helps to resolve the apparent discrepancy described above?

(A)   Laboratory studies on animals with kidney stones reveal that they rarely get additional stones once calcium supplements are added to the diet.

(B)   Increasing dietary oxalate while reducing dietary calcium does not reduce the chances of kidney stone recurrence.

(C)   Kidney stone development is sometimes the result of an inherited disorder that can result in excessive production of calcium and oxalate.

(D)   Increasing calcium intake increases the amount of calcium eliminated through the intestines, which decreases the amount to be filtered by the kidneys.

(E)   Some kidney stones are composed of uric acid rather than a combination of calcium and oxalate.

4. PT29, S4, Q19

In the decade from the mid-1980s to the mid-1990s, large corporations were rocked by mergers, reengineering, and downsizing. These events significantly undermined employees' job security. Surprisingly, however, employees' perception of their own job security hardly changed over that period. Fifty-eight percent of employees surveyed in 1984 and 55 percent surveyed in 1994 stated that their own jobs were very secure.

Each of the following contributes to an explanation of the surprising survey results described above EXCEPT:

(A)   A large number of the people in both surveys work in small companies that were not affected by mergers, reengineering, and downsizing.

(B)   Employees who feel secure in their jobs tend to think that the jobs of others are secure.

(C)   The corporate downsizing that took place during this period had been widely anticipated for several years before the mid-1980s.

(D)   Most of the major downsizing during this period was completed within a year after the first survey.

(E)   In the mid-1990s, people were generally more optimistic about their lives, even in the face of hardship, than they were a decade before.

Solutions: Explain a Result Questions

Answer Key

1. A

2. E

3. D

4. B

1. PT30, S4, Q5

In a poll of eligible voters conducted on the eve of a mayoral election, more of those polled stated that they favored Panitch than stated that they favored any other candidate. Despite this result, another candidate, Yeung, defeated Panitch by a comfortable margin.

Each of the following, if true, contributes to a resolution of the discrepancy described above EXCEPT:

(A)   Of Yeung's supporters, a smaller percentage were eligible to vote than the percentage of Panitch's supporters who were eligible to vote.

(B)   A third candidate, Mulhern, conducted a press conference on the morning of the election and withdrew from the race.

(C)   The poll's questions were designed by staff members of Panitch's campaign.

(D)   Of the poll respondents supporting Yeung, 70 percent described the election as "important" or "very important," while 30 percent of respondents supporting Panitch did the same.

(E)   The poll, conducted on a Monday, surveyed persons in the downtown area, and the percentage of Yeung's supporters who work downtown is lower than that of Panitch's supporters.

Answer choice (A) is correct.

What would be expected: Panitch wins the election (because the polls showed him in the lead).
The unexpected result: Yeung defeats Panitch by a comfortable margin.

Remember our buckets: 1) further evidence for the EXPECTED, 2) evidence for the UNEXPECTED, and 3) irrelevant. For this EXCEPT question, we'll have four answers that explain the unexpected result and one that either provides further evidence for the expected result or is irrelevant.

(B) explains the unexpected result. If a third candidate dropped out, and his supporters went to Yeung, those two blocs combined could have added up to more votes than Panitch's supporters.

(C) explains the unexpected result. Panitch's staff would have a clear motive for designing a skewed poll that would show Panitch in the lead, and this design could explain the poll results.

(D) explains the unexpected result. If a larger percentage of Yeung's supporters considered the election "very important" or "important," then those people may have been more likely to cast votes.

(E) explains the unexpected result. This choice provides another explanation for the poll's results: An unrepresentative sample of people were polled. The actual number of Yeung's supporters in the general population may have been higher, but these people could have been underrepresented if this choice were true.

If choice (A) had said "eligible to participate in the poll" rather than "eligible to vote," this answer would have been incorrect. As it stands, however, this answer choice goes in Bucket 1, and thus is the correct answer. It provides further evidence for the *expected* result: that Panitch would win. If a smaller percentage of Yeung's supporters were able to cast a vote, then we would

MANHATTAN
PREP

expect Yeung to have a smaller number of votes than Panitch.

2. PT31, S2, Q11

Several thousand years ago, people in what is now North America began to grow corn, which grows faster and produces more food per unit of land than do the grains these people had grown previously. Corn is less nutritious than those other grains, however, and soon after these people established corn as their staple grain crop, they began having nutrition-related health problems. Yet the people continued to grow corn as their staple grain, although they could have returned to growing the more nutritious grains.

Which one of the following, if true, most helps to explain why the people mentioned continued to grow corn as their staple grain crop?

(A)   The variety of corn that the people relied on as their staple grain produced more food than did the ancestors of that variety.

(B)   Modern varieties of corn are more nutritious than were the varieties grown by people in North America several thousand years ago.

(C)   The people did not domesticate large animals for meat or milk, either of which could supply nutrients not provided by corn.

(D)   Some grain crops that could have been planted instead of corn required less fertile soil in order to flourish than corn required.

(E)   The people discovered some years after adopting corn as their staple grain that a diet that supplemented corn with certain readily available nongrain foods significantly improved their health.

Answer choice (E) is correct.

The wording of this question explicitly gives us our paradox: Why did people continue to grow corn as their staple crop even after they started having nutrition-related health problems?

Here are our buckets again: 1) further evidence for the EXPECTED, 2) evidence for the UNEXPECTED, and 3) irrelevant.

(A) is tempting because a higher yield might seem to be a good thing, but look closely—this answer is irrelevant to the unexpected result. The ability to produce more corn relative to ancestral times does not give us any reason why these people would continue to grow corn, since the nutritional problems occurred "soon after these people established corn as their staple grain crop." A comparison to ancestral times is out of scope. This answer also does not address the main element of the paradox: the weaker nutrition of corn relative to other grains.

(B) is irrelevant to the unexpected result. The nutrition of "modern" corn would not have affected the decisions of people thousands of years ago.

(C) provides further evidence for the expected result by removing an alternate source of nutrients not provided by corn.

(D) provides further evidence for the expected result. If corn required more fertile soil than some of the other grain crops, then we would expect that growing these other crops would be easier.

(E) explains the unexpected result. The major problem with corn was that it led to nutrition-related health problems—if nongrain foods could be used to supplement nutrition and improve health, then there would be less of a need to switch from corn as the staple grain crop. This is our answer.

13

3. PT31, S3, Q2

One way kidney stones can form is when urine produced in the kidneys is overly concentrated with calcium or oxalate. Reducing dietary calcium has been thought, therefore, to decrease the likelihood that calcium will concentrate and form additional stones. Oddly enough, for many people the chances of recurrence are decreased by increasing calcium intake.

Which one of the following, if true, most helps to resolve the apparent discrepancy described above?

(A)   Laboratory studies on animals with kidney stones reveal that they rarely get additional stones once calcium supplements are added to the diet.

(B)   Increasing dietary oxalate while reducing dietary calcium does not reduce the chances of kidney stone recurrence.

(C)   Kidney stone development is sometimes the result of an inherited disorder that can result in excessive production of calcium and oxalate.

(D)   Increasing calcium intake increases the amount of calcium eliminated through the intestines, which decreases the amount to be filtered by the kidneys.

(E)   Some kidney stones are composed of uric acid rather than a combination of calcium and oxalate.

Answer choice (D) is correct.

What would be expected: Increasing calcium intake shouldn't decrease chance of stones recurring (because decreasing calcium intake is thought to decrease chances for stones, and stones can be formed from calcium).

The unexpected result: For many people, increasing calcium intake decreases chance of recurring stones.

Let's think of our buckets: 1) further evidence for the EXPECTED, 2) evidence for the UNEXPECTED, and 3) irrelevant.

(A) seems like evidence for the unexpected result. It shows that what's true for humans seems to be similarly true in experiments with animals. Let's keep it for now.

(B) is related to the conclusion in a very confusing and ultimately unhelpful way. We'd need more information to see how this relates to the unexpected result.

(C) is irrelevant to the conclusion. It does not have any direct relation to the impact of calcium intake.

(D) is clearly evidence for the unexpected result. It explains why increased calcium intake can decrease the likelihood of recurring stones—because it decreases the amount of calcium the kidneys are required to filter.

(E) is irrelevant to the conclusion. The fact that some kidney stones are composed of something else does not impact our discussion.

Both choices (A) and (D) seem to be evidence for the unexpected result. However, choice (D) explains clearly why the unexpected may occur, whereas choice (A) does not. Answer choice (A) does not help to resolve the discrepancy. Like the additional lazy, muscular animals we encountered in the cat problem, it only helps to confirm that the discrepancy exists. Therefore, choice (D) is the correct answer.

4. PT29, S4, Q19

In the decade from the mid-1980s to the mid-1990s, large corporations were rocked by mergers, reengineering, and downsizing. These events significantly undermined employees' job security. Surprisingly, however, employees' perception of their own job security hardly changed over that period. Fifty-eight percent of employees surveyed in 1984 and 55 percent surveyed in 1994 stated that their own jobs were very secure.

Each of the following contributes to an explanation of the surprising survey results described above EXCEPT:

(A)   A large number of the people in both surveys work in small companies that were not affected by mergers, reengineering, and downsizing.

(B)   Employees who feel secure in their jobs tend to think that the jobs of others are secure.

(C)   The corporate downsizing that took place during this period had been widely anticipated for several years before the mid-1980s.

(D)   Most of the major downsizing during this period was completed within a year after the first survey.

(E)   In the mid-1990s, people were generally more optimistic about their lives, even in the face of hardship, than they were a decade before.

Answer choice (B) is correct.

For Explain a Result questions, first identify the paradox by figuring out the expected and the unexpected results. Given the fact that employees' job security was significantly undermined from the mid-'80s to mid-'90s, we can say the following:

What would be expected: The survey would show that fewer employees thought their jobs were "very

secure" in 1994 than in 1984 (because downsizing, etc. undermined job security).

The unexpected result: Employees' perception hardly changed.

You know your buckets by now! Since this is an EXCEPT question, you want the one answer that is not in Bucket 2.

(A) explains the unexpected result. If the survey sample contained a disproportionate number of employees whose jobs were not "rocked by mergers, reengineering, and downsizing," these employees' perceptions may not have been affected and the survey results make sense.

(C) explains the unexpected result. If the downsizing were anticipated, then perceptions may have shifted before the survey period rather than during it.

(D) explains the unexpected result. If most of the major downsizing happened immediately after the first survey (at the beginning of the period we're concerned with), then perceptions of job security may have fallen quickly, then had years to recover in time for the next survey in 1994. People who were employed in 1994 may have had good reason to believe their jobs were secure, especially if they weren't laid off in that first year!

(E) explains the unexpected result. If people were generally more optimistic in 1994 than in 1984, then even though their job security may have changed, their perception of that security may have been buoyed by this new optimism.

Answer choice (B) contains a small but critical shift in language—"the jobs of others." The passage only discusses employees' feelings about their own jobs, so this choice is irrelevant. This is our answer.

13

Conclusion

In This Chapter...

Conclusion

Congratulations on making it to the end of this book! We know it's been a challenge, but we expect that you'll be far better off for it on test day. In terms of your study timeline, we expect that most of you are about here:

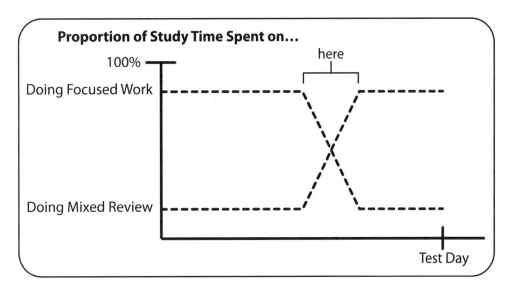

At this point, we have three primary suggestions:

1. Prioritize mixed review.
2. Wrap up your focused work.
3. Finalize your timing strategy.

Let's discuss these three areas in depth.

Prioritize Mixed Review

As we've discussed elsewhere, preparing for the exam by doing only mixed review is not recommended. It is an inefficient way to improve your skills and get better at solving problems. However, it's also a mistake to focus only on content-specific work.

In large part, this is because your LSAT score is based not only on your understanding or your abilities, but also on your *performance*. That is, your score is based on how well you represent your understanding and your talents in a specific context and in one moment in time. As we know from real life, when confronted with pressure situations, two people with the same abilities can have drastically different experiences.

Often, the difference in the performances can be attributed to mind-set and preparation. Consider the mixed review in the final part of your training as preparation for performing at your best on test day.

The More Like Test Day, the Better

Thinking about your review in those terms, it makes sense that as you get closer and closer to the exam, you ought to try to make your practice as representative of the real thing as you can.

The LSAT is administered digitally, so if you're practicing questions on paper, limit yourself to the kind of in-question annotation that you're allowed on the digital platform: highlighting, underlining, eliminating answers, selecting answers, and flagging questions. Any free-hand notations such as diagramming and short-hand notes should be relegated to your scratch paper. If you're someone who does a lot of diagramming and note-taking, you may not want to use the stylus end of the pen provided by the test center because you'll have to flip it around every time you want to write something down. When you practice on digital exams, figure out how you're most comfortable holding your writing utensil and which finger is available to make on-screen selections, eliminations, and annotations.

The digital platform also has a built-in timer. If you find a countdown timer helpful, use one in any paper-based practice you do, too. If you find a countdown timer distracting and stress inducing, don't worry—remember that you can hide it on the digital test platform by clicking on it.

In general, we recommend that a substantial amount of your mixed review come in the form of full, timed LSAT sections and complete LSAT practice exams. Again, the more realistic the better. If you have gotten accustomed to giving yourself extra breaks during your practice tests, or if you've allowed yourself to spread a single test out over multiple days, chances are high that the real thing is going to feel much tougher, and much more exhausting, than you anticipated. Your final practice exams should take place under test-like conditions, as closely as you can re-create them.

Finally, you may want to do some mixed review that specifically targets certain groups of question types. These subsets can group questions that have great commonality, such as those belonging to the Assumption Family, or those that are easily mistaken for one another, such as Identify the Conclusion and Inference. Doing mixed review of these subgroups can be very beneficial. As you did after Chapter 7 and Chapter 11, take an LR section of an official PrepTest and use your question stem identification skills to isolate the kind of questions you want to review. Make note of what kind of questions you pulled from the section so you can mine it for other questions later.

Use Your Practice Tests to. . . Practice

We know that when you take your practice exams, especially right before the actual exam, what's probably going to be most important to you is the overall scaled score. That's natural, and pretty much everyone feels the same way. You want to know how you are doing!

However, keep in mind that the benefit of these exams is supposed to be that of *practicing*. Make sure to use these exams to practice your test-day strategy. Here are two specific areas where practice can have a significant impact on your performance:

1. **Timing strategy.** In just a bit, we'll talk in detail about designing a personalized and optimal timing strategy. One of the most important things you can do is practice implementing this strategy so that you are *completely* comfortable with it before the exam. That means two things specifically: You are confident that you can and will stay balanced and finish on schedule, and you also know how to adjust as need be in case things happen to go awry.

MANHATTAN
PREP

2. **Your ability to smoothly shift gears.** If you've been following our recommendations up to this point, most of your work has been focused on one question type at a time. We feel this is the best way to improve your understanding and skill level in the initial stages of your practice. However, on the exam, you will have to be comfortable switching from one problem type to another, over and over again. This is a significant challenge, and one that you ought to prepare for.

The most essential key to success is that you have a clear plan for how to attack each type of problem. Here is a quick list of the major question types that you have just studied in depth:

Analyze Argument Structure	Necessary Assumption
Explain a Result	Principle Example
Flaw	Principle Support
Inference	Strengthen the Argument
Match the Flaw	Sufficient Assumption
Match the Reasoning	Weaken the Argument

Take a moment to reflect on each question type on the list. Does a clear process quickly come to mind? Do you have a clear sense of the most important issues to consider? If not, and if you don't, you will definitely want to revisit those particular chapters to reinforce the primary takeaways.

The other key, which many test-takers fail to consider, is to be *active* about shifting gears from problem to problem. Force yourself to think about it! Use the question stem to categorize the problem, and use the category to remind yourself of your process. Use your practice exams to build this into your mental routine.

The reason we stress the above is that we know it's very easy, once you get into the rhythm of the exam, to lose sight of the unique task that each question presents. All these questions look alike! An obvious and dangerous consequence can be that you pick the right answer for the wrong question type; for example, you pick a Weaken answer for a Strengthen question. A more subtle, but perhaps more pervasive, consequence of losing sight of your task is that it causes you to waste time. Without a clear sense of what you need to do, you will find yourself thinking about things that do not lead to the right answer. Actively concentrate on shifting gears during your practice exams so that it is second nature by test day.

Use Your Practice Exams to Evaluate and Fine-Tune

Again, we know and understand that you will focus a great deal on your scaled score, but we want to make sure that you also use your exams to get a better sense of more specific strengths and weaknesses. Take notice of one or two question types, or subsets of question types, that seem to cause you the most trouble, and make sure to emphasize these in the focused work that you do. Also try to notice any general skills, such as being able to identify the correct conclusion to any argument, that might need fine-tuning before test day. Isolate these issues and do some focused work on them, then apply this work to your other practice exams.

When you're reviewing your practice test, it's dangerously easy to review only the questions you got wrong. But what about the questions where you picked correctly between two attractive choices but lacked confidence in your decision? These need to be reviewed as well. To make it easier to review these questions, develop a system for marking problems to return to. If you're practicing on paper, circle the questions that you don't feel 100% about, and make it clear which

answers were easy eliminations and which were part of your final, agonizing, they-both-look-great moments. If you're taking a digital practice exam, use the flagging tool to mark questions to return to, and only use the elimination function on answer choices you're confident about eliminating. Also—and this will take some willpower—remember that we recommend you review flagged questions and any answer choices *before* you score your test so that you can continue to grapple with them and improve your analysis skills before finding out the answers.

Wrap Up Your Focused Work

Though you will want to spend a majority of your remaining study hours on mixed review, it will also be extremely beneficial to do some more focused work. Here are two general suggestions:

1. Review Individual Question Types

For most of you, it's probably been at least a few weeks since you last spent a significant amount of time focused on, say, Flaw questions, and perhaps you don't feel as automatic in thinking about them as you did back then. If that's the case, it's okay! That mastery is still in you. It's just time to review.

One suggestion we have is to resist the temptation to review every single unusual and super-difficult challenge that the LSAT might throw your way. The temptation is understandable. Let's call it "Noah's Ark Syndrome": Just before the moment of truth, you try to get your hands, or mind, on everything you think could possibly be of use. This type of studying rarely has much positive benefit.

Instead, we encourage you to try to simplify your understanding. Consider carefully what it is that is most important to know about each problem type, and consider carefully what is most important to remember about the process you need to use to get to the right answer. For each question type, make sure that you have a clear understanding of the key decisions that will need to be made and that you have confidence in your ability to make them.

For question types in which you are strong, we imagine the above review can be fairly quick and automatic—it will just be reinforcement of what you already know and do in solving problems. You will want to spend more time on the areas where you felt weakest. Often, there is great value in revisiting a lesson that you originally found challenging. This can be especially true now that you have more experience with the test as a whole.

2. Firm Up Sagging Skills

It's very common for students to end up being very strong in a variety of areas, but somehow markedly weaker in one particular and fundamental area, such as being able to separate supporting and opposing evidence in an argument. If you have a general area like that where you lack confidence, make sure to address it quickly. Don't let it prevent you from making the best of the rest of your abilities.

You probably already know if you have a weakness in one or two of these areas, and if you do, chances are it impacts your performance on a variety of questions. Make sure to do whatever you can to shore up these issues. Practice just identifying conclusions or cores, or review wrong answers to Inference questions to sharpen your sense of faulty reasoning.

Your Optimal Timing Strategy

It's an unfortunate truth that the test is *designed* to not give you enough time. The vast majority of us would perform better if we had unlimited time, but the exam is meant to test our ability to evaluate arguments *efficiently,* and it wouldn't be able to test that if there weren't time pressure.

What this means is that how you utilize your time is an important component of your overall score. We've actually been talking about this on a microlevel for the entire book; much of what we discuss in terms of *process* can be thought of in terms of *how you should use your time during a problem.* Now, let's talk about it in greater detail.

Your timing strategy should take into consideration two factors: 1) your goal score, and 2) the typical construction of each Logical Reasoning section.

Assuming that your strengths and weaknesses are balanced evenly across Logical Reasoning, Logic Games, and Reading Comprehension—and we understand that this is a huge assumption—here are the approximate number of "misses" you can afford per section to get to your goal score:

If your goal score is...	You can afford to miss...
150	10 questions per section
155	8 questions per section
160	6 questions per section
165	4 questions per section
170	2 or 3 questions per section
175	1 question per section
177+	0 or 1 question per section

Again, these are just approximations, and the scoring scale for every exam will be slightly different. But at this point, it's helpful to think about the number of misses you can live with, and, ideally, you want to make sure that these misses coincide with questions you expect to find most difficult. You don't want to miss problems you can and should get right, and, in terms of your timing, you want to make sure that you don't waste time on the problems that are least likely to reward you with a point.

So think now, if you haven't already, about the types of questions that cause you the most difficulty. If you find Match the Reasoning problems to be the most difficult, and you know that you can afford a few misses in a section, then you should know, going into the exam, that that's a question type you won't spend extra time on. That doesn't mean you won't try your best to get the question correct—it simply means you will go in knowing that you will not spin your wheels on a Match the Reasoning question.

It's also helpful to be mindful of the natural progression of a typical section. The Logical Reasoning section has a tendency to go through certain "zones" of difficulty, and these tendencies are fairly consistent from exam to exam. Here is a rough diagram of these tendencies:

MANHATTAN

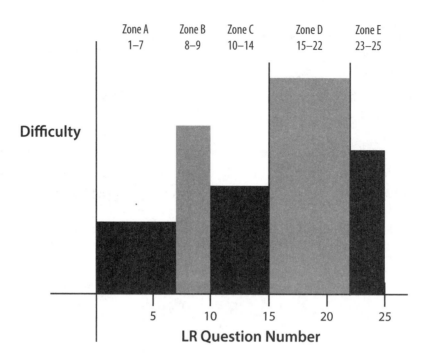

It's important to note, once again, that these are tendencies and not absolutes. Please do not contact us irate if you happen to run into a fourth problem in a section that happens to be particularly difficult; we know that can happen. However, these tendencies are consistent enough that it's helpful to know about them and use them in your planning.

Per the natural ebb and flow of the section, here are some very general timing recommendations that are meant to keep you balanced throughout:

After question…	You should be at about…
5	5 minutes
10	11 minutes
15	18 minutes
20	26 minutes

Again, keep in mind that the above recommendations are meant to be as general as possible and that, ideally, we are hoping that you will adjust these recommendations to fit your toolset and goals.

If you feel that you miss a lot of questions because you rush, and if you know you can afford, say, five misses in a section, you may want to devote more time to the earlier problems so that you can make sure you get them correct, knowing that you may have to cut bait on some more difficult problems later, or even skip them entirely.

If, as you approach test day, you still can't seem to finish the LR section on time, you'll want to carve out a strategic skipping strategy. Some students find they can improve their scores by employing a "scan and guess" strategy on questions that sound like they were written in another language. If you can't even untangle the argument, the question is unlikely to reward you with a point, so saving that time for questions that suit you better may be the best move.

Other students find that they need to skip some problems in their entirety, without taking the time to even read them. This type of strategic skipping strategy could include skipping the longest problems, skipping problems of question

types that you consistently struggle with, skipping problems in the most difficult "zone," or some combination of the three. Experiment with different strategies in practice until you find one that lands you the most points, then practice with that strategy until it's automatic for test day. If you do need to skip questions, remember to always select an answer for questions that you skip. There's no penalty for a wrong answer, and hey, you might nail it on a lucky guess!

If, on the other hand, you are aiming for a 180 sort of score and are concerned about the idea of getting stuck and having to rush on one or two particularly challenging problems, we recommend that you build in an extra "bank" of time. Design your timing strategy so that it adds up to, say, 30 minutes instead of 35. That way, you know that you have 5 extra minutes in the "bank" that you can feel free to spend whenever certain problems happen to come up and bite you in ways you didn't expect. This is where the flagging function of the digital testing platform comes in handy. If you perform extremely well in LR and execute most questions with a high degree of confidence, flag any question about which you are uncertain. The navigation bar at the bottom of the screen makes it easy to click on your flagged questions and come back to them at the end of the section when you know exactly how much time you have for your deep dive.

Another simple way to gauge timing for those who are seeking an extremely high-level score (and aren't prone to reading or reasoning errors when moving quickly) is to aim to solve the first 15 questions in 15 minutes. That should leave plenty of time to carefully reason through the remaining problems.

Make sure to practice these strategies as you take your practice exams so that you can adjust them as need be, and so that you can implement them automatically on test day. Get comfortable with the pace that is required to stay on schedule, and consider carefully what your plan will be if you get slightly behind on time. Ideally, once you've gotten into the exam, timing is something that you monitor, but not something that takes away from your focus and energy.

Final Thoughts: Be the QB

Let's finish by talking about a real-life situation that requires quick and accurate decision making in a stressful situation. Consider the position of a football quarterback. The position of quarterback has evolved, in our modern age, to be something akin to that of a rocket scientist. Every play has dozens of variables that need to be considered, decisions that need to be made in split seconds, and the added pressure of elite athletes running toward you with the goal of hitting you as hard as possible. Are the best quarterbacks the ones who try to think about every possible variable all at once? No. We've seen those quarterbacks, and they are typically the ones who trip over their own feet. The best ones see and understand what is most important to consider in any situation, and they have a system for thinking about these things in an organized manner. They've prepared enough to be confident in their decision making. So confident that, when they inevitably make mistakes, they don't get shaken and abandon their process or worry about the last play instead of focusing on the next.

It's easy to get overwhelmed by the intricacies of the exam, and it's easy to fall into the trap of thinking about too much at once. Mistakes happen, and when they do, it's also easy to abandon ship—to stress about that last hard question instead of clearing your mind and using all your hard-won skills to tackle the next. For every question you attempt, try to use all of your experience and understanding to focus on what each problem is really about and the most efficient process for arriving at the right answer. This simple and strong compass will be your most important tool for success on test day. With it, we are confident that you will represent your abilities at their best.

14

Go beyond books.
Try us for free.

In Person

Find an LSAT course near you and attend the first session free, no strings attached.

**Find your city at
manhattanprep.com/lsat/classes**

Online

Enjoy the flexibility of prepping from home or the office with our online course.

**See the full schedule at
manhattanprep.com/lsat/classes**

On Demand

Prep where you are, when you want with LSAT Interact™— our on-demand course.

**Try multiple full lessons for free at
manhattanprep.com/lsat/interact**

Not sure which is right for you? Try all three! Or, give us a call, and we'll help you figure out which program fits you best.

Toll-Free U.S. Number 800.576.4628 | International 001 212.721.7400 | Email lsat@manhattanprep.com